Jewish, Christian, and Muslim Travel Experiences

Judaism, Christianity, and Islam – Tension, Transmission, Transformation

---

Edited by Patrice Brodeur, Alexandra Cuffel,
Assaad Elias Kattan, and Georges Tamer

Volume 16

Jewish, Christian, and Muslim Travel Experiences

3rd century BCE – 8th century CE

Edited by
Susanne Luther, Pieter B. Hartog, and Clare E. Wilde

DE GRUYTER

ISBN 978-3-11-071741-9
e-ISBN (PDF) 978-3-11-071748-8
e-ISBN (EPUB) 978-3-11-071751-8
ISSN 2196-405X

Library of Congress Control Number: 2023939099

Bibliographic information published by the Deutsche Nationalbibliothek
The Deutsche Nationalbibliothek lists this publication in the Deutsche Nationalbibliografie;
detailed bibliographic data are available on the internet at http://dnb.dnb.de.

© 2023 Walter de Gruyter GmbH, Berlin/Boston
Typesetting: Integra Software Services Pvt. Ltd.
Printing and binding: CPI books GmbH, Leck

www.degruyter.com

Contents

List of Contributors —— VII

Pieter B. Hartog and Susanne Luther
Jewish, Christian, and Muslim Travel Experiences —— 1

Robin B. Ten Hoopen
"And as They Travelled Eastward" (Gen 11:2): Travel in the Book of Genesis and the Anonymous Travelers in the Tower of Babel Account —— 11

Christoph Jedan
The Consolations of Travel: Reading Seneca's *Ad Marciam* vis-à-vis Paul of Tarsus —— 33

Nils Neumann
The (Missing) Motif of "Returning Home" from an Otherworldly Journey in Menippean Literature and the New Testament —— 55

Sigurvin Lárus Jónsson
The Educational Aspect of the Lukan Travel Narrative: Jesus as a Πεπαιδευμένος —— 73

Pieter B. Hartog
Acts of the Apostles—A Celebration of Uncertainty? Constructing a Dialogical Self for the Early Jesus Movement —— 97

Susanne Luther
"Today or Tomorrow We Will Go to Such and Such a City" (Jas 4:13): The Experience of Interconnectivity and the Mobility of Norms in the Ancient Globalized World —— 113

Theo Witkamp and Jan Krans
Heavenly Journey and Divine Epistemology in the Fourth Gospel —— 145

Eelco Glas
Following Vespasian in His Footsteps: Movement and (E)motion Management in Josephus' *Judean War* —— 161

Gert van Klinken
Religion on the Road—Nehalennia Revisited: Voyagers Addressing a North Sea Deity in the Second Century CE —— 181

Benjamin Lensink
Mapping Cosmological Space in the Apocalypse of Paul and the *Visio Pauli*: The Actualization of Virtual Spatiality in Two Pauline Apocalyptical Journeys based on 2 Cor 12:2–4 —— 189

Tobias Nicklas
The Travels of Barnabas: From the Acts of the Apostles to Late Antique Hagiographic Literature —— 229

Catherine Hezser
Rabbinic Geography: Between the Imaginary and Real —— 251

Paul L. Heck
The Journey of Zayd Ibn ʿAmr: In Search of True Worship —— 269

Reuven Kiperwasser and Serge Ruzer
Nautical Fiction of Late Antiquity: Jews and Christians Traveling by Sea —— 295

Clare E. Wilde
Monasteries as Travel Loci for Muslims and Christians (500–1000 CE) —— 313

Sachregister —— 337

Stellenregister —— 341

List of Contributors

Eelco Glas, Postdoctoral Researcher, Aarhus University (Denmark)

Pieter B. Hartog, Assistant Professor of Ancient Judaism, Protestantse Theologische Universiteit (Netherlands)

Paul Heck, Professor of Theology and Islamic Studies, Georgetown University (USA)

Catherine Hezser, Professor of Jewish Studies, School of Oriental and African Studies, University of London (UK)

Christoph Jedan, Professor of Ethics and Comparative Philosophy of Religion, University of Groningen (Netherlands)

Sigurvin Lárus Jónsson, Postdoctoral Researcher, Westfälische Wilhelms-Universität Münster (Germany)

Reuven Kiperwasser, Research Associate and Lecturer at Ariel University and Research Associate at the Hebrew University of Jerusalem (Israel)

Gert J. van Klinken, Assistant Professor of Church History, Protestantse Theologische Universiteit (Netherlands)

Jan L.H. Krans, Assistant Professor of New Testament Studies, Protestantse Theologische Universiteit (Netherlands)

Benjamin Lensink, Doctoral Researcher, Georg-August-Universität Göttingen (Germany)

Susanne Luther, Professor of New Testament, Georg-August-Universität Göttingen (Germany)

Nils Neumann, Professor of Biblical Theology, Leibniz Universität Hannover (Germany)

Tobias Nicklas, Professor of Exegesis and Hermeneutics of the New Testament, University of Regensburg (Germany) and Adjunct Ordinary Professor, Catholic University of America (USA)

Serge Ruzer, Professor of Comparative Religion, Hebrew University (Israel)

Robin B. Ten Hoopen, Doctoral Researcher, Protestantse Theologische Universiteit (Netherlands)

Clare Wilde, Honorary Research Fellow, University of Auckland (New Zealand)

Theo Witkamp, Head of the Center for Professional Formation and Spirituality Emeritus, Protestantse Theologische Universiteit (Netherlands)

Pieter B. Hartog and Susanne Luther
Jewish, Christian, and Muslim Travel Experiences

Abstract: This chapter introduces the theme of the volume and the contributions it seeks to make to the study of ancient travel. Such contributions are twofold. First, this volume is the first to include early Islamic travel within the comparative study of travel in antiquity. Second, our focus on experiential aspects of ancient journeying break new ground in demonstrating the variety of experiences travelling may evoke and in leading the way in the application of new methods in the study of ancient travel. This introduction ends with suggestions for future research, for which the articles collected here set the stage.

Travel, pilgrimage, and migration are well-established themes in the study of antiquity. Due in no small part to Lionel Casson's groundbreaking *Travel in the Ancient World*,[1] classicists, archaeologists, scholars of religion, theologians, and ancient historians all acknowledge the importance of mobility and related themes in the lives and literature of a notable subset of people in the ancient world.[2] An extensive overview of the developments in each of these fields would be beyond the scope of this introduction.[3] Instead, we will limit ourselves to outlining the specific contributions that this volume aims to make to the study of ancient travel, supplemented with suggestions for future research.

Before doing so, however, it is our pleasure to thank those who have contributed to this volume. Most contributions find their origin in a 2020 conference in Gronin-

---

[1] Lionel Casson, *Travel in the Ancient World* (London: George Allen & Unwin, 1974).
[2] As will be explored further below, it should be emphasized that travel in the ancient world was often a privilege of the elite or of those travelling in a professional capacity (merchants, soldiers). For many in antiquity, travel was out of the question, and passing travellers could even prove a serious burden. On the latter topic see Laura Nasrallah, "Imposing Travellers: An Inscription from Galatia and the Journeys of the Earliest Christians," in *Journeys in the Roman East: Imagined and Real*, ed. Maren R. Niehoff, Culture, Religion, and Politics in the Greco-Roman World 1 (Tübingen: Mohr Siebeck, 2017), 273–86; Laura Salah Nasrallah, *Archaeology and the Letters of Paul* (Oxford: Oxford University Press, 2019).
[3] Such overviews are available elsewhere. Particularly thorough is Maren R. Niehoff, "Journeys on the Way to This Volume," in Niehoff, *Journeys in the Roman East*, 1–20. See also Philip A. Harland, "Pausing at the Intersection of Religion and Travel," in *Travel and Religion in Antiquity*, ed. Philip A. Harland, Studies in Christianity and Judaism/Études sur le christianisme et le judaïsme 21 (Waterloo: Wilfrid Laurier Press, 2011), 1–26; Pieter B. Hartog and Elisa Uusimäki, "Introduction: Views on the Mediterranean," *NTT JTSR* 75 (2021): 153–60.

https://doi.org/10.1515/9783110717488-001

gen, which was organised jointly by the Department of Jewish, Christian and Islamic Origins in the Faculty of Theology and Religious Studies of the University Groningen and the Protestant Theological University. We look back to three inspiring days of scholarly exchange and thank our (then) host institutions for their financial and practical support. We are particularly thankful to the participants in the conference for their contributions, both on site and in this volume. We also owe gratitude to those colleagues who were not part of the conference in Groningen, but were willing to contribute to this volume. Finally, several people have been instrumental in getting this volume in its current shape. We thank Forrest Kentwell and Jonas Hiese for their expertise and commitment in editing the first batch of articles that reached us, and Marie Raschner for seeing the publication all the way through with great dedication and diligence.

Travel in Judaism, Christianity, and Islam

Bringing together scholars of Judaism, Christianity, and Islam, this volume foregrounds the role that travel plays in each of these religious traditions. By so doing, our volume joins a growing body of scholarly literature developing a comparative approach to ancient journeying, both religious and other. Jaś Elsner and Ian Rutherford, for instance, presented a collection of essays dealing with Greco-Roman, Jewish, and Christian pilgrimage.[4] The same comparative outlook underlies Philip Harland's volume *Travel and Religion in Antiquity*, which deals specifically with the religious aspects of travel and includes an article on ancient Mesopotamia and one on the Nabataeans.[5] Pilgrimage, of course, gets its fair share of attention in that volume as well, but, as its contributions show, the gods often also had a significant role to play in journeys that served another purpose than visiting a shrine. Finally, Maren Niehoff's 2017 volume *Journeys in the Roman East* moves beyond pilgrimage to analyze journeys of various kinds in Jewish, Christian, and Greco-Roman sources ranging from the early Roman empire up until late antiquity.[6]

Our focus in the pages that follow is both narrower and broader than that of these earlier volumes. In contrast to these previous works, this volume draws particular attention to the role of travel in three monotheistic traditions. As a result, themes such as ancient philosophical reflection on travel or military travel are absent from this volume. Greek and Roman views on travel do appear, but nearly

---

[4] Jaś Elsner and Ian Rutherford, eds., *Pilgrimage in Graeco-Roman and Early Christian Antiquity: Seeing the Gods* (Oxford: Oxford University Press, 2005).
[5] Harland, *Travel and Religion*.
[6] Niehoff, *Journeys in the Roman East*.

exclusively in a comparative context. The contributions of Pieter B. Hartog, Christoph Jedan, and Nils Neumann, for instance, contextualize travel experiences in several New Testament writings (or, in the case of Christoph Jedan's treatment of Paul, the lack of such experiences) by comparing them with Pausanias' *Perigesis Hellados*, Philostratus' *Life of Apollonius of Tyana*, Seneca's *Ad Marciam*, or Menippean literature. The only exception to our focus on Judaism, Christianity, and Islam is Gert van Klinken's analysis of the goddess Nehalennia, who was venerated in what is now the Dutch province of Zeeland and served as a patron for merchants who travelled the Scheldt River.

At the same time, this volume moves beyond previous comparative work by bringing early Islam into the picture. While similarities between Jewish, Christian, and Greco-Roman travelling have been noted in earlier studies, Islam has been all but ignored by scholars of ancient journeying. This oversight is particularly remarkable given the long-standing study of Christian pilgrimage and the increasing attention being given to travel in rabbinic literature, for which Catherine Hezser's 2011 monograph *Jewish Travel in Antiquity* was instrumental.[7] Against this backdrop, early Islam presents itself as another late antique religious tradition in which travel occupied a central role. The significance of mobility in the formative stage of Islam speaks already from its expansion through conquest.[8] Yet travel continued to occupy a key role in Islam and offered ways of contact with other cultures and religions. Thus, Zayd Ibn 'Amr's journey in search for true worship, which Paul Heck discussed in his contribution, brings him into contact with Jewish, Christian, and other religionists. At a later period, Clare E. Wilde shows, Muslim travelers of various kinds would regularly lodge in Christian monasteries. The contacts between Jews, Christians, and Muslims in late antiquity, therefore, call for a comparative approach to travelling that treats these three traditions together in their intricate connectedness.

Adopting such a comparative approach does not entail restricting oneself to religious travel or pilgrimage. Nor does it imply a focus on earthly travels. The travelers who appear in this volume, travelled for various reasons: merchants feature prominently in contributions by van Klinken, Susanne Luther, and Wilde; Heck's protagonist is a pilgrim in search of true worship; Hartog, Jedan, Sigurvin Lárus

---

7 Catherine Hezser, *Jewish Travel in Antiquity*, TSAJ 144 (Tübingen: Mohr Siebeck, 2011). On the contribution that Hezser's book makes in laying to rest the image of the Jews as a largely sedimentary culture see Pieter B. Hartog and Lieve Teugels, "Jews on the Move: Catherine Hezser's *Jewish Travel in Antiquity*," *NTT JTSR* 75 (2021): 275–81.
8 See D.R. Hill, "The Mobility of the Arab Armies in the Early Conquests" (MA Thesis, Durham University, 1963), http://etheses.dur.ac.uk/9863/; Gudrun Krämer, *Geschichte des Islam* (Munich: Beck, 2005), 27–68 (esp. 29–34).

Jónsson, and Tobias Nicklas write about travelling teachers and apostles; and a traveling emperor appears in Eelco Glas' article. Nor did all travelers in this volume traverse geographical spaces: contributions by Benjamin Lensink, Neumann, and Theo Witkamp and Jan Krans show how religious experiences can take the shape of otherworldly journeys. Even while travelers remain geographically in place, their heavenly journeys provide them access to trans-earthly knowledge. Like the sage who traverses the earth in search of wisdom—think of Zayd Ibn ʿAmr, for instance—the protagonists of Lensink's and Witkamp and Krans' articles traverse the cosmos in pursuit of knowledge.

Travel and Experience

This brings us to a second contribution that this volume makes to the study of ancient travel. In much previous scholarship, the focus has been on either the practicalities and materiality of travel or on literary and narratological depictions of space and travel. Thus, the Roman road network, often perceived as a catalyst for increased mobility, has been the subject of extensive study.[9] The same holds for Roman travel management: as Claudia Moatti has shown, the Roman empire was a world of extensive mobility, but the Romans also regulated this mobility.[10] The study of Jewish and Christian travel, too, is often practically inclined, raising questions such as: where would travelers stay during their journeys? or: How would they deal with the dangers that awaited them en route?[11]

---

9 Casson, *Travel* explicitly identifies the Roman empire as a turning point in the development of ancient mobility, and his findings have greatly influenced subsequent scholarship. On Roman roads see, in addition to Casson's work, Thomas Pekáry, *Untersuchungen zu den römischen Reichsstrassen* (Bonn: Habelt, 1968); Raymond Chevallier, *Les voies romaines* (Paris: Armand Colin, 1972); Hans Christian Schneider, *Altstraßenforschung* (Darmstadt: Wissenschaftliche Buchgesellschaft, 1982); Cornelis van Tilburg, *Traffic and Congestion in the Roman Empire* (London: T&T Clark, 2006); Anne Kolb, ed., *Roman Roads: New Evidence—New Perspectives* (Berlin: De Gruyter, 2019).

10 Claudia Moatti, "Le contrôle de la mobilité des personnes dans l'empire romain," *Mélanges de l'École française de Rome—Antiquité* 112 (2000): 925–58; Claudia Moatti, "Roman World, Mobility," in *Encyclopedia of Global Human Migration*, ed. Immanuel Ness, Saër Maty Bâ, Michael Borgolte, Donna Gabaccia, Dirk Hoerder, Alex Julca, Cecilia Menjivar, Marlou Schrover, and Gregory Woolf (Oxford: Wiley Blackwell, 2013), 1–14; Claudia Moatti, "Migration et droit dans l'Empire Romain: Catégories, contrôles et integration," in *The Impact of Mobility and Migration in the Roman Empire: Proceedings of the Twelfth Workshop of the International Network Impact of Empire (Rome, June 17–19, 2015)*, ed. Elio Lo Cascio and Laurens Ernst Tacoma, Impact of Empire 22 (Leiden: Brill, 2016), 222–45.

11 See, for instance, the large amount of practical information gathered in Hezser, *Jewish Travel*, 19–196.

In addition to these practical matters, literary depictions of space and travel have been prominent in previous studies on ancient journeying. Hezser, for instance, devotes the larger part of her monograph on Jewish travel to literary portrayals of travel in Jewish (mostly rabbinic) sources.[12] Many contributions in the comparative volumes mentioned above also focus on the aims and effects of literary representations of travel. Moreover, travel is, understandably, an important theme in narratologically informed studies of space in ancient literature.[13] Most contributions to this volume join the choir of those who study literary portrayals of travel, as their focus is on travel in literature. This literary focus speaks most clearly from those contributions that explore literary aspects of the travel topos. Neumann compares literary descriptions of otherworldly journeys in the New Testament with those in Menippean literature. Heszer shows how rabbinic literature offers geographical imaginations rather than real-life geography, writing that the rabbis' "geographical references and descriptions should ... be considered a mixture of daily life (e.g., travel) experiences, biblical reminiscences, hearsay, and wishful thinking" (265). Reuven Kiperwasser and Serge Ruzer, finally, draw attention to a common core of "sailor-yarn traditions" (307) in Jewish, Christian, and other travel narratives, on which each of these narratives builds to fulfil its specific purposes.

At the same time, this volume adds a specific dimension: it concentrates particularly on the experiences of the traveler and how these are managed by, and serve the purposes of, the authors of literary travel accounts. Such an experiential perspective is not entirely novel: Jean-Marie André and Marie-Françoise Baslez include a small section on "l'experience du voyage" in their monograph *Voyager dans l'Antiquité*, and Silvia Montiglio details how wandering in Greek literature is accompanied with "pains and privations" and so is informative of "the human condition."[14] Even so, the study of travel and experience remains strongly indebted to narratological and literary approaches, despite the potential application of social-scientific (e.g., psychological) methods in this field of study. The notion of the dialogical self, for instance, may prove helpful in understanding how the experiences of uncertainty shapes identity, as Hartog argues in his contribution. What is more, studies on travel and experience tend to foreground the intricate connection between travel and uncertainty and, related to it, the quest for wisdom. The contributions in

---

12 Hezser, *Jewish Travel*, 197–440.
13 See, e.g., Irene J.F. de Jong, ed., *Space in Ancient Greek Literature*, MnS 339 (Leiden: Brill, 2012); Maximilian Benz and Katrin Dennerlein, eds., *Literarische Räume der Herkunft: Fallstudien zu einer historischen Narratologie* (Berlin: De Gruyter, 2016).
14 Jean-Marie André and Marie-Françoise Baslez, *Voyager dans l'Antiquité* (Paris: Fayard, 1993), 66–70; Silvia Montiglio, *Wandering in Ancient Greek Culture* (Chicago: The University of Chicago Press, 2005), 24–61.

this volume confirm this link, but also add other experiences to the picture. In this way, we aim to broaden the study of travel and experience in antiquity.

The contributions in this volume address four main themes. First, the articles by Robin B. Ten Hoopen, Hartog, and Nicklas explore how journeys create uncertainty. This uncertainty, in turn, offers a canvas to develop one's identity. Building on this dynamics, authors of literary sources dig into the travel motif to promote their own agendas. Concentrating on Gen 11 and the unknown "travelers" in Gen 11:2, Ten Hoopen shows how travel is central to Israel's foundation narratives. Thus, he concludes, "the human itinerary towards Babel is to be taken as a theological journey that founds Israel's history in Mesopotamia," but "the divine descent of the universal Israelite deity YHWH depreciates Babel's role as the center of the world" (28). Hartog shows how uncertainty about one's sense of belonging is a key experience for travelers, and how the book of Acts explores this uncertainty to create a dialogical self for the early Jesus movement. Nicklas, lastly, shows how various literary writings touch on the image of the apostles of Barnabas as a traveler. By so doing, they write the churches that Barnabas visited—particularly the church of Cyprus—into early Christian narrative space.

Second, the experience of danger and uncertainty is central to Glas' article. Yet as Glas shows, Josephus' portrayal of Vespasian's indecisiveness to travel to Rome and claim power (*JW* 4.588–663) does not serve the construction of identity. Instead, Vespasian's hesitancy to journey during the winter season—in itself a sensible decision, given the dangers ancient literature associated with journeying in winter[15]—characterizes the emperor doubtful, and so offers a subtle critique of the Flavian dynasty. In this case, then, features that may at first glance appear fortuitous—the ability to restrain one's impulses and a judicious calculation of danger—appear in a context where they serve not only to commend, but simultaneously to criticize, the character of a protagonist.

Third, journeys provide access to true worship, wisdom, or knowledge. The experiences of the traveler thus entail the transformation of either the traveler or his audience—or both. Through his journey in search of true worship, Zayd Ibn ʿAmr, whom Heck discusses, transformed earlier forms of worship at the Meccan Kaʿba. Whilst Zayd was on a search to learn wisdom, Luke's Jesus rather appears as one who teaches wisdom. As Jónsson shows, the *Reisebericht* in Luke's gospel (Luke 9:51–19:40) portrays Jesus as a πεπαιδευμένος who teaches while travelling. "Throughout the Travel Narrative," Jónsson concludes, "we are reminded that Jesus is travelling. . ., to where he is travelling . . ., that he is teaching. . . and most impor-

---

15 See, e.g., Philo, *Leg.* 190, with comments by Pieter B. Hartog, "Space and Travel in Philo's *Legatio ad Gaium*," *SPhiloA* 30 (2018): 71–92 (85–87).

tantly that his influence grows both geographically . . .and with regard to the size of the crowds" (91). In addition to these earthly journeys, heavenly journeys also offer access to knowledge. Visionary experiences that take the shape of otherworldly journeys are a welcome source for literary description. Lensink shows how two early Christian apocalypses—the Apocalypse of Paul and the Visio Pauli—take up 1 Cor 12:2–4 and actualize the virtual meaning of the Pauline passage in different ways. Each writing offers its own spatial description, even if both emphasize the importance of the visionary experience for obtaining wisdom. Witkamp and Krans recognize a similar dynamics in the Gospel of John. Drawing out similarities and differences between the gospel and Jewish apocalypses, Witkamp and Krans demonstrate how "[t]he visionary is given extraordinary heavenly knowledge and insight which only he can receive" (157).

Fourth, the experiences associated with travel can bring about consolation, as Jedan's contribution demonstrates. Offering a detailed reading of the travel motif in Seneca's *Ad Marciam*, Jedan shows how an extended analogy between life and an imagined journey to Syracuse, his description of which Seneca lards with touristic information, is to bring consolation to Marcia after the loss of her son Metilius. Moreover, Seneca describes Metilius' afterlife as a journey and an ascent to the sphere of the heavenly bodies. The centrality of travel in Seneca's *Ad Marciam* contrasts, so Jedan argues, with the absence of explicit travel motifs in the Pauline literature. Jedan explains this difference by pointing to the different cosmological views of Paul and Seneca and by exploring "the possibility of Paul expressing aspects of what he could achieve with travel motifs by other linguistic means" (49).

Journeys Beyond This Volume

We hope and expect that the contributions in this volume contribute to the advancement of the comparative study of travel in the ancient world. Notwithstanding the contributions that this volume aims to make, many themes remain rather underexplored in the study of ancient travel. By means of concluding this introduction, we therefore take the opportunity to reflect on the directions which future research on this important theme may take.

To begin with, this journey does not make explicit the question who travelled in the ancient world. As Laura Nasrallah has shown, travel often was the prerequisite of the elite or those who travelled in a professional capacity.[16] For the majority of inhabitants of the Hellenistic, Roman, and Byzantine worlds—in larger part regard-

---

16 Nasrallah, "Imposing Travellers."

less of their religious or cultural affiliations—extensive journeying was out of the question, and travelers could even prove a burden on local communities.[17] These important observations invite the application of socio-historical models in the study of ancient travel. Such models have, of course, extensively proven useful for the study of the ancient world, but they rarely feature in studies on ancient travel.

This plea for exploring new methodological frameworks can be extended to the specific focus of this volume: the experience of travel. Psychological concepts and methodological lenses have been put to good use in the study of antiquity, but have not really made an impact in the study of ancient travel. Seeing however that journeys—as this volume shows—entailed a variety of psychological and other experiences, their study may well benefit for applying such concepts and lenses more fully in future years.

Finally, this volume confirms the value of developing a longue durée approach to travel and its various aspects. The volumes by Harland and Niehoff already lead the way in this regard, and this volume—with its inclusion of early Islam—demonstrates once more the intricate cross-connection between different religious and cultural traditions in the ancient world. Moreover, contributions in this volume testify to continuities between ancient and modern travel: consider, for instance, Jedan's observation that "Seneca's list parallels what today's travel guidebooks still highlight as Syracuse's key sights" (38). A long-term perspective remains a desideratum, therefore, for all who wish to trace continuities and ruptures in the development of travel and mobility, from antiquity up until the modern day.

References

André, Jean-Marie, and Marie-Françoise Baslez. *Voyager dans l'Antiquité*. Paris: Fayard, 1993.
Benz, Maximilian, and Katrin Dennerlein, eds. *Literarische Räume der Herkunft: Fallstudien zu einer historischen Narratologie*. Berlin: De Gruyter, 2016.
Casson, Lionel. *Travel in the Ancient World*. London: George Allen & Unwin, 1974.
Chevallier, Raymond. *Les voies romaines*. Paris: Armand Colin, 1972.
Elsner, Jaś, and Ian Rutherford, eds. *Pilgrimage in Graeco-Roman and Early Christian Antiquity: Seeing the Gods*. Oxford: Oxford University Press, 2005.
Harland, Philip A., ed. *Travel and Religion in Antiquity. Travel and Religion in Antiquity*. Studies in Christianity and Judaism/Études sur le christianisme et le judaïsme 21. Waterloo: Wilfrid Laurier Press, 2011.

---

[17] See the works quoted in n. 2 above.

Harland, Philip A. "Pausing at the Intersection of Religion and Travel." Pages 1–26 in *Travel and Religion in Antiquity*. Edited by Philip A. Harland. Studies in Christianity and Judaism/Études sur le christianisme et le judaïsme 21. Waterloo: Wilfrid Laurier Press, 2011.

Hartog, Pieter B. "Space and Travel in Philo's *Legatio ad Gaium*." *SPhiloA* 30 (2018): 71–92.

Hartog, Pieter B., and Elisa Uusimäki. "Introduction: Views on the Mediterranean." *NTT JTSR* 75 (2021): 153–60.

Hartog, Pieter B., and Lieve Teugels. "Jews on the Move: Catherine Hezser's Jewish Travel in Antiquity." *NTT JTSR* 75 (2021): 275–81.

Hezser, Catherine. *Jewish Travel in Antiquity*. TSAJ 144. Tübingen: Mohr Siebeck, 2011.

Hill, D.R. "The Mobility of the Arab Armies in the Early Conquests." MA Thesis, Durham University, 1963. Http://etheses.dur.ac.uk/9863/.

Jong, Irene J.F. de, ed. *Space in Ancient Greek Literature*. MnS 339. Leiden: Brill, 2012.

Kolb, Anne, ed., *Roman Roads: New Evidence—New Perspectives*. Berlin: De Gruyter, 2019.

Krämer, Gudrun. *Geschichte des Islam*. Munich: Beck, 2005.

Moatti, Claudia. "Le contrôle de la mobilité des personnes dans l'empire romain." *Mélanges de l'École française de Rome—Antiquité* 112 (2000): 925–58.

Moatti, Claudia. "Roman World, Mobility." Pages 1–14 in *Encyclopedia of Global Human Migration*. Edited by Immanuel Ness, Saër Maty Bâ, Michael Borgolte, Donna Gabaccia, Dirk Hoerder, Alex Julca, Cecilia Menjivar, Marlou Schrover, and Gregory Woolf. Oxford: Wiley Blackwell, 2013.

Moatti, Claudia. "Migration et droit dans l'Empire Romain: Catégories, contrôles et integration." Pages 222–45 in *The Impact of Mobility and Migration in the Roman Empire: Proceedings of the Twelfth Workshop of the International Network Impact of Empire (Rome, June 17–19, 2015)*. Edited by Elio Lo Cascio and Laurens Ernst Tacoma. Impact of Empire 22. Leiden: Brill, 2016.

Montiglio, Silvia. *Wandering in Ancient Greek Culture*. Chicago: The University of Chicago Press, 2005.

Nasrallah, Laura. "Imposing Travellers: An Inscription from Galatia and the Journeys of the Earliest Christians." Pages 273–86 in *Journeys in the Roman East: Imagined and Real*. Edited by Maren R. Niehoff. Culture, Religion, and Politics in the Greco-Roman World 1. Tübingen: Mohr Siebeck, 2017.

Nasrallah, Laura. *Archaeology and the Letters of Paul*. Oxford: Oxford University Press, 2019.

Niehoff, Maren R., ed. *Journeys in the Roman East: Imagined and Real*. Culture, Religion, and Politics in the Greco-Roman World 1. Tübingen: Mohr Siebeck, 2017.

Niehoff, Maren R. "Journeys on the Way to This Volume." Pages 1–20 in *Journeys in the Roman East: Imagined and Real*. Edited by Maren R. Niehoff. Culture, Religion, and Politics in the Greco-Roman World 1. Tübingen: Mohr Siebeck, 2017.

Pekáry, Thomas. *Untersuchungen zu den römischen Reichsstrassen*. Bonn: Habelt, 1968.

Schneider, Hans Christian. *Altstraßenforschung*. Darmstadt: Wissenschaftliche Buchgesellschaft, 1982.

Tilburg, Cornelis van. *Traffic and Congestion in the Roman Empire*. London: T&T Clark, 2006.

Robin B. Ten Hoopen
"And as They Travelled Eastward" (Gen 11:2): Travel in the Book of Genesis and the Anonymous Travelers in the Tower of Babel Account

Abstract: This article studies the role of travel and the identity of the travelers in Gen 11:1–9, the Tower of Babel story. The introduction reflects on Genesis as a book of travels and lists the various occurrences of travelling in the Primeval History. The main part of the article discusses Genesis 11. This narrative presents YHWH as a travelling deity and commences and ends with the migration of a group of unidentified travelers. Who are they? Where did they go to and where have they come from? How did their journey change them? By identifying the travelers as primeval humanity, the author illustrates that Genesis 11 is a theological and sociological story concerning identity formation in which travel plays a prominent role. The journey to and from Sinear prefigures the itineraries of the patriarchs, founds Israel's history in Mesopotamia, but also mocks the role of Mesopotamia for the identity of the Israelites. In Genesis 11, Babel functions as a transient place for a pre-Abrahamic humanity that will be dispersed to allow Abraham, and the Israelites, to enter the stage. The conclusion illustrates how reflection on (modern) travel experiences and the study of biblical itineraries could fertilize each other.

Introduction

The first book of the Hebrew Bible already illustrates that travel is part of the biblical DNA.[1] The book of Genesis not only contains the raison d'être for the journey of the Israelites to the promised land (Genesis 12), but also narratives in which journeys express what life is about.[2] In search for food: Josephs brothers (Gen 42:3). In search for love: Abraham's servant (Genesis 24). Going to work: Joseph

---
[1] Other famous examples include the Exodus, the wandering in the desert, and the exile. The Israelites have even been designated as transitory by nature by connecting the root עבר ("to pass over") to the עברי ("Hebrews" or "nations descending from Shem"). See, e.g., Gen 10:21–24 and cf. HALOT, "עֶבֶר II."
[2] With the exception of holidays or leisure travelling, all modern types of travelling are attested.

and his brothers (Gen 37:12–17). To escape from an enemy: Jacob and Esau (Gen 27:43ff). Reuniting the family: Jacob and his children (Gen 46:1–4). A forced migration: Cain and Joseph (Gen 4:12–16; 37:28, 36). And a voluntary migration (Genesis 12–13).[3]

In all cases, these itineraries are not only related to the larger story of Israel,[4] but also mark or generate life experiences. Travel implies transition, a loss of habits and gaining of new ones, a transient experience leading to an unknown future. Hence, the Genesis itineraries provide a rich source of reflection for character development, family relations, and religious experiences.[5] Yet, although both ancient and modern scholars have dealt with the notions of walking with God (Gen 5:21–24; 6:9; 17:1), the calling of Abraham (Gen 12:1–4), or even travel narratives,[6] I am unaware of social scientific or philosophical approaches that have related the Genesis itineraries to (modern) experiences of travel. This contribution may function as a first attempt to do so. Although it's focus will be on the historical and ideological context of Genesis 11, it will illustrate how reflection on (modern) travel experiences and biblical itineraries could fertilize each other. Ancient stories may be read in new ways, and modern travel habits may be reconsidered with biblical itineraries in mind.

Genesis as a Book of Travels

Although Genesis is foremost a book of generations, itineraries make up an important part of the book. The semantic field of travelling and settling in the book of Genesis includes the verbs: to go (הלך), to descend (ירד), to dwell or settle (ישב),

---

[3] Starting from a call of YHWH in Gen 12:1–3, Abraham's migration is voluntary. Note also Lot's settlement in the Jordan valley in Genesis 13.
[4] As noted by Yairah Amit, these travels have "theological, national and historical purposes." Yairah Amit, "Travel Narratives and the Message of Genesis," in *The Formation of the Pentateuch: Bridging the Academic Cultures of Europe, Israel, and North America*, ed. Jan C. Gertz et al., FAT 111 (Tübingen: Mohr Siebeck, 2016), 223–42 (242).
[5] Although often without explicit attention for travel, scholars and novelist have reflected on well-known characters from the book of Genesis. See some of the chapters in J. Harold Ellens and Wayne G. Rollins, *Psychology and the Bible: From Genesis to Apocalyptic Vision* (Westport, CT: Praeger Publishers, 2004). And for a narrative approach Thomas Mann, *Joseph und seine Brüder: Vier Romane in einem Band*, 6th ed. (Frankfurt am Main: S. Fischer, 2007). See also the psychoanalytical reflection on Genesis 11 in André LaCocque, *The Captivity of Innocence: Babel and the Yahwist* (Eugene, OR: Cascade Books, 2010).
[6] See for example Gen. Rab. 30:10; Philo, *De Abrahamo*; Walter Vogels, "Enoch Walked with God and God Took Enoch," *Theoforum* 34 (2003): 283–303; Amit, "Travel Narratives."

to come (בוא), to move out (יצא), to go up (עלה), to travel (נסע), to separate (פרד), to be dispersed (פוץ), to move (עתק), to pitch a tent (נטה, אהל), to flee (ברך), and to return (שוב).

The most extensive examples are found in the narratives of the patriarchs. Terah leaves Ur (יצא), goes (הלך), comes (בוא), and settles (ישב) in Haran (Gen 11:31). Abraham[7] moved his tent (אהל), comes (בוא), and settles (ישב) near the oaks of Mamre (Gen 13:18). Jacob/Israel travels (נסע) and pitches his tent (אהל) at Migdal Eder (Gen 35:21). Also, Lot (Gen 13:11–12), Hagar (Gen 16:6–8), Abraham's servant (Gen 24:4, 61), Isaac (Gen 26:1–23), Esau (Gen 33:12), and even YHWH and his messengers (מלכים) are reported travelling (Gen 11:5, 7; Gen 18:21–22, Gen 19:1; Gen 28:12–13). Yet, the example par excellence is attested in Gen 12:1–9. YHWH commands Abraham to go (הלך) to the land. Abraham goes (הלך) and Lot goes (הלך) with him when he leaves (יצא) Haran. Abraham and his company go out (יצא הלך) and arrive (בוא) in Canaan. Abraham traverses (עבר) the land towards Shechem, from where he moves again (עתק) and pitches his tent (נטה) east of Betel and west of Ai. Finally, he travels in the direction of the Negev (הלך, נסע).

Travelling does not start with the patriarchs, however. The Primeval History (Genesis 1–11) already contains both implicit and explicit itineraries. God's call to spread out over the earth (Gen 1:28) suggests travel to be the second commandment, after procreation. And the non-P creation story refers both to YHWH's placing of the human in the garden (Gen 2:8, 15), and the couple's forced migration from the garden (Gen 3:22–24). Yet, it is Cain who figures in the first short travel story. Banned to a life of wandering (Gen 4:12, 14), he goes out (יצא) and settles (ישב) in Nod, east of Eden (Gen 4:16).

The list of references continues with Enoch who, in the death-oriented and staccato genealogy of Genesis 5, is taken by God to dwell at the ends of the earth.[8] Together with Noah, Enoch is also attributed the metaphorical notion of walking with God (התהלך האלהים, Gen 5:21–24, 6:9).[9]

Genesis 6–10, moreover, contains two implicit journeys, those of the sons of God (בני האלהים, Gen 6:1–4) and the sons of Noah (Gen 9:19; 10:5, 32), yet both are

---

[7] For convenience, I will use the name Abraham also in stories where the patriarch is still called Abram.
[8] See Robin B. Ten Hoopen, "Genesis 5 and the Formation of the Primeval History: A Redaction Historical Case Study," *ZAW* 129 (2017): 177–93; Robin B. Ten Hoopen, "Where Are You, Enoch? Why Can't I Find You? Genesis 5:21–24 Reconsidered," *JHS* 18.4 (2018): 1–24.
[9] This combination attests the motif of *Gottesnähe* and may echo the description of YHWH's strolling in the Garden in Eden (3:8). See Erhard Blum, *Studien zur Komposition des Pentateuch*, BZAW 189 (Berlin: De Gruyter, 1990), 289–93; Ten Hoopen, "Genesis 5."

not explicitly referenced.[10] The most extensive itinerary of the Primeval History, however, is located in its final chapter. Commonly known as the Tower of Babel story,[11] Gen 11:1–9 not only describes YHWH himself as descending (ירד) to inspect the tower and city (Gen 11:5, 7), but starts and ends with the migration (נסע), settlement (ישב), and dispersion (פוץ) of an unidentified group of travelers. Once identified as "humanity" (בני האדם) in Gen 11:5, these travelers, later construction workers, are primarily referred to as "they" or "them" (Gen 11:2–4, 6–9). The first and final reference to these travelers reads:

וַיְהִי בְּנָסְעָם מִקֶּדֶם וַיִּמְצְאוּ בִקְעָה בְּאֶרֶץ שִׁנְעָר וַיֵּשְׁבוּ שָׁם:

And as they travelled eastward[12] they found a valley in the land of Shinar and settled there (Gen 11:2)

וּמִשָּׁם הֱפִיצָם יְהוָה עַל־פְּנֵי כָל־הָאָרֶץ:

And from there YHWH scattered them over the face of the whole earth (Gen 11:9b)

The main part of this contribution will deal with these travelers and their travelling deity. Who are they? Where did they go to and where have they come from? Did they go on a planned trip or were they wandering around in search for a new home? What would they have imagined of their journey? And how did it change them? With these and other questions in mind, we will look afresh at the famous narrative of Genesis 11.

---

10 In Genesis 6, we may assume that the בני האלהים descended to have intercourse with the daughters of men (בנות האדם). In Genesis 6–9, the ark is described as moving towards the Ararat mountains.
11 As is well-known this title overlooks the importance of the city. See Benno Jacob, *Das erste Buch der Tora: Genesis* (Berlin: Schocken, 1934), 301.
12 See for this rendering the next section.

Genesis 11 and Its Travelers

Gen 11:1–9 contains a narrative full of etiologies, wordplay and humor, all in a dense style.[13] It forms a coherent text[14] and has both a concentric and a parallel structure, the latter contrasting the act of the humans (Gen 11:1–4) with the act of YHWH (Gen 11:5–9).[15] The story is part of the non-P or J strand which can at least be identified in the Primeval History (Genesis 1–11).[16]

As many of the stories in the non-P Primeval History, Genesis 11 is not merely a story of progress.[17] Although the dispersion of humanity ends their conglomerating in Babel and leads to the rich world of peoples and a plurality of languages,

---

13 See the commentaries of Umberto Cassuto, *A Commentary on the Book of Genesis: Part II: From Noah to Abraham: Genesis VI 9–XI 32*, trans. Isaac Abrahams (Jerusalem: Magnes Press, 1964); Claus Westermann, *Genesis 1–11*, BKAT I/1 (Neukirchen-Vluyn: Neukirchener Verlag, 1974); Gordon J. Wenham, *Genesis 1–15*, WBC 1 (Dallas, TX: Word, 1987); Andreas Schüle, *Der Prolog der hebräischen Bibel: Der literar- und theologiegeschichtliche Diskurs der Urgeschichte* (Zürich: TVZ, 2006). And the monographs of Christoph Uehlinger, *Weltreich und «eine Rede»: Eine neue Deutung der sogenannten Turmbauerzählung (Gen 11, 1–9)*, OBO 101 (Freiburg: Universitätsverlag; Göttingen: Vandenhoeck & Ruprecht, 1990); LaCocque, *Captivity of Innocence*. A choice of other recent works includes: Ellen J. van Wolde, "The Tower of Babel as Lookout of Genesis 1–11," in *Words Become Worlds: Semantic Studies of Genesis 1–11*, BIS 6 (Leiden: Brill, 1994), 84–109; Thedore Hiebert, "The Tower of Babel and the Origin of World's Cultures," *JBL* 126 (2007): 29–58; Arie van der Kooij, "The City of Babel and Assyrian Imperialism: Genesis 11:1–9 Interpreted in the Light of the Mesopotamian Sources," in *Congress Volume Leiden 2004*, ed. André Lemaire, VTSup 109 (Leiden: Brill, 2006), 1–18; John Day, *From Creation to Babel: Studies in Genesis 1–11* (London: T&T Clark International, 2013), 166–88.
14 See van der Kooij, "City of Babel," 1–7; Day, *From Creation*, 166–70. An extensive redaction-historical hypothesis is found in Uehlinger, *Weltreich*. Yet, although earlier forms of this story may have existed, I agree with van der Kooij and Day that no coherent layers can be reconstructed from the text.
15 See Cassuto, *From Noah*, 232.
16 Scholarship is divided over whether the non-P strand continues in Genesis 12–50. For different views see Christoph Levin, *Der Jahwist*, FRLANT 157 (Göttingen: Vandenhoeck & Ruprecht, 1993); David M. Carr, *Reading the Fractures of Genesis: Historical and Literary Approaches* (Louisville: Westminster John Knox, 1996); Jan C. Gertz, "Babel im Rücken und das Land vor Augen: Anmerkungen zum Abschluss der Urgeschichte und zum Anfang der Erzählungen von den Erzeltern Israels," in *Die Erzväter in der Biblischen Tradition: Festschrift für Matthias Köckert*, ed. Anselm Hagedorn and Henrik Pfeiffer, BZAW 400 (Berlin: De Gruyter, 2009), 9–34; Ronald S. Hendel, "Is the 'J' Primeval Narrative an Independent Composition? A Critique of Crüsemann's 'Die Eigenständigkeit der Urgeschichte,'" in *The Pentateuch: International Perspectives on Current Research*, ed. Thomas B. Dozeman, Konrad Schmid, and Baruch J. Schwarz, FAT 78 (Tübingen: Mohr Siebeck, 2011), 181–205.
17 See especially Genesis 2–3 and Gen 6:1–4. Here I agree with interpreters as John Day and Ron Hendel. See Day, *From Creation*; Ron S. Hendel, "Genesis 1–11 and Its Mesopotamian Problem," in *Cultural Borrowings and Ethnic Appropriations in Antiquity*, ed. Erich Gruen (Stuttgart: Steiner, 2005), 23–36.

the story also contains a border-crossing. Humanity's fear to be spread out over the earth, leads to a "we-oriented action"[18]: "Come let *us* bake bricks ... come let *us* build *ourselves* a city and a tower ... and let *us* make a name for *ourselves*" (Gen 11:3–4). As often in our own world, it is fear that causes hubris.[19] The search for a name, the increased power of the humans (Gen 11:6), and the self-centered "we" of the builders (Gen 11:3–4) form a tread to YHWH. This 'we' is countered in the narrative by YHWH's emphatically formulated plural (Gen 11:5, 7) and descent. Hence, YHWH's (vertical) descent and horizontal dispersion show a rejection of the name-making and alleged vertical movement of the humans.

The importance of the motif of movement is not only emphasized by locating the descent of YHWH in the stylistic center of the story (Gen 11:5),[20] but also by the role granted to travelers in verses 2 and 9. Gen 11:2 contains a short itinerary introducing them: "And as they travelled eastward they found a valley in the land of Shinar and settled there." Although itineraries are often used to create a continuous narrative and have a bridge function,[21] this example leaves much to the imagination of the reader. The final part of Gen 11:2 is clear. The group of travelers is described as settling in a בקע, a valley or a plain, in the land Shinar (שנער), an equivalent for southern Mesopotamia or Babylonia. Yet, what about the first part of Gen 11:2: "and as they travelled eastward." Where did these people come from and what did their travelling look like? Three hints are provided by reading the verse in the larger context.

First, the root נסע, to travel, primarily occurs in narrative texts where temporary dwelling in tents may be assumed.[22] These unidentified travelers thus likely take up their belongings to settle elsewhere. The root נסע also relates their movement to that of the tent-dwelling patriarchs and the Israelites.[23] In the book of Genesis, the connection with the former stands out. Of the thirteen occurrences of the root (Gen 11:2; 12:9 twice; 13:3, 11; 20:1; 33:12, 17; 35:5,16, 21; 37:17; 46:1), this is the only attestation in the Primeval History. As Abraham and Jakob, these travelers take up their belongings and hit the road.

---

18 Van Wolde, "Tower of Babel," 97.
19 As noted by Day, the motif of hubris is present, but so is the emphasis on one place and the expressed fear of humanity. See Day, *From Creation*, 182–85.
20 Gen 11:5 is the center of the story in the concentric structure. See note 15.
21 See Amit, "Travel Narratives," 226.
22 This corresponds to the suggested meaning "to pull out tent pegs"; see *HALOT*, s.v. "נסע." Although נסע does not always denote a movement in which all belongings were taken (e.g., Gen 37:17; Exod 14:10, 19), most occurrences do and are related to the itineraries of the Israelites (e.g., Exod 12:37; 17:1; Num 9:18; 12:16; 33:3–48).
23 See the previous note. While this connection is certainly present from a synchronic perspective, also diachronic scholarship has related the occurrences of נסע in Gen 11:2, the patriarchal narratives, and the desert wanderings. See, for example, Levin, *Der Jahwist*, 128.

Second, in the remainder of Gen 11:2 the travelers are described as moving מקדם: "from the east" or "eastward." While the former is suggested by LXX and Vulgate, the latter is supported by all other occurrences of מקדם in the book of Genesis (Gen 2:8; 3:24; 12:8 twice; 13:11a, all non-P) and by the pattern of eastward movement attested in Gen 3:24; 4:16; 10:30 (all non-P). Additional support for this reading is provided by noting that מקדם contains a double entendre in Genesis 2–13. The designation is positive in Gen 2:8, signifying a location where YHWH walks and immortality could be found, but negative when suggesting exile from the place where YHWH dwells in Gen 3:24.[24] Similarly, Gen 12:8 describes an eastward movement by which Abraham prefigures the track of Jacob,[25] but Gen 13:10–11 represents a negative move eastward.[26] Here, Lot decides to move towards a land that looks like the garden of YHWH, but ends up near Sodom. From a synchronic perspective, the occurrence of מקדם in Gen 11:2 is sandwiched between Eden and Abraham and Lot, and may be interpreted with these passages in mind. Will the journey of the travelers be towards Eden or away from Eden? Will it look like that of Abraham or will it reflect Lot's desire to go to Eden, but end up in Sodom?[27]

Third, the location in the east (מקדם) is also part of a larger group of references in Genesis 1–11 that contain a Mesopotamian motif: the Garden in the East (Gen 2:8), the use of a version of the Mesopotamian flood story (Genesis 6–9), and the references to Mesopotamian cities (Gen 10:8–12).[28] While we return to the importance of this aspect in section 5, we note here that the eastward movement of Gen 11:2 does not imply a start in the west, but rather describes their destination. The movement מקדם, is a journey towards the cradle of civilization.

Having introduced the travelers in the, now dissected, Gen 11:2, the narrator grants them the role of construction workers in the main part of the narrative (Gen 11:3–9). Once identified as "humanity" (בני האדם) in Gen 11:5, these anonymous "they" (3pl verb) or "them" (3mp suffix), as they are coined in Gen 11:2–4, 6–9,

---

24 See for a discussion of some of these aspects Robin B. Ten Hoopen, "The Garden in Eden: A Holy Place?" in *Jerusalem and Other Holy Places as Foci of Multireligious and Ideological Confrontation*, ed. Pieter B. Hartog et al., JCP 37 (Leiden: Brill, 2021), 170–92.
25 See Gen 28:10–20; 35:1–7. For connections between the itineraries of Jacob and Abraham, see Matthias Köckert, "Wie wurden Abraham- und Jakobüberlieferung zu einer 'Vätergeschichte' verbunden?" *HEBAI* 3 (2014): 43–66.
26 In seven other cases קדם designates the east in the Book of Genesis. Gen 2:14 locates the Tigris east of Assyria. Gen 4:16 and 10:30 are part of the motif of eastward movement. Gen 13:14 and 28:14 contain the blessing of an extensive territory in all directions. Gen 25:6 and 29:1 refer to places where the relatives of Abraham and Jacob live.
27 We return to this aspect at pp. 24–26 below. I hope to work out the implications of these remarks for Genesis 11–13 in a future article.
28 See pp. 25–26 below and Hendel, "Genesis 1–11."

build the city and tower of Babel. Their vertical construction work evokes YHWH's vertical movement, leading to a renewed horizontal movement of humanity (Gen 11:8–9). In the end, the dispersion of humanity turns the construction workers into travelers again (Gen 11:9).

In sum, Genesis 11 refers to a group of unidentified travelers who turn into construction workers, but end up as travelers. Although their role as travelers may at first sight be marginal in a story dealing with the construction of a city and tower, the central role of the descent of YHWH in Gen 11:5 and the emphasis granted to horizontal and vertical movement (Gen 11:2, 5, 7–9) suggests that their identity as construction workers is transient or liminal. Starting of as unidentified travelers, they turn into dispersed travelers. Enough reason to take a closer look at the alleged identity of these travelers.

The Anonymous Travelers of Gen 11:2

In a 1966 article, Gerhard Wallis summarizes an common conclusion at the time by stating: "Die Notiz, daβ die Bewohner des mesopotamischen Tiefebene aus den ostwärts angrenzend Bergländern stammen, mag als bestätigt gelten."[29] The position that Wallis sees as commonly accepted, argued that the travelers of Gen 11:2 were nomadic mountain dwellers who settled on the Mesopotamian plain.[30] Most recently this position has been developed by anthropologists Karel van Schaik and Kai Michel in their *Good Book of Human Nature* as well as by Dutch geologist Salomon Kroonenberg in his *De Binnenplaats van Babel*.[31] By using evolutionary, geological, and anthropological insights, Kroonenberg for example suggests that the travelers of Genesis 11 are a group of hunter-gatherers who moved from the Zagros mountains to settle at the plain of Mesopotamia (between 6000–5500 BCE) and later build the city of Uruk in the 4th millennium BCE.[32] Thus assuming that Genesis 11 tells 2000 years history in one verse.

---

29 Gerhard Wallis, "Die Stadt in den Überlieferungen der Genesis," *ZAW* 78 (1966): 133–48 (141–42).
30 Note already Josephus, *A.J.* 1.109–10, who assumes that Noah's sons descended from the mountains to the plain.
31 Salomon Kroonenberg, *De binnenplaats van Babel: Het raadsel van de spraakverwarring* (Amsterdam: Atlas Contact, 2014), 25–26, 40–41; Carel van Schaik and Kai Michel, *The Good Book of Human Nature: An Evolutionary Reading of the Bible* (New York: Basic Books, 2016), 96–101.
32 Kroonenberg, *De binnenplaats van Babel*. See also van Schaik and Michel, *Evolutionary Reading*, 96. Similar suggestions have been coined by confessional scholars, e.g., John H. Walton, "The Mesopotamian Background of the Tower of Babel Account and Its Implications," *BBR* 5 (1995): 155–75.

The identification of the travelers as nomadic settlers is part of an extensive reception-history in which the protagonists of Genesis 11 have both been identified with a specific group and with humanity at large.[33] Suggestions for a specific group include Noah and his sons,[34] the Chamites[35] or Babelites lead by Nimrod,[36] and the generation of the dispersion.[37] In contrast, other voices in the reception historical choir, as well as most recent scholarship, have identified the travelers with all of humanity.[38] In their view, the subject of Gen 11:2 is the subject of Gen 11:1: "the whole earth" (כל־הארץ). Hence, when Gen 11:2 reads "as they travelled," this "they" is "the whole earth" or humanity as a whole.[39] The reference to the builders as humanity (בני האדם, 11:5) as well the motifs of the unity of languages (Gen 11:1) and one people (עם, Gen 11:6) certainly support the suggestion that all humanity was on the move in Gen 11:2.

Yet, although I agree that both the narrative as a whole and its current context in the Primeval History suggest that the travelers should be taken as the whole of humanity, this does not solve the question of their alleged identity. In fact, it asks for an answer on two questions:
1. Who could have been implied with 'all humanity'?
2. Why does the narrator refer to these travelers as "they" and "them"?

Two subsections aim to do answer these questions. Their goal is not to provide dogmatic answers, but rather to illustrate and explicate a more synchronic or contextual reading and a more diachronic reading of the text. While the former approach is found in literary or religious readings, the latter is primarily historical-critical.

---

33 I hope to provide a more extensive overview in a future article.
34 Jub. 10:19–36; Joseph., *AJ* 1.109–10.
35 See for example, Martin Luther, *Lectures on Genesis*, ed. Jaroslav Pelikan and Daniel E. Poellot, trans. George V. Schick, Luther's Works 2 (St. Louis: Concordia, 1960), 212, 216.
36 On the role of Nimrod see Karel van der Toorn and Pieter W. van der Horst, "Nimrod before and after the Bible," *HTR* 83 (1990): 1–29.
37 See Gen. Rab. 36:1; 38:1–9.
38 E.g., Jacob, *Genesis*, 297; Schüle, *Prolog*, 382; Gertz, "Babel," 27. The reading is already attested in the Targum Neofiti. Note also the identification with Noah and his sons (cf. n. 34), who are the assumed humanity from a narrative perspective.
39 See Uehlinger, *Weltreich*, 317. While ארץ is mostly feminine it is sometimes masculine and could be the subject of the 3pl. masculine verb and suffix in Gen 11:2. Note that כל־הארץ is also the subject of the (fem) verb נפץ/פוץ in Gen 9:19.

Who would have been implied with 'humanity'?

Here, I suggest to distinguish between a contextual reading and a diachronic reading of an older non-P version of the text.

In the larger context of the book of Genesis, the whole of humanity has either to be taken as the sons of Noah and some of their descendants, or a later generation of the descendants of Noah. This view is both attested in the earliest recensions of the story,[40] and amongst medieval interpreters as Ibn Ezra.[41] While the amount of people needed to build a large city likely presumes that Genesis 11 is set several generations after that of Noah's sons,[42] the combination of the genealogical remarks in Genesis 9–11 show that Noah and his sons would have been present if the building project was carried out before the birth of Abraham.[43] This implies that Genesis 11 either has to precede the table of nations of Genesis 10 in time, or assumes that the nations of Genesis 10 have joined themselves to be dispersed once again.[44] In both cases the identification of 'humanity' is the same: Noah, his sons, and their descendants.

A different outcome is reached when a diachronic approach is pursued. As noted above, Genesis 11 belongs to the non-P strand of the Primeval History. In the final version of Genesis 1–11, this strand has been combined with a Priestly strand.[45] Although the order in which these strands were broad together is highly contested, I have argued elsewhere that in my view the non-P strand preceded the priestly strand.[46] Hence, we may ask who would have been implied with all humanity in the non-P version of Genesis 1–11.

The answer depends on one's reconstruction of the textual history.[47] As stated above, I maintain that Gen 11:1–9 does not contain different redactions,[48] but was inserted as a whole in the current version of Genesis. Within the non-P version

---

40 Jub. 10:19–36; Joseph., *AJ* 1.109–10.
41 See Abraham ben Meir Ibn Ezra, *Ibn Ezra's Commentary on the Pentateuch*, trans. H. Norman Strickman and Arthur M. Silver (New York: Menorah, 1988), 137–38.
42 Hence, it does not surprise that some traditions have ascribed the building of Babel to giants, with the giant Nimrod (גבר or γίγας) as their leader. Their help would surely have speeded up the building.
43 See Ibn Ezra, *Commentary on the Pentateuch*, 137–38.
44 See on this already Joseph., *AJ* 1.109–10.
45 See for possible scenario's Carr, *Reading the Fractures*. And now David M. Carr, *The Formation of Genesis 1–11: Biblical and Other Precursors* (New York: Oxford University Press, 2020).
46 Ten Hoopen, "Genesis 5."
47 For different positions, see Hermann Gunkel, *Genesis: Übersetzt und erklärt*, 3rd ed., GHAT 1.1 (Göttingen: Vandenhoeck & Ruprecht, 1910), 92–96; Uehlinger, *Weltreich*, 318–23, 559; Gertz, "Babel."
48 See notes 13–14.

of the Primeval History, Genesis 11 likely preceded the non-P verses of Genesis 10 (Gen 10:8–19, 21, 25–30)[49] and followed upon the narrative of Noah's Vineyard (Gen 9:18–27).[50] This final non-P Primeval History thus either assumed a gap in time between the latter story and Genesis 11 (allowing for humanity to increase) or contained a short transition which has now been lost. Since this non-P version did (probably) not contain extensive genealogies, we cannot be certain whether Noah and his sons would have been involved in the building project. Yet since the non-P version of Genesis 10 would have dealt with Cham/Canaan and Shem, it may be assumed that the generation of the flood was still there. Hence, also in the final non-P version humanity would have existed of Noah and his descendants, although not identified as such.

Yet, we may even go a step further. As suggested by Reinhard Kratz, and followed in adjusted form by David Carr and John Day, it seems likely that an older version of the non-P narrative did not contain the story of the flood,[51] thus excluding the destruction of all humanity except for Noah and his sons.[52] This allows for a larger group of humans to be involved in the construction work. If I am correct that Genesis 11 was part of this earlier strand,[53] the travelers of Genesis 11 would have consisted of the humans originating from Gen 4:17–26* and Gen 6:1–4*, possibly including the mighty heroes of old (Gen 6:4).[54]

---

[49] Of which Gen 10:16–18a might be an addition. See Carr, *Reading the Fractures*, 161–63.
[50] Wellhausen already suggested that some parts of Gen 10 followed upon 11. Yet, he assumed that Gen 9:20–27 was from a later hand. See Julius Wellhausen, *Die Composition des Hexateuchs und der historischen Bücher des Alten Testaments*, 4th ed. (Berlin: De Gruyter, 1876), 12.
[51] Reinhard G. Kratz, *The Composition of the Narrative Books of the Old Testament*, trans. John Bowden (London: T&T Clark, 2005); Carr, *The Formation of Genesis 1–11*, 159–77; John Day, *From Creation to Abraham: Further Studies in Genesis 1–11* (London: Bloomsbury T&T Clark, 2021). Note already the discussion by Wellhausen, *Composition*, 10–12. I thank John Day for sharing and discussing some of his forthcoming work with me.
[52] In this earlier version of the strand, Gen 5:29 and the story of Noah and the Vineyard (Gen 9:20–28) were present but illustrated a focus on a particular protagonist and family, rather than on the mere survivor of the flood. The "whole earth" of Genesis 11 may have included Noah, but this remains uncertain. In any case, the use of נפץ/פוץ in Gen 9:19 may be seen as a connective thread after the insertion of the non-P Flood story to connect the flood, the story of the vineyard, and Genesis 11.
[53] Here I agree with John Day. Yet, note that Carr and Gertz hold that Genesis 11 is a later addition to either the Primeval History as a whole (Gertz) or to the non-P layer (Carr). Gertz, "Babel"; Carr, *The Formation of Genesis 1–11*. I hope to work out my views in a future article.
[54] The connections between Genesis 6 and 11 are well-known: the motif of border-crossing, the soliloquy of YHWH (Gen 6:3; 11:5–7), but also the motif of the name (Gen 6:4; 11:5–7). Most interesting for this chapter is the usage of בני האדם in Gen 11:5 and the בני האלהים and בנות האדם in Gen 6:1–4 to denote members of the species humanity (or divinity). If I am correct, the suggestion that giants helped to build Babel may even go back to earliest context of the story.

In sum, both in the final canonical text and in the final non-P version, the unspecified humanity of Genesis 11 existed of Noah, his sons, and his descendants.[55] In an older version, however, Genesis 11 was concerned with the whole of humanity, which may or may not have included Noah.[56] Finally, my diachronic reconstruction explains the lack of contextual references in Genesis 11 to the surrounding stories, its connections with Genesis 2–3 and Gen 6:1–4, and the focus on the whole of humanity in Gen 2–3; 4:17–26*; 6:1–4*; 11:1–9.

Why does the narrative contain so many references to "they" and "them"?

If the travelers of Genesis 11 are to be identified as the whole of humanity, why does the narrator only identify them once as such (in Gen 11:5), but prefers references to "they" and "them"? According to André LaCocque, the author (J) does so because he "wants his readers to realize that, among others things they participate in Babel's building."[57] While I agree with LaCocque that the anonymity of the text provides current readers with an opportunity to identify themselves with the travelers or construction workers, I doubt whether ancient authors would have provided such a mere open reading of the text in which the subject remains unclear. In my view, the use of "they" and "them" rather fits the agenda of the non-P strand in Genesis 1–11 and identifies the developing identity of these humans. My argument runs as follows.

First, the characters in the non-P strand are often paradigmatic or archetypical,[58] as is demonstrated by the strand's prominent use of etiologies (e.g., the enmity between serpent and humans) and the names given to the protagonists (e.g., Adam, Eve, Abel). Individual characters or groups are not merely individuals, but represent types, structures, or humans at large. This *double entendre* could also explain the unexplicit identity of the travelers. One the one hand, they are "the whole earth" implying both the concrete group and an archetype for humanity as such.

---

55 As noted, Gen 9:19 may suggest an identification between the sons of Noah and the travelers.
56 See note 52.
57 LaCocque, *Captivity of Innocence*, 21 (note also pp. 49, 70, 82).
58 These terms are also used by LaCoque, *Captivity of Innocence*, 69–75. Yet he suggests an intended ambiguity without concrete protagonists.

On the other hand, they are "them" or "they," a specific group of humans living at the narrated time.[59]

Second, their designation as "they" and "them" may emphasize their developing identity. These travelers, turned into construction workers to become travelers again, are not yet a clear people with a home. In order to become such a people, they need to move to Babel and then move on to leave Babel again. Hence, the use of "they" and "them" may emphasize their liminality or transience. They are not yet who they will become.

Why Travel to Babel? The Travelers as Nomads, Exiles, or Theological Constructs of Identity Formation

Having shown that travel is an important motif in Genesis 11 and that the itinerary of the whole of humanity towards Babel leads to another journey, we may now ask why humanity travels to Babel to leave the city again? Does their movement reflect a nomadic motif that aims to criticize city life, as suggested by several authors?[60] Does it reflect the exile and the dispersion of the Israelites as others have suggested?[61] Or is an alternative reading more likely?

Although there is certainly reason to assume a critical perspective on city life in the book of Genesis,[62] Genesis 11 nor the book of Genesis as a whole presents a general conflict between city life and nomadic life in my view. I will elaborate my critique on this view in three points.

---

59 In this sense the story may contain a notion of "othering" that is also attested in the reception history which identified the Babelites as the nations, or even sinners. See the start of this section. Yet, note that this othering is compensated by the role of humanity at large and the emphatic use of "us" in verses 3–4.
60 E.g. Wallis, "Die Stadt." See also Walton, "Tower of Babel"; Van Schaik and Michel, *Evolutionary Reading*. See recently Arie C. Leder, "'There He Built an Altar to the Lord' (Gen 12:8): City and Altar Building in Genesis," *OTE* 32 (2019): 58–83. A contrast between the settling of the travelers and the sojourning of the patriarchs had already been noted by Philo, *Conf.* 76-82.
61 See for example, Schüle, *Prolog*; LaCocque, *Captivity of Innocence*.
62 The city is often related to images of violence (Gen 4:17–24; 18–19) and of a closed society with fear for others (Gen 11; 18–19). Yet note that in Gen 10:8–12 cities have a positive or neutral function. Also, the city of Cain (Gen 4:17) does not have to be framed negatively. This frame is derived from Cain's fratricide (Gen 4:1–16).

First, the alleged contrast between nomads and city-dwellers often depends on the idea that Abraham and the patriarchs were akin to the Arabian nomads known from oral traditions and anthropological studies. Yet, the patriarchs combine farming and herding (a mixed-economy), have clear residences, and are in contact with cities, not living an isolated life.[63]

Second, more important for a rejection of the view that the book of Genesis elevated nomadic life are the reasons for travelling. In the non-P narrative, the itinerary to Canaan does not reflect a nomadic desire for wandering, but rather a divine calling (Gen 12:1–4a; 13:17). Moreover, the shorter itineraries in the book of Genesis are concerned with cult sites or locations that play a large part in later biblical narratives.[64] Abraham's travels to the area of Bethel (Gen 12:8–9) and Egypt (Gen 12:10ff) are related to the Northern Empire and the Exodus from Egypt. Hence, the patriarchal narratives do not tell the story of nomads but of the Israelites, incorporated in Abraham as corporate personality. These Israelites are called by YHWH to became a people that needs to travel before it reaches their destination. So even though Abraham moves away from cities (Ur and Haran), he does so in order to follow the voice of his deity, not to become a nomad. In the words of theologian Miroslav Volf, "departure is here a temporary state, not an end in itself."[65]

Third, as suggested in section 3, the short itinerary of Genesis 11 does not contrast the itineraries of the patriarchs, but rather prefigures them. Similarly, the movement towards Babel can be related to the patriarchal crossing of the promised land to visit the places that would become central to Israel's history: Egypt and Bethel. While Abraham prefigures the narrative of Jacob, Joseph, and the Israelites by stopping in Egypt and Bethel (Gen 12:1–20), the whole of humanity in Genesis 11 heads to Mesopotamia, the other place so central to Israel's identity. Yet, it leaves Babel not because the narrator despises city life (although he might have done) and wants humanity to become nomads, but to illustrate humanity's spreading out over the earth and get the journey to Canaan going. It is in Canaan where Abraham will settle and where YHWH will be involved with his people. Hence, it is Canaan that Abraham does not build to make a name for himself, but builds an altar to call on the name of YHWH (Gen 12:8; 13:18).[66]

---

[63] Hendel, "J Primeval Narrative," 193–95; Amit, "Travel Narratives," 232.
[64] Hendel, "J Primeval Narrative," 194; Amit, "Travel Narratives," 232–35.
[65] Miroslav Volf, *Exclusion and Embrace: A Theological Exploration of Identity, Otherness, and Reconciliation* (Nashville, TN: Abingdon Press, 1996), 40.
[66] Leder, "City and Altar Building." Yet in contrast to Leder, I do not think that this illustrates the contrast between city and altar, but rather between Babel and promised land as set out below.

According to other scholars, the dispersion from Babel prefigures the exile and even the (desire for) diaspora.[67] If accepted, this interpretation could provide the ancient Israelites with a model of identification and contrast for their own journey. The exiles found themselves on the road to Babel and later left it to spread out over the face of the earth, some returning to Israel (as Abraham), others settling in other places. Yet, although the exiles may even have contributed to building projects, they were in bonds and did not come to make a name for their themselves, but were taken to a foreign empire to contribute to its reputation. Depending on the alleged dating of Genesis such a reading can either be seen as reception-historical or historical. In my view, a reception-historical connection is more probable. Not only do I think the non-P stories date to the pre-exilic period,[68] it also seems unlikely to me that an Israelite author presents humanity, including Israel, as constructing Babel after having faced the trauma of the exile through the hands of the Babylonians.[69] Hence, although the journey towards Mesopotamia and dispersion from Babel could have been imaginable for businessman and members of the royal court, I do not think that it was drawn up to reflect the exile.

Yet, if the journeys of Genesis 11 do not reflect a tension between nomads and city dwellers nor a prefiguration of the exile, what do they reflect? Following the lead of Ronald Hendel, I suggest they reflect the identity of the Israelites. As noted in section 3 and set out more fully by Hendel, the non-P narratives of Genesis 1–11 show a tendency to found Israel's history in Mesopotamia, but also provide a counternarrative to what can be seen as "the Mesopotamian Primeval History."[70] The location in the east (Gen 2:8), the use of the Mesopotamian flood story, the references to Mesopotamian cities in Gen 10:8–12, and the reference to Shinar and Babel are all part of an encompassing strategy to provide an identity for the Israelites

---

67 See for example Schüle, *Prolog*; LaCocque, *Captivity of Innocence*.
68 See for the dating of Genesis 11 (and the whole J source or non-P strand of Primeval History) to the Neo-Assyrian Period van der Kooij, "City of Babel"; Day, *From Creation*, 48–49; Ron Hendel and Jan Joosten, *How Old Is the Hebrew Bible: A Linguistic, Textual, and Historical Study*, AYBRL (New Haven: Yale University Press, 2018), 108–13.
69 The knowledge of Mesopotamian construction work is well-attested throughout the Ancient Near East and does not have to derive from personal experience. While the location and the dispersion may remind of the exilic period, both can be explained otherwise. As for the location, the choice for Babel was part of a larger strategy enfolded below. As for the dispersion, it fits the etiological focus of non-P and concerns the whole world and not merely the Israelites. In my view, a date for Genesis 11 to the exilic or post-exilic period can thus only be considered convincing on other grounds, while a reading as suggested below makes most sense in the Neo-Babylonian or Neo-Assyrian period.
70 See Hendel, "Genesis 1–11," 24–25.

by making them part of a humanity that originated in Mesopotamia, the cradle of civilization.

Yet, at the same time, these stories create a counter narrative through the subversion of the Mesopotamian notion of the ascent from nature to culture.[71] Genesis 11 functions to close this motif. While Babel was considered the summum of what humanity could reach from a Mesopotamian perspective, the biblical authors use it to tell their story of the dispersion of humanity and the confusion of the languages. Hence, the journey to Shinar is in Genesis 11 primarily theological and sociological. Babel is not depicted negatively because it was a city nor because it was related to the exile, but to mock its status as imperial center of the world and contrast it to promised land. Babel is the transient place for a pre-Abrahamic humanity that will be dispersed to allow Abraham, and the Israelites, to enter the stage.[72] This motif is further developed in the role of YHWH as travelling deity in Genesis 11.

A Travelling Humanity and a Travelling Deity

As noted above, not only humans but also YHWH is depicted as travelling in the book of Genesis. Having been described as walking in the Garden in Eden (Gen 3:8), Gen 11:5–7 tells how YHWH, and his heavenly court, descend(s) to see[73] the tower and the city,[74] turning YHWH into a traveler. While both ancient and modern commentators have felt unease with this movement of God,[75] the non-P author and many of his Ancient Near Eastern colleagues clearly had no problem presenting a deity as a traveler between heaven and earth.[76]

---

[71] Hendel, "Genesis 1–11," 29. For an illustration of this motif see tablets I–IV of the SB Gilgamesh Epic.
[72] See for a modern discussion of transient places and their importance Alain de Botton, *The Art of Travel*, (London: Penguin, 2003).
[73] Either in the sense of "inspect" or "to notify himself about." Also often read as an anachronistic remark: YHWH having to descend to see the tower with its head into the heavens.
[74] Two other passages might be relevant here. In Gen 18:21–22, YHWH announces in language similar to Genesis 11 that he will descend to Sodom and Gomorrah (ירד and ראה, but 1cs). In Gen 28:12–13, God's messengers descend (and go up) on the stairs near Bethel while YHWH stands next to Jacob in his dream.
[75] Philo, *Conf.* 134–139; Cassuto, *From Noah*, 247. But see Jub. 10:23 where both YHWH and his angels descend. The observation that the descent motif is a stylistic way to mock the tower's top into heaven, does not contradict my point.
[76] Note for example, Genesis 18, 32; Exod 33:18–23. Yet other Biblical authors certainly did have problems with these assumptions. See the fine discussion of the bodies of God in Mark S. Smith, "The Three Bodies of God in the Hebrew Bible," *JBL* 134 (2015): 471–88. In Ancient Near Eastern

The importance of YHWH's travel for the narrative of Genesis 11, can be illustrated by following the common view that the tower of Babel represented a ziqqurrat.[77] Although the exact function of the ziqqurrat remains unknown, it is assumed to be a temple tower which functioned as stairs between the cosmic regions of heaven, earth, and the netherworld. The deity descended these stairs to enjoy a meal at the top of the ziqqurrat.[78] Hence, its function was not to create a way for humans to go up, but a place for gods to come down. While most exegetes assume this view was mocked or neglected in Genesis 11, John Walton has argued that the intention of the building project was exactly to bring YHWH down to earth.[79] Walton's view provides an interesting perspective on the notion of travel. If the intention of the builders was to bring YHWH down to earth, they aimed to reside together with him in Babel to receive his divine protection. Yet, when YHWH descends, he does not intend to dwell in Babel, but rather comes to visit and disperse humanity. In this way, illustrating that YHWH is not to be limited to one place, especially not to Babel, but prefers movement. Yet, even when Walton is wrong and the builders did want to reach heaven, the "centripetal uniformity" in which tower and city function like a "beehive,"[80] stills contrasts YHWH's act of dispersion. Hence, in either reading, movement is the medicine against cessation. Humanity needs to move in order to open up the story of Abraham and his travel to the land of Canaan.[81]

In sum, Genesis 11 presents YHWH as the moving and travelling deity of all humanity who prefers movement above cessation in Babel. This "universalistic" outlook emphasizes that YHWH is the God of all the earth. Although YHWH creates vertical borders, he opens up horizontal horizons. These horizons are invitations to travel, especially in the direction of the promised land.

---

texts, traveling deities are broadly attested. In narrative texts, deities could for example travel to visit humans or fellow deities. Also, the practice of "godnap," the removal and return of divine statues, has been interpreted as a form of divine travel. In the Marduk Prophecy, for example, Marduk himself tells how he traveled to Hatti to establish trade routes between the Hittites and Babylon. See for the latter Erika D. Johnson, "Time and Again: Marduk's Travels," in *Time and History in the Ancient Near East: Proceedings of the 56th Rencontre Assyriologique Internationale at Barcelona 26-30 July 2010*, ed. Lluís Feliu et al. (Winona Lake, IN: Eisenbrauns, 2013), 113–16.

77 For discussion see Day, *From Creation*, 171–75.
78 See Claus Ambos, "Ziqqurrat A," *RlA* 15 5/6:323–25.
79 Walton, "Tower of Babel."
80 LaCocque, *Captivity of Innocence*, 53.
81 It is possible to relate this remark to the priestly blessing to fill the earth (Gen 1:28; 9:1). Yet, note that the contrast between fear and YHWH's plans is already present in Genesis 11.

Towards a Conclusion: The Travelers, Transient Places, and Genesis 1–11

My contribution has focused on the role of travel in Gen 11:1–9. Having illustrated the importance of the motif of movement in this story, I have argued that the human itinerary towards Babel is to be taken as a theological journey that founds Israel's history in Mesopotamia. In contrast, the divine descent of the universal Israelite deity YHWH depreciates Babel's role as the center of the world. It stops human's cessation in Babel and allows for human dispersion from this alleged center. This motif of movement over cessation is buttressed by the role of the travelers in Gen 11:2, 9. In Gen 11:2, their image is quickly painted. There is no need to inform us on how they anticipated their journey, who they met on the road, or even how the experience changed them, they merely need to arrive in Shinar. Yet, what seemed to be the destination, turns out to be a transient place. In liminal Babel, the construction workers turn again into travelers when YHWH descends. Not to become nomads or the move away from city life as such, but rather to spread out over the earth in order for a new journey to begin: the itinerary towards the promised land. Starting of as travelers in Gen 11:2, their journey continues in Gen 11:9 and will be resumed in the remainder of the book of Genesis.

Having showed how a focus on movement and travel contributes to a new understanding of Genesis 11, I conclude with a short reflection on what this story may teach modern travelers. Let me start by noting some similarities and differences between modern notions of travel and Genesis 11. The experiences described in Genesis 11 are comparable to modern experiences in that travelers learned a new language, lost something they had when they started, found a new identity, and hoped that their deity or protective spirit would join them on the road and at their destination. They are incomparable in that this journey was merely a tool to reach a destination, while modern reflection emphasizes the importance of the journey itself, sometimes even above the destination.[82] Moreover, the itinerary of Genesis 11 is incomparable in that humans were dispersed by YHWH and could not understand each other anymore. The latter aspects show that this travel story rightly belongs to the Primeval History. It both concerns the world we live in and the world that came before this world.

From a normative perspective, the itinerary of Genesis 11 illustrates that travel is an important way for humans to construct and develop an identity, as a group

---

82 In Genesis 11, the emphasis is on movement, but the in- and outsights of journey itself are of no interest to the narrator. See for (a critical discussion of) this modern insight, but above all a fine book on why we travel and how we might be more fulfilled in doing so De Botton, *The Art of Travel*.

and as an individual. On an ecological note, this story teaches that journeys do not have to be by plain and can even be imaginary to still have (this) impact. While the climate crisis has pressed these issues for the last decades, the Covid-19 pandemic both illustrates what is possible without regular long-distance travelling as well as the importance of short journeys, or at least a stroll or a hike, to keep a balanced life.[83] In the end, these current insights may be very similar to those from the biblical stories. Travel is necessary for a human being, but a plain does not have to bring us to the other side of the world to help develop our identity, find food, or love. Especially when an intended journey contributes to a world where power is conglomerated and resources not equally shared, Genesis 11 may suggest to reconsider it.

References

Ambos, Claus. "Ziqqurrat A." Pages 323–25 in vol. 15 5/6 of *RlA*. 16 vols. Berlin: De Gruyter, 2017.
Amit, Yairah. "Travel Narratives and the Message of Genesis." Pages 223–42 in *The Formation of the Pentateuch: Bridging the Academic Cultures of Europe, Israel, and North America*. Edited by Jan C. Gertz, Bernard M. Levinson, Dalit Rom-Shiloni, and Konrad Schmid. FAT 111. Tübingen: Mohr Siebeck, 2016.
Blum, Erhard. *Studien zur Komposition des Pentateuch*. BZAW 189. Berlin: De Gruyter, 1990.
Carr, David M. *Reading the Fractures of Genesis: Historical and Literary Approaches*. Louisville, KY: Westminster John Knox, 1996.
Carr, David M. *The Formation of Genesis 1–11: Biblical and Other Precursors*. New York: Oxford University Press, 2020.
Cassuto, Umberto. *A Commentary on the Book of Genesis: Part II: From Noah to Abraham: Genesis VI 9–XI 32*. Translated by Isaac Abrahams. Jerusalem: Magnes Press, 1964.
Day, John. *From Creation to Babel: Studies in Genesis 1–11*. London: Bloomsbury T&T Clark, 2013.
Day, John. *From Creation to Abraham: Further Studies in Genesis 1–11*. London: Bloomsbury T&T Clark, 2021.
De Botton, Alain. *The Art of Travel*. London: Penguin, 2003.
Ellens, J. Harold, and Wayne G. Rollins, eds. *Psychology and the Bible: From Genesis to Apocalyptic Vision*. Westport, CT: Praeger Publishers, 2004.
Gertz, Jan C. "Babel im Rücken und das Land vor Augen: Anmerkungen zum Abschluss der Urgeschichte und zum Anfang der Erzählungen von den Erzeltern Israels." Pages 9–34 in *Die Erzväter in der Biblischen Tradition: Festschrift für Matthias Köckert*. Edited by Anselm Hagedorn and Henrik Pfeiffer. BZAW 400. Berlin: De Gruyter, 2009.
Gunkel, Hermann. *Genesis: Übersetzt und erklärt*. 3rd ed. GHAT 1.1. Göttingen: Vandenhoeck & Ruprecht, 1910.

---

[83] As in many countries, the government in the Netherlands allowed only "necessary traveling" for several months in 2020.

Hendel, Ron, and Jan Joosten. *How Old Is the Hebrew Bible: A Linguistic, Textual, and Historical Study*. AYBRL. New Haven: Yale University Press, 2018.

Hendel, Ronald S. "Genesis 1–11 and Its Mesopotamian Problem." Pages 23–36 in *Cultural Borrowings and Ethnic Appropriations in Antiquity*. Edited by E. Gruen. Stuttgart: Steiner, 2005.

Hendel, Ronald S. "Is the 'J' Primeval Narrative an Independent Composition? A Critique of Crüsemann's 'Die Eigenständigkeit der Urgeschichte.'" Pages 181–205 in *The Pentateuch: International Perspectives on Current Research*. Edited by Thomas B. Dozeman, Konrad Schmid, and Baruch J. Schwarz. FAT 78. Tübingen: Mohr Siebeck, 2011.

Hiebert, Theodore. "The Tower of Babel and the Origin of World's Cultures." *JBL* 126 (2007): 29–58.

Ibn Ezra, Abraham ben Meir. *Ibn Ezras Commentary on the Pentateuch*. Translated by H. Norman Strickman and Arthur M. Silver. New York: Menorah, 1988.

Jacob, Benno. *Das erste Buch der Tora: Genesis*. Berlin: Schocken, 1934.

Johnson, Erica D. "Time and Again: Marduk's Travels." Pages 113–16 in *Time and History in the Ancient Near East: Proceedings of the 56th Rencontre Assyriologique Internationale at Barcelona 26–30 July 2010*. Edited by Lluís Feliu, Jaume Llop, Adelina Millet-Albà, and Joaquín Sanmartín. Winona Lake, IN: Eisenbrauns, 2013.

Köckert, Matthias. "Wie wurden Abraham- und Jakobüberlieferung zu einer „Vätergeschichte" verbunden?" *HEBAI* 3 (2014): 43–66.

Kooij, Arie van der. "The City of Babel and Assyrian Imperialism: Genesis 11:1–9 Interpreted in the Light of the Mesopotamian Sources." Pages 1–18 in *Congress Volume Leiden 2004*. Edited by André Lemaire. VTSup 109. Leiden: Brill, 2006.

Kratz, Reinhard G. *The Composition of the Narrative Books of the Old Testament*. Translated by John Bowden. London: T&T Clark, 2005.

Kroonenberg, Salomon. *De binnenplaats van Babel: Het raadsel van de spraakverwarring*. Amsterdam: Atlas Contact, 2014.

LaCocque, André. *The Captivity of Innocence: Babel and the Yahwist*. Eugene, OR: Cascade Books, 2010.

Leder, Arie C. "'There He Built an Altar to the Lord' (Gen 12:8): City and Altar Building in Genesis." *OTE* 32 (2019): 58–83.

Levin, Christoph. *Der Jahwist*. FRLANT 157. Göttingen: Vandenhoeck & Ruprecht, 1993.

Luther, Martin. *Lectures on Genesis*. Edited by Jaroslav Pelikan and Daniel E. Poellot. Translated by George V. Schick. Luther's Works 2. St. Louis: Concordia, 1960.

Mann, Thomas. *Joseph und seine Brüder: Vier Romane in einem Band*. 6th ed. Frankfurt am Main: S. Fischer, 2007.

Schaik, Carel van, and Kai Michel. *The Good Book of Human Nature: An Evolutionary Reading of the Bible*. New York: Basic Books, 2016.

Schüle, Andreas. *Der Prolog der hebräischen Bibel: Der literar- und theologiegeschichtliche Diskurs der Urgeschichte*. Zürich: TVZ, 2006.

Smith, Mark S. "The Three Bodies of God in the Hebrew Bible." *JBL* 134 (2015): 471–88.

Ten Hoopen, Robin B. "Genesis 5 and the Formation of the Primeval History: A Redaction Historical Case Study." *ZAW* 129 (2017): 177–93.

Ten Hoopen, Robin B. "Where Are You, Enoch? Why Can't I Find You? Genesis 5:21–24 Reconsidered." *JHS* 18.4 (2018): 1–24.

Ten Hoopen, Robin B. "The Garden in Eden: A Holy Place?" Pages 170–92 in *Jerusalem and Other Holy Places as Foci of Multireligious and Ideological Confrontation*. Edited by Pieter B. Hartog, Shulamit Laderman, Vered Tohar, and Archibald L.H.M. van Wieringen. JCP 37. Leiden: Brill, 2021.

Toorn, Karel van der, and Pieter W. van der Horst. "Nimrod before and after the Bible." *HTR* 83 (1990): 1–29.

Uehlinger, Christoph. *Weltreich und «eine Rede»: Eine neue Deutung der sogenannten Turmbauerzählung (Gen 11, 1–9)*. OBO 101. Freiburg: Universitätsverlag; Göttingen: Vandenhoeck & Ruprecht, 1990.
Vogels, Walter. "Enoch Walked with God and God Took Enoch." *Theoforum* 34 (2003): 283–303.
Volf, Miroslav. *Exclusion and Embrace: A Theological Exploration of Identity, Otherness, and Reconciliation*. Nashville, TN: Abingdon Press, 1996.
Wallis, Gerhard. "Die Stadt in den Überlieferungen der Genesis." *ZAW* 78 (1966): 133–48.
Walton, John H. "The Mesopotamian Background of the Tower of Babel Account and Its Implications." *BBR* 5 (1995): 155–75.
Wellhausen, Julius. *Die Composition des Hexateuchs und der historischen Bücher des Alten Testaments*. 4th ed. Berlin: De Gruyter, 1876.
Wenham, Gordon J. *Genesis 1–15*. WBC 1. Dallas, TX: Word, 1987.
Westermann, Claus. *Genesis 1–11*. BKAT I/1. Neukirchen-Vluyn: Neukirchener Verlag, 1974.
Wolde, Ellen J van. "The Tower of Babel as Lookout of Genesis 1–11." Pages 84–109 in *Words Become Worlds: Semantic Studies of Genesis 1–11*. BIS 6. Leiden: Brill, 1994.

Christoph Jedan
The Consolations of Travel: Reading Seneca's *Ad Marciam* vis-à-vis Paul of Tarsus

Abstract: The chapter compares the use of travel vocabulary and imagery in Seneca, with a specific focus on the *Ad Marciam*, and Paul. It also discusses comparative methodology. Two extended travel narratives take a surprising space in Seneca's *Ad Marciam* (nearly a fifth of the text), while there is a surprising scarcity of travel vocabulary in Paul. The chapter argues that we cannot explain this difference by interpreting Paul as mostly interested in the journeys of "the inner human being" and Seneca as mostly interested in the "superficially visible." It explains the key role of the two travel narratives in the context of Seneca's consolatory project, aimed at the spiritual transformation of his addressee. The chapter argues for a properly contextualized, bi-directional comparative strategy, which investigates not only the underpinning world views that might lead to contrasting motifs and concepts, but also how different concepts and theories fulfil comparable functions in the context of different world views. In this vein the chapter points to fundamental differences between Seneca and Paul regarding the nature and scope of cosmic permanence and human immortality, but also to differences between Seneca's and Paul's axiologies, as factors determining the relative neglect of travel motifs in Paul compared to Seneca. The structure of Paul's overall theology and mission allow us to understand why he tends to avoid travel metaphors, since they aggregate positive and negative aspects of travel. Paul "offloads" the negative aspects of travelling on to the word field of "work," and is thus able to address his communities with a more positive, flattering message than could be achieved with the word field of "travel."

A comparative reading of Seneca's *Ad Marciam* vis-à-vis the Pauline epistles on the theme of travel is not entirely new. In his wide-ranging *Tria Corda* lectures at the University of Jena, New Testament scholar Knut Backhaus has taken first steps towards such a comparison. The main motif behind his (cursory) discussion is the fact that in Paul's writings travel metaphors are scarce or "underdeveloped" ("nicht ausgeprägt").[1] Given the importance of travel in Paul's life, this is a fact in need of explanation. Backhaus suggests that Paul was not interested in "outward travel" ("die äußere Reise") but in the journeys of the inner human being; he was not interested in the "superficially visible," but the true home of the baptized

---

[1] Knut Backhaus, *Religion als Reise: Intertextuelle Lektüren in Antike und Christentum* (Tübingen: Mohr Siebeck, 2014).

(Phil 3:20). In Paul, the individual journey in this world is no more than necessary toil; it is characterized by "nomadism." By implication, the reader is led to believe that Seneca would have to be located at the opposite, unflattering extreme: only concerned with the superficially visible, with this-worldly experience, and not at all with the inner human being. Such an interpretation, however, is implausible, since it does not allow us to understand how Stoicism could have been a viable contender of the nascent Christian movement in the religio-philosophical market place.[2] It runs the risk of defending a questionable *interpretatio Christiana* of Stoicism that precludes rather than aids fuller understanding of the context of early Christian writings.

In this chapter I offer an alternative reading of Seneca vis-à-vis Paul that contributes to ongoing efforts at comparing the two authors.[3] However, the focus of my discussion is on strategy as much as on content. At stake is, ultimately, how we conduct comparison as an interpretive tool. The discussion proceeds in five steps: (1) A brief introduction of the background to and content of the *Ad Marciam* will establish the surprising importance of the theme of travel, especially in two extended "travel narratives" that account for nearly a fifth of the whole text. I shall then offer an interpretation of those two travel narratives, already looking across the fence at Pauline theology (2) and (3). This is followed (4) by suggestions for an interpretation of Paul centring on the remarkable scarcity of travel motifs in a narrow sense. Finally (5), I shall offer a brief discussion of comparative strategy, centring on comparison as bi-directional, reflective interpretation.

Context and Content of the *Ad Marciam*

It may be useful to begin our discussion with a few remarks on the context and content of the *Ad Marciam*. The *Ad Marciam* is a consolation and such texts seem to have become culturally quite alien to us today. We tend to look with some suspicion at the argumentative thrust of consolations, their attempt to reason the bereaved into less extreme forms of mourning and towards a constructive engagement with their lives without the deceased. Against the background of such an attitude of suspicion it is understandable that even philologists, who are supposed to be the

---

[2] See Christoph Jedan, "Antike Philosophie als Gegenstand religionswissenschaftlicher Analyse: Plädoyer für eine neue Historiographie," *Journal of Ethics in Antiquity and Christianity* 1 (2019): 55–69.
[3] See most recently Joseph R. Dodson and David E. Briones, eds., *Paul and Seneca in Dialogue* (Leiden: Brill, 2017).

guardians of ancient culture, have sometimes responded with undisguised ridicule to the *Ad Marciam*.[4] To prevent misunderstanding: I am by no means suggesting to simply ignore such feelings of uneasiness. As it will turn out, they may be useful heuristically, allowing us to understand something important about the difficulties of writing a consolation. As Seneca's text will show (see below on *Marc.* 16.8), he must have been painfully aware of similar reservations against consolations, and tries to achieve his goal of comforting his addressee in spite of them.

The circumstances of Seneca's addressee can be reconstructed from the text.[5] Marcia is a Roman noblewoman, the daughter of Roman senator and historian Cremutius Cordus. In 25 CE Cordus had felt obliged to commit suicide because he had snubbed emperor Tiberius' henchman Sejanus. He either could not or would not mend fences and he clearly wanted to avoid being executed for treason with the concomitant public disgrace of his family. In this situation, suicide appears to have been the best way out. After his death, Cordus' historical works were ordered to be burnt. His daughter Marcia must have been remarkably resilient. As soon as the political tide turned (early in Caligula's reign), she republished her father's works from a few hidden copies. However, she was hit by disaster again. Her second son Metilius, then a young adult, died prematurely. Grief-stricken, Marcia was unable to reengage with her surroundings. Marcia was three years into that debilitating form of mourning, when Seneca wrote his consolation for her.

It is notoriously difficult to give an exact date for the latter events and for the composition of *Ad Marciam*,[6] but the most likely scenario is that the text was written at some point between 37 and 41 CE.[7] The ascension of Caligula in 37 CE is a reasonable *terminus post quem* since the republication of Cordus' works mentioned

---

[4] See e.g., Johann F. Schinnerer, Über Senecas Schrift an Marcia: Programm der Königlichen Studienanstalt Hof für das Schuljahr 1888/89 (Hof: Mintzel 1889), 18: "Eine so beschaffene Schrift, deren Verfasser nur darauf ausgeht zu täuschen und eine Menge gelehrten Stoffes aufzutischen, dürfte wenig geeignet sein, ein niedergeschlagenes Herz aufzurichten." Another example is Marcus Wilson, "Seneca the Consoler? A New Reading of his Consolatory Writings," in Greek and Roman Consolations: Eight Studies of a Tradition and its Afterlife, ed. Han Baltussen (Swansea: The Classical Press of Wales, 2013), 93–121.
[5] In the following, I use L.D. Reynolds' OCT edition of Seneca's dialogues. Translations are my own, unless stated otherwise.
[6] Proposed dates vary enormously: Jane Bellemore argues for a date between 34 and 37 CE, and thus during the late reign of Tiberius, on account of rather positive mentions of Tiberius in the *Ad Marciam* that serve to curry favor with the emperor. Léon Herrmann, by contrast, has suggested a date after February 62 CE, at a time when Seneca had fallen out of Nero's grace and had ample time for writing: Léon Herrmann, "La date de la Consolation à Marcia," *REA* 31 (1929): 21–28.
[7] For overviews of Seneca's life see Miriam Griffin, *Seneca: A Philosopher in Politics* (Oxford: Oxford University Press, 1976) and Emily Wilson, *Seneca: A Life* (New York: Oxford University Press, 2014).

in the text seems to have depended on a regime change. Also, thematically, the *Ad Marciam* has much in common with the first two books of *De ira*, clearly among Seneca's early extant writings.[8] Seneca's exile in 41 CE is a reasonable *terminus ante quem*, since the text seems to suggests that at the time of writing, Seneca and Marcia are both in Rome (*Marc.* 16.2).[9] Internal evidence would suggest, moreover, that a late date within the window 37–41 CE is more likely: we have to square the text conveying the impression of Marcia still being a rather young woman at the time of her father's death with the report that Metilius, who had died very young, was already the father of two children. To accommodate all of this on a timeline, a late date for the *Ad Marciam* is preferable. Moreover, even if this is highly speculative, a date late in the window 37–41 CE would provide Seneca with powerful additional motives for writing to Marcia, above and beyond the likelihood of Seneca's feeling genuine sympathy for her. Seneca seems to know quite a bit about Marcia and her family history, their paths may even have crossed. The relationship between Marcia and her son Metilius had been such that Marcia had done a lot to advance Metilius' public career. Seneca must have felt in a similar position as Metilius, because for years he was looked after by his aunt in Egypt. Upon their return to Rome his aunt helped Seneca to launch his career. Also, at the time of writing the *Ad Marciam* Seneca's own father had recently died, a historian and writer just as Marcia's father. While a genuine feeling of sympathy thus need not be doubted, against the background of all those similarities and connections, a date close to Seneca's own exile— at a time when he could already feel the net of prosecution closing on him for the supposed adultery with Julia Livilla, the sister of Caligula and niece of Claudius— would suggest two additional powerful motives for writing the text: (1) The feeling of personal danger would have increased Seneca's sense that Cordus, who had been hunted down in the power struggles during Tiberius' reign, had experienced a predicament similar to his own. (2) The writing of a consolation might project an image of Seneca as a (sexually) disinterested and legitimate *confidant* of highly placed Roman women, an especially attractive role to adopt in those circumstances.

Be that as it may, Seneca's interest in offering a genuine and intellectually credible consolation based on broader cultural conventions as well as his own Stoic convictions need not be doubted on account of those additional motives. In what

---

[8] See, e.g., Janine Fillion-Lahille, "La production littéraire de Sénèque sous les règnes de Caligula et de Claude, sens philosophique et portée politique: Les 'Consolations' et le 'De ira'," in *Teilband Philosophie, Wissenschaften, Technik. Philosophie (Stoizismus)*, ed. Wolfgang Haase, ANRW 36/3 (Berlin: De Gruyter, 1989), 1606–38.

[9] *Pace* C.W. Marshall, "The Works of Seneca the Younger and their Dates," in *Brill's Companion to Seneca: Philosopher and Dramatist*, ed. Andreas Heil and Gregor Damschen (Leiden: Brill, 2014), 33–44.

follows, I shall focus on the consolatory purpose of the *Ad Marciam*. In light of this consolatory purpose, we should examine the extraordinary role played in the text of the *Ad Marciam* by two passages providing travel narratives. In *Marc.* 17.2–18, human life is compared to a sea journey to Syracuse: just as such a sea voyage is attractive in spite of all the risks and inconveniences to be endured, so human life is worth living. In *Marc.* 24.5–26.7, Metilius' afterlife is described in terms of a journey: an ascent to the sphere of the heavenly bodies, the subsequent encounter with other deceased and the effortless moving around among the stars, with an easy overview of natural and human history and an insight into the inner workings of the cosmos. The length of the two passages alone—taken together, they account for more than 18% of the text—signals their importance for the overall argument. The passages are way too long to reproduce in their entirety here. In the next two sections, I shall offer an interpretation of the passages in the wider context of the *Ad Marciam*.

The Sea Voyage to Syracuse (*Marc.* 17.2–18)

In the *Ad Marciam*, Seneca uses frequently the literary device of an imagined dialogue with Marcia, in which Marcia states the reasons for viewing the loss of her son as an injustice that rightly undermines her trust in the providential governance of the cosmos. Seneca takes upon himself the role of refuting Marcia's imagined arguments, thus defending a worldview that is compatible with Stoic ideas of a fundamental goodness and reasonableness of the cosmos. Such an exchange precedes our first travel passage (*Marc.* 17.2–18) and thus elucidates the function of the travel narrative in the overall argument. At *Marc.* 16.8, Seneca reminds Marcia that she focuses in an unbalanced way on her loss (as humans generally do). Instead, she should also be mindful of the goods that even a raging Fortune left untouched for Marcia to enjoy:

> [I]niquiores sumus aduersus relicta ereptorum desiderio. Sed si aestimare uolueris quam ualde tibi fortuna, etiam cum saeuiret, pepercerit, scies te habere plus quam solacia: respice tot nepotes, duas filias.
>
> We are all unfair towards what is left due to our desire for what has been snatched away. But if only you were prepared to appreciate how much lenient Fortune has been with you, even when she raged, you would know that you have more than words of comfort: Look at your many grandchildren and your two daughters! (*Marc.* 16.8)

The reference to her grandchildren and daughters is a clear signal that Seneca is aware of, and wishes to avoid, critiques of consolation (see above). Seneca underscores by that Fortune tosses around good and bad people in an indiscriminate way (*exempto discrimine eodem modo malos bonosque iactari*: *Marc.* 16.8). Again, this is in line with Stoic axiology which sees virtue as the only good and discards non-moral goods as irrelevant.[10] Stating that Fortune "tosses around" human beings irrespective of their moral status is therefore a plausible rejoinder (for a Stoic) to the charge that fortune treats Marcia unfairly. The imagined dialogue is continued with a reply by Marcia, that even if the charge against Fortune does not stick, it is nonetheless hard to lose a son whom one has raised and to whom one is attached. Seneca replies:

> Who would deny that it is hard? But it is the human condition. To this end you are born: that you lose, that you die, that you hope, that you fear, that you make others worry as well as yourself, that you fear as well as long for death and, what is worst, that you never know what you really are (*cuius esses status*). (*Marc.* 17.1)

Immediately after this response begins our first travel passage. From the above, the readers are made to expect an argument to the effect that life is valuable overall, in spite of the hardships it entails and in spite of the utterly frustrating human condition. The passage begins with the words:

> Suppose someone said to a man who desired to go to Syracuse: "Take advance note (*ante cognosce*) of all the inconveniences, all the enjoyments of your future journey, then set sail under those conditions (*ita*). These are the things that you can marvel at" (*Marc.* 17.2)

In literary terms, the whole passage takes the shape of an extended analogy, in which Seneca likens the entry into life to a difficult but rewarding sea journey to Syracuse. Marcia is invited to regard entry into life as the entry into the dazzling cosmic city: a "journey" which knows dangers and inevitable loss, but is ultimately worth it.

Seneca begins by inviting Marcia to imagine someone who thinks about travelling to Syracuse. Seneca offers a description of what the traveller might see. He begins with the positive things and he names, in order: (1) The location of the island of Sicily, which lets one grasp its geological development (in former times, it was obviously connected to the mainland), (2) the famous whirlpool of Charybdis, (3) the fountain of Arethusa, (4) the peaceful harbour, (5) the ancient quarries where captives were held to do forced labour. Finally (6) the great city itself with its phantastic climate during winter (*Marc.* 17.2–4). It is striking how Seneca's list parallels what today's travel guidebooks still highlight as Syracuse's key sights, including

---

10 An excellent introduction to Stoic ethics is Tad Brennan, *The Stoic Life: Emotions, Duties, and Fate* (Oxford: Oxford University Press, 2005). For my own interpretation highlighting the religious aspect of ancient Stoicism, see Christoph Jedan, *Stoic Virtues: Chrysippus and the Religious Character of Stoic Ethics* (New York: Continuum, 2009), esp. 110–18.

rather detailed accounts of the stone quarries (*latomie*) and their alleged use as a prison for Athenian prisoners of war under Dionysius. To quote as an example from a Dutch travel guide:

> The *latomie* [quarries] served sometimes as prison. There are many such quarries in Syracuse, but due to safety concerns only a few of them can be visited. One of the largest is the *Latomia del Paradiso*, opposite the Greek theatre. One of the stone pits there is the so-called *Orecchio di Dionisio*, the Ear of Dionysius. This strange name derives from the painter Caravaggio; according to him the acoustics in the pit was so good that the tyrant Dionysius the Elder could eavesdrop on the conversation of the prisoners. The strange, high, narrow and tapered form of the *Orecchio di Dionisio* reminds one of a Gothic cathedral.... Along the *via Bassa Acradina*, there are more stone quarries, the *latomie dei Cappucini*. It is said that in ancient times 7000 Athenian prisoners of war were locked up there, having been taken captive during their hapless expedition in 415–413 BCE. Thucydides, the fifth-century Athenian historian, talks about the abysmal conditions in which the prisoners of war had to work. Many fell ill due to the unhealthy climate, by daytime very hot, humid at night; above all, the prisoners were given no more than a little water and corn each day.[11]

We can glean from this example how an ancient quarry, the memory of the ill-fated Athenian expedition against Syracuse and of intense human suffering can combine to exert touristic appeal, even after a lapse of more than 2400 years. Curiously, while the name "Ear of Dionysius" was invented much later, by the Baroque painter Caravaggio, such touristic details have inspired even professional historians to re-imagine the past. In the comments to his translation of Seneca's *Ad Marciam*, John W. Basore explains our passage with a reference to the Ear of Dionysius (see Figure 1), even if it is unlikely that the Athenian soldiers were held at the site.[12]

Seneca continues by conjuring up the negative aspects: "But, having experienced (*cognoueris*) all these things, the heavy and unhealthy summer climate will ruin[13] the benefits (*corrumpet*). Even worse, there will be (*erit*) Dionysius the tyrant, the destroyer of freedom, justice and the law, desiring domination even after Plato, and life even after exile" (*Marc.* 17.5).

Seneca goes on to evoke some of the worst excesses of the tyrant (all in the future tense): "Some he will burn, others he will flog" (*Marc.* 17.5). Seneca then draws a first conclusion: "If, after such a warning, someone said he wanted to enter Syra-

---

11 Ernest Kurpershoek, *Reisgids Sicilië*, 2nd ed. (Utrecht/Antwerp: Kosmos 1989), 98–99 (my translation).
12 John W. Basore, *Seneca: Moral Essays*, 3 vols. (Cambridge, MA: Harvard University Press 1932), 2:56 (note a).
13 Note the transition into the future tense, which helps to blur distinctions between past, present and future (for more on this, see below).

Figure 1: The "Ear of Dionysius," Syracuse (photo by Christoph Jedan).

cuse, isn't it the case that he could only have a justified complaint against himself, who did not stumble into all this but came knowingly?" (*Marc.* 17.6)[14]

---

[14] Two remarks are in order here. First, it is important to realize that Seneca presupposes a positive answer throughout: the journey to Syracuse is worth the trouble and the risk. Second, it is significant that Seneca aggregates historically very different phases in a single moment: persistent facts of natural history blend with the memory of the forced labor in Syracuse's quarries and of the long-gone tyrant Dionysius. Seneca thus evokes the continued presence of the past; in part this can be explained as a literary strategy to increase the urgency of his description beyond a dry summary. However, the literary strategy might also serve the purpose of evoking the possibility of a synthesizing view beyond the normal confines of human history, which—as Seneca will claim in the second travel passage—is available to the souls in the celestial afterlife (see below).

This remark concludes the first part of the analogy, the journey to Syracuse. What readers expect now is an application of the imagery of the journey to Syracuse to the more abstract theme of human life. And in fact, we are offered exactly this application at *Marc.* 18.1: "Come on, apply this image to the entry into the whole of human life (<*Ad*> *hanc imaginem agedum totius uitae introitum refer*)." This means that the flow of the argument is interrupted by the passage *Marc.* 17.6–7, which focuses on a prosopopoeia of Nature, offering the same "deal" to every parent that entails no single guarantee as to the fate of their offspring (*dicit omnibus nobis natura . . . qui tibi nihil certi sponderunt*): one's future children may be beautiful or deformed, they may be saviors of the country or its betrayers, they may outlive oneself or one has to bury them. If, Seneca has Nature say, after these laws have been declared, you decide to have children, free the gods of blame completely, because they haven't promised you anything for certain. The passage sounds odd in its current position, which has been maintained by modern editions.[15] Scholars such as Johan Nicolai Madvig and Eugène Albertini have suggested to transpose the passage to the beginning of the analogy (i.e., immediately after *Marc.* 17.1);[16] Martin Clarence Gertz has proposed its placement at the end of the analogy (i.e., immediately after *Marc.* 18.8).[17] While both transpositions make perfect sense, Gertz' proposal does have the edge: at *Marc.* 17.1, the discussion was about the human condition and the uncertainty of life prospects in general. Placing the passage immediately after *Marc.* 17.1 would again disrupt the flow of the argument, which elaborates with the sea voyage to Syracuse on the mixed bag of experiences one will have to make in life; the discussion will have to return to parenthood ultimately, but doing this right after *Marc.* 17.1 with a prosopopoeia of Nature would be completely unprepared and would moreover give the point away prematurely. Far better, therefore, to transpose the offending passage behind *Marc.* 18.8. At *Marc.* 18.8, the topic of parenthood is brought up, so the prosopopoeia is not only prepared, it offers the fitting finale of the analogy, in which Nature addresses all parents, and Marcia with them. In line with these considerations, I shall interpret the passage as the analogy's conclusion.

As stated above, Seneca elaborates the second part of the analogy from *Marc.* 18.1 onwards. The person deliberating on whether or not to travel to Syracuse is in the exact same situation as a person who were to deliberate, before birth, whether

---

15 Cf. the discussion in C.E. Manning, *On Seneca's "Ad Marciam"* (Leiden: Brill, 1981), 96–97 (with literature).
16 Johan Nicolai Madvig, *Adversaria critica ad scriptores graecos et latinos*, 3 vols. (Copenhagen 1871–1884; repr., Hildesheim: Olms, 1967), 2:354–55; Eugène Albertini, *La composition dans les ouvrages philosophiques de Sénèque* (Paris: Boccard 1923), 171–73.
17 Martin Clarence Gertz, *Studia critica in Annaei Senecae dialogos* (Copenhagen: Guldendal, 1874), 11.

or not entering life would be worth it on the whole. In this context, Seneca introduces the Stoic concept of the world as a city of gods and humans: just as the sea voyage to Syracuse allows one to visit a fascinating city, so entering life is tantamount to visiting the cosmic city of gods and humans, which affords views and experiences of unparalleled grandeur. There are cosmic marvels to be seen in the planets, but also Earth itself presents a fascinating spectacle: large-scale geographical structures, cities, the effects of human agriculture, even a sight of humans travelling is afforded, conquering the world. On the negative side, of course, it is clear that life will have to end—and a painful end it will be, involving illness, loss and ultimately death. Nonetheless, the opportunity of entering the cosmic city is entirely worth all disadvantages: Seneca claims that a person put before this choice would evidently choose life under such conditions.

However, Seneca's argument does not pre-empt a Kantian transcendental-philosophical argument that rests on the need to presuppose such a choice on the part of the person about to enter life. In Seneca's argument the fact that the person about to enter life is not asked, does not face that choice, can be considered a relevant counterargument. Seneca thus brings up this counterargument on behalf of Marcia: "but nobody, you say, has consulted us!" (*Marc.* 18.8). Seneca replies that our parents—who can be counted on to have a modicum of experience with life's terms—have made the choice vicariously for us (*Marc.* 18.8).[18] In this way, the analogy invokes explicitly the topic of parenthood. It is obvious that Marcia should apply the general lesson to herself: she had given birth to Metilius knowing the terms of life and—in spite of the early death of her son—she was right to do so, since Metilius has been able to make the marvellous experience of entering the cosmic city of gods and humans. The argument has a clear consolatory focus: even in retrospect, Marcia need not feel guilty. The prosopopoeia of Nature—the passage from *Marc.* 17.6–7 that should, as I have argued, be transposed to the end of the analogy—draws out the analogy's lesson: having children comes with no guarantees as to their lot. The analogy concludes, therefore, with the statement: "If, after these laws have been set out, you decide to take children, you must free the goods from all blame, because they really have not given you any promises" (*Marc.* 17.7). The statement brings home the message the whole extended analogy was designed to convey: the early death of Metilius is no reason to doubt the fundamental goodness and reasonableness of the divinely administered cosmos.

---

18 It is clear that Seneca proceeds from contemporary cultural expectations that differ markedly from those in early Christianity: pregnancy, birth and the survival of a child and admission into a family are not a divine gift, but are a matter of human control.

As I noted above, the fact that Seneca uses the simile of a sea voyage to Syracuse as the first part of the extended analogy has stimulated Léon Herrmann to consider the *Ad Marciam* a late work of Seneca's. According to Herrmann, the very detailed description of the trip to Syracuse must be indebted to Seneca's friend and correspondent Lucilius, who was—or so Herrmann believed—thinking at the time about taking up the position of a procurator in Syracuse. The extended analogy would thus be the recycling of a deliberation between the two friends.[19] However, Herrmann's suggestion is unconvincing, not only due to the obvious thematic overlap of the *Ad Marciam* with the first two books of *De ira*, one of Seneca's earliest surviving texts (see above), but also because there is a less far-fetched explanation for the great detail of the description of the voyage to Syracuse: it is very likely that Seneca himself had visited Syracuse on a sea voyage. The background to this probable visit was that Seneca suffered from a young age from a chronic disease, very likely tuberculosis. He was in a bad state, even thought about suicide. For more than ten years, he was looked after by his aunt, married to Gaius Galerius, the Roman prefect of Egypt between 16 and 31 CE. The climate of Egypt was considered healthy for such illnesses. Now, the sea voyage between Ostia and Alexandria would very likely have taken place during winter, the preferred route being from Ostia southwards, circumnavigating the south of Sicily, heading upwards again to Syracuse, before making the crossing to the Greek coast, circumnavigating Crete before heading south to Alexandria, and vice versa.[20] It is notable that Seneca's "touristic" description of Syracuse places the description of its winter climate before the summer climate, thus assuming a journey in wintertime. All in all, it is likely that Seneca would have visited Syracuse himself on his journey to and from Alexandria. As to the risks involved, he was fully aware of them: the ship that carried his uncle home to Italy in 31 CE sank and he did not survive the shipwreck. We cannot be sure whether or not Seneca and his aunt were travelling with the same ship,[21] but the events certainly induced the realization of a narrow escape. In sum, the great detail of Seneca's description of the journey to Syracuse was very likely based on first-hand experience.

---

19 Curiously, Herrmann maintained the late date of the *Ad Marciam* in a subsequent publication, even if he changed the date of Lucilius' envoy to Syracuse to a time prior to 58 CE; see Léon Herrmann, "Chronologie des oeuvres en prose de Sénèque," *Latomus* 2 (1937): 94–112.
20 For itineraries, see the Stanford ORBIS tool (https://orbis.stanford.edu/; last accessed 20 April 2023); see also Wilson, *Seneca*, 62.
21 Some commentators automatically assume that they did. See, e.g., Griffin, *Seneca*, 43; but more careful is Wilson, *Seneca*, 62. The textual evidence is inconclusive: see Sen., *Helv.* 19.2.

The Afterlife as a Journey (*Marc.* 24.5–26.7)

Let us proceed to the second travel narrative, which marks the end of the *Ad Marciam* (*Marc.* 24.5–26.7). It describes the afterlife of Metilius as an ascent to, and sojourn in, the sphere of the heavenly bodies. It is important to stress that the topic of Metilius' afterlife is introduced in a conditional way that is characteristic for the bulk of extant ancient "philosophical" consolations. The consolations tend to follow the template of Socrates' speech in Pl., *Ap.* 40A–41D, which has variously been referred to as the "Socratic paradox" or the "Socratic alternative."[22] Socrates distinguishes two scenarios: either death is the end of his consciousness, in which case it should be likened to a deep, dreamless sleep. Else, death marks the transition to a highly attractive meeting place of the good. Whatever scenario will turn out to be true, both are supremely attractive in Socrates' view, so in neither case will death harm him; his friends and supporters need not grieve for him. In the *Phaedo* (114C–115A), Socrates pronounces that his hopes are all for the afterlife scenario, but the agnostic attitude in respect of the two scenarios remains a significant characteristic, particularly when compared to fully-fledged afterlife beliefs in early Christian writings.[23] The Socratic alternative also structures Seneca's *Ad Marciam*. The first part of the *Ad Marciam* appears to argue from the assumption that Metilius has ceased to exist and that his early death has spared him a lot of suffering (see especially *Marc.* 19.4–21.1); at *Marc.* 23.1, however, Seneca switches gears and argues from the second scenario of the Socratic alternative, yet without highlighting the transition at all. It seems a matter of course that Metilius has a soul that survives death. The death of Metilius leaves only the unimportant outer shell behind. His true self, his soul, is first lingering above to be cleansed of contamination by his mortal, bodily existence (*Marc.* 25.1). His soul then reaches its natural habitat, a place between the stars. A "saintly band" (*coetus sacer*: *Marc.* 25.1) welcomes him there: heroes of the past, including Cordus, Marcia's father. He introduces Metilius into the secrets of nature (*in arcana naturae libens ducit*: *Marc.* 25.2), which are a matter not of reasoning but of experience up there. In the whole passage, the

---

22 See e.g., Horst-Theodor Johann, *Trauer und Trost: Eine quellen- und strukturanalytische Untersuchung der philosophischen Trostschriften über den Tod* (Munich: Fink, 1968), esp. 120–26; Karlhans Abel, *Bauformen in Senecas Dialogen: Fünf Strukturanalysen: dial. 6, 11, 12, 1 und 2* (Heidelberg: Winter, 1967), 29; Christoph Jedan, "Troost door argumenten: Herwaardering van een filosofische en christelijke traditie," *NTT* 68 (2014): 7–22.

23 An interesting exception to the general trend will be Plutarch's *Consolatio ad uxorem*, in which Plutarch can fall back on afterlife beliefs which he and his wife happen to share, supported by their initiation in the Dionysiac mysteries (611C–F). This common background, however, must have been an exceptional commonality between consoland and consoler, which makes the modus operandi of the *Consolatio ad uxorem* far more akin to that of early Christian treatises.

motif of travel remains important: not only is the ascent to the (heavenly) afterlife a journey, also in the sphere of the stars, travel is the mode of existence:

> They [the souls] are set free to explore among the unlimited and vast space of the eternal things. There are no seas spread out between those that could hinder them, nor the height of mountains, pathless rock faces or the uncertain ground of sandbars. Everything is even there and through their moving easily and quickly, they are permeable for, and mixed with, the stars. (*Marc.* 25.3)[24]

Just as the final paragraphs of the first travel section, so the final paragraphs of the present travel narrative contain a prosopopoeia; this time, it is not Nature, but Marcia's father who lays down the lesson to be learnt from this travel narrative:

> It was once my delight to compile the history of what took place in a single epoch in the most distant region of the universe and among the merest handful of people. Now I may have the view of countless centuries, the succession and traits of countless ages, the whole array of years: I may behold the rise and fall of future kingdoms, the downfall of great cities and new invasions of the sea.. . . And when the time shall come for the world to be blotted out in order that it may begin its life anew, these things will destroy themselves by their own power, and stars will clash with stars, and all the fiery matter of the world that now shines in orderly array will blaze up in a common conflagration. Then also the souls of the blest, who have partaken of immortality, when it shall seem best to God to create the universe anew—we, too, amid the falling universe, shall be added as a tiny fraction to this mighty destruction and shall be changed again into our former elements. Happy, Marcia, is your son, who already knows these mysteries! (*Marc.* 26.5–7, trans. Basore)

Here we find a sophisticated combination of biographical information and a general Stoic world-view. Three points are particularly notable: (1) The view from above underscores the transitoriness of human existence vis-à-vis the immense timeframe of the cosmic process. It dwarfs parochial allegiances and thus supports Stoic cosmopolitanism. (2) The cosmos as a whole is a divine creation, but it will not persist in its current shape. The only permanence can be found in the divine control in or over the ever-changing cosmos. (3) This cyclical world view implies

---

24 It is obvious that the afterlife section is heavily indebted to early Greco-Roman philosophy. Seneca himself signals as much by invoking the authority of Plato near the beginning of the section (*Marc.* 25.2). It is most likely that Seneca would have taken inspiration from Cicero's writings (especially the final section of the *De republica*, i.e., the so-called "Somnium Scipionis," and the fifth and final book of the *Tusculanae disputationes*), which display a characteristic blend of Stoic and Platonic motifs. In the literature, Cicero's eschatological descriptions have been taken to derive from Posidonius (135–51 BCE), a Stoic philosopher with Platonic sympathies, whose lectures Cicero had attended as a young man (see, e.g., Karlhans Abel, "Poseidonios und Senecas Trostschrift an Marcia (dial. 6, 12, 5 ff.)," *RMP* 107 [1964]: 221–60). While such questions of tradition are interesting in their own right, they are beside the point here. Seneca's interest in producing an effective consolation does not commit him to philosophical originality.

that even the afterlife of virtuous human beings is limited to the present world cycle.[25] Importantly, the limitation of the soul's afterlife is not deplored; it is fully embraced as part and parcel of adoring the mightiness of the divinely administered cosmic process.

The fact that those Stoic doctrines are presented as based on the experience of Cordus, the beloved father of Marcia, and are, moreover, presented as a personal communication from him, serves to increase their credibility and status in the eyes of Marcia. This is important considering the consolatory purpose of the *Ad Marciam* in its historical context. I have already alluded above to a widespread cultural suspicion against consolation as a mechanical, impersonal affair. As Seneca sees it, Marcia's prolonged mourning stems from a mistaken judgment: she thinks that she has a complaint against fortune. She was singled out unfairly, having to witness the premature death of her son Metilius. Clearly, this charge goes against the core of the Stoic world view: the whole of nature is a divinely controlled, providential process. For the Stoics, only personal virtue matters or matters fully, other things such as length of life, health, family, honours etc. are adiaphora. Seneca's reply could have consisted in launching into a full defence of Stoic philosophy. But how effective a consolation would that have been? Seneca would have appeared as a philosophical salesman, preaching to a grieving woman. Not she and her grief, but a defence of the Stoic school would have taken centre stage. So, the prosopopoeia of Cordus as the finale of the consolation increases the acceptability and credibility of the highly sophisticated philosophical doctrines for Marcia.

The realization that consolatory efficacy is key to Seneca's literary approach in the *Ad Marciam* can also help us to answer two pressing questions. First, why would Seneca have chosen to put so much emphasis on the motif of travel? And, second, why would Seneca have chosen to include not one but two travel narratives?

As to the first question, invoking travel motifs allows Seneca to connect to experiences Marcia may have had or can easily relate to. Seneca uses the experience of travel to bring up key Stoic doctrines, the world as a cosmic city made up of gods and humans and the idea of a divinely controlled, providential world cycle that will recurrently be destroyed in a conflagration, while backgrounding their nature of abstract philosophical doctrines. Moreover, the experience of travel allows Seneca to appeal to a feeling that we today still refer to with an ancient word as

---

[25] It is hardly necessary to underscore that this cyclical view of cosmic history stands in marked contrast to (later to be canonized) early Christian views of a linear salvation history. In the context of a linear salvation history, the afterlife is tantamount to an end of history. I shall return to the issue below.

"the sublime."[26] The experience of travel can be comforting insofar as it conveys a sense of the sublime: Through drawing on the experience of travel, Seneca invokes the grandeur of nature, and a frisson of danger, Seneca thus shows that nature is so much bigger than we are. Nature dwarfs us. However, we are not simply crushed. In reflexively beholding the grandeur of nature, we are at the same time elated: we are not only small compared to nature, we are made significant by seeing the whole and by realizing our smallness in comparison with it. This consolatory togetherness of feeling small and grand at the same time is what the travel experience is about.

This leads up directly to our second question. If the extended analogy of the first travel narrative already offers a fine consolation, and conveys very similar messages to the second, why concluding with a second travel narrative? Again, consolatory efficacy is the key to an answer. The first travel narrative has the function of preparing the ground for the second. This preparation is necessary considering the cultural background to ancient consolations: As pointed out above, the frequent use of the Socratic alternative as a structuring device in consolations highlights their context of religio-philosophical fluidity and pluralism. Ancient consolers would have been hard pressed to pin down their consolands to a specific belief regarding the afterlife. The afterlife, in short, was a possibility, perhaps a probability, but never a certainty which a consoler could take for granted.

Seneca's repeated use of the travel motif works around this difficulty. The first travel narrative is utilized in the context of the first leg of the Socratic alternative: death has annihilated Metilius. The extended analogy invokes a mundane travel experience that is well-known and eminently credible in all its detail. However, Seneca combines this with a summary in the form of a prosopopoeia of Nature, an entity that was not self-evidently acceptable outside the Stoic school. The accessible, mundane character of the journey to Syracuse thus increases the credibility of the Stoic lesson to be drawn from the first travel narrative. The first travel narrative strategically blurs boundaries Marcia would normally take for granted, for instance between past, present and future, and between the real and the imagined (see above).

Seen against the background of this preparation, the second travel narrative, detailing the metaphysically even less self-evidently acceptable ascent of the soul to

---

26 See, e.g., Alain de Botton, *The Art of Travel* (London: Penguin, 2003), 178: "Sublime landscapes, through their grandeur and power, retain a symbolic role in bringing us to accept without bitterness or lamentation the obstacles we cannot overcome and events we cannot make sense of.. . . If the world is unfair or beyond our understanding, sublime places suggest it is not surprising things should be thus. We are the playthings of the forces that laid out the oceans and chiselled the mountains. Sublime places gently move us to acknowledge limitations that we might otherwise encounter with anxiety or anger in the ordinary flow of events."

a heavenly afterlife and the nature of the afterlife as continuous change, thus appears far less problematic. Its acceptability is strengthened further by invoking with the final prosopopoeia not an abstract entity, but Cordus, Marcia's beloved father, as the spokesman of the Stoic world-view. His speech deepens out the Stoic message conveyed before (the goodness of the cosmos and Stoic axiology, i.e., the indifference of non-moral goods, such as health and length of life, and the value of virtue), conjuring up the large-scale cosmological background to the Stoic world-view.

In short, the use of two travel narratives must be considered a skilful rhetorical stratagem that increases the plausibility and thus the consolatory efficacy of the *Ad Marciam* with respect to her primary addressee.

From Seneca to Paul

Now that we have discussed the two "travel narratives" it is time to engage with Paul. Within the limitations of this chapter, I cannot even begin to do justice to any single Pauline writing, let alone several (Deutero-)Pauline writings. What I shall do instead is to mark possible pathways for an analysis, taking my cue from Backhaus' pertinent question: why is the motif of travel so surprisingly unimportant in Paul, especially when compared to Seneca? In my view, a satisfactory answer should contain at least the following three elements.

(1) The two authors have markedly different views of the cosmos and of time and teleology (see above). Key for Seneca is that the cosmos is divinely administered, but evolves cyclically in a process of creative construction and destruction. The individual human being may have a certain permanence beyond mundane life, but nothing in the way of an eternal life. We might refer to this view of human life in the cosmos as "life in transit." If the afterlife is a fulfilment of cherished activities and of lifelong ambition, the best Seneca can envision for Cordus and Metilius is a life of learning and understanding, looking around, observing the world and large-scale cosmic secrets. Travel motifs ideally express Seneca's views of "life in transit," of cosmic history as cyclical and of the afterlife as observing and learning about the reasonable structure of the cosmos. They are, in the context of Seneca's thought, supremely consolatory.

Paul, by contrast, appears to entertain views of the cosmos (and human life in it) as teleologically structured towards a single goal. With the rupture of the second coming of Christ, the world ends in a final, stable destination, enabling the transformed human beings' vision of God in an afterlife (1 Cor 13:9–12).[27] Change and impermanence are thus kept away from the fulfilment of human life and history; their importance can at the most be instrumental, characterizing the route towards the final destination.

This means, of course, that travel motifs cannot have the same high status and importance in Paul's theology as in Seneca to begin with, and cannot fulfil the consolatory function they have in Seneca. It is no coincidence, therefore, that Paul does not use a travel metaphor but a sports metaphor when he wants to express his orientation towards the fulfilment of his life (Phil 3:10–14)—the crossing of a finish line symbolizes a stable destination.[28]

(2) We should be open to the possibility of Paul expressing aspects of what he could achieve with travel motifs by other linguistic means. What would be needed, then, is a clear-headed answer as to why it would have been preferable for Paul to use such different linguistic means. In this respect it is important to note that Seneca's travel motifs express the positive as well as the negative aspects of travelling, especially in the first travel narrative. One has to endure a lot in return for the positive aspects of travel, which include learning new things and meeting people one cannot normally see (for instance, Cremutius Cordus in the second travel narrative).

This goes towards showing that travel motifs can be deeply ambivalent. Wishing to avoid the risk of conflating the two aspects of travel metaphors might therefore be a valid reason for avoiding travel metaphors. It seems that this is the case in Paul. He avoids travel metaphors because he wants to separate the positive and negative aspects usually expressed by such metaphors. The wish to spend time with the communities he has founded does thus get an unambivalently positive connotation, the hardship and risks incurred a clearly negative one. It is also important to note that many of the functions fulfilled by travel metaphors in Seneca and other authors are fulfilled in Paul by the word field of "work." Thus separating out the positive and negative functions allows Paul to defend his status as apostle, as the one who has worked, suffered, incurred risks, in short: humiliated himself more than any other apostle (2 Corinthians 11). This allows him also to underscore his independence from a community, because he is self-supporting through his work (1 Thess 2:9, perhaps echoed in 2 Thess 3:6–11), and he does so for the sake of the credibility of his teaching, his exemplary function. Conversely, his addressees can feel taken seriously, special and beloved, just because Paul takes upon him all those negatives in order to

---

[27] It remains a matter of dispute how exactly that transformation is conceptualized in Paul. See, e.g., James P. Ware, "The Salvation of Creation: Seneca and Paul on the Future of Humanity and of the Cosmos," in Dodson und Briones, *Paul and Seneca*, 285–306.

[28] As Backhaus, *Religion als Reise*, 229, notes himself, yet without reflecting further on this.

be with them, preach to them, and so forth. It also increases the credibility of Paul's message, because he is prepared to go to such lengths to spread it.

All of this could hardly be expressed using travel metaphors, which would have risked lumping together positive and negative aspects that must be kept apart for Paul to be able to make those points. In short, the thrust of Paul's theological messages makes it hard to imagine how he could have used travel metaphors in continuity with ancient literary conventions.

(3) Ultimately, we need to realize that comparison must not and cannot be too narrowly focused.[29] Analyzing the motif of travel in Seneca vis-à-vis Paul should reflectively reconstruct two distinct linguistic tapestries and the functions they fulfil in their respective contexts. This means that we have to look beyond the narrow motif of travel, as Backhaus unwittingly underscores in his discussion of a sports metaphor (see above). For instance, in order to defend Fortune against Marcia's charge that members of her family have been struck down, Seneca uses the simile of an advancing army that has come under enemy fire: every dart makes a victim, and Marcia should be happy that so many of her children and grandchildren are still alive (*Marc.* 16.5).

It would be too easy to note that there is no such simile in Paul, and explain its absence by a contrast between Paul's idea of providence versus the supposed absence of it in Stoicism. The Stoics, too, entertain a notion of providence, only that they expect different things from it. We can learn about the subtle differences once we reflect on the function of Seneca's simile. Seneca maintains the ultimate reasonableness of life. He needs to point out that suffering loss does not contradict that reasonableness. The motif of Fortune shooting arrows at the advancing army of human beings, including Marcia's family, is designed to bring home the fact that life is ultimately about something else than non-moral goods such as health and duration of life. The motif thus aims at a profound change of Marcia's attitude vis-à-vis the divine cosmos, making her give up her imagined right to make special demands for herself and those dear to her.[30]

Paul, by contrast, believes that non-moral goods can be trumped by a spiritual or religious good (e.g., Gal 4:13–14; Phil 1:19–25; 3:7–11); this is a far cry, however, from believing that non-moral goods are irrelevant. Paul will thus hope for a com-

---

29 *Pace* Troels Engberg-Pedersen, "Paul in Philippians and Seneca in *Epistle* 93 on Life after Death and Its Present Implications," in Dodson und Briones, *Paul and Seneca*, 267–84.
30 This is not to deny, however, that Seneca elaborates in other writings a point that is *secondary* compared to the one made here: hardships are important, character-building challenges; cf. on this aspect Brian J. Tabb, "Paul and Seneca on Suffering," in Dodson und Briones, *Paul and Seneca*, 88–108. It is clear that such a message would not have helped his case with Marcia.

pensatory spiritual good for his or anyone else's suffering, whereas Seneca does not expect any such gain from divine providential guidance. The lesson conveyed by divine Nature, which we might variously characterize as spiritual, religious or philosophical, is there for human beings to reap, but this is ultimately their responsibility alone. It is important to realize, however, that Paul, too, appears to share Seneca's concern about the problem of special pleading, in line with many other religio-philosophical worldviews. The simile of the potter summarizes Paul's rejoinder (Rom 9:14–24). Perhaps it is no coincidence that Paul does not use military imagery in this context; after all, his God has more anthropomorphic traits and is emotionally engaged with his chosen people. It might have been harder to square this with the simile of an enemy force striking indiscriminately.

If this is right, the key difference between Paul's and Seneca's theologies is not one of providence versus its absence, but different degrees of anthropomorphism in their image of God, different expectations regarding providential governance and, ultimately, different axiologies.

Conclusion: Comparison as Bi-Directional, Reflective Interpretation

Travel metaphors are surprisingly scarce in Paul, considering the centrality of travel in his life (e.g., Acts 9:1–9 and 22:6–11 on the apparition of Christ on the road to Damascus, 2 Cor 11:25–26 and Acts 27–28 on travelling and being shipwrecked). Yet, it would be too easy to explain this surprising fact by the Paul's focus on the "inner being," presumably in sharp contrast to Seneca, to whom would then be attributed a rather shallow philosophy. On the contrary, if we consider how strategically Seneca goes about his consolatory project in the *Ad Marciam*, we should say that that text is all about the "inner being," especially Marcia's as Seneca's primary addressee.

However, let there be no misunderstanding. I have not been concerned with scoring easy points at the expense of Backhaus' (cursory) discussion of Seneca vis-à-vis Paul. As I have made clear right from the outset, I consider Backhaus' work a valuable attempt at grappling with the sprawling theme of travel in the New Testament and (part of) its cultural context. It cannot come as a surprise if Backhaus considers some authors in less detail than other specialists with different interests would have wished.

The reason why Backhaus' interpretation has served as a contrast, is that it exemplifies a widespread use of comparison in New Testament Studies (and, presumably, way beyond). Significant in this regard is Backhaus' defence of his approach in the introductory lecture. He presents his approach on the one hand as "comparative profiling," on the other hand he excuses himself ("as a biblicist") from the expectation of offering scholarly contributions to the study of nonbiblical texts and suggests instead that his readings will lead to a better understanding of the *specificum Christianum* in New Testament texts.[31] Conceived of in this way, comparison is given a curiously one-sided mission: mining ancient Greco-Roman texts for better literary classifications and interpretations of New Testament texts. In this vein, Backhaus classifies literary motifs in Greco-Roman culture to offer a literary analysis of New Testament texts. Let me hasten to add that this approach is not only widespread, but also has undoubted merits in allowing us to (re-)appreciate the literary richness of those texts, the many ways in which they were functioning against a background of cultural knowledge that we today need to (re-)acquire in order to better understand them. However, what this does not deliver is comparison in the straightforward sense of a "reciprocal illumination" (to use Arvind Sharma's fortuitous phrase).[32]

If the outlines of the interpretation offered above appear convincing, this should make us pause and reconsider the use of comparison. Comparison should be conceived of as a bi-directional affair, in which both sides of the comparison are contextualized and held up against each other to gain deepened understanding of both. Such comparison requires repeated "flips" between the two *comparanda*, to ascertain whether or not plausible aggregates of motifs (matching or otherwise) have been built. Such a procedure is by no means new. In the realm of political philosophy, American philosopher John Rawls famously suggested the search for a "reflective equilibrium" as the best way of building general conceptual schemata and theories.[33]

This goes to the heart of any comparative enterprise: we need to interrogate evolving categories all the way during our analysis, asking ourselves not only where possible matches and mismatches can be found, but also where different conceptual structures serve similar purposes. It is for this reason that this chapter has contextualized the travel episodes in Seneca's *Ad Marciam* in such detail and has tried to explain their consolatory purpose as well as their philosophical and theological underpinnings, all the while flagging important differences between Seneca's Stoic worldview and Paul's theology. And it is for this reason that we have inquired into concepts and theories in Paul that do similar work as the travel motifs in Seneca.

I acknowledge that a plea for such bi-directional, reflective comparison may be deeply unfashionable, since it may be perceived as potentially undermining the disciplinary independence of New Testament Studies as opposed to, for instance,

---

[31] Backhaus, *Religion als Reise*, 10–16.
[32] Arvind Sharma, Religious Studies and Comparative Methodology: The Case for Reciprocal Illumination (Albany: State University of New York Press, 2005).
[33] John Rawls, *A Theory of Justice* (Cambridge MA: Harvard University Press, 1971).

classical philology and ancient history. Moreover, such a style of comparative work would make large-scale thematic work even harder. However, if scholarship and the acquisition of knowledge are our primary goal, I cannot see how we could be content with anything less complex.

References

Abel, Karlhans. *Bauformen in Senecas Dialogen: Fünf Strukturanalysen: dial. 6, 11, 12, 1 und 2*. Heidelberg: Winter, 1967.
Abel, Karlhans. "Poseidonios und Senecas Trostschrift an Marcia (dial. 6, 12, 5 ff.)." *RMP* 107 (1964): 221–60.
Albertini, Eugène. *La composition dans les ouvrages philosophiques de Sénèque*. Paris: Boccard, 1923.
Backhaus, Knut. *Religion als Reise: Intertextuelle Lektüren in Antike und Christentum*. Tübingen: Mohr Siebeck, 2014.
Basore, John W., ed. and trans. *Seneca: Moral Essays*. 3 vols. Cambridge, MA: Harvard University Press 1932.
Bellemore, Jane. "The Dating of Seneca's Ad Marciam De Consolatione." *CQ* 42 (1992): 219–34.
Brennan, Tad. *The Stoic Life: Emotions, Duties, and Fate*. Oxford: Oxford University Press, 2005.
De Botton, Alain. *The Art of Travel*. London: Penguin 2003.
Dodson, Joseph R., and David E. Briones, eds. *Paul and Seneca in Dialogue*. Leiden: Brill, 2017.
Engberg-Pedersen, Troels. "Paul in Philippians and Seneca in *Epistle* 93 on Life after Death and Its Present Implications." Pages 267–84 in *Paul and Seneca in Dialogue*. Edited by Joseph R. Dodson and David Briones. Leiden: Brill, 2017.
Fillion-Lahille, Janine. "La production littéraire de Sénèque sous les règnes de Caligula et de Claude, sens philosophique et portée politique: Les 'Consolations' et le 'De ira'." Pages 1606–38 in *Teilband Philosophie, Wissenschaften, Technik. Philosophie (Stoizismus)*. Edited by Wolfgang Haase. ANRW 36/3. Berlin: De Gruyter, 1989.
Gertz, Martin Clarence. *Studia critica in Annaei Senecae dialogos*. Copenhagen: Gyldendal 1874.
Griffin, Miriam. *Seneca: A Philosopher in Politics*. Oxford: Oxford University Press, 1976.
Hermann, Léon. "La date de la Consolation à Marcia." *REA* 31 (1929): 21–28.
Herrmann, Léon. "Chronologie des oeuvres en prose de Sénèque." *Latomus* 2 (1937): 94–112.
Jedan, Christoph. "Antike Philosophie als Gegenstand religionswissenschaftlicher Analyse: Plädoyer für eine neue Historiographie." *Journal of Ethics in Antiquity and Christianity* 1 (2019): 55–69.
Jedan, Christoph. "The Rapprochement of Religion and Philosophy in Ancient Consolation: Seneca, Paul, and Beyond." Pages 159–84 in *Religio-Philosophical Discourses in the Mediterranean World: From Plato, through Jesus, to Late Antiquity*. Edited by Anders Klostergaard Petersen and George van Kooten. Leiden: Brill, 2017.
Jedan, Christoph. "Troost door argumenten: Herwaardering van een filosofische en christelijke traditie." *NTT* 68 (2014): 7–22.
Jedan, Christoph. *Stoic Virtues: Chrysippus and the Religious Character of Stoic Ethics*. New York: Continuum, 2009.
Johann, Horst-Theodor. *Trauer und Trost: Eine quellen- und strukturanalytische Untersuchung der philosophischen Trostschriften über den Tod*. Munich: Fink, 1968.
Kurpershoek, Ernest. *Reisgids Sicilië*. 2nd ed. Utrecht/Antwerp: Kosmos, 1989.

Madvig, Johan Nicolai. *Adversaria critica ad scriptores graecos et latinos.* 3 vols. Copenhagen, 1871–84. Repr., Hildesheim: Olms, 1967.

Manning, C.E. *On Seneca's "Ad Marciam."* Leiden: Brill, 1981.

Marshall, C.W. "The Works of Seneca the Younger and their Dates." Pages 33–44 in *Brill's Companion to Seneca: Philosopher and Dramatist.* Edited by Andreas Heil and Gregor Damschen. Leiden: Brill, 2014.

Reynolds, L.D., ed. *L. Annaei Senecae Dialogorum libri duodecim.* Oxford: Oxford University Press, 1977.

Rawls, John. *A Theory of Justice.* Cambridge MA: Harvard University Press, 1971.

Schinnerer, Johann F. *Über Senecas Schrift an Marcia: Programm der Königlichen Studienanstalt Hof für das Schuljahr 1888/89.* Hof: Mintzel, 1889.

Sharma, Arvind. *Religious Studies and Comparative Methodology: The Case for Reciprocal Illumination.* Albany: State University of New York Press, 2005.

Tabb, Brian J. "Paul and Seneca on Suffering." Pages 88–108 in *Paul and Seneca in Dialogue.* Edited by Joseph R. Dodson and David Briones. Leiden: Brill, 2017.

Ware, James P. "The Salvation of Creation: Seneca and Paul on the Future of Humanity and of the Cosmos." Pages 285–306 in *Paul and Seneca in Dialogue.* Edited by Joseph R. Dodson and David E. Briones. Leiden: Brill, 2017.

Wilson, Emily. *Seneca: A Life.* New York: Oxford University Press, 2014.

Wilson, Marcus. "Seneca the Consoler? A New Reading of his Consolatory Writings." Pages 93–121 in *Greek and Roman Consolations: Eight Studies of a Tradition and Its Afterlife.* Edited by Han Baltussen. Swansea: The Classical Press of Wales, 2013.

Nils Neumann
The (Missing) Motif of "Returning Home" from an Otherworldly Journey in Menippean Literature and the New Testament

Abstract: Visionary accounts of otherworldly journeys form a well-known segment of ancient literature. Narrations of different cultural provenance describe how a hero travels to heaven or to the netherworld and in doing so gains some sort of boon that he or she carries back to the earthly sphere. Otherworldly journeys typically feature the elements of the narrative scheme of the so-called "Monomyth," which Joseph Campbell described in his 1949 book *The Hero with a Thousand Faces*. The present chapter analyzes two prominent otherworldly journeys from the New Testament: one journey to Hades (Luke 16:19–31) and one to heaven (Rev 4:1–11). In comparing these biblical texts to narrations from the Menippean tradition (journeys to Hades in Lucian's *Cataplus* and *Necyomantia*; journeys to heaven in Lucian's *Icaromenippus* and Seneca's *Apocolocyntosis*) it will be seen that unlike many of their ancient parallels the New Testament accounts lack the motif of "returning home" from the journey. How can this be explained?

Journeys to the otherworld represent a common narrative topic, both in New Testament and other Greco-Roman writings (as well as in the Hebrew Bible and Ancient Near Eastern literature). A hero somehow manages to cross the boundary between the earthly and the heavenly or underworld spheres and in doing so gains access to impressions or knowledge that normally is unavailable to mortal humans. One might think of, e.g., the journeys to Hades that the ancient Greek heroes Odysseus, Heracles and Orpheus undertake. Or, consider king Gilgamesh' journey to the waters of death or the journeys to heaven that are bestowed on the prophets Ezekiel or Daniel in the Hebrew Bible.[1]

---

[1] Ancient Near Eastern and Greco-Roman cosmologies share the notion that there is both a heavenly sphere above the earthly realm as home of the gods and an underworld below the earth where the dead and other spirits dwell. On Ancient Near Eastern cosmology that often envisages more than one heaven see Wilhelm Bousset, "Die Himmelsreise der Seele," *AR* 4 (1901): 136–69 and 229–73 (esp. 248–49); Adela Yarbro Collins, "The Seven Heavens in Jewish and Christian Apocalypses," in *Death, Ecstasy and Other Worldly Journeys*, ed. John J. Collins and Michael Fishbane (Albany: State University of New York Press, 1995), 59–93 (64). For a discussion of Greco-Roman accounts see Martha Himmelfarb, "The Practice of Ascent in the Ancient Mediterranean World," in Collins and Fishbane, *Death, Ecstasy and Other Worldly Journeys*, 123–37. See also Alan F. Segal, "Heavenly Ascent in Hellenistic Judaism, Early Christianity and their Environment," *ANRW* 2.23.2 (1980):

The Analysis of Narrative Schemes

The present chapter focuses on otherworldly journeys in the New Testament and in Menippean literature, a genre of ancient satire that is preserved mainly in the writings of Lucian of Samosata. The particular choice of Menippean material is due to the fact that Menippean literature features obvious parallels to the writings of the New Testament and is thus well-suited to illustrate the rootedness of the early Christian texts within their overall literary context. The genre of Menippean literature goes back to the Cynic writer Menippos of Gadara (3rd century BCE), whose works have been lost entirely. But luckily his way of writing has found a number of imitators: the Roman authors Varro and Seneca, as well as Lucian, who writes in Greek.[2] In comparing New Testament text sequences to these Menippean narra-

---

1333–94; Kelley Coblentz Bautch, "Spatiality and Apocalyptic Literature," *HeBAI* 5 (2016): 273–88 (276–79). Pilar Gómez Cardó offers a short overview about accounts of descents to Hades from Homer onwards. See Pilar Gómez Cardó, "Menippus, a Truly Living Ghost in Lucian's Necromancy," in *Visitors from Beyond the Grave: Ghosts in World Literature*, ed. Dámaris Romero-González, Israel Muñoz-Gallarte and Gabriel Laguna-Mariscal (Coimbra: Coimbra University Press, 2019), 47–64 (48). Cf. also Martha Himmelfarb, *Tours of Hell: An Apocalyptic Form of Jewish and Christian Literature* (Philadelphia: University of Pennsylvania Press, 1983); John C. Stephens, *Journeys to the Underworld and Heavenly Realm in Ancient and Medieval Literature* (Jefferson: McFarland & Co., 2019); Richard Bauckham, "Descents to the Underworld," in *The Fate of the Dead: Studies in the Jewish and Christian Apocalypses*, ed. Richard Bauckham (Leiden: Brill, 1998), 9–48; Meghan Henning, *Educating Early Christians through the Rhetoric of Hell: "Weeping and Gnashing of Teeth" as Paideia in Matthew and the Early Church*, WUNT 2/382 (Tübingen: Mohr Siebeck, 2014); Jan N. Bremmer, "Descents to Hell and Ascends to Heaven in Apocalyptic Literature," in *The Oxford Handbook of Apocalyptic Literature*, ed. John J. Collins (Oxford: Oxford University Press, 2014), 340–57.

2 The Cynic philosopher Menippos from Gadara is said to have coined the genre, combining poetic and prosaic passages within the form of philosophical dialogue. Cf. Joel C. Relihan, *Ancient Menippean Satire* (Baltimore: John Hopkins University Press, 1993), 17–21. In its satirical nature Menippean literature oftentimes mocks human pursuit of wealth and reputation, arguing in a Cynic manner that wealth and reputation cannot make anybody happy, but—on the contrary—only cause people to lie, steal and use all sorts of violence. In order to prove this point Menippean literature frequently narrates of otherworldly journeys. The otherworldly point of view reveals the fugacity of earthly possessions and esteem (concerning the typical narrative plots in Menippean literature see Relihan, *Ancient Menippean Satire*, 21–25). Although none of Menippos' works have survived, the impact of his way of writing can be seen from its resonances in Varro, Seneca, and most prominently Lucian. On the reception of Menippos in Lucian's writings see Rudolf Helm, *Lucian und Menipp* (Leipzig: Teubner, 1906), 14–15. On main characteristics of Menippean literature also see Barbara P. McCarthy, "Lucian and Menippus," *YCS* 4 (1934): 3–55; Nils Neumann, *Lukas und Menippos: Hoheit und Niedrigkeit in Lk 1,1–2,40 und in der menippeischen Literatur*, NTOA 68 (Göttingen: Vandenhoeck & Ruprecht, 2008), 205–209 und 267–87.

tions, special attention needs to be dedicated to the narrative deep structures that underlie their accounts of otherworldly journeys.

Describing literary deep structures is not a new approach in literary criticism. A century ago, in 1923, the Russian structuralist Vladímir Propp published the original Russian edition of his book on folk tales that became influential within western scholarship from the middle of the 20th century on.[3] In his study, Propp examines a large number of Russian folk tales and comes to the conclusion that an overall literary scheme exists that underlies all concrete narrations. The scheme consists of 31 events altogether—Propp calls them "functions"—the sequence of which forms the entire tale. The functions range from "one of the members of a family absents himself from home" (no. 1), via "the hero leaves home" (no. 11), "the hero acquires the use of a magical agent" (no. 14) and "the hero returns" (no. 20), to "the hero is married and ascends the throne" (no. 31). It is important to note that according to Propp the scheme is open to a degree of flexibility: not every concrete folk tale must include all of the 31 functions. In fact, oftentimes a tale will only exhibit a smaller number of elements. The present functions, however, will always remain in the exact order that Propp identifies.

In the middle of the 20th century, in 1949, the American writer Joseph Campbell, maybe under the influence of Propp's work, publishes his study on mythological narrations.[4] From the functions in Propp's book cited above it already becomes clear that a Russian folk tale basically narrates of a hero who must leave his home in order to accomplish a quest and then returns home again. A very similar scheme, according to Campbell, can be found in mythological narrations from all ages and cultures. Since in his view most concrete myths can be traced back to one and the same narrative pattern, Campbell calls this scheme the "Monomyth."[5] The mythological narration mainly consists of three stages: first, the hero needs to leave home and cross the border into an unknown and insecure terrain ("separation"); second, the hero encounters an adventure that results in their achieving special knowledge or powers, gaining a "boon" that enables them to help and support their fellow people ("initiation"); and third, the hero comes back home, brings the boon and lives happily ever after ("return"). Since the myth starts and ends at home, Camp-

---

3 See Vladímir Propp, *Morphology of the Folktale*, 2nd ed. (Austin: University of Texas Press, 1968), 25–65.
4 In identifying a pattern of narrated events the approaches of Propp and Campbell are similar, although there is no explicit reference to Propp in Campbell's work *The Hero with a Thousand Faces*, as far as I can see. Cf. Joseph Campbell, *The Hero with a Thousand Faces*, 3rd ed. (Novato: New World Library, 2008). The English translation of Propp's *Morphology of the Folktale* did not appear until 1958.
5 Campbell, *Hero*, 23.

bell visualizes the scheme by the form of a circle, one half of which represents the home space, whereas the other half is the dangerous and foreign land. Campbell's circle is divided into these two halves by a straight horizontal line that represents the threshold between home and the "region of supernatural wonder."[6] In order to solve the quest and achieve the boon, the hero accordingly must cross this threshold twice: the first time as he leaves from home and then the second time as he returns.

This narrative scheme of "The Hero's Journey" also forms the basis of ancient narrations of otherworldly journeys, because obviously a human has to leave the earthly sphere in order to travel to the otherworld, and is then consequently expected to return as soon as his mission is accomplished.[7] If this turns out to be correct, the elements of the scheme can be seen as recurring "motifs," which fulfill a certain narrative function within the journey account. To test this hypothesis, otherworldly journeys from Menippean literature will be examined first, before turning to the New Testament afterwards. A main focus of the analysis that follows will be directed to the crossing of the threshold between earth and the otherworld.

Otherworldly Journeys in Menippean Literature

A main trait of Menippean narrations lies in the frequent crossing of the borders between heaven, earth and Hades. Not only do humans travel to the heavenly realm or to the underworld, but characters from heaven or Hades also show up on the surface of the earth in several instances. The following analysis, however, will concentrate on the writings that depict a human hero traveling the otherworld.

Journeys to Hades

The majority of Lucian's *The Downward Journey* (*Cataplus*) deals with the travel from the earthly sphere to the land of the dead. Hermes, the heavenly messenger, accompanies a group of people who have died a short time before and leads them to the place where they are to enter the boat of Charon the ferryman who wants to take them across the river Lethe to the underworldly court. They have already

---

[6] See Campbell, *Hero*, esp. 23–31.
[7] The boundary that divides the earthly sphere from the otherworldly realm forms a major structural marker of the narrated cosmological space. On narrations of heavenly ascensions as accounts of boundary crossing see Himmelfarb, "Practice," 123.

passed the entrance (Lucian, *Catapl.* 4, στόμιον) to the netherworld and now face the major transit to their eternal dwelling place, because nobody is allowed to travel there on their own.

During the process of boarding the boat a long dialogue emerges between Hermes and Charon, who discuss the awkward behavior of three travelers in particular who take very different views on their fate: a rich tyrant (Megapethes), a poor cobbler (Mikyllos) and a Cynic philosopher (Cyniscus).[8] As his name already indicates, the tyrant laments his death all the time. He cannot stand the fact that he has to leave all his possessions behind and even sees his enemies inheriting what he once owned. Megapethes even tried to run away from the group so that Hermes by the help of the Cynic had to run after him and catch him again (*Catapl.* 4). Due to his unwillingness to come to terms with his death the formerly rich man had to be put in fetters and is now tied to the mast of Charon's boat (*Catapl.* 13). The Cynic, on the contrary, laughs all the time, makes fun of the tyrant and takes everything very easy. Similarly, the formerly poor shoemaker arrives at Charon's boat happily. Being asked why he is so happy about his death, Mikyllos explains that now he does not have to suffer from hunger and toil anymore.[9] Later he puts the obvious contrast between himself and the tyrant into words by the punchline: "We, the poor people, laugh, whereas the rich grieve and lament" (*Catapl.* 15).[10] The reversal of statuses through death is illustrated vividly and embodied in the consequent narration of the transit. The cobbler is the last one to enter the boat that happens to be already out of seats, so Mikyllos is allowed to sit on the shoulders of the tyrant (*Catapl.* 19).

Having arrived at the other side, the darkness of the underworld makes everybody look alike; no social differences and hierarchies exist anymore (*Catapl.* 22). All the dead then must be brought before the seat of the judge Rhadamanthys who examines the deeds that they have done during their lifetimes. Again, the narration makes use of a graphic illustration, for the sins are visible as marks (στίγματα) on the souls and bodies of the dead (*Catapl.* 24).[11] Everybody is stripped of their clothes and judged by Rhadamanthys.[12] The judge sends the Cynic and the cobbler to the island of the blessed, because they have lead virtuous lives. But the tyrant, who has gained his wealth by committing all sorts of fraud, sexual abuse, and murder,

---

[8] On Lucian's selection of his main characters see Helm, *Lucian*, 66.
[9] Seen this way, death is liberation from life's hardship. See Gómez Cardó, "Menippus," 51.
[10] The more a person possessed at lifetime, the more intense the lament about the loss. Cf. Gómez Cardó, "Menippus," 50.
[11] Cf. Ronald F. Hock, "Lazarus and Mikyllus: Greco-Roman Backgrounds to Luke 16:19–31," *JBL* 106 (1987): 447–63 (459).
[12] On the historical background of the motives of the otherworldly judgment and the visible marks on the mortals' souls see Helm, *Lucian*, 31–32.

putting people to death without hearing them in the trial, is punished eternally. He is not allowed to drink from the water of Lethe that makes people forget everything about their past, so that he has to remember his former wealth and will grieve for it in all eternity (*Catapl.* 28). Nobody returns to the earthly sphere. Megapenthes' begging and flight attempt proved unsuccessful.

In another work, called *Menippus* (or *Necyomantia*), the Cynic philosopher and inventor of the genre plays the main role.[13] Without dying he has managed to pay a visit to the netherworld and tells his friend everything about the journey after his return. In order to gain access to Hades, Menippos undergoes a lengthy procedure by the help of a Babylonian magician (*Nec.* 6–7).[14] Additionally, he dresses himself up with a lion's skin and felt cap and takes a lyre with him to fool the guard of the netherworld and make him think he was Herakles (*Nec.* 8).[15] In this masquerade he actually passes the entrance, transits the chasm that the magician summoned up for him (*Nec.* 9) and convinces Charon to allow him on the ferry. In the dark of Hades they arrive at the court where the judge—this time it is Minos—sits on his throne (*Nec.* 11).[16]

Similarly to the narrative plot of the *Cataplus*,[17] the work describes a reversal of statuses that mainly affects the wealthy who are sentenced to eternal punishment because of all the crimes they committed during their lives.[18] The poor on the other hand receive a less severe punishment (*Nec.* 14). All earthly beauty is lost, too, after death. Seeing the dead being stripped of their wealth makes Menippos, the Cynic laugh, whereas all the formerly wealthy people lament over their loss (*Nec.* 17).[19]

Returning from Hades is easy. The magician shows Menippos a shortcut that brings him quickly back to earth where he now informs his friend about his insight

---

[13] The appearance of Menippos as a literary character in Lucian's work is usually seen as a proof that Lucian follows his *Vorlage* of the philosopher from Gadara particularly closely here. The same applies to Lucian's *Icaromenippus* (see 2.2). Cf. Relihan, *Ancient Menippean Satire*, 104; McCarthy, "Lucian," 10.

[14] See Bousset, "Himmelsreise," 246; Gómez Cardó, "Menippus," 57. The procedure reminds of initiation rites in the Mystery Religions (cf. Helm, *Lucian*, 22–23) or necromancy (cf. Bauckham, "Descents," 26). On ritual preparation for the experience of an ascent in the mysteries see Martha Himmelfarb, *Ascent to Heaven in Jewish and Christian Apocalypses* (New York: Oxford University Press, 1993), 108.

[15] The narration draws upon Homer's story of Herakles (cf. Gómez Cardó, "Menippus," 54–55), combining it with elements from the descents of Orpheus and Theseus (cf. Bauckham, "Descents," 23).

[16] Cf. Bousset, "Himmelsreise," 250–51 on the motif of the otherworldly judges that forms the basis of Lucian's accounts. Bousset traces it back to Plato's so-called *Apocalypse of Er* (Pl., *Plt.* 10.14–15).

[17] On the similarities in the last judgment see Helm, *Lucian*, 68–69.

[18] Cf. Helm, *Lucian*, 51.

[19] The seer Teiresias conforms the insight that accordingly a simple life without luxury is the best life a person can lead. On the roots of the motif cf. Bauckham, "Descents," 22.

that a simple and modest life is the best. The underworld has even passed a new law that the souls of the rich must return to earth after death again, while their bodies are punished, and will be reborn as donkeys so that they may serve the poor (*Nec.* 20). By this measure the reversal of statuses becomes obvious.

Journeys to Heaven

A very similar plot underlies Lucian's work *Icaromenippus*. Again, Menippos holds a conversation with his friend, albeit this time the hero has just returned from his trip to heaven. Of course the journey requires quite a bit of preparation. Modeled on the example of Daedalus, Menippos builds himself a pair of wings, but avoiding wax as glue, not to get himself into the same trouble that caused Daedalus' adventure to fail (*Icar.* 2–3).[20]

Equipped like this, Menippos makes his way to the moon and consequently to heaven where he meets Zeus and the other gods. Again, the journey helps the protagonist to regard earthly conditions from a new point of view. This time the insight mainly exposes the philosophers' folly, who are greedy and unreliable, teaching in an opportunistic way without even believing themselves what they preach.[21] Their natural philosophy lacks all evidence, as Menippos now finds out by visiting the moon (*Icar.* 20).[22] But the wealthy and powerful also get criticized for their vicious habits that Menippos can clearly see from above (*Icar.* 15–17). The work ends with Menippos' visiting the council of the gods where Zeus grants his wish to punish the philosophers. The highest of gods decides to crush them all soon with his thunderbolt (*Icar.* 33). The short closing remark narrates how Hermes takes Menippos back to earth, where he meets his friend (*Icar.* 34).

A somewhat special case can be found in Seneca's *Apocolocyntosis*, because although the main character dies, he does not go to Hades immediately, but travels to heaven first.[23] The protagonist is not just any person, but the emperor Claudius, who accordingly wants to be consecrated as a god himself after death, like his ancestor Augustus already was. Seneca, however, describes the traverse between

---

20 Helm, *Lucian*, 105–106 offers a discussion of the motific background of the procedure.
21 See Helm, *Lucian*, 90–91 on the general criticism in the *Icaromenippus*.
22 Cf. Catherine Hezser, "Ancient 'Science Fiction': Journeys into Space and Visions of the World in Jewish, Christian, and Greco-Roman Literature of Antiquity," in *Christian Origins and Hellenistic Judaism: Social and Literary Contexts for the New Testament*, ed. Stanley E. Porter and Andrew W. Pitts (Leiden: Brill, 2013), 397–438 (415–16).
23 The dialogue differs from other Menippean works in including both a journey to Heaven and a journey to Hades afterwards. Cf. also Relihan, *Ancient Menippean Satire*, 76.

the spheres in much less detail than does Lucian. Seneca does describe the circumstances and reliability of Claudius' death at length, though. Partly, the author uses the narration of Claudius' final breath to make fun of the emperor's bodily flaws[24] in order to show how bad a person he is. On the other hand the emphasis that Seneca lays on the reliability of his account (*Apocol.* 1.1–3) also stresses the satirical quality of his narration,[25] because no mortal would have been able to attend the heavenly proceedings of course.

After his death, Claudius makes his way to the citadel of the gods, who do not want to grant him access at first. Only after winning over Hercules, Claudius can enter the gathering of gods, because Hercules forced their way in (*Apocol.* 8.1).[26] The main reason why the heavenly council decides against Claudius' application is that Claudius was an unjust judge during the time of his reign, pronouncing death sentences without even listening to what the accused had to say (*Apocol.* 10.3–4),[27] very much like the charge against the rich tyrant in Lucian's *Cataplus*.[28]

Once more it is Mercury's job (Greek Hermes) to guide the dead person to Hades (*Apocol.* 11.6). On his arrival there, Claudius is accused of murdering innumerable adversaries without proper trials. The judge refuses to listen to Claudius' plea, just as the former emperor had always put those to death whom he wanted to get rid of, without listening to possible defenses (*Apocol.* 14.2).[29] In the end, Claudius becomes a servant himself and has to work as a court usher in the underworld (*Apocol.* 15.2). This work, too, culminates in the reversal of fortunes and statuses, accordingly.

---

24 The emperor is known to have suffered from flatulence, so Seneca has his soul leave the body through the anus, and not, as would be the usual notion, through the mouth (*Apocol.* 4.2–3). On this much discussed detail see Relihan, *Ancient Menippean Satire*, 81. Furthermore Claudius exhibits severe walking problems and an inarticulate way of talking.
25 Cf. also Allan A. Lund, *[L. Annaeus Seneca] Apocolocyntosis Divi Claudii* (Heidelberg: Universitätsverlag C. Winter, 1994), 61.
26 The sequence of events is not altogether clear at this point of the narration, because the handwritten tradition has a—probably small—gap at this place. Cf. Joachim Adamietz, "Senecas 'Apocolocyntosis'," in *Die römische Satire*, ed. Joachim Adamietz (Darmstadt: Wissenschaftliche Buchgesellschaft, 1986), 356–82 (373); Detlev Dormeyer, "Die Apotheose in Seneca 'Apocolocyntosis' und die Himmelfahrt Lk 24,50–53; Apg 1,9–11," in *Testimony and Interpretation: Early Christology and Its Judeo-Hellenistic Milieu*, ed. Jiri Mrázek and Jan Roskovec, JSNTSup 272 (London: T&T Clark, 2004), 125–42 (134).
27 On the moral criteria of Menippean judgments see Relihan, *Ancient Menippean Satire*, 86. On the criticism against the regime and the importance of Seneca's work with this respect cf. also Dormeyer, "Apotheose," 140.
28 The parallel in characterization between Seneca's Claudius and Lucian's Megapenthes is also observed by Helm, *Lucian*, 72.
29 Cf. Lund, *Apocolocyntosis*, 122.

The Narrative Scheme

Each of the four narrations dedicates much attention to the outward journey to Hades or heaven.[30] Getting there is not easy. It takes a trip on Charon's boat (*Cataplus* and *Necyomantia*), special preparations (*Necyomantia* and *Icaromenippus*), help (*Necyomantia*) or tools (*Necyomantia* and *Icaromenippus*), or even force (Seneca's *Apocolocyntosis*) to gain access to the otherworldly spheres.

Much shorter are the endings of these Menippean writings. The main character either takes a shortcut back home (*Necyomantia*) or is quickly guided by Hermes (*Icaromenippus*). Two works, however, do not narrate the option of getting back home at all, namely the works in which the main characters have died. Once you are dead there is no return (*Cataplus* and *Apocolocyntosis*). Whereas the outward journey is difficult and needs to be described in detail, the way back is either easy or impossible. Oftentimes the dead struggle to accept their fate. Those who used to be rich or powerful during their earthly lives do not want to let go of their former privileges.[31] Because of their struggle they are given a companion on their way to Hades—mostly in the person of Hermes—who explains the procedure to them and also uses slight force if necessary.[32] Special assistance is needed by Menippos, who manages to access Hades without even dying by the help of the Babylonian magician.[33] Humans on their way to heaven, however, are not always reliant on an otherworldly guide or travel companion.

---

[30] Interestingly, in his comparison of Lucian's *Menippus* and *Icaromenippus*, Relihan also identifies a number of recurring traits, the pattern of which in other words forms a deep structure of these Menippean narrations. Relihan's scheme includes the following elements: (1) the protagonist returns from an otherworldly journey and (2) tells his friend about it in some detail. (3) His decision to travel Hades or Heaven is due to Menippos' observations that many philosophers are charlatans, not practicing what they preach. (4) Some preparation is necessary in order to make sure the journey will be successful. (5) Seen from below or above human egocentrism proves to be folly, (6) as trustworthy inhabitants of the otherworldly sphere confirm. (7) The dialogue thus ends with a confirmation of the newly learned re-evaluation of earthly priorities. See Relihan, *Ancient Menippean Satire*, 105–14.

[31] Ancient Jewish and Early Christian apocalyptic texts, too, show a vast interest in otherworldly punishment and reward. Cf. Himmelfarb, *Tours*, 169–70.

[32] On the relevance of a tour guide in Apocalyptic literature see Meghan Henning, "Hell as 'Heterotopia': Edification and Interpretation from Enoch to the Apocalypses of Peter and Paul," in *Between Canonical and Apocryphal Texts: Processes of Reception, Rewriting, and Interpretation in Early Judaism and Early Christianity*, ed. Jörg Frey, Claire Clivaz and Tobias Nicklas, WUNT 419 (Tübingen: Mohr Siebeck, 2019), 309–31 (317–18). The Menippean travel guides are distinct from the apocalyptic ones in that they not only wait for the human arrivals within the otherworld but also support them crossing the threshold between earth and the otherworldly sphere.

[33] Cf. Gómez Cardó, "Menippus," 57–58.

As long as the protagonists are still alive, they can return from the journey—and tell their friend what they just experienced. Each of the four texts under consideration tells the story of a reversal of statuses in the otherworld. Seen from heaven or from the perspective of death, earthly power, prestige and wealth are no desirable achievements.[34] On the contrary, wealth and power are usually founded on unjust behavior and will be lost after death, so that the loss causes great pain to the formerly rich people. Furthermore all unjust behavior will be punished by the gods or in the last judgment.

In the *Necyomantia* and the *Icaromenippus* the main character makes his way back to earth after his otherworldly journey, bringing the knowledge to his friend.[35] These two Menippean works, thus, fit well within the narrative scheme of Campbell's Monomyth. But the *Cataplus* and the *Apocolocyntosis* end in Hades.[36] There is no return, although everybody has learned their lessons here as well.

Otherworldly Journeys in the New Testament

In the New Testament, elaborate accounts of otherworldly journeys are rare. The most lengthy text that deals with a journey to Hades is the Lukan parable of Dives and Lazarus (Luke 16:19–31). The most detailed journey to heaven by far is of course Revelation. The vision of the trip starts with the assumption of the seer into heaven in Rev 4:1.

A Journey to Hades: Luke 16:19–31

The Lukan parable of the rich man and Lazarus includes striking parallels to the Menippean writings and especially to the *Cataplus*. In the New Testament account, after living very different lives, both the rich and the poor man die and consequently end up in the otherworld.[37] Lazarus who suffered from hunger during his earthly life is carried to Abraham's bosom by angels, where he finds comfort.[38] But

---

34 See Neumann, *Lukas und Menippos*, 275–79.
35 The feature of sharing the message with the fellow humans can also be found in the apocalyptic book of Third Baruch. Cf. Yarbro Collins, "Seven Heavens," 77.
36 See Bauckham, "Descents," 10, 16 and 21–22 on the inescapability of Hades.
37 On the sharp contrast the parable uses see Hans-Georg Gradl, "Von den Kosten des Reichtums: Die Beispielerzählung vom reichen Mann und armen Lazarus (Lk 16,19–31) textpragmatisch gelesen," *MThZ* 56 (2005): 305–17 (309).
38 Cf. Bauckham, "Descents," 36 on the recognition of this motif.

the rich man who enjoyed a luxury lifestyle wearing purple clothes and dining opulently must suffer from Hades' unbearable heat (see esp. Luke 16:25).[39] Traditional interpretations often assume that the bosom of Abraham where angels carry the poor man must be located in the heavenly sphere. This is, however, debatable, since Abraham and the rich man can easily communicate in the otherworld and are only separated by a chasm (χάσμα, Luke 16:26; cf. Lucian, *Nec.* 9). Clearly and explicitly the rich man goes to Hades after death (Luke 16:23), where he suffers from flames and great heat. Against the backdrop of ancient Hellenistic cosmology—with which Luke and his audience are obviously familiar—it would be natural to think that both Lazarus and the formerly rich man dwell in Hades after death, but within different areas that are strictly separated.[40]

There is a lesson to learn from their fate, because Luke, too, describes a reversal of fortunes.[41] The formerly rich man must suffer, whereas the formerly poor man finds comfort at Abraham's bosom. When Abraham turns down the rich man's request to send Lazarus and bring him some water to cool his tongue and ease his pain, the rich man finally understands this dynamics of status reversal. It becomes clear from the wish that he utters consequently: to warn his brothers, so that they might change their lives as long as that is still possible and escape their eternal punishment.[42] But they do have Moses and the prophets, which must suffice, as Abraham states (Luke 16:27–31). As in Lucian's *Cataplus*, there is no return from the journey in this account.[43]

---

[39] The description of his life forms a close parallel to the characterizations of the rich and unjust in Lucian's Menippean works. Cf. Hock, "Lazarus," 458.

[40] Cf. Hock, "Lazarus," 456 on aspects of the parable's cosmology. See also Outi Lehtipuu, "The Imagery of the Lukan Afterworld in the Light of Some Roman and Greek Parallels," in *Zwischen den Reichen: Neues Testament und römische Herrschaft*, ed. Michael Labahn and Jürgen Zangenberg, TANZ 36 (Tübingen: Francke, 2002), 133–46 (136). In Lucian all the dead are carried to Hades, crossing the river Lethe. Those who have lead a morally good life are allowed to enter the Isle of the Blessed, whereas the wicked have to dwell in eternal darkness (see the judgment scene Lucian, *Catapl.* 24 and 28). Thus, the plot of Lucian's *Cataplus* suggests that both the places for the good and for the wicked are parts of Hades. On the extensive description of the Isles of the Blessed in Lucian's *Verae historiae* see Heinz-Günther Nesselrath, "Die Reise zu den Inseln der Seligen von Hesiod bis Lukian," in *Between the Worlds: Contexts, Sources, and Analogues of Scandinavian Otherworld Journeys*, ed. Matthias Egeler and Wilhelm Heizmann (Berlin: De Gruyter, 2020), 373–88 (384).

[41] Gradl, "Kosten," 312 offers a helpful schematic that illustrates both, the contrast between the poor and the rich man in their earthly lives and in the otherworld, and the reversal of fortunes that death brings for them.

[42] It is absolutely plausible when Gradl, "Kosten," 314 assumes that this warning ultimately addresses the Lukan audience. Also see Henning, *Educating Early Christians*, 125.

[43] Cf. Gradl, "Kosten," 316.

A Journey to Heaven: Rev 4:1–11

The book of Revelation narrates a lengthy vision that starts in chapter 1 and then stretches all over the course of the writing that ends in chapter 22. Interestingly, with the beginning of Revelation 4 the seer John changes his location. Whereas the events of Revelation 1–3 happened within the earthly sphere, chapters 4 and following take place in heaven. Through a door that opens in heaven (Rev 4:1, θύρα ἠνεῳγμένη ἐν τῷ οὐρανῷ),[44] John enters the heavenly realm, as the trumpet-like voice has ordered him to do.[45] This is possible "in the spirit" (ἐν πνεύματι, Rev 4:2). From now on the seer remains in heaven and watches the events that are going on in heaven as well as the catastrophes on earth from his heavenly point of view.

Revelation 4 introduces the heavenly setting by underscoring the central position of God's throne, the power he possesses over all the world—including not only heaven but also earth and the netherworld (Rev 5:13), as well as the reverence he receives from all living creatures.[46] The heavenly scenery is organized in concentric circles of groups of creatures, all of which point towards the throne in the middle.[47] God is enthroned in the center and his radiant "glory" can be perceived visually by John the seer.[48] The description moves from the center to the outside step by step, mentioning the four living beings and 24 elders, and then later in Revelation 5 myriads of angels that join the heavenly worship. By falling to the ground before the throne and honoring the one who sits on it (Rev 4:10), the living beings and 24 elders also establish an obvious hierarchy. God, who sits on the throne is the

---

[44] The motif of the heavenly door recurs in Third Baruch (see Yarbro Collins, "Seven Heavens," 77–78) and also has parallels in 1 Enoch and the Testament of Abraham (see Heszer, "Ancient 'Science Fiction'," 433). On the seer's ascent in Revelation 4 cf. also Nils Neumann, "Der Thron und die δόξα: Die anschauliche Charakterisierung Gottes in der Johannesoffenbarung," in *Gott als Figur: Narratologische Analysen biblischer Texte und ihrer Adaptionen*, ed. Ute E. Eisen and Ilse Müllner, HBS 82 (Freiburg: Herder, 2016), 374–94 (379–80).
[45] This feature closely parallels the ascension in Test. Levi 2:6. Cf. Yarbro Collins, "Seven Heavens," 63.
[46] On the similarity between the notion of heaven in Revelation and in Lucian's *Icaromenippus* see Heszer, "Ancient 'Science Fiction'," 432–33.
[47] On the origin of the ancient Jewish notion that the believers, too, will be seated on heavenly thrones in eternity, and on the interconnectedness of heavenly visions and notions of the afterlife see John J. Collins, "A Throne in the Heavens: Apotheosis in Pre-Christian Judaism," in Collins and Fishbane, *Death, Ecstasy and Other Worldly Journeys*, 43–58.
[48] The Greek term δόξα occurs explicitly only in the lists of predicates that the creatures give to the one on the throne (Rev 4:9, 11; 5:12, 13; 7:12; 19:1) and then later in the description of the new creation (Rev 21:23; see also 22:4). The context in Revelation 4 suggests that the radiance that emerges from the throne forms the visible aspect of God's glory.

one and only authority, and all creatures owe him their reverence.⁴⁹ This emphasis is of particular interest, because within the earthly realm of Revelation's time God's authority seems to be highly controversial. The book is full of hidden or sometimes even quite obvious criticism against those who claim that Christian faith is compatible with loyal citizenship within the Roman empire. No, says the author of Revelation, you have to decide: either you stay loyal to God and worship him alone, or you pay loyalty to the emperor, but this in fact means to worship the satanic beast.⁵⁰ The heavenly perspective thus reveals an insight into the true hierarchies of the whole world with God's authority that exceeds all earthly and human powers by far.

The seer John does not return from his journey to heaven. Within Relevation's narrative dynamic this is due to the fact that the border between heaven and earth is overturned in the final section of the book. In the end heaven and earth flee from God's face (Rev 20:11), and the new creation joins heaven and earth into one new unity where God himself dwells among men. According to this narrative logic there is no possibility and no necessity for John to return from his trip. Revelation's closing verses do, however, reflect on the communication between the seer and the Christian communities within the earthly realm. Quite like the returning Menippos in Lucian's satiric writings, the seer John has a message to convey to his fellows. Although Revelation does not narrate of the seer's return from his journey explicitly, at the beginning of the work the main character has already received the order to write down what he saw and heard, so that the Christian churches in the province of Asia can learn about the apocalyptic announcement (see Rev 1:19). Now, the end of the text underscores the necessity to deliver all these words faithfully (Rev 22:7, 18–19). The work must not be sealed, because the events that it describes are about to begin immediately (Rev 22:10).

The New Testament Journeys

The Lukan parable as well as Revelation's vision both represent somewhat incomplete versions of Campbell's scheme. For different reasons neither Lazarus or the rich man nor the seer John can return to the sphere where they started their journeys. But still, both examples stress the fact that on the outward journey there is

---

49 See Neumann, "Thron," 386–87 on the concentric spatiality of Revelation's heavenly realm and its implications.
50 On the anti-imperial line of attack in Revelation see Darrell D. Hannah, "The Throne of His Glory: The Divine Throne and Heavenly Mediators in Revelation and the Similitudes of Enoch," *ZNW* 94 (2003): 68–96 (70); Marianne Meye Thompson, "Worship in the Book of Revelation," *Ex Auditu* 8 (1992): 45–54 (46–47).

a threshold between the earthly sphere and the otherworld, which can only be crossed under special circumstances. This applies to the threshold between earth and Hades in Luke 16 as well as to the chasm that separates the place of the blessed from the eternal punishment of the wicked, and it also applies to the threshold between earth and heaven, which the seer John is allowed to cross through a door in Revelation 4.

Furthermore, both journeys enable the main characters to examine earthly life from a new point of view: in Hades the rich man soon finds out that he should have lived a different life in order to escape his horrible punishment. And John the seer gains insight into God's majesty that excels all earthly authority and by this vision immediately settles the question of whether or not one should be loyal to the Roman emperor and worship him.

Conclusion

Apart from their obviously very different religious propositions, the comparison of the narrative schemes shows that there are similarities as well as differences between the Menippean and New Testament accounts of otherworldly journeys.[51] Firstly, all texts discussed above dedicate some attention to the possibilities of crossing the threshold between this world and heaven or Hades. Secondly, the journey gives the main characters the opportunity to see the earth—and human life—from a new and different perspective. What seems valuable, desirable and powerful from an earthly point of view, turns out to be frail, undesirable and even harmful when examined from the perspective of the otherworld. This leads to a new and different evaluation of earthly values that includes a reversal of statuses between rich and poor, between mighty and weak. Thirdly, not all heroes return from their journeys. Especially those who die can never come back to life. Death is irreversible. Only one character in the Menippean writings discussed above manages to make his way back to earth, namely Lucian's Menippos who found a way of traveling Hades without dying. That is why he can return to earth in the end. The threshold between earth and heaven is permeable in both directions,[52] whereas the threshold between earth and Hades is only semi-permeable: humans usually can only cross it in downward direction once they have died.

---

[51] Very convincingly Ronald F. Hock has emphasized the parallels between the Lukan parable and Menippean literature. See Hock, "Lazarus."
[52] Very similarly Himmelfarb, *Ascent*, 4.

Because the borders are hard to cross, the travelers between the spheres oftentimes need assistance by otherworldly characters that serve as helpers, guides or travel companions. Accessing heaven is sometimes easier than entering Hades.[53] At times humans can make their way to heaven on their own without a helper, like Lucian's Menippos in the *Icaromenippus*[54] or Revelation's John,[55] unless they are rascals like Seneca's emperor Claudius. Especially those who have to die and adjourn to Hades against their will need a guide who hinders them from escaping their fate. This applies to Lucian's tyrant Megapenthes, as well as to Seneca's Claudius and Luke's rich man. The dead can never return to their earthly lives. Accordingly, some of Lucian's Menippean writings exhibit the full "circle" of a hero's journey as described by Campbell, whereas other texts, seen against this foil seem incomplete.

This raises the question what does happen or does not happen after the hero's (un)successful return from an otherworldly journey. This question is answered very clearly in Lucian's *Necyomantia* and *Icaromenippus*: the main character comes back to the earthly sphere and immediately shares his new gained insight about the reversal of statuses with his friend. Similarly, the rich man in Hades in the Lukan parable expresses the wish to send a messenger to his brothers in order to warn them from the fate that awaits them once they die. The rich tyrant of the *Cataplus*—although he makes a number of attempts to run away and return to earth—is not allowed to get back to life. He must watch how others inherit his possessions, unable to change a thing about it.

Thus, altogether the journeys under consideration here do not bring up their ethical implications only modestly.[56] The "boon" that the heroes bring back from

---

[53] This feature in the sources considered here parallels Martha Himmelfarb's observation that in the Hellenistic world humans are not always clearly distinguished from the gods. See Himmelfarb, *Ascent*, 47.
[54] Lucian's main character does, however, meet a counselor. Menippos makes all the way to the moon on his own, where he encounters the philosopher Empedocles who gives him good advice that helps Menippos to continue his journey successfully. Cf. Heszer, "Ancient 'Science Fiction'," 417.
[55] On Christ's role as a mediator in the heavenly throne scene of Revelation cf. Hannah, "Throne." It is obvious that in Revelation, too, there are heavenly agents who help the seer John to understand what he experiences—most notably in the function of an *angelus interpres*. These mediators, however, are not directly involved in the process of John's ascension into heaven. Bauckham, "Descents," 29 spots a historical development at this point: according to his view the older Greek accounts feature guides who help the dead find the way to Hades, whereas the later apocalyptic texts have the guides welcome the visitors in Hades, showing them around and explaining them what they see. On the role of the *angelus interpres* see also Bremmer, "Descents," 343–45. Martha Himmelfarb considers apocalyptic descents to the world of the dead to be "demonstrative explanations." See Himmelfarb, *Tours*, esp. 66–67.
[56] Bart D. Ehrman also underscores the ethical impetus that shapes Ancient Jewish and Early Christian accounts of otherworldly journeys. See, e.g., Bart D. Ehrman, *Heaven and Hell: A History*

their journeys is their ethical message, the re-evaluation of earthly values from the perspective of the otherworld.[57] In fact, some of the sources considered here have otherworldly authorities confirm this insight, like the underworldly judge Radamanthys in Lucian's *Cataplus*. But his authority is hardly necessary to get the point; human common sense suffices in order to rethink earthly priorities when seen from an otherworldly angle.[58] Even if the hero does not return from his journey, as in the *Cataplus* or the New Testament sequences, this ethical boon is available to the texts' readers who in the process of reading have the chance of taking in the otherworldly perspective. The Menippean dialogues as well as the New Testament examples make it quite explicit and obvious what their readers are supposed to learn from the narrations.[59] Death is irreversible. Hence, it is the readers' responsibility to bring the message and its ethical postulations to life within the earthly realm.[60]

---

of the Afterlife (London: Oneworld, 2020), 5, 13, 15. With regard to the Matthean notion of the sphere of death and descriptions of the underworld in Jewish apocalypses see most prominently Henning, *Educating Early Christians*, 41 and esp. 153–56. On the pedagogical function of Lucian's otherworldly journey accounts see Gómez Cardó, "Menippus," 53. For apocalyptic literature cf. Henning, "Hell," 321 and 330–31. Meghan Henning underscores the fact that apocalyptic descriptions of the otherworld create "heterotopias," spaces that are different from but not altogether incomparable to the readers' real world experiences so that the heterotopia allows the addressees to view their everyday world in a new light.

57 Accordingly, these narrations fit within John C. Stephens' category of journeys to "moral awareness." See Stephens, *Journeys*, esp. 123–24. In his book Stephens groups otherworldly journey accounts into six kinds, differentiating between "mystical" journeys and journeys that lead to "spiritual transformation," "philosophic wisdom," etc. These categories, however, should not be taken as indicating strict separations. The texts considered in the present contribution in fact show that their heroes often also undergo a spiritual change and gain philosophic wisdom.

58 Cf. Gómez Cardó, "Menippus," 60.

59 In contrast to the sources considered here, many ancient accounts of heavenly ascensions result in the protagonist gaining immortality, as Himmelfarb underscores. See Himmelfarb, "Practice," 124–25. Neither Lucian's Menippos nor the seer John of Revelation become immortal by traveling heaven. And the emperor Claudius, who does expect to become a god by the means of his journey to heaven, is turned down and sent to Hades. Accordingly, the boon that the hero brings back home to the audience in the Menippean and biblical accounts is of a different quality, because it serves an ethical reevaluation of earthly priorities. From their journeys the heroes return bringing a message that is of relevance for the whole world, as Campbell observes with regard to his "Monomyth." See Campbell, *Hero*, 30.

60 With respect to Revelation Carol J. Rotz and Jan A. du Rand convincingly argue that this work mainly aims at forming the relation between God and its readers. Cf. Carol J. Rotz and Jan A. du Rand, "The One Who Sits on the Throne: Towards a Theory of Theocentric Characterisation According to the Apocalypse of John," *Neotest* 33 (1999): 91–111 (esp. 107). Within the historical context in Early Christianity this relation does bear a clear ethical implication. Those who worship the

References

Adamietz, Joachim. "Senecas 'Apocolocyntosis'." Pages 356–82 in *Die römische Satire*. Edited by Joachim Adamietz. Darmstadt: Wissenschaftliche Buchgesellschaft, 1986.

Bauckham, Richard. "Descents to the Underworld." Pages 9–48 in *The Fate of the Dead: Studies in the Jewish and Christian Apocalypses*. Edited by Richard Bauckham. Leiden: Brill, 1998.

Bousset, Wilhelm. "Die Himmelsreise der Seele." *AR* 4 (1901): 136–69 and 229–73.

Bremmer, Jan N. "Descents to Hell and Ascends to Heaven in Apocalyptic Literature." Pages 340–57 in *The Oxford Handbook of Apocalyptic Literature*. Edited by John J. Collins. Oxford: Oxford University Press, 2014.

Campbell, Joseph. *The Hero with a Thousand Faces*. 3rd ed. Novato: New World Library, 2008.

Coblentz Bautch, Kelley. "Spatiality and Apocalyptic Literature." *HeBAI* 5 (2016): 273–88.

Collins, John J. "A Throne in the Heavens: Apotheosis in pre-Christian Judaism." Pages 43–58 in *Death, Ecstasy and Other Worldly Journeys*. Edited by John J. Collins and Michael Fishbane. Albany: State University of New York Press, 1995.

Dormeyer, Detlev. "Die Apotheose in Seneca 'Apocolocyntosis' und die Himmelfahrt Lk 24,50–53; Apg 1,9–11." Pages 125–42 in *Testimony and Interpretation: Early Christology and Its Judeo-Hellenistic Milieu*. Edited by Jiri Mrázek and Jan Roskovec. JSNTSup 272. London: T&T Clark, 2004.

Ehrman, Bart D. *Heaven and Hell: A History of the Afterlife*. London: Oneworld, 2020.

Gómez Cardó, Pilar. "Menippus, a Truly Living Ghost in Lucian's Necromancy." Pages 47–64 in *Visitors from Beyond the Grave: Ghosts in World Literature*. Edited by Dámaris Romero-González, Israel Muñoz-Gallarte and Gabriel Laguna-Mariscal. Coimbra: Coimbra University Press, 2019.

Gradl, Hans-Georg. "Von den Kosten des Reichtums: Die Beispielerzählung vom reichen Mann und armen Lazarus (Lk 16,19–31) textpragmatisch gelesen." *MThZ* 56 (2005): 305–17.

Hannah, Darrell D. "The Throne of His Glory: The Divine Throne and Heavenly Mediators in Revelation and the Similitudes of Enoch." *ZNW* 94 (2003): 68–96.

Helm, Rudolf. *Lucian und Menipp*. Leipzig: Teubner, 1906.

Henning, Meghan. *Educating Early Christians through the Rhetoric of Hell: "Weeping and Gnashing of Teeth" as Paideia in Matthew and the Early Church*. WUNT 2/382. Tübingen: Mohr Siebeck, 2014.

Henning, Meghan. "Hell as 'Heterotopia': Edification and Interpretation from Enoch to the Apocalypses of Peter and Paul." Pages 309–31 in *Between Canonical and Apocryphal Texts: Processes of Reception, Rewriting, and Interpretation in Early Judaism and Early Christianity*. Edited by Jörg Frey, Claire Clivaz and Tobias Nicklas. WUNT 419. Tübingen: Mohr Siebeck, 2019.

Heszer, Catherine. "Ancient 'Science Fiction': Journeys into Space and Visions of the World in Jewish, Christian, and Greco-Roman Literature of Antiquity." Pages 397–438 in *Christian Origins and Hellenistic Judaism: Social and Literary Contexts for the New Testament*. Edited by Stanley E. Porter and Andrew W. Pitts. Leiden: Brill, 2013.

Himmelfarb, Martha. *Ascent to Heaven in Jewish and Christian Apocalypses*. New York: Oxford University Press, 1993.

Himmelfarb, Martha. "The Practice of Ascent in the Ancient Mediterranean World." Pages 123–37 in *Death, Ecstasy and Other Worldly Journeys*. Edited by John J. Collins and Michael Fishbane. Albany: State University of New York Press, 1995.

---

enthroned God must not participate in the satanic idolatry that Revelation sees in any reverence to the Roman emperor and his empire. See Thompson, "Worship," 46.

Himmelfarb, Martha. *Tours of Hell: An Apocalyptic Form of Jewish and Christian Literature*. Philadelphia: University of Pennsylvania Press, 1983.

Hock, Ronald F. "Lazarus and Mikyllus: Greco-Roman Backgrounds to Luke 16:19–31." *JBL* 106 (1987): 447–63.

Lehtipuu, Outi. "The Imagery of the Lukan Afterworld in the Light of Some Roman and Greek Parallels." Pages 133–46 in *Zwischen den Reichen: Neues Testament und römische Herrschaft*. Edited by Michael Labahn and Jürgen Zangenberg. TANZ 36. Tübingen: Francke, 2002.

Lund, Allan A. *[L. Annaeus Seneca] Apocolocyntosis Divi Claudii*. Heidelberg: Universitätsverlag C. Winter, 1994.

McCarthy, Barbara P. "Lucian and Menippus." *YCS* 4 (1934): 3–55.

Nesselrath, Heinz-Günther. "Die Reise zu den Inseln der Seligen von Hesiod bis Lukian." Pages 373–88 in *Between the Worlds: Contexts, Sources, and Analogues of Scandinavian Otherworld Journeys*. Edited by Matthias Egeler and Wilhelm Heizmann. Berlin: De Gruyter, 2020.

Neumann, Nils. "Der Thron und die δόξα: Die anschauliche Charakterisierung Gottes in der Johannesoffenbarung." Pages 374–94 in *Gott als Figur: Narratologische Analysen biblischer Texte und ihrer Adaptionen*. Edited by Ute E. Eisen and Ilse Müllner. HBS 82. Freiburg: Herder, 2016.

Neumann, Nils. *Lukas und Menippos: Hoheit und Niedrigkeit in Lk 1,1–2,40 und in der menippeischen Literatur*. NTOA 68. Göttingen: Vandenhoeck & Ruprecht, 2008.

Propp, Vladímir. *Morphology of the Folktale*. 2nd ed. Austin: University of Texas Press, 1968.

Relihan, Joel C. *Ancient Menippean Satire*. Baltimore: John Hopkins University Press, 1993.

Rotz, Carol J., and Jan A. du Rand. "The One Who Sits on the Throne: Towards a Theory of Theocentric Characterisation According to the Apocalypse of John." *Neotest* 33 (1999): 91–111.

Segal, Alan F. "Heavenly Ascent in Hellenistic Judaism, Early Christianity and their Environment." *ANRW* 2.23.2 (1980): 1333–94.

Stephens, John C. *Journeys to the Underworld and Heavenly Realm in Ancient and Medieval Literature*. Jefferson: McFarland & Co., 2019.

Thompson, Marianne Meye. "Worship in the Book of Revelation." *Ex Auditu* 8 (1992): 45–54.

Yarbro Collins, Adela. "The Seven Heavens in Jewish and Christian Apocalypses." Pages 59–93 in *Death, Ecstasy and Other Worldly Journeys*. Edited by John J. Collins and Michael Fishbane. Albany: State University of New York Press, 1995.

Sigurvin Lárus Jónsson
The Educational Aspect of the Lukan Travel Narrative: Jesus as a Πεπαιδευμένος

Abstract: This article approaches the Lukan travel narrative (Luke 9:51–19:27) from the perspective of ancient travel, first exploring the questions of why, if and how this section is designated as a travel narrative and then reflecting on the topic of education as it connects to the narrative strategy of Luke. The *why* is explored in relation to research history, that despite different aspects inevitably returns to the topic of travel in the section, the *if* in comparison to contemporary literature where travel is a predominant topic across genres and the *how* in light of the sources that the Gospel of Luke builds upon, predominantly the ὁδός theme from the Gospel of Mark and the Septuagint. Finally, attention is given to the connection between travel and education in contemporary literature, where the identity of educated persons, πεπαιδευμένοι, are bound up with travel in that travel is a mode of and prerequisite for education. The educational portrait of Paul in Acts as educated has been highlighted in recent scholarship, where travel plays an important part, yet the portrait of Jesus in the Gospel of Luke as a teacher and prophet is also supported through the travel narrative. Instead of depicting Jesus' travel to Jerusalem as a straightforward journey, Luke expands his influence geographically and includes teaching material that builds up the image of Jesus as a πεπαιδευμένος. This educational aspect serves at least two purposes, to establish his authority and to serve as an *exemplum* for early Christians who themselves travel and teach.

Any introduction to the New Testament will contain a discussion of "the travel narrative"[1] or "der Reisebericht"[2] as a descriptive for the section in the Gospel of Luke

---

[1] Examples abound. To name a few, Carl R. Holladay writes: "Especially remarkable in Luke ... is the lengthy Travel Narrative, occupying almost a third of the Gospel (9:51–19:27)" (*Introduction to the New Testament: Reference Edition* [Waco: Baylor University Press, 2017], 50). Luke Timothy Johnson writes: "To accommodate the great amount of new material, Luke ... takes Mark's mention of Jesus' traveling to Jerusalem (Mk 11:1) and opens it up into a ten-chapter 'journey narrative' (9:51–19:44), in which Jesus addresses in turn the crowds, his opponents, and his disciples, as he makes his way toward his destiny in Jerusalem" (*The New Testament: A Very Short Introduction* [Oxford: Oxford University Press, 2010], 49).
[2] David C. Bienert, *Bibelkunde des Neuen Testaments*, 3rd ed. (Gütersloh: Gütersloher Verlagshaus, 2021), 80: "In seinem *großen Reisebericht* (Lk 9,51–19,27) bietet Lukas das Material aus Q und aus seinem »Sondergut« (S^Lk) dar." Udo Schnelle, *Einleitung in das Neue Testament*, 9th rev. ed., UTB 1830 (Göttingen: Vandenhoeck & Ruprecht, 2017), 321: "Den größten Einschnitt gegenüber Mk stellt der

https://doi.org/10.1515/9783110717488-005

that starts with Jesus setting his face to go up to Jerusalem (αὐτὸς τὸ πρόσωπον ἐστήρισεν τοῦ πορεύεσθαι εἰς Ἰερουσαλήμ, Luke 9:51) and ends, in different places according to scholarship,[3] as he reaches his destination with a triumphal entry into the city (Luke 19:28–40 par.). This article will approach the travel narrative from the perspective of ancient travel. We first explore the questions of why, if and how this section is designated as a travel narrative: *why* it is called a travel narrative with regard to research history, *if* it should be described as a travel narrative in comparison to contemporary writings and *how* the author of Luke-Acts receives the topic of travel from his sources and develops it in his narrative to describe the early Christian movement as the "way"—ὁδός (Acts 9:2; 24:14, 22). The Lukan travel narrative serves many theological and narrative purposes for the Gospel, and we conclude with a reflection on the topic of education as it connects to the narrative strategy of a travel narrative. The result of this study is that the author emphasizes the portrait of Jesus as an ideal educated teacher, a πεπαιδευμένος, to establish his authority and to serve as an *exemplum* for early Christians.

A Research History of the *Reisebericht*

Our discussion begins with some considerations about why the designation 'travel narrative' is the predominant descriptive for Luke 9:51–19:27. The Lukan travel narrative has been the subject of discussion in critical biblical scholarship from its inception, on the one hand from a source critical perspective and on the other with regard to content. Johann Jakob Griesbach, in his synopsis published in 1774–1775,[4]

Reisebericht (Lk 9,51–19,27) dar, in den Lukas ausschließlich Sondergut und Q-Überlieferungen integriert, ehe er in 18,15 die markinische Erzählfolge wieder aufnimmt."
3 Filip Noël, *The Travel Narrative in the Gospel of Luke: Interpretation of Lk 9,51–19,28*, Collectanea Biblica et Religiosa Antiqua 5 (Brussel: KVAB, 2004), 249–82 provides a good overview of the different hypotheses. See also Michael Wolter, *Das Lukasevangelium*, HNT 5 (Tübingen: Mohr Siebeck, 2008), 365–68. Wolter summarizes the discussion as: "the spectrum of proposals ... reaches from 18.30 (e.g., Zahn) via 18.35 (e.g., Nolland), 19.10 (e.g., Marshall ...), 19.27/28 (e.g., Bovon; ... F. Noël) and 19.44 (e.g., ... Moessner) to 19.46 ..., 19.48 (e.g., Schleiermacher ...) or even 21.38 (e.g., Meynet)" (*The Gospel According to Luke*, trans. Wayne Coppins, 2 vols. [Waco: Baylor University Press, 2017], 2:41).
4 *Libri historici Novi Testamenti graece 1: Synopsis evangeliorum Matthaei, Marci et Lucae: Textum ad fidem codicum, versionum, et patrum emendavit et lectionis varietatem adiecit J.J. Griesbach* (Halle: Curt, 1774–1775). On the publication history of this synopysis see J.J. Griesbach and Bo Reicke, "Commentatio qua Marci Evangelium totum e Matthaei et Lucae commentariis decerptum esse monstratu," in *J.J. Griesbach: Synoptic and Text-Critical Studies 1776–1976*, ed. Bernard Orchard and Thomas R. W. Longstaff, SNTSMS (Cambridge: Cambridge University Press, 1978), 68–102 (68–69).

as well as in a following commentary on the synoptic Gospels,[5] already discusses Luke 10:1–18:14 as a unit.[6] Griesbach contends that Mark was the latest synoptic Gospel written, employing both Matthew and Luke, and that Mark had left out Luke 10:1–18:14. Griesbach does not use the term "travel narrative",[7] although his modern translator does,[8] yet he highlights the sayings (and thus educational) aspect of the section (*sermonibus Christi*). In English-speaking scholarship of the 19th century the designation "great insertion" or "long insertion"[9] describes this section from a source-critical perspective, corresponding to the "great omission" in Luke (Mark 6:45–8:26). Burnett Hillman Streeter in his influential *Four Gospels* discusses the "great Central Section of Luke, ix.51–xviii.14", thus focusing solely on source-critical observations: "The only safe name by which one can call it is the 'Central Section'—a title which states a fact but begs no questions."[10] The source-critical connection between the Synoptic Gospels (*Literarkritik*) remains an open question in scholarship, although the Two-Source Hypothesis continues to be the dominant model (Luke employs Mark and Q).[11]

From this viewpoint one observes that Luke follows the text of Mark (with modifications) from Luke 3 onward.[12] This dependence on Mark is then abruptly halted in Luke 9:51[13] and resumed in Luke 18:15[14] and finally in Luke 19:28ff. with the entry into Jerusalem.[15] The competing models in the 19th century also served as

---

5 *Commentatio qua Marci evangelium totum e Matthaei et Lucae commentariis decerptum esse monstratur*, 2 vols. (Jena: Officina Stranckmannio-Fickelscherria, 1789–1790), https://www.digitale-sammlungen.de/view/bsb10353846?page=6. On the publication history of this commentary see Griesbach and Reicke, "Commentatio," 70–71.
6 "By leaving out the travel narrative in Luke 10:1–18:14, Mark even sacrificed about one-third of the Gospel of Luke, since this section of the Gospel consists almost entirely of speeches of Christ" (Bo Reicke, "Griesbach's Answer to the Synoptic Question," in Orchard and Longstaff, *J.J. Griesbach*, 50–67 [54]).
7 "[I]mo inde a Luc. 10,1 ad cap. 18,14. Tertiam fere Evangelii Lucae partem intactam praetermitteret, quoniam tota fere sermonibus Christi constat" (Griesbach, *Commentatio*, 4).
8 Reicke, "Griesbach's Answer," 54.
9 See, e.g., Lester Bradner Jr., "The First Written Gospel: Results of Some of the Recent Investigations," *The Biblical World* 1 (1893): 432–44 (433): "Luke's long insertion 9:51–18:14."
10 Burnett Hillman Streeter, *The Four Gospels: A Study of Origins*, 4th rev. ed. (London: Macmillan, 1930), 203.
11 For an overview see John S. Kloppenborg, *Excavating Q: The History and Setting of the Sayings Gospel* (Edinburgh: T&T Clark, 2000).
12 *Synopsis quattuor evangeliorum*, ed. Kurt Aland, 15th ed., 4th corr. Print. (Stuttgart: Deutsche Bibelgesellschaft, 2005), §§13, 20–22; §§16, 24–25; ff.
13 Aland, *Synopsis* §§174, 255.
14 Aland, *Synopsis* §§251–53, 334–37.
15 Aland, *Synopsis* §§269, 365–68ff.

explanations for the travel narrative, on the one hand the Griesbach hypothesis discussed above, Mark is an epitome of both Matthew and Luke,[16] and the hypothesis that Luke knew Matthew, a precursor to the Farrer-Goulder hypothesis.[17] August Jacobsen, for instance, published an article in the *ZWT* in 1886 where he discusses "die Zusammenhangslosigkeit"[18] of the travel narrative (Luke 9:51–18:14) and proposes as an explanation that Luke is following Matthew as a source.[19] Jacobsen cites the KEK commentary of Heinrich Meyer and Bernhard Weiss as a point of contrast, who explain this incoherence on the basis of Luke collecting different sources in chronological order.[20] The scholarly dissention regarding the scope of the travel narrative can in part be explained by whether the focus is on source critical observations (Luke 18:14) or on the content as a journey that reaches its destination in Jerusalem (19:28–41).

Already with Friedrich Schleiermacher do we find both an emerging consensus regarding the designation *Reisebericht* and doubts as to whether this is a fitting description. In 1817, Schleiermacher describes Luke 9:51 as the start of the third *Hauptmasse* and criticises the contemporary consensus that Luke 9:51–19:48 is a separate source and a gnomology:

> Die meisten neueren Kritiker, welche mit IX,51 eine eigene Denkschrift angehn lassen, die Lukas, wie sie war, seinem Buch einverleibt habe, nennen diese eine Gnomologie und endigen sie mit XVIII,14. Beides scheint mir nicht ganz richtig.[21]

While Schleiermacher notes the unity of this *Hauptmasse* and the delineating marker in Luke 9:51, he acknowledges neither "gnomology" nor "Reisebericht" as fitting descriptions of the unit and states that even though it begins with a statement about

---

16 For a discussion of its modern relevance see Christopher M. Tuckett, *The Revival of the Griesbach Hypothesis: An Analysis and Appraisal*, SNTSMS 44 (Cambridge: Cambridge University Press, 1983).
17 For a discussion of its modern relevance see e.g. Mark Goodacre, *Goulder and the Gospels: An Examination of a New Paradigm*, LNTS 133 (Sheffield: Sheffield Academic Press, 1996).
18 August Jacobsen, "Der lukanische Reisebericht," *ZWT* 29 (1886): 152–79 (153).
19 Jacobsen, "Der lukanische Reisebericht," 156: "Die folgende Untersuchung wird sich zu einem vollständigen Indicienbeweise dafür gestalten, dass Lukas in den Reiseberichte dem Matthäus-Evangelium gefolgt ist. Er schliesst sich ihm Schritt für Schritt in ganz genauer Folge an: der Hauptanlass, eine oder mehrere umfassendere Quellen daneben anzunehmen, fällt nach diesem Nachweis fort."
20 Heinrich August Wilhelm Meyer and Bernhard Weiss, *Kritisch exegetisches Handbuch über die Evangelien des Markus und Lukas*, 8th ed., KEK 2 (Göttingen: Vandenhoeck & Ruprecht, 1878), 398.
21 Friedrich Schleiermacher, *Ueber die Schriften des Lukas: Ein kritischer Versuch* (Berlin: Reimer, 1817), 158.

Jesus travelling to Jerusalem, this is coincidental "ganz zufällig."[22] Alternative designations for this section highlight the geography described, such as the title "Perean section",[23] that stems from the hypothesis that Jesus travelled east of the Jordan river based on Mark 10:1 parr. (ἔρχεται εἰς τὰ ὅρια τῆς Ἰουδαίας [καὶ] πέραν τοῦ Ἰορδάνου, Mark 10:1) and the title "Samaritan section",[24] stressing Samaria as the first destination (εἰσῆλθον εἰς κώμην Σαμαριτῶν, Luke 9:52)[25] and references to Samaritans.[26] The designation *Reisebericht* has been the standard descriptive of the section starting with Luke 9:51 since the 19th century. Examples abound, such as Karl Wilhelm Stein's 1830 commentary that discusses the "Reise Jesu nach Jerusalem, Kap. 9,51–19,28"[27] as a unit and Christian Hermann Weisse's *Die evangelische Geschichte* from 1838 that delineated the "sogenannte Reisebericht" as Luke 9:51 "wenigstens bis" 18:15.[28] This consensus regarding the start of the Lukan unit (9:51) and dissension regarding its conclusion that is reflected in modern scholarship,[29] is already in place in the 19th century. The discussion about its content also shares elements with modern scholarship and the KEK commentary from 1878 doubts that the narrative can be called an "actual travel narrative," since the descriptions of destination are so vague.[30]

---

22 Schleiermacher, *Schriften des Lukas*, 247: "Wenn die besondere Schrift vor der Erzählung von Segnung der Kinder zu Ende war, so hatte sie gar keinen Schluß; sie war eine vielleicht noch unbeendigte auf jeden Fall noch ungestaltete Sammlung, die eben so wenig ein Reisebericht als eine Gnomologie heißen konnte, und bei der gar kein Plan ersichtlich ist, so dass man es als ganz zufällig ansehn müßte, daß sie grade mit Ankündigung einer Reise nach Jerusalem anfing."
23 See e.g., Frédéric Godet, *Kommentar zu dem Evangelium des Lucas*, trans. E.R. Wunderlich (Hannover: Meyer, 1872), 251–54; Dean Rockwell Wickes, ed., *The Sources of Luke's Perean Section* (Chicago: University of Chicago Press, 1912). For references see also Noël, *The Travel Narrative in the Gospel of Luke*, 161 (n. 575).
24 See e.g., William Sanday, "A Survey of the Synoptic Question: III: Points Proved or Probable (continued)," *The Expositor* Fourth Series 3 (1891): 302–16 (308): "This 'Great Insertion,' or 'Journal of Travel' (Reisebericht), or 'Peræan Section,' or 'Samaritan Section,' as it has been variously called." For references see also Noël, *The Travel Narrative in the Gospel of Luke*, 162 (nn. 576–577).
25 See also the reference "between Samaria and Galilee" (διὰ μέσον Σαμαρείας καὶ Γαλιλαίας, Luke 17:11).
26 Luke 10:33; 17:16.
27 Karl Wilhelm Stein, *Kommentar zu dem Evangelium des Lucas, nebst einem Anhange über den Brief an die Laodiceer* (Halle: Gebauer-Schwetschke, 1830), 8.
28 Christian Hermann Weisse, *Die evangelische Geschichte: Kritisch und philosophisch bearbeitet*, 2 vols. (Leipzig: Breitkopf und Härtel, 1838), 1:88.
29 For an overview of scholarly opinions see Wolter, *Lukasevangelium*, 364–68.
30 Meyer and Weiss, *Markus und Lukas*, 396: "Aber es ist zu erwägen, dass zu einem eigentlichen „Reisebericht" doch jedenfalls das Markiren von einzelnen Stationen gehören würde, das hier vor 18,35, wo es durch Mark. bedingt ist, gänzlich fehlt, da selbst 17,11 offenbar nur die Absicht hat, das Zusammensein eines Samariters mit Juden in der folgenden Erzählung (v.16) zu erklären."

Modern scholarship has revisited the questions of the 19th century about the delineation, content and source-critical origins of the travel narrative, yet the descriptive remains universal. Attempts to read Luke without Q, following the Farrer-Goulder hypothesis,[31] have no less focused on the topic of travel. Mark Goodacre, for instance, following Streeter discusses the "central section"[32] as "a rather sophisticated narrative" where the "journeying motif is a literary conceit that allows Luke to draw in the best of the Matthean material while integrating it into a structure that is inspired by Mark."[33] Filip Noël provides a valuable delineation of the research history,[34] where the discussion has centred on theological issues,[35] intertextuality[36] and discussion about genre.[37] An important exception is Reinhard von Bendemann,[38] who according to Markus Öhler "successfully proves that it [the travel narrative] does not exist."[39] Bendemann employs both source critical observations[40] and content, where he argues for a differentiation between travel and wandering:

> Es besteht eine grundlegende Differenz zwischen der Wanderschaft Jesu im dritten Evangelium und dem »Reisen« im zweiten Band des Doppelwerkes. . . . Gegenüber den verschiedenen in der Forschung unternommenen Versuchen, die Stoffe eines postulierten »Reiseberichts« im Lukasevangelium vor dem Hintergrund antiker Reiseliteratur zu erschließen, ist festzuhalten, daß der lukanische Jesus nicht im antiken Sinn »reist«. . . . Das Bild des wan-

---

[31] Goodacre, *Goulder and the Gospels*.
[32] Streeter, *The Four Gospels*, 203.
[33] Mark Goodacre, "Re-Walking the 'Way of the Lord': Luke's Use of Mark and His Reaction to Matthew," in *Luke's Literary Creativity*, ed. Jesper Tang Nielsen and Mogens Müller, LNTS 550 (London: Bloomsbury, 2016), 39.
[34] Noël, *The Travel Narrative in the Gospel of Luke*.
[35] Noël, *The Travel Narrative in the Gospel of Luke*, 23–36: "§3 [. . .] Christological and Ecclesiological Themes."
[36] Noël, *The Travel Narrative in the Gospel of Luke*, 63–139: "III. Old Testament Interpretation Models for the Lukan Travel Narrative."
[37] Noël, *The Travel Narrative in the Gospel of Luke*, 140–82: "IV. Return to the Historical and Biographical Interpretation?"
[38] Reinhard von Bendemann, *Zwischen ΔΟΞΑ und ΣΤΑΥΡΟΣ: Eine exegetische Untersuchung der Texte des sogenannten Reiseberichts im Lukasevangelium*, BZNW 101 (Berlin: De Gruyter, 2001).
[39] Markus Öhler, review of Reinhard von Bendemann, *Zwischen ΔΟΞΑ und ΣΤΑΥΡΟΣ*, *JBL* 123 (2004): 167–69 (168).
[40] Bendemann, *Zwischen ΔΟΞΑ und ΣΤΑΥΡΟΣ*, 51: "Entgegen allen Hypothesen, die für die Stoffe in Lk 9,51–18,14 kategorisch mit besonderen Quellenverhältnissen rechnen, ist aber festzustellen: Auch in den Teilen des dritten Evangeliums, die als die ›große Einschaltung‹ in den Markusrahmen und damit als Nicht-Markus-Stoff gelten, ist eine kontinuierliche Berücksichtigung und Rezeption des zweiten Evangeliums aufweisbar." His arguments are listed on pages 52–55 and 415–39.

dernden Jesus im ersten Band des lukanischen Doppelwerkes ist von solchen Darstellungen kategorial unterschieden. Es entspricht grundsätzlich dem des durch die Lande wandernden Jesus im Markusevangelium.[41]

Importantly, Bendemann's conclusion is that the image of Jesus in Luke 11:1–18:30 highlights his role(s) as a teacher to disciples (Jüngerinstruktion), leading figures in the community (Μαθηταί mit besonderer Autorität und Verantwortung), Pharisees and scribes (Pharisäer und Schriftgelehrten) and the crowds (Umkehrforderung und Gerichtsrede an die ὄχλοι).[42]

What is a Travel Narrative?

We next turn to the question if the section should be described as a travel narrative in comparison to contemporary writings. When discussing narrative, it is important to distinguish between travel as a narrative device, as a story moves through space in a narrative, and travel-writing as a distinct genre. The abundance of travel writings in antiquity and the presence of travel descriptions across genres attest to the importance of travel as an inherent part of Mediterranean society. Historically the Hellenistic and the early imperial periods facilitated travel in the Mediterranean world, due to the spread of Greek as a common language, infrastructure and stability as summarised by Jonathan S. Burgess:

> War and trade were always prime causes of mobility in the ancient Mediterranean world. In the Hellenistic Age, following the military campaigns of Alexander the Great, the spread of Greek culture and language throughout the eastern Mediterranean facilitated travel. During the Roman empire, the Pax Romana enabled relatively safe transportation throughout the Mediterranean.[43]

The most influential travel descriptions of antiquity are the voyages of the Homeric epics, which have inspired countless travel narratives from ancient literature to modern travel guides.[44] Strabo begins his *Geography*, written between 18 and 23

---

41 Bendemann, *Zwischen ΔΟΞΑ und ΣΤΑΥΡΟΣ*, 95–97.
42 Bendemann, *Zwischen ΔΟΞΑ und ΣΤΑΥΡΟΣ*, 208–353: "VI. Jüngerinstruktion, Umkehrforderung und Gerichtsansage zwischen ΔΟΞΑ und ΣΤΑΥΡΟΣ."
43 Jonathan S. Burgess, "Travel Writing and the Ancient World," in *The Cambridge History of Travel Writing*, ed. Nandini Das and Tim Youngs (Cambridge: Cambridge University Press, 2019), 19–32 (19).
44 John Freely, *A Travel Guide to Homer: On the Trail of Odysseus Through Turkey and the Mediterranean* (New York: Tauris, 2014).

CE,⁴⁵ with an homage to Homer,⁴⁶ and his work is explicitly based on the portrait of Homer as historian and traveller: "Strabo speaks of the poet's 'love of learning' (τό φιλείδημον), coupling it ... with his 'love of travel' (τό φιλέκδημον), using two words that are unique to this text."⁴⁷ The Roman epics are based on Homeric voyages, from Virgil's *Aeneid* ⁴⁸ to the Flavian Epics, such as Statius' *Silvae*, which both present a geographical ideology⁴⁹ and travel narratives,⁵⁰ praising, e.g., the Flavian roads (*via Domitiana*).⁵¹ Similarly Pausanias' *Description of Greece* or Ἑλλάδος Περιηγήσις, is "by far our best surviving example of a *periegesis*, a genre of descriptive [travel] writing which is mostly lost."⁵² Pausanias' work, written in the 2nd century CE,⁵³ based its world of myth and landscape on the descriptions of Homer.⁵⁴

Homer's portrait set the standard for the Greco-Roman literary world and Odysseus became "the appropriate archetype for the traveller, and by extension for the travel writer."⁵⁵ Despite this influence of the Homeric journeys on travel litera-

---

45 Daniela Dueck, "Introduction," in *The Routledge Companion to Strabo*, ed. Daniele Dueck (London: Routledge, 2017), 1–6 (1).
46 Strabo, *Geogr.* 1.1: "The science of Geography, which I now propose to investigate, is, I think, quite as much as any other science, a concern of the philosopher; and the correctness of my view is clear for many reasons. In the first place, those who in earliest times ventured to treat the subject were, in their way, philosophers—Homer" (trans. H.L. Jones, LCL).
47 Lawrence Kim, "The Portrait of Homer in Strabo's Geography," *CP* 102 (2007): 363–88 (366).
48 Benj. L. D'Ooge, "The Journey of Aeneas," *The Classical Journal* 4 (1908): 3–12 (3): "The wily Ulysses filled ten years with travel and adventure while returning to his island home. As is well known, the dutiful Aeneas travels over much of the same course and consumes almost as much time in journeying from Ilium's strand to the Oenotrian Land."
49 Christopher Alan Parrott, "The Geography of the Roman World in Statius' Silvae" (Ph.D. diss., Harvard University, 2013).
50 Michael C.J. Putnam, "Statius *Siluae* 3.2: Reading Travel," *Illinois Classical Studies* 42 (2017): 83–139.
51 Statius, *Silvae* 4.3.
52 K.W. Arafat, *Pausanias' Greece: Ancient Artists and Roman Rulers* (Cambridge: Cambridge University Press, 1996), 2.
53 A majority of scholars believed it to have been completed before 180 CE. On the discussion see Ewen Bowie, "Inspiration and Aspiration: Date, Genre, and Readership," in *Pausanias: Travel and Memory in Roman Greece*, ed. Susan E. Alcock, John F. Cherry, and Jaś Elsner (Oxford: Oxford University Press, 2001), 21–32 (21–24).
54 "Pausanias ransacks the epic tradition, fragmenting it and taking what is relevant for the place he is in here, now. Homer for him is not a tradition of performance. Homer does not 'make' or 'sing' poetry, rather he 'has said' it, and so it exists now as an archive of data" (Greta Hawes, *Pausanias in the World of Greek Myth* [Oxford: Oxford University Press, 2021], 19).
55 Peter Hulme and Tim Youngs, "Introduction," in *The Cambridge Companion to Travel Writing*, ed. Peter Hulme and Tim Youngs (Cambridge: Cambridge University Press, 2002), 1–13 (2).

ture,⁵⁶ Burgess contends that "it is awkward to ascribe travel *writing* to Homer."⁵⁷ This "awkwardness" stems on the one hand from the oral nature of Homeric composition according to Burgess, but also from his definition of the genre. Despite this reservation Burgess argues that "fantastic and fictitious travel tales such as the Odyssey, Lucian's *True History*, ancient novels, and Alexander romances ... should be included in the study of the field."⁵⁸ A concise definition of a text that belongs to the genre of travel writing is that it "consists of predominantly factual, first-person prose accounts of travels that have been undertaken by the author-narrator."⁵⁹ Some ancient texts focused exclusively on travel, such as "the periodos ('way about') and periegesis ('leading about') [which] provided practical directions for a route over land, [or] periplus ('sailing about') [which] gave navigational instruction."⁶⁰

In addition to providing practical information about travel, travel narratives often had ethical and educational elements. This aspect is found across genres and relates on the one hand to the expectation that the educated elites (the πεπαιδευμένοι) were expected to travel widely as part of their education and on the other to the importance of eyewitness accounts (αὐτόπται) as authorial.⁶¹ Herodotus employs the language of travel as he asserts his authority as a historiographer: He will "go forward [προβήσομαι] in his account, going through [ἐπεξιών] the small and large cities of men alike [ὁμοίως]."⁶² With travel comes perspective and Herodotus both presents himself directly as an ideal traveller and through characters, such as "Solon the Athenian sage"⁶³—"the paradigmatic travelling wise man"⁶⁴—of course with an evocation of the *Odyssey* in mind.⁶⁵ Likewise in the Roman epics "Aeneas grows ... by gaining

---

56 Edith Hall, *The Return of Ulysses: A Cultural History of Homer's Odyssey* (Baltimore, MD: Johns Hopkins University Press, 2008).
57 Burgess, "Travel Writing and the Ancient World," 32.
58 Burgess, "Travel Writing and the Ancient World," 32.
59 Tim Youngs, "Introduction: Defining the Terms," in *The Cambridge Introduction to Travel Writing*, ed. Tim Youngs (Cambridge: Cambridge University Press, 2013), 1–16 (3).
60 Burgess, "Travel Writing and the Ancient World," 23.
61 Maria Pretzler, "Greek Intellectuals on the Move: Travel and *Paideia* in the Roman Empire," in *Travel, Geography and Culture in Ancient Greece, Egypt and the Near East*, ed. Colin Adams and Jim Roy, Leicester Nottingham Studies in Ancient Society 10 (Oxford: Oxbow Books, 2007), 123–38 (123–24, 130–31).
62 Hdt., *Hist.* 1.5, trans. Rachel Friedman, "Location and Dislocation in Herodotus," in *The Cambridge Companion to Herodotus*, ed. Carolyn Dewald and John Marincola (Cambridge: Cambridge University Press, 2006), 165–77 (166).
63 Hdt., *Hist.* 1.29–33.
64 Friedman, "Location and Dislocation," 173.
65 Friedman, "Location and Dislocation," 166: "As is frequently noted, the language of his first statement of authorial method is the language of travel: Once he identifies the man who first wronged the Greeks, he will 'go forward in his account, going through the small and large cities of men alike'

knowledge and experience..., at the beginning of his travels, Aeneas is *incertus quo fata ferant* [Vergil, *Aen.* 3.57]... but at the end he is *certus quo fata ferant* [Vergil. *Aen.* 5.704ff.; 8.530ff]."[66] Pausanias is indebted to Herodotus in his descriptions,[67] the author himself "obviously, well-travelled and well-read",[68] but the fabric of his subject matter of putting "Greece into words... is woven tight with *paideia*, living knowledge of Homer, Euripides, and Cornutus et al."[69]

Travel is no less a topic in Jewish literature as Catharine Hezser has shown in her *Jewish Travel in Antiquity*, which studies both "the material basis of travel within Roman Palestine and between Palestine and the Jewish Diaspora in antiquity"[70] and the "narrative depiction of Jewish mobility in the literary sources of the Hellenistic and Roman period."[71] Pilgrimages to Jerusalem were a fundamental part of the expectation for Diaspora Jews and especially so in the century preceding the Jewish War.[72] Pilgrimage should be understood as a widespread phenomenon in Greco-Roman antiquity[73] and one that belonged to the educational habitus of the elite.[74] Hezser argues that "[a]fter 70 C.E., when rabbis and Torah study replaced priests and sacrifices within Judaism, [educational forms] of religious travel became

---

(1.5.3). With this sentence, evocative of the opening of the ancient travel tale *par excellence*, the *Odyssey*, where the poet asks the Muse to sing of the man who 'wandered much... and saw the cities of many men and knew their minds' (*Od.* 1.1–3), Herodotus introduces his authorial persona as that of a traveller."

[66] Michael Erler, "Educational Travels and Epicurean *Prokoptontes*: Vergil's Aeneas as an Epicurean Telemachus," in *Ethics in Ancient Greek Literature: Aspects of Ethical Reasoning from Homer to Aristotle and Beyond*, ed. Maria Liatsi, TCSV 102 (Berlin: de Gruyter, 2020), 193–204 (199–200).

[67] Hawes, *Pausanias in the World of Greek Myth*, 8.

[68] Hawes, *Pausanias in the World of Greek Myth*, 4.

[69] Hawes, *Pausanias in the World of Greek Myth*, 19.

[70] Catharine Hezser, *Jewish Travel in Antiquity*, TSAJ 144 (Tübingen: Mohr Siebeck, 2011), 19.

[71] Hezser, *Jewish Travel in Antiquity*, 197.

[72] See, e.g., Daniel R. Schwartz, "Pilgrimage to Jerusalem in Antiquity," in *Routledge Handbook on Jerusalem*, ed. Suleiman A. Mourad, Naomi Koltun-Fromm, and Bedross Der Matossian (London: Routledge, 2019), 269–75 (269): "Jewish pilgrimage to Jerusalem was a massive phenomenon, especially in the last century of the Temple's existence—the century that began with Herod the Great's rise to power and ended with the Roman destruction of Jerusalem and the Temple in 70 CE.... This was a century in which, between the *pax Romana* that facilitated travel and Herod's huge investment in the Temple and the city itself—Jerusalem became 'by far the most famous city of the Orient' (Pliny, *Natural History* 5.70)."

[73] Jaś Elsner and Ian Rutherford, "Introduction," in *Pilgrimage in Graeco-Roman & Early Christian Antiquity: Seeing the Gods*, ed. Jaś Elsner and Ian Rutherford (Oxford: Oxford University Press, 2005), 1–38 (1–9).

[74] Marco Galli, "Pilgrimage as Elite *Habitus*: Educated Pilgrims in Sacred Landscape During the Second Sophistic," in Elsner and Rutherford *Pilgrimage*, 253–90 (253–56).

a substitute for pilgrimages to the Temple. Like the earlier pilgrimages, they created *communitas* amongst rabbis and their students and adherents."[75]

The Gospel of Luke uniquely contains multiple travel narratives in the second chapter that has the parents of Jesus travelling to Bethlehem from Nazareth for his birth (Luke 2:1–21), to Jerusalem to have him presented in the Temple (Luke 2:22–39) and finally for the annual Passover in Jerusalem (Luke 2:41) where he returns to the Temple while his parents look for him (Luke 2:42–51). Luke-Acts is in itself a narrative of how the message reaches Rome (Acts 28:16–31), to where all roads lead, through the travels of Paul. The we-passages in Acts are the closest parallel in the New Testament to the genre of travel writing. This section in the latter half of Acts (16:10–17; 20:5–21:18; 27–28) "consists of predominantly factual, first-person prose accounts of travels that have been undertaken by the author-narrator",[76] claims that the author of Luke-Acts specifically makes: the factual in his introduction to the Gospel (Luke 1:1–4) and the first-person travel account in the we-passages of Acts (16:12ff). Acts finally defines early Christians as those who "belong to the ὁδός," those who are on the "road" or "way."[77]

Travel as a Topic in Luke-Acts

Thirdly we ask how the author of Luke-Acts receives the topic of travel from his sources and develops it in his narrative. The Gospel of Luke employs the earliest Gospel as a source and thus his descriptions of travel. Travel is a central concern in the Gospel of Mark, the narrative opens with quotes from Isaiah (and Malachi) introducing the messenger (ἄγγελος, Mark 1:2), John the Baptist, who is to make straight the way of the Lord (τὴν ὁδὸν κυρίου, Mark 1:3). The ὁδός theme then runs through the Gospel, both metaphorically as the way of the Lord to be imitated by readers and literally as Jesus travels the ὁδός from "Nazareth of Galilee" (Mark 1:9) to Jerusalem. "Mark ... captures the double meaning of way as a path or journey (2:23; 4:4, 15; 6:8; 8:3; 10:17; 10:46) and as the journey toward discipleship (8:27; 9:33–34; 10:32; 10:52; 11:8; 12:14)."[78] Adela Yarbro Collins summarizes the distinctiveness of this portrait in connection to the scriptural background of the Gospel:

---

[75] Hezser, *Jewish Travel in Antiquity*, 385.
[76] Youngs, "Introduction," 3.
[77] The term ὁδός is used five times in Acts as a designation for early Christians (Acts 9:2; 19:9, 23; 22:4; 24:22).
[78] John R. Donahue and Daniel J. Harrington, *The Gospel of Mark*, Sacra Pagina 2 (Collegeville, MN: Liturgical Press, 2005), 61.

One of the most striking characteristics of the presentation of Jesus as a teacher in the Gospel of Mark is the itinerant character of his teaching activity. Jesus' traveling from place to place is explained in 1:38 in terms of his intention to proclaim the good news of God in various places (cf. 1:14–15). It is difficult to find analogies to this activity and its rationale. The prophet Elijah went from place to place, sometimes in the normal way, but at the direct command of God or the angel of the Lord for some specific reason, and sometimes transported by the spirit of God (1 Kgs 18: 12, 46). . . . Elisha moves from place to place independently, but it is not to proclaim a message to all the people, as is the case with Jesus.[79]

Jesus' wandering activity in Mark 1:35–8:26 does not aim toward a specific destination, but beginning with 8:27, "Jesus' movement follows the pilgrimage route from Caesarea Philippi to Jerusalem."[80] The watershed moment in the Markan plot is chapter 10, where Jesus goes on the road (ἐν τῇ ὁδῷ, Mark 10:32) to travel up to Jerusalem with his disciples. "See, we are going up to Jerusalem, and the Son of Man will be handed over" (Mark 10:33, NRSV). The noun ὁδός appears 15 times in the Gospel[81] and the last occurrence is a reference to Jesus teaching the way of God (τὴν ὁδὸν τοῦ θεοῦ, Mark 12:14), albeit from the mouth of his opponents (τινας τῶν Φαρισαίων καὶ τῶν Ἡρῳδιανῶν, Mark 12:13). Metaphorical use of a ὁδός theme is well known in Greek literature, both gentile and Jewish, and the figure of the "way of the Lord" is common in Mark's source text, Second Isaiah.[82] Non-Jewish examples include ὁδός depicting a "way or manner," such as in Pindar and Euripides,[83] a "way of doing or speaking," such as in Herodotus,[84] and a method μέθοδος (μετά, ὁδός), such as in Aristotle.[85]

The idea of discipleship is reflected in the ὁδός theme in Mark, where the verb ἀκολουθέω ("to follow") is a key lexeme that runs through the Gospel narrative. Jesus is introduced in the opening chapter as travelling in Galilee, where he calls

---

79 Adela Yarbro Collins, *Mark: A Commentary*, Hermeneia (Minneapolis: Fortress, 2007), 77.
80 Yarbro Collins, *Mark*, 77 (n. 35).
81 Mark 1:2, 3; 2:23; 4:4, 15; 6:8; 8:3, 27; 9:33, 34; 10:17; 10:32, 46, 52; 11:8; 12:14.
82 Donahue and Harrington, *The Gospel of Mark*, 61: "Isaiah (40.3; 42.16; 43.16, 19; 48.17; 49.11; 51.10) for the path by which God will bring back the people from exile."
83 LSJ s.v. ὁδός III.1: "way or manner, πολλαὶ δ' ὁ . . . εὐπραγίας Pi.O.8.13; γλώσσης ἀγαθῆς ὁδός A.Eu.989 (anap.); θεσπεσία ὁ. the way or course of divination, Id.Ag.1154 (lyr.); μαντικῆς ὁ. S.OT311; οἰωνῶν ὁδοῖς Id.OC1314; σῶν ὁ. βουλευμάτων E.Hec.744; γνώμης Id.Hipp.290; λογίων ὁ. their way, intent, Ar.Eq.1015; εὐτελείας ὁ. Jul.Or.6.198d."
84 LSJ s.v. ὁδός III.2: "a way of doing, speaking, etc., τῇσδ' ἀφ' ὁδοῦ διζήσιος Parm.1.33, cf. 8.18; τριφασίας ἄλλας ὁ. λόγων ways of telling the story, Hdt.1.95, cf. 2.20,22; but τριφασίας ὁ. τρέπεται turns into three forms, Id.6.119; ἄδικον ὁ. ἰέναι Th.3.64; ὁ. ἥντιν' ἰών by what course of action, Ar.Pl.506, cf. Nu.75; ἣν ἔχομεν ὁ. λόγων Id.Pax733; μία δὴ λείπεται . . ὁ. Pl.Smp.184b."
85 LSJ s.v. ὁδός III.3: "method, system, Id.Sph.218d, Arist.APr.53a2, al.; ὁδῷ methodically, systematically, Pl.R.533b, Stoic.2.39, etc.; so καθ' ὁδόν Pl.R.435a; τὴν διὰ τοῦ στοιχείου ὁ. ἔχων ἔγραφεν Id.Tht.208b (cf. διέξοδον 208a)."

his first disciples and they follow him (ἠκολούθησαν αὐτῷ, Mark 1:18) and as the number of disciples grows on Jesus' travels the call ἀκολούθει μοι is repeated.[86] Those that follow him go from specific disciples (1:18; 2:14), to many (πολλοί, Mark 2:15), to great crowds (πολὺ πλῆθος, Mark 3:7; ὄχλος πολύς, Mark 5:24) and all follow him on his travels. Insightful passages include Mark's definition of discipleship in 8:34,[87] "let them deny themselves and take up their cross and follow me" (NRSV), and the story of Bartimaeus, who first waits by the ὁδός (Mark 10:46) and then follows Jesus on the ὁδός (ἠκολούθει αὐτῷ ἐν τῇ ὁδῷ, Mark 10:52).

Itinerancy is fundamental to the early Christian movement, and Gerd Theissen famously proposed that radical itinerancy "Wanderradikalismus"[88] lay at the heart of the transmission and preservation of Jesus logia.[89] This emphasis can be seen in the extensive missionary travels of Paul and the theme of itinerancy in the synoptic double tradition (Q 10:4–19)[90] and Mark (6:8).[91] The other New Testament Gospels pick up on the ὁδός theme in different ways. The noun is found 22 times in Matthew, in both a literal and metaphorical sense, yet in John the term is exclusively used metaphorically, first in the Isaiah quote preserved in all four Gospels[92] and then in Jesus' dialogue with Thomas where he describes himself as the ὁδός.[93] From chapter 3 onward Luke follows the Markan storyline and thus the ὁδός theme, beginning with an allusion in the Benedictus to Isa 40:3 (Καὶ σὺ δέ, παιδίον, προφήτης ὑψίστου κληθήσῃ, προπορεύσῃ γὰρ ἐνώπιον κυρίου ἑτοιμάσαι ὁδοὺς αὐτοῦ, Luke 1:76) that is then repeated as he picks up the prophetic citation in Mark 1:1–2:

Mark 1:2c: ὃς κατασκευάσει τὴν ὁδόν σου·   Luke 7:27: ὃς κατασκευάσει τὴν ὁδόν σου
Mark 1:3: φωνὴ βοῶντος ἐν τῇ ἐρήμῳ·   Luke 3:4: φωνὴ βοῶντος ἐν τῇ ἐρήμῳ·
ἑτοιμάσατε τὴν ὁδὸν κυρίου,   ἑτοιμάσατε τὴν ὁδὸν κυρίου

---

86 Mark 1:17–18; 2:14, 15; 3:7; 5:24; 6:1; 8:34; 10:21, 28, 52; 11:19; 15:41.
87 Εἴ τις θέλει ὀπίσω μου ἀκολουθεῖν, ἀπαρνησάσθω ἑαυτὸν καὶ ἀράτω τὸν σταυρὸν αὐτοῦ καὶ ἀκολουθείτω μοι, Mark 8:34.
88 Gerd Theissen,"Wanderradikalismus: Literatursoziologische Aspekte der Überlieferung von Worten Jesu im Urchristentum," ZTK 70 (1973): 245–71.
89 Theissen,"Wanderradikalismus," 270: "Verfolgt man die Überlieferung der Worte Jesu im Urchristentum, so stößt man auf drei Sozialformen urchristlichen Glaubens: Wanderradikalismus, Liebespatriarchalismus und gnostischen Radikalismus."
90 Μὴ βαστάζετε βαλλάντιον, μὴ πήραν, μὴ ὑποδήματα, καὶ μηδένα κατὰ τὴν ὁδὸν ἀσπάσησθε, Luke 10:4.
91 Καὶ παρήγγειλεν αὐτοῖς ἵνα μηδὲν αἴρωσιν εἰς ὁδὸν εἰ μὴ ῥάβδον μόνον, μὴ ἄρτον, μὴ πήραν, μὴ εἰς τὴν ζώνην χαλκόν, Mark 6:8.
92 Εὐθύνατε τὴν ὁδὸν κυρίου, John 1:23; see Mark 1:3; Matt 3:3; Luke 3:4.
93 Λέγει αὐτῷ [ὁ] Ἰησοῦς· ἐγώ εἰμι ἡ ὁδός … οὐδεὶς ἔρχεται πρὸς τὸν πατέρα εἰ μὴ δι' ἐμοῦ, John 14:6.

The noun ὁδός appears 20 times in the Gospel,[94] with Luke intermittently omitting it from his Markan source,[95] yet preserving it in key sections such as the parable of the sower (ὃ μὲν ἔπεσεν παρὰ τὴν ὁδόν, Mark 4:4//Luke 8:5; οἱ (δὲ) παρὰ τὴν ὁδόν, Mark 4:15//Luke 8:12), the Bartimaeus narrative (ἐκάθητο παρὰ τὴν ὁδόν, Mark 10:46//Luke 18:35),[96] the entry into Jerusalem (πολλοὶ τὰ ἱμάτια αὐτῶν ἔστρωσαν εἰς τὴν ὁδόν, Mark 11:8//ὑπεστρώννυον τὰ ἱμάτια αὐτῶν ἐν τῇ ὁδῷ, Luke 19:36) and finally in the admission (or accusation) that Jesus teaches the 'way' of God (ἐπ' ἀληθείας τὴν ὁδὸν τοῦ θεοῦ διδάσκεις, Mark 12:14//Luke 20:21). The concluding Emmaus narrative has the post-resurrection Jesus on the road (ἐν τῇ ὁδῷ, Luke 24:32, 35) with his disciples, where Jesus summarizes the message of Luke's Gospel. The travel narrative contains six references to ὁδός, Luke adds a ὁδός reference to the Q saying about Jesus not having anywhere to rest his head (πορευομένων αὐτῶν ἐν τῇ ὁδῷ, Luke 9:57)[97] and changes its position in the saying about settling out of court compared to Matthew (ἐν τῇ ὁδῷ δὸς ἐργασίαν ἀπηλλάχθαι ἀπ' αὐτοῦ, Luke 12:58).[98] In the Lukan parables we find it in the parable of the good Samaritan (ἱερεύς τις κατέβαινεν ἐν τῇ ὁδῳ, Luke 10:31), the parable of the friend at midnight (φίλος μου παρεγένετο ἐξ ὁδοῦ, 11:6), and in the Q parable of the great dinner

---

94 Luke 1:76, 79; 2:44; 3:4–5; 7:27; 8:5, 12; 9:3, 57; 10:4, 31; 11:6; 12:58; 14:23; 18:35; 19:36; 20:21; 24:34–35.

95 Mark 2:23 has the construct ὁδὸν ποιεῖν, which neither Luke 6:1 nor Matt 12:1 preserve. A TLG textual search for "ὁδὸν ποιεῖν" retrieves no parallels from antiquity for the phrase. Mark 8:3 belongs to Luke's "Great omission" (Mark 6:45–8:26) and is thus omitted in its entirety. In the narrative about Peter's confession, Luke changes the context in Mark from Jesus asking his disciples "on the way" (καὶ ἐν τῇ ὁδῷ, Mark 8:27) to Jesus praying (προσευχόμενον, Luke 9:18). In the discussion about who is the greatest among the disciples (τίς μείζων, Mark 9:34), Luke 9:46 removes both the geography (Καφαρναούμ, Mark 9:33) and the references that they were "on the way" (ἐν τῇ ὁδῷ, Mark 9:33–34). The same is true for the narrative about the rich young man (εἰς ὁδὸν, Mark 10:17) in Luke 18:8 and the third prediction of the passion (*Leidensankündigung*) (Ἦσαν δὲ ἐν τῇ ὁδῷ ἀναβαίνοντες εἰς Ἱεροσόλυμα, Mark 10:32) in Luke 17:25 and 18:31–34 (ἰδοὺ ἀναβαίνομεν εἰς Ἰερουσαλήμ, Luke 18:31).

96 In the parallel to Mark 10:52 ἠκολούθει αὐτῷ ἐν τῇ ὁδῷ, Luke 18:43 only has ἠκολούθει αὐτῷ omitting the ὁδός reference.

97 The ὁδός reference is not found in Matt 8:18 and is thus not considered as part of Q by the IQP. James M. Robinson, Paul Hoffmann, and John S. Kloppenborg, eds., *The Critical Edition of Q: A Synopsis Including the Gospels of Matthew and Luke, Mark and Thomas* (Leuven: Peeters, 2000), 150–51.

98 Matt 5:25b reads ἕως ὅτου εἶ μετ' αὐτοῦ ἐν τῇ ὁδῷ. Robinson, Hoffmann, and Kloppenborg, *The Critical Edition of Q*, 395 (n 8): "The position of ἐν τῇ ὁδῷ where the main clause and the subordinate clause meet (Luke), or at the conclusion of the subordinate clause that itself follows the main clause (Matthew)."

(ἔξελθε εἰς τὰς ὁδοὺς . . ., Luke 14:23).⁹⁹ Finally, Luke 10:4 receives from Q a programmatic statement about travel that contains a ὁδός reference, (μηδένα κατὰ τὴν ὁδὸν ἀσπάσησθε, Luke 10:4). The topic of travel in the Gospel of Mark is on the one hand a narrative marker connected to the destination of Jerusalem, foreshadowed through the passion predictions (Mark 8:31; 9:31; 10:32–34), and on the other hand a metaphorical reference to the ὁδός as the path of following Jesus – ἀκολούθει μοι. This is the background through which Luke expands both the journey to Jerusalem and the portrait of Jesus as a πεπαιδευμένος, topics that are connected in antiquity as we will see.

Education and Travel in the Lukan Travel Narrative

Finally, we explore how the author of Luke-Acts connects the topic of education to his travel narrative and why. So far, we have highlighted the role of the "way" as a topic that the author received from both the Septuagint and his Markan source and its connection on the one hand to the theme of discipleship and on the other hand to Jesus logia. The teachings of Jesus are in the Gospel of Luke concentrated in the travel narrative, especially the Lukan *Sondergut* tradition in chapters 10–12 and 15–19, with its distinctive parables[100] and emphasis on the topic of wealth.[101] Numerous scholars have discussed the teaching aspect of the Jesus logia found in the Travel Narrative, among them David Moessner, who connects the image of Jesus as a teacher in Luke to a Deuteronomistic prophet, citing Luke 13:23–33 where Jesus is "sent to instruct and admonish the people in god's will."[102] Similarly, two recent monographs address the educational ideals of Luke-Acts in relation to Hellenistic paideia. Katja Hess explores the portrait of Paul in Acts in relation to both Greek and Jewish paideia and concludes that the author explicitly presents him as a

---

99 Matt 22.9a reads: πορεύεσθε οὖν ἐπὶ τὰς διεξόδους τῶν ὁδῶν, Q 14:23 [ἔξελθε] [εἰς] τὰς ὁδοὺς (IQP).
100 The Lukan parables of the good Samaritan (10:25–37), the friend at night (11:5–8), the rich fool (12:16–21), the lost coin (15:8–9), the prodigal son (15:11–32), the unjust steward (16:1–13), the rich man and Lazarus (16:19–31), the master and servant (17:7–10), the unjust judge (18:1–8), and the Pharisee and the publican (18:9–14).
101 Helga Kramer, *Lukas als Ordner des frühchristlichen Diskurses um „Armut und Reichtum" und den „Umgang mit materiellen Gütern": Eine überlieferungsgeschichtliche und diskurskritische Untersuchung zur Besitzethik des Lukasevangeliums unter besonderer Berücksichtigung des lukanischen Sonderguts*, NET 21 (Tübingen: Francke, 2015).
102 David Paul Moessner, *Lord of the Banquet: A Literary and Theological Investigation of the Lukan Travel Narrative* (Minneapolis: Fortress, 1989), 120–27.

rhetorician, philosopher and "Geistträger."[103] Michael Becker extensively compares Luke-Acts to the writings of Dio of Prusa to ask if the writings were comprehensible to a Greek educated audience.[104] His conclusion is that the Gospel of Luke and the Acts of the Apostles have quantitatively more material to offer than the other Synoptic Gospels that show linguistic and discursive overlap with the textual products of educated pagan contemporaries.[105] Both studies are in line with the current trend to view Christianity as a "Bildungsreligion"[106] due to the extensive literary production of early Christianity, yet the connection between travel and education is addressed in neither study.

The lack of attention to travel narrative as part of ancient genres is noted by Moessner, who argues that "much work is still needed in comparing the role of journeying in the Gospels and Acts to the journey accounts . . . in the popular Greco-Roman biography."[107] The same is true for the Greek and Roman novels, as "travel is one of the main ingredients of the ancient novelistic genre, [where] the plot is immediately connected with changes in geographical setting."[108] An important study of the connection between education and travel in the 1st through 4th centuries CE focuses on the Second Sophistic as exemplary authors, because of their explicit educational identity.[109] Christian Fron begins his discussion of *Bildung*

---

103 Katja Hess, *Rhetor, Philosoph, Geistträger: Die Bildungsthematik in der lukanischen Paulusdarstellung*, FZB 137 (Würzburg: Echter, 2019), 391: "Im Rahmen der Untersuchung hat sich gezeigt, dass Lukas ein sichtbares Interesse daran hat, Paulus in der Apostelgeschichte mit dem antik-paganen Bildungsideal und der jüdisch-hellenistischen Bildungstradition in Verbindung zu bringen."
104 Matthias Becker, *Lukas und Dion von Prusa: Das lukanische Doppelwerk im Kontext paganer Bildungsdiskurse*, SCCB 3 (Leiden: Brill, 2020), 1: "dass die christliche Botschaft in besonderem Maße für ein urbanes christliches Publikum mit paganem Bildungshintergrund verständlich und plausibel wird?"
105 Becker, *Lukas und Dion von Prusa*, 634.
106 Exemplary is Udo Schnelle, *Die ersten 100 Jahre des Christentums 30–130 n. Chr.: Die Entstehungsgeschichte einer Weltreligion*, 2nd ed., UTB 4411 (Göttingen: Vandenhoeck & Ruprecht, 2016), 501–5: "Das frühe Christentum als Bildungsreligion." For an evaluation of this research trend see Samuel Vollenweider, "Bildungsfreunde oder Bildungsverächter? Überlegungen zum Stellenwert der Bildung im frühen Christentum," in *Was ist Bildung in der Vormoderne?*, ed. Peter Gemeinhardt SERAPHIM 4 (Tübingen: Mohr Siebeck, 2019), 283–304 (284–86).
107 David Paul Moessner, *Luke the Historian of Israel's Legacy, Theologian of Israel's Christ: A New Reading of the "Gospel Acts" of Luke*, BZNW 182 (Berlin: De Gruyter, 2016), 206 (n. 8).
108 Koen de Temmerman, "The Novel: Chariton," in *Space in Ancient Greek Literature*, ed. Irene J.F. de Jong, MnS 339 (Leiden: Brill, 2012), 483–502 (488). See James Romm, "Travel," in *The Cambridge Companion to the Greek and Roman Novel*, ed. Tim Whitmarsh (Cambridge: Cambridge University Press, 2008), 109–26.
109 See, e.g., the volume Barbara E. Borg, ed., *Paideia: The World of the Second Sophistic*, Millennium 2 (Berlin: De Gruyter, 2004).

und Reisen[110] with Philostratus, who while comparably late for our purposes (born in 170),[111] is important in three respects:
1) as the major source on the Second Sophistic (βίοι σοφιστῶν)[112] and the author who coined the term "Second Sophistic" (δευτέρα σοφιστική);[113]
2) as the biographer of Apollonius of Tyana, whose *Vita* has often been compared to the Gospels[114] and whose genre has been described as a *Reiseroman*;[115]
3) as an author who exploits the theme of travel in multiple ways.[116] Fron's argument is that the identity of the educated, the πεπαιδευμένοι, was bound up with travel, in that travel was a mode of and prerequisite for education,[117] that centres of learning (*Einzugsgebiete*) attracted students[118] and that educated professional, such as sophists, philosophers, physicians and jurists travelled as part of their educational identity.[119]

---

110 Christian Fron, *Bildung und Reisen in der römischen Kaiserzeit: Pepaideumenoi und Mobilität zwischen dem 1. und 4. Jh. n. Chr.*, UALG 146 (Berlin: De Gruyter, 2021).
111 For discussion about his life, see Graham Anderson, *Philostratus: Biography and Belles Lettres in the Third Century A.D.* (London: Croom Helm, 1986) and Ewen Bowie and Jaś Elsner, eds., *Philostratus*, GCRW (Cambridge: Cambridge University Press, 2009).
112 For discussion about the *Vitae sophistarum* see Kendra Eshleman, *The Social World of Intellectuals in the Roman Empire: Sophists, Philosophers, and Christians*, GCRW (Cambridge: Cambridge University Press, 2012), 125–48 and Jaś Elsner, "A Protean Corpus," in Bowie and Elsner, *Philostratus*, 3–18.
113 Philostr., *V S* 480–481: Τὴν ἀρχαίαν σοφιστικὴν ῥητορικὴν ἡγεῖσθαι χρὴ φιλοσοφοῦσαν· ... ἡ δὲ μετ' ἐκείνην, ἣν οὐχὶ νέαν, ἀρχαία γάρ, δευτέραν δὲ μᾶλλον προσρητέον (TLG).
114 Richard A. Burridge, *What Are the Gospels? A Comparison with Graeco-Roman Biography*, 2nd ed. (Grand Rapids: Eerdmans, 2004), 156, for bibliography see n. 19. Especially important is Gerd Petzke, *Die Traditionen über Apollonius von Tyana und das Neue Testament*, SCHNT 1 (Leiden: Brill, 1970).
115 Eduard Meyer, "Apollonios von Tyana und die Biographie des Philostratos," *Hermes* 52 (1917): 371–424 (384): "[M]it dem Idealbild dieses übermenschlichen Theosophen verbindet er als gebildeter Literat allerlei interessante Belehrung, die den Leser fesseln und die Monotonie der Darstellung beleben soll, und so wird sein Werk zugleich ein phantastischer Reiseroman nach Art derer, die Lucian in der Ἀληθὴς ἱστορία so geistvoll verspottet."
116 John Elsner, "Hagiographic Geography: Travel and Allegory in the Life of Apollonius of Tyana," *JHS* 117 (1997): 22–37 (24): "The theme of travel is exploited in a number of ways by Philostratus. He uses it to establish the credentials of his holy man in a world of sophists, wise men and teachers, part of whose identity was defined by travel (not least as they are presented in Philostratus' own *Lives of the Sophists*)."
117 Fron, *Bildung und Reisen*, chapter 1, 135–215, esp. "Die Notwendigkeit des Reisens für den Erwerb von Paideia", 84–101.
118 Fron, *Bildung und Reisen*, chapter 2, with a specific focus on Alexandria, Antioch, Athens, Beirut, Ephesus, Pergamon, Rome and Smyrna, 135–215.
119 Fron, *Bildung und Reisen*, chapter 3, "Auf der Suche nach einem Platz in der Gelehrtenwelt: Reisen für die Karriere sowie zum Erwerb von Ruhm und Ehre", 216–80.

Philostratus himself had the opportunity to travel extensively[120] and boasted in the conclusion to the *Vita* that he had seen most of the known world: καίτοι τῆς γῆς, ὁπόση ἐστίν, ἐπελθὼν πλείστην.[121] Apollonius' travels are a dominant feature of the narrative and an emphasis is laid upon the extent of his journeys, "follow[ing] in the footsteps of Alexander the Great and Dionysus" and surpassing the extent of their travels.[122] While the metaphorical theme of ὁδός is not present in the *Vita* in a similar way to the Gospels, there are interesting parallels. In the first book for example, Apollonius travels to Nineveh where he visits the barbarous idol of Ion (Ἰὼ ἡ Ἰνάχου) and shows himself wiser than the priests and prophets (οἱ ἱερεῖς καὶ προφῆται) of her cult.[123] One among them, Damis, becomes Apollonius' disciple and having a taste for the ὁδός (ζηλώσας τῆς ὁδοῦ) he joins him with the words "You follow God, but I you" (σὺ μὲν θεῷ ἐπόμενος, ἐγὼ δὲ σοί).[124] The idea of discipleship thus involves a metaphorical ὁδός, following God's follower, as well as actual itinerancy.

The educational markers of travel that Fron highlights are certainly present in the portrait of Paul in Acts, as he presumably travelled to Jerusalem for his education with Gamaliel (Acts 22:3),[125] Jerusalem being a Jewish *Einzugsgebiet*,[126] and he subsequently travelled extensively as part of his intellectual profession. Much work has been done on the travels of Paul since the landmark *Paul the Traveller*,[127] yet the travel element of his educational portrait seems underdeveloped.[128] The similarities between the portrait of Paul in Acts and the *Life of Apollonius of Tyana* were noted by John Esler:

---

120 Philostr., *V A* 5.2.
121 Philostr., *V A* 8.31.
122 Romm, "Travel," 277. See also Elsner, "Hagiographic Geography."
123 Philostr., *V A* 1.19.
124 Philostr., *V A* 1.19.
125 See Hess, *Rhetor, Philosoph, Geistträger*, chapter 1.2, esp. "Tarsus als Geburtsort und Jerusalem als Erziehungs- und Ausbildungsort", 192ff.
126 Discussing the connection to Gamaliel, Bruce Chilton argues that "the cultural reality [was] that Jerusalem, and Jerusalem alone, was the place to be for any Pharisee who considered himself advanced" (*Rabbi Paul: An Intellectual Biography* [New York: Doubleday, 2004], 32).
127 William Mitchell Ramsay, *St. Paul the Traveller and the Roman Citizen* (London: Hodder and Stoughton, 1895).
128 Hess, *Rhetor, Philosoph, Geistträger*, does not address this aspect of Paul's portrait and Ryan S. Schellenberg laments that since "Paul is among the most famous of ancient travellers ... it is ... surprising to note how superficially New Testament scholarship has sought to understand Paul's travels" ("Danger in the Wilderness, Danger at Sea: Paul and the Perils of Travel," in *Travel and Religion in Antiquity*, ed. Philip A. Harland, Studies in Christianity and Judaism/Études sur le christianisme et le judaïsme 21 [Waterloo: Wilfrid Laurier University Press, 2011], 141–61 [141]).

> [T]he geographic frame is more than a 'mere' narrative device – it is an essential strategy of the argument which propels the sage into divinity. Here the parallel is less with Jesus than (strikingly) with St Paul in the last third of Acts. In the case of Paul too, travel – including visits to the cardinal centres of ancient religion, like Athens, as well as to the sites of the new Christian cult which he propagates – establishes a hagiographic superiority which culminates in a triumphant journey to Rome, where the Apostle teaches unmolested for two years with no hint of his impending martyrdom (Acts 28.30–1). While geography is indeed a principal means of encapsulating Apollonius' acts, it is also – as it reaches outside the empire, within the empire and into even Rome itself – a way of defining Apollonian holiness.[129]

Travel is according to Esler an essential strategy that ensures the construction of an idealized portrait, i.e. holiness.

The Lukan travel narrative does not refer to travel for education, similarly to Paul in Acts presumably visiting Jerusalem to study with Gamaliel and visiting the educational centres of the ancient world, the gentile *Einzugsgebiete*[130] and Jerusalem as the centre of learning, but the travel narrative does portray Jesus as an educated travelling teacher. Throughout the travel narrative, we are reminded that Jesus is travelling (Luke 9:52, 56; 10:38; 13:22; 14:25; 17:11), to where he is travelling (9:51, 53; 13:22, 33; 17:11; 18:31; 19:11, 28), that he is teaching (διδάσκαλος, 10:25; 11:45; 12:13; 18:18; διδάσκω, 11:1; 13:10, 22) and most importantly that his influence grows both geographically (Samaria, 9:51–56; Jericho, 18:30; 19:1) and with regard to the size of the crowds (τῶν δὲ ὄχλων ἐπαθροιζομένων, 11:29; ἐν οἷς ἐπισυναχθεισῶν τῶν μυριάδων τοῦ ὄχλου, 12:1; συνεπορεύοντο δὲ αὐτῷ ὄχλοι πολλοί, 14:25). The author receives and expands the latter aspect from his source the Gospel of Mark, but the former is a distinctively Lukan narrative device. Instead of depicting Jesus' travel to Jerusalem as a straightforward journey (Mark 10:32–52), Luke expands his influence geographically and includes teaching material (*Sondergut*) that builds up the image of Jesus as a πεπαιδευμένος. This educational aspect serves at least two purposes, to establish the authority of Jesus as a teacher (or prophet[131]), and as an *exemplum* for early Christians who themselves travel and teach the gospel entrusted to them as members of the ὁδός movement.

---

129 Elsner, "Hagiographic Geography," 35.
130 Fron, *Bildung und Reisen*, 135ff.
131 Moessner, *Lord of the Banquet*, 207–10: "The Story of the Deuteronomistic Journeying-Guest Prophet."

References

Anderson, Graham. *Philostratus: Biography and Belles Lettres in the Third Century A.D.* London: Croom Helm, 1986.
Arafat, Karim W. *Pausanias' Greece: Ancient Artists and Roman Rulers.* Cambridge: Cambridge University Press, 1996.
Becker, Matthias. *Lukas und Dion von Prusa: Das lukanische Doppelwerk im Kontext paganer Bildungsdiskurse.* SCCB 3. Leiden: Brill, 2020.
Bendemann, Reinhard von. *Zwischen ΔΟΞΑ und ΣΤΑΥΡΟΣ: Eine exegetische Untersuchung der Texte des sogenannten Reiseberichts im Lukasevangelium.* BZNW 101. Berlin: De Gruyter, 2001.
Bienert, David C. *Bibelkunde des Neuen Testaments.* 3rd ed. Gütersloh: Gütersloher Verlagshaus, 2021.
Borg, Barbara E., ed. *Paideia: The World of the Second Sophistic.* Millennium 2. Berlin: De Gruyter, 2004.
Bowie, Ewen. "Inspiration and Aspiration: Date, Genre, and Readership." Pages 21–32 in *Pausanias: Travel and Memory in Roman Greece.* Edited by Susan E. Alcock, John F. Cherry, and Jaś Elsner. Oxford: Oxford University Press, 2001.ss
Bowie, Ewen, and Jaś Elsner, eds. *Philostratus.* GCRW. Cambridge: Cambridge University Press, 2009.
Bradner, Lester, Jr. "The First Written Gospel: Results of Some of the Recent Investigations." *The Biblical World* 1 (1893): 432–44.
Burgess, Jonathan S. "Travel Writing and the Ancient World." Pages 19–32 in *History of Travel Writing.* Edited by Nandini Das and Tim Youngs. Cambridge: Cambridge University Press, 2019.
Burridge, Richard A. *What Are the Gospels? A Comparison With Graeco-Roman Biography.* 2nd ed. Grand Rapids, MI: Eerdmans, 2004.
Chilton, Bruce. *Rabbi Paul: An Intellectual Biography.* New York: Doubleday, 2004.
Collins, Adela Yarbro. *Mark: A Commentary.* Hermeneia. Minneapolis: Fortress Press, 2007.
Donahue, John R., and Daniel J. Harrington. *The Gospel of Mark.* SP 2. Collegeville, MN: Liturgical Press, 2005.
D'Ooge, Benj. L. "The Journey of Aeneas." *The Classical Journal* 4 (1908): 3–12.
Dueck, Daniela. "Introduction." Pages 1–6 in *The Routledge Companion to Strabo.* Edited by Daniela Dueck. London: Routledge, 2017.
Elsner, Jaś. "A Protean Corpus." Pages 3–18 in *Philostratus.* Edited by Ewen Bowie and Jaś Elsner. GCRW. Cambridge: Cambridge University Press, 2009.
Elsner, Jaś, and Ian Rutherford. "Intoduction." Pages 1–38 in *Pilgrimage in Graeco-Roman & Early Christian Antiquity: Seeing the Gods.* Edited by Jaś Elsner and Ian Rutherford. Oxford: Oxford University Press, 2005.
Elsner, John. "Hagiographic Geography: Travel and Allegory in the Life of Apollonius of Tyana." *JHS* 117 (1997): 22–37.
Erler, Michael. "Educational Travels and Epicurean *Prokoptontes*: Vergil's Aeneas as an Epicurean Telemachus." Pages 193–204 in *Ethics in Ancient Greek Literature: Aspects of Ethical Reasoning from Homer to Aristotle and Beyond.* Edited by Maria Liatsi. TCSV 102. Berlin: De Gruyter, 2020.
Eshleman, Kendra. *The Social World of Intellectuals in the Roman Empire: Sophists, Philosophers, and Christians.* GCRW. Cambridge: Cambridge University Press, 2012.
Freely, John. *A Travel Guide to Homer: On the Trail of Odysseus Through Turkey and the Mediterranean.* New York: Tauris, 2014.
Friedman, Rachel. "Location and Dislocation in Herodotus." Pages 165–77 in *The Cambridge Companion to Herodotus.* Edited by Carolyn Dewald and John Marincola. Cambridge: Cambridge University Press, 2006.

Fron, Christian. *Bildung und Reisen in der römischen Kaiserzeit: Pepaideumenoi und Mobilität zwischen dem 1. und 4. Jh. n. Chr.* UALG 146. Berlin: De Gruyter, 2021.
Galli, Marco. "Pilgrimage as Elite Habitus: Educated Pilgrims in Sacred Landscape During the Second Sophistic." Pages 253–90 in *Pilgrimage in Graeco-Roman & Early Christian Antiquity: Seeing the Gods*. Edited by Jaś Elsner and Ian Rutherford. Oxford: Oxford University Press, 2005.
Godet, Frédéric. *Kommentar zu dem Evangelium des Lucas*. Translated by E. R. Wunderlich. Hannover: Meyer, 1872.
Goodacre, Mark. *Goulder and the Gospels: An Examination of a New Paradigm*. LNTS 133. Sheffield: Sheffield Academic Press, 1996.
Goodacre, Mark. "Re-walking the 'Way of the Lord': Luke's Use of Mark and His Reaction to Matthew." Pages 26–43 in *Luke's Literary Creativity*. Edited by Jesper Tang Nielsen and Mogens Müller. LNTS 550. London: Bloomsbury, 2016.
Griesbach, Johann Jacob. *Commentatio qua Marci evangelium totum e Matthaei et Lucae commentariis decerptum esse monstratur*. Jena: Officina Stranckmannio-Fickelscherria, 1789. https://www.digitale-sammlungen.de/view/bsb10353846?page=6.
Hall, Edith. *The Return of Ulysses: A Cultural History of Homer's Odyssey*. Baltimore, MD: Johns Hopkins University Press, 2008.
Hawes, Greta. *Pausanias in the World of Greek Myth*. Oxford: Oxford University Press, 2021.
Hess, Katja. *Rhetor, Philosoph, Geistträger: Die Bildungsthematik in der lukanischen Paulusdarstellung*. FZB 137. Würzburg: Echter, 2019.
Hezser, Catherine. *Jewish Travel in Antiquity*. TSAJ 144. Tübingen: Mohr Siebeck, 2011.
Holladay, Carl R. *Introduction to the New Testament: Reference Edition*. Waco: Baylor University Press, 2017.
Hulme, Peter and Tim Youngs. "Introduction." Pages 1–13 in *The Cambridge Companion to Travel Writing*. Edited by Peter Hulme and Tim Youngs. Cambridge: Cambridge University Press, 2002.
Jacobsen, August. "Der lukanische Reisebericht." *ZWT* 29 (1886): 152–79.
Johnson, Luke Timothy. *The New Testament: A Very Short Introduction*. Very Short Introductions. Oxford: Oxford University Press, 2010.
Kim, Lawrence. "The Portrait of Homer in Strabo's Geography." *CP* 102 (2007): 363–88.
Kloppenborg, John S. *Excavating Q: The History and Setting of the Sayings Gospel*. Edinburgh: T&T Clark, 2000.
Kramer, Helga. *Lukas als Ordner des frühchristlichen Diskurses um „Armut und Reichtum" und den „Umgang mit materiellen Gütern": Eine überlieferungsgeschichtliche und diskurskritische Untersuchung zur Besitzethik des Lukasevangeliums unter besonderer Berücksichtigung des lukanischen Sonderguts*. NET 21. Tübingen: Francke, 2015.
Meyer, Eduard. "Apollonios von Tyana und die Biographie des Philostratos." *Hermes* 52 (1917): 371–424.
Meyer, Heinrich August Wilhelm and Bernhard Weiss. *Kritisch exegetisches Handbuch über die Evangelien des Markus und Lukas*. 8th ed. KEK 2. Göttingen: Vandenhoeck & Ruprecht, 1878.
Moessner, David Paul. *Lord of the Banquet: A Literary and Theological Investigation of the Lukan Travel Narrative*. Minneapolis: Fortress, 1989.
Moessner, David Paul. *Luke the Historian of Israel's Legacy, Theologian of Israel's Christ: A New Reading of the "Gospel Acts" of Luke*. BZNW 182. Berlin: De Gruyter, 2016.
Noël, Filip. *The Travel Narrative in the Gospel of Luke: Interpretation of Lk 9,51–19,28*. CBRA 5. Brussel: KVAB, 2004.
Öhler, Markus. Review of Reinhard von Bendemann. "Zwischen ΔΟΞΑ und ΣΤΑΥΡΟΣ: Eine exegetische Untersuchung der Texte des sogenannten Reiseberichts im Lukasevangelium." *JBL* 123 (2004): 167–69.

Parrott, Christopher Alan. "The Geography of the Roman World in Statius' Silvae." Ph.D. diss., Harvard University, 2013.
Petzke, Gerd. *Die Traditionen über Apollonius von Tyana und das Neue Testament*. SCHNT 1. Leiden: Brill, 1970.
Pretzler, Maria. "Greek Intellectuals on the Move: Travel and *Paideia* in the Roman Empire." Pages 123–38 in *Travel, Geography and Culture in Ancient Greece, Egypt and the Near East*. Edited by Colin Adams and Jim Roy. Leicester Nottingham Studies in Ancient Society 10. Oxford: Oxbow Books, 2007.
Putnam, Michael C.J. "Statius *Siluae* 3.2: Reading Travel." *Illinois Classical Studies* 42 (2017): 83–139.
Ramsay, William Mitchell. *St. Paul the Traveller and the Roman Citizen*. London: Hodder and Stoughton, 1895.
Reicke, Bo. "Commentatio qua Marci Evangelium totum e Matthaei et Lucae commentariis decerptum esse monstratu." Pages 68–102 in *J. J. Griesbach: Synoptic and Text-Critical Studies 1776–1976*. Edited by Bernard Orchard and Thomas R. W. Longstaff. SNTSMS. Cambridge: Cambridge University Press, 1978.
Reicke, Bo, and Ronald Walls. "Griesbach's answer to the Synoptic Question." Pages 50–67 in *J.J. Griesbach: Synoptic and Text – Critical Studies 1776–1976*. Edited by Bernard Orchard and Thomas R.W. Longstaff. SNTSMS. Cambridge: Cambridge University Press, 1978.
Robinson, James M., Paul Hoffmann, and John S. Kloppenborg, eds. *The Critical Edition of Q: A Synopsis Including the Gospels of Matthew and Luke, Mark and Thomas*. Leuven: Peeters, 2000.
Romm, James. "Travel." Pages 109–26 in *The Cambridge Companion to the Greek and Roman Novel*. Edited by Tim Whitmarsh. Cambridge: Cambridge University Press, 2008.
Sanday, William. "A Survey of the Synoptic Question: III: Points Proved or Probable (continued)." *The Expositor* Fourth Series 3 (1891): 302–16.
Schellenberg, Ryan S. "Danger in the Wilderness, Danger at Sea: Paul and the Perils of Travel." Pages 141–61 in *Travel and Religion in Antiquity*. Edited by Philip A. Harland. Studies in Christianity and Judaism/Études sur le christianisme et le judaïsme 21. Waterloo: Wilfrid Laurier University Press, 2011.
Schleiermacher, Friedrich. *Ueber die Schriften des Lukas: Ein kritischer Versuch*. Berlin: Reimer, 1817.
Schnelle, Udo. *Die ersten 100 Jahre des Christentums 30–130 n. Chr.: Die Entstehungsgeschichte einer Weltreligion*. 2nd ed. UTB 4411. Göttingen: Vandenhoeck & Ruprecht, 2016.
Schnelle, Udo. *Einleitung in das Neue Testament*. 9th rev. ed. UTB 1830. Göttingen: Vandenhoeck & Ruprecht, 2017.
Schwartz, Daniel R. "Pilgrimage to Jerusalem in Antiquity." Pages 269–75 in *Routledge Handbook on Jerusalem*. Edited by Suleiman A. Mourad, Naomi Koltun-Fromm, and Bedross Der Matossian. London: Routledge, 2019.
Stein, Karl Wilhelm. *Kommentar zu dem Evangelium des Lucas, nebst einem Anhange über den Brief an die Laodiceer*. Halle: Gebauer-Schwetschke, 1830.
Streeter, Burnett Hillman. *The Four Gospels: A Study of Origins*. 4th rev. ed. London: Macmillan, 1930.
Temmerman, Koen de. "The novel: Chariton." Pages 483–502 in *Space in Ancient Greek Literature*. Edited by Irene J.F. de Jong. MnS 339. Leiden: Brill, 2012.
Theissen, Gerd. "Wanderradikalismus: Literatursoziologische Aspekte der Überlieferung von Worten Jesu im Urchristentum." *ZTK* 70 (1973): 245–71.
Tuckett, Christopher M. *The Revival of the Griesbach Hypothesis: An Analysis and Appraisal*. SNTSMS 44. Cambridge: Cambridge University Press, 1983.
Vollenweider, Samuel. "Bildungsfreunde oder Bildungsverächter? Überlegungen zum Stellenwert der Bildung im frühen Christentum." Pages 283–304 in *Was ist Bildung in der Vormoderne?* Edited by Peter Gemeinhardt. SERAPHIM 4. Tübingen: Mohr Siebeck, 2019.

Weisse, Christian Hermann. *Die evangelische Geschichte: Kritisch und philosophisch bearbeitet*. 2 vols. Leipzig: Breitkopf und Härtel, 1838.
Wickes, Dean Rockwell, ed. *The Sources of Luke's Perean Section*. Chicago, IL: University of Chicago Press, 1912.
Wolter, Michael. *Das Lukasevangelium*. HNT 5. Tübingen: Mohr Siebeck, 2008.
Wolter, Michael. *The Gospel according to Luke*. Translated by Wayne Coppins. 2 vols. Waco: Baylor University Press, 2017.
Youngs, Tim. "Introduction: Defining the Terms." Pages 1–16 in *The Cambridge Introduction to Travel Writing*. Edited by Tim Youngs. Cambridge: Cambridge University Press, 2013.

Pieter B. Hartog
Acts of the Apostles—A Celebration of Uncertainty? Constructing a Dialogical Self for the Early Jesus Movement

Abstract: In the ancient world, travel was often a source of anxiety and uncertainty. This uncertainty pertained both to the practical aspects of traveling and to the experience of being away from one's own land and culture. This chapter explores how the latter type of uncertainty can inspire new formulations of self and identity. Employing the modern-day psychological notion of the dialogical self and paying particular attention to the apostolic meeting in Acts 15, I aim to show how the development of the Way, as Acts of the Apostles describes it, evoked uncertainty among its members. As a response to this uncertainty, the book of Acts suggests overarching categories to describe the Way as a movement that is both familiar and new.

Among the many experiences that travelers in the first centuries of our era may have had, uncertainty can perhaps claim pride of place. Its most tangible expression concerned the practicalities of travel. On the roads, robbers were a constant risk (cf. Luke 10:25–37), and pirates posed a threat at sea.[1] Nature also often caused trouble: heat or cold could make overland travel a tricky business, while changing winds could put sea travelers in peril—the winter season was particularly notorious in this regard.[2] As a result, traveling was often a communal effort, and ancient travelers depended on others—fellow travelers and facilitators—to ensure the success of their journeys.[3]

---

1 On robbers and bandits see Brent D. Shaw, "Bandits in the Roman Empire," *PaP* 105 (1984): 3–52. On pirates and the image of the Romans as putting an end to piracy in the Mediterranean see David Braund, "Piracy under the Principate and the Ideology of Imperial Eradication," in *War and Society in the Roman World*, ed. John Rich and Graham Shipley (London: Routledge, 1993), 195–212; Philip de Souza, *Piracy in the Graeco-Roman World* (Cambridge: Cambridge University Press, 1999).
2 Veg., *Mil.* 4.39. See also Philo, *Legat.* 190, where wintery sea storms symbolize the storms Gaius has in store for the Judaean people.
3 Cf. Vernon K. Robbins, "By Land and By Sea: The We-Passages and Ancient Sea Voyages," in *Perspectives on Luke-Acts*, ed. Charles H. Talbert (Macon, GA: Mercer University Press; Edinburgh: T&T Clark, 1978), 215–42, who argues that this communal aspect of travelling provides the socio-cultural background to the use of first person speech (often in the plural) in sea voyage narratives. Those who facilitated travel have often escaped the attention of scholars, but see the insightful analysis of Laura Nasrallah, "Imposing Travelers: An Inscription from Galatia and the Journeys of the Earliest Christians," in *Journeys in the Roman East: Imagined and Real*, ed. Maren R. Niehoff, Culture, Religion, and Politics in the Greco-Roman World 1 (Tübingen: Mohr Siebeck, 2017), 273–96.

Uncertainty did not end there, though: their dependency made ancient travelers vulnerable, and inn keepers, boat captains, and unknown others on the road had to be greeted with healthy suspicion.[4] The omnipresent risks of travel were well-known and made lasting impressions in ancient literature across cultural and ethnic boundaries: no desert journey narrative is complete without a lack of water, no ancient novel without pirates, and no sea travel episode without shipwreck.

Aside from these "obvious and practical hardships of travel," writes Steven Muir, travelers faced yet another type of uncertainty. This second sort of anxiety "has to do with how one's social identity becomes precarious when one is separated from the primary social groupings of family and fellow citizens."[5] What is more, the exposure to novel cultural and ethnic groups on one's journeys—facilitated in the Roman period by the construction of substantive road and waterway networks[6]—triggered travelers to rethink their own senses of belonging. As an increasing number of scholars has come to realize, the Roman world witnessed several developments reminiscent of the modern globalized West, such as sudden increases in connectivity and growing intercultural and transcultural awareness among its inhabitants.[7] As a result, cultural and ethnic self-presentations in the first centuries CE—as they are expressed in literary writings from these periods—often reflect what Jan Nederveen Pieterse has called a "diversification and amplification of 'sources of the self'."[8] This proliferation of a range of sources of the self offers valuable new opportunities for individuals in globalized contexts to forge multi-lev-

---

[4] See e.g. Catherine Hezser, *Jewish Travel in Antiquity*, TSAJ 144 (Tübingen: Mohr Siebeck, 2011), 89–119, who describes how Jewish travelers would often rather spend the night with fellow Jews than in public hostels.
[5] Steven Muir, "Religion on the Road in Ancient Greece and Rome," in *Travel and Religion in Antiquity*, ed. Philip A. Harland, Studies in Christianity and Judaism/Études sur le christianisme et le judaïsme 21 (Waterloo: Wilfrid Laurier University Press, 2011), 29–47 (30).
[6] On the prominence of travel in the Roman world see Lionel Casson, *Travel in the Ancient World* (London: Allen & Unwin, 1974); Jean-Marie André and Marie-Françoise Baslez, *Voyager dans l'Antiquité* (Paris: Fayard, 1993), 77–166.
[7] See Robert Witcher, "Globalisation and Roman Imperialism: Perspectives on Identities in Roman Italy," in *The Emergence of State Identities in Italy in the First Millennium BC*, ed. Edward Herring and Kathryn Lomas (London: Accordia Research Institute, University of London, 2000), 213–25; Andrew Gardner, "Thinking about Roman Imperialism: Postcolonialism, Globalisation and Beyond?" *Brittania* 44 (2013): 1–25; Martin Pitts and Miguel John Versluys, eds., *Globalisation and the Roman World: World History, Connectivity and Material Culture* (Cambridge: Cambridge University Press, 2014). See also Susanne Luther's contribution in this volume.
[8] Jan Nederveen Pieterse, *Globalization and Culture: Global Mélange*, 3rd ed. (Lanham, MD: Rowman & Littlefield, 2016), 74.

elled identities for themselves.[9] In this contribution, I draw attention to processes of developing what I shall call "dialogical selves," which are triggered by the anxiety faced by travelers to manage the variegated sources of the self with which their journeys bring them into contact.

Theorizing Uncertainty Through Dialogical Self Theory

To approach this topic, I have found the methodological framework of Dialogical Self Theory particularly helpful. Developed by Dutch psychologist Hubert Hermans, Dialogical Self Theory approaches the human mind as consisting of a variety of self-positions (cf. Nederveen Pieterse's "sources of the self"), which are in dialogue with each other and between which the self can alternate.[10] These self-positions are both internal and external; they incorporate the social context of the self into the self, so that the self takes the shape of a micro-society. In other words, the self, for Hermans, is not unchanging over time, but is *"extended* in space and time" and affected by the various contexts in which it finds itself.[11] As a result, dialogues between different self-positions take place at the levels of both communal and individual selves.

In the study of New Testament literature, the notion of the dialogical self has been used most fruitfully to account for processes of self-formation that those who joined the early Jesus movement underwent. Kobus Kok and Dieter Roth offer the example of a student "who is an executive in a large consulting firm in Pretoria," but "has to take part in 'pagan' African rituals in the rural area of Natal where his father is a traditional African chief." This example, Kok and Roth propose, may be illustrative of the tensions that those who joined the Jesus movement experienced: on the one hand they adopted a new self-understanding grounded in their faith, on the other they remained closely tied to their previous cultural ties and practices. "In

---

9 I have argued elsewhere that such multi-levelled identities can be recognized in the book of Acts and other writings from the early Roman empire. See Pieter B. Hartog, "Where Shall Wisdom be Found? Identity, Sacred Space, and Universal Knowledge in Philostratus and the Acts of the Apostles," in *Jerusalem and Other Holy Places as Foci of Multireligious and Ideological Confrontation*, ed. Pieter B. Hartog et al., Jewish and Christian Perspectives 37 (Leiden: Brill, 2021), 131–49.
10 Hubert J. M. Hermans and Harry J. G. Kempen, *The Dialogical Self: Meaning as Movement* (San Diego, CA: Academic Press, 1993); Hubert J. M. Hermans and Agnieszka Hermans-Konopka, *Dialogical Self Theory: Positioning and Counter-Positioning in a Globalizing Society* (Cambridge: Cambridge University Press, 2010).
11 Quote from Hermans and Hermans-Konopka, *Dialogical Self Theory*, 82.

such a negotiation," Kok and Roth conclude, "the separation between 'Christianity' and previous socio-cultural identities may not have been as definitive and clear-cut as once thought."[12]

In this example, the student's education and working environment provide him with novel self-positions, which interact with those with which he was familiar from his upbringing. This results in a dialogical self, in which these various self-positions interact in complex ways and work together to inspire a rich self-image. In similar vein, the notion of a dialogical self illustrates the nexus between travel and self-formation—a role travel has played throughout much of ancient and less ancient history.[13] As individuals find themselves in new contexts as a result of their journeys, their selves obtain access to novel self-positions. Through this amplification of self-positions these selves gain in breadth and depth.

Applied to the literary level, travel motifs in ancient literature are excellently suited to construct layered and multi-faceted dialogical selves for the protagonists of the narratives in which these motifs occur. This is indeed what we see happening in the book of Acts, as well as in contemporaneous travel narratives. What is more, these individual dialogical selves often serve as exemplars of group identity. In the book of Acts, for instance, Peter and Paul—the book's main protagonists—exemplify the ethos of the Way as a movement in which Jews and non-Jews are united.[14] Ascribing dialogical selves to these protagonists—in particular Paul, who features as a seasoned traveler—therefore promotes a dialogical understanding of the group to which they belong.

The experience of uncertainty rarely appears explicitly in studies on the dialogical self in ancient literature. Yet in Hermans and Hermans-Konopko's account

---

12 All quotation from Jacobus Kok and Dieter T. Roth, "Sensitivity towards Outsiders and the Dynamic Relationship between Mission and Ethics/Ethos," in *Sensitivity towards Outsider: Exploring the Dynamic Relationship between Mission and Ethics in the New Testament and Early Christianity*, ed. Jacobus Kok et al., WUNT 2/364 (Tübingen: Mohr Siebeck, 2014), 1–23 (7). Cf. how Gerd Theissen evokes the dialogical self to account for Paul's ongoing engagement with different strands of Judaism after joining the Jesus movement: Gerd Theissen, "The Letter to the Romans and Paul's Plural Identity," in *The Making of Christianity: Conflicts, Contacts, and Constructions: Essays in Honor of Bengt Holmberg*, ed. Magnus Zetterholm and Samuel Byrskog, ConBNT 47 (Winona Lake, IN: Eisenbrauns, 2012), 301–22.
13 See, e.g., Karlpeter Elis, ed., *Bildungsreise—Reisebildung* (Vienna: LIT, 2004); Christian Fron, *Bildung und Reisen in der römischen Kaiserzeit: Pepaideumenoi und Mobilität zwischen dem 1. und 4. Jh. n. Chr.*, UALG 146 (Berlin: De Gruyter, 2021).
14 See Acts 20:17–38, where Paul sets aspects of his previous life as an example to the recipients of his message. More broadly see Robert C. Tannehill, *The Narrative Unity of Luke-Acts: A Literary Interpretation*, 2 vols. (Minneapolis: Fortress Press, 1986, 1990), 2:328, who writes: "Heroic figures (like Paul in Acts) inevitably become models of behavior, and Paul's farewell to the Ephesian elders (20:18–35) indicates awareness that Paul could be an effective model for the later church."

of the dialogical self, this experience plays a central role. In the process of developing a dialogical self, these authors stress, uncertainty is unavoidable. They distinguish four aspects of such uncertainty:

> (i) *complexity*, referring to a great number of parts (of self and society) that have a variety of interconnections; (ii) *ambiguity*, referring to a suspension of clarity, as the meaning of one part is determined by the flux and variation of the other parts; (iii) *deficit knowledge*, referring to the absence of a superordinate knowledge structure that is able to resolve the contradictions between the parts; and (iv) *unpredictability*, implying a lack of control of future developments.[15]

For Hermans and Hermans-Konopko, this uncertainty is not necessarily a negative experience, provided it is carefully managed and reduced. In those cases, uncertainty can provide a stimulus to engage in new contacts and modes of cooperation or serve "as a definitive farewell to the dogmas and ideologies of institutions that restricted and confined the self in earlier times."[16] Yet it can also cause serious problems when those who experience such uncertainty are unable to reduce it. Reductions can take place in different ways, but Hermans and Hermans-Konopko present the option of "going into this uncertainty rather than avoiding it" as the most preferable option.[17] In this way, they argue, one deals with the uncertainty which modern-day globalized spaces may evoke in a truly dialogical fashion, that is, by incorporating a wide range of self-positions into a coherent yet open whole. Hence, "certainty does not result from avoiding uncertainty but from *entering* it."[18]

In what follows, I intend to show that one purpose of the book of Acts is to reduce the uncertainty that comes with the development of the Way as a novel, multi-ethnic and trans-ethnic, movement.[19] To do so, I analyze Acts' account of the apostolic council (Acts 15:1–35) from the perspective of Hermans and Hermans-Konopko's description of uncertainty, wondering how in this episode the four aspects of this type of uncertainty are upheld and reduced.

---

[15] Hermans and Hermans-Konopko, *Dialogical Self Theory*, 3 (cf. 28) (italics theirs).
[16] Hermans and Hermans-Konopko, *Dialogical Self Theory*, 28.
[17] Hermans and Hermans-Konopko, *Dialogical Self Theory*, 46, 77 (italics omitted). Other ways of reducing uncertainty are "a reduction of the number and heterogeneity of positions in the repertoire"; "giving the lead to one powerful position that is permitted to dominate the repertoire as a whole"; "sharpening the boundaries between oneself and the other"; "adding instead of diminishing the number of positions in the self." See Hermans and Hermans-Konopko, *Dialogical Self Theory*, 44–47.
[18] Hermans and Hermans-Konopko, *Dialogical Self Theory*, 28 (italics theirs).
[19] On the book of Acts as negotiating the novelty of the Way see also Pieter B. Hartog, "Noah and Moses in Acts 15: Group Models and the Novelty of The Way," *NTS* 67 (2021): 496–513.

The Apostolic Council: A Celebration of Uncertainty?

Acts' description of the apostolic council occupies a central place in the narrative, occurring in the middle of Paul's first (Acts 13–14) and second (Acts 15:36–17:22) missionary journeys.[20] In the chapters leading up to Acts 15, Jesus' prediction that his disciplines should bear witness "in Jerusalem, in the whole of Judaea and Samaria, and until the end of the earth" (1:8) begins to be realized, as "Judaeans from every nation under heaven" (Acts 2:5), Samaritans (Acts 8:4–8, 14–18, 25), and individuals and groups from various *ethnê* (Acts 8:26–40, 10–11, 13–14) come to join the Jesus movement. Thus, beginning from Jerusalem the disciples' forced (Acts 8:1–4) and voluntary (Acts 13:1–3) travels made sure that the circles of those who joined this new movement grew wider and wider.

Encouraging as these developments may be, they are paired with increasing uncertainty about the character of the Jesus movement. In Hermans and Hermans-Konopka's terms, the first chapters of Acts display an increase in complexity and ambiguity. As a varied assemblage of non-Judaeans join the Jesus movement, the range of self-positions available to this movement—as it were[21]—increases. This creates the type of complexity in which "a great number of parts (of self and society) that have a variety of interconnections" must be managed.[22] Seeing that these potential self-positions are intrinsically related to one another through their common acceptance of the apostles' message, the multiplication of these self-positions breeds ambiguity about the terms by which they should go together.

This type of complexity and ambiguity, Hermans and Hermans-Konopka point out, results in deficit knowledge about "a superordinate knowledge structure that

---

20 Cf. how Hermann Wolfgang Beyer, *Die Apostelgeschichte* (Göttingen: Vandenhoeck & Ruprecht, 1932), 91 describes the apostolic meeting as Acts' "Herzstück." Beyer is quoted with approval by Charles K. Barrett, *A Critical and Exegetical Commentary on the Acts of the Apostles*, ICC (London: T&T Clark, 1994, 1998), 696.
21 As a psychological notion, the concept of the dialogical self is not straightforwardly applicable to a societal group instead of an individual human being. At the same time, in its conception of the self as a "micro-society" in which a range of self-positions is in dialogue with one another, Dialogical Self Theory draws an explicit parallel between dialogical society and the dialogical self. If what happens in society happens on a micro-level in the self, the reverse may also be true: what we see happening in individuals reflects broader societal developments. Applied to the topic of this paper, the dialogical selves of Peter and Paul as Acts constructs them can be taken as symbols for the type of group the book wishes to promote. On the self as a micro-society see, e.g., Hubert J. M. Hermans, "Dialogical Self Theory in a Boundary-Crossing Society," in *Moral and Spiritual Leadership in an Age of Plural Moralities*, ed. Hans Alma and Ina ter Avest (London: Routledge, 2019), 27–47.
22 Hermans and Hermans-Konopka, *Dialogical Self Theory*, 3.

is able to resolve the contradictions between the parts."[23] Providing such a structure, I would argue, is one of the key purposes of the book of Acts. The only New Testament writing to employ the term "the Way" as a self-designation,[24] Acts sets out to build a self-understanding for this novel movement in which its various self-positions are in a healthy dialogue with one another. At the same time, the overarching structures Acts proposes are nowhere fully fledged, and a certain amount of uncertainty and unpredictability—Hermans and Hermans-Konopka's fourth characteristic of uncertainty—remains.

The apostolic council illustrates the tension between reducing and upholding uncertainty, which runs throughout the book of Acts. The decree that results from the apostolic meeting has often been taken to serve a legislative function, providing a list of minimum requirements which non-Jewish members of the Way would have to fulfil (cf. Acts 15:5, 20).[25] Yet such a legislative reading of the decree is not self-evident. To begin with, the terms of the decree do not amount to clear-cut regulations. The two versions of the decree (Acts 15:20, 29) differ in the order and formulation of their terms, and the exact meaning of the individual terms remains disputed, as the history of interpretation evidences.[26] Second, Acts 15 has apparently undergone a process of redaction, with Acts' author including an earlier source (or sources)—probably reflected in Acts 15:29 (par. 21:25)—into his narrative. In that case, while the original source may have served some legislative purpose, in the hands of Acts' author, it becomes a token of identity for the Way.[27] Third, the letter that communicates the apostles' decision explicitly acknowledges its limited geographical validity

---

23 Hermans and Hermans-Konopka, *Dialogical Self Theory*, 3.
24 Though the term may have its roots in Luke's gospel. On the term see Paul Trebilco, *Self-Designations and Group Identity in the New Testament* (Cambridge: Cambridge University Press, 2012), 247–71; Pieter B. Hartog, "Reading Acts in Motion: Motion and Glocalisation in the Acts of the Apostles," in *Mediterranean Flows: People, Ideas and Objects in Motion*, ed. Anna Usacheva and Emilia Mataix Ferrándiz, Contexts of Ancient and Medieval Anthropology 3 (Leiden: Brill, 2023), 96–110 (100–102).
25 See. e.g. Markus Bockmuehl, "The Noahide Commandments and New Testament Ethics: With Special Reference to Acts 15 and Pauline Halakhah," *RevB* 102 (1995): 72–101 (93); Richard Bauckham, "James and the Gentiles (Acts 15.13–21)," in *History, Literature, and Society in the Book of Acts*, ed. Ben Witherington, III (Cambridge: Cambridge University Press, 1996), 154–84 (154); Jürgen Wehnert, *Die Reinheit des »christlichen Gottesvolkes« aus Juden und Heiden: Studien zum historischen und theologischen Hintergrund des sogenannten Aposteldekrets*, FRLANT 173 (Göttingen: Vandenhoeck & Ruprecht, 1997); John van Eck, *Handelingen: De wereld in het geding* (Kampen: Kok, 2003), 317–37, esp. 327–31.
26 Space does not permit a full discussion; see Hartog, "Noah and Moses," 501–7 for references.
27 On the literary history of Acts 15 see, e.g., Ernst Haenchen, *The Acts of the Apostles: A Commentary* (Philadelphia: Westminster, 1971), 455–72; Gerhard Schneider, *Die Apostelgeschichte: II. Teil* (Freiburg: Herder, 1982), 174–77, 187, 189–92; Wehnert, *Reinheit*, 33–55; Lutz Doering, *Ancient*

to Jesus followers "in Antioch and Syria and Cilicia" (Acts 15:23).[28] Finally, the four requirements in the decree are rather one-sided as a legislative program: three of the four requirements (idols, blood, and strangled things) appear to have a cultic background, while only one term (sexual misconduct) governs human interaction. It appears, therefore, that Acts' story about the apostolic meeting is not so much about what members of the Way should *do*, but about how they should *understand* the movement to which they now belong. The central question this chapter (and, by extension, the entire book of Acts[29]) seeks to answer, is: what type of movement is the Way?[30]

As I have argued elsewhere,[31] Acts 15 answers this question in two ways. First, the decree's terms πορνεία and αἷμα, as well as the command to abstain from idolatry—if that is what ἀλίσγημα in Acts 15:20 means—seem to evoke commandments associated with Noah in Gen 8–9, which are to govern human life after the flood. Second, the terms πορνεία, ἀλίσγημα, and πνικτόν suggest a connection between the decree and laws pertaining to the *gerim* as they feature in the Levitical Holiness Code (Lev 17–26). In both cases, the universalist appeal of the group model involved—the laws in Gen 8–9 apply to all human beings who are to inhabit the earth anew, those alluded to from Lev 17–26 to Israelites and *gerim* together—makes these models well-suited to characterize the Way, in which Jews and non-Jews from a broad range of ethnic and cultural backgrounds come together.

At the same time, neither the connection with Noah-related commandments nor that with the Holiness Code are spelled out explicitly and in full. The background of most terms in the decree remains highly ambiguous, and the names of

---

Jewish Letters and the Beginnings of Christian Epistolography, WUNT 298 (Tübingen: Mohr Siebeck, 2012) 464–65.

28 Cf. Helmut Löhr, "'Unzucht': Überlegungen zu einer Bestimmung der Jakobus-Klauseln im Aposteldekret sowie zu den Geltungsgründen von Normen frühchristlicher Ethik, " in *Aposteldekret und antikes Vereinswesen: Gemeinschaft und ihre Ordnung*, ed. Markus Öhler, WUNT 280 (Tübingen: Mohr Siebeck, 2011), 49–64.

29 Cf. Barrett, *Acts of the Apostles*, xxxvi, who describes how the purpose of Acts 15 symbolizes that of Acts as a whole.

30 For readings of Acts 15 that emphasize the chapter's identity-constructive rather than legislative purposes see Luke Timothy Johnson, *The Acts of the Apostles*, SaPaSe 5 (Collegeville, MN: Liturgical Press, 1992), 270; Burkhard Jürgens, *Zweierlei Anfang: Kommunikative Konstruktionen heidenchristlicher Identität in Gal 2 und Apg 15*, BBB 120 (Berlin: Philo, 1999); Roland Deines, "Das Aposteldekret—Halacha für Heidenchristen oder christliche Rücksichtnahme auf jüdische Tabus?" in *Jewish Identity in the Greco-Roman World: Jüdische Identität in der griechisch-römischen Welt*, ed. Jörg Frey, Daniel R. Schwartz, and Stephanie Gripentrog, AJEC 71 (Leiden: Brill, 2007), 323–95; Markus Öhler, "Das Aposteldekret als Dokument ethnischer Identität im Spiegel antiker Vereinigungen," in Öhler, *Aposteldekret und antikes Vereinswesen*, 341–82.

31 Hartog, "Noah and Moses."

Noah and Moses are absent as sources for the decree's contents.[32] The literary effect of this play between aligning the Way with and distancing it from the generation of human beings after the flood and the legal unity of Israelites and *gerim* in some of the regulations from the Holiness Code is to portray this movement at the same time as a group reminiscent of earlier groups in Israel's history and as something fundamentally new. In Hermans and Hermans-Konopka's terms, therefore, Acts 15 both reduces uncertainty—by offering models by which to make sense of the complexity and ambiguity that surrounds the Jesus movement—and fosters it—by not fully aligning the Jesus movement with these models. Throughout Acts, an amount of unpredictability persists.

This unpredictability plays out on the literary level as well. As I pointed out, Acts 15 offers an interlude in between Paul's unabated travels. As Paul's journeys continue in Acts 16 and take a turn to Macedonia (Acts 16:6–10), Acts allows for the possibility of discovering new self-positions and, in their wake, new overarching structures in which they fit. This is not merely a hypothetical possibility, as Paul's speech in Athens (Acts 17:16–34) demonstrates. In that speech, Paul portrays the Way not in terms of post-flood humanity or a group of Israelites and *gerim*, but—through an Aratus quotation—as the offspring of God/Zeus, the father of all (Acts 17:25–28). In this particular case, Paul's acquaintance with a new group he encounters on his journeys triggers him to find a new conceptual framework to make sense of the type of group that the followers of the Way constitute.

Ultimately, Paul's travels take him to Rome, and this is where the book of Acts ends off (Acts 28:11–31). As several scholars have argued, Acts' sudden end captures the openness of the book as a whole.[33] If Acts reads as a search for categories to make sense of the early Jesus movement, its final sentence about Paul proclaiming God's kingdom in Rome reads as an invitation to Acts' readers to continue that search. Seeing that the book of Acts was written quite some time after Paul's alleged

---

[32] Moses in mentioned in Acts 15:21, but not as inspiration for the terms of the apostolic decree. Noah is entirely absent from Acts. On the background of the terms of the decree see—from different perspectives—Terence Callan, "The Background of the Apostolic Decree (Acts 15:20, 29; 21:25)," *CBQ* 55 (1993): 284–97; Friedrich Avemarie, "Die jüdischen Wurzeln des Aposteldekrets: Lösbare und ungelöste Probleme," in Öhler, *Aposteldekret und antikes Vereinswesen*, 5–32.

[33] See most notably Daniel Marguerat, *The First Christian Historian: Writing the "Acts of the Apostles"*, SNTSMS 121 (Cambridge: Cambridge University Press, 2004), 205–30. See also Pieter B. Hartog, "*Ioudaioi* and Migrant Apostles in the book of Acts," in *Migration und biblische Theologie: Positionen und theologische Herausforderungen aus Perspektive der alt- und neutestamentlichen Wissenschaft*, ed. Benedikt Hensel and Christian Wetz, Arbeiten zur Bibel und ihrer Geschichte (Leipzig: Evangelische Verlagsanstalt, 2023), 479–94 (488–90). For a survey of different views see Karl L. Armstrong, "The End of Acts and the Jewish Response: Condemnation, Tragedy, or Hope?" *CBR* 17 (2019): 209–30.

arrival in Rome,[34] the end of the book opens up a space for readers to reflect on the development of the Way after Paul—a development of which they themselves have been a part. In the ongoing development of the early Jesus movement and the related move towards a dialogical self-understanding, Paul's arrival and proclamation in Rome inaugurates a new episode. Only this episode has not finished, and Acts' readers are exhorted to reflect on and take their place within the Way.

To sum up, the experience of uncertainty that accompanies ancient travelers finds literary expression in the book of Acts, where the spread of the apostles' message results in an increase of complexity and ambiguity within the Jesus movement. The apostolic meeting in Acts 15 addresses this complexity and ambiguity and reduces uncertainty by offering humanity in the time of Noah and joint legislation for Israelites and *gerim* as frameworks for understanding the Way. At the same time, Acts 15 does not fully resolve the uncertainty that shines through in Acts' earlier chapters, in that none of the groups models this chapter offers is fully developed. Thus the chapter sets the stage for the journeys that follow and, eventually, for Acts' open end, which exhorts it readers to reflect on and take their place within the Way.

Constructing Group Identity Through Travel Narratives

As I have sought to show, Acts of the Apostles testifies to the transformative potential of travel narratives for the construction of both personal and communal identities. This transformative potential results from the uncertainty that accompanies one's travels. As Hermans and Hermans-Konopka argue, one can react in various ways when one finds themselves in a situation of a sudden proliferation of self-po-

---

[34] The date of Acts is a notorious point of contention among New Testament scholars. Not only do many scholars consider the dates of Luke and Acts in tandem, therefore tending to deny a late date for the latter writing, but even those scholars who take Acts on its own differ greatly in their datings. Arguing for a date in the 2nd century are the contributions to Rubén R. Dupertuis and Todd Penner, eds., *Engaging Early Christian History: Reading Acts in the Second Century* (Oxford: Routledge, 2013). Arguing for an early date is Karl L. Armstrong, *Dating Acts in its Jewish and Greco-Roman Contexts*, LNTS 637 (London: T&T Clark, 2021). Arguing for a middle position because of Acts' alleged reflection of Roman imperial policies is Drew W. Billings, *Acts of the Apostles and the Rhetoric of Roman Imperialism* (Cambridge: Cambridge University Press, 2017). I tend to agree with Matthias Klinghardt's argument that Acts serves as an *Integrationstext*; this would suggest a later rather than earlier date, though perhaps not as late as Klinghardt proposes. See Matthias Klinghardt, "Das Apostledekret als kanonischer Integrationstext: Konstruktion und Begründung von Gemeinsinn," in Öhler, *Aposteldekret und antikes Vereinswesen*, 91–112; Hartog, "Noah and Moses."

sitions. For some individuals, such situations can result in a loss of self and a painful process of recovering a sense of self. A better reaction, write the two authors, is to embrace the uncertainty, manage and reduce it, and so arrive at a new selves in which old and new self-positions are in dialogue with one another.

The Roman empire facilitated travel in unprecedented fashion, and it is no surprise that processes similar to the ones described by Hermans and Hermans-Konopka and featuring in Acts of the Apostles can be recognized in literary writings from the first centuries of our era. In the Hellenistic and Roman periods, study journeys and touristic travels were well-known phenomena among the societal elites and aided those who undertook them to gain in knowledge, wisdom, and a deepened sense of belonging in the world.[35] One representative of this phenomenon is Pausanias (2nd century CE), who offers an account of his journey across Greece in his *Periegesis Hellados*. Yet Pausanias' Greece is, as Jaś Elsner remarks, "a fantasy."[36] Pausanias' depiction of Greece turns the territory into a symbol of what once was, reviving those aspects of the past which Pausanias deems fitting for his own understanding as a Greek author living under Rome.[37] In this way, Pausanias' travel account offers fruitful opportunities for constructing Greekness. In Elsner's words, "[Pausanias'] collection of *hellenika* ... makes every object or event, as Pausanias meets it in his time, into a direct channel to the myths and histories in which Greek identity is represented as inhering for all time."[38]

Another witness to travel as a source of constructing cultural identity is Philostratus' *Life of Apollonius of Tyana*. Philostratus (2nd–3rd century CE) writes not about his own journeys, but about those of Pythagoraean philosopher-cum-wonderworker Apollonius, who lived in the first century CE. A prolonged journey to India occupies a central place in Philostratus' narrative (*V A* 2–3).[39] India, for Philostra-

---

35 On educational journeys see André and Baslez, *Voyager dans l'Antiquité*, 297–315. On tourism see André and Baslez, *Voyager dans l'Antiquité*, 317–72; René Bloch, *Andromeda in Jaffa: Mythische Orte als Reiseziele in der jüdischen Antike*, Franz-Delitzsch-Vorlesung 2015 (Münster: Institutum Judaicum Delitzschianum, 2017).
36 Jaś Elsner, "Structuring 'Greece': Pausanias' *Periegesis* as a Literary Construct," in *Pausanias: Travel and Memory in Roman Greece*, ed. Susan E. Alcock, John F. Cherry, and Jaś Elsner (Oxford: Oxford University Press, 2001), 3–20 (18).
37 On Pausanias' project see Maria Pretzler, *Pausanias: Travel Writing in Ancient Greece* (London: Duckworth, 2007); Janick Auberger, "Pausanias le Périégète et la Seconde Sophistique," in *Perceptions of the Second Sophistic and Its Times—Regards sur la Seconde Sophistique et son époque*, ed. Thomas Schmidt and Pascale Fleury, Phoenix Supplementary Volume 49 (Toronto: University of Toronto Press, 2011), 133–45.
38 Elsner, "Structuring 'Greece'," 19.
39 For a more elaborate analysis of Apollonius' visit to the Brahmins see Hartog, "Where Shall Wisdom be Found?" 135–42.

tus, counts as the zenith of wisdom and Apollonius' journey there is the final step in reaching the status of sage. Yet Philostratus' India is an ambiguous place. On the one hand, it represents Greek culture, as all individuals Apollonius encounters on his journeys speak Greek, and king Phraotes of Taxila practices sports "in the Greek way" (*V A* 2.27) and offers a meal reminiscent of Greek symposia (*V A* 2.27–28). To an extent, India here "serves only to comment on Greek practice and enhance the superlative Greekness of Apollonius."[40] On the other hand, India remains a distinctly non-Greek place. Phraotes, for all his Greek behavior, apologizes for having been born a barbarian (*V A* 2.27); the Brahmins explicitly criticize Greek wisdom (*V A* 3.18, 3.25); and Philostratus makes a point of India's location beyond the river Hyphasis—the traditional eastern border of the Hellenistic empire.[41] The literary effect of this ambiguous portrayal of India and Greekness is the promotion of a new understanding of what it means to be culturally Greek. As Janet Downie argues, "one of the central concerns of the *Life of Apollonius* [is]: what is the nature and value of Hellenism in a cosmopolitan, imperial world?"[42] The outcome of Apollonius' quest is a dialogical sense of Greekness, in which the wisdom of a wide range of cultural traditions which Apollonius encountered on his journeys is in dialogue with one another. The phrase "to a wise man Greece is everywhere" (*V A* 1.35)—sometimes taken as the motto of the *Life of Apollonius*—aptly captures this dialogical understanding of Greekness: if Greekness can be found everywhere, all localities, vice versa, have something to contribute to Greekness as an overarching dialogical category.

A final example is Philo of Alexandria, a Judaean philosopher and politician, who lived in 1st-century CE Alexandria. In his *Legatio ad Gaium*, Philo narrates how he travelled to Rome to plead the case for the Alexandrian Judaeans. The cause for this embassy was the riots that had broken out in Alexandria in 38 CE between Judaean and Greek inhabitants of the city. Philo's account of these riots and his journey to Rome are, just as Pausanias' Greece, a fantasy that serves specific goals. As I have shown elsewhere, the *Legatio* offers an understanding of the *Ioudaios ethnos* as upholding traditional Roman values (that is, values that characterized the rule of the first emperors Augustus and Tiberius) at a time when the entire

---

40 Kendra Eshleman, "Indian Travel and Self-Location in the *Life of Apollonius* and the *Acts of Thomas*," in *Journeys in the Roman East: Imagined and Real*, ed. Maren R. Niehoff, Culture, Religion, and Politics in the Greco-Roman World 1 (Tübingen: Mohr Siebeck, 2017), 183–201 (191).
41 See Arr., *Anab*. 5.28.1–29.1.
42 Janet Downie, "Palamedes and the Wisdom of India in Philostratus' *Life of Apollonius of Tyana*," *Mouseion* 13 (2016): 65–83 (65).

empire is under threat as a result of young Caligula's reckless actions.[43] This notion of Judeans as faithful Romans bolsters the rationale for the embassy in which Philo partakes: as he journeys to Rome, Philo participates in the structures of the Roman empire, just as loyal inhabitants of that empire would.[44]

In these three examples, literary depictions of travel serve to promote particular constructions of identity. Pausanias' journey to Greece revives the Greek past as Pausanias understood it; Apollonius' travels across and beyond the Roman empire embody a cosmopolitan, dialogical understanding of Greekness; and Philo's journey to Rome enables him to portray the *Ioudaios ethnos* as a guardian of Roman values. The book of Acts thus fits the literary culture of the first centuries of our era: its emphasis on travel enables its author to construct the Way as the realization of eschatological predictions in Israel's Scriptures, which had foreseen the joining together of Jews and non-Jews at the end of times.[45] Thus, in Acts too, travel motifs offer fruitful opportunities to construct group identity and position one's group within the globalized Roman empire.

Conclusion

In the ancient world, travel was often a source of anxiety and uncertainty. Employing the modern-day psychological notion of the dialogical self, I have attempted to show how narrated travel experiences can also inspire new or altered constructions of personal and group identity. In the book of Acts, the apostles' journeys and the consequent spread of their message raises the question how the early Jesus movement should be understood. Acts as a whole, but especially chapter 15, can be read as an attempt to reduce that uncertainty, while also leaving some uncertainty and appealing to its readers to take their position within the Way. As it employs travel

---

43 Pieter B. Hartog, "Contesting *Oikoumene*: Resistance and Locality in Philo's Legatio ad Gaium," in *Intolerance, Polemics, and Debate in Antiquity: Politico-Cultural, Philosophical, and Religious Forms of Critical Conversation*, ed. George van Kooten and Jacques van Ruiten, TBN 25 (Leiden: Brill, 2019), 205–31.
44 This Roman portrayal of the Judaeans may correlate with a broader development in Philo's thinking. In her intellectual biography of Philo, Maren Niehoff argues that the journey to Rome had a lasting impact on his thinking, as is evident not only from the *Legatio* and *In Flaccum*, but also from other writings that stem from the later stages of Philo's life. See Maren R. Niehoff, *Philo of Alexandria: An Intellectual Biography*, AYBRL (New Haven: Yale University Press, 2018), 25–46.
45 Acts' indebtedness to these predictions is evident from the central place that eschatologically oriented quotations from Israel's Scriptures occupy in the Acts narrative. See, e.g., quotations from Joel 3:1 in Acts 2:28 or Amos 9:11–12 in Acts 15:16–17. Cf. Hartog, "Reading Acts in Motion," 107–10.

experiences, coined in literary writing, to promote a particular sense of belonging in the world, the book of Acts can be seen to join the ranks of other writings from the Roman imperial period, both Jewish and other.

References

André, Jean-Marie, and Marie-Françoise Baslez. *Voyager dans l'Antiquité*. Paris: Fayard, 1993.
Armstrong, Karl L. "The End of Acts and the Jewish Response: Condemnation, Tragedy, or Hope?" *CBR* 17 (2019): 209–30.
Armstrong, Karl L. *Dating Acts in its Jewish and Greco-Roman Contexts*. LNTS 637. London: T&T Clark, 2021.
Auberger, Janick. "Pausanias le Périégète et la Seconde Sophistique." Pages 133–45 in *Perceptions of the Second Sophistic and Its Times—Regards sur la Seconde Sophistique et son époque*. Edited by Thomas Schmidt and Pascale Fleury. Phoenix Supplementary Volume 49. Toronto: University of Toronto Press, 2011.
Avemarie, Friedrich. "Die jüdischen Wurzeln des Apostoldekrets: Lösbare und ungelöste Probleme." Pages 5–32 in *Aposteldekret und antikes Vereinswesen: Gemeinschaft und ihre Ordnung*. Edited by Markus Öhler. WUNT 280. Tübingen: Mohr Siebeck, 2011.
Barrett, Charles K. *A Critical and Exegetical Commentary on the Acts of the Apostles*. ICC. London: T&T Clark, 1994, 1998.
Bauckham, Richard. "James and the Gentiles (Acts 15.13–21)." Pages 154–84 in *History, Literature, and Society in the Book of Acts*. Edited by Ben Witherington, III. Cambridge: Cambridge University Press, 1996.
Beyer, Hermann Wolfgang. *Die Apostelgeschichte*. Göttingen: Vandenhoeck & Ruprecht, 1932.
Billings, Drew W. *Acts of the Apostles and the Rhetoric of Roman Imperialism*. Cambridge: Cambridge University Press, 2017.
Bloch, René. *Andromeda in Jaffa: Mythische Orte als Reiseziele in der jüdischen Antike*. Franz-Delitzsch-Vorlesung 2015. Münster: Institutum Judaicum Delitzschianum, 2017.
Bockmuehl, Markus. "The Noahide Commandments and New Testament Ethics: With Special Reference to Acts 15 and Pauline Halakhah." *RevB* 102 (1995): 72–101.
Braund, David. "Piracy under the Principate and the Ideology of Imperial Eradication." Pages 195–212 in *War and Society in the Roman World*. Edited by John Rich and Graham Shipley. London: Routledge, 1993.
Callan, Terence. "The Background of the Apostolic Decree (Acts 15:20, 29; 21:25)." *CBQ* 55 (1993): 284–97.
Casson, Lionel. *Travel in the Ancient World*. London: Allen & Unwin, 1974.
Deines, Roland. "Das Aposteldekret—Halacha für Heidenchristen oder christliche Rücksichtnahme auf jüdische Tabus?" Pages 323–95 in *Jewish Identity in the Greco-Roman World: Jüdische Identität in der griechisch-römischen Welt*. Edited by Jörg Frey, Daniel R. Schwartz, and Stephanie Gripentrog. AJEC 71. Leiden: Brill, 2007.
Doering, Lutz. *Ancient Jewish Letters and the Beginnings of Christian Epistolography*. WUNT 298. Tübingen: Mohr Siebeck, 2012.
Downie, Janet. "Palamedes and the Wisdom of India in Philostratus' *Life of Apollonius of Tyana*." *Mouseion* 13 (2016): 65–83.

Dupertuis, Rubén R., and Todd Penner, eds. *Engaging Early Christian History: Reading Acts in the Second Century*. Oxford: Routledge, 2013.
Eck, John van. *Handelingen: De wereld in het geding*. Kampen: Kok, 2003.
Elis, Karlpeter, ed. *Bildungsreise—Reisebildung*. Vienna: LIT, 2004.
Elsner, Jaś. "Structuring 'Greece': Pausanias' Periegesis as a Literary Construct." Pages 3–20 in *Pausanias: Travel and Memory in Roman Greece*. Edited by Susan E. Alcock, John F. Cherry, and Jaś Elsner. Oxford: Oxford University Press, 2001.
Eshleman, Kendra. "Indian Travel and Self-Location in the *Life of Apollonius* and the *Acts of Thomas*." Pages 183–201 in *Journeys in the Roman East: Imagined and Real*. Edited by Maren R. Niehoff. CRPG 1. Tübingen: Mohr Siebeck, 2017.
Fron, Christian. *Bildung und Reisen in der römischen Kaiserzeit: Pepaideumenoi und Mobilität zwischen dem 1. und 4. Jh. n. Chr.* UALG 146. Berlin: De Gruyter, 2021.Gardner, Andrew. "Thinking about Roman Imperialism: Postcolonialism, Globalisation and Beyond?" *Brittania* 44 (2013): 1–25.
Haenchen, Ernst. *The Acts of the Apostles: A Commentary*. Philadelphia: Westminster, 1971.
Hartog, Pieter B. "Contesting *Oikoumene*: Resistance and Locality in Philo's *Legatio ad Gaium*." Pages 205–31 in *Intolerance, Polemics, and Debate in Antiquity: Politico-Cultural, Philosophical, and Religious Forms of Critical Conversation*. Edited by George van Kooten and Jacques van Ruiten. TBN 25. Leiden: Brill, 2019.
Hartog, Pieter B. "Noah and Moses in Acts 15: Group Models and the Novelty of The Way." *NTS* 67 (2021): 496–513.
Hartog, Pieter B. "Where Shall Wisdom be Found? Identity, Sacred Space, and Universal Knowledge in Philostratus and the Acts of the Apostles." Pages 131–49 in *Jerusalem and Other Holy Places as Foci of Multireligious and Ideological Confrontation*. Edited by Pieter B. Hartog, Shulamit Laderman, Vered Tohar, and Archibald L.H.M. van Wieringen. Jewish and Christian Perspectives 37. Leiden: Brill, 2021.
Hartog, Pieter B. "Reading Acts in Motion: Motion and Glocalisation in the Acts of the Apostles." Pages 96–110 in *Mediterranean Flows: People, Ideas and Objects in Motion*. Edited by Anna Usacheva and Emilia Mataix Ferrándiz. Contexts of Ancient and Medieval Anthropology 3. Leiden: Brill, 2023.
Hartog, Pieter B. "*Ioudaioi* and Migrant Apostles in the book of Acts." Pages 479–94 in *Migration und biblische Theologie: Positionen und theologische Herausforderungen aus Perspektive der alt- und neutestamentlichen Wissenschaft*. Edited by Benedikt Hensel and Christian Wetz. Arbeiten zur Bibel und ihrer Geschichte. Leipzig: Evangelische Verlagsanstalt, 2023.
Hermans, Hubert J.M. "Dialogical Self Theory in a Boundary-Crossing Society." Pages 27–47 in *Moral and Spiritual Leadership in an Age of Plural Moralities*. Edited by Hans Alma and Ina ter Avest. London: Routledge, 2019.
Hermans, Hubert J.M., and Agnieszka Hermans-Konopka. *Dialogical Self Theory: Positioning and Counter-Positioning in a Globalizing Society*. Cambridge: Cambridge University Press, 2010.
Hermans, Hubert J.M., and Harry J.G. Kempen. *The Dialogical Self: Meaning as Movement*. San Diego, CA: Academic Press, 1993.
Hezser, Catherine. *Jewish Travel in Antiquity*. TSAJ 144. Tübingen: Mohr Siebeck, 2011.
Johnson, Luke Timothy. *The Acts of the Apostles*. SaPaSe 5. Collegeville, MN: Liturgical Press, 1992.
Jürgens, Burkhard. *Zweierlei Anfang: Kommunikative Konstruktionen heidenchristlicher Identität in Gal 2 und Apg 15*. BBB 120. Berlin: Philo, 1999.
Klinghardt, Matthias. "Das Aposteldekret als kanonischer Integrationstext: Konstruktion und Begründung von Gemeinsinn." Pages 91–112 in *Aposteldekret und antikes Vereinswesen: Gemeinschaft und ihre Ordnung*. Edited by Markus Öhler. WUNT 280. Tübingen: Mohr Siebeck, 2011.

Kok, Jacobus, and Dieter T. Roth. "Sensitivity towards Outsiders and the Dynamic Relationship between Mission and Ethics/Ethos." Pages 1–23 in *Sensitivity towards Outsider: Exploring the Dynamic Relationship between Mission and Ethics in the New Testament and Early Christianity*. Edited by Jacobus Kok, Tobias Nicklas, Dieter T. Roth, and Christopher M. Hays. WUNT 2/364. Tübingen: Mohr Siebeck, 2014.

Löhr, Helmut. "'Unzucht': Überlegungen zu einer Bestimmung der Jakobus-Klauseln im Aposteldekret sowie zu den Geltungsgründen von Normen frühchristlicher Ethik." Pages 49–64 in *Aposteldekret und antikes Vereinswesen: Gemeinschaft und ihre Ordnung*. Edited by Markus Öhler. WUNT 280. Tübingen: Mohr Siebeck, 2011.

Marguerat, Daniel. *The First Christian Historian: Writing the "Acts of the Apostles"*. SNTSMS 121. Cambridge: Cambridge University Press, 2004.

Muir, Steven. "Religion on the Road in Ancient Greece and Rome." Pages 29–47 in *Travel and Religion in Antiquity*. Edited by Philip A. Harland. Studies in Christianity and Judaism/Études sur le christianisme et le judaïsme 21. Waterloo: Wilfrid Laurier Press, 2011. Nasrallah, Laura. "Imposing Travellers: An Inscription from Galatia and the Journeys of the Earliest Christians." Pages 273–86 in *Journeys in the Roman East: Imagined and Real*. Edited by Maren R. Niehoff. Culture, Religion, and Politics in the Greco-Roman World 1. Tübingen: Mohr Siebeck, 2017.

Nederveen Pieterse, Jan. *Globalization and Culture: Global Mélange*. 3rd ed. Lanham, MD: Rowman & Littlefield, 2016.

Niehoff, Maren R. *Philo of Alexandria: An Intellectual Biography*. AYBRL. New Haven: Yale University Press, 2018.

Öhler, Markus. "Das Aposteldekret als Dokument ethnischer Identität im Spiegel antiker Vereinigungen." Pages 341–82 in *Aposteldekret und antikes Vereinswesen: Gemeinschaft und ihre Ordnung*. Edited by Markus Öhler. WUNT 280. Tübingen: Mohr Siebeck, 2011.

Pitts, Martin, and Miguel John Versluys, eds. *Globalisation and the Roman World: World History, Connectivity and Material Culture*. Cambridge: Cambridge University Press, 2014.

Pretzler, Maria. *Pausanias: Travel Writing in Ancient Greece*. London: Duckworth, 2007.

Robbins, Vernon K. "By Land and By Sea: The We-Passages and Ancient Sea Voyages." Pages 215–42 in *Perspectives on Luke-Acts*. Edited by Charles H. Talbert. Macon, GA: Mercer University Press; Edinburgh: T&T Clark, 1978.

Schneider, Gerhard. *Die Apostelgeschichte: II. Teil*. Freiburg: Herder, 1982.

Shaw, Brent D. "Bandits in the Roman Empire." *PaP* 105 (1984): 3–52.

Souza, Philip de. *Piracy in the Graeco-Roman World*. Cambridge: Cambridge University Press, 1999.

Tannehill, Robert C. *The Narrative Unity of Luke-Acts: A Literary Interpretation*. 2 vols. Minneapolis: Fortress Press, 1986, 1990.

Theissen, Gerd. "The Letter to the Romans and Paul's Plural Identity." Pages 301–22 in *The Making of Christianity: Conflicts, Contacts, and Constructions: Essays in Honor of Bengt Holmberg*. Edited by Magnus Zetterholm and Samuel Byrskog. ConBNT 47. Winona Lake, IN: Eisenbrauns, 2012.

Trebilco, Paul. *Self-Designations and Group Identity in the New Testament*. Cambridge: Cambridge University Press, 2012.

Wehnert, Jürgen. *Die Reinheit des »christlichen Gottesvolkes« aus Juden und Heiden: Studien zum historischen und theologischen Hintergrund des sogenannten Aposteldekrets*. FRLANT 173. Göttingen: Vandenhoeck & Ruprecht, 1997.

Witcher, Robert. "Globalisation and Roman Imperialism: Perspectives on Identities in Roman Italy." Pages 213–25 in *The Emergence of State Identities in Italy in the First Millennium BC*. Edited by Edward Herring and Kathryn Lomas. London: Accordia Research Institute, University of London, 2000.

Susanne Luther
"Today or Tomorrow We Will Go to Such and Such a City" (Jas 4:13): The Experience of Interconnectivity and the Mobility of Norms in the Ancient Globalized World

Abstract: The ethics of speech is a central aspect of ancient ethics. The New Testament writings engage in this ancient discourse by receiving and creatively adapting speech-ethical norms and values from the ancient Jewish and Greco-Roman contexts as well as by introducing their individual positions back into the ancient discourse. This flow of early Christian norms and notions between regions and cultures in the Roman Empire has been examined from a tradition-historical perspective. This contribution explores the issues from the perspective of globalization studies in order to gain new insights into the interconnectivity of the networks that enabled the mobility of norms and the emergence of common traditional milieus based on the ancient perception of a "globalized world."

For the ancient Mediterranean region, there is ample evidence of a high level of connectivity and mobility of people, goods, and ideas. This was due to the good economic, social and communicative infrastructure in the Roman Empire, resulting from the predominantly peaceful political conditions, but also due to the well-developed road system and the advances in seafaring,[1] which—despite the considerable dangers of travel and transportation, e.g., from bandits, pirates, accidents, storms and shipwrecks[2]—provided convenient travel routes and the possibility of rapid communication:

---

[1] Cf. Laura Nasrallah, "Imposing Travellers: An Inscription from Galatia and the Journeys of the Earliest Christians," in *Journeys in the Roman East: Imagined and Real*, ed. Maren R. Niehoff, Culture, Religion, and Politics in the Greco-Roman World 1 (Tübingen: Mohr Siebeck, 2017), 273–96, 274–275 on the Roman road system; cf. also Irmgard Männlein-Robert, "Move Your Self: Mobility and Migration of Greek Intellectuals to Rome," in *Self, Self-Fashioning, and Individuality in Late Antiquity New Perspectives*, ed. Maren R. Niehoff and Joshua Levinson (Tübingen: Mohr Siebeck, 2019), 331–52 (332).
[2] Cf. Ryan S. Schellenberg, "'Danger in the Wilderness, Danger at Sea': Paul and the Perils of Travel," in *Travel and Religion in Antiquity*, ed. Philip Harland, Studies in Christianity and Judaism/Études sur le christianisme et le judaïsme 21 (Waterloo: Wilfrid Laurier University Press, 2011), 141–61; for ancient literature on sea travels cf. Jens Börstinghaus, *Sturmfahrt und Schiffbruch: Zur lukanischen Verwendung eines literarischen Topos in Apostelgeschichte 27,1–28,6*, WUNT 2/274 (Tübingen: Mohr Siebeck, 2010).

https://doi.org/10.1515/9783110717488-007

Travel . . . was a natural part of the ancient world, since merchants sailed between the major seaports of the Eastern Mediterranean region around 500 BCE and most Greek city-states were founded along the coast. Inland, key centres were linked by common road networks, for which carts and beasts of burden were available for transportation. Travel was expensive but essential for warfare, diplomacy, trade, and social life. Greeks visited religious sites, festivals, and health-related sanctuaries, and travelling actors were known for organising theatre performances in various locations.[3]

Travel made up an inherent part of life—especially in elite circles: people traveled to explore the world; traveled as merchants[4] and as tourists; traveled to religious events and to pilgrimage sites;[5] and embarked on journeys to visit family or to gain knowledge, e.g., by studying with renowned rhetors and teachers in cities such as Athens or Rome.[6] It is therefore appropriate to speak of a "culture voyageuse"[7] in the 1st and 2nd centuries CE, which developed as a result of the close and diverse interconnections around the Mediterranean[8] and generated a perception of the *oikumene* of the time as a globalized world—a perception also shared by ancient

---

[3] Elisa Uusimäki, "Itinerant Sages: The Evidence of Sirach in its Ancient Mediterranean Context," *JSOT* 44 (2020): 315–36 (326–27). Cf. the Stanford ORBIS tool (https://orbis.stanford.edu/; last accessed 20 April 2023).

[4] Cf. Kenn Hirth, *The Organization of Ancient Economies: A Global Perspective* (Cambridge: Cambridge University Press, 2020), 194–235; for the ancient merchant diaspora cf. Hirth, *The Organization of Ancient Economies*, 218–25.

[5] Cf. Susan Alcock and Robin E. Osborne, eds., *Placing the Gods: Sanctuaries and Sacred Space in Ancient Greece* (Oxford: Clarendon, 1994); Matthew Dillon, *Pilgrims and Pilgrimage in Ancient Greece* (London: Routledge, 1997); Jás Elsner and Ian Rutherford, eds., *Pilgrimage in Graeco-Roman and Early Christian Antiquity: Seeing the Gods* (Oxford: Oxford University Press, 2005); Steven Muir, "Religion on the Road in Ancient Greece and Rome," in Harland, *Travel and Religion in Antiquity*, 29–47; René Bloch, "Show and Tell: Myth, Tourism, and Jewish Hellenism," in René Bloch, *Ancient Jewish Diaspora: Essays on Hellenism*, JSJSup 206 (Leiden: Brill, 2022), 101–27.

[6] Marie Pretzler, "Greek Intellecutals on the Move: Travel and Paideia in the Roman Empire," in *Travel, Geography and Culture in Ancient Greece, Egypt and the Near East*, ed. Colin Adams and Jim Roy (Oxford: Oxbow, 2007), 123–38; cf. also Lesley Adkins and Roy A. Adkins, *Handbook of Life in Ancient Rome* (New York: Oxford University Press, 1994), 167–200; Jean Marie André and Marie Françoise Baslez, *Voyager dans l'Antiquité* (Paris: Fayard, 1993), 224–29 and 309–12; on the parody of such educational journeys cf. Maren R. Niehoff, "Parodies of Educational Journeys in Josephus, Justin Martyr, and Lucian," in *Journeys in the Roman East: Imagined and Real*, ed. Maren R. Niehoff, CRPG 1 (Tübingen: Mohr Siebeck, 2017), 203–24.

[7] André and Baslez, *Voyager dans l'Antiquité*, 7. For a survey of ancient literature on travel see Jan Willem Drijvers, "Travel and Pilgrimage Literature," in *A Companion to Late Antique Literature*, ed. Scott McGill and Edward J. Watts (Hoboken: Wiley, 2018), 359–72.

[8] Michael Sommer, "OIKOYMENH: Longue Durée Perspectives on Ancient Mediterranean 'Globality'," in *Globalisation and the Roman World: World History, Connectivity and Material Culture*, ed. Martin Pitts and Miguel John Versluys (Cambridge: Cambridge University Press, 2014), 175–97.

Judaism[9] and early Christianity.[10] The Epistle of James, which is addressed to "the twelve tribes scattered among the nations" (Jas 1:1), illustrates this perception beautifully when it formulates the attitude of the merchant travelers in Jas 4:13–15:

> [13] Come now, you who say, "Today or tomorrow we will go (πορευσόμεθα) to such and such a city and spend a year there and engage in business (ἐμπορευσόμεθα) and make profit (κερδήσομεν)" [14] yet you do not know what will be tomorrow, what your life will be like; for you are mist that appears for a little while and then vanishes. [15] Instead, you should say, "If the Lord wills, we will live and do this or that."

This passage portrays (one group among the) addressees of the letter, namely, merchants who consider taking advantage of the excellent travel routes and well-developed trade networks of the ancient Mediterranean world in order to travel to a city, or perhaps from city to city, for trade and profit. Their self-confidence in making travel plans is exposed by the author of the Letter of James as presumptuous and insolent toward God. In doing so, he is not criticizing the travel plans or even the pursuit of profit per se. Rather, he cautions against reckoning one's ambitious and presumptuous plans, especially concerning such dangerous and unpredictable undertakings as long-distance travel, as being within one's own sphere of influence instead of in the hands of the Lord who governs all things. It is precisely the experience of traveling that should teach merchants to be prudent and God-fearing in their planning, and it is wisdom literature, a tradition of great importance to the author of the Letter of James, that reinforces the awareness of the uncertainty of human plans for the future (cf., e.g., Prov 16:9; Sir 11:18–19). And yet, it seems that James's addressees lack practical wisdom: the author characterizes their conduct—knowing the right action (καλὸν ποιεῖν) and yet not following it—as a sin (Jas 4:17).

In this study, the focus will not be on the misconduct of the merchants or on the *conditio Jacobaea*, but rather on the question of how travelers in antiquity, e.g.,

---

9 On Jewish travel in antiquity cf. Catherine Hezser, *Jewish Travel in Antiquity*, TSAJ 144 (Tübingen: Mohr Siebeck, 2011); cf. also René Bloch, "What If the Temple of Jerusalem Had Not Been Destroyed by the Romans?" in Bloch, *Ancient Jewish Diaspora*, 128–49 (137–39); cf. also Wayne O. McCready, "Pilgrimage, Place, and Meaning Making by Jews in Greco-Roman Egypt," in Harland, *Travel and Religion in Antiquity*, 69–81.
10 Cf., e.g., Pieter B. Hartog, "Reading Acts in Motion: Movement and Glocalisation in the Acts of the Apostles," in *Mediterranean Flows: People, Ideas and Objects in Motion*, ed. Anna Usacheva and Emilia Mataix Ferrándiz, Contexts of Ancient and Medieval Anthropology 3 (Leiden: Brill Schöningh, 2023), 96–110, who points out that early Christianity was a "thoroughly translocal movement" (109), "a movement on a par with the Roman Empire, whose networks and power structures it reflects" (110). Cf. also Susan Haber, "Going Up to Jerusalem: Pilgrimage, Purity, and the Historical Jesus," in Harland, *Travel and Religion in Antiquity*, 49–67; Loveday Alexander, "Mapping Early Christianity: Acts and the Shape of Early Church History," *Interpretation* 57 (2003): 163–73.

as merchants, transported knowledge and how networks, e.g., the networks of merchant travelers, promoted the mobility of knowledge, ideas, and wisdom. The reference to merchant travelers in James 4 provides grounds for assuming that the addressees were widely connected and integrated into the networks of the Roman Empire. Which new insights might be gained, based on this perception, with regard to the involvement of the Letter of James in ancient and early Christian discourses? In the following, I will explore this question with reference to a concrete example: the ancient discourse on speech ethics.

Merchants in Antiquity and the "Acquisition" of Wisdom through Traveling

The verb used for the merchants' planned actions, ἐμπορεύομαι (Jas 4:13), refers to their manner of trading, for it describes the work of wholesalers (ἔμποροι) who traded goods overseas, who may have been ship owners, or may have been businessmen traveling on merchant ships. The goods—wine, oil, grain, spices, precious metals, wood, pottery, textiles, and so forth—were then sold locally either by the ἔμποροι themselves or by local retail merchants (κάπηλοι).[11] Although the two terms, ἔμποροι and κάπηλοι, came to be used increasingly interchangeably in the Roman imperial period, the terminology used in the Letter of James, in conjunction with its argumentative context, suggests that the author does not have itinerant craftsmen or small retailers in mind, but rather merchants on a larger scale who engaged in long-distance overseas commerce and spent extended periods of time in a foreign place, e.g., for wintering purposes.[12]

A central aspect of trade was profit. Although "[m]erchants without question performed important economic functions for society," it is evident that "[t]he fact that they often are perceived as doing so for self-gain rather than as benefactors for the communities in which they lived resulted in merchants being held in low esteem."[13] Overseas merchants often formed syndicates of countrymen and lived

---

[11] Cf. Wiard Popkes, *Der Brief des Jakobus*, ThHKNT 14 (Leipzig: Evangelische Verlagsanstalt, 2001), 288–90. On market places and the structure of the ancient economy cf. Hirth, *The Organization of Ancient Economies*. For Roman seafaring and laws relating to Roman maritime commerce cf. Peter Candy and Emilia Mataix Ferrandis, eds., *Roman Law and Maritime Commerce* (Edinburgh: Edinburgh University Press, 2022).
[12] Cf. Rainer Metzner, *Der Brief des Jakobus*, ThHKNT 14 (Leipzig: Evangelische Verlagsanstalt, 2017), 244–46.
[13] Hirth, *The Organization of Ancient Economies*, 206.

abroad for extended periods of time to trade their goods, thus forming "trade diasporas," which were "communities of merchants living among aliens in associated networks."[14] Trade diasporas

> [s]hared social ties provided the network through which information flowed . . . . As autonomous groups in the societies where they resided, diaspora communities maintained internal order, protected themselves, and disciplined members who deviated from established moral or economic practices . . . . Trade diasporas have been found in one form or another everywhere where long-distance trade occurred on a large scale. They were a driving force behind the dispersal of minorities throughout the ancient and premodern worlds.[15]

The basis "for the success of a trade diaspora was the maintenance of trust and shared cultural values between its members."[16] This reality becomes relevant when considering that the Letter of James presents itself as a diaspora letter,[17] communicating cultural, religious, and ethical values to its readers, who are envisioned as living "scattered among the nations" (Jas 1:1).

Philo of Alexandria parallels merchants with those who seek to attain wisdom through travel. He states that just as merchants travel far across land and sea for the sake of gain, letting no person, adverse circumstances or hazards prevent them from traveling, so should those who want to gain wisdom, travel far and wide for the sake of gaining this most desirable of all possessions. They are to be like merchant travelers. Philo describes them as explorers—curious, investigative and insa-

---

14 Philip Curtin, *Cross-Cultural Trade in World History* (Cambridge: Cambridge University Press, 1984), 3. Cf. also Hirth, *The Organization of Ancient Economies*, 218: "Conquest was one way that people could be relocated from their native homeland. But it was not the most common. While many factors were involved in the dispersal of ethnic populations around the globe, economic motivations including trade were particularly important. Here the discussion focuses on the trade diaspora, which was both the Internet of ancient commerce and the highway along which goods moved and commercial relationships were structured. Philip Curtin (1984) first identified the importance of the trade diaspora as one of the most widespread human institutions and a primary mechanism for long-distance trade in the ancient and premodern world."
15 Hirth, *The Organization of Ancient Economies*, 219–20. Cf. at 219: "Trade diasporas typically share three important characteristics in common with one another. First, the trade diaspora was made up of merchants, or at least groups of individuals whose primary objective was to enhance their economic well-being through trade.... A second feature is that the diaspora group often represents a minority group in the land that they occupy. They frequently represent . . . middleman minorities based on the economic role they play in the societies where they are found. And third, diaspora groups were not isolated. Rather, they were part of a system of interconnected communities that formed a network-based economy that operated through personal and established economic relationships."
16 Hirth, *The Organization of Ancient Economies*, 220.
17 Cf. Karl-Wilhelm Niebuhr, "Der Jakobusbrief im Licht frühjüdischer Diasporabriefe," *NTS* 44 (1998): 420–43.

tiable for the gain of knowledge (*Migr.* 216–218). The motives for setting out on a journey are diverse, but mostly focus on gain, whether expressed in the intention to make profit as traders or in the desire to acquire wisdom and knowledge for one's own pleasure or in order to benefit one's home community (*Abr.* 65).[18] This close correlation of traveling merchants and educational travelers coincides with the portrayal of travel as an educational experience. For example, the translator of the Book of Sirach draws on his own experience of travel when he acknowledges the intrinsic value of travel and states in 34:9–13:[19]

> Since a man roamed (ἀνὴρ πεπλανημένος), he knew many things, and he who is experienced will tell with understanding. He who had no experience knows few things, but he who has roamed (πεπλανημένος) will increase cleverness (πανουργίαν). I have seen many things in my wandering (ἐν τῇ ἀποπλανήσει μου), and more than my words is my understanding. Frequently I was in danger of death, and I was saved because of these things.[20]

The traveler thus gains knowledge and wisdom, although he "may not be traveling primarily for the sake of wisdom ... the travel motif is linked with his capability to distinguish good from bad. This implies that the traveller is expected to deliberate, making observations and judgements on what he encounters away from home."[21] And, according to Sirach, his travels gain him πανουργία, which is precisely the character trait that also characterizes the "cunning" Odysseus.[22] Sir 34:14ff. implies

---

18 Cf. for Philo Uusimäki, "Itinerant Sages," 325; cf. also Pieter B. Hartog, "Space and Travel in Philo's *Legatio ad Gaium*," *SPhiloA* 30 (2018): 71–92; Pieter B. Hartog, "Contesting *Oikoumenē*: Resistance and Locality in Philo's *Legatio ad Gaium*," in *Intolerance, Polemics, and Debate in Antiquity. Politico-Cultural, Philosophical, and Religious Forms of Critical Conversation*, ed. George van Kooten and Jacques van Ruiten, TBN 25 (Leiden: Brill, 2019), 205–231. For the aspect of migration cf. also Maren R. Niehoff, "Wie wird man ein mediterraner Denker? Der Fall Philon von Alexandria," in *Ein pluriverses Universum. Zivilisationen und Religionen im antiken Mittelmeerraum*, ed. Richard Faber and Achim Lichtenberger, Mittelmeerstudien 7 (Paderborn: Schöningh, 2015), 355–367.
19 Cf. also Sir 8:15; 26:12; 33:2; 36:31; 42:3. For the translator of Ben Sira as traveler from Israel to Egypt cf. Elisa Uusimäki, "The Formation of a Sage according to Ben Sira," in *Second Temple Jewish 'Paideia' in Context*, ed. Jason M. Zurawski and Gabriele Boccaccini, BZNW 228 (Berlin: De Gruyter, 2017), 59–69; Elisa Uusimäki, "The Rise of the Sage in Greek and Jewish Antiquity," *JSJ* 49 (2018): 1–29; Frank Ueberschaer, *Weisheit aus der Begegnung: Bildung nach dem Buch Ben Sira*, BZNW 379 (Berlin: De Gruyter, 2007).
20 Trans. Albert Pietersma and Benjamin G. Wright, eds., *A New English Translation of the Septuagint* (Oxford: Oxford University Press, 2007).
21 Uusimäki, "Itinerant Sages," 319.
22 Cf. Burkard M. Zapff, "Normenbegründung vor gewandeltem Hintergrund: Jesus Sirach als Vermittler zwischen traditionellem jüdischem Glauben und hellenistischem Geist," in *Athen, Rom, Jerusalem: Normentransfers in der antiken Welt*, ed. Gian Franco Chiai, Eichstätter Studien Neue Folge 66 (Regensburg: Pustet, 2012), 25–40 (36): "Der Vielgereiste erwirbt also nach Sirach gerade den Charakterzug, der auch den 'listenreichen' Odysseus auszeichnet! Hier folgt also Sirach in ganz

that the God-fearing traveler is armed against the dangers of travel (cf. Sir 1:11–20; 40:26–27); the ideal of the God-fearing traveler is also taken up in Jas 4:13–15 and, in line with the wisdom tradition, the merchant travelers in James are reproached for their self-confidence and their lack of the fear of God (cf. Jas 1:5).[23]

These thoughts from Philo and Sirach, both associated with ancient Alexandria, are adopted and adapted in the passage on merchant travelers in the Letter of James. Alexandria was a major cultural and intellectual center, the city was a prime destination for educational travel, and as one of the great commercial ports of the ancient Mediterranean world, it was also the gateway for trade voyages.[24] Do these common traditions allow for the assumption, that the Letter of James also originated in Alexandria? The place of composition of the Letter of James is disputed; but wherever it originated, whether in Alexandria,[25] or, e.g., in Antioch on the Orontes,[26] or in one of the other centers of the early Christian world, the author engaged with a wide variety of different traditions.

---

positiver Weise hellenistischem Zeitgeist, praktiziert diesen nicht nur im eigenen Leben, sondern empfiehlt dieses Tun auch heranwachsenden jungen Juden weiter." For the reception of Hellenism and Greek literature cf. Erich S. Gruen, *Diaspora: Jews amidst Greeks and Romans* (Cambridge: Harvard University Press, 2002), 213–31.

23 However, in the *conditio Jacobaea* the Letter of James takes up tradition from ancient practical philosophical ethics and refocuses it in a Jewish-Christian theocentric way. For this observation as well as for parallels in the Greco-Roman, Jewish and Jesus traditions cf. Knut Backhaus, "Conditio Jacobaea: Jüdische Weisheitstradition und christliche Alltagsethik nach Jak 4,13–17," in *Schrift und Tradition: Festschrift für Josef Ernst zum 70. Geburtstag*, ed. Knut Backhaus and Franz G. Untergaßmair (Paderborn: Schöningh, 1996), 135–58.

24 For the Jewish diaspora in Alexandria cf. John M.G. Barclay, *Jews in the Mediterranean Diaspora from Alexander to Trajan (323 BCE–117 CE)* (Edinburgh: T&G Clark, 1999), 19–81; a reevaluation of the sources on the Jewish diaspora in Alexandria presents cf. Erich S. Gruen, *Diaspora*, 54–83. Cf. also Benjamin Schliesser et al., eds., *Alexandria: Hub of the Hellenistic World*, WUNT 460 (Tübingen: Mohr Siebeck, 2021).

25 For the reason of common traditions, but also because James employs maritime metaphors (cf., e.g., Jas 1:6; 3:4, 7), scholars have argued for Alexandria as place of origin. Cf., e.g., Franz Schnider, *Der Jakobusbrief*, RNT (Regensburg: Pustet, 1987), 18; James Moffatt, *The General Epistles James, Peter, and Judas*, MNTC, 7th ed. (London: Hodder & Stoughton, 1953), 1; Udo Schnelle, *Einleitung in das Neue Testament*, 8th ed. (Göttingen: Vandenhoeck & Ruprecht, 2013), 466.

26 For Antiochia (or Syria) as place of origin cf., e.g., Matthias Konradt, *Christliche Existenz nach dem Jakobusbrief: Eine Studie zu seiner soteriologischen und ethischen Konzeption*, StUNT 22 (Göttingen: Vandenhoeck & Ruprecht, 1998), 317–38; Matthias Konradt, "Der Jakobusbrief im frühchristlichen Kontext: Überlegungen zum traditionsgeschichtlichen Verhältnis des Jakobusbriefes zur Jesusüberlieferung, zur paulinischen Tradition und zum 1Petr," in *The Catholic Epistles and the Tradition*, ed. Jacques Schlosser, BETL 176 (Leuven: Peeters, 2004), 171–212; Patrick J. Hartin, *James and the Q-Sayings of Jesus*, JSNTSup 47 (Sheffield: Sheffield Academic, 1991), 233–40; Massey H. Shepherd, "The Epistle of James and the Gospel of Matthew," *JBL* 75 (1956): 40–51 (49–51).

The speech-ethical traditions received in the Letter of James, which will be of specific interest in this study, contain close parallels to the speech ethics in the Gospel of Matthew. While different places of origin have been suggested for the Gospel of Matthew, such as Alexandria, Caesarea Maritima, Caesarea Philippi, Transjordan, Damascus, Phoenicia, Galilee and Edessa, Syria—or more specifically Antioch—is still favored by many scholars.[27] The close parallels between the teachings on speech ethics in Matthew's Gospel, possibly inspired by Syrian traditions, and the Letter of James testify to another line of reception for the author of James.[28]

Whereas common traditions often serve as evidence for a common place of origin or at least for a common milieu, the perspective of ancient global mobility challenges this argumentation by assuming an embeddedness within a transcultural environment with a constant flow of ideas, traditions and knowledge.[29] And while the various issues concerning the provenance of the Letter of James and the Gospel of Matthew cannot be pursued further here, the question arises whether the mobility of ideas and concepts in the ancient globalized world can shed new light on the diverse arguments concerning the place of composition or provide a compelling explanation for the common traditions and the similarities in emphasis—especially with a view to speech-ethical traditions—between the Gospel of Matthew and the Letter of James.

Speech Ethics in Early Christianity from the Perspective of Tradition and Reception History

The term "speech ethics" describes the discourse on ethical paradigms and moral instruction concerning verbal communication in interpersonal relationships as well as ethical reflection on anthropological and theological preconditions and consequences of the use of language and its significance for the relationship between God and humans.[30] In ancient literature, issues of speech ethics were prevalent in

---

[27] Cf. for an overview David C. Sim, "Reconstructing the Social and Religious Milieu of Matthew: Methods, Sources, and Possible Results," in *Matthew, James, and Didache: Three Related Documents in Their Jewish and Christian Settings*, ed. Huub van de Sandt and Jürgen K. Zangenberg, SymS 45 (Atlanta: Society of Biblical Literature, 2008), 13–32, esp. 19–25.

[28] Cf. Susanne Luther, *Sprachethik im Neuen Testament: Analyse des frühchristlichen Diskurses im Matthäusevangelium, im Jakobusbrief und im 1Petrusbrief*, WUNT 2/394 (Tübingen: Mohr Siebeck, 2015).

[29] Cf. also the concept of "migrant literature." For a recent approach cf. Casper C. de Jonge, "Greek Migrant Literature in the Early Roman Empire," *Mnemosyne* 75 (2022): 10–36.

[30] Luther, *Sprachethik im Neuen Testament*, 9–11.

all literary genres (e.g., comedy, drama, epigrams, letters, treatises, handbooks) and many fields of life (e.g., law, ethics, rhetoric, religion, philosophy). A broad spectrum of topoi was addressed: examples of adequate as well as inadequate uses of speech, insulting language; judging and correction; oath taking and oath formulas; angry, jocular, humorous and obscene speech; aesthetics of language; silence and refraining from speaking; ethical aspects of rhetoric and elocution; possibilities and preconditions of controlling speech; the truthfulness and the integrity of the person in speech and action; and many others.

From the very beginning, early Christianity was familiar with and in their literary writings participated in the broad ancient discourse on the ethics of speech.[31] Among the New Testament writings, especially the Gospel of Matthew and the Letters of James are indicative of an interest in speech ethics. The topoi discussed in the New Testament show broad thematic overlap with the contemporary discourse: angry speech, the aspect of the evil of the tongue, control of the tongue, examples of inadequate or wrong use of speech, truthfulness and integrity of the person in speech and action, as well as the complementary topoi of judging and *correctio fraterna* are taken up and form the pillars of the New Testament speech-ethical discourse. And yet, the New Testament writings only receive certain speech-ethical topoi from the contemporary discourse, while others are not addressed, such as reflections on obscene speech, on humorous language, on aesthetics of language, silence and refraining from speaking, polemics, language philosophy, *Streitkultur,* or rhetoric. The topoi that are addressed in the New Testament writings, however, are not only adopted, but also reinterpreted within the Christian worldview, thus forming separate, distinctive but uniform discourse positions within the contemporary speech-ethical discourse. The New Testament writings demand speech-ethical conduct which is characterized by specific re-accentuations, radicalizations, and reorientations compared to the speech ethics of the ancient context. New Testament speech ethics focuses on the speakers' predisposition for appropriate speech as well as on the effects of such speech on the speakers and their relation to the divine. One can observe a tendency to align the desired speech-ethical conduct with the ethical norms of credibility, truth, usefulness, and the inherently positive use of language as well as the notional ideals of holiness and perfection. Especially in the Gospel of Matthew and the Letter of James, speech-ethical *topoi* are taken up in distinctive ways and with distinctive emphases that are embedded in the broader ethical argumentation and intricately linked with

---

31 The following observations are based on Luther, *Sprachethik im Neuen Testament,* passim, esp. 405–39. For the terminology of discourse analysis, based on Achim Landwehr, *Historische Diskursanalyse,* 2nd ed., Historische Einführungen 4 (Frankfurt: Campus, 2009), 91–131 and Siegfried Jäger, *Kritische Diskursanalyse: Eine Einführung,* 6th ed. (Münster: Unrast, 2012), cf. Luther, *Sprachethik im Neuen Testament,* 32–40.

anthropological and theological teachings. Other New Testament writings, such as the First Letter of Peter, the Epistles to the Ephesians and the Colossians as well as the Pastoral Epistles, show only peripheral interest in speech-ethical aspects and adopt only individual topoi of the ancient discourse.[32]

New Testament speech ethics features a number of correlations and discourse entanglements that suggest extra-discursive influences: there are frequent interconnections with (a) the inner-Christian discourse of the Christ event, as the ability to appropriate speech-ethical conduct is found in the indicative of the Gospel and is often linked to the theme of the new creation; (b) the ancient discourse of character formation, which is taken up in the aspect of the formation of the inner disposition; (c) the ancient discourse of anthropology, which emerges in statements that recognize speech as an expression of the human constitution; (d) the discourse of eschatology, which is received from the Hebrew Bible and early Jewish tradition, and which motivates speech ethics and attributes a soteriological significance to it; and (e) the discourse of identity construction of early Christian groups in their encounter with the world around them. Thus, speech ethics in the New Testament writings is integrated into the context of different discourses that influence, justify, motivate, and guide the discourse. The interconnectedness with other ancient speech-ethical discourses indicates the receptiveness of early Christianity and their willingness to engage with contemporary discourses. It can be assumed that the twofold trend involving adoption as well as creative appropriation and reshaping of speech-ethical tradition arose out of the early Christian need to develop and establish their own identity, to constitute a community, and, at the same time, to integrate themselves into ancient society.[33]

The question arising from these findings is: Why do these and only these few and late New Testament writings engage in the discourse on speech ethics? In antiquity, the discourse on speech ethics was prevalent in the Hebrew Bible and ancient Jewish writings as well as in Greco-Roman literature.[34] But in the New Testament, it is the Gospel of Matthew and the Letter of James in particular that bear witness to the reception, transmission, and distinctive transformation of these specific traditions.

---

[32] Cf. Luther, *Sprachethik im Neuen Testament*, 12–13.
[33] Although it is of course not possible to determine with certainty the degree to which the decision to engage with different discourses was conscious, the observation that some New Testament authors engaged more intensely with particular traditions than with others, while other New Testament authors refrained from engaging with a particular discourses, suggests that early Christian authors were very much aware of the availability of traditions within the ancient translocal network and of the options arising from the flow of ideas and concepts for the processes of reception. Cf. Luther, *Sprachethik im Neuen Testament*, 436.
[34] For examples from Jewish and Graeco-Roman traditions cf. Luther, *Sprachethik im Neuen Testament*, passim.

An attempt to explain these findings from the perspective of tradition and reception history could be based on the assumption that speech ethics played a more significant role in the ancient Jewish wisdom literature than in Greco-Roman literature, even though speech-ethical topoi are received and reflected in all genres and traditions of ancient literature. It is then possible to assume that the authors of those New Testament writings that are closely related to the ancient Jewish context—such as the Gospel of Matthew and the Letter of James—took over the acute awareness of the significance of speech-ethical issues from Jewish writings, complemented them with ethical argumentation and motifs from Greco-Roman writings, and inscribed their own speech-ethical instructions into the context of the early Christian self-understanding and worldview.

This explanation might also point to a common background of shared traditions between the Gospel of Matthew and the Letter of James.[35] Although no literary dependencies or direct references can be constructed between these early Christian writings, it has been assumed that they draw on common traditions, were written in a common milieu, and adapted these common traditions according to their respective concerns, interests, and situations.[36] Although it cannot be determined with certainty whether these New Testament writings belong to one specific "text group" due to the lack of historical information, a relationship between the

---

[35] Cf. especially van de Sandt and Zangenberg, *Matthew, James, and Didache*, on a common tradition-historical background of the Gospel of Matthew, the Letter of James and the Didache; on the recurrence to common tradition by the Gospel of Matthew, the Letter of James and the Letter of 1 Peter cf. Peter H. Davids, "James and Peter: The Literary Evidence," in *The Missions of James, Peter, and Paul*, ed. Bruce Chilton and Craig Evans, NovTSup 115 (Leiden: Brill, 2005), 29–52 (33–46); cf. also Gunnar Garleff, *Urchristliche Identität in Matthäusevangelium, Didache und Jakobusbrief*, BVB 9 (Münster: LIT-Verlag, 2004). Jürgen K. Zangenberg, "Matthew and James," in *Matthew and his Christian Contemporaries*, ed. David C. Sim (London: T&T Clark, 2008), 104–22 (115–116) points out common topics in Matthew and James, such as "(1) endurance of trials and prayer in faith without doubt (Jas. 1.6; Mt. 5.10–12; 6.13; 21.21); (2) rich and poor (Jas. 4.13–5.6; Mt. 6.19, 34); (3) respect of persons (Jas. 2.1–13; Mt. 19.16–30); (4) evil-speaking (Jas. 3.1–12; Mt. 7.16–20; 12.33, 36; 15.11); (5) wrathful man (Jas. 1.19–20; Mt. 5.21–22), and (6) oaths (Jas. 5.12; Matt [sic] 5.34–37)."

[36] Cf. Zangenberg, "Matthew and James," 104: "The question of whether James is 'dependent' upon Matthew or vice versa is not the issue here, since such questions can hardly be answered with any degree of certainty. Despite rare occasions of explicit referentiality in early Christian literature, we usually have to operate with similarities and convergences of very different kinds. These include, for example, simultaneous adoption of seemingly identical background traditions and the use of similar terminologies (or the lack thereof)." Zangenberg explains the differences between the writings as "due to difference in genres, to the divergent availability of early Christian traditions and to the diverse situations of their addressees", Zangenberg, "Matthew and James," 121. Cf. also Konradt, "Der Jakobusbrief im frühchristlichen Kontext," 206–207.

texts has often been assumed.[37] Can the perspective of interconnectivity and mobility in the globalized world of antiquity shed new light on these uncertainties? Does the perspective of globalization underscore these uncertainties, in that it emphasizes the fact that common traditions do not imply common origin?

The Experience of Globalization in Early Christianity and in the Roman Empire

Although network theory and analysis have been helpful tools in describing and evaluating the interconnectivity and exchange in the ancient Mediterranean and in early Christianity within this context,[38] the focus of the present study is specifically on the *perception* and *experience* of the world at that time due to these networks and on the effects these networks, including trade networks, had on local communities.

In recent years it has been established that globalization theory not only applies to modern societies, but can also be applied fruitfully to historical periods such as the era of the Roman Empire.[39] In general terms, "globalisation can be described as processes by which localities and people become increasingly interconnected and interdependent."[40] It is "the trend of growing worldwide interconnectedness."[41]

---

[37] Cf. van de Sandt and Zangenberg, *Matthew, James and Didache*, passim.
[38] Anna Collar, *Religious Networks in the Roman Empire: The Spread of New Ideas* (Cambridge: Cambridge University Press, 2013); István Czachesz, "Women, Charity and Mobility in Early Christianity: Weak Links and the Historical Transformation of Religions," in *Changing Minds: Religion and Cognition Through the Ages*, ed. István Czachesz and Tamás Biró, Groningen Studies in Cultural Change 42 (Leuven: Peeters, 2011), 129–54; István Czachesz, "The Evolutionary Dynamics of Religious Systems: Laying the Foundations of a Network Model," in *Origins of Religion, Cognition and Culture*, ed. Armin W. Geertz (Durham: Acumen, 2013), 98–120; István Czachesz, "Network Science in Biblical Studies: Introduction," *Annali di storia dell'esegesi* 39 (2022): 9–26; Dennis C. Duling, "Paul's Aegean Network: The Strength of Strong Ties," *BTB* 43 (2013): 135–54.
[39] Cf. Martin Pitts and Miguel John Versluys, "Globalisation and the Roman World: Perspectives and Opportunities," in *Globalisation and the Roman World: World History, Connectivity and Material Culture*, ed. Martin Pitts and Miguel John Versluys (Cambridge: Cambridge University Press, 2014), 3–31; Justin Jennings, "Distinguishing Past Globalizations," in *The Routledge Handbook of Archaeology and Globalization*, ed. Tamar Hodos (London: Routledge, 2017), 12–28; Justin Jennings, *Globalizations and the Ancient World* (Cambridge: Cambridge University Press, 2011); Robert Witcher, "The Globalized Roman World," in Hodos, *Routledge Handbook of Archaeology and Globalization*, 634–51.
[40] Pitts and Versluys, "Globalisation and the Roman World: Perspectives and Opportunities," 11.
[41] Jan Nederveen Pieterse, "Ancient Rome and Globalisation: Decentring Rome," in Pitts and Versluys, *Globalisation and the Roman World*, 225–39 (235); cf. also Jan Nederveen Pieterse, *Globalization and Culture: Global mélange*, 2nd ed. (Lanham: Rowman and Littlefield, 2009), 43.

Moreover, globalization has been defined as "processes of increasing connectivities that unfold and manifest as social awareness of those connectivities."[42] As has already been indicated above, recent research on mobility, migrations, and the travel of knowledge and wisdom has shown that "with regard to mobility, the Roman world breaks with stereotypical representations of the past as immobile, fragmented, segmented, sheltered, closed off."[43] It can be stated that

> The institutionalisation of the Hellenistic system over the whole oikumene resulted in an unparalleled circulation of goods and peoples and common practices. Along with that came the stress on local identities that is characteristic of a globalised world. The global culture itself was Hellenistic, but it was only through the Roman conquest of the known world that, from a contemporary perspective, the world also literally became global. From the period of 200 BC onwards, therefore, the whole oikumene is one "hyper-network", which we should call "global" to better indicate the degree of connectivity and time-space compression we are talking about.[44]

The applicability of the concept of globalization to the Roman world has, of course, been challenged. From a geographical perspective, for instance, the Roman Empire was never "global"—in the sense of world-spanning—in its expanse, and while Roman imperialism may have increased connectivity by reducing the costs of travelling and transportation and providing more security and information as well as legal structures in order to support economic enterprises, innovations in Roman transport and communication do not testify to a noticeable time-space compression as we experience it in the modern globalized world.[45] However, it has also been stated that

> until well into the Principate, the Roman world was effectively growing rather than shrinking, albeit in fits and starts, as new regions were incorporated into its political, economic and social space. In cultural and conceptual terms, this might be seen as a kind of spatial compression, experienced as such by the inhabitants of newly incorporated areas as they came to think of themselves as part of a wider world.[46]

---

42 Tamar Hodos, "Globalization: Some Basics: An Introduction to The Routledge Handbook of Archaeology and Globalization," in Hodos, *Routledge Handbook of Archaeology and Globalization*, 3–11 (4).
43 Nederveen Pieterse, "Ancient Rome and Globalisation," 231.
44 Miguel John Versluys, "Roman Visual Material Culture as Globalising *Koine*," in Pitts and Versluys, *Globalisation and the Roman World*, 141–74 (163).
45 The concept of "space-time compression" describes the perception of the world getting smaller due to the multitude of "global" interconnections. For a critical perspective on the concept of globalization cf. Neville Morley, "Globalisation and the Roman Economy," in Pitts and Versluys, *Globalisation and the Roman World*, 49–68.
46 Morley, "Globalisation and the Roman Economy," 57.

This means, that with a view to the Roman Empire, the focus for globalization has to be "on social relationships, cultural practices and above all individual subjectivities" rather than on "physical structures and processes."[47] What is "globalized" in the Roman world is the "imaginative construction," the ideology of the Roman Empire as a "global" structure:

> It is not just that individuals are increasingly integrated into wider social networks, and that local events are shaped by things happening many miles away and vice versa. It is the extent to which, in a globalised or globalising world, individuals increasingly view themselves in relation to a global rather than local context; they choose a social identity rather than simply accepting it as a given, and they do this in full awareness of and with reference to the whole range of possibilities that have now become available through the proliferation of knowledge of the world as a whole.[48]

What can be detected, therefore, is the change of perception in individuals and groups within the Roman Empire, who experience themselves as being part of a globalized world and react by constructing an identity for themselves as members of this globalized world, not only of their own community, region, or nation. It is therefore not the modern perception of time-space compression arising through travelling by plane instead of on foot or through communicating via the internet instead of the postal service, but for antiquity it is rather "an acceleration of long-distance economic, political, and social processes that shrinks one's *experience* of space and time."[49] What has been of special interest in literature on globalization, therefore, is the impact it has on cultures. The focus here is, on the one hand, on the homogenization that occurs, and, on the other hand, on the heterogeneity that arises: "a general consensus is that globalisation is an uneven process, reconfiguring social relations and political institutions, and fostering cultural diversity and social inequality."[50] As Martin Pitts and Miguel John Versluys observe,

> [t]his viewpoint is encapsulated in the term "glocalization", deriving from the Japanese *dochakuka*, loosely translating as "global localization". The concept of glocalization helps to emphasise how the homogenising elements of global culture (from institutions and commodities to social practices and ideas) are differentially incorporated into local cultures, which are in turn altered in the process.[51]

---

[47] Morley, "Globalisation and the Roman Economy," 59.
[48] Morley, "Globalisation and the Roman Economy," 59.
[49] Jennings, "Distinguishing Past Globalizations," 14 (my italics).
[50] Pitts and Versluys, "Globalisation and the Roman World: Perspectives and Opportunities," 14.
[51] Pitts and Versluys, "Globalisation and the Roman World: Perspectives and Opportunities," 14. The central elements to be identified and analyzed in this approach are therefore power, resources and identity, which determine the process of global intermingling of cultures.

Glocalization is thus an effect of the interconnectedness and interchange of the ancient globalized world, it describes "the ways in which broadly shared ideas, goods, and practices are modified and adapted locally to accord with local practice, customs, habits, and beliefs,"[52] for

> [a]s those globally common practices reverberate through a cultural group—in the form of new shapes, styles, or goods—social practices within that group evolve to build upon the initial thread that facilitated global-level understanding in the first place. Often, such evolutions are adapted in a way that speaks directly and explicitly to that group, which increases their appeal locally. This is the idea of glocalization, or the local adaptation of those widely shared practices and values, which appears in the convergence most popularly associated with globalization.[53]

This strong interconnectedness of the Roman world led to the experience of living in a globalized world: "[T]he Greco-Roman world is significant in relation to globalisation as subjectivity, or world consciousness, and the evolution of cosmopolitanisms.... Orbis terrarum is an early world consciousness."[54] The Roman Empire was perceived as an "integrated, well-connected and, as it were, 'global' oikoumene."[55] This perception however, is primarily founded on the strong connectivity through inter-regional as well as global networks, which emerged all over the Roman Empire, e.g., with a view to religion, trade,[56] or migration and were based on the adoption of and adherence to particular standards and norms.

> What Rome brought to the rest of its world were standards with ever wider global reach and, arguably, much richer ideological content; these standards helped to promote economic activity by lowering costs, but at the same time they were more likely to be adopted in regions that were already more closely involved in extra-regional trade – which in turn helped to promote processes of broader cultural change as their users absorbed something of the wider values of the network and made their own contributions to its development. The processes of

---

52 Hodos, "Globalization: Some Basics," 6.
53 Hodos, "Globalization: Some Basics," 6.
54 Nederveen Pieterse, "Ancient Rome and Globalisation," 231–32; cf. also Jan Nederveen Pieterse, *Ethnicities and Global Multiculture: Pants for an Octopus* (Lanham: Rowman & Littlefield, 2007), 9: "King Herod, who was appointed King of Judea by the Romans, was 'by birth an Idumean (i.e. Edomite), by profession a Jew, by necessity a Roman, by culture and by choice a Greek'. Multiple and intersecting cultural layers and overlapping jurisdictions, then as now, generate multiple identities."
55 Sommer, "OIKOYMENH," 175–79 (176), who gives an overview over ancient perceptions of globalization, e.g., by Aelius Aristides in Arist. 26.101–2.
56 For the effect of globalization on everyday life on a local and regional level through research into mass consumption in the Roman empire cf. Martin Pitts, "Globalisation, Circulation and Mass Consumption in the Roman World," in Pitts and Versluys, *Globalisation and the Roman World*, 69–98.

the economic, the political and the cultural integration of the empire appear to be far more interdependent than is generally recognised.[57]

Justin Jennings has formulated eight criteria that characterize a "global culture," a term used "to encapsulate all of the ways that people's lives are fundamentally transformed by the increased flow of long-distance goods, people, and ideas"[58] and thus help to identify instances of "globalization":

> The first of the trends is *time-space compression*, an acceleration of long-distance economic and social processes that shrinks one's experience of space and time. With time-space compression, the world feels smaller and smaller. The second hallmark of globalization is *deterritorialization*, the sense that many places seem unconnected to their local cultural context.. . . *Standardization* is the third trend. Since globalization brings diverse groups together, there is a need to operate on a common footing through the use of shared language, economic structures, etc. The fourth trend in globalization is *unevenness*. Global networks are not the same across the world. Some places . . . are highly connected, whereas other places have very few connections to the outside world. *Homogenization*, the fifth trend, is perhaps the most well-known of changes occurring in globalization. Homogenization is the process through which foreign, often Western, goods and ideas are adopted by other groups. This process is often balanced by the sixth trend, *cultural heterogeneity*, as new ways of living are generated through the mixing of various global flows. . . . The *re-embedding of local culture* is the seventh trend seen in globalization. The social changes that occur because of global flows can be traumatic, and some groups react to these changes by returning to local traditions. This embrace of the past, often reimagined for the present, is sometimes explicitly done to reject foreign influence. *Vulnerability* is the last trend. As global networks connect people together in more numerous and deeper ways, groups become increasingly interdependent. When things go wrong,. . . everyone is affected.[59]

These eight characteristics that are associated with globalization can prove useful for the understanding of early Christianity within the Roman Empire as an agent within a globalized world. With this theoretical background, the question can be reformulated as: Would it change our perception if these categories were used to reconsider the historical context of early Christianity within the globalized world of the Roman Empire?

---

57 Morley, "Globalisation and the Roman Economy," 65.
58 Jennings, *Globalizations and the Ancient World*, 31.
59 Jennings, *Globalizations and the Ancient World*, 30–31; for a detailed discussion of the criteria cf. Jennings, *Globalizations and the Ancient World*, 121–42; cf. also Versluys, "Roman Visual Material Culture as Globalising *Koine*," 161.

Speech Ethics in Early Christianity from the Perspective of Globalization Studies

More concretely, would it change our perception if we read early Christian texts like the Letter of James from the perspective of globalization? Could the focus on the ancient experience of living in a globalized world with regular long-distance movements of people, goods, and ideas contribute to our understanding of the mobility of ancient discourses, specifically the discourse on speech ethics, in early Christianity?

Time-space compression, i.e., the perception of the world getting smaller due to the multitude of global interconnections, is considered as being the effect of the "growing worldwide interconnectedness" that defines globalization.[60] It has been established in previous scholarship that the Roman Empire can be considered in terms of globalization. Studies focusing "on ancient mobility, on migrations and on the spread of religion and the travel of knowledge and technology"[61] in the Roman Empire testify to an increasing connectivity, "of a type that encompasses a wide-scale flow of ideas and knowledge."[62] At the same time, however, it has been recognized that "the Greco-Roman world is significant in relation to globalisation as subjectivity, or world consciousness," meaning that the perception of the *orbis terrarum* has to be considered as "an early world consciousness" and that the Roman world—considered from the perspective of contemporaries—can be described as global, although, in this case, "global" does not necessarily need to comprise the entire world.[63] The Roman Empire has been described as an "integrated, well-connected and, as it were, 'global' oikoumene"[64] and the lively travel activity and strong networking ambitions of early Christianity testify to their partaking in this perception.[65] The Letter of James indicates an awareness of the connectivity of its world and constructs its own place and role in this connectivity. It presupposes a (fictive?) network spread throughout the globalized world, maintained or enhanced by merchant travelers, where this letter will be received and unfold its influence.[66] The author seems to rely on this "global" network of communication and interaction

---

60 Nederveen Pieterse, "Ancient Rome and Globalisation," 235.
61 Nederveen Pieterse, "Ancient Rome and Globalisation," 231.
62 Hodos, "Globalization: Some Basics," 4.
63 Nederveen Pieterse, "Ancient Rome and Globalisation," 231.
64 Sommer, "OIKOYMENH," 176.
65 Cf. Duling, "Paul's Aegean Network," 135–54.
66 But cf. also Matthias Klinghardt, "Wie und warum ist der Jakobusbrief ins Neue Testament gekommen? Der Jakobusbrief als kanonisches Pseudepigraph," *ZNT* 50 (2022): 85–95, who argues that the Letter of James never circulated as an independent letter, but suggests that it was composed

in order to reach his addressees, the representatives of the "twelve tribes scattered among the nations" (Jas 1:1), i.e., those groups of early Christ-followers envisioned to live "all over the place."

This perception, in turn, is closely linked with the second characteristic of globalization, deterritorialization, i.e., the observation that "culture becomes increasingly abstracted from a local, geographically fixed context."[67] Indications for deterritorialization can be found in the Letter of James with regard to the scope of the received tradition as well as to the scope of the intended dissemination of the letter.

First, the traditions received are not local traditions, but the Letter of James draws on a broad spectrum of philosophical and ethical ideas and motifs. The speech-ethical topoi taken up in the New Testament can be found, e.g., in Plato and Aristotle, Plutarch, Seneca, Epictetus, Philo, the Hebrew Bible, the writings from Qumran, and early Jewish literature.[68] What this perspective on the Greco-Roman world as a global οἰκουμένη emphasizes is the strong intermingling of norms and ethical ideals, of motifs and traditions, of persuasive and educational strategies, of motivations for action as well as of genres of instruction at that time. The overarching discourse on speech ethics in antiquity was fed by different traditions and groups, that—although for the New Testament writings we cannot claim literary dependency—seem to interact with or react to each other.

Second, the Letter of James presents itself as a diaspora letter, i.e., traditionally a letter written from Israel to the Jewish people scattered all over the world in order to encourage them and remind them of their ancestral customs and traditions.[69] As a Christian writing,[70] the Letter of James adapts this genre and its

---

as a "canonical pseudepigraphon," specifically for the inclusion in canonical edition of the New Testament.

67 Versluys, "Roman Visual Material Culture as Globalising *Koine*," 161. Jennings, *Globalizations and the Ancient World*, 125: "Although deterritorialization does not lead to a complete unmooring of culture from local affairs . . ., the ties to a single location are weakened as a result of the myriad of long-distance interactions that connect that place to other regions." And Jennings, *Globalizations and the Ancient World*, 126: "Deterritorialization does not only occur through the stretching of social networks. It also occurs when foreign people, products, and ideas are incorporated into a place."

68 For examples cf. Luther, *Sprachethik im Neuen Testament*, 67–404.

69 Cf. Niebuhr, "Der Jakobusbrief im Licht frühjüdischer Diasporabriefe," 424–31.

70 Cf. Maren Niehoff, "The Implied Audience of the Letter of James," in *New Approaches to the Study of Biblical Interpretation in Judaism of the Second Temple Period and in Early Christianity*, ed. Gary A. Anderson, Ruth A. Clements, and David Satran, STDJ 106 (Leiden: Brill, 2013), 57–77, in support of Oda Wischmeyer ("Reconstructing the Social and Religious Milieu of James: Methods, Sources, Possible Results," in van de Sandt and Zangenberg, *Matthew, James, and Didache*, 33–41), who reads the letter as an early Christian text not comparable with diaspora letters, but against John Kloppenborg (John S. Kloppenborg, "Diaspora Discourse: The Construction of Ethos in James,"

claim for his purpose of writing to early Christians settled far from their ancestral homelands. The letter has to be read as a text addressed to people living scattered across the known ancient world, even if the question of whether the homeland is connected with a specific place on the map or whether this is a metaphorical reference to the Christians' heavenly home and their dissociation with the world has to remain unresolved.[71] Although the text addresses a broad group of people, it does not provide concrete information about the historical profile of the addressees or their possible local background. It indicates the presupposition of reaching a large group of addressees, i.e., of his text being distributed across a vast area through networks of interconnected congregations. Therefore, what is relevant with regard to the perspective of globalization studies is the *literary claim* of this writing to send out teaching and admonition, not to a specific community, but to a broader, more global audience, so to speak, and to addressees living scattered "all over the world."

Moreover, through the reception, evaluation, and reinterpretation of a broad spectrum of Jewish as well as Greco-Roman traditions; through the literary presentation as wisdom teaching; and through the integration of a broad spectrum of intellectual-historical, cultural, religious and ethical aspects of the broader ancient discourse on speech ethics, the author of the Letter of James lays claim to the universal validity of his teaching,[72] and in doing so aims to appeal to an even wider audience, even beyond early Christian circles.[73]

Further characteristics of globalization, standardization, i.e., the emergence of a common way of envisioning the world, and cultural homogenization, i.e., the reliance on similar ideas and products that occurs with the flow between groups, nations, and cultures, are intricately linked and involve "interpretation, translation, mutation, adaptation and 'indigenization' as the receiving culture brings its

---

NTS 53 [2007]: 242–70), who argues that James is addressing a Jewish audience and that early Christianity was a movement within Judaism; similarly Niebuhr, "Der Jakobusbrief im Licht frühjüdischer Diasporabriefe," 420–43, who reads James as comparable to diaspora letters, but addressed to a group of Jewish and gentile Christians.

71 Cf. Metzner, *Brief des Jakobus*, 54–55.

72 Cf. Gerd Theissen, "Weisheit als Mittel sozialer Abgrenzung und Öffnung: Beobachtungen zur sozialen Funktion frühjüdischer und urchristlicher Weisheit," in *Weisheit*, ed. Aleida Assmann, ALK 3 (München: Fink, 1991), 193–203, who points to the openness of wisdom traditions in early Christianity—in contrast to the (social) demarcation by status and ethnos of wisdom teaching in early Judaism.

73 Cf. Susanne Luther, "Profiling the Author of the Letter of James: Dealing with Traditions in the Light of Epistolary Authorship Conceptions," in *Who was James? Essays on the Letter's Authorship and Provenance*, ed. Eve-Marie Becker, Sigurvin Lárus Jónsson and Susanne Luther, WUNT 485 (Tübingen: Mohr Siebeck, 2022), 29–55 (esp. 47–50); cf. also Dale C. Allison, "The Fiction of James and Its *Sitz im Leben*," *RB* 108 (2001): 529–70 (569–70).

own cultural resources to bear, in dialectical fashion, upon 'cultural imports'."[74] With regard to these characteristics, the findings presented above concerning the New Testament discourse on speech ethics have shown that the New Testament texts recur to a number of topoi of the contemporary discourse, receive a selection of them, adapt them to their specific needs and incorporate them into the Christian worldview and eschatological timeframe.[75] Of course, these aspects—the preconditions, processes and effects of the transfer of norms—have already been taken into account by past research.[76] What comes into clearer focus through the perspective of globalization is the influence of the broader perspective and the close contact between different places within the Roman world. The awareness of this constant exchange of ideas and traditions points, on the one hand, to the importance of analyzing the individual traits of the speech-ethical positions within the discourse, and, on the other hand, to the significance of each group for voicing their specific position. Through engaging the broader ancient discourse on speech ethics, the contributors of individual early Christian discourse positions achieve integration into this globalized world, and through their individual positioning and specific emphases from the early Christian perspective, they are able to establish a distinct (moral) identity of their own group. From a sociological perspective, therefore, the embedding into the contemporary discourse as well as the emphasis on boundaries and individual traits play a central role.

Globalization is also characterized by unevenness, i.e., the existence of power imbalances between the different regions of interregional networks. The early Christian network consisted on the geographical level of larger, more powerful agents like the communities in Jerusalem, Alexandria, Antioch, Ephesus, or Rome and a great number of smaller communities.[77] On the level of personal agency, a number of prominent agents—like Paul, Peter, James, but also Paul's co-workers—are known from the New Testament texts, who, through their spoken or written word and through their interconnectedness with different geographical centers of the early Christian network exerted influence on the development of early Chris-

---

[74] John Tomlinson, *Globalization and Culture* (Chicago: University of Chicago Press, 1999), 84. Cf. also Jennings, *Globalizations and the Ancient World*, 132: "Homogenization, therefore, is not so much about the spread of a single way of life as it is about how people come into contact with widely shared ideas and products and make them their own."

[75] Cf. Susanne Luther, "Von Feigenbäumen und Oliven: Die Rezeption, Transformation und Kreation sprachethischer Traditionen im Jakobusbrief," *Annali di Storia dell'Esegesi* 34 (2017): 381–401; Luther, "Profiling the Author of the Letter of James," 29–55.

[76] Cf. Chiai, *Athen, Rom, Jerusalem*.

[77] Duling, "Paul's Aegean Network," 135–54.

tian theology, ethics, and the spread of the movement.[78] The authority of—later normative—early Christian writings is usually ascribed to either the orthonymous or pseudonymous authorship of one of these eminent figures or to the prominence of one of the larger, more influential communities.

The Letter of James fits into this profile. Its ethical directive power is based on the premise that a certain speech-ethical conduct is required for partaking in the community which authored and authorized the speech-ethical admonitions. This authority to issue ethical directives is closely related to the power of interpretation and teaching, which allows for a free and creative reception and adaption and for a new interpretation of common speech-ethical topoi within the framework of the Christian worldview and their authoritative communication. The Letter of James bases its authoritative teaching on the reference to an eminent person of early Christianity through the pseudonymous ascription of the teaching on specific traditions on speech ethics to James, the brother of Jesus.[79] Moreover, its composition is usually located in one of the large centers of early Christianity, e.g., in Alexandria, Rome, or Antioch.[80]

And the broad discourse on speech ethics interacts with social issues in that all New Testament texts concerned with speech-ethical topics deal with the relationship between early Christianity and its historical context, i.e., with its engagement with the societal and political situation. These texts, especially the Gospel of Matthew and the Letter of James, prescribe norms of behavior, avoidance strategies, and alternative courses of action that are informed by the worldview of early Christianity and that stand in opposition to the conventional norms of conduct of the world around them. At the same time, the discourse exerts power in that the New Testament discourse concerning speech ethics helps to construct a worldview that prescribes both categories of perception and constructions of meaning and foundations of identity in relation to the appropriate use of speech and its soteriological significance, and disseminates these in the early Christian networks. It thus establishes and shapes a community that bases affiliation with the community on the acceptance of the discourse.[81]

---

[78] With a view to Antioch cf., e.g., Martin Hengel and Anna Maria Schwemer, *Paulus zwischen Damaskus und Antiochien: Die unbekannten Jahre des Apostels*, WUNT 108 (Tübingen: Mohr Siebeck, 1998), 423–61.
[79] Cf. Susanne Luther, "Strategies of Authorizing Tradition in the Letter of James," in *Authoritative Writings in Early Judaism and Early Christianity: Their Origin, Collection and Meaning*, ed. Tobias Nicklas and Jens Schröter, WUNT 441 (Tübingen: Mohr Siebeck, 2020), 209–23.
[80] See above footnotes 25 and 26.
[81] Cf. for the methodological framework Landwehr, *Historische Diskursanalyse*, 128–29.

Concerning the geographical aspect, it has been argued that the speech-ethical traditions used and the way they are integrated into the early Christian eschatological worldview suggest a common milieu of the New Testament texts mainly concerned with speech ethics, namely, the Letter of James and the Gospel of Matthew.[82] But can—or even should—this milieu be more clearly located geographically?

It has rightly been stated that "[i]t is important to recognize that this general uncertainty and ambiguity with regard to rather fundamental issues within the field of New Testament Studies reflects the normal situation. Authorship is a complex matter. The communication situation is often quite unclear, as is dating and the redaction history of many texts."[83] Of course, this observation is also true for questions concerning the historical origin and composition of the writings:

> The situation described above is certainly relevant when it comes to the Didache, James, and Matthew, which are all characterized by numerous isagogic problems. We cannot be sure when and where these documents were written or by whom . . . We should not rule out the possibility of finding evidence that could bring more clarity to the historical setting of these documents, but it may be wise not to expect too much in this regard. Perhaps it is more realistic to try to find the most efficient methodological strategy for using these documents without being absolutely certain of their geographical location, dating, or specific communication situation.[84]

Nevertheless, in current research the composition of the Gospel of Matthew is predominantly located in Syria, often more concretely in Antioch on the Orontes.[85] Let us work with this hypothesis and see which role this metropolis, according to

---

[82] Huub van de Sandt and Jürgen K. Zangenberg, "Introduction," in van de Sandt and Zangenberg, *Matthew, James, and Didache*, 1–9 (1–2): "Matthew, James, and the Didache are writings that most certainly span the worlds of Judaism and Christianity. . . . The three documents could reflect various stages in the development of a network of communities that shared basic theological assumptions and expressions, or they may represent contemporaneous strands or different regional forms of the same wider phenomenon we now call Jewish Christianity. . . . We believe that in addition to the Pauline and Johannine 'schools,' Matthew, James, and the Didache represent a third important religious milieu within earliest Christianity, which is characterized by its distinct connections to a particular ethical stream of contemporary Jewish tradition. This is so even if cohesion between these three documents is less distinct and constituted differently compared to the Pauline and Johannine corpora and would certainly not exclude possible affinities to other early Christian documents. This is why we prefer the somewhat more vague term 'milieu' to the sociologically more definitive 'school' with all its problems, assumptions, and implications."
[83] Magnus Zetterholm, "The Didache, Matthew, James—and Paul: Reconstructing Historical Developments in Antioch," in van de Sandt and Zangenberg, *Matthew, James, and Didache*, 73–90 (75).
[84] Zetterholm, "The Didache, Matthew, James," 75.
[85] Cf., e.g., David C. Sim, "Reconstructing the Social and Religious Milieu of Matthew," 19–25; cf. also Raymond E. Brown and John P. Meier, *Antioch and Rome: New Testament Cradles of Catholic Christianity* (London: Chapman, 1983), 18–27.

Josephus the third largest city of the Roman Empire (*B.J.* 3.29), could have played. Located on the river Orontes, and "only a day's sail from the Mediterranean, Antioch lay at a crossroads between the cultures of the classical world and those that flourished along the Tigris and Euphrates. With its connection to the caravan routes to the Red Sea and the Persian Gulf, it played a vital role in Rome's expanding interests in the Near East in the early years of the first millennium."[86] The city was populated by Greeks, Romans, and Syrians, and had a large Jewish diaspora community.[87] Antioch was a Greco-Roman melting pot with Cyprian, Egyptian and Persian influences. The city was one of the hubs of the Roman Empire and it was still a center of intellectual life in the early Christian era.[88] The early Jewish-Christian community in Antioch is reported to have had strong interests in pagan mission as early Christians that fled Jerusalem found refuge in Antioch. There was also a strong connection between Antioch and Paul, Peter and James according to the testimony of the New Testament writings.[89] If we imagine Syria, or more specifically Antioch, as the origin and center of the early Christian speech-ethical discourse, this can be made plausible by other writings that probably originated in Syria and that are, to a certain extent, concerned with speech-ethical topics, such as—with much hesitation as to a definite location of its composition—the Didache.[90] Due to the strong Jewish presence in Antioch, the recurrence of an Antiochene speech-ethical

---

[86] Angela M. H. Schuster, "Antioch in Antiquity," *Archaeology* 53/6 (2000): 69–70 (69). Cf. on the same page: "For nearly a millennium the city of Antioch, located on the Syrian border of southern Turkey, reigned as one of the ancient world's great cities, renowned for its sophistication, the opulence of its buildings and broad avenues, its markets filled with exotic and luxurious goods, and, perhaps more important, its artistic and intellectual life".

[87] Cf. Barclay, *Jews in the Mediterranean Diaspora*, 242–58; Magnus Zetterholm, *The Formation of Christianity in Antioch: A Social-Scientific Approach to the Separation between Judaism and Christianity* (London: Routledge, 2003), esp. 18–52.

[88] For early Christian Antioch cf. Brown and Meier, *Antioch and Rome*; cf. also Jan W. Drijvers, "Syrian Christianity and Judaism," in *History and Religion in Late Antique Syria*, ed. Jan W. Drijvers, Variorum Collected Studies Series 464 (Aldershot: Variorum, 1994), 124–46; Andreas Feldtkeller, *Identitätssuche des syrischen Urchristentums: Mission, Inkulturation und Pluralität im ältesten Heidenchristentum*, NTOA 25 (Göttingen: Vandenhoeck & Ruprecht, 1993).

[89] Cf. Michelle Slee, *The Church in Antioch in the First Century CE: Communion and Conflict*, LNTS 244 (London: Sheffield Academic Press, 2003).

[90] Cf. Jürgen K. Zangenberg, "Reconstructing the Social and Religious Milieu of the Didache: Observations and Possible Results," in van de Sandt and Zangenberg, *Matthew, James, and Didache*, 43–69 (69): "From what Didache tells us directly, we can only conclude that the text came from anywhere in the Greek-speaking (eastern) Mediterranean, that it was deeply rooted in Judaism and shows striking similarities with Matthew and—to a lesser but still significant degree—with James, and all three might very well have come from a common 'milieu.'" Much more certain is Zetterholm, "The Didache, Matthew, James," 73–90.

discourse to Jewish wisdom traditions, which emphasized the topic of appropriate speech as central to the ethical discussion, could easily be explained.

However, the perspective of globalization provides an opportunity to draw a larger picture: it is not necessary to localize the common historical context of early Christian speech-ethical traditions on the map. It can rather be observed, that wherever the Letter of James was composed, the interconnectivity and interaction of the globalized Roman world made it easy for ideas to travel and the connections between the author of James and Syria or even Antioch seem to have been strong enough for these possibly specific Syrian or even Antioch ethical traditions to travel and reach any place of the composition of the Letter of James.[91]

Here two further aspects associated with globalization studies come into view: the trend to cultural heterogeneity, i.e., "the way that global flows are significantly different from one region to another"[92] and the re-embedding into local culture, i.e., the trend to react to the emergence of the global culture by enhancing cultural variation on a local level and to protect or reconstruct local uniqueness.[93] These phenomena emphasize "the fact that global and local trends belong intrinsically together, whilst also indicating that something new emerges from global-local interactions: a 'glocal' cultural expression, which combines global and local elements in new and creative ways."[94] The Letter of James can be considered as an ancient "glocal writing," as it reflects the "global intellectual context of the Hellenistic world,"[95] while at the same time the author underscores the local traditions and builds on them. And in this we might find an explanation as to why only a few and relatively late New Testament writings were concerned with speech ethics, each having its own specific emphases in its teaching. We can read speech ethics as reflecting a specific local interest, a distinct form of early Christian ethics that was perhaps characteristic for the Syrian or Antioch local milieu. Yet, it also imported ideas and norms from the ancient global discourse and exported its own adapted ideas and norms back into the global network. It also exported ideas within the early Christian network which caused single topoi to be taken up by other New Testament writings.

The eighth criterion of globalization, vulnerability, describes the phenomenon of increasing dependence of places on other places in the global interaction, "combined with the related erosion of the local," which leads to insecurity and "to a heightened awareness of possible risks and to a fixation on these risks and how to

---

91 Cf. here also Hartog, "Reading Acts in Motion."
92 Jennings, *Globalizations and the Ancient World*, 135.
93 Cf. Jennings, *Globalizations and the Ancient World*, 136.
94 Pieter B. Hartog, "Jubilees and Hellenistic Encyclopaedism," *JSJ* 50 (2019): 1–25 (18).
95 Cf. Hartog, "Jubilees and Hellenistic Encyclopaedism," 18.

avert them."⁹⁶ The Letter of James—just like the Gospel of Matthew—speaks into this situation of insecurity by providing comprehensive and clear ethical instructions, that are the precondition of the affiliation with the group.

Conclusions: The Mobility of Ideas in the Ancient Globalized World

Let me summarize: What does globalization theory have to offer for the questions addressed in this essay? Do we need globalization theory to reach these conclusions? The answer is "yes" and "no."⁹⁷ Many aspects that globalization theory addresses have already been in the focus of earlier analyses. But the above explorations have shown that globalization theory encourages the identification and appreciation of networks based on the Roman imperial infrastructure beyond the physical level. In doing so, globalization theory can bring new aspects into focus and increase the awareness of aspects that were not given much prominence before. This awareness relates, in particular, to the universal reception, transfer, and dissemination of speech-ethical teaching, "notably the 'universalisation of the particular' hand-in-hand with the 'particularisation of the universal'."⁹⁸ Globalization theory can thus shed new light on contentious issues and offer new perspectives on unresolved questions in New Testament scholarship.

Moreover, the perspective of globalization "has the potential to provide detailed insights into degrees of global consciousness, participation and exclusion from aspects of global culture, and the general experiences of living in the Roman world for all social groups, especially non-elites."⁹⁹ This approach therefore takes the "world consciousness" of individuals and groups and their experience of cosmopolitanism within the ancient "globalized world" into account. In this way, the approach allows for a bigger picture as the intense inter- and intra-cultural as well as inter- and intra-regional connectivities and pluriform "global" interactions are applied to illuminate our understanding of the complex amalgamation of discourse traditions and the striking congruences of common milieus of early Christian writings like the Letter of James and the Gospel of Matthew.¹⁰⁰

---

96 Cf. Jennings, *Globalizations and the Ancient World*, 139.
97 Versluys, "Roman Visual Material Culture as Globalising *Koine*," 164.
98 Pitts, "Globalisation, Circulation and Mass Consumption," 93.
99 Pitts, "Globalisation, Circulation and Mass Consumption," 93.
100 What Versluys claims for objects also applies to ideas, cf. Versluys, "Roman Visual Material Culture as Globalising *Koine*," 167: "[I]n cultural terms the Roman oikumene was a global ethnos-

The approach of globalization studies invites a perception of early Christianity as an active agent within this cultural, social, religious and intellectual hyper-network of the ancient Mediterranean, in dependence on and autonomy from the surrounding world, in integration and demarcation from their historical context. Therefore, the form of communication of the Letter of James, its intended dissemination as a diaspora letter, receiving material from different traditions and using a kind of global rhetoric that allows for an embedding of its teaching within the wider ancient discourse as well as a reception of the wisdom conveyed by a broad audience within the global οἰκουμένη,[101] allows for the assumption that the practice of letter writing with a broader audience in view and the dissemination of authorial teaching to the global οἰκουμένη, can—just like traveling—be considered as one of the practices that trigger globalization.

References

Adkins, Lesley and Roy A. Adkins. *Handbook of Life in Ancient Rome*. New York: Oxford University Press, 1994.
Alcock, Susan and Robin E. Osborne, eds. *Placing the Gods: Sanctuaries and Sacred Space in Ancient Greece*. Oxford: Clarendon, 1994.
Alexander, Loveday. "Mapping Early Christianity: Acts and the Shape of Early Church History." *Interpretation* 57 (2003): 163–73.
Allison, Dale C. "The Fiction of James and Its *Sitz im Leben*." *RB* 108 (2001): 529–70.
André, Jean Marie and Marie Françoise Baslez. *Voyager dans l'Antiquité*. Paris: Fayard, 1993.
Backhaus, Knut. "Conditio Jacobaea: Jüdische Weisheitstradition und christliche Alltagsethik nach Jak 4,13–17." Pages 135–58 in *Schrift und Tradition: Festschrift für Josef Ernst zum 70. Geburtstag*. Edited by Knut Backhaus and Franz G. Untergaßmair. Paderborn: Schöningh, 1996.
Barclay, John M.G. *Jews in the Mediterranean Diaspora from Alexander to Trajan (323 BCE–117 CE)*. Edinburgh: T&T Clark, 1999.

---

cape characterised by continuous cultural circularity. If we see objects as actants in this circular system—and if we think about how humans depend on these things and how these things depend on other things—a rather different picture of the Roman world emerges than usually imagined. A picture fundamentally characterised by objects in motion.... Thus, many more actants than ever before were added to the hyper-network we call the (globalised) Roman world. As things with agency these objects would indeed strongly influence the people around them. If we decide to place most emphasis in our understanding of the Roman world on these objects in motion, we could perhaps even say that all political and social developments traditionally employed to describe it are just structures built around these circulating things."
101 Cf. Gian Franco Chiai and Andreas Hartmann, "Athen, Rom, Jerusalem: Normentransfers in der Alten Welt," in Chai, *Athen, Rom, Jerusalem*, 11–24 (esp. 20–21).

Bloch, René. "Show and Tell: Myth, Tourism, and Jewish Hellenism." Pages 101–27 in *Ancient Jewish Diaspora: Essays on Hellenism*. JSJSup 206. Leiden: Brill, 2022.

Bloch, René. "What If the Temple of Jerusalem Had Not Been Destroyed by the Romans?" Page 128–49 in *Ancient Jewish Diaspora: Essays on Hellenism*. JSJSup 206. Leiden: Brill, 2022.

Börstinghaus, Jens. *Sturmfahrt und Schiffbruch: Zur lukanischen Verwendung eines literarischen Topos in Apostelgeschichte 27,1–28,6*. WUNT 2/274. Tübingen: Mohr Siebeck, 2010.

Brown, Raymond E., and John P. Meier. *Antioch and Rome: New Testament Cradles of Catholic Christianity*. London: Chapman, 1983.

Candy, Peter, and Emilia Mataix Ferrándis, eds. *Roman Law and Maritime Commerce*. Edinburgh: Edinburgh University Press, 2022.

Chiai, Gian Franco, and Andreas Hartmann. "Athen, Rom, Jerusalem: Normentransfers in der Alten Welt." Pages 11–24 in *Athen, Rom, Jerusalem: Normentransfers in der antiken Welt*. Edited by Gian Franco Chiai. Eichstätter Studien Neue Folge 66. Regensburg: Pustet, 2012.

Chiai, Gian Franco, ed. *Athen, Rom, Jerusalem: Normentransfers in der antiken Welt*. Eichstätter Studien Neue Folge 66. Regensburg: Pustet, 2012.

Collar, Anna. *Religious Networks in the Roman Empire: The Spread of New Ideas*. Cambridge: Cambridge University Press, 2013.

Curtin, Philip. *Cross-Cultural Trade in World History*. Cambridge: Cambridge University Press, 1984.

Czachesz, István. "Network Science in Biblical Studies: Introduction." *Annali di storia dell'esegesi* 39 (2022): 9–26.

Czachesz, István. "The Evolutionary Dynamics of Religious Systems: Laying the Foundations of a Network Model." Pages 98–120 in *Origins of Religion, Cognition and Culture*. Edited by Armin W. Geertz. Durham: Acumen, 2013.

Czachesz, István. "Women, Charity and Mobility in Early Christianity: Weak Links and the Historical Transformation of Religions." Pages 129–54 in *Changing Minds: Religion and Cognition Through the Ages*. Edited by István Czachesz and Tamás Biró. Groningen Studies in Cultural Change 42. Leuven: Peeters, 2011.

Davids, Peter H. "James and Peter: The Literary Evidence." Pages 29–52 in *The Missions of James, Peter, and Paul*. Edited by Bruce Chilton and Craig Evans. NovTSup 115. Leiden: Brill, 2005.

Dillon, Matthew. *Pilgrims and Pilgrimage in Ancient Greece*. London: Routledge, 1997.

Drijvers, Jan W. "Syrian Christianity and Judaism." Pages 124–46 in *History and Religion in Late Antique Syria*. Edited by Jan W. Drijvers. Variorum Collected Studies Series 464. Aldershot: Variorum, 1994.

Drijvers, Jan Willem. "Travel and Pilgrimage Literature." Pages 359–72 in *A Companion to Late Antique Literature*. Edited by Scott McGill and Edward J. Watts. Hoboken: Wiley, 2018.

Duling, Dennis C. "Paul's Aegean Network: The Strength of Strong Ties." *BTB* 43 (2013): 135–54.

Elsner, Jás and Ian Rutherford, eds. *Pilgrimage in Graeco-Roman and Early Christian Antiquity: Seeing the Gods*. Oxford: Oxford University Press, 2005.

Feldtkeller, Andreas. *Identitätssuche des syrischen Urchristentums: Mission, Inkulturation und Pluralität im ältesten Heidenchristentum*. NTOA 25. Göttingen: Vandenhoeck & Ruprecht, 1993.

Garleff, Gunnar. *Urchristliche Identität in Matthäusevangelium, Didache und Jakobusbrief*. BVB 9. Münster: LIT-Verlag, 2004.

Gruen, Erich S. *Diaspora: Jews amidst Greeks and Romans*. Cambridge: Harvard University Press, 2002.

Haber, Susan. "Going Up to Jerusalem: Pilgrimage, Purity, and the Historical Jesus." Pages 49–67 in *Travel and Religion in Antiquity*. Edited by Philip Harland. Studies in Christianity and Judaism/Études sur le christianisme et le judaïsme 21. Waterloo: Wilfrid Laurier University Press, 2011.

Hartin, Patrick J. *James and the Q-Sayings of Jesus*. JSNTSup 47. Sheffield: Sheffield Academic, 1991.

Hartog, Pieter B. "Space and Travel in Philo's *Legatio ad Gaium*." *SPhiloA* 30 (2018): 71–92.

Hartog, Pieter B. "Jubilees and Hellenistic Encyclopaedism." *JSJ* 50 (2019): 1–25.
Hartog, Pieter B. "Contesting *Oikoumenē*: Resistance and Locality in Philo's *Legatio ad Gaium*." Pages 205–231 in *Intolerance, Polemics, and Debate in Antiquity. Politico-Cultural, Philosophical, and Religious Forms of Critical Conversation*. Edited by George van Kooten and Jacques van Ruiten. TBN 25. Leiden: Brill, 2019.
Hartog, Peter B. "Reading Acts in Motion: Movement and Glocalisation in the Acts of the Apostles." Pages 96–110 in *Mediterranean Flows: People, Ideas and Objects in Motion*. Edited by Anna Usacheva and Emilia Mataix Ferrándiz. Contexts of Ancient and Medieval Anthropology 3. Leiden: Brill Schöningh, 2023.
Hengel, Martin, and Anna Maria Schwemer. *Paulus zwischen Damaskus und Antiochien: Die unbekannten Jahre des Apostels*. WUNT 108. Tübingen: Mohr Siebeck, 1998.
Hezser, Catherine. *Jewish Travel in Antiquity*. TSAJ 144. Tübingen: Mohr Siebeck, 2011.
Hirth, Kenn. *The Organization of Ancient Economies: A Global Perspective*. Cambridge: Cambridge University Press, 2020.
Hodos, Tamar. "Globalization: Some Basics: An Introduction to The Routledge Handbook of Archaeology and Globalization." Pages 3–11 in *The Routledge Handbook of Archaeology and Globalization*. Edited by Tamar Hodos. London: Routledge, 2017.
Jäger, Siegfried. *Kritische Diskursanalyse: Eine Einführung*. 6th ed. Münster: Unrast, 2012.
Jennings, Justin. *Globalizations and the Ancient World*. Cambridge: Cambridge University Press, 2011.
Jennings, Justin. "Distinguishing Past Gobalizations." Pages 12–28 in *The Routledge Handbook of Archaeology and Globalization*. Edited by Tamar Hodos. London: Routledge, 2017.
Jonge, Casper C. de. "Greek Migrant Literature in the Early Roman Empire." *Mnemosyne* 75 (2022): 10–36.
Klinghardt, Matthias. "Wie und warum ist der Jakobusbrief ins Neue Testament gekommen? Der Jakobusbrief als kanonisches Pseudepigraph." *ZNT* 50 (2022): 85–95.
Kloppenborg, John S. "Diaspora Discourse: The Construction of Ethos in James." *NTS* 53 (2007): 242–70.
Konradt, Matthias. *Christliche Existenz nach dem Jakobusbrief: Eine Studie zu seiner soteriologischen und ethischen Konzeption*. StUNT 22. Göttingen: Vandenhoeck & Ruprecht, 1998.
Konradt, Matthias. "Der Jakobusbrief im frühchristlichen Kontext: Überlegungen zum traditionsgeschichtlichen Verhältnis des Jakobusbriefes zur Jesusüberlieferung, zur paulinischen Tradition und zum 1Petr." Pages 171–212 in *The Catholic Epistles and the Tradition*. Edited by Jacques Schlosser. BETL 176. Leuven: Peeters, 2004.
Landwehr, Achim. *Historische Diskursanalyse*. 2nd ed. Historische Einführungen 4. Frankfurt: Campus, 2009.
Luther, Susanne. *Sprachethik im Neuen Testament: Analyse des frühchristlichen Diskurses im Matthäusevangelium, im Jakobusbrief und im 1Petrusbrief*. WUNT 2/394. Tübingen: Mohr Siebeck, 2015.
Luther, Susanne. "Von Feigenbäumen und Oliven: Die Rezeption, Transformation und Kreation sprachethischer Traditionen im Jakobusbrief." *Annali di Storia dell'Esegesi* 34 (2017): 381–401.
Luther, Susanne. "Strategies of Authorizing Tradition in the Letter of James." Pages 209–23 in *Authoritative Writings in Early Judaism and Early Christianity: Their Origin, Collection and Meaning*. Edited by Tobias Nicklas and Jens Schröter. WUNT 441. Tübingen: Mohr Siebeck, 2020.
Luther, Susanne. "Profiling the Author of the Letter of James: Dealing with Traditions in the Light of Epistolary Authorship Conceptions." Pages 29–55 in *Who was James? Essays on the Letter's Authorship and Provenance*. Edited by Eve-Marie Becker, Sigurvin Lárus Jónsson and Susanne Luther. WUNT 485. Tübingen: Mohr Siebeck, 2022.

Männlein-Robert, Irmgard. "Move Your Self: Mobility and Migration of Greek Intellectuals to Rome." Pages 331–52 in *Self, Self-Fashioning, and Individuality in Late Antiquity New Perspectives*. Edited by Maren R. Niehoff and Joshua Levinson. Tübingen: Mohr Siebeck, 2019.

McCready, Wayne O. "Pilgrimage, Place, and Meaning Making by Jews in Greco-Roman Egypt." Pages 69–81 in *Travel and Religion in Antiquity*. Edited by Philip Harland. Studies in Christianity and Judaism/Études sur le christianisme et le judaïsme 21. Waterloo: Wilfrid Laurier University Press, 2011.

Metzner, Rainer. *Der Brief des Jakobus*. ThHKNT 14. Leipzig: Evangelische Verlagsanstalt, 2017.

Moffatt, James. *The General Epistles James, Peter, and Judas*. MNTC. 7th ed. London: Hodder & Stoughton, 1953.

Morley, Neville. "Globalisation and the Roman Economy." Pages 49–68 in *Globalisation and the Roman World: World History, Connectivity and Material Culture*. Edited by Martin Pitts and Miguel John Versluys. Cambridge: Cambridge University Press, 2014.

Muir, Steven. "Religion on the Road in Ancient Greece and Rome." Pages 29–47 in *Travel and Religion in Antiquity*. Edited by Philip Harland. Studies in Christianity and Judaism/Études sur le christianisme et le judaïsme 21. Waterloo: Wilfrid Laurier University Press, 2011.

Nasrallah, Laura. "Imposing Travellers: An Inscription from Galatia and the Journeys of the Earliest Christians." Pages 273–96 in *Journeys in the Roman East: Imagined and Real*. Edited by Maren R. Niehoff. Culture, Religion, and Politics in the Greco-Roman World 1. Tübingen: Mohr Siebeck, 2017.

Nederveen Pieterse, Jan. "Ancient Rome and Globalisation: Decentring Rome." Pages 225–39 in *Globalisation and the Roman World: World History, Connectivity and Material Culture*. Edited by Martin Pitts and Miguel John Versluys. Cambridge: Cambridge University Press, 2014.

Nederveen Pieterse, Jan. *Ethnicities and Global Multiculture: Pants for an Octopus*. Lanham: Rowman & Littlefield, 2007.

Nederveen Pieterse, Jan. *Globalization and Culture: Global Mélange*. 2nd ed. Lanham: Rowman and Littlefield, 2009.

Niebuhr, Karl-Wilhelm. "Der Jakobusbrief im Licht frühjüdischer Diasporabriefe." *NTS* 44 (1998): 420–43.

Niehoff, Maren R. "The Implied Audience of the Letter of James." Pages 57–77 in *New Approaches to the Study of Biblical Interpretation in Judaism of the Second Temple Period and in Early Christianity*. Edited by Gary A. Anderson, Ruth A. Clements, and David Satran. STDJ 106. Leiden: Brill, 2013.

Niehoff, Maren R. "Wie wird man ein mediterraner Denker? Der Fall Philon von Alexandria." Pages 355–367 in *Ein pluriverses Universum. Zivilisationen und Religionen im antiken Mittelmeerraum*. Edited by Richard Faber and Achim Lichtenberger. Mittelmeerstudien 7. Paderborn: Schöningh, 2015.

Niehoff, Maren R. "Parodies of Educational Journeys in Josephus, Justin Martyr, and Lucian." Pages 203–24 in *Journeys in the Roman East: Imagined and Real*. Edited by Maren R. Niehoff. Culture, Religion, and Politics in the Greco-Roman World 1. Tübingen: Mohr Siebeck, 2017.

Pietersma, Albert and Benjamin G. Wright, eds. *A New English Translation of the Septuagint*. Oxford: Oxford University Press, 2007.

Pitts, Martin and Miguel John Versluys. "Globalisation and the Roman World: Perspectives and Opportunities." Pages 3–31 in *Globalisation and the Roman World: World History, Connectivity and Material Culture*. Edited by Martin Pitts and Miguel John Versluys. Cambridge: Cambridge University Press, 2014.

Pitts, Martin. "Globalisation, Circulation and Mass Consumption in the Roman World." Pages 69–98 in *Globalisation and the Roman World: World History, Connectivity and Material Culture*. Edited by Martin Pitts and Miguel John Versluys. Cambridge: Cambridge University Press, 2014.

Popkes, Wiard. *Der Brief des Jakobus*. ThHKNT 14. Leipzig: Evangelische Verlagsanstalt, 2001.
Pretzler, Marie. "Greek Intellecutals on the Move: Travel and Paideia in the Roman Empire." Pages 123–38 in *Travel, Geography and Culture in Ancient Greece, Egypt and the Near East*. Edited by Colin Adams and Jim Roy. Oxford: Oxbow, 2007.
Sandt, Huub van de, and Jürgen K. Zangenberg, eds. *Matthew, James, and Didache: Three Related Documents in Their Jewish and Christian Settings*. SymS 45. Atlanta: Society of Biblical Literature, 2008.
Sandt, Huub van de and Jürgen K. Zangenberg. "Introduction." Pages 1–9 in *Matthew, James, and Didache: Three Related Documents in Their Jewish and Christian Settings*. Edited by Huub van de Sandt and Jürgen K. Zangenberg. SymS 45. Atlanta: Society of Biblical Literature, 2008.
Schellenberg, Ryan S. "'Danger in the Wilderness, Danger at Sea': Paul and the Perils of Travel." Pages 141–61 in *Travel and Religion in Antiquity*. Edited by Philip Harland. Studies in Christianity and Judaism/Études sur le christianisme et le judaïsme 21. Waterloo: Wilfrid Laurier University Press, 2011.
Schliesser, Benjamin, Jan Rüggemeier, Thomas J. Kraus and Jörg Frey, with the assistance of Daniel Herrmann, eds. *Alexandria: Hub of the Hellenistic World*. WUNT 460. Tübingen: Mohr Siebeck, 2021.
Schnelle, Udo. *Einleitung in das Neue Testament*. 8th ed. Göttingen: Vandenhoeck & Ruprecht, 2013.
Schnider, Franz. *Der Jakobusbrief*. RNT. Regensburg: Pustet, 1987.
Schuster, Angela M.H. "Antioch in Antiquity." *Archaeology* 53/6 (2000): 69–70.
Shepherd, Massey H. "The Epistle of James and the Gospel of Matthew." *JBL* 75 (1956): 40–51.
Sim, David C. "Reconstructing the Social and Religious Milieu of Matthew: Methods, Sources, and Possible Results." Pages 13–32 in *Matthew, James, and Didache: Three Related Documents in Their Jewish and Christian Settings*. Edited by Huub van de Sandt and Jürgen K. Zangenberg. SymS 45. Atlanta: Society of Biblical Literature, 2008.
Slee, Michelle. *The Church in Antioch in the First Century CE: Communion and Conflict*. LNTS 244. London: Sheffield Academic Press, 2003.
Sommer, Michael. "OIKOYMENH: Longue Durée Perspectives on Ancient Mediterranean 'Globality'." Pages 175–97 in *Globalisation and the Roman World: World History, Connectivity and Material Culture*. Edited by Martin Pitts and Miguel John Versluys. Cambridge: Cambridge University Press, 2014.
Theissen, Gerd. "Weisheit als Mittel sozialer Abgrenzung und Öffnung: Beobachtungen zur sozialen Funktion frühjüdischer und urchristlicher Weisheit." Pages 193–203 in *Weisheit*. Edited by Aleida Assmann. ALK 3. München: Fink, 1991.
Tomlinson, John. *Globalization and Culture*. Chicago: University of Chicago Press, 1999.
Ueberschaer, Frank. *Weisheit aus der Begegnung: Bildung nach dem Buch Ben Sira*. BZNW 379. Berlin: De Gruyter, 2007.
Uusimäki, Elisa. "The Formation of a Sage according to Ben Sira." Pages 59–69 in *Second Temple Jewish 'Paideia' in Context*. Edited by Jason M. Zurawski and Gabriele Boccaccini. BZNW 228. Berlin: De Gruyter, 2017.
Uusimäki, Elisa. "The Rise of the Sage in Greek and Jewish Antiquity." *JSJ* 49 (2018): 1–29.
Uusimäki, Elisa. "Itinerant Sages: The Evidence of Sirach in its Ancient Mediterranean Context." *JSOT* 44 (2020): 315–36.
Versluys, Miguel John. "Roman Visual Material Culture as Globalising *Koine*." Pages 141–74 in *Globalisation and the Roman World: World History, Connectivity and Material Culture*. Edited by Martin Pitts and Miguel John Versluys. Cambridge: Cambridge University Press, 2014.
Wischmeyer, Oda. "Reconstructing the Social and Religious Milieu of James: Methods, Sources, Possible Results." Pages 33–41 in *Matthew, James, and Didache: Three Related Documents in their Jewish and Christian Settings*. Edited by Huub van de Sandt and Jürgen K. Zangenberg. SymS 45. Atlanta: Society of Biblical Literature, 2008.

Witcher, Robert. "The Globalized Roman World." Pages 634–51 in *The Routledge Handbook of Archaeology and Globalization*. Edited by Tamar Hodos. London: Routledge, 2017.

Zangenberg, Jürgen K. "Matthew and James." Pages 104–22 in *Matthew and his Christian Contemporaries*. Edited by David C. Sim. London: T&T Clark, 2008.

Zangenberg, Jürgen K. "Reconstructing the Social and Religious Milieu of the Didache: Observations and Possible Results." Pages 43–69 in *Matthew, James, and Didache: Three Related Documents in Their Jewish and Christian Settings*. Edited by Huub van de Sandt and Jürgen K. Zangenberg. SymS 45. Atlanta: Society of Biblical Literature, 2008.

Zapff, Burkard M. "Normenbegründung vor gewandeltem Hintergrund: Jesus Sirach als Vermittler zwischen traditionellem jüdischen Glauben und hellenistischem Geist." Pages 25–40 in *Athen, Rom, Jerusalem: Normentransfers in der antiken Welt*. Edited by Gian Franco Chiai. Eichstätter Studien Neue Folge 66. Regensburg: Pustet, 2012.

Zetterholm, Magnus. *The Formation of Christianity in Antioch: A Social-Scientific Approach to the Separation between Judaism and Christianity*. London: Routledge, 2003.

Zetterholm, Magnus. "The Didache, Matthew, James—and Paul: Reconstructing Historical Developments in Antioch." Pages 73–90 in *Matthew, James, and Didache: Three Related Documents in Their Jewish and Christian Settings*. Edited by Huub van de Sandt and Jürgen K. Zangenberg. SymS 45. Atlanta: Society of Biblical Literature, 2008.

Theo Witkamp and Jan Krans

Heavenly Journey and Divine Epistemology in the Fourth Gospel

Abstract: The Fourth Gospel has two travel scenarios, one mundane or earthly, the other heavenly or spiritual. On the earthly level Jesus travels from and to Jerusalem, on the spiritual level he travels from and to heaven. The first level is real, but the second level shows us what really is at stake. What is more, the mundane is there not for its own sake, but in order to direct us towards the heavenly spheres. The dialogue with Nicodemus (John 3) is crucial in this respect. Here it becomes clear that the way in which Jesus is depicted as a traveler from and to heaven, as the one who is sent by the Father and who will return to his Father, is closely intertwined with the question of epistemology. In other words, here we see what it means that "no one has ever seen God" and that "the only son has made him known" (John 1:18). We analyze the logic of the dialogue and its background in (mostly) Jewish apocalypticism. This results in a "thick" interpretation of the words "no one has ascended into heaven" (John 3:13) and what these imply for claims to spiritual knowledge. It is argued that the dialogue with Nicodemus centers around such claims. What is more, the theme runs through the gospel as a whole. The implications for Johannine sectarianism and the didactic outlook of the Fourth Gospel are discussed in the final section of the paper.

Travel Images

The focus in this chapter is not on literal, but on spiritual traveling. Our main source is the gospel of John. We shall speak of heavenly journeying and study its connections to Johannine epistemology. In the case of the Fourth Gospel this means that we should without further ado start in heaven. This is where the story begins, "in the beginning." It is the place where the λόγος is, from where he descends to earth and to which he returns at the end of his career (John 1:1–18; 13:1, 3; 20:17). In other words, we encounter the descent/ascent pattern of Johannine Christology. The Logos, who was with God in the beginning, descends from on high, becomes flesh as the man Jesus and lives on earth in order to accomplish the works of God, his Father. He leaves when the work is finished and he returns to his sender. This travel motif with its descent/ascent pattern is fundamental and can be seen as the backbone of the Johannine messenger Christology, as has often been recognized.[1]

It is remarkable, though, that neither the descent nor the ascent itself is part of John's narrative. The descent of the logos is declared, not narrated. We also do not have a story of Jesus' ascension, comparable to, e.g., Luke 24 or Acts 1. The last reference to Jesus' ascension is the cryptic remark to Mary Magdalene in John 20:17: "Do not hold on to me, because I have not yet ascended to the Father. But go to my brothers and say to them, 'I am ascending to my Father and your Father, to my God and your God'."[2] But we do not hear anything about the heavenly journey itself and how it happened. A description of what is to be seen in heaven, such as we encounter in the visions of Isaiah 6, Ezekiel 1, Daniel 7–8, and so often in the Old Testament Pseudepigrapha or in the book of Revelation, with their myriads of angels and their heavenly liturgy, is also completely lacking. We read only about the "that" of the descent and the ascension and nothing about the "how" and the "what."

Besides the spiritual journey there is also a mundane travel scenario. The Johannine Jesus does not only travel from heaven to earth and back again, he also travels quite much on earth. Most of all he goes to Jerusalem to attend one of the Jewish festivals (three Passovers and two other festivals are mentioned),[3] or he leaves Jerusalem and Judea again, often (but not always) because of the hostilities he encounters there. His usual destination in this case is Galilee,[4] but after John 7:10 he remains somewhere in Judea or Jerusalem.[5] The verb which is used for his travel to Jerusalem, is ἀναβαίνειν ("to go up, to ascent"; see John 2:13; 5:1; 7:8, 10, 14; 11:55; 12:20 [other literal uses in John 10:1 and 21:11 "to climb"]). It fits the geographic situation of Jerusalem: one has to go up to get there. Jerusalem is more than geography, however. It is the holy city. To travel to Jerusalem is to travel to the sanctuary, the temple, where the presence of God abides. Jerusalem is also the center of the Jewish nation, the hometown of the people of God, the πατρίς, the place of origin for everybody who wants to regard himself a member of the chosen people (John 4:20, 22, 44).[6] John is very much aware of this. But he accepts it only to oppose it. The Johannine Jesus consistently acts in such a way and says such things

---

[1] Cf. e.g., the opening paragraph of Wayne A. Meeks, "The Man from Heaven in Johannine Sectarianism," *JBL* 91 (1972): 44–72.
[2] Bible translations are taken from the *New Revised Standard Version*.
[3] John 2:13; 5:1; 7:2, 8, 10, 14; 11:55; 12:12.
[4] John 2:1, 12; 4:3, 46, 54; 6:1; 7:1, but 3:22 mentions "the Judean countryside."
[5] Jesus is in Judea, but outside Jerusalem in John 10:40 "across the Jordan to the place where John had been baptizing earlier"; John 11:1, 15 "Bethany"; and John 11:54 "a town called Ephraim in the region near the wilderness."
[6] Cf. Wayne A. Meeks, "Galilee and Judea in the Fourth Gospel," *JBL* 85 (1966): 159–69 who argues cogently that for John Jerusalem is the true πατρίς of the Messiah. C.H. Dodd, *Historical Tradition*

that Jerusalem with its temple loses its religious importance. The point John wants to make is that with the coming of Jesus the role of the temple has been superseded. The locus of God's presence is not to be found in the literal Jewish temple anymore, but in the body of Jesus, the place where the logos found an abode (ἐσκήνωσεν, John 1:14) and which can also be called a temple itself (ναός, John 2:21; 4:21, 23; cf. John 1:51; 14:6 etc.). Time and again Jesus speaks words at the festivals which show that the real meaning of Passover (John 2:13 etc.), Tabernacles/Booths (John 7:2), or Dedication (John 10:22) is to be found in him and not elsewhere. He is the lamb, the light, the one who is sanctified, just as it is he who is the manna, the real bread from heaven which God gives (John 6:32–35).[7] The implication is that from now on one's religious identity is not determined by one's loyalty to Jerusalem, the law, or the temple anymore but by one's loyalty to, or belief in, Jesus, the Messiah, the Son of Man, the Son of God.

This means that geography and theology are closely linked. We can even see a symbolic interplay between the literal and the spiritual journey in Jesus' going up to Jerusalem and his going up to heaven, which is Jesus' final destiny. The same verb ἀναβαίνειν can be used for both and John 7:8 gives a hint that there is a word play on these to different meanings of the verb. Here Jesus says: "I am not going up to this feast, for my time has not yet fully come." He means that he will not yet go up now, but only at the time of the Pesach of his death, as the perceptive reader of the gospel knows (cf. John 12:55 *et seq*.). And then it will be much more than a going up to Jerusalem, it will be Jesus' ascent to heaven, when he really "goes up" (John 3:13; 6:62; 20:17; cf. 1:51) and "returns" to his Father's house (John 13:1–3 etc.).[8] The riddles later on in John 7–8 confirm the double meaning: Jesus' interlocutors are not able to understand what he means by "going away" and are only able to hear in it a crude, literal sense, which results in curious misunderstandings (John 7:33–36; 8:21–22) from which no advance is possible for them (cf. John 8:21, 43; 12:39 οὐ

---

in the Fourth Gospel (Cambridge: Cambridge University Press, 1963), 240 saw this possibility, but remained undecided.

7 In the same sense the role of Torah has been changed from "giver of life" to "witness to Jesus who gives real life" (John 5:39, cf. John 1:17), cf. Severino Pancaro, *The Law in the Fourth Gospel*, NovTSup 42 (Leiden: Brill, 1975).

8 That is why there is only a superficial contradiction between John 7:8 ("I am not going") and 10 ("he also went"). Its goal is to challenge the reader to probe deeper. The same kind of wordplay can be seen with regard to ὑπάγειν, "to leave," cf. John Ashton, *Understanding the Fourth Gospel*, 2nd ed. (Oxford: Oxford University Press, 2007), 132. To be sure, John can use different verbs for this "going away" or "leaving" (cf. John 13:1–3: μεταβαίνειν, ὑπάγειν; 17:11, 13 ἔρχεσθαι; also in the literal sense of going to Judea or Jerusalem as in John 7:33 or 12:12), so it is not the verb per se which is important to him, but its semantic possibilities.

δύνασθε). Readers of the gospel, however, are supposed to be in the privileged position of potential comprehension.[9]

Nevertheless, John's Gospel can hardly be called a travel narrative: it is not traveling as such which is important to him, but location, i.e., location in its spiritual sense. Just as Jerusalem is the location of the house of God, so Jesus is the location of the presence of God and heaven is the location of God himself. It is important to get there (John 14:2) and to know how to get there (John 14:6), just as it is important to know where one's origins are (e.g., John 6:42; 8:14). As we said before, the κατάβασις and the ἀνάβασις of Jesus are not part of John's narrative. After the stage setting in the prologue, they are only mentioned in the discourses. But here they are repeatedly referred to and here they receive their real meaning. All of this means that the travel accounts function within the broader scope of spiritual epistemology and not the other way round. Jesus has seen what the truth is and he can testify to the truth because of what he has seen. He is a traveler from above, a divine messenger. The first time Jesus' ἀνάβασις in the sense of "going up to heaven" is mentioned is in John 3:13 and this is an excellent place to get to the heart of the matter, because here we will see how much this talking about descent and ascent has to do with epistemology.

Divine Epistemology

John 3 contains the famous and difficult conversation between Jesus and Nicodemus.[10] We will start in verse 13 and work our way back to the beginning. In this verse Jesus utters a striking claim: "No one has ascended into heaven except the one who descended from heaven, the Son of Man." Adele Reinhartz, who commented on the gospel of John in *The Jewish Annotated New Testament*, rightly remarked that this statement "seems to ignore Enoch (Gen 5:22, 24) and Elijah (2 Kings 2:11), both of whom were taken up to heaven instead of undergoing death."[11] She could have added that it also seems to contradict other stories of heavenly voyages of Abraham, Levi, Isaiah and others, such as we can find in a number of Jewish apocalypses.[12]

---

9 Cf. Ashton, *Understanding*, 130–33 on the Johannine riddle.
10 Cf. Ashton, *Understanding*, 277–80, who feels the need for an excursus on the structure of John 3: "The sequence of thought in John 3 is notoriously hard to follow" (277). He himself does not see the epistemological issue at hand clearly enough in our eyes, however.
11 Amy-Jill Levine and Marc Zvi Brettler, eds., *The Jewish Annotated New Testament* (Oxford: Oxford University Press, 2011), 164.
12 Cf. 1 En. 1–36; 37–71; 2 Enoch; Testament of Levi 2–5; 3 Baruch; Ascension of Isaiah; Apocalypse of Abraham; Apocalypse of Zephaniah; Testament of Abraham and the author of the self-glorification

From a Johannine point of view the most important among them is the figure of Moses, who, according to many sources, ascended to heaven at the time he went up to God on Mount Sinai.[13] This means that the Johannine Jesus makes an exclusive claim: only one has ascended to heaven and nobody else, not even Moses.

John 1:18, "No one has ever seen God," should be understood in the same vein, i.e., with a polemical twist, because heavenly ascent often entailed a vision of God in Jewish tradition (cf. also John 6:46 and 14:9). In the longer version of the Hellenistic Jewish *Orphica*, for instance, we read that God is not to be seen by mortal eyes (20–24), which is common Jewish knowledge at the time.[14] The *Orphica* continues: "And no one has seen the ruler of mortal men, except a certain unique man" (i.e., Moses).[15] In Philo, too, Moses is granted a vision of God, or, rather, not the Existent (ὁ ὤν) himself, but the Image, the Logos.[16] Even within the Tenach itself the words from Exod 33:20 ("no one shall see me and live") are not as unequivocal as they

---

hymn from the Qumran (4Q491: "none shall be exalted save me"). Cf. Peter Schäfer, *The Origins of Jewish Mysticism* [Tübingen: Mohr Siebeck, 2007], 146–51).

13 Invoked by Exod 19:3, 20-25; 34:2, 28, 29–35; cf. Exod 20:21. See, e.g., Ezek. Trag. 68–81 (where Moses is even invited by God himself to mount his throne, be it only in his dream). For Philo, Moses's going up at Mount Sinai and his entering into the "darkness where God was" (Exod 20:21) was "an ethereal and heavenly journey" (*QE* 2.44), "a proleptic experience of deification," as M. David Litwa says ("The Deification of Moses in Philo of Alexandria," *SPhiloA* 26 [2014]: 1–27 [14]; more references can be found here). From later time, 3 En. 15B:2 "When Moses ascended to the height ... the dwellings of the *ḥašmal* (i.e., the innermost of the celestial palaces) were opened to him" (trans. Philip Alexander, "3 (Hebrew Apocalypse of) Enoch," in *The Old Testament Pseudepigrapha*, ed. James H. Charlesworth, 2 vols. [New Haven: Yale University Press, 1983; repr., Peabody: Hendrickson, ²2011], 1:223–15 [303]). See further Peder Borgen, "Some Jewish Exegetical Traditions as Background for Son of Man Sayings in John's Gospel (John 3,13-14 and context)," in *L'Évangile de Jean: Sources, rédaction, théologie*, ed. Marinus de Jonge, BETL 44 (Gembloux: Leuven University Press, 1977), 243–58 and Abraham J. Heschel, *Heavenly Torah: As Refracted through the Generations*, ed. and trans. Gordon Tucker (New York: Continuum, 2005), 341–57 (with many rabbinic references and discussions on the theme) who traces the origin of this tradition to apocalyptic literature.

14 In his introduction to *The Old Testament Pseudepigrapha*, Charlesworth draws attention to the fact that after the exile God's transcendence is the default modus: "God is usually seen as one who is above ... far removed from the earth" and mostly acts only through intermediaries (James H. Charlesworth, "Introduction for the General Reader," in Charlesworth, *Old Testament Pseudepigrapha*, 1:xxi–xxxiv [xxxi]).

15 Trans. Michael Lafargue, "Orphica," in *The Old Testament Pseudepigrapha*, ed. James H. Charlesworth, 2 vols. (New Haven: Yale University Press, 1983; repr., Peabody: Hendrickson, ²2011), 2:795–801 (799), who thinks of a heavenly ascent of Moses (Lafargue, "Orphica," 797, 799). The *Orphica*'s shorter version does not mention Moses' special position (see Lafargue, "Orphica," 800–801).

16 E.g., Litwa, "Deification," 17–18 mentions Philo, *Post.* 13–16, *Leg.* 97–103, *Conf.* 95–97, and *Mos.* 2.71. More can be found in Scott D. Mackie, "Seeing God in Philo of Alexandria: The Logos, the Powers, or the Existent One?" *SPhiloA* 21 (2009): 25–47 and Scott D. Mackie, "Seeing God in Philo of Alexandria: Means, Methods, and Mysticism," *JJS* 43 (2012): 147–79.

often seem to be. Num 12:8 ("with him [=Moses] I speak face to face") gives another impression already.[17] But the explicit vision of God in Isa 6:1–5; Ezek 1:26–28[18] and Dan 7:9–10 certainly contradict Exod 33:20. Traditions about the legendary Enoch and some other pseudepigrapha testify to the same phenomenon in a heightened fashion.[19]

---

[17] Ps.-Philo, LAB 11:4 seems to contradict Exod 33:20 right away, on the basis of Num 12:8, when the author recounts that at the occasion of the giving of the Law at the mountain (cf. Exodus 20) the people said to Moses: "Do not let God speak to us lest perhaps we die. For behold today we know that God speaks to a man face to face *and that man may live*" (our italics, trans. Daniel J. Harrington, "Pseudo-Philo," in *The Old Testament Pseudepigrapha*, ed. James H. Charlesworth, 2 vols. [New Haven: Yale University Press, 1983; repr., Peabody: Hendrickson, ²2011], 2:297–377 [319]).

[18] With its very circumspect language, cf. Schäfer, *Origins*, 34–52.

[19] In 1 Enoch 17–19 we read how Enoch is "lifted up" and receives visions of the secrets of heaven and earth: "I, Enoch, I saw the vison of the end of everything alone; and none among human beings will see as I have seen" (1 En. 19:3). According to the opening section of the Similitudes, Enoch receives even more astounding privileges: "I am one who has seen the face of the Lord ... I have gazed into the eyes of the Lord ... I have seen the right hand of the Lord ... I have seen the scope of the Lord ... I have heard the Lord speaking" (1 En. 39:5–6). And in 1 En. 71:1 we are told how Enoch "ascended into the heavens" and is shown all the secrets. In "the heaven of heavens" (1 En. 91:5) he even saw "the Antecedent of Time: his head is white and pure like wool and his garment is indescribable" (1 En. 91:10, trans. Ephraim Isaac, "1 [Ethiopic Apocalypse of] Enoch," in *The Old Testament Pseudepigrapha*, ed. James H. Charlesworth, 2 vols. [New Haven: Yale University Press, 1983; repr., Peabody: Hendrickson, ²2011], 1:5–90). The same note is struck in 2 Enoch. According to 2 En. 22:1–6 rec. J, Enoch is allowed to see "the view of the face of the Lord" and to stand in front of his face forever (trans. Frances I. Andersen, "2 [Slavonic Apocalypse of] Enoch," in *The Old Testament Pseudepigrapha*, ed. James H. Charlesworth, 2 vols. [New Haven: Yale University Press, 1983; repr., Peabody: Hendrickson, ²2011], 1:91–221 [136–38]). Schäfer, *Origins*, 81, aptly concludes that this means that he "is greater than Moses." Cf. also Test. Levi 5:1: "I saw the holy Temple and the Most High upon a throne of glory" (trans. Schäfer, *Origins*, 70 [Howard C. Kee, "Testaments of the Twelve Patriarchs," in *The Old Testament Pseudepigrapha*, ed. James H. Charlesworth, 2 vols. (New Haven: Yale University Press, 1983; repr., Peabody: Hendrickson, ²2011), 1:775–828 (789) differs], who stresses that neither in Ezekiel or in Henoch, nor here the vision of God "is the primary goal ... but the message conveyed by God during the vision"). In Mart. Ascen. Isa. 9:37–38, we read that the prophet is taken up into the seventh heaven in a vision and saw "the Great Glory" (trans. Michael A. Knibb, "Martyrdom and Ascension of Isaiah," in *The Old Testament Pseudepigrapha*, ed. James H. Charlesworth, 2 vols. [New Haven: Yale University Press, 1983; repr., Peabody: Hendrickson, ²2011], 2:143–76 [172], cf. Schäfer, *Origins*, 97–99). But it also says that Isaiah is (falsely) accused of having said: "'I see more than Moses the prophet.' Moses said, 'There is no man who can see the Lord and live.' But Isaiah has said, 'I have seen the Lord, and behold I am alive.'" (Mart. Ascen. Isa. 3:8–9; Knibb, "Martyrdom and Ascension of Isaiah," 160). E.g., Apoc. Ab. 16 is more restrained: "You (Abraham) will not look at him (the Eternal One) himself" (trans. Ryszard Rubinkiewicz, "Apocalypse of Abraham," in *The Old Testament Pseudepigrapha*, ed. James H. Charlesworth, 2 vols. [New Haven: Yale University Press, 1983; repr., Peabody: Hendrickson, ²2011], 1:681–705 [696]).

This means that John seems to contradict vehemently certain (apocalyptic) traditions about ascending to heaven and seeing God, especially with regard to Moses, even when they originated from within Scripture itself. As a matter of fact, he does not only contradict them, he is also is able to incorporate (some of) them by reinterpreting them. We see this happen when he quotes directly from the relevant chapter Isaiah 6 and mentions the vision the prophet has had. He admits that Isaiah had a vision of the divine, but, says John, "he saw *his* glory and spoke about *him*" (John 12:41), i.e., he saw Jesus, the Messiah, the Son of God, the Light (John 12:34–36). This can only mean that Isaiah did not only foresee Christ's future, but that he also had experienced a vision of the preexistent Christ, just as Abraham before him had seen him, as Jesus had said in John 8:56–58 ("before Abraham was, I am").[20]

We should add that not only Jewish, but non-Jewish ascension traditions, too, are ruled out by the apodictic wording of John 3:13. Alan Segal showed how pervasive and how variegated these traditions were in the Greco-Roman world. He also showed how much they had to do with different forms of post-mortem ascent in astral journeys and with ruler cults.[21] He mentions, e.g., Hercules, Castor and Pollux, and Aridaeus/Thespesius (from Plutarch's *Moralia*), but also the "The dream of Scipio" in Cic., *Rep.* 6.9–26, which speaks of the ascension of the souls of the rulers. Apart from the story of the ascension of Romulus, he draws attention to Vergil's famous "Fourth Eclogue," which knows a complete ascent-descent mythology ("a new offspring is sent down from heaven"). It is a telling piece of evidence for the cult of the emperor which becomes more important with the death of Julius Caesar and the rise of Augustus.[22] Segal also reminds us of a fragment at the beginning of Parmenides' epic poem where it is told how the philosopher is carried away by "immortal charioteers" in order to learn "all things," which provides his philosophy with "the authority of a revelation."[23] This quotation reminds us that the whole idea of a heavenly ascent should be seen in relation to the question where people receive

---

20 On John's use of Isaiah see now the insightful article from Catrin H. Williams, "Johannine Christology and Prophetic Traditions: The Case of Isaiah," in *Reading the Gospel of John's Christology as Jewish Messianism: Royal, Prophetic, and Divine Messiahs*, ed. Benjamin E. Reynolds and Gabriele Boccaccini, AGJU 106 (Leiden: Brill, 2018), 92–123.
21 Alan F. Segal, "Heavenly Ascent in Hellenistic Judaism, Early Christianity and their Environment," *ANRW* 2.23.2 (1980): 1333–94. The examples are taken from this article.
22 Roman ideas on deification of the ruler are part of the religious history of the Mediterranean as a whole, of course, as can be seen, e.g., by Isaiah's prophecy on the king of Babylon: "You said in your heart: I will ascend to heaven; I will raise my throne above the stars of God; I will sit on the mount of assembly on the heights of Za'phon . . . I will make myself like the Most High." The point being made here is that the deified king must die like any other human being: "But you are brought down to She'ol, to the depths of the Pit" (Isa 14:13–15). He is nothing but ordinary flesh and blood.
23 Segal, "Heavenly Ascent," 1344.

knowledge, both the knowledge to rule as a king, and the comprehensive knowledge of the secrets of heaven and earth.

Interestingly, the Johannine Jesus seems not to be interested in the possibility of a heavenly journey as such. He grants that it is possible, but that only one is capable of having really done it.[24] The pivotal issue, however, is about knowledge. The question at stake, as the preceding verse makes clear, is: Who has knowledge of the heavenly things? In verse 10 Nicodemus is reproached because he, a teacher of Israel, God's chosen people, is without understanding: he only knows earthly things, but is ignorant of spiritual realities. Jesus, on the other hand, claims, "we know" what we are talking about, "we have seen" (John 3:11), which implies that he has knowledge of the heavenly things (τὰ ἐπουράνια, John 3:12)[25], that is: he and the Spirit, and nobody else.[26] The mentioning of the title of Son of Man in John 3:13 underscores his authority in dealing with these heavenly issues.[27]

---

[24] There is an old problem with the form ἀναβέβηκεν in John 3:13, because the perfect tense would imply that there has been an ascension of Jesus *prior* to his descent from heaven. This problem has found many intriguing and ingenious answers, such as from Peder Borgen, "Some Jewish Exegetical Traditions" (ascent means enthronement before descent to earth) or, to our knowledge, the latest one from John Ashton, "The Johannine Son of Man: A New Proposal," *NTS* 57 (2011): 508–29 (the merging of two traditions of heavenly voyages in this single verse: one angelic, starting in heaven, concerned with the emissary, the Son of God; one mystical, starting from earth, concerned with the Son of Man; cf. already his *Understanding the Fourth Gospel*, 251–59). The discussion might in the end be unsubstantial, however; that is to say, when Madison N. Pierce and Benjamin R. Reynolds, "The Perfect Tense-Form and the Son of Man in John 3.13: Developments in Greek Grammar as a Viable Solution to the Timing of the Ascent and Descent," *NTS* 60 (2014): 149–55, are right that "time value is *not* the primary feature of the verbal form" (153) but "aspect, which is the author's viewpoint of the action" (152–53). According to this view, ἀναβέβηκεν in John 3:13 "describes a unique *quality* of the Son of Man" (Pierce and Reynolds, "Perfect Tense-Form," 154, our italics) and can be translated as a timeless present: "No one ascends to heaven." On this account there is no strong reason to interpret ἀναβέβηκεν in the sense that Jesus' ascension *precedes* his descent (or that Jesus already has ascended to heaven at the time of his dialogue with Nicodemus), as traditional grammar would have it.

[25] "The heavenly things" (John 3:12) are an equivalent of "the kingdom of God" (John 3:5), cf. Sap. Sal. 10:10; another reminder of the tradition of heavenly voyages here.

[26] We concur with Benjamin E. Reynolds who understands the "we" in John 3:11 as referring to Jesus and the Spirit, see "The Testimony of Jesus and the Spirit: The 'We' of John 3:11 in its Literary Context," *Neotest* 41 (2007): 157–72. But this will automatically include the believers, because they will be inhabited by the Spirit; and so they will share in Jesus' knowledge (cf. John 14:17; 16:13).

[27] Glory and authority are always the issue in the Johannine Son of Man sayings (John 1:51; 3:13; 5:27; 6:27, 62; 8:28; 9:35; 12:23, 34 and 13:31). This verse also opens up the question of the relationship between ἀναβαίνειν (John 3:13) and ὑψωθῆναι (John 3:14). Francis J. Moloney, "The *Parables of Enoch* and the Johannine Son of Man," in *Johannine Studies 1975–2017*, WUNT 372 (Tübingen: Mohr Siebeck, 2017), 233–60, shows that our verses deal with revelation and knowledge of the mysteries of the heavenly with the Son of Man as *locus revelationis* (246–48), but his claim that "[t]

Our contention that the Nicodemus story is about epistemology (i.e., that it hinges on the questions: How do you know? Who has knowledge?) is confirmed by its beginning, to which we now turn. Nicodemus starts his dialogue with Jesus politely by saying, "Rabbi, we know that you are a teacher who has come from God; for no one can do these signs that you do apart from the presence of God" (or: "if God were not with him" [NIV]). Polite as it is, it also contains a claim to knowledge: "we know (οἴδαμεν)." By using these words Nicodemus shows himself to be the representative of the "many" who believed in Jesus "because they saw the things that he was doing" (2:23). From other texts in John's gospel, we know that, taken in itself, Nicodemus is not wrong: indeed, Jesus' signs do identify him as the one who is sent by God and it is correct to say that they show that God is with him (e.g., John 2:11; 4:54; 15:24; 20:30; especially telling is the reaction of the man born blind in John 9:30–33). Nevertheless, his claim to knowledge or, in other words, Nicodemus' epistemological claim is sharply opposed by Jesus. His reaction ("very truly, I tell you, no one can see the kingdom of God without being born again/from above") is blunt and seems at first sight to hit an entirely different note than Nicodemus' polite opening words. But it is, in fact, a completely adequate reply once we notice that Jesus wants to state that the only real knowledge a man can have about him have comes from above (ἄνωθεν). In order to "see" or to "enter" the kingdom of God, that is, have spiritual insight and knowledge and to be able to identify Jesus reliably, it is absolutely necessary to receive a new beginning "from above" of "from the spirit." This stands over again all earthly knowledge which is only "flesh." Humans can only beget humans, human knowledge can only create human knowledge (cf. John 3:31; 1:12–13). That is why it is crucial to realize that as a human being it is absolutely impossible to draw any firm conclusions about heavenly things, i.e., Jesus' identity.

We could ask, what should Nicodemus have said in order not to be criticized by Jesus? My suggestion is that he should have asked a question, such as: "Tell me, rabbi, who are you really? Are we right when we hail you as a teacher who has come from God, because we see the miracles that you do? Teach us the truth, for as

---

he Johannine use of *hypsoo* should not be associated with ascension" (253), is not to be accepted; the very sequence from verse 13 to verse 14 makes this already difficult to believe. In our eyes ὑψωθῆναι in John's gospel is first of all exaltation to heaven and only secondarily exaltation on the cross. The Isaianic substratum of John's way of speaking of exaltation and glorification, as comes to light (again) in Williams's article "Johannine Christology and Prophetic Traditions," clearly shows this, but it can also be reached on merely exegetical grounds. See the insightful monograph of Benjamin E. Reynolds, *The Apocalyptic Son of Man in the Gospel of John*, WUNT 2/249 (Tübingen: Mohr Siebeck, 2008).

humans we are born blind and are in need of a spiritual birth before we can say anything about you which is true."

The epistemological question is addressed more often. In fact, it runs through the Gospel as a whole. We often read about the fact that Jesus is a stranger to the people, starting in John 1:26 when John the Baptist speaks about someone "whom you do not know." At first sight we might think that he means, "whom you do not know *yet*," but only later we will understand that it was meant in a much more fundamental way. In John 6:42, for instance, the people claim to know (οἴδαμεν) who Jesus' father is, but they do not realize that knowing something about his earthly origin is nothing compared to having knowledge about his heavenly origin. When you do not know where he really comes from, he remains unknown. Here, too, lines are drawn sharply: only people who have been "drawn" or "taught" by God (διδακτοὶ θεοῦ John 6:44–46), to whom it has been given by God (John 6:65), can know who he is and are able to come to Jesus.

The difference between earthly and heavenly origins is also the subject of the discussion between Jesus and the people in Jerusalem in John 7:27–29. Here, too, they claim to know something important about Jesus ("we know where he is from"), but they only talk about his earthly roots, so they do not understand him in the least and even become aggressive towards Jesus in the end. Jesus himself is also very explicit at another occasion in John 8:14–15 ("I know . . . you do not know") and John 8:19 ("you know neither me nor my father").[28] There is a vital and painful truth to be learned: Jesus comes to give heavenly truth, but people do not recognize him, the Son, they do not understand what he says, they do not acknowledge his words, they do not understand his acts, in short, they do not know where he comes from (πόθεν); so they refuse and reject him (cf. John 1:10–11; 3:11, 32), even when they initially feel sympathetic towards him. That is why our writer had warned his readers already, that Jesus "would not entrust himself to them" (John 2:24) right at the beginning of the Nicodemus story. He wants to drive this lesson home in showing that Jesus cannot entrust himself to any ordinary human being, even not to one of the best among them, represented by Nicodemus here, who, being a teacher of Israel, is, alas, not able to understand him.

It has often been asked why Nicodemus comes at night.[29] When all his appearances in John's gospel are taken into account (John 3:1–9; 7:50–52; 19:39–40), opin-

---

28 Cf. also John 15:21 they will persecute you "because they do not know the one/him who sent me." The impotence of hearing Jesus' words and knowing him when people have another origin than God is the harsh thrust of the fierce discussion in John 8:39–59.
29 Numerous proposals have been given such as: he does not want to be seen with Jesus; may be out of fear (cf. John 20:19); rabbis liked to have discussions at night; night means darkness (cf. John 13:30) etc.

ions waver: should he be interpreted in a positive or in a negative way? The best position in our eyes is still the one taken long ago by Marinus de Jonge.[30] He called him a representative of the group of "sympathizers," i.e., people who are attracted to Jesus and who have a positive attitude towards him in principle, but who do not belong to the inner circle and lack deeper insight. In fact, it is a dangerous in-between position, as is stressed in John 12:35–36, "Walk while you have the light, so that the darkness may not overtake you. If you walk in the darkness, you do not know where you are going." This verse seems apt to characterize Nicodemus: despite his sympathetic behavior, he does not really know where he is going and so he is in constant danger.

Johannine Sectarianism and Spiritual Didactics

John 3 was the central text in Wayne Meeks' famous article "The Man from Heaven in Johannine Sectarianism."[31] According to Meeks, the metaphor of descent and ascent most of all shows Jesus as the stranger from heaven, who is fundamentally misunderstood by his interlocutors. The descent/ascent pattern serves as the warrant for the esoteric revelation which Jesus brings. According to Rudolf Bultmann's famous dictum, Jesus only revealed that he was the revealer. According to Meeks this is even too much. It is more to the point to say: "[H]e reveals rather that he is an enigma."[32] Jesus is an incomprehensible foreigner on this earth and his esoteric knowledge does not connect him to, but distinguishes him from the men of this world.[33] Meeks contended that this way of speaking served a social function and revealed the self-consciousness of the Johannine believers. The incomprehensible strangeness of Jesus represents the esoteric strangeness of the Johannine believer community. It is estranged from its own Jewish world. The gospel reflects a sectarian consciousness and one of its primary functions must have been "to provide a reinforcement for the community's social identity, which appears to have been largely negative. It provided a symbolic universe which gave religious

---

[30] Marinus de Jonge, *Jesus, Stranger from Heaven and Son of God: Jesus Christ and the Christians in Johannine Perspective*, ed. and trans. John E. Steely (Missoula, MT: Society of Biblical Literature, 1977).
[31] Meeks, "The Man from Heaven." Cf. John Ashton's verdict: "the most significant single essay" written on the Fourth Gospel since Rudolf Bultmann's commentary from 1941 (*Understanding the Fourth Gospel*, 250).
[32] Meeks, "The Man from Heaven," 57.
[33] Meeks, "The Man from Heaven," 61.

legitimacy, a theodicy, to the group's actual isolation form the larger society."[34] They do not belong to this world, just as their hero does not belong there.

There is still much to be said in favor of this conclusion. When only heavenly knowledge can count as real knowledge and when only the one who has come down from heaven can reveal it to whomever he wants it to, there seems not to be much room for ordinary ways of knowing or for critical discussions about the question whether this knowledge is true or false. Moreover, Jesus' disciples, those who believe in him, share in his experiences, the gospel says. They are not recognized or understood, just as Jesus was not (John 3:8; 15:20–21). John 5 and 9 reflect negative experiences of the Johannine Christians with their Jewish environment. They run the risk of excommunication.[35] As people who are "healed" by Jesus they even run the risk of becoming martyrs, just like their hero (John 12:10, 24–26, 15:20). And also, just like him, they are not "from below" but "from above" (John 1:12–13; 3:8; 15:19; 17:14, 16).[36]

Nevertheless, Meeks' contention that John's gospel reflects a sectarian consciousness also has some weaknesses. First of all, we should probably show some restraint in drawing sociological conclusions about the intended audience from a text like the gospel of John. The text does not address problems of the Johannine community directly, so we should leave some room for the difference between their hero and the community. Experiences of the Johannine community are reflected in the story, but they are not depicted. We have glimpses, not the whole picture.[37]

Most of all, however, we want to draw attention to the didactic character of the Fourth Gospel. In our eyes, the κατάβασις/ἀνάβασις structure of its Christology and its concomitant epistemology does not only reflect a sectarian consciousness, but must primarily be seen as a didactic means, a sharply formulated invitation for its readers. Remarkably, Meeks himself realizes this sometimes, as when he states that the theme of exaltation in John 3:14 not only results in misunderstanding, but is at the same time "an occasion for advancing his (=John's) didactic purpose."[38]

---

[34] Meeks, "The Man from Heaven," 70.
[35] The classic text on this is James L. Martyn, *History and Theology in the Fourth Gospel*, 3rd ed. (Louisville: John Knox, 2003).
[36] But in the case of the disciples, it is a *conferred* status, not an ontological one, as Meeks, "Man from Heaven," 68 aptly remarks, pointing to John 15:19; 17:6, 14 ("given").
[37] Cf. the section on the Johannine community in Stanley E. Porter and Hughson T. Ong, eds., *The Origins of John's Gospel*, Johannine Studies 2 (Leiden: Brill, 2016), with articles from Hunghson T. Ong ("The Gospel from a Specific Community but for All Christians: Understanding the Johannine Community as a 'Community of Practice'," 101–23), Marc-André Argentino and Guy Bonneau ("The Function of Social Conflict in the Gospel of John," 124–41) and Ruth Sheridan ("Johannine Secatarianism: A Category Now Defunct?" 142–66).
[38] Meeks, "The Man from Heaven," 64.

So, he acknowledges that there is a didactic purpose. Elsewhere he challenges his own reading when he says that "neither they (sc. Nicodemus et al.), *nor we*" could possibly know the rules of the language-game Jesus is playing.³⁹ This, however, cannot possibly be true, because the whole point is that readers *can* learn to understand them. John wants to lead his readers into a deeper understanding, but in order to do this, he makes it hard to get in. The misunderstandings continually challenge the reader to be more perceptive than the people who inhabit the narrative. The author wants his readers to catch the spiritual meaning of what they are reading. In fact, this is what happens in the text when John tests his readers time and again to understand a word or a situation better than the characters in his story do. Sometimes he helps them, sometimes not. But on the whole readers are supposed to be in a position where they can be more perceptive than, e.g., Nicodemus, the Jews, or even the disciples (e.g., John 6:1–5). We are given clues in order to be able to understand what is the case and to do it better than Jesus' interlocutors. The main clue is given in the prologue already, but clues can be found throughout the Gospel (e.g., John 2:21–22).⁴⁰ Its pneumatology provides a theological rationale for the phenomenon.

It is a literary device which can also be detected in the apocalyptic tradition of Judaism. The visionary is given extraordinary heavenly knowledge and insight which only he can receive, but by writing it down he paradoxically shares his knowledge with his readers who by proxy become shareholders in this heavenly knowledge. It is by no means exclusively Jewish apocalypticism, though. The Platonic tradition also knows it as when in Plato's dialogues the readers are invited to move beyond their first impressions and to see the real light.⁴¹ The works of Philo of Alexandria would not have existed without it, either. Spiritual didactics as a way to real life, this is the theme of John's Gospel. Just as Jesus challenges Nicodemus, so John challenges his readers. Readers are invited to accept the humble position of spiritual students instead of acting like would-be teachers who claim to have

---

39 Meeks, "The Man from Heaven," 68 (our italics).
40 Reader-response criticism, beginning with R. Alan Culpepper, *Anatomy of the Fourth Gospel: A Study in Literary Design* (Philadelphia: Fortress Press, 1983), has given ample evidence of this.
41 For a comparison of Johannine and Platonic thinking see the two interesting articles by George H. van Kooten, "The 'True Light Which Enlightens Everyone' (John 1:9): John, *Genesis*, the Platonic Notion of the 'True, Noetic Light,' and the Allegory of the Cave in Plato's *Republic*," in *The Creation of Heaven and Earth: Re-Interpretation of Genesis I in the Context of Judaism, Ancient Philosophy, Christianity, and Modern Physics*, ed. George H. van Kooten (Leiden: Brill, 2005), 149–94; and "The Last Days of Socrates and Christ: *Euthrypho, Apology, Crito*, and *Phaedo* Read in Counterpoint with John's Gospel," in *Religio-Philosophical Discourses in the Mediterranean World: From Plato, through Jesus, to Late Antiquity*, ed. A. Klostergaard Pedersen and George H. van Kooten (Leiden: Brill, 2017), 219–43.

knowledge, but in reality know nothing. So, the Fourth Gospel is an ambivalent text. It can result in sectarian consciousness, but it can also create humble critical religious acumen. It depends on what kind of readers it finds.

References

Alexander, Philip. "3 (Hebrew Apocalypse of) Enoch." Pages 1:223–15 in *The Old Testament Pseudepigrapha*. Edited by James H. Charlesworth. 2 vols. New Haven: Yale University Press, 1983. Repr., Peabody: Hendrickson, ²2011.

Anderson, Frances I. "2 (Slavonic Apocalypse of) Enoch." Pages 1:91–221 in *The Old Testament Pseudepigrapha*. Edited by James H. Charlesworth. 2 vols. New Haven: Yale University Press, 1983. Repr., Peabody: Hendrickson, ²2011.

Argentino, Marc-André, and Guy Bonneau. "The Function of Social Conflict in the Gospel of John." Pages 124–41 in *The Origins of John's Gospel*. Edited by Stanley E. Porter and Hughson T. Ong. Johannine Studies 2. Leiden: Brill, 2016.

Ashton, John. "The Johannine Son of Man: A New Proposal." *NTS* 57 (2011): 508–29.

Ashton, John. *Understanding the Fourth Gospel*. 2nd ed. Oxford: Oxford University Press, 2007.

Borgen, Peder. "Some Jewish Exegetical Traditions as Background for Son of Man Sayings in John's Gospel (John 3,13–14 and context)." Pages 243–58 in *L'Évangile de Jean: Sources, rédaction, théologie*. Edited by Marinus de Jonge. BETL 44. Gembloux: Leuven University Press, 1977.

Charlesworth, James H., ed. *The Old Testament Pseudepigrapha*. 2 vols. New Haven: Yale University Press, 1983. Repr., Peabody: Hendrickson, ²2011.

Charlesworth, James H. "Introduction for the General Reader." Pages 1:xxi–xxxiv in *The Old Testament Pseudepigrapha*. Edited by James H. Charlesworth. 2 vols. New Haven: Yale University Press, 1983. Repr., Peabody: Hendrickson, ²2011.

Culpepper, R. Alan. *Anatomy of the Fourth Gospel: A Study in Literary Design*. Philadelphia: Fortress Press, 1983.

Dodd, C.H. *Historical Tradition in the Fourth Gospel*. Cambridge: Cambridge University Press, 1963.

Harrington, Daniel J. "Pseudo-Philo." Pages 2:297–377 in *The Old Testament Pseudepigrapha*. Edited by James H. Charlesworth. 2 vols. New Haven: Yale University Press, 1983. Repr., Peabody: Hendrickson, ²2011.

Heschel, Abraham J. *Heavenly Torah: As Refracted through the Generations*. Edited and translated by Gordon Tucker. New York: Continuum, 2005.

Isaac, Ephraim. "1 (Ethiopic Apocalypse of) Enoch." Pages 1:5–90 in *The Old Testament Pseudepigrapha*. Edited by James H. Charlesworth. 2 vols. New Haven: Yale University Press, 1983. Repr., Peabody: Hendrickson, ²2011.

Jonge, Marinus de. *Jesus, Stranger from Heaven and Son of God: Jesus Christ and the Christians in Johannine Perspective*. Edited and translated by John E. Steely. Missoula, MT: Society of Biblical Literature, 1977.

Kee, Howard C. "Testaments of the Twelve Patriarchs." Pages 1:775–82 in *The Old Testament Pseudepigrapha*. Edited by James H. Charlesworth. 2 vols. New Haven: Yale University Press, 1983. Repr., Peabody: Hendrickson, ²2011.

Knibb, Michael A. "Martyrdom and Ascension of Isaiah." Pages 2:143–76 in *The Old Testament Pseudepigrapha*. Edited by James H. Charlesworth. 2 vols. New Haven: Yale University Press, 1983. Repr., Peabody: Hendrickson, ²2011.

Kooten, George H. van. "The 'True Light Which Enlightens Everyone' (John 1:9): John, *Genesis*, the Platonic Notion of the 'True, Noetic Light,' and the Allegory of the Cave in Plato's *Republic*." Pages 149–94 in *The Creation of Heaven and Earth: Re-Interpretation of Genesis I in the Context of Judaism, Ancient Philosophy, Christianity, and Modern Physics*. Edited by George H. van Kooten. Leiden: Brill, 2005.

Kooten, George H. van. "The Last Days of Socrates and Christ: *Euthrypho, Apology, Crito*, and *Phaedo* Read in Counterpoint with John's Gospel." Pages 219–43 in *Religio-Philosophical Discourses in the Mediterranean World: From Plato, through Jesus, to Late Antiquity*. Edited by Anders Klostergaard Petersen and George van Kooten. Leiden: Brill, 2017.

Lafargue, Michael. "Orphica." Pages 2:795–801 in *The Old Testament Pseudepigrapha*. Edited by James H. Charlesworth. 2 vols. New Haven: Yale University Press, 1983. Repr., Peabody: Hendrickson, ²2011.

Levine, Amy-Jill, and Marc Zvi Brettler, eds. *The Jewish Annotated New Testament*. Oxford: Oxford University Press, 2011.

Litwa, M. David. "The Deification of Moses in Philo of Alexandria." *SPhiloA* 26 (2014): 1–27.

Mackie, Scott D. "Seeing God in Philo of Alexandria: The Logos, the Powers, or the Existent One?" *SPhiloA* 21 (2009): 25–47.

Mackie, Scott D. "Seeing God in Philo of Alexandria: Means, Methods, and Mysticism." *JJS* 43 (2012): 147–79.

Martyn, James L. *History and Theology in the Fourth Gospel*. 3rd ed. Louisville: John Knox, 2003.

Meeks, Wayne A. "Galilee and Judea in the Fourth Gospel." *JBL* 85 (1966): 159–69.

Meeks, Wayne A. "The Man from Heaven in Johannine Sectarianism." *JBL* 91 (1972): 44–72.

Moloney, Francis J. "The Parables of Enoch and the Johannine Son of Man." Pages 233–60 in *Johannine Studies 1975–2017*. WUNT 372. Tübingen: Mohr Siebeck, 2017.

Ong, Hunghson T. "The Gospel from a Specific Community but for All Christians: Understanding the Johannine Community as a 'Community of Practice.'" Pages 101–23 in *The Origins of John's Gospel*. Edited by Stanley E. Porter and Hughson T. Ong. Johannine Studies 2. Leiden: Brill, 2016.

Pancaro, Severino. *The Law in the Fourth Gospel*. NovTSup 42. Leiden: Brill, 1975.

Pierce, Madison N., and Benjamin R. Reynolds. "The Perfect Tense-Form and the Son of Man in John 3.13: Developments in Greek Grammar as a Viable Solution to the Timing of the Ascent and Descent." *NTS* 60 (2014): 149–55.

Reynolds, Benjamin E. *The Apocalyptic Son of Man in the Gospel of John*. WUNT 2/249. Tübingen: Mohr Siebeck, 2008.

Reynolds, Benjamin E. "The Testimony of Jesus and the Spirit: The 'We' of John 3:11 in its Literary Context." *Neotest* 41 (2007): 157–72.

Rubinkiewicz, Ryszard. "Apocalypse of Abraham." Pages 1:681–705 in *The Old Testament Pseudepigrapha*. Edited by James H. Charlesworth. 2 vols. New Haven: Yale University Press, 1983. Repr., Peabody: Hendrickson, ²2011.

Schäfer, Peter. *The Origins of Jewish Mysticism*. Tübingen: Mohr Siebeck, 2007.

Segal, Alan F. "Heavenly Ascent in Hellenistic Judaism, Early Christianity and their Environment." *ANRW* 2.23.2 (1980): 1333–94.

Sheridan, Ruth. "Johannine Secatarianism: A Category Now Defunct?" Pages 142–66 in *The Origins of John's Gospel*. Edited by Stanley E. Porter and Hughson T. Ong. Johannine Studies 2. Leiden: Brill, 2016.

Williams, Catrin H. "Johannine Christology and Prophetic Traditions: The Case of Isaiah." Pages 92–123 in *Reading the Gospel of John's Christology as Jewish Messianism: Royal, Prophetic, and Divine Messiahs*. Edited by Benjamin E. Reynolds and Gabriele Boccaccini. AGJU 106. Leiden: Brill, 2018.

Eelco Glas
Following Vespasian in His Footsteps: Movement and (E)motion Management in Josephus' *Judean War*

Abstract: This chapter examines Josephus' account of the Year of the Four Emperors in book 4 of the *Judean War*, and in particular Vespasian's response to the prospect of having to undertake a sea voyage from Judea to Rome to deal with the vicious Vitellius. Scholars have often taken the details of Josephus' account as highly favorable to the Flavians. Consequently, they have argued that Josephus' version of the events is arguably the most pro-Flavian version to survive from antiquity. Drawing on Greek and Roman views of narrative composition and arrangement, the present chapter challenges this view by examining Josephus' characterization of Vespasian's emotions and disposition as part of its wider literary context. The analysis suggests, first, that through his use of recognizable literary topoi related to sea travel, Josephus offers his readers interpretative clues for implicit criticism of the Flavians. The language and narrative structure of the *War* encourage comparisons between Vespasian and other characters staged in the narrative, such as Herod the Great. Second, the analysis sheds light on the rationale and patterns underlying the literary representation of travel and travel experiences in Josephus' histories. Motifs of "travel" and "travel experiences" are not as incidental as they often seem to be. They can have important functions as literary devices in the narrative. Their paradigmatic nature allows readers to discover thematic structures and relationships between exemplary scenes for themselves.

Note: This research was initiated as part of my PhD project at the University of Groningen and developed with funding from the European Research Council grant 948264 (ANINAN). I am grateful to the audience at the conference "Jewish, Christian and Muslim Travel Experiences (3th BCE-8th CE)" (Groningen, 27–29 March 2020) for their valuable questions and suggestions. In particular, I would like to thank Steve Mason, Elisa Uusimäki, and Gillian R. Glass for their extensive feedback on earlier versions of my text, Jon Davies for sharing the proofs of his monograph, the editors of this volume for the suggested textual improvements, and Forrest Kentwell for correcting my English. Any remaining errors are my own.

Preliminaries: Travel and Travel Experiences in the *Judean War*

At first sight, reflections on travel experiences do not feature centrally in Josephus' treatises.[1] Josephus does make reference to a few journeys, but he rarely explains their details or the experiences of the individuals and groups undertaking them.[2] Consequently, while the subject of travel is booming business in scholarship of early Judaism, Christianity, and Islam, they have rarely pursued anything in such directions in relation to Josephus' corpus.[3]

However, since Josephus does not often elaborate on travel or travel experiences as such, we should be alert in the few cases where he offers more detailed descriptions of certain journeys or the experiences of individuals or groups undertaking them. By analyzing Josephus' presentation of the Year of the Four Emperors (esp. *B.J.* 4.588–663), this chapter will illustrate the literary functions of travel and travel experiences in Josephus' narratives. One of the most striking features of Josephus' narrative of this Roman civil war is, as Tessa Rajak notes, the fact that he structures it "by keeping track of Flavian movements."[4] Moreover, in the beginning of the narrative, Josephus offers his readers a glimpse into Vespasian's mind when hearing the news of Vitellius' accession to power. Vespasian is outraged, but he considers the distance and the prospect of a hazardous sea journey in the midst of winter. These considerations force him to keep his emotions in check and to postpone further action (*B.J.* 4.588–591). Josephus' choice to slow down at this point of the narrative, offering reflections on the inner motions of one of *War*'s most important characters and his decision *not* to make a move, is most certainly not inciden-

---

1 In contrast to the related subjects of space and geography, which seem to play a rather important role, on which see, e.g., Yuval Shahar, *Josephus Geographicus: The Classical Context of Geography in Josephus*, TSAJ 98 (Tübingen: Mohr Siebeck, 2004); John M. Vonder Bruegge, *Mapping Galilee in Josephus, Luke, and John: Critical Geography and the Construction of an Ancient Space*, AJEC 93 (Leiden: Brill, 2016), 32–90; Zeev Safrai, *Seeking Out the Land: Land of Israel Traditions in Ancient Jewish, Christian and Samaritan Literature (200 BCE–400 CE)*, JCPS 32 (Leiden: Brill, 2018), 43–75.
2 Catherine Hezser, *Jewish Travel in Antiquity*, TSAJ 144 (Tübingen: Mohr Siebeck, 2011), 209–13.
3 One of the few focused studies is Maren R. Niehoff, "Parodies of Educational Journeys in Josephus, Justin Martyr, and Lucian," in *Journeys in the Roman East: Imagined and Real*, ed. Maren R. Niehoff, Culture, Religion, and Politics in the Greco-Roman World 1 (Tübingen: Mohr Siebeck, 2017), 203–22 (206–10). See also Daniel R. Schwartz, "'Going up to Rome' in Josephus's *Antiquities*," in Niehoff, *Journeys*, 373–88, who examines the diction of travel in *Antiquities* 18–20 in order to identify the sources underlying Josephus' account. Also instructive is René Bloch, *Andromeda in Jaffa: Mythische Orte als Reiseziele in der jüdischen Antike*, Franz-Delitzsch-Vorlesung 2015 (Münster: Institutum Judaicum Delitzschianum, 2017).
4 Tessa Rajak, *Josephus: The Historian and His Society*, 2nd ed. (London: Duckworth, 2002), 213–14.

tal. Considering the military-political nature of the *War* and the fact that this work was written to target an elite audience in the city where Vespasian resided as the new emperor, Josephus will have been very much aware of the words he put on paper and their potential effects on his readers.[5]

The central question of this chapter is how Josephus communicated such moral and political lessons in the *War* and what he may have communicated when elaborating on Vespasian's response to the prospect of travelling. Greeks and Romans did not always explicate the plain meaning of a narrative text (= "telling"), but very often hid them in choices of disposition and narrative arrangement (= "showing").[6] Given that Josephus described the individuals and groups stages in his work in accordance with Greco-Roman rhetorical conventions, we should be sensitive to hidden meanings conveyed through allusive hints in his narrative web. The significance of this point is illustrated in a contribution of Nicolas Wiater, who examines the two main narrative strands of the *War*—waging war against the Romans and *stasis*—and argues that Josephus uses a technique, which he calls "interpretation through juxtaposition," that is also found in Thucydides' *Histories*. Wiater shows that the *War* is structured in a way that enables its readers to discover interrelations between events on their own. Thus, the full meaning of one event becomes clear only when reading it alongside another.[7]

Using a similar approach, this chapter will foreground the literary functions of Vespasian's display of emotions in response to the prospect of having to undertake a sea journey from Judea to Rome.[8] Specifically, it will investigate the narrative

---

[5] For further discussion and scholarship on this subject see Eelco Glas, "Flavius Josephus' Self-Characterization in First-Century Rome: A Literary Analysis of the Autobiographical Passages in the *Bellum Judaicum*" (PhD. diss., University of Groningen, 2020); Eelco Glas, "Josephus between Jerusalem and Rome: Cultural Brokerage and the Rhetoric of Emotion in the *Bellum Judaicum* (1.9–12)," *Histos* 14 (2020): 275–99.

[6] A point made in Frederick Ahl and Hanna M. Roisman, *The Odyssey Re-formed* (Ithaca, NY: Cornell University Press, 1996), 14. Relevant ancient discussions are, for example, Demetr. *Eloc.* 288; Quint., *Inst.* 9.2.65. On the distinction between showing and telling among ancient scholia see René Nünlist, *The Ancient Critic at Work: Terms and Concepts of Literary Criticism in Greek Scholia* (Cambridge: Cambridge University Press, 2009), 32, 246, 248. On the importance of ancient rhetoric for the literary presentation in Greek narrative see Koen De Temmerman, *Crafting Characters: Heroes and Heroines in the Ancient Greek Novel* (Oxford: Oxford University Press, 2014), 31–41.

[7] Nicolas Wiater, "Reading the *Jewish War*: Narrative Technique and Historical Interpretation in Josephus's *Bellum Judaicum*," *Materiali e Discussioni per l'analisi dei testi classici* 64 (2010): 145–85.

[8] The centrality of the Rome-Judea axis in Josephus' *Antiquities* is also recognized in Schwartz, "'Going up to Rome'," 373: "Josephus's frequent references to travel back and forth between Judea and Rome in the first century constitute the structural backbone of his narrative for this period in the last three books of his *Jewish Antiquities*." Cf. Tamar Landau, *Out-Heroding Herod: Josephus, Rhetoric, and the Herod Narratives*, AJEC 63 (Leiden: Brill, 2006), 115–86.

relationship between Vespasian's emotion management and his movement patterns, attending to the immediate literary context and the broader compositional structures of the *War*. We will see that Josephus structures the *War* in a way that encourages comparison with other statesmen in book 4 (e.g., Vitellius, Mucianus), but also elsewhere in the *War* (Herod the Great, *B.J.* 1.274–285). By using a variety of literary motifs as structuring devices, he invites his readers to bestow praise and blame on the characters staged in his narrative without having to spell everything out explicitly as a narrator.

The main aim of this interpretative attempt is to shed light on the rationale and patterns underpinning the literary representation of travel experiences in Josephus' histories.[9] Motifs of "travel" and "travel experiences" are not as incidental as they often seem to be. They can have important functions as literary devices in the narrative. Their paradigmatic nature allows readers to discover the thematic structures of and relationships between exemplary scenes on their own. Furthermore, other than increasing our understanding of Josephus' descriptions of travel experiences, the results of my analysis have significant ramifications for a major discussion in Josephus studies, namely, his literary depiction of the Flavians. Considering that the Flavian dynasty had used and continued to use the Judean-Roman conflict to establish their imperial authority,[10] Josephus' description of the Flavians, and especially his narrative of the year of the emperors, would have caught the immediate attention of his audience, eager to learn about the steps their emperor had taken to assume power. Rajak and many others have suggested that the details of Josephus' account are highly favorable towards the Flavians, resulting in a more pro-Flavian version "than any other that survives."[11] Taking the scholarship of Steve Mason as

---

[9] My contribution does not focus on the historical events underpinning Josephus' narrative, such as the impact of Josephus' migration experiences after the Judean revolt on his intellectual development. This subject has been discussed in Michael Tuval, "A Jewish Priest in Rome," in *Flavius Josephus: Interpretation and History*, ed. Jack Pastor, Pnina Stern, and Menahem Mor, JSJSup 146 (Leiden: Brill, 2011), 397–411; Michael Tuval, *From Jerusalem Priest to Roman Jew*, WUNT 2/357 (Tübingen: Mohr Siebeck, 2013).

[10] On Flavian propaganda see, e.g., Martin Goodman, *Rome and Jerusalem: The Clash of Ancient Civilizations* (London: Allen Lane, 2007), 428–33; Samuele Rocca, *In the Shadow of the Caesars: Jewish Life in Roman Italy*, BRLA 74 (Leiden: Brill, 2022), 241–77. For an extensive analysis of the Flavian monuments of the Judean-Roman conflict in Rome, see Fergus Millar, "Monuments of the Jewish War in Rome," in *Flavius Josephus and Flavian Rome*, ed. Jonathan Edmondson, Steve Mason, and James Rives (Oxford: Oxford University Press, 2005), 101–28.

[11] See Rajak, *Josephus*, 213–15. See more recently, for example, Jonathan Davies, *Representing the Dynasty in Flavian Rome: The Case of Josephus'* Jewish War (Oxford: Oxford University Press, 2023), 98–127 (esp. 109–27): Josephus' description of the Year of the Four Emperors is "a highly convenient version of events from Vespasian's perspective" and "in many ways [the] most consistently pro-Flavian" that can be found in the *War* (quotes from 192 and 193). See also, e.g., Gerda de Kleijn,

point of departure, my analysis questions the view still common among specialists and non-specialists that Josephus' intellectual agenda was to a large extent determined by his Flavian patrons, or at least that he used his literary abilities to depict the Flavians in the best possible light. It suggests that Josephus, by implementing the aforementioned structuring devices, offers his readers interpretative clues for implicit criticism of the Flavians through his presentation of Vespasian's motivations and movement patterns.[12]

Reading Vespasian's Travel Narrative in the *Judean War*

Taking these considerations as a starting point, the following offers reflections on how Josephus uses the motif of sea voyages during winter season to set up subtle juxtapositions between different characters. It is striking how frequently Josephus narrates very similar circumstances and records in detail how individuals respond to these circumstances. Comparing these cases potentially explains aspects of characterization that we might otherwise not have been able to extract from Josephus' narrative. The responses of different individuals to similar experiences in similar situations gives the reader essential information about their virtues (or the lack thereof).

To realize this, I propose to begin the discussion with investigating Vespasian's responses to challenges in the context of Josephus' narrative of the Year of the Four Emperors. This order of discussion is informed by my suspicion that the episodes narrating the experiences of Herod and Mucianus are specifically designed to offer indirect reflections on the character of Vespasian, who would obviously have been the character drawing the most interest in Flavian Rome. The full meaning of Josephus' characterization of Vespasian becomes evident only when reading his experiences alongside those of other characters in the *War*. My arguments suggest that Josephus

---

"C. Licinius Mucianus, Vespasian's Co-ruler in Rome," *Mnemosyne* 66 (2013): 433–59 (437); Frédéric Hurlet, "Sources and Evidence," in *A Companion to the Flavian Age of Imperial Rome*, ed. Andrew Zissos (Malden, MA: Blackwell, 2016), 17–39 (21–22); Adam Kemezis "Flavian Greek Literature," in Zissos, *Companion*, 450–68 (460).
12 Cf. Steve Mason, "Figured Speech and Irony in T. Flavius Josephus," in Edmondson, Mason, and Rives, *Flavius Josephus and Flavian Rome*, 243–88. See more recently, e.g., Steve Mason, "Vespasian's Rise from Civil War in Josephus's *Bellum Judaicum*," in *After 69 CE: Writing Civil War in Flavian Rome*, ed. Lauren Donovan Ginsberg and Darcy Anne Krasne, TCSV 63 (Berlin: De Gruyter, 2018), 199–226.

was much more subtle in his presentation of the Flavians than often assumed, and perhaps even (silently) critical, allowing his Roman audience to explore dangerous and, by necessity, hidden meanings of the narrative.[13]

Vespasian's Moderation

Let us begin with looking at Josephus' description of Vespasian's response to Vitellius' accession to power (*B.J.* 4.588–591), which because of its centrality will be given in Greek and in translation:

> Οὐεσπασιανὸς δὲ ὡς τὰ πλησίον Ἱεροσολύμων καταστρεψάμενος ὑπέστρεψεν εἰς Καισάρειαν, ἀκούει τὰς κατὰ τὴν Ῥώμην ταραχὰς καὶ Οὐιτέλλιον αὐτοκράτορα. τοῦτο αὐτόν, καίπερ ἄρχεσθαι καθάπερ ἄρχειν καλῶς ἐπιστάμενον, εἰς ἀγανάκτησιν προήγαγεν, καὶ τὸν μὲν ὡς ἐρήμου καταμανέντα τῆς ἡγεμονίας ἡδόξει δεσπότην, περιαλγήσας δὲ τῷ πάθει καρτερεῖν τὴν βάσανον οὐχ οἷός τε ἦν καὶ τῆς πατρίδος πορθουμένης ἑτέροις προσευσχολεῖν πολέμοις. ἀλλ' ὅσον ὁ θυμὸς ἤπειγεν ἐπὶ τὴν ἄμυναν, τοσοῦτον εἶργεν ἔννοια τοῦ διαστήματος· πολλὰ γὰρ <ἂν> φθάσαι πανουργήσασαν τὴν τύχην πρὶν αὐτὸν εἰς τὴν Ἰταλίαν περαιωθῆναι, καὶ ταῦτα χειμῶνος ὥρᾳ πλέοντα, <καὶ> σφαδάζουσαν ἤδη κατεῖχεν τὴν ὀργήν.

> When Vespasian had destroyed all places near Jerusalem and had returned to Caesarea, he heard of the disturbances in Rome and that Vitellius had become emperor. Even though he knew both how it was to be ruled as to rule himself, this caused indignation. He could not honor a master who had so madly seized imperial government as if simply vacant. He was so greatly pained by his passion that he was not able to fully endure the torment, nor to give his attention to another war when his country was destroyed. However, as great as the wrath urged him forward to its defence, so much was he restrained by the thought of the great distance. For before he could successfully make it to Italy, fortune could catch him with some villainy, especially because he had to sail in time of winter. Thus, while he struggled to do so, he held back his wrath.

Josephus describes Vespasian's internal struggles when he is forced to witness "the destruction of his country" in the context of his extended narrative of the Year of the Four Emperors and the civil war in Rome (esp. *B.J.* 4.440–441, 494–502, 545–549, 585–588, 631–657), which he deliberately places alongside the *stasis* in Jerusalem.[14]

---

[13] On the classical context of implicit and figurative characterization practices in Josephus see Mason, "Figured Speech and Irony"; Glas, "Josephus' Self-Characterization," 65–69. For the classical context more generally see Frederick Ahl, "The Art of Safe Criticism in Greece and Rome," *AJP* 105 (1984): 174–208; Shadi Bartsch, *Actors in the Audience: Theatricality and Doublespeak from Nero to Hadrian* (Cambridge: Harvard University Press, 1994).

[14] On the theme of civil war as a structuring device in the *War*, see Eelco Glas, "Overcoming Otherness in Flavian Rome: Flavius Josephus and the Rhetoric of Identity in the *Bellum Judaicum*," in *Roman Identity: Between Ideal and Performance*, ed. F. Lautaro Roig Lanzillotta et al. (Turnhout: Brepols, 2023), 163–84 (esp. 171–80).

In the context of this narrative framework, Josephus consistently tracks down the movements of Vespasian and his representatives. While Vespasian travels quite a bit between different places, most of the long-distance travelling is done by Vespasian's representatives. Briefly after Nero's suicide, Vespasian sends his son Titus and Agrippa II from Caesarea to Rome to greet Galba as the new emperor (*B.J.* 4.498–502). However, after Galba's assassination Titus is prompted to return "through some divine impulse" (*B.J.* 4.501). Vespasian himself moves to and from Caesarea on multiple occasions (*B.J.* 4.486, 550, 588, 620), campaigns in the surroundings of Jerusalem (*B.J.* 4.550–555), sends letters to Egypt (*B.J.* 4.616), moves to Berytus (*B.J.* 4.620), and then proceeds to Antioch (*B.J.* 4.630). In Antioch, he sends his trusted general Mucianus to Italy with a substantial force to take on Vitellius and his German legions. Mucianus decides to march (rather than to sail) to Italy through Cappadocia and Phrygia (*B.J.* 4.630–632). Antonius Primus, loyal to Vespasian but working on his own initiative, also hastens himself and the Third Legion of Moesia to give battle to Vitellius' army in Cremona (*B.J.* 4.633–644). Immediately afterwards, he marches to Rome and destroys Vitellius and his army (*B.J.* 4.650–654), only one day after the destruction of the Temple of Jupiter Capitolinus and the murder of Vespasian's brother Sabinus (*B.J.* 4.645–649). Vespasian's appointed representative Mucianus arrives on the following day and stops Antonius' troops from further slaughter, relieving the citizens of Rome from their fears and confirming Vespasian's accession to power (*B.J.* 4.654–655). At this point, Vespasian reappears as victor in Alexandria (*B.J.* 4.656) and makes plans to travel to Rome (*B.J.* 4.658), only to disappear again until the beginning of *War* 7, where we find Vespasian still on his journey to Rome (*B.J.* 7.21–22). The movement patterns of military leaders and their troops thus form an important ingredient of Josephus' presentation of the Year of the Four Emperors.

In this narrative, Josephus foregrounds Vespasian's victorious rise from the Roman civil war and places it alongside the (self-)destruction of Vitellius, who demonstrates a barbarian-like disposition throughout the narrative.[15] Josephus foregrounds Vitellius' greed and rashness on several occasions, using it to establish a contrast with Vespasian's character. For example, in the passage just cited we see how he, paraphrasing Vespasian's thoughts on the matter (but not necessarily committing himself to Vespasian's viewpoint), stresses how Vitellius "madly seized" the imperial government (*B.J.* 4.589). Vespasian's legions in Judea compare the temperance of their leader to the depravity of Vitellius (*B.J.* 4.596), a judgment that is emphatically confirmed by the narrator close to the end of the volume (*B.J.* 4.652). Josephus emphasizes Vitellius' rashness on several occasions, but most emphatically when describing his drunkenness and gluttony after an extravagantly luxu-

---

15 Davies, *Representing the Dynasty*, 114–15.

rious meal served on the day that his "throat was cut in the centre of Rome" (*B.J.* 4.652; cf. 4.318, 349). He characterizes Vitellius as a "savage tyrant" (*B.J.* 4.596) who in his "natural cruelty thirsts for noble blood" (*B.J.* 4.647). In many regards, Vitellius' character closely resembles that of the Judean tyrants responsible for the destruction of the Jerusalem and the temple by beginning a civil war.[16]

When compared to Vitellius' villainy, it is easy to see why scholars have frequently taken Josephus' narrative of the Year of the Four Emperors as saturated with pro-Flavian bias. Overall, the overt comments in the narrative suggest that Vespasian counterbalances Vitellius' viciousness and is cherished by Josephus as a protector of the interests of the Roman people (cf. *B.J.* 4.588–591, 593–594, 596, 616, 630, 544, 654–656). Considering this, the passage cited above can be interpreted as confirming this picture, indicating Vespasian's mental strength and self-control throughout the narrative: despite the overwhelming strength of his emotions, Vespasian has the ability to keep his composure and take balanced decisions based on reasonable considerations, *such as* the risks involved in sailing the Mediterranean in time of winter (*B.J.* 4.591: χειμῶνος ὥρᾳ πλέοντα).[17]

The picture of a moderate and sensible Vespasian is further backed when looking at the literary topos of the sea voyage, and the dangers accompanying such a voyage. Josephus' use of this topos would most certainly have alerted his readers and stimulated their imagination.[18] To give an idea, in Homer's *Odyssey*, storms feature prominently in the wanderings of Odysseus (*B.J.* 5.291–387; *B.J.* 12.403–425) and the story of Ajax' death (*B.J.* 4.499–511). Hesiod describes the sea as something evil (*Op.* 617–695): if one cares about life and limbs, sea voyages outside of the sailing season should be avoided, unless one longs for "storm-tossed seafaring" (Hes., *Op.* 618: ναυτιλίης δυσπεμφέλου).[19] The motif also features prominently in the New Testament, with

---

16 Cf. Mason, "Vespasian's Rise," 215–17; Glas, "Rhetoric of Identity," 177. On Josephus' characterization of Vitellius see also Davies, *Representing the Dynasty*, 114–15.
17 According to Thackeray, Josephus invokes Thucydides' description of the naval battle between the Athenian and the Spartan fleet in book 4 of the *Histories* (Thuc. 4.14–15). While the Spartans rush forward headlong without thinking about the potential consequences and the fortune of the Athenians on this occasion, Vespasian holds back his anger and shows awareness that fortune might turn against him when taking unnecessary risk. Vespasian remains in control, whereas the Spartans lose it. See the note *ad loc.* in Henry St.J. Thackery, trans., *Josephus: The Jewish War, Volume 2: Books 3–4*, LCL (Cambridge: Harvard University Press, 1927).
18 For a general historical discussion of seafaring in the ancient world, see F.J. Meijer, "Mare Clausum aut Mare Apertum: Een beschouwing over zeevaart in de winter," *Hermeneus* 55 (1983): 2–20.
19 Cf. M.P.O. Morford, *The Poet Lucan: Studies in Rhetorical Epic* (Oxford: Basil Blackwell, 1967), 20–23. On the motif of a sea-storm in ancient epic see more recently the essays in Thomas Biggs and Jessica Blum, eds., *The Epic Journey in Greek and Roman Literature* (Cambridge: Cambridge University Press, 2019).

Jesus' stilling of the storm in the Gospels (Matt 8:23–27 par. Mark 4:35–41; Luke 8:22–25) and, more elaborately, Paul's shipwreck during his voyage to Rome (Acts 27, esp. verses 9–12).[20] According to his own claims, Josephus experienced similar dangers himself when travelling to Rome in 64 CE (*Vita* 13–16).

The importance of seafaring and the dangers inherent to it become especially apparent when looking at Caesar's crossing of the Adriatic from Brundisium to Epirus as described in Caes., *Civ.* 3.6 and the reception of this passage. Caesar does not stress the unusualness of his decision, but casually remarks that he "sailed on the 4th of January" (*Civ.* 3.6.1). He adds that he took no less than seven legions with him and found calm anchorage without losing a single ship (*Civ.* 3.6.3).[21] Notably, Caesar's voyages became famous and sparked the imagination of later authors. Lucan takes this to an extreme, devoting more than 50 lines to the event (*Phars.* 5.403–460).[22] Lucan develops this motif further by describing Caesar, who is convinced of his own indestructibility, overplaying his hand by trying his fortune a second time in another storm (*Phars.* 5.504–677). During this crossing, which is not mentioned in Caesar's *De bello civili*, Caesar delivers two speeches in which he defies the power of the sea (Luc., *Phars.* 5.577–593 and 5.653–671) and is almost killed because of this, making his survival a miracle (Luc., *Phars.* 5.671–677). Thus, in Lucan's *Pharsalia*, the sea serves as an important characterizing device, used to illustrate the limits of human power and Caesar's insight.[23]

Considering that seafaring, especially during winter season, inspired fear and was considered extremely dangerous, we might interpret Josephus' emphasis on Vespasian's hesitance to undertake such a sea voyage as underscoring his moderate

---

20 On Paul's shipwreck in Acts see Susan Marie Praeder, "Acts 27:1–28:16: Sea Voyages in Ancient Literature and the Theology of Luke-Acts," *CBQ* 46 (1984): 683–706; Dennis R. MacDonald, "The Shipwrecks of Odysseus and Paul," *NTS* 45 (1999): 88–107; Troy M. Troftgrüben, "Slow Sailing in Acts: Suspense in the Final Sea Journey (Acts 27:1–28:15)," *JBL* 136 (2017): 949–68. On Jesus stilling the storm in the Gospels see Charles H. Talbert and J.H. Hayes, "A Theology of Sea Storms in Luke-Acts," in *Society of Biblical Literature Seminar Papers* 34, ed. E. H. Lovering, Jr. (Atlanta: Scholars Press, 1995), 321–36; Rick Strelan, "A Greater Than Caesar: Storm Stories in Lucan and Mark," *ZNW* 91 (2000): 166–79.

21 This daring move underlines Caesar's incredible speed, which enables him to be a step ahead of Pompeius, who just tried to block him from crossing the Adriatic (Caes., *Civ.* 3.5.2). Caesar's speed (*celeritas*) is awed in, for example, Cic., *Att.* 7.22.1, 8.9a.2. On Caesar's *celeritas* in the *De bello civili* see Luca Grillo, *The Art of Caesar's Bellum Civile: Literature, Ideology, and Community* (Cambridge: Cambridge University Press, 2012), 14–36.

22 In addition to Lucan cf. Plut., *De fort. Rom.* 319B-D; *Caes.* 37–38; App., *B Civ.* 2.56–58; Suet., *Iul.* 58; Val. Max. 9.8.2; Cass. Dio 41.46.

23 The classical treatment of storms in Lucan's *Pharsalia* is Morford, *The Poet Lucan*, 37–58. For a detailed commentary on the second storm see Monica Matthews, *Caesar and the Storm: A Commentary on Lucan*, De Bello Civili, Book 5, Lines 476–721 (Bern: Lang, 2008).

character. This reading, which is clearly discernible when looking at the themes and structure of Josephus' text, emphasizes Vespasian's role as a beacon of rest, who would become the statesman to save the empire from Vitellius' rash and greedy impulses. Vespasian's display of self-control and his ability to cure Rome from the disease of *stasis* qualify him as the only true leader of the Roman nation.[24]

The Swift and the Slow: Herod's Energy

But other aspects of Josephus' narrative might qualify this glowing picture.[25] Greeks and Romans would have recognized the logic of a general taking care of his personal safety.[26] At the same time, quickness and energy are qualities that are often praised in Greco-Roman literature. For example, in spite of the display of hubris in Lucan's version of Caesar's crossings of the Adriatic, Caesar's speed (*celeritas*) is a character trait awed by, for example, Cicero (*Att.* 7.22.1; 8.9a.2). This is the character trait that underscores his ability to be a step ahead of his enemies.[27] In view of Caesar's quickness, Vespasian's caution might be seen as a lack of determination, especially because the fate of the whole empire depends on Vespasian's decisions.

The ambiguity of sailing in the midst of the χειμών, the Greek word for both "winter" and "storm," can be illustrated by looking at Philo's use of the theme.[28] In his *In Flaccum*, Philo relates how Flaccus was "destined to have his fill of the frightening dangers of the sea" because he decided to embark on a sea voyage in early winter (*Flacc.* 125: ἀρχομένου χειμῶνος) to Italy, a decision that underscores his foolishness.[29] However, in the *Legatio ad Gaium*, the motif is used in the opposite

---

24 So also, e.g., Davies, *Representing the Dynasty*, 115–16.
25 In agreement with Mason, "Vespasian's Rise."
26 See, for example, Polybius' ruthless judgment about M. Claudius Marcellus for acting "more like a simpleton than a general" (*Hist.* 10.32.7–12) and his praise for Hannibal for the great care he took to provide for his own safety (*Hist.* 10.33.2). Both examples are discussed in Arthur M. Eckstein, *Moral Vision in the Histories of Polybius* (Berkeley: University of California Press, 1995), 28–29.
27 On Caesar's *celeritas* in the *Civil War* see Grillo, *The Art of Caesar's Bellum Civile*, 14–36.
28 Motifs of travel in Philo's *Legatio ad Gaium* are discussed more extensively in Pieter B. Hartog, "Space and Travel in Philo's *Legatio ad Gaium*," *SPhiloA* 30 (2018): 71–92; and Pieter B. Hartog, "Joodse reizigers in het Romeinse Rijk: Tussen globalisering en zelfbehoud," *NTT JTSR* 74 (2020): 23–38 (29–33). For a more elaborate discussion of Philo's *Legatio* see Pieter B. Hartog, "Contesting *Oikoumene*: Resistance and Locality in Philo's *Legatio ad Gaium*," in *Intolerance, Polemics, and Debate in Antiquity: Politico-Cultural, Philosophical, and Religious Forms of Critical Conversation*, ed. George van Kooten and Jacques van Ruiten, TBN 25 (Leiden: Brill, 2019), 205–31.
29 See the commentary *ad loc.* in Pieter W. van der Horst, *Philo's Flaccus: The First Pogrom: Introduction, Translation and Commentary*, PACS 2 (Leiden: Brill, 2003).

way. When receiving the news of Gaius' order to set up a statue in the temple of Jerusalem, the Judean emissaries (including Philo) exclaim that they "decided to sail in the midst of the winter, not knowing how great a storm was awaiting us, a land storm far more dangerous than that of the sea" (*Legat*. 190: χειμῶνος μέσου διεπλεύσαμεν ἀγνοοῦντες, ὅσος χειμὼν ἔφεδρός ἐστιν ὁ κατὰ γῆν ἀργαλεώτερος πολλῷ τοῦ κατὰ θάλατταν). The emissaries willingly took the risk of sailing the Mediterranean in the midst of winter, knowing that storms are the rule rather than the exception in winter season, to save themselves from "fatal acts of lawlessness." This risk is presented as evident, but also as predictable and necessary considering the high stakes of the mission, in contrast with the unpredictability of the χειμών unleashed by Gaius.[30] Thus, Philo's use of sea voyaging in winter times shows that such an act is foolish on account of the dangers involved, *except* in case of emergencies.

Whatever we can say about Josephus' literary representation of Vespasian, he is not the kind of character that takes immediate action in the case of emergencies, even when the fate of the whole empire is at stake. This becomes especially apparent when reading Vespasian's lack of immediate activity alongside Herod the Great's response to a similar challenge. In the first half of the Herod narrative in Book 1 (*B.J.* 1.204–430),[31] Josephus presents Herod as the embodiment of ideal leadership. Herod possesses an energetic disposition and the ability to get things done (δραστήριος). His strong sense of purpose as general and politician greatly contributes to his successes. This becomes evident in numerous episodes, but especially in the episode describing the perils Herod faces when seizing his kingdom (*B.J.* 1.277–285). Along general lines, the setting, the stakes, and the language are remarkably similar to the narrative setting at the end of *War* 4, so much so that we could call it a narrative doublet.[32] Both Herod and Vespasian are under significant political pressure, with respectively the kingdom of Judea and the Roman Empire at stake. Emotion management occupies a significant place in both episodes: Herod experiences strong emotions when receiving the news about the death of his brother (*B.J.* 1.277–278); Vespasian experiences strong emotions when receiving the news about

---

30 On this passage and its literary function cf. Hartog, "Space and Travel," 85–86.
31 For a brief discussion on the structure and themes of the Herod narrative, including further references, see Glas, "Josephus' Self-Characterization," 70–71.
32 The use of such devices was common in ancient literature. On the use of narrative doublets in the *Odyssey* see K. O'Nolan, "Doublets in the Odyssey," *CQ* 28 (1978): 23–37. On the use of such doublets in classical historiography see, e.g., Christina S. Kraus, "Repetition and empire in the *Ab urbe condita*," in *Style and Tradition: Studies in Honor of Wendell Clausen*, ed. Clive Foss and Peter Knox (Stuttgart: Teubner, 1998), 264–83. On the ancient Greek novel see John R. Morgan, "Narrative Doublets in Heliodorus' Aithiopika," in *Studies in Heliodorus*, ed. Richard Hunter (Cambridge: Cambridge Philological Society, 1998), 60–78; Saiichiro Nakatani, "Doublings in Achilles Tatius," *JCS* 49 (2001): 74–85.

the disturbances in Rome (*B.J.* 4.588–589). Most conspicuously, both characters are facing the unattractive prospect of having to sail the Mediterranean during winter season. If Josephus structured the *War* in a way that enables his readers to discover interrelations between events on their own, as Wiater suggests, reading both episodes alongside each other might render interesting results.

Let us have a closer look at Vespasian's response to the bad tidings that receive him in Caesarea. Vespasian is hardly able to bear the torment of his emotion (πάθος). It urges him forward, but he succeeds in holding back his anger (κατεῖχεν τὴν ὀργήν) and do nothing. The distance (διάστημα) and the fact that it is winter season (χειμῶνος ὥρᾳ πλέοντα), knowing that fortune (τύχη) might trick him on his way, stop him from urging forward (ἐπείγω). Considering how ancient authors often foreground the role of fortune in wintry seafaring, Vespasian's judgment seems reasonable. However, as Mason notes, the attitude of waiting and seeing characterizes Vespasian's behavior throughout the narrative. For example, when receiving the news of Nero's death, Vespasian's first response is to delay (ἀνεβάλλετο) his expedition to Jerusalem and wait for the outcome (καραδοκῶν) of the power struggle (*B.J.* 4.497). In the passage cited above, he is subject to unbearable torment, anger, and rage but is unable to act on his own initiative. Immediately after this, his soldiers and officers take control of the situation and force Vespasian to accept his responsibility, threatening to kill him if he refuses (*B.J.* 4.592–604). Even after accepting his responsibility, he needs Mucianus and the other generals to get him moving (προτρεπομένων) and act as an emperor (*B.J.* 4.605). Vespasian uses the winter season as an excuse not to take action, even though the fate of the entire empire is at stake.

As will become evident from the following paraphrase, the path taken by Herod—he continues on his path in response to his emotion, accomplishes this with Caesar-like speed, and does not allow external circumstances to stop his motion—diametrically opposes the choices of Vespasian. When Herod is put under military and political pressure by Antigonus and his Parthian allies, he realizes the need for external help to secure Judea. The Arabs, which Herod assumed to be friends, are unwilling to offer any (*B.J.* 1.274–276) and so Herod decides to retreat to Egypt. At this point, he receives the news about the death of his brother Phasael (B.J. 1.277). Herod is hurled from anxiety to grief, but nevertheless decides to continue on his way (ἤει προσωτέρω). Herod's speed of movement is further emphasized by Josephus' casual remark about the belated (βραδύς) change of mind of the Arab king, who regrets his decision and sends messengers to Herod. However, Herod outstrips (φθάνω) these messengers and reaches Pelusium. Having arrived there, he is denied access to any of the ships, but nonetheless succeeds in arranging an escort to Alexandria after taking his case to the higher authorities (*B.J.* 1.278). He sails to Rome, undeterred by the fact that it is midwinter and that there are the problems in Italy (*B.J.* 1.279: μήτε τὴν ἀκμὴν τοῦ χειμῶνος ὑποδείσας μήτε τοὺς κατὰ τὴν Ἰταλίαν θορύβους ἐπὶ Ῥώμης ἔπλει), to gain Roman support against his enemies. Herod evades Cleopatra's impertinent request to become her general; he is almost shipwrecked and strands at Pamphylia, lacking the funds to build a new ship. He nonetheless manages to get one and sails to Brundisium, from where he finishes his journey to Rome. In Rome he makes his appeal to Mark Antony and Octavian. The deliberateness of his actions becomes apparent in his remark that he had "sailed midwinter to secure [Mark Antony's] protection" (*B.J.* 1.281: διὰ χειμῶνος πλεύσειεν ἐπ' αὐτὸν ἱκέτης): Herod is fully aware of the risks involved, but considers his cause too important to be delayed. His great efforts have considerable payoff: Mark Antony pities Herod and greatly admires his virtue (ἀρετή). Octavian recognizes his energetic disposition (δραστήριος). They lead him before the Senate and crown him king of Judea (*B.J.* 1.282–285).

Given that Herod secures his kingdom under very similar circumstances, even if it is necessary to take risks, Herod comes off much better in this remote comparison. When the stakes and pressure are high, Vespasian is stationary and slow to take action. External circumstances make him pause and unwilling to take any risk. By contrast, the grieving Herod displays a determination that only seems to grow after bad tidings reach him. His actions bear witness to a Caesar-like speed and an incredible ability to achieve his purposes in spite of considerable setbacks and difficult external circumstances.

Vespasian's Tardiness and the Chronology of Rome's Destruction

Given the remoteness of the comparison, we should be careful not to read the passage as a direct criticism on Vespasian's course of action. Simultaneously, it is now becoming clear that, at the very least, Josephus may not have been a major fan of Vespasian's leadership style. We might carry this point one step further by taking Vespasian's tardiness as a clue for interpreting the movement patterns of Vespasian's agents and the timing of their arrival in Rome.

As various scholars have pointed out, the chronology of Josephus' account is of crucial importance for understanding his presentation of the Flavian accession to power.[33] In particular, he makes the news of Vitellius' actions in Rome the beginning of Vespasian's imperial ambitions (*B.J.* 4.586–587). The problem of this claim is that Vespasian and his supporters could not have heard of the behavior of Vitellius

---

33 The most elaborate treatment is Davies, *Representing the Dynasty*, 116–17.

and his troops on the 1st of July, the day of Vespasian's acclamation, because they could not have arrived in Rome before that date. It is probable that the Flavians used the misbehavior of the Vitellians to justify their coup from hindsight.[34] By contrast, later Greek and Roman authors suggest that Vespasian's ambitions must have taken shape shortly after the death of Galba, while Otho was still emperor (Suet., *Vesp.* 5.1; Tac., *Hist.* 2.6–7; Cass. Dio 65.8).[35] According to most scholars, this means that Josephus deliberately adjusted his narrative in trying to adhere to the official Flavian story.

This reading can be questioned on various grounds.[36] Most essential for my current purpose: if Josephus deliberately places the beginning of Vespasian's pretensions before the 1st of July, that is, late spring or early summer, what does that tell us about Vespasian's response to the news of Vitellius' accession as emperor and his decision not to travel to Rome because he had to sail in time of *winter*? As Mason aptly remarks, Vespasian "would have sailed and his army would have marched in the most favourable season possible."[37] Because the whole narrative would probably still be fresh in the mind of Josephus' readers, Josephus' presentation of the episode may have struck them as an attempt to find excuses on Vespasian's part and wiggle himself out of the most important task possible, namely, jumping to the rescue of his πατρίς.

While scholars have noted the importance of chronology in the beginning of the account of the Year of the Four Emperors in *War* 4, the end of Josephus' narrative has never been explored in any systematic fashion. My observations on Vespasian's inactiveness, tardiness, and immobility early in the account have significant ramifications for Josephus' emphasis on the chronology at the narrative's end. While Josephus narrates most of his account of the Year of the Four Emperors in a rather quick pace and without caring too much about the details, he slows down to a day-by-day pace at the climax of the narrative.[38] This feature, which is not found in any other account of the same events, might be crucial for understanding Josephus' version.

---

34 See, for example, Gwyn Morgan, *69 A.D.: The Year of Four Emperors* (Oxford: Oxford University Press, 2006), 181–82; Rhiannon Ash, *Tacitus* Histories *Book 2* (Cambridge: Cambridge University Press, 2007), 231; Davies, *Representing the Dynasty*, 100–102, 117.
35 See, e.g., Rajak, *Josephus*, 214; Ash, *Tacitus* Histories, 33; Davies, *Representing the Dynasty*, 117. Possible continuities between the accounts of Josephus and Tacitus are discussed in Mason, "Vespasian's Rise," 217–18.
36 Cf. Mason, "Vespasian's Rise," 218–20.
37 Mason, "Vespasian's Rise," 222.
38 Cf. Steve Mason, "Of Audience and Meaning: Reading Josephus's *Judean War* in the Context of a Flavian Audience," in *Josephus and Jewish History in Flavian History and Beyond*, ed. Joseph Sievers and Gaia Lembi, JSJSup 104 (Leiden: Brill, 2005), 71–100 (98).

As discussed above, Vespasian accepts imperial rule only after his soldiers threaten to kill him (*B.J.* 4.603–604) and is forced into motion by his commanders, most notably Mucianus (*B.J.* 4.605). After a digression on Egypt's geography, Josephus tells the reader that Vespasian secures that region by dispatching a letter to the Judean governor Tiberius Alexander (*B.J.* 4.616–619). He also receives support from the legions in Moesia and Pannonia (*B.J.* 4.619), and the Syrian and other provinces (*B.J.* 4.620–621). After having received tremendous support from different sides, Vespasian finally gets on the move and travels to Antioch (*B.J.* 4.630). Upon his arrival there, his thoughts are disclosed by Josephus: "Moreover, when considering in which direction to turn, he judged that going to Rome, which was thrown into disorder under Vitellius, was more important than a rapid motion to Alexandria, which he perceived to be secure already" (*B.J.* 4.631). In brief: Rome is Vespasian's priority, not Alexandria. He decides to send his trusted general Mucianus to Rome. Josephus does not inform his audience about why Vespasian does not go himself, nor what kind of extremely important business kept him from going to Rome. Vespasian disappears from view until the end of *War* 4 (*B.J.* 4.656–663). In turn, also Mucianus is anxious about sailing in midwinter (ὁ δὲ διὰ τὴν τοῦ χειμῶνος ἀκμὴν δείσας τὸ πλεῖν), one of the major reasons that apparently kept Vespasian from going himself when he heard about Vitellius' accession. However, he solves the problem by travelling over land via Cappadocia and Phrygia (*B.J.* 4.632), whereas Vespasian decided not to take action at all.

The subsequent narrative subtly suggests that Vespasian's tardiness in the beginning may have had destructive consequences in Rome. Civil war develops fully between Mucianus' departure from Antioch and his arrival in Rome. Troops led by Antonius Primus, loyal to the Flavians but acting without Vespasian's consent, battle and defeat the legions of Vitellius near Cremona. Vespasian's brother Sabinus is killed in an attempt to defend the Capitol against Vitellius. Domitian barely escapes. The temple of Jupiter Optimus Maximus is destroyed in the skirmishes (*B.J.* 2.649). Only one day later (μετὰ μίαν ἡμέραν) Antonius' men march into the city and annihilate Vitellius' troops (*B.J.* 4.650). Vitellius himself is butchered in the center of Rome, presumably on the third of Apellaeus (21st of December, 69 CE). Thousands are killed, and they even turn against the innocent citizens of Rome. Mucianus and his army arrive on the following day (*B.J.* 4.654: τῇ δ'ὑστεραίᾳ) and hence two days after the great clash between Sabinus' revolutionaries and Vitellius' troops (*B.J.* 4.645–649).[39] Josephus' emphasis on the precise moment of Mucianus'

---

39 This peculiarity in Josephus' narrative is also observed in de Kleijn, "C. Licinius Mucianus," 439.

arrival, which is not emphasized at all in other sources,[40] prompts a fundamental question: would Mucianus and his troops have been able to prevent this disaster if Vespasian had not lingered and taken up his responsibilities immediately? The narrative framing suggests that the worst of the civil war in Rome could have been prevented if Vespasian had acted more decisively, like Herod, or even Mucianus.

The closing scene of *War* 4 sheds light on Vespasian's whereabouts. Vespasian receives the news of his great victory in Rome upon his arrival in—of all places—Alexandria (*B.J.* 4.656), the city that had no priority for Vespasian because it had already been secured. Upon receiving the good news from Rome, "he was setting himself in motion (ὥρμητο) to undertake a sea voyage to Rome as soon as the winter was over and was quickly (τάχος) administering affairs in Alexandria" (*B.J.* 4.658). Now that all the dangers and risks are removed, Vespasian finds his energy back and suddenly makes haste to travel to Rome and secure the position others have acquired for him. The irony is subtle but unmistakable.

Implications and Conclusions

This chapter has shown how Josephus sets up his descriptions of travel experiences in a way that invites his audience to draw moral-political lessons from them. This setup corresponds to the broader military-political purposes of his historical narratives and resembles Greco-Roman historiographical conventions of his days. To substantiate this point, this chapter has analyzed the complex and multi-layered nature of Vespasian's emotion management in response to the prospect of undertaking a dangerous sea voyage from Judea to Rome in the midst of winter.

The deeper meaning of Vespasian's emotion management and subsequent actions becomes clear only when reading them in the context of similar events narrated elsewhere in the *War*. On the one hand, the immediate attention of the reader is drawn to the obvious contrast between the cautious and moderate Vespasian and the rash and immoderate Vitellius, the scapegoat in Josephus' narrative of the Year of the Four Emperors. Interpreted this way, Vespasian stands out as the savior of Rome and the empire. On the other hand, a complementary reading is plausible in consideration of Josephus' use of the motif of wintry seafaring, a standard theme in classical

---

40 Tac., *Hist.* 4.1–11; Suet., *Vesp.* 7.1; Cass. Dio 64.22. Tacitus' account assumes considerable a considerable temporal gap between the death of Vitellius and the arrival of Mucianus. See, e.g., Tac., *Hist.* 4.4. Cf. de Kleijn, "C. Licinius Mucianus," 439–42. Also note that Tacitus suggests that Mucianus was a major factor delaying the Flavian forces (e.g., *Hist.* 3.78), something passed over entirely by Josephus.

literature that would have been recognizable for Josephus' audience, and Vespasian's tardiness: he literally freezes and needs the urging of his subordinates to get himself moving. Vespasian's indecisiveness becomes evident when considering that he will have received the news of Vitellius' accession in the spring or the early summer, at the very latest, and would not have needed to sail in winter at all. Josephus presents alternative paths of action elsewhere in the *War*, for example, when describing Herod's emotion management and determined response to setbacks under very similar circumstances, including undertaking a sea journey in the midst of winter. Herod's case shows that Vespasian's estimation of the risks involved is justified, but also that a readiness to take risk in case of emergencies can be rewarding and result in considerable strategic advantages. Moreover, Vespasian's second-in-command, Mucianus, immediately decides to travel by land instead of undertaking a sea voyage. When read in light of Vespasian's tardiness in the beginning of the narrative, we might take Josephus' emphasis on the timing of Mucianus' arrival in Rome, only two days after the murder of Vespasian's brother, as a subtle attempt to invite his readers to judge Vespasian's accession to power along more critical lines than the official story constructed by the Flavians would have allowed, while maintaining the possibility of giving a different and much more positive interpretation.

If my arguments concerning Vespasian's emotional response to the prospect of travelling are accepted, it is difficult to see this narrative as an unqualified praise of Vespasian. Setting his narrative up in an ambiguous fashion would have allowed Josephus to avoid the danger of offending the emperor (and, by extension, certain death). The immediate attention is drawn towards the contrast between the vicious Vitellius and the virtuous Vespasian. However, when looking closely at Josephus' carefully spun web of narrative actions and decisions, it appears that more unconventional and urbanely critical messages are hidden underneath the surface of the narrative.

References

Ahl, Frederick. "The Art of Safe Criticism in Greece and Rome." *AJP* 105 (1984): 174–208.
Ahl, Frederick, and Hanna M. Roisman. *The Odyssey Re-formed*. Ithaca, NY: Cornell University Press, 1996.
Ash, Rhiannon. *Tacitus* Histories *Book 2*. Cambridge: Cambridge University Press, 2007.
Bartsch, Shadi. *Actors in the Audience: Theatricality and Doublespeak from Nero to Hadrian*. Cambridge: Harvard University Press, 1994.
Biggs, Thomas, and Jessica Blum, eds. *The Epic Journey in Greek and Roman Literature*. Cambridge: Cambridge University Press, 2019.
Bloch, René. *Andromeda in Jaffa: Mythische Orte als Reiseziele in der jüdischen Antike*. Franz-Delitzsch-Vorlesung 2015. Münster: Institutum Judaicum Delitzschianum, 2017.

Davies, Jonathan. *Representing the Dynasty in Flavian Rome: The Case of Josephus' Jewish War*. Oxford: Oxford University Press, 2023.

De Temmerman, Koen. *Crafting Characters: Heroes and Heroines in the Ancient Greek Novel*. Oxford: Oxford University Press, 2014.

Eckstein, Arthur M. *Moral Vision in the Histories of Polybius*. Berkeley: University of California Press, 1995.

Glas, Eelco. "Flavius Josephus' Self-Characterization in First-Century Rome: A Literary Analysis of the Autobiographical Passages in the *Bellum Judaicum*." PhD diss., University of Groningen, 2020.

Glas, Eelco. "Josephus between Jerusalem and Rome: Cultural Brokerage and the Rhetoric of Emotion in the *Bellum Judaicum* (1.9–12)." *Histos* 14 (2020): 275–99.

Glas, Eelco. "Overcoming Otherness in Flavian Rome: Flavius Josephus and the Rhetoric of Identity in the *Bellum Judaicum*." Pages 163–84 in *Roman Identity: Between Ideal and Performance*. Edited by F. Lautaro Roig Lanzillotta, José L. Brandão, Cláudia Teixeira, and Ália Rodrigues. Turnhout: Brepols, 2023.

Goodman, Martin. *Rome and Jerusalem: The Clash of Ancient Civilizations*. London: Allen Lane, 2007.

Grillo, Luca. *The Art of Caesar's Bellum Civile: Literature, Ideology, and Community*. Cambridge: Cambridge University Press, 2012.

Hartog, Pieter B. "Space and Travel in Philo's *Legatio ad Gaium*." *SPhiloA* 30 (2018): 71–92.

Hartog, Pieter B. "Contesting *Oikoumene*: Resistance and Locality in Philo's *Legatio ad Gaium*." Pages 205–31 in *Intolerance, Polemics, and Debate in Antiquity: Politico-Cultural, Philosophical, and Religious Forms of Critical Conversation*. Edited by George van Kooten and Jacques van Ruiten. TBN 25. Leiden: Brill, 2019.

Hartog, Pieter B. "Joodse reizigers in het Romeinse Rijk: Tussen globalisering en zelfbehoud." *NTT JTSR* 74 (2020): 23–38.

Hezser, Catherine. *Jewish Travel in Antiquity*. TSAJ 144. Tübingen: Mohr Siebeck, 2011.

Horst, Pieter W. van der. *Philo's Flaccus: The First Pogrom: Introduction, Translation and Commentary*. PACS 2. Leiden: Brill, 2003.

Hurlet, Frédéric. "Sources and Evidence." Pages 17–39 in *A Companion to the Flavian Age of Imperial Rome*. Edited by Andrew Zissos. Malden, MA: Blackwell, 2016.

Kleijn, Gerda de. "C. Licinius Mucianus, Vespasian's Co-Ruler in Rome." *Mnemosyne* 66 (2013): 433–59.

Kemezis, Adam. "Flavian Greek Literature." Pages 450–68 in *A Companion to the Flavian Age of Imperial Rome*. Edited by Andrew Zissos. Malden, MA: Blackwell, 2016.

Kraus, Christina S. "Repetition and Empire in the *Ab urbe condita*." Pages 264–83 in *Style and Tradition: Studies in Honor of Wendell Clausen*. Edited by Clive Foss and Peter Knox. Stuttgart: Teubner, 1998.

Landau, Tamar. *Out-Heroding Herod: Josephus, Rhetoric, and the Herod Narratives*. AJEC 63. Leiden: Brill, 2006.

MacDonald, Dennis R. "The Shipwrecks of Odysseus and Paul." *NTS* 45 (1999): 88–107.

Mason, Steve. "Figured Speech and Irony in T. Flavius Josephus." Pages 243–88 in *Flavius Josephus and Flavian Rome*. Edited by Jonathan Edmondson, Steve Mason, and James Rives. Oxford: Oxford University Press, 2005.

Mason, Steve. "Of Audience and Meaning: Reading Josephus's *Judean War* in the Context of a Flavian Audience." Pages 71–100 in *Josephus and Jewish History in Flavian History and Beyond*. Edited by Joseph Sievers and Gaia Lembi. JSJSup 104. Leiden: Brill, 2005.

Mason, Steve. "Vespasian's Rise from Civil War in Josephus's *Bellum Judaicum*." Pages 199–226 in *After 69 CE: Writing Civil War in Flavian Rome*. Edited by Lauren Donovan Ginsberg and Darcy Anne Krasne. TCSV 65. Berlin: De Gruyter, 2018.

Matthews, Monica. *Caesar and the Storm: A Commentary on Lucan,* De Bello Civili, *Book 5, Lines 476–721.* Bern: Lang, 2008.
Meijer, F.J. "Mare Clausum aut Mare Apertum: Een beschouwing over zeevaart in de winter." *Hermeneus* 55 (1983): 2–20.
Millar, Fergus. "Monuments of the Jewish War in Rome." Pages 101–28 in *Flavius Josephus and Flavian Rome.* Edited by Jonathan Edmondson, Steve Mason, and James Rives. Oxford: Oxford University Press, 2005.
Morford, M.P.O. *The Poet Lucan: Studies in Rhetorical Epic.* Oxford: Basil Blackwell, 1967.
Morgan, Gwyn. *69 A.D.: The Year of Four Emperors.* Oxford: Oxford University Press, 2006.
Morgan, John R. "Narrative Doublets in Heliodorus' Aithiopika." Pages 60–78 in *Studies in Heliodorus.* Edited by Richard Hunter. Cambridge: Cambridge Philological Society, 1998.
Nakatani, Saiichiro. "Doublings in Achilles Tatius." *JCS* 49 (2001): 74–85.
Niehoff, Maren R. "Parodies of Educational Journeys in Josephus, Justin Martyr, and Lucian." Pages 203–22 in *Journeys in the Roman East: Imagined and Real.* Edited by Maren R. Niehoff. Culture, Religion, and Politics in the Greco-Roman World 1. Tübingen: Mohr Siebeck, 2017.
Nünlist, René. *The Ancient Critic at Work: Terms and Concepts of Literary Criticism in Greek Scholia.* Cambridge: Cambridge University Press, 2009.
O'Nolan, K. "Doublets in the Odyssey." *CQ* 28 (1978): 23–37.
Praeder, Susan Marie. "Acts 27:1–28:16: Sea Voyages in Ancient Literature and the Theology of Luke-Acts." *CBQ* 46 (1984): 683–706.
Rajak, Tessa. *Josephus: The Historian and His Society.* 2nd ed. London: Duckworth, 2002.
Rocca, Samuele. *In the Shadow of the Caesars: Jewish Life in Roman Italy.* BRLA 74. Leiden: Brill, 2022.
Safrai, Zeev. *Seeking Out the Land: Land of Israel Traditions in Ancient Jewish, Christian and Samaritan Literature (200 BCE–400 CE).* JCPS 32. Leiden: Brill, 2018.
Schwartz, Daniel R. "'Going up to Rome' in Josephus's *Antiquities.*" Pages 373–88 in *Journeys in the Roman East: Imagined and Real.* Edited by Maren R. Niehoff. Culture, Religion, and Politics in the Greco-Roman World 1. Tübingen: Mohr Siebeck, 2017.
Shahar, Yuval. *Josephus Geographicus: The Classical Context of Geography in Josephus.* TSAJ 98. Tübingen: Mohr Siebeck, 2004.
Strelan, Rick. "A Greater Than Caesar: Storm Stories in Lucan and Mark." *ZNW* 91 (2000): 166–79.
Talbert, Charles H., and J.H. Hayes. "A Theology of Sea Storms in Luke-Acts." Pages 321–36 in *Society of Biblical Literature Seminar Papers* 34. Edited by E.H. Lovering, Jr. Atlanta: Scholars Press, 1995.
Troftgrüben, Troy M. "Slow Sailing in Acts: Suspense in the Final Sea Journey (Acts 27:1–28:15)." *JBL* 136 (2017): 949–68.
Thackery, Henry St.J., trans. *Josephus: The Jewish War, Volume 2: Books 3–4.* LCL. Cambridge: Harvard University Press, 1927.
Tuval, Michael. "A Jewish Priest in Rome." Pages 397–411 in *Flavius Josephus: Interpretation and History.* Edited by Jack Pastor, Pnina Stern, and Menahem Mor. JSJSup 146. Leiden: Brill, 2011.
Tuval, Michael. *From Jerusalem Priest to Roman Jew.* WUNT 2/357. Tübingen: Mohr Siebeck, 2013.
Vonder Bruegge, John M. *Mapping Galilee in Josephus, Luke, and John: Critical Geography and the Construction of an Ancient Space.* AJEC 93. Leiden: Brill, 2016.
Wiater, Nicolas. "Reading the *Jewish War*: Narrative Technique and Historical Interpretation in Josephus's *Bellum Judaicum.*" *Materiali e Discussioni per l'analisi dei testi classici* 64 (2010): 145–85.

Gert van Klinken
Religion on the Road—Nehalennia Revisited: Voyagers Addressing a North Sea Deity in the Second Century CE

Abstract: Connections between travel and religion are discussed by an analysis of the seafarers' cult of Nehalennia during the early Roman Empire in a region that now belongs to the seaboard of the Dutch province of Zeeland. Veneration of Nehalennia exemplifies an important aspect of transition, not only for those who made the perilous journey between Britain and the European mainland so many years ago, but also for those who study religious history from a modern perspective. The cult of Nehalennia demonstrates the impact of Mediterranean concepts of the divine on local culture in the North, a dissemination that clearly received an impetus from travel between different regions of the vast Roman Empire.

It is noticed that some aspects that are commonly attributed to the era of Christianization during Frankish rule can already be observed in pagan form in the Nehalennia cult during the second century CE. In order to understand the formative process that was to shape the Christian culture of the Middle Ages, this case study suggests that many of its characteristics were brought in during the preceding Roman era, when paganism in the form of fusion between Greco-Roman and native Germanic motives was still the norm. Despite massive demographic and political change, continuity in the religious developments during the first millennium CE deserves academic attention. Both in the Roman and in the early Medieval era ideas used to be exchanged via networks of trading connections, and not only by the agency of religious professionals.

At the Crossroads

In Roman times it was not unusual to find the shrines of the gods on crossroads. Wayfarers and sailors were well-acquainted with the tendency of temple complexes to spring up at the same site as fairs, markets and other examples of economic activity. As Wim van Es remarks in his books on the Romans in the Netherlands, spiritual and material interests were intertwined.[1] It was natural for both commercial and religious spheres of activity to be located at sites that were being

---

[1] Wim A. van Es, *De Romeinen in Nederland* (Bussum: Fibula-Van Dishoeck, 1973), 152.

https://doi.org/10.1515/9783110717488-010

frequented by travellers. The sacred and the mundane were not taken as mutually exclusive, in the sense that they were prohibited to interconnect. As Guy de la Bédoyère put it: "There is no doubt that travelling, and the passage from one place to another, represented an important spiritual experience."[2]

A well-known example is provided by the temples dedicated to Nehalennia at the Scheldt estuary, in what is now the province of Zeeland at the Dutch seaboard between Walcheren and Schouwen-Duiveland. Both shrines flourished between the second and early third century CE, only to be claimed by the shifting seabed later. Paradoxically it may be argued that the rich trove of texts and statuaries retrieved from these sites in modern times and now cared for in Leiden, would probably have been lost for posterity if they had not been engulfed by the sea. Until their demise, both temples used to stand at the Southern bank of the Scheldt estuary. The remains of the Domburg temple ended up in the North Sea and the better-known examples of Colijnsplaat (*Ganuenta*) in the Eastern Scheldt. The Roman toponym for Domburg is unknown. Naval shrines of this type are especially common at the Western seaboards of the Roman Empire. We even find them in the far West, such as Nornour in the Isles of Scilly.[3]

It is assumed that both temples at the Scheldt estuary belonged to the so-called Gallo-Roman type, which is also known from France, Belgium, Great-Britain and the Western fringe of Germany. A central tower-like *cella*, which used to contain the image of the deity, was surrounded by a concentric ambulatory with a pitched roof built into the *cella* walls. It is not uncommon for the revered deity to have a native name combined with Roman symbolism and of course an accompanying text in Latin—an obvious example of the *interpretatio Romana*, where autochthonous and Roman conceptions of the divine are fused together.

Native elements, also found at Domburg and Ganuenta, are the presence of a grove of trees (*nemus, nemeton*) and the stylistic phenomenon of triplication. A charming detail in these local deities was their dress, designed in a way that is specific for these two locations. Similar examples of local costume (*klederdracht*) can be found in the attire of the Matrones in the Cologne region, especially in their caps modelled after those worn by the female members of the Ubii tribe.

Though mostly presented as an individual, it is not uncommon to find Nehalennia triplicated, while maintaining her name in the plural form: *Neihalenninis*. As a single person, Nehalennia can be referred to in terms of an intimate relationship between the deity and the dedicant. When triplicated, there is a sense of numen

---

[2] Guy de la Bédoyère, *Gods with Thunderbolts: Religion in Roman Britain* (Tempus: Stroud, 2007), 105.
[3] Jeanette Ratcliffe and Charles Johns, *Scilly's Archaeological Heritage* (Truro: Twelveheads Press, 2003), 13, 31.

rather than individuality: presence of the divine power that is often associated with a specific spot on the map (as *genius loci*) but not as a personal presence.

Travelers came to visit the Nehalennia shrines as part of their commercial travels via the seaways between Germania Inferior and Britannia. Most of the individuals we know by name were merchants and sea captains from the Rhine and Moselle valleys, exporting goods that had been manufactured in Cologne and Treves to the British market. During the outward-bound leg of their journey, they would make a promise (*votum*) to set up an altar to the deity, on the condition that they and their loads would return safely. If this came to pass (and as far as we can see: only then!), they would set up their votive altar, delicately carved and with words of thanks to Nehalennia. In his analysis of Roman culture in the Rhineland, Michael Zelle remarks that this was common practice in their region of origin.[4] Similar votive altars were raised in honor of Jupiter Conservator in Colonia Ulpia Traiana at the left bank of the river Rhine. Such stones, known as *Weihesteine* in the Rhineland, also show female goddesses such as the Matres or Matrones. Another similarity to Nehalennia are the fruits (pears and apples) that were deposited on top of some of the votive altars and that were also rendered in stone. We also find fruit in the hands of the male Batavian god Hercules Magusanus (Empel; Xanten). Zelle believes that the Matrones were essentially benign, unlike the warlike Hercules Magusanus.[5] Nevertheless, their goodwill did not come cheap: even for a well-established trading firm, a votive stone of the quality that is in evidence in Domburg and Ganuenta would require substantial investments. Limestone, and more rarely sandstone, blocks had been brought in from the South via the rivers Meuse and Rhine, most likely already chiseled into the required general form. Individual touches, especially the votive texts, would be added on site, in accordance with the wishes of each dedicant. A veneration of this type depended on an economy that was producing a decent surplus.

The Matres are often perceived as native in their origin (compared to the Frisian Hludana). However, as is typical for the *interpretatio Romana*, Nehalennia is simultaneously styled in the guise of the goddess Fortuna, as known from Italy. She represents Fortuna Redux, the guarantee of a safe return of the traveler on land and sea. Iconographical markers for Fortuna Redux are the cornucopia and the ship rudder, which draw attention to Fortuna's positive influence at land and sea. This is not to say that they are addressed in a way that is fully anthropological. Roland Geschlößl rightly remarks that the ambiguity between a personalized god and *numina loci* is an element of what he calls *Götterverschmelzung*.[6]

---

4 Michael Zelle, *Götter und Kulte: Colonia Ulpia Traiana* (Cologne: Rheinland, 2000), 93.
5 Zelle, *Götter und Kulte*, 95.
6 Roland Gschlößl, *Im Schmelztiegel der Religionen: Göttertausch bei Kelten, Römern und Germanen* (Mainz: Wissenschaftliche Buchgesellschaft, 2006).

Addressing a North Sea Deity

The making of an offering to a god must be considered as an unusual event, outside the normal routine of daily life. It can be noted that the rich correspondence from Vindolanda (more than eight hundred partially preserved letters from Northumbria, early second century BCE) refers to a shrine in just one instance, where a load of wheat was to be delivered to a certain Amabilis, *ad fanum*. The mention of the shrine is preceded by a delivery to "the oxherds at the wood (*bubulcaris in siluam*)," which is suggestive of a rustic setting of this special shrine.[7] References to transport and travel, on the other hand, are quite common in Vindolanda. Travelers were quite aware of the problems they might encounter on the road. However, apart from a few oblique references, they preferred to address difficulties connected to travel as a matter of fact, rather than connect them to any religious invocation. The letter of Octavius to Candidus offers an example of this approach:

> *Mitte coria que scribis esse Cataractonio scribe denture mi et karrum de quo scribis et quit sit cum eo karro mi scribe iam illec petissem nissi iumenta non curavi uexsare dum uiae male sunt.*

> The hides which you write [about] are at Cataractonium—write that they be given to me and the waggon about which you write. Write to me what is with that waggon. I would have already been to collect them except that I did not care to injure the animals while the roads are bad.[8]

This represents the rather matter-of-fact way in which the residents of Vindolanda used to ponder on the realities of travel in their daily correspondence. It was possible to add a reference to unspecified deities: "If the gods (*di*) are propitious." However, the editors of the Vindolanda correspondence take this as no more than a "standard expression of optimism."[9]

It seems that religious discourse belonged to a special niche, rather than to the common occurrences of daily life. How was the deity addressed by her travelling devotees? In his reflection on this general theme, Jörg Rüpke defends the proposition that doing for Roman religion is of more importance than believing. He makes his point in a discussion of Cicero's *De natura deorum*:

---

7 Alan K. Bowman and J. David Thomas, eds., *The Vindolanda Writing Tablets*, Tabulae Vindolandenses 2 (London: Trustees of the British Museum, 1994), 123–24 (180: 10–11).
8 Bowman and Thomas, *Vindolanda*, 321–29 (343: 15–21).
9 Bowman and Thomas, *Vindolanda*, 339 (349: 2).

Religio in the singular in Cicero's argument is a necessary consequence of any belief in a god, and finds its expression, as also its limits, in various feelings of religious obligation: *religiones*.[10]

So, there was a contract, in written form:

> There is no doubt that in the Imperial Age more people acquired the ability to read written characters, even though advanced textual competence remained an elite phenomenon. Against this background, religion was increasingly regarded not only as something knowable, but also something that had to do with texts.[11]

But Rüpke is rather more hesitant about the element of piety, at least in the early modern sense of the word:

> Whereas both the request ... and the thanks promised were embedded in a full and enduring communication, in the context of the votum institution they became discrete events in time. Once the obligation incurred by the vow had been made good, the tie binding the two parties in mutual responsibility was loosed.[12]

The dedication texts of the Nehalennia cult in Domburg and Colijnsplaat have been published by Petrus Stuart. Names of dedicants include at least the praenomen and nomen gentile of the dedicant, and often, also the cognomen and father's name. Fairly typical is the dedication of Sumaronius Primanus, who made good on his promise to Nehalennia and did so gladly and willingly: *Deae Nehalenniae Sumaronius Primanus v(otum) s(olvit) l(ibens) m(erito)*.[13]

In other cases, we find an explicit statement that this was being done by putting up a votive altar: *aram posuit*.[14] This is not to say that Nehalennia could claim exclusivity. Even within her own temenos or temple grounds, dedications to Jupiter Optimus Maximus, Neptune and the native Burorina—though less common—could also be found. Of all these deities it is said that they are venerated by travelers for their protective aspects, for instance in the phrase (note the plural): *Diis deabusque praesidibus provinciarum* (protectors).[15]

The procedure is traced back to the vow, made at the beginning of the journey, *ex voto susceptor*. In many cases the tone is almost business-like, especially when the dedicant refers to his thanks for better results (*ob meliores actus*) or refers to the

---

[10] Jörg Rüpke, *Pantheon: A New History of Roman Religion* (Princeton: Princeton University Press, 2018), 181.
[11] Rüpke, *Pantheon*, 336.
[12] Rüpke, *Pantheon*, 336.
[13] Petrus Stuart, *Nehalennia van Domburg: Geschiedenis van de stenen monumenten*, 2 vols. (Utrecht: Matrijs, 2013), 1:83–85 (24).
[14] Stuart, *Nehalennia van Domburg*, 86 (26).
[15] Stuart, *Nehalennia van Domburg*, 102–103 (38).

safe landing of his cargo (*ob merces bene conservatas*, in the wordings of a negotiator cretarius Britannicus (a merchant who specializes in exporting ceramics from the mainland to Britain).

More personal are the references to a feeling of obligation toward the deity, for instance in the phrase *ex precepto aram posuit pro salute filii sui*—an altar has been set up at her command and for the benefit of a son of the dedicant. The same idea can be expressed as *ex iussu, ex imperio ipseus* (ipsius) or *ex imperio eius*. In some cases, the actual year of the proceedings was noted, by adding a consular date.

Meaning

Finally, we may ask what meaning the making and fulfilling of a vow may have had for the dedicant. The most plausible explanation, still to be found in many books, is of course that of *do ut des*. In this way of thinking, it is commonly assumed that people invest in religion on the assumption of making a net profit in the end. The argument can be extended to presume that this assumption is grounded in a supernatural belief in divine powers that are both able to influence the human fate and open for negotiation. However, we have good reason to question the basic elements of this explanatory model. First, we may ask where the material gain is. Dedicants have no guarantee of a safe return while making his vow. All they know is that they have pledged to honor the deity in the hypothetic case of such a safe return. Apart from that, it should be noted that the Nehalennia corpus dates from the declining years of the classic Roman pantheon. As Neil Bernstein remarks in his discussion of Publius Papinius Statius' epical poem *Thebaid*, it was no longer possible for the cultured upper strata of society to believe in the simpler and supernatural versions of *do ut des*:

> The *Thebaid* presents its readers with a series of difficult questions regarding the relationship between ritual, agency, and power. What is the point of engaging in ritual if it cannot certify a positive relationship with the gods? What is the point of moral decision-making in a world where the gods (i) deliberately conceal essential facts from human beings and (ii) remove agency from human beings by manipulating their emotions to the point where they are no longer capable of making rational choices?[16]

In fact, it may be that the *do ut des* explanation is not necessary at all to explain the veneration of seafarers for Nehalennia. Rather, we may speculate that for these dedicants, experience of life as such offered the impetus for their *religio*, instead of the

---

[16] Neil Bernstein, "Ritual Murder and Suicide in the *Thebaid*," in *Ritual and Religion in Flavian Epic*, ed. Antony Augoustaki (Oxford: Oxford University Press, 2013), 233–48 (247).

hope of gain or even an articulated belief in the supernatural. What we know is that we are people on the road, vulnerable and under the doom that we will die sooner or later. It is worth noting that a basic pattern found in the Nehalennia inscriptions is being repeated in post-Roman times. Memorial stones for the dead in early Christian Scandinavia typically maintain the importance of mentioning the dedicant's name, together with the person for whom the monument is being constructed in the first place. A reference to the Christian God may be added ("God is one"), but not in the form of any specific favors being asked.[17] This is an indication of a form of awareness beyond *do ut des*, in our efforts during our everyday lives and also in our feelings of thanks for generosities offered to us even by a finite existence. Thanks are offered out of our free will, and perhaps also in the faint hope that our words may be read and registered by posterity.

A final question is how different this dedicatory spirituality is when compared to later developments in Christianity. Reflecting on this subject, I was struck by the similarity between the basic layout of the Nehalennia texts and that of Christian funerary inscriptions in the early modern era.[18]

CINERIBUS ET MEMORIAE
GULEILMI CARWITHEN A.B.
HUIUS ECCLESIAE
ANN XLIV RECTORIS
FILII NATU MAXIMI
IOANNIS CARWITHEN A.B.

We can hardly fail to note the similarities: after having addressed the divine name, the text turns to a mortal man, recorded with some basic detail of family, profession and date. Also, the last words on a Christian headstone are often reserved for an expression of thanks.

---

17 Terje Spurkland, *Norwegian Runes and Runic Inscriptions* (Woodbridge: Boydell Press, 2005), 96–98.
18 John Parker, *Reading Latin Epitaphs* (Exeter: Exeter Press, 2008), 5.

References

Bédoyère, Guy de la. *Gods with Thunderbolts: Religion in Roman Britain*. Stroud: Tempus, 2007.
Bernstein, Neil. "Ritual Murder and Suicide in the *Thebaid*." Pages 233–48 in *Ritual and Religion in Flavian Epic*. Edited by Antony Augoustakis. Oxford: Oxford University Press, 2013.
Bowman, Alan K., and Thomas, J. David eds. *The Vindolanda Writing Tablets*. Tabulae Vindolandenses 2. London: Trustees of the British Museum, 1994.
Es, Wim A. van. *De Romeinen in Nederland*. Bussum: Fibula-Van Dishoeck, 1973.
Gschlößl, Roland. *Im Schmelztiegel der Religionen: Göttertausch bei Kelten, Römern und Germanen*. Mainz: Wissenschaftliche Buchgesellschaft, 2006.
Parker, John. *Reading Latin Epitaphs*. Exeter: Exeter Press, 2008.
Ratcliffe, Jeanette and Charles Johns. *Scilly's Archaelogical Heritage*. Truro: Twelveheads Press, 2003.
Rüpke, Jörg. *Pantheon: A New History of Roman Religion*. Princeton: Princeton University Press, 2018.
Spurkland, Terje. *Norwegian Runes and Runic Inscriptions*. Woodbridge: Boydell Press, 2005.
Stuart, Petrus. *Nehalennia van Domburg: Geschiedenis van de stenen monumenten*. 2 vols. Utrecht: Matrijs, 2013.
Zelle, Michael. *Götter und Kulte: Colonia Ulpia Traiana*. Cologne: Rheinland, 2000.

Benjamin Lensink
Mapping Cosmological Space in the Apocalypse of Paul and the *Visio Pauli*: The Actualization of Virtual Spatiality in Two Pauline Apocalyptical Journeys based on 2 Cor 12:2–4

Abstract: This chapter discusses how two early Christian texts, the Apocalypse of Paul (NH V,2) and the *Visio Pauli*, took up the ascension account written by the Apostle Paul in 2 Cor 12:2–4, and how they provided their own interpretation of this heavenly journey. More specifically, it focuses on how both texts use space and spatiality in order to show how they have taken up the sparse details regarding space in 2 Cor 12:2–4. After a discussion of the spatial frames and the narrative world of both texts based on the narratological methodology into spatiality as introduced by Marie-Laure Ryan combined with a Deleuzian framework for reception history as pioneered by Brennan Breed, this chapter presents a three-fold conclusion. (1) While basing themselves on the same biblical passage, the two texts present different spatial frames and narrative worlds. (2) Both texts are best understood as differing actualizations of the virtual potential of space in 2 Cor 12:2–4. (3) They use space to present an ethical message: the Apocalypse of Paul aims to show its readers the dangers of escaping the material realm and the hostilities during the heavenly ascent while attempting to become a psychic being; the *Visio Pauli* uses the far shores of the river Ocean as revelatory lands, telling its readers what might wait for them in the afterlife depending on what life they decide to live on earth.

Introduction

The apostle Paul wrote an ascension account in 2 Cor 12:2–4. He mentions a certain "person in Christ" (ἄνθρωπον ἐν Χριστῷ) who was taken up as far as the third heaven and into paradise. It is a brief story—it takes up only two sentences in the NA[28]—embedded in a section of 2 Corinthians in which Paul tries to defend his apostolic authority against his boasting opponents.[1]

---

1 2 Corinthians 10–13, see also pp. 192–94 below.

https://doi.org/10.1515/9783110717488-011

Two early Christian texts, both called the Apocalypse of Paul, took up this Pauline account and provided their own versions of the heavenly journey. In order to differentiate between the two, I call the shorter apocalypse found in Nag Hammadi Codex V,2 the Apocalypse of Paul (*ApocPaul*), and the longer apocalypse transmitted in a multitude of manuscripts and languages the *Visio Pauli* (*Visio*). The main focus of this article lies on the narratological description of the space(s) through which Paul travels in *ApocPaul* and *Visio*, based on the method for narrative spatiality by Marie-Laure Ryan. How do their descriptions of space shape their respective travel accounts, and how do they relate to the heavenly ascent in 2 Cor 12:2–4? I combine this narrative method with a Deleuzian framework for reception history as introduced by Brennan Breed, to examine how *ApocPaul* and *Visio* as hypertexts have taken up the rather sparse details regarding space in their hypotext 2 Cor 12:2–4, arguing that *ApocPaul* and *Visio* are two actualizations of virtual spatial possibility of the heavenly journey found in 2 Corinthians.[2]

In order to do this properly, I first present the narratological methodology of spatiality as introduced by Ryan. Then I focus on Paul's own ascension account as we find it in 2 Cor 12:2–4 with special attention to spatiality. After this, I briefly discuss the theory of reception introduced by Breed, to then analyze how both *ApocPaul* and *Visio* used 2 Cor 12:2–4 to write their own ascension account. The article closes with a conclusion discussing the findings.

Space

The notion of spatiality is an important category within the broader framework of narratology, since "[e]vents happen somewhere."[3] Narratives always imply space, even if spatial information is sparse: "When the location has not been indicated, readers will simply supply one. *They* will imagine the scene, and in order to do so, they have to situate it somewhere, however vague the imaginary place may

---

[2] For other studies comparing *ApocPaul* and *Visio*, focusing on different other aspects, cf., e.g., J.R. Harrison, "In Quest of the Third Heaven: Paul and His Apocalyptic Imitators," *VC* 58 (2004): 24–55; Riemer Roukema, "Paul's Rapture to Paradise in Early Christian Literature," in *The Wisdom of Egypt: Jewish, Early Christian, and Gnostic Essays in Honour of Gerard P. Luttikhuizen*, ed. Anthony Hilhorst and George H. van Kooten, AJEC 59 (Leiden: Brill, 2005), 267–83; Hans-Josef Klauck, "With Paul through Heaven and Hell: Two Apocryphal Apocalypses," *BR* 52 (2007): 57–72.

[3] Mieke Bal, *Narratology: Introduction to the Theory of Narrative*, 4th ed. (Toronto: University of Toronto Press, 2017), 182. Cf., e.g., Marie-Laure Ryan, "Space," in *The Living Handbook of Narratology*, ed. Peter Hühn et al., § 1, https://www-archiv.fdm.uni-hamburg.de/lhn/node/55.html (last accessed 11 November 2022).

be."[4] Readers thus make a mental map of the space described (or not described) in the narrative: "As readers or spectators progress through the narrative text, they gather spatial information into a cognitive map or mental model of narrative space.... The various landmarks shown or mentioned in the story are made into a coherent world through an awareness of the relations that situate them with respect to each other."[5] The narrative analysis of space sets out to examine what is told in narratives in terms of its spatial dimensions.

Narrative space, or space as described in a narrative, can be created in several ways. One could refer to geographical spaces such as "Rome" or "Judea," or name concrete spaces like "the Temple in Jerusalem" or "the house of Zacchaeus the tax collector," or use descriptive ("inside," "outside") or deictic ("here," "there") language.[6] It should thus not come as a surprise that space can be analyzed in different ways. In this paper, I base myself on the methodological framework introduced by Ryan, who differentiates between five categories of analyzing narrative space:[7]

1. Spatial frames: the locations where the narrative takes place.
2. Setting: the socio-historico-geographic "background" of the narrative.
3. Story space: all space mentioned and referred to in the narrative, including but not limited to spatial frames.
4. Narrative (or story) world: the world of the narrative as created by the readers' imagination, based on cultural knowledge and real world experience. Information not supplied by the text is supplied by the reader as "a coherent, unified, ontologically full, and materially existing geographical entity."[8] The creation of a narrative world also happens in fictional stories such as the two apocalypses on which this article focuses. In these kinds of texts, "readers assume that the narrative world extends beyond the locations named in the text and that there is continuous space between them, even though they cannot fill out this space with geographic features."[9]
5. Narrative universe: this universe includes both the world presented by the text, as well as "all the counterfactual worlds constructed by characters as beliefs, wishes, fears, speculations, hypothetical thinking, dreams and fantasies."[10]

---

[4] Bal, *Narratology*, 182–83.
[5] Ryan, "Space," § 21.
[6] Susanne Luther, "Space," in *How John Works: Storytelling in the Fourth Gospel*, ed. Douglas Estes and Ruth Sheridan, RBS 86 (Atlanta: Society of Biblical Literature, 2016), 59.
[7] Cf. Ryan, "Space," §§ 5–11; Marie-Laure Ryan, Kenneth Foote, and Maoz Azaryahu, *Narrating Space/Spatializing Narrative: Where Narrative Theory and Geography Meet*, Theory and Interpretation of Narrative (Columbus: Ohio State University Press, 2016), 23–25.
[8] Ryan, Foote, and Azaryahu, *Narrating Space*, 24.
[9] Ryan, "Space," § 9.
[10] Ryan, "Space," § 10.

In what follows, I specifically focus on the spatial frames and narrative world of the Pauline ascension accounts. Treating the spatial frames, such as individual heavens in *ApocPaul* or the heavenly Jerusalem in *Visio*, makes it possible to discuss the text per se: since the spatial frames are described using written language, they are semantic in nature. The narrative world is treated because it encapsulates both spatial frames and story space, and because it enables me to tie all individual spatial frames together into a coherent whole. The narrative world of *ApocPaul*, for example, exists of earth and ten vertically consecutive heavens, of which heavens one and two are not mentioned. Still, the acknowledgement of heavens three through ten by the text implies the existence of these first two. They are thus part of the narrative world presented by the text.

Both apocalypses have the same setting: they refer to the historical figure Paul and present the first-century apostle traveling through the Mediterranean world, during which he is taken on a heavenly journey.

The Apostle Paul

Paul's Account of a Heavenly Journey in 2 Cor 12:2–4

Paul's own account of a heavenly journey is brief. He wrote it down in 2 Cor 12:2–4, which can be structured as two tricola (vv. 2a–c; 3a–4a) with a conclusion (v. 4b):

2a   Οἶδα ἄνθρωπον ἐν Χριστῷ πρὸ ἐτῶν δεκατεσσάρων,
2b   εἴτε ἐν σώματι οὐκ οἶδα, εἴτε ἐκτὸς τοῦ σώματος οὐκ οἶδα, ὁ θεὸς οἶδεν,
2c   <u>ἁρπαγέντα</u> τὸν τοιοῦτον <u>ἕως τρίτου οὐρανοῦ</u>.
3a   Καὶ οἶδα τὸν τοιοῦτον ἄνθρωπον,
3b   εἴτε ἐν σώματι εἴτε χωρὶς τοῦ σώματος οὐκ οἶδα, ὁ θεὸς οἶδεν,
4a   <u>ὅτι ἡρπάγη εἰς τὸν παράδεισον</u>
4b   καὶ ἤκουσεν ἄρρητα ῥήματα ἃ οὐκ ἐξὸν ἀνθρώπῳ λαλῆσαι.

2a I know a person in Christ who fourteen years ago,
2b   *whether in the body I do not know, whether out of the body I do not know; God knows,*
2c   that such a person <u>was snatched up as far as the third heaven.</u>
3a And I know that such a person,
3b   *whether in the body or without the body I do not know; God knows,*
4a   <u>was snatched up into paradise</u>
4b and heard unspeakable words, which no person is allowed to speak.[11]

---

11 Translations from ancient languages are mine, unless indicated otherwise.

The current scholarly consensus is that this "person in Christ" (ἄνθρωπον ἐν Χριστῷ, v. 2a), of whom Paul speaks refers to Paul himself.[12] That he does not indicate that he himself is the protagonist in this brief passage is understandable when we assess it in its broader context of 2 Corinthians 10–13, polemic chapters in which Paul discusses boasting in order to defend his ministry and apostolic power.[13] Whereas Paul's opponents boast about their accomplishments and strengths, the only way Paul boasts is "in the Lord" (ἐν κυρίῳ, 2 Cor 10:17). Since it would be inconsistent and against his own argumentation to say that he himself made this journey, he speaks about himself as "a person in Christ."

It remains unclear whether or not Paul meant to make a distinction between the third heaven in v. 2c and paradise in v. 4a. This ambiguity is reflected in modern scholarship, which generally can be divided into two sides. On the one side, there

---

12 Cf. Thomas Schmeller, *Der zweite Brief an die Korinther*, EKK VIII/2 (Göttingen: Vandenhoeck & Ruprecht, 2015), 282: "Mit sehr wenigen Ausnahmen vertreten alle neueren Ausleger/innen die Auffassung, dass Paulus in V. 2–4 von sich selbst spricht." Cf. furthermore, for scholars arguing that Paul refers to himself in the third person, C.K. Barrett, *The Second Epistle to the Corinthians*, BNTC (London: Adam & Charles Black, 1973), 307; Rudolf Bultmann, *Der zweite Brief an die Korinther*, KEK 8 (Göttingen: Vandenhoeck & Ruprecht, 1976), 221; Christian Wolff, *Der zweite Brief des Paulus an die Korinther*, ThHK 8 (Leipzig: Evangelische Verlagsanstalt, 1989), 242–43; Hans-Josef Klauck, *2. Korintherbrief*, NEBNT 8 (Würzburg: Echter Verlag, 1994), 91; Victor Paul Furnish, *II Corinthians*, AB 32A (New Haven: Yale University Press, 1995), 543–45; Jan Lambrecht, *Second Corinthians*, SP 8 (Collegeville, MN: Liturgical Press, 1999), 200–201; Paul Barnett, *The Second Epistle to the Corinthians*, NICNT (Grand Rapids: Eerdmans, 1997), 567 (esp. n. 27); Margaret Thrall, *The Second Epistle to the Corinthians*, 2 vols., ICC (London: Bloomsbury, 2001), 2:772–82; Erich Gräßer, *Der zweite Brief an die Korinther: Kapitel 8,1–13,13*, ÖTK 8/2 (Gütersloh: Gütersloher Verlagshaus, 2005), 182–87; Craig S. Keener, *1–2 Corinthians*, NCBiC (Cambridge: Cambridge University Press, 2005), 238–39. A handful of scholars has proposed someone else as protagonist: Léon Herrmann argues that it is Paul's companion Apollos ("Apollos," *RevScRel* 50 [1976]: 330–36); Morton Smith reads it as an ascension of Jesus ("Ascent to the Heavens and the Beginning of Christianity," in *Aufstieg und Abstieg—Vorträge gehalten auf der Eranos Tagung in Ascona vom 19. bis 27. August 1981*, ed. Adolf Portmann and Rudolf Ritsema [Ascona: Eranos Foundation; Frankfurt: Insel, 1982], 403–29); Michael Goulder mentions a Christian friend from Paul ("Visions and Knowledge," *JSNT* 56 [1994]: 53–71); Hans Dieter Betz has proposed that we should take the ascension account *cum grano salis*, as he thinks it is best explained as a parody (*Der Apostel Paulus und die sokratische Tradition: Eine exegetische Untersuchung zu seiner "Apologie" 2 Korinther 10–13*, BHT 45 [Tübingen: Mohr Siebeck, 1972], 72–73, 82–85, 89–95).
13 On Paul's strategy, defense and enemies in 2 Corinthians 10–13 cf., e.g., Dustin W. Ellington, "Not Applicable to Believers? The Aims and Basis of Paul's 'I' in 2 Corinthians 10–13," *JBL* 131 (2012): 325–40; Akira Satake, "Schritt für Schritt: Die Argumentation des Paulus in 2Kor 10–13," in *Der zweite Korintherbrief: Literarische Gestalt—Historische Situation—Theologische Argumentation: Festschrift zum 70. Geburtstag von Dietrich-Alex Koch*, ed. Dieter Sänger, FRLANT 250 (Göttingen: Vandenhoeck & Ruprecht, 2012), 283–99; Udo Schnelle, "Der 2. Korintherbrief und die Mission gegen Paulus," in Sänger, *Der zweite Korintherbrief*, 300–22.

is the group that thinks that the third heaven and paradise are two expressions for the same place. This one is by far the largest.[14] The other group argues that they are two separate spaces, and that Paul first went to the third heaven and then to paradise during one journey. A third option, that Paul here describes two separate journeys, does not seem to be held by any scholar.[15]

When analyzing this passage regarding space and spatiality, it is noteworthy that there are no real descriptions of space. The "third heaven" and "paradise" are mentioned, but Paul does not seem to be interested in giving the Corinthians an explanation of his journey or a description of the dimensions and contents of these spaces, wherefore they are not developed. We as readers, however, imagine that they occupy space, since—as I indicated above—events have to take place somewhere.

Other Important Pauline Texts for *ApocPaul* and *Visio*

Next to 2 Cor 12:2–4, the main influence for the authors of *ApocPaul* and *Visio*, there are other New Testament texts that have influenced our apocalypses. These are especially Galatians 1–2, where Paul tells the Galatians that he went to Jerusalem to meet with the other apostles, and Acts 9, where Paul's ecstatic conversion on the road to Damascus is described.[16] These pieces of information were all of importance to sketch the two heavenly journeys:

> Die Entrückung in den dritten Himmel, die ekstatische Erfahrung auf dem Weg nach Damaskus und die Lebenswende des Paulus in Folge einer Offenbarung werden sehr früh in

---

[14] Cf., e.g., Barrett, *The Second Epistle to the Corinthians*, 310; Maurice Carrez, *La deuxième épitre de Saint Paul aux Corinthiens*, Commentaire du Nouveau Testament—Deuxième série 8 (Geneva: Labor et Fides, 1986), 228; Wolff, *Der zweite Brief des Paulus an die Korinther*, 244; Furnish, *II Corinthians*, 544; Barnett, *The Second Epistle to the Corinthians*, 560; Lambrecht, *Second Corinthians*, 201; Thrall, *The Second Epistle to the Corinthians*, 785–92; Gräßer, *Der zweite Brief an die Korinther*, 187–91; Schmeller, *Der zweite Brief an die Korinther*, 288. Somewhat more tentatively also Klauck, *2. Korintherbrief*, 92; Keener, *1–2 Corinthians*, 239.

[15] Cf. for a discussion of these three options, especially the last two ones, Christopher Rowland, *The Open Heaven: A Study of Apocalyptic in Judaism and Early Christianity* (London: SPCK, 1982), 381–86. Cf. also Paula R. Gooder, *Only the Third Heaven? 2 Corinthians 12:1–10 and Heavenly Ascent*, LNTS 313 (London: T&T Clark, 2006), 172–75. For ancient interpretations of these possibilities cf. esp. James Buchanan Wallace, *Snatched into Paradise (2 Cor 12:1–10): Paul's Heavenly Journey in the Context of Early Christian Experience*, BZNW 179 (Berlin: De Gruyter, 2011), 289–331; Gerald Bray, ed., *1–2 Corinthians*, ACCS New Testament 7 (New York: Routledge, 1999), 301–3.

[16] On the importance of Galatians 1–2 for *ApocPaul* cf., e.g., Jacques van der Vliet, "Paul and the Others: Rereading the Gnostic Apocalypse of Paul (NHC V,2)," *Gnosis* 7 (2022): 127–50 (132–36).

Zusammenhang mit einander gesehen, obwohl man nicht weiß, ob es um das gleiche oder verschiedene Ereignisse geht. Die Vielzahl der Hinweise im Neuen Testament lässt die Fakten nicht klarer werden—und macht einen Samen fruchtbar, aus dem weitere Entwicklungen hervorgehen.[17]

In this paper, I analyze two of these "weitere Entwicklungen," namely *ApocPaul* and *Visio*.

The Use of Space in *ApocPaul* and *Visio*: Two Actualizations of Virtual Spatial Possibilities of 2 Cor 12:2–4

The Virtual and the Actual: Reception History

As we have seen, there is a distinct lack of spatial description in Paul's own account of his heavenly ascent. In what follows, I analyze *ApocPaul* and *Visio* while focusing on spatiality. How do their descriptions of space shape their respective travel accounts? I use Ryan's above-mentioned methodological framework for the study of space and combine it with the theory of reception history as proposed by Hebrew Bible scholar Brennan Breed as he presents it in his book *Nomadic Text: A Theory of Biblical Reception History*. In the fifth chapter of this book, he employs the thoughts of French philosopher Gilles Deleuze in his search for an understanding of reception history. Of the three Deleuzian concepts he introduces, I am especially interested in the first, namely the distinction between the virtual and the actual.[18] This is a departure from other approaches within biblical studies, which normally try to differentiate between the possible and real. Such positions assume that there are many possible explanations of a text, but that only one is both possible and real. Breed, on the other hand, differentiates between the virtual and actual. To illustrate this, he refers to the color of the sky: "Whenever a thing changes, we may think of

---

17 Charlotte Touati, "Das Schweigen sprechen lassen: Von 2 Kor 12,2–4 zu den apokryphen Apokalypsen," in *Christian Apocrypha: Receptions of the New Testament in Ancient Christian Apocrypha*, ed. Tobias Nicklas and Jean-Michel Roessli, NTP 26 (Göttingen: Vandenhoeck & Ruprecht, 2014), 301–12 (302).
18 The other two concepts that Breed treats are the inversion of the relationship between problems and solutions, and a topological approach to structure. Because of limited space, and because these concepts are of lesser importance for the goal of this current paper, they are left out. Cf. Brennan W. Breed, *Nomadic Text: A Theory of Biblical Reception History* (Bloomington: Indiana University Press, 2014), 124–31.

this change as the virtual dimension of the object generating a new actual state of affairs from its potential powers. When the sky turns from blue to yellow, the potential yellowing power of the sky emerges."[19] This process is called "the actualization of the virtual"[20] by Deleuze. Breed argues that this model is useful in the study of the reception history of the Bible by thinking of biblical texts as dynamic virtual fields, generating different actualizations when different criteria are met: "[E]ach reading actualizes a text, giving it local significance by making manifest a particular construction, or determination, of the various elements that compose a particular edition of a text."[21] This approach implies, among other things,[22] that no particular actualization is intrinsically better than another and that there is not one "real" actualization since the virtual conditions a process and not a finalized product.[23] In what follows, I take over this terminology and its conceptual framework in interpreting both *ApocPaul* and *Visio* as different actualizations of the virtual

---

[19] Breed, *Nomadic Text*, 122. He continues on this same page: "[T]he virtual multiplicity that conditions the actual coloring of the sky is not identifiable with any particular color, nor is it merely a tracing of all colors the sky has turned to in the recent past. Neither is it a monstrous agglomeration of all the colors the sky might turn. Rather, the virtual is the structure by which the sky has color at all."

[20] Cf. Gilles Deleuze, *Difference and Repetition*, trans. Paul Patton (New York: Columbia University Press, 1995), 185–86. where he uses these concepts in the context of evolutionary biology.

[21] Breed, *Nomadic Text*, 124.

[22] In total, Breed presents five implications. (1) No single form or reading of a text exhausts that text's potential force. (2) The virtual text is determinable but not given as determined. (3) This virtual text can actualize in a multitude of divergent ways. (4) The virtual conditions a process instead of a final product. (5) Each reading of a text actualizes it, giving it local significance by making apparent a construction or determination of the elements that make up a particular version of a particular text. See Breed, *Nomadic Text*, 123–24.

[23] This does not mean that every reading is valid or successful according to Breed—some readings can be classified as failures. He bases himself on the Deleuzian use of the mathematical term "topology": "Euclidean geometry assumes that all shapes exist within the featureless space of a flat plane. Topology, on the other hand, asks about the ways a form changes as it is embedded within a variety of curved and folded spaces. Thus, topology gives us a way to imagine one form as it traverses a series of different contexts" (Breed, *Nomadic Text*, 130). Breed adapts the concept of topology for the use of text interpretation: "Instead of asking whether a commentator has provided the correct meaning of the text or whether a translator has given the right translation, one could ask a more topological question, namely, how one might bend, stretch, and fold this text in order to read it differently without destroying its form" (Breed, *Nomadic Text*, 131). By bending a text too far, for example by claiming that Paul strictly remains on earth in *ApocPaul*—a statement that can be dismissed on a semantic as well as narrative level—the reading actualizes a different text than the *ApocPaul*, or no text at all.

potential inherent in 2 Cor 12:2–4.[24] Combined with the aforementioned human need for a space in which a narrative takes place, it should come as no surprise that both texts actualize virtual spatial potential in which their stories take place, to answer (some of) the unclarities in Paul's own ascension account, and to fill in the perceived spatial gaps in the Pauline narrative.

Paul's Journey in *ApocPaul*

This text has survived in one Coptic copy as the second text from codex V[25] of the Nag Hammadi library. It is a relatively short story, only taking up pages 17–24. Several sections of the text are badly damaged, which has resulted in significant lacunae. The beginning lines of the story, about four to eight lines of text, are now lost, and only a few letters of the title of the work remain.[26] The last six to ten lines of page eighteen—the second page of *ApocPaul*—are also lacking.[27] The story switches between first- and third-person narration. This is most likely a scribal error and serves no narratological goals.[28] Nowadays, most scholars agree that *ApocPaul* is Valentinian[29] in nature,[30] and was originally written in Greek around

---

24 I am aware that there are of course a lot of other biblical and non-biblical texts that have influenced how both apocalypses have taken shape. Still, I believe 2 Cor 12:2–4 to be the main interest of both writers, which is why I think it is justified to present the relation between these three texts in this Deleuzian model.

25 This codex sometimes is called the "apocalyptic codex" because all but one text (V,1) are apocalyptic in nature. *Eugnostos* (V,1), 1st Apoc. Jas. (V,3), 2nd Apoc. Jas. (V,4), and Apoc. Adam (V,5). On this name cf. Jean-Marc Rosenstiehl and Michael Kaler, *L'Apocalypse de Paul (NH V, 2)*, BCNHT 31 (Québec: Les presses de l'Université Laval, 2005), 149–51.

26 William Murdock and George MacRae argue that there are four lines that lack at the end of page seventeen, whereas Rosenstiehl and Kaler in their critical edition argue that there are a total of about eight lines now lost. Cf. William R. Murdock and George W. MacRae, "The Apocalypse of Paul: V,2: 17,19–24,7," in *Nag Hammadi Codices V, 2–5 and VI with Papyrus Berolinensis 8502, 1 and 4*, ed. Douglas M. Parrott (Leiden: Brill, 1979), 50; Rosenstiehl and Kaler, *L'Apocalypse de Paul*, 98.

27 Murdock and MacRae think there are four lines wanting, Rosenstiehl argues for about ten. Cf. Murdock and MacRae, "The Apocalypse of Paul," 52; Rosenstiehl and Kaler, *L'Apocalypse de Paul*, 100.

28 Murdock and MacRae, "The Apocalypse of Paul," 48; Cf. also Rosenstiehl in Rosenstiehl and Kaler, *L'Apocalypse de Paul*, 20–22.

29 On Valentinianism in general cf. Einar Thomassen, *The Spiritual Seed: The Church of the "Valentinians,"* Nag Hammadi and Manichaean Studies 60 (Leiden: Brill, 2006); Christoph J. Markschies and Einar Thomassen, eds., *Valentinianism: New Studies*, NHMS 96 (Leiden: Brill, 2020).

30 Cf. most recently Matthew Twigg, *The Valentinian Temple: Visions, Revelations, and the Nag Hammadi Apocalypse of Paul* (New York: Routledge, 2022), 20 (n. 79): "In many cases, *ApocPaul*'s Valentinianism is no longer something to be argued for at all, but rather safely assumed without

the late second or early third century.³¹ It describes how Paul travels from the so-called "mountain of Jericho" to the tenth heaven.

Spatial Frames in *ApocPaul*

The beginning of the text tells how Paul meets the Holy Spirit in the form of a young boy (ⲕⲟⲩⲉⲓ ϣⲏⲙ, 18:6, 8, 13–14).³² The Holy Spirit functions as *angelus interpres*—Paul's guide through the heavens, of which there are ten in total. The Spirit tells Paul he has come to take him up to Jerusalem to meet his fellow apostles (19:17–19). The journey starts on earth, in a place the text calls "the mountain of Jericho" (ⲡⲧⲟⲟⲩ ⲛ̅ϩⲓⲉⲣⲓⲭⲱ):³³

> ⲙⲁⲧⲟⲩⲛⲟⲥ ⲡⲉⲕⲛⲟⲩⲥ ⲡⲁ[ⲩⲗ]ⲟⲥ· ⲁⲩⲱ ⲉⲛⲁⲩ ϫⲉ ⲡⲓⲧⲟⲟⲩ ⲉⲧⲉⲕϩⲱⲙ ⲉϫⲱϥ ⲛ̅ⲧⲟϥ ⲡⲉ ⲡⲧⲟⲟⲩ ⲛ̅ϩⲓⲉⲣⲓⲭⲱ· ϫⲉ ⲉⲕⲉⲥⲟⲩⲱⲛ ⲛⲉⲧ ϩⲏⲡ ⲉϩⲣⲁⲓ̈ ϩⲛ̅ ⲛⲉⲧⲟⲩⲟⲛϩ̅ ⲉⲃⲟⲗ.
>
> Wake up your mind (νοῦς), Paul, and see that the mountain on which you tread is the mountain of Jericho, so that you know the hidden things in those that are visible.³⁴

For those familiar with the geography of Israel, the text mentioning a mountain of Jericho can be confusing, as the city is not built on a mountain, nor is there any mountain in its vicinity. Several scholars have offered different interpretations to explain this mountain. Jean-Marc Rosenstiehl argues that the mountain from *ApocPaul* can be identified with the mountain Nebo based on Deut 32:49 and

---

any defence required." Here, he also provides a brief bibliography of recent works claiming the Valentinianism of the *ApocPaul*. Cf. also pp. 115–208. Cf. also Michael Kaler, *Flora Tells a Story: The Apocalypse of Paul and Its Contexts*, Studies in Christianity and Judaism/Études sur le christianisme et le judaïsme 19 (Waterloo, Ontario: Wilfrid Laurier University Press, 2008), 63–72; However, compare Jean-Daniel Dubois, who claims that no consensus has been reached yet: "What Is 'Gnostic' within Gnostic Apocalypses?" in *Dreams, Visions, Imaginations: Jewish, Christian and Gnostic Views of the World to Come*, ed. Tobias Nicklas, Jens Schröter, and Armand Puig i Tàrrech, BZNW 247 (Berlin: De Gruyter, 2021), 385–410. He refers to Dylan M. Burns, "Is the *Apocalypse of Paul* a Valentinian Apocalypse? Pseudepigraphy and Group Definition in NHC V,2," in *Die Nag-Hammadi-Schriften in der Literatur- und Theologiegeschichte des frühen Christentums*, ed. Jens Schröter, Konrad Schwarz, and Clarissa Paul, STAC 106 (Tübingen: Mohr Siebeck, 2017).
31 Cf. Kaler, *Flora Tells a Story*, 47–76. However, compare van der Vliet, who proposes a fourth-century date: van der Vliet, "Paul and the Others," 145–47.
32 Cf. here Rosenstiehl in Rosenstiehl and Kaler, *L'Apocalypse de Paul*, 70–77.
33 All Coptic quotes from *ApocPaul* are taken from Murdock and MacRae, "The Apocalypse of Paul."
34 *ApocPaul* 19:10–14.

34:1, where this mountain is portrayed as "across from Jericho" (על פני ירחו).³⁵ Furthermore, the "Mountain of Jericho" is mentioned in the *History of the Capture in Babylon*, a late-antique pseudepigraphic work.³⁶ Rosenstiehl identifies this mountain of Jericho with the Nebo, also in the *ApocPaul*.³⁷

A different identification is offered by Matthew Twigg, who disagrees with Rosenstiehl. He argues that the meaning of "mountain of Jericho" in the *History of the Capture in Babylon* does not influence the one found in the *ApocPaul*.³⁸ What he does argue, is that Jericho was often used as negative example in early Christianity. In the story of the good Samaritan, the man who was being ambushed descended from Jerusalem to Jericho.³⁹ This was allegorized in early Christianity, so that the man descending to Jericho became the human soul, the robbers earthly powers, and Jesus the Samaritan.⁴⁰ Paul, in contrast, travels the other way. He ascends from Jericho to Jerusalem. Since there is no physical mountain close to Jericho, Twigg suggests that the mountain should be seen metaphorically, as the peak and epitome of the things it represents. In the case of Jericho, that is the material world.⁴¹ The verb used for Paul's trampling on the mountain, ϩⲱⲙ, is the Coptic equivalent of the Greek πατεῖν⁴² that is used by Jesus in Luke 10:19 when he tells that he gives the disciples the power to trample on snakes, scorpions, and enemies.⁴³ These

---

35 Deut 32:49a: [YHWH speaks:] "Go up to the mountain of the Abarim, this is the mountain Nebo, which is in the land Moab, which is across from Jericho" (על פני ירחו); Deut 34:1: "And Moses went from the desert of Moab towards the mountain Nebo, the top of Pisgah, which is across from Jericho (על פני ירחו). And YHWH showed him all the land of Gilead, as far as Dan." Cf. Jean-Marc Rosenstiehl, "La montagne de Jéricho (NH V,2,19,11–13)," in *Coptica—Gnostica—Manichaia: Mélanges offerts à Wolf-Peter Funk*, BCNHE 7 (Québec: Les presses de l'Université Laval, 2006), 885–92.
36 Cf. History of the Capture in Babylon 25: "on top of the mountain of Jericho (ϩⲓϫⲙ̄ⲡⲧⲟⲟⲩ ⲛ̄ⲛⲓϩⲉⲣⲓⲭⲱ)," in K.H. Kuhn, *A Coptic Jeremiah Apocryphon* (Louvain: Le Muséon, 1970). Kuhn points out the challenges that come trying to date the work. He himself remains cautious by stating that a date sometime between the second and seventh centuries belongs to the realm of possibilities (p. 104).
37 Rosenstiehl, "La montagne," 890: "[I]l faut se rendre à l'évidence: si la montagne de Jéricho désigne le mont Nebo dans l'apocryphe copte de Jérémie, il faudrait une certaine dose d'inconséquence pour s'obstiner à donner à la même expression un sens différent dans l'Apocalypse copte de Paul."
38 Matthew Twigg, "The Mountain of Jericho in the Nag Hammadi *Apocalypse of Paul*: A Suggestion," *VC* 69 (2015): 422–42 (427).
39 Luke 10:30: "A certain person descended from Jerusalem to Jericho" (ἄνθρωπός τις κατέβαινεν ἀπὸ Ἱεροθσαλὴμ εἰς Ἱεριχώ).
40 Riemer Roukema, "The Good Samaritan in Ancient Christianity," *VC* 57 (2003): 56–74.
41 Twigg, "The Mountain of Jericho," 434.
42 Cf. W.E. Crum, *A Coptic Dictionary* (Oxford: Oxford University Press, 1939), 674.
43 Luke 10:19: "See, I have given you the power to trample upon snakes and scorpions, and on every power of the enemy, and nothing will wrong you" (ἰδοὺ δέδωκα ὑμῖν τὴν ἐξουσίαν τοῦ πατεῖν ἐπάνω ὄφεων καὶ σκορπίων, καὶ ἐπὶ πᾶσαν τὴν δύναμιν τοῦ ἐχθροῦ, καὶ οὐδὲν ὑμᾶς οὐ μὴ ἀδικήσῃ).

enemies were interpreted as heavenly or celestial powers in early Christianity.[44] Twigg concludes: "In other words, 'see that this mountain upon which you trample upon is the mountain of Jericho' becomes something like, *see that this devil which you overcome is the devil of the material world.*"[45] The spatial frame described here thus is metaphorical in order to portray the material world in a negative way. This is consistent with how the text presents the material world in general.[46]

Hereafter, the Spirit tells Paul about the goal of their journey: Jerusalem. He takes him up into the heavens in order to bring him there:

ⲧⲟⲧⲉ ⲡⲓ[ⲡⲛⲁ] ⲉⲧ[ⲟⲩⲁⲁⲃ] ⲉⲧⲉ ⲛⲉϥϣⲁϫⲉ ⲛⲙ̄[ⲙⲁϥ ⲁϥ]ⲧⲱⲣⲡ̄ ⲙ̄ⲙⲟϥ ⲉϩⲣⲁⲓ̈ ⲉⲡ.ⲭ.ⲓⲥ.ⲉ, ϣⲁϩⲣⲁⲓ̈ ⲉϯⲙⲉ[ϩϭⲟⲙ]ⲧⲉ ⲙ̄ⲡⲉ· ⲁⲩⲱ ⲁϥⲟⲩⲱϣ[ⲧⲃ̄ ⲉ]ϩⲣⲁⲓ ⲉϯⲙⲉϩϥⲧⲟ ⲙ̄[ⲡⲉ].

Then (τότε) the Holy Spirit (πνεῦμα), who was speaking with him, seized him upwards to the third heaven and he passed upwards to the fourth heaven.[47]

The second spatial frame is the fourth heaven. The third heaven is only mentioned here, and the first two heavens are omitted. I discuss these particularities below. The description of the fourth heaven is longer, but still quite sparse:

ⲁⲓ̈ⲛⲁⲩ ⲇⲉ ϩⲛ̄ ϯⲙⲉϩϥⲧⲟ ⲙ̄ⲡⲉ ⲕⲁⲧⲁ ⲅⲉⲛⲟⲥ ⲁⲓ̈ⲛⲁⲩ ⲇⲉ ⲉⲛⲓⲁⲅⲅⲉⲗⲟⲥ ⲉⲩⲉⲓⲛⲉ ⲛ̄ⲛⲟⲩⲧⲉ· ⲉⲛⲓⲁⲅⲅⲉⲗⲟⲥ ⲉⲩ[ⲉ]ⲓⲛⲉ ⲛ̄ⲛⲟⲩⲯⲩⲭⲏ ⲉⲃⲟⲗ ϩⲙ̄ ⲡⲕⲁϩ ⲛ̄ⲧⲉ ⲛⲉⲧⲙⲟⲟⲩⲧ· ⲁⲩⲕⲁⲁⲥ ϩⲛ̄ ϯⲡⲩⲗⲏ ⲛ̄ⲧⲉ ϯⲙⲉϩϥⲧⲟ ⲙ̄ⲡⲉ.

And (δέ) I saw in the fourth heaven, according to (κατά) race (γένος). And I saw the angels (ἄγγελος), being in the likeness of gods, angels (ἄγγελος) bringing a soul (ψυχή) from the land of the dead. They placed it in the gate (πύλη) of the fourth heaven.[48]

We learn from this quote that the fourth heaven contains angels, and that it has a gate. In this heaven, the judgment of a soul takes place. It has to defend itself, but ultimately fails to convince its accusers of its innocence. Its punishment is reincarnation (*ApocPaul* 20:5–21:22).[49] The gate, which functions as an entrance to the

---

44 Twigg, "The Mountain of Jericho," 440.
45 Twigg, "The Mountain of Jericho," 442 (italics original). Cf. here also Lautaro Roig Lanzillotta, "The Apocalypse of Paul (NHC V,2): Cosmology, Anthropology, and Ethics," *Gnosis* 1 (2016): 110–31 (115): "Paul's point of departure is the lower realm, the sphere of influence of the Devil."
46 Cf. pp. 204–5 below.
47 *ApocPaul* 19:20–25.
48 *ApocPaul* 20:5–11.
49 On the sequence of events in the fourth heaven cf., e.g., Jean-Marc Rosenstiehl, "Crime et châtiment au quatrième ciel: NH V,2: 20,5–21,21," in *L'Évangelie selon Thomas et les textes de Nag Hammadi*, ed. Louis Painchaud and Paul-Hubert Poirier, BCNHE 8 (Québec: Les presses de l'Université Laval, 2007), 559–83; Roig Lanzilotta, "The Apocalypse of Paul," 119–20; Kaler in Rosenstiehl and Kaler, *L'Apocalypse de Paul*, 209–35; Cf. for a comparison of this scene with judgment scenes in other apocalyptic works van der Vliet, "Paul and the Others," 136–39.

heaven, is not exclusive to the fourth heaven, as also the fifth[50] and sixth[51] heaven are described as having a gate. The fourth and sixth heavens also have a toll-collector (ⲧⲉⲗⲱⲛⲏⲥ, *ApocPaul* 20:16; 22:20) acting as gatekeeper. The idea that heavens have gates is not new. William Murdock gives an overview of the motif in Egyptian, Greek, Mithraic, and Sumerian texts, as well as in Jewish traditions.[52] Toll collectors as gatekeepers is a motif not exclusive to Nag Hammadi texts, as it is found in Egyptian sources,[53] as well as in early Jewish texts.[54]

The Greek *Tabula Cebetis*, a pseudonymous work probably dated to the first century CE,[55] describes a journey—an allegory for true education[56]—in which travelers pass through the gates of three walls that circle the castle of happiness (εὐδαιμονία) which is the goal of the voyage. These gates are occupied by gate keepers: the keeper of the first gate, named δαίμων, looks like an old man and is full of wisdom and deceit (*Tab. Ceb.* 4.2–3); the second gate keeper is False Culture (*Tab. Ceb.* 12.1–3), and at the third gate travelers meet True Culture (*Tab. Ceb.* 18.2). Only after passing through these gates does one enter the acropolis with the castle where happiness waits for them (*Tab. Ceb.* 21.3). In the lands between the rings of walls roam personifications of powers that try to lead voyagers astray and keep them from traveling further. Travelers must be able to distinguish between good and evil in order to resist these temptations and continue through the gates to arrive at the castle of happiness. Thus, "[t]he gates play a central role because passing through them—crossing the threshold into a new realm of being—forms the heart of the pedagogy of the text."[57] According to Michael Kaler, the significance of the gates in *ApocPaul* and other Nag Hammadi texts "lies in the fact that they impede the

---

50 *ApocPaul* 21:26–28: "And (δέ) I went, and the gate (πύλη) opened. And I went upwards to the fifth heaven" (ⲁⲛⲟⲕ ⲇⲉ ⲉⲓⲙ[ⲟⲟϣ]ⲉ ⲁⲥⲟⲩⲱⲛ ⲛϭⲓ ⲧⲡⲩⲗ[ⲏ ⲁⲩⲱ] ⲁⲓⲉⲓ ⲉϩⲣⲁⲓ ⲉⲧⲙⲉϩϯ ⲙ̄[ⲡⲉ]).
51 *ApocPaul* 22:11–13: "And (δέ) I went with the spirit, and the gate (πύλη) opened for me. Then (τότε) we went upwards to the sixth heaven" (ⲁⲛⲟⲕ ⲇⲉ ⲛⲉⲓⲙⲟⲟϣⲉ ⲙⲛ ⲡⲉⲡⲛ̄ⲁ̄ ⲁⲩⲱ ⲁⲥⲟⲩⲱⲛ ⲛⲁⲓ ⲛϭⲓ ⲧⲡⲩⲗⲉ ⲧⲟⲧⲉ ⲁⲛⲉⲓ ⲉϩⲣⲁⲓ ⲉⲧⲙⲉϩⲥⲟ ⲙ̄ⲡⲉ).
52 William R. Murdock, "The Apocalypse of Paul from Nag Hammad Codex V: A Translation and Interpretation" (PhD diss., School of Theology at Claremont, 1968). Cf. also Rosenstiehl in Rosenstiehl and Kaler, *L'Apocalypse de Paul*, 53 (n. 334). He refers to several Jewish texts that mention heavenly gates.
53 O.H.E. Burmester, "Egyptian Mythology in the Coptic Apocrypha," *Orientalia* 7 (1938): 355–67.
54 Cf., e.g., the Mart. Ascen. Isa. 10:24–27 and 3 En. 18:3–4. Cf. for a brief discussion of the word ⲧⲉⲗⲱⲛⲏⲥ in the Nag Hammadi Corpus Kaler in Rosenstiehl and Kaler, *L'Apocalypse de Paul*, 223–25.
55 Rainer Hirsch-Luipold, "Einleitung," in *Die Bildtafel des Kebes: Allegorie des Lebens*, ed. Rainer Hirsch-Luipold et al., SAPERE 8 (Darmstadt: Wissenschaftliche Buchgesellschaft, 2005), 11–37 (29).
56 Hirsch-Luipold, "Einleitung," 22.
57 Susanne Luther, "Topographies of Conduct? Ethical Implications of the Ekphrastic Description of Jerusalem in Rev 21," in *Vivid Rhetoric in the New Testament*, ed. Meghan Henning and Nils Neumann (Atlanta: Society of Biblical Literature, forthcoming). Cf. furthermore Reinhard Feldmeier,

soul's ascension out of the cosmos. The focus is on their status as potential obstacles which are nonetheless overcome, thanks to the enlightenment or power of the soul or of its guide."[58] The narrative purpose of the gates in these texts thus function similarly, in that in both the *Tabula* and *ApocPaul*, gates are obstacles that need to be overcome in order to reach the goal, either true happiness through education in the *Tabula* or psychic existence in the tenth heaven in *ApocPaul*.

After the visit to the fourth heaven, the Spirit, Paul and the Apostles go through to the gate of the fifth heaven where they see a great angel holding an iron rod in his hand (ⲉⲩⲛⲟϭ ⲛⲁⲅⲅⲉⲗⲟⲥ . . . ⲉϥⲁⲙⲁϩⲧⲉ ⲛⲛⲟⲩϭⲉⲣⲱⲃ, *ApocPaul* 22:2–4). This angel, together with three other angels wielding whips, goads souls to their judgment, presumably the judgment in the fourth heaven.[59] Paul and his companions travel onwards to the sixth heaven rather quickly, where he sees a great light shining down[60] before confronting the toll collector of the sixth heaven:

ⲁⲉⲓ[ⲟ]ⲩⲱϣⲃ ⲉⲓ̈ϫⲱ ⲙⲙⲟⲥ ⲙⲡⲧⲉⲗⲱ[ⲛⲏ]ⲥ ⲉⲧϩⲛ ⲧⲙⲉϩⲥⲟ ⲙⲡⲉ [ϫⲉ ⲁⲟⲩⲱⲛ] ⲛⲁⲓ̈ ⲁⲩⲱ ⲡⲓⲡⲛ̅ⲁ̅ ⲉⲧⲟ[ⲩⲁⲁⲃ ⲉⲧϩⲁⲧⲁ]ϩⲏ ⲁϥⲟⲩⲱⲛ ⲛ[ⲁⲓ̈ ⲧⲟⲧⲉ ⲁⲛⲉⲓ̈ ⲉϩⲣⲁⲓ̈ ⲉⲧⲙⲉϩⲥⲁ[ϣϥⲉ ⲙⲡⲉ].

And I conversed, I spoke to the toll-collector (τελώνης), who was in the sixth heaven: "open to me and the Holy Spirit (πνεῦμα), who is in front of me." He opened for me. Then (τότε) I went up to the seventh heaven.[61]

A lacunous parchment makes it challenging to decipher what exactly happens with our delegation in the seventh heaven, which is disappointing because the seventh heaven receives quite some attention in *ApocPaul*. In terms of space, it describes a throne that shines seven times as bright as the sun, on which an "old man" (ⲉⲩϩⲗⲗⲟ ⲛ̅ⲣⲱ[ⲙⲉ]) sits:

[ⲧⲟⲧⲉ ⲁⲛⲉⲓ̈] ⲉϩⲣⲁⲓ̈ ⲉⲧⲙⲉϩⲥⲁ[ϣϥⲉ ⲙⲡⲉ ⲁⲓ̈ⲛⲁ]ⲩ ⲉⲩϩⲗⲗⲟ ⲛ̅ⲣⲱ[ⲙⲉ . . .]ⲉ ⲙⲡⲟⲩⲉⲓⲛ [ⲁⲩⲱ ⲉⲣⲉ ⲡⲉϥϩⲟⲉⲓ]ⲧⲉ ⲟⲩⲟⲃⲉϣ ⲛⲉⲣ[ⲉⲡⲉϥⲑⲣⲟⲛⲟⲥ ⲉ]ⲧϩⲛ̅ ⲧⲙⲉϩⲥⲁϣϥⲉ ⲙⲡⲉ [ⲛⲉϥ]ⲣ̅ ⲛ̅ⲟⲩⲟⲉⲓⲛ ⲛ̅ⲣⲟⲩⲟ ⲉⲡⲣⲏ ⲛ̅[ⲥⲁϣ]ϥ̅ ⲛ̅ⲕⲱⲃ ⲛ̅ⲥⲟⲡ.

Then (τότε) we went upwards to the seventh heaven. I saw an old man . . . the light, and whose garment was white. The light of his throne (θρόνος), which was in the seventh heaven, was seven times greater than the sun.[62]

"Paedeia Salvatrix: Zur Anthropologie und Soteriologie der Tabula Cebetis," in Hirsch-Luipold et al., *Die Bildtafel des Kebes*, 149–63.
58 Kaler in Rosenstiehl and Kaler, *L'Apocalypse de Paul*, 220. Other Nag Hammadi texts that describe heavenly gates are the Pistis Sophia (*passim*); Great Power 41:7; Treatise of the Sethians 56:25–26.
59 Cf. for a brief interpretation of the journey through this heaven Kaler in Rosenstiehl and Kaler, *L'Apocalypse de Paul*, 236–44.
60 This is the light of the seventh heaven that is so bright that it lightens up the sixth heaven as well. Cf. below.
61 *ApocPaul* 22:19–24.
62 *ApocPaul* 22:23–30.

The passage shows parallels to the description of God in Daniel 7, especially vv. 9–10, where he is described as "the Ancient of Days" (עַתִּיק יוֹמִין), who wears white clothing and sits on a flaming throne. It also shows similarities to "the one sitting on the throne" (ὁ καθημένος ἐπὶ τοῦ θρόνου), i.e. God, in Revelation 4–5. The old man in *ApocPaul* shows Paul his principalities and authorities ruling the world, the ⲚⲒⲀⲢⲬⲎ and ⲚⲒⲈⲜⲞⲨⲤⲒⲀ. This is a reference to Eph 6:12, where the text warns the community that their struggle is not against flesh and blood, but "against the principalities, against the powers, against the earthly governors of this darkness, against the spiritual forces of evil in the heavenly regions."[63] This entity is clearly meant to be the demiurge, the evil or incapable creator of the material realm, here polemically portrayed as the God of the Old Testament.[64] The demiurge does treat Paul respectfully as he calls him blessed and set apart, repeating what the Spirit said to Paul at the beginning of the text:[65] "Where are you going Paul, the one who is blessed and the one who is set apart from his mother's womb?"[66] Paul's answer is that he goes "to the place (τόπος) from which I came" (*ApocPaul* 23:9–10). When the demiurge inquires where that place is, Paul answers with a polyptoton:

ⲈⲒⲚⲀⲂⲰⲔ ⲈϨⲢⲀⲒ ⲈⲠⲔⲞⲤⲘⲞⲤ ⲚⲦⲈ ⲚⲈⲦⲘⲞⲞⲨⲦ ϪⲈⲔⲀⲀⲤ ⲈⲒⲚⲀⲢⲀⲒⲬⲘⲀⲖⲰⲦⲒⲌⲈ Ⲛ†ⲀⲒⲬⲘⲀⲖⲰⲤⲒⲀⲦⲎ ⲈⲦⲀⲨⲢⲀⲒⲬⲘⲀⲖⲰⲦⲒⲌⲈ ⲘⲘⲞⲤ ϨⲚ †ⲀⲒⲬⲘⲀⲖⲰⲤⲒⲀ ⲚⲦⲈ ⲦⲂⲀⲂⲨⲖⲰⲚ.

I am going down towards the world (κόσμος) of the dead, in order to lead captive (αἰχμαλωτίζειν) the captivity (αἰχμαλωσία) that was led captive (αἰχμαλωτίζειν) in the captivity (αἰχμαλωσία) of Babylon.[67]

---

63 Πρὸς τὰς ἀρχάς, πρὸς τὰς ἐξουσίας, πρὸς τοὺς κοσμοκράτορας τοῦ σκότους τούτου, πρὸς τὰ πνευματικὰ τῆς πονηρίας ἐν τοῖς ἐπουρανίοις. Cf. also *ApocPaul* 19:3–5.
64 For an overview of the demiurge in antiquity cf. Carl Séan O'Brien, *The Demiurge in Ancient Thought: Secondary Gods and Divine Mediators* (Cambridge: Cambridge University Press, 2015). For the demiurge in gnostic thought cf., e.g., Ingvild Sælid Gilhus, "The Gnostic Demiurge—An Agnostic Trickster," *Religion* 14 (1984): 301–11; Jarl E. Fossum, "The Origin of the Gnostic Concept of the Demiurge," *ETL* 61 (1985): 142–52; Gerard P. Luttikhuizen, "The Demonic Demiurge in Gnostic Mythology," in *The Fall of the Angels*, ed. Cristoph Auffarth and Loren T. Stuckenbruck, TBN 6 (Leiden: Brill, 2004), 148–60.
65 *ApocPaul* 18:16–17.
66 *ApocPaul* 23:2–4: ⲈⲔⲚⲀⲂⲰⲔ ⲈⲦⲰⲚ ⲠⲀⲨⲖⲞⲤ ⲠⲈⲦⲤⲘⲀⲘⲀⲀⲦ· ⲀⲨⲰ ⲠⲈⲚⲦⲀ[Ⲩ] ⲠⲞⲢϪϤ ⲈⲂⲞⲖ ϪⲒⲚ ⲚϨⲢⲎⲦⲤ ⲚⲦⲈϤⲘⲀⲀⲨ. Cf. Gal 1:15: "the one who set me [Paul] apart from my mother's womb" (ὁ ἀφορίσας με ἐκ κοιλίας μητρός μου). Cf. also Murdock and MacRae, *The Apocalypse of Paul*, 60–61.
67 *ApocPaul* 23:13–17. Cf. Eph 4:8: "he ascended to the height and led captivity captive" (ἀναβὰς εἰς ὕψος ᾐχμαλώτευσεν αἰχμαλωσίαν; modified quote from Ps 67:19 LXX). See also van der Vliet, "Paul and the Others," 135–36.

Paul is ordered by the Spirit to show the old man his "sign,"[68] after which the old man gives them permission to travel on ahead into the eighth heaven the ogdoad, the eighth heaven. The last ten lines of the text then rather sparingly describe the journey through the last three remaining heavens:

ⲁⲩⲱ ⲧⲟⲧⲉ [ⲁ]ⲥⲟⲩⲱⲛ ⲛ̄ϭⲓ ⲧⲙ̄[ⲉϩ]<ⲥⲁϣϥⲉ>[69] ⲙ̄ⲡ[ⲉ] ⲁⲩⲱ ⲁⲛⲉ̄ⲓ ⲉϩⲣⲁⲓ̈ [ⲉⲧ]ϩⲟⲅⲇⲟⲁⲥ, ⲁⲓ̈ⲛⲁⲩ ⲇⲉ ⲉⲡⲓⲙⲛ̄ⲧⲥⲛⲟⲟⲩⲥ ⲛ̄ⲛⲁⲡⲟⲥⲧⲟⲗⲟⲥ· ⲁⲩⲣ̄ⲁⲥⲡⲁⲍⲉ ⲙ̄ⲙⲟⲓ̈ ⲁⲩⲱ ⲁⲛⲉ̄ⲓ ⲉϩⲣⲁⲓ̈ ⲉ†ⲙⲉϩⲯⲓⲧⲉ ⲙ̄ⲡⲉ· ⲁⲓ̈ⲣ̄ⲁⲥⲡⲁⲍⲉ ⲛ̄ⲛⲏ ⲧⲏⲣⲟⲩ ⲉⲧϩⲛ̄ †ⲙⲁϩⲯⲓⲧⲉ ⲙ̄ⲡⲉ, ⲁⲩⲱ ⲁⲛⲉ̄ⲓ ⲉϩⲣⲁⲓ̈ ⲉ†ⲙⲉϩⲙⲏⲧⲉ ⲙ̄ⲡⲉ· ⲁⲩⲱ ⲁⲓ̈ⲣ̄ⲁⲥⲡⲁⲍⲉ ⲛ̄ⲛⲁϣⲃⲏⲣ ⲙ̄ⲡⲛ̅ⲁ̅.

And then (τότε) the seventh heaven opened, and we went upwards to the Ogdoad. And (δέ) I saw the twelve apostles (ἀπόστολος). They greeted (ἀσπάζεσθαι) me and we went upwards to the ninth heaven. I greeted (ἀσπάζεσθαι) all those who were in the ninth heaven, and we went upwards towards the tenth heaven. And I greeted (ἀσπάζεσθαι) my fellow spirits (πνεῦμα).[70]

Here again the heavens are only mentioned. On the level of space, they are part of the frames since at least we learn that our travelers traverse through them and that these heavens have inhabitants, so they must have some layout or room for the residents to live in and our delegation to travel through. Direct descriptions of these three heavens are however lacking.

The Narrative World of *ApocPaul*

The narrative world of *ApocPaul* is a tripartite cosmos, divided into an earthly, a celestial, and a heavenly realm.[71] The earthly realm is described as "earth" (*ApocPaul* 19:29), "world of the dead" (*ApocPaul* 20:19–20; 23:13–14), "creation" (*ApocPaul* 20:4; 23:27) or as "the world" (*ApocPaul* 21:5).[72] It is also the space that contains the Mountain of Jericho, where Paul's heavenly journey begins. *ApocPaul* sees this realm as only negative:

---

68 Showing signs is common among ancient ascension stories. Cf., e.g., Kaler in Rosenstiehl and Kaler, *L'Apocalypse de Paul*, 266–68; van der Vliet, "Paul and the Others," 139. Michael Domeracki argues that the sign in *ApocPaul* is Valentinian baptism. This seems a bit overblown to me, as there is not a lot of information to work with. Michael S. Domeracki, "The Apocalypse of Paul (NHC V,2) as a Valentinian Baptismal Liturgy of Ascent," *Gnosis* 2 (2017): 212–34.
69 This emendation is suggested by Murdock and MacRae, as the text itself reads †ⲙⲉϩⲥⲟ ⲙ̄ⲡ[ⲉ], "the sixth heaven." Since it is clearly stated before that they entered the seventh heaven, and continue onwards towards the eighth heaven, this emendation is justified. Cf. Murdock and MacRae, "The Apocalypse of Paul," 60.
70 *ApocPaul* 23:29–24:8.
71 Roig Lanzillotta, "The Apocalypse of Paul," 114–21.
72 Cf. Roig Lanzillotta, "The Apocalypse of Paul," 115.

From an anthropological perspective, this region is associated with the body, which is mentioned three times and is always equated with sin. From an ethical perspective, it is the scenario in which lawless deeds, murder, and concupiscence take place. From an epistemological one, finally, we may say that it is the realm of darkness, where torpor of the mind obstructs knowledge and from which consequently one must awake.[73]

The general view of the text towards the earthly realm thus strengthens Twigg's interpretation of the mountain of Jericho as epitome of the realm of the Devil.

The second realm, the celestial realm, is made up of the first seven heavens. Although the first two are not mentioned at all, it is clear that they do exist, as Paul's journey starts in the third heaven, which presumes the existence of another two below it. The heavens do not receive equal attention, as the third heaven is only mentioned in passing and Paul is almost immediately taken to the fourth heaven, which gets quite a bit of attention from our scribe. The omission of the first two and brief mention of the third heaven are aptly explained by Kaler, who argues that this text was written as what he calls a "heterodox" polemic piece to contend with "orthodox" Christianity. Since both sides could agree on the fact that Paul indeed traveled to the third heaven, as we learn from 2 Cor 12:2c, the first three heavens needed no explanation. *ApocPaul* seems to have taken the first three heavens for granted, and omitted them for this reason.[74]

Something similar then happens in the fifth and sixth heavens, as spatial information, or any information at all, is scarce. The text describes that there are four angels goading souls to their judgment in the fifth heaven, and that there is a bright light in the sixth heaven, which is a preview to the bright light in the seventh heaven. Then in the seventh heaven, where Paul has his confrontation with the demiurge, the text describes the old man wearing white robes sitting on a throne that is seven times as bright as the sun. This all obviously presumes some kind of space, but this again is not developed at all.

Lastly, the eighth, ninth, and tenth heaven as the highest, heavenly realm are mentioned. Here as well there is no real spatial information or rather no information at all apart from the fact that we learn that these heavens have inhabitants who are being greeted by Paul. Kaler, who sees this text as a polemic work, argues as follows: since the author proved that Paul rose above the demiurgic realm by showing the sign of the Spirit, the author of the text made his—or, following Kaler,

---

73 Roig Lanzillotta, "The Apocalypse of Paul," 115–16.
74 Kaler, *Flora Tells a Story*, 61–62. Cf. also Roig Lanzillotta, "The Apocalypse of Paul," 116; Twigg, "The Mountain of Jericho," 424: "[T]he ambiguity between the 'third heaven' (12:2) and 'Paradise' (12:4) could easily be exploited by later interpreters to the effect that Paul ascended past the third heaven into some unspecified higher region."

her—point that one needs to conquer the demiurge in order to get to the heavenly realm. A description of these heavens is therefore not needed, and thus omitted.[75]

Still, this option offered by Kaler—the text as a polemical work—seems a bit too speculative to me, and I think this explanation also works with leaving polemics out, as does for example Lautaro Roig Lanzillotta: "[T]he ascension in Apocalypse of Paul is presented as an ethical progress, which begins upon his leaving Jericho, the realm of the body and physical existence, and culminates in Jerusalem, the higher psychic level."[76] This explanation, the ascent as an ethical progress, is more successful in explaining the relative emptiness of the heavens, as the writer was simply not interested in giving a detailed overview of the cosmos, but rather in the dangers one might encounter during their ascension. They achieve this by describing the terrors, challenges, and toll collectors in the fourth, fifth, sixth, and seventh heaven. After entering the eighth heaven, there is no need for further descriptions, as the goal of the text is met: the soul can become one with God.[77]

Be that as it may, the lack of any additional information likely was less of a problem for readers in antiquity, as Kaler points out:

> The lack of description does not impair the overall coherence and continuity of the ascent. Also, the original readers of the text would have had an idea of the sort of things that go on in the various heavens in the ascension apocalypse tradition. Thus the lack of detail would be less disconcerting to them than it is to us.[78]

There is one remaining unclarity in the narrative world, namely the location of Jerusalem. In my opinion, this depends on two elements in the text. First, where the mountain of Jericho is located. I have already indicated that I think that the mountain of Jericho is to be read metaphorically, as the epitome of materiality. Second, how the role which the apostles play is interpreted. At the beginning of our text, the Spirit tells Paul that he has come to take him up to Jerusalem where he will meet his fellow apostles in *ApocPaul* 18:17–19: "For (ἐπειδή) I came to you so that you might go upwards to Jerusalem to your fellow apostles (ἀπόστολος)."[79] In other words, where the apostles are, there Jerusalem can be found. April DeConick points out

---

75 Kaler, *Flora Tells a Story*, 60–62.
76 Roig Lanzillotta, "The Apocalypse of Paul," 125.
77 Roig Lanzillotta, "The Apocalypse of Paul," 125. For a more radical view cf. Michael Kaler, "The Intriguing Absence of God in the *Apocalypse of Paul*," *ETL* 34 (2018): 235–40 (esp. 238): "What we are left with, then, is an apocalyptic text that takes its protagonist up through the heavens, has him overcome the demiurgic God, and then, in the very highest level of the cosmos, shows him simply joining his 'fellow spirits,' with no other deity present.... There is no true king. There is simply an elite group of spirits sitting at the top of the universe, at peace and together."
78 Kaler in Rosenstiehl and Kaler, *L'Apocalypse de Paul*, 236.
79 ⲉⲡⲓⲇⲏ ⲁⲓ[ⲉⲓ] ⲉⲣⲟⲕ ϫⲉ ⲉⲕⲛⲁ[ⲃⲱⲕ ⲉϩⲣⲁ]ⲓ [ⲉⲉ]ⲓ[ⲏ̄ⲙ̄] ϣⲁ ⲛⲉⲕϣⲃⲏ[ⲣ ⲁⲡⲟⲥⲧⲟⲗⲟⲥ].

that in other gnostic texts the apostles are often positioned in the celestial realm, under the power of the demiurgic god.[80] With this in mind, Roig Lanzillotta goes on to argue that the same relation between Paul and the apostles can be found in *ApocPaul*. He connects this with the argument that Paul "looks (back)" to greet the apostles when he enters the eighth heaven:

ⲁⲩⲱ ⲧⲟⲧⲉ [ⲁ]ⲥⲟⲩⲱⲛ ⲛ̄ϭⲓ ⲧⲙ[ⲉϩ] <ⲥⲁϣϥⲉ>[81] ⲙ̄ⲡ[ⲉ] ⲁⲩⲱ ⲁⲛⲉ̂ⲓ ⲉϩⲣⲁⲓ̈ [ⲉⲧ] ϩⲟⲅⲇⲟⲁⲥ ⲁⲓ̈ⲛⲁⲩ ⲇⲉ ⲉⲡⲙⲛ̄ⲧⲥⲛⲟⲟⲩⲥ ⲛ̄ⲁⲡⲟⲥⲧⲟⲗⲟⲥ· ⲁⲩⲣⲁⲥⲡⲁⲍⲉ ⲙ̄ⲙⲟⲓ ⲁⲩⲱ ⲁⲛⲉ̂ⲓ ⲉϩⲣⲁⲓ̈ ⲉⲧⲙⲉϩⲯⲓⲧⲉ ⲙ̄ⲡⲉ.

And then (τότε) it opened, that is the seventh heaven, and we went upwards to the Ogdoad. And I saw the twelve apostles (ἀπόστολος), and they greeted (ἀσπάζεσθαι) me and we went upwards to the ninth heaven.[82]

This, together with the fact that Paul is able to see them when he looks up from the earth (*ApocPaul* 19:18–20), which Roig Lanzillotta interprets as them being in psychic form, leads him to conclude that the apostles, like Jerusalem, are part of the celestial realm under the influence of the demiurge.[83] I do not agree with this position for two reasons. First, the text does not clearly indicate that Paul looked back, nor that the apostles stayed in the demiurgic realm, only that he saw and greeted the apostles after entering the Ogdoad. Moreover, the text is also not clear about who continue the journey from the Ogdoad onwards, because the first-person plural (ⲁⲛⲉⲓ, *we* went) used in the passage can on the one hand refer to Paul and the Spirit, or on the other to Paul, the Spirit, and the apostles. Secondly and more importantly, just before Paul greets the apostles for the first time when he is still on earth, the Spirit calls them "elect spirits" (ϩⲉⲛⲡ̄ⲛ̄ⲁ̄ ⲅⲁⲣ ⲉⲩⲥⲟⲧⲡ̄ ⲛⲉ, "for they are elect spirits [πνεῦμα]," *ApocPaul* 19:17–18). Since the apostles are said to be elect spirits, the apostles are clearly intended to be pneumatic beings, who reside in the divine regions, just as the spirits living in the tenth heaven, whom Paul greets: ⲁⲩⲱ ⲁⲛⲉⲓ ⲉϩⲣⲁⲓ ⲉⲧⲙⲉϩⲙⲏⲧⲉ ⲙ̄ⲡⲉ ⲁⲩⲱ ⲁⲓⲣⲁⲥⲡⲁⲍⲉ ⲛ̄ⲛⲁϣⲃⲏⲣ ⲙ̄ⲡ̄ⲛ̄ⲁ̄, "And we went upwards to the tenth heaven, and I greeted (ἀσπάζεσθαι) my fellow spirits (πνεῦμα)," *ApocPaul* 24:6–8. The apostles therefore have to reside in the *pleroma*, the divine and pneumatic realm. What these two arguments then imply about the location of the heavenly Jerusalem in *ApocPaul* is clear. It is the antithesis of the earthly Jericho, which is—in the words of Twigg—the realm of the devil in the material world. The Spirit

---

80 April D. DeConick, "Apostles as Archons: The Fight for Authority and the Emergence of Gnosticism in the Tchacos Codex and Other Early Christian Literature," in *Codex Judas Paper: Proceedings of the International Congress on the Tchacos Codex Held at Rice University, Houston, Texas, March 13–16, 2008*, ed. April D. DeConick, NHMS 71 (Leiden: Brill, 2009), 243–88.
81 See n. 69 where I argue that this is a scribal error.
82 *ApocPaul* 23:29–24:4.
83 Roig Lanzillotta, "The Apocalypse of Paul," 117–18.

has come to take Paul from this earthly Jericho to the splendor of the divine and pneumatic Jerusalem, the realm where the apostles reside as elect spirits.[84]

The *Visio Pauli*

Visio originates from the fourth century CE, and was most likely composed in Egypt.[85] It describes a detailed journey of Paul through heaven and hell. *Visio* has had tremendous influence in both the late antique and medieval periods: the Greek composition has been translated in Latin, Coptic, Arabic, Armenian, Ethiopic, Georgian, Old Church Slavonic and Syriac. There have been multiple Latin redactions made,[86] and the Latin translations also spawned many translations into vernacular European languages such as German, Czech and French.[87] Singular episodes, stories and anecdotes from this apocalypse were adapted in many works, most notably in Dante's *Divine Comedy*.[88] It is thus important to clarify which version is used when

---

[84] For arguments similar to mine cf. van der Vliet, "Paul and the Others," 134, where he points out that Paul's visit to Jerusalem to meet the other apostles in Galatians 1–2 is important for the structure of the text as well. For his argument that Jerusalem must be in the ogdoad or a higher heaven cf. van der Vliet, "Paul and the Others," 141–42. Cf. also Kaler, *Flora Tells a Story*, 11; Kaler in Rosenstiehl and Kaler, *L'Apocalypse de Paul*, 271–74.

[85] For some discussions regarding date and place of composition of *Visio* cf. Robert P. Casey, "The Apocalypse of Paul," *JTS* 34 (1933): 1–32 (1–2), who held a now outdated opinion that it was written in the third and expanded in the fourth century. Theodore Silverstein, "The Date of the 'Apocalypse of Paul'," *Mediaeval Studies* 24 (1962): 335–48; Lenka Jiroušková, *Die Visio Pauli: Wege und Wandlungen einer orientalischen Apokryphe im lateinischen Mittelalter: Unter Einschluß der alttschechischen und deutschsprachigen Textzeugen*, MLST 34 (Leiden: Brill, 2006), 7–9; Emiliano Fiori, "A Reactivation of the Apocalyptic Genre in Early Egyptian Monasticism: The *Apocalypse of Paul*," in *Wissen in Bewegung: Institution—Iteration—Transfer*, ed. Eva Cancik-Kirschbaum and Anita Traninger, Episteme in Bewegung: Beiträge zu einer transdiziplinären Wissensgeschichte 1 (Wiesbaden: Harrassowitz, 2015), 307–22 (307); Lautaro Roig Lanzillotta and Jacques van der Vliet, *The Apocalypse of Paul (Visio Pauli) in Sahidic Coptic: Critical Edition, Translation and Commentary*, With an Appendix by Jos van Lent. SVigChr 179 (Leiden: Brill, 2023), 152–166.

[86] Cf., e.g., Theodore Silverstein, *Visio Sancti Pauli: The History of the Apocalypse in Latin Together with Nine Texts* (London: Christophers, 1935).

[87] Casey made an overview of versions of the text in ancient languages that remains relevant to this day: "The Apocalypse of Paul." See for more specialized discussions Jiroušková, *Die Visio Pauli*, who presents a reception history of *Visio* focused on Latin, Czech and German translations.

[88] Cf., e.g., Theodore Silverstein, "Did Dante Know the Vision of St. Paul?" in *Harvard Studies and Notes in Philology and Literature 19* (Cambridge: Harvard University Press, 1936), 231–47.

working with this text. For this analysis, I base myself on the Coptic version of the text, and cite the new critical edition by Roig Lanzillotta and van der Vliet.[89]

The Coptic version of *Visio* has survived in one codex, British Library Ms Or 7023.[90] Since the first fifteen of the total 78 pages of this only Coptic version of *Visio* are missing, and Ernest Budge's *editio princeps* from 1915 makes it seem as if there are more pages missing than actually is the case, this version is often overlooked in scholarly research. Apart from this lacuna at the start of *Visio*, the first eight folios, there is only one more lacuna of two pages—one folio—instead of the 52 pages Budge suggested. Overall, the Coptic version of *Visio* should be regarded as one of the most important witnesses of *Visio* as it is in many cases better understandable than the best Latin version, L¹ Paris.[91]

Spatial Frames in *Visio*

Since the first fifteen pages are lost, there is no information on where this text had Paul take off on his journey.[92] Let us commence by following the journey Paul makes in the Coptic *Visio*, which can be divided into eight sections.[93]

---

89 Roig Lanzillotta and van der Vliet, *The Apocalypse of Paul*, 170–223. I thank them both for making the critical edition available to me before publication.
90 For a codicological description of this text, cf. Roig Lanzillotta and Van der Vliet, *The Apocalypse of Paul*, 19–39. There are also some smaller fragments described by them, cf. 39–50.
91 For the critical edition of Budge cf. Ernest A.T.W. Budge, *Miscellaneous Coptic Texts in the Dialect of Upper Egypt* (London: British Museum Press, 1915), 534–74 (Coptic text), 1043–84 (English translation). For a careful and comprehensive comparison of the different editions of *Visio* cf. Lautaro Roig Lanzillotta, "The Coptic 'Apocalypse of Paul' in Ms Or 7023," in *The Visio Pauli and the Gnostic Apocalypse of Paul*, ed. Jan N. Bremmer and István Czachesz, Studies on Early Christian Apocrypha 9 (Leuven: Peeters, 2007), 158–97. On the lacunae see Roig Lanzillotta, "The Coptic 'Apocalypse of Paul'," 160–168; on the Coptic version as the best version, see Roig Lanzillotta, "The Coptic 'Apocalypse of Paul'," 168–193 (esp. 193), as well as Roig Lanzillotta and van der Vliet, *The Apocalypse of Paul*, *passim*. The most recent edition of L¹ Paris can be found in Theodore Silverstein and Anthony Hilhorst, *Apocalypse of Paul: A New Critical Edition of Three Long Latin Versions*, COr 21 (Geneva: Patrick Cramer, 1997).
92 On the beginning of *Visio* in the Latin witnesses cf., e.g., Pierluigi Piovanelli, "The Miraculous Discovery of the Hidden Manuscript, or the Paratextual Function of the Prologue to the *Apocalypse of Paul*," in Bremmer and Czachesz, *The Visio Pauli and the Gnostic Apocalypse of Paul*, 23–49; Jiroušková, *Die Visio Pauli*.
93 These overarching spatial frames as I call them here are: the place where the sinners get judged (*Visio* 15–18); the third heaven (twice: *Visio* 19–20; 55); the Land of Inheritance, containing among other things the City of Christ (*Visio* 21–30); the Land of the Wicked (*Visio* 30–44); the earthly paradise (*Visio* 45–54); the heavenly paradise (*Visio* 56–62); the Mountain of Olives (*Visio* 64).

(1) *The Judgment of Two Sinful Souls* (*Visio* 16–18). The beginning of the extant Coptic text places Paul in the middle of the judgment of a soul (ⲯⲩⲭⲏ, ψυχή). It gets accused by its angel (ⲁⲅⲅⲉⲗⲟⲥ, ἄγγελος) and its spirit (ⲡⲛⲉⲩⲙⲁ, πνεῦμα).[94] Before the soul is taken up to heaven to be judged by God, the soul gets tortured by the "powers," (ⲛⲉⲝⲟⲩⲥⲓⲁ, ἐξουσία): "As soon as it reached the powers (ἐξουσία) that should bring it upwards to heaven, one suffering followed another" (*Visio* 16:2).[95] These powers are described as terrible animalistic figures, with the faces of lions, bulls, bears, dragons, serpents, donkeys and crocodiles wearing armor and wielding weapons.[96] Beast-faced creatures with fiery tongues and iron teeth chew on the soul for about an hour.[97] Regarding space, not much is revealed. The beginning of the text is missing, so we do not know whether it would have been mentioned there where Paul was transported to by his *angelus interpres*. The only certainty is that this episode takes place in a space that is on a lower plane than heaven, as the powers torture the soul before they bring it *up* (ⲉⲩⲛⲁϫⲓⲧⲥ̄ ⲉϩⲣⲁⲓ) to the heaven in order for it to be judged. Although direct descriptions are not given, the text communicates that the heaven must take up an impressive amount of space, because there are myriads and myriads of angels and archangels: "As soon as it [the soul] was inside the heaven, I heard angels (ἄγγελος) and archangels (ἀρχάγγελος), numbering myriads upon myriads" (*Visio* 16:4).[98] The soul is judged by God and handed over to Aftemelouchos, the angel in charge of punishment (*Visio* 16:7). A second soul is also judged and sent to the "Tartarouchos of hell" (ⲡⲧⲁⲣⲧⲁⲣⲟⲩⲭⲟⲥ [ταρταροῦχος] ⲛ̄ⲁⲙⲛ̄ⲧⲉ, *Visio* 18:2).[99]

---

94 Cf. on the spirit judging its soul Casey, who claims that *Visio* "considered [the spirit] as a quasi-angelic being, residing in each man as a kind of super-soul, not unlike the Egyptian *ka*" ("The Apocalypse of Paul," 13).
95 ⲛ̄ⲧⲉⲩⲛⲟⲩ ⲛ̄ⲧⲁⲥⲧⲁϩⲉ ⲛⲉⲝⲟⲩⲥⲓⲁ ⲉⲩⲛⲁϫⲓⲧⲥ̄ ⲉϩⲣⲁⲓ ⲉⲧⲡⲉ, ϩⲓⲥⲉ ⲉⲭⲛ̄ ϩⲓⲥⲉ.
96 These seven animalistic figures might refer to the seven theriomorphic planetary rulers in Origen, *Contra Celsum* 6.30–31. For details, cf. Roig Lanzillotta and van der Vliet, *The Apocalypse of Paul*, 234–237.
97 These powers with animalistic creatures, especially the ones with crocodile faces, could point toward Egyptian origins of the text: Jan N. Bremmer, "Christian Hell: From the Apocalypse of Peter to the Apocalypse of Paul," *Numen* 56 (2009): 298–325 (306–9). On early Christian incorporation of Egyptian afterlife motives cf. David Frankfurter, "Amente Demons and Christian Syncretism," *ARelG* 14 (2013): 83–102.
98 ⲛ̄ⲧⲉⲩ[ⲛ]ⲟⲩ ⲛ̄ⲧⲁⲥⲣ̄ ⲡϩⲟⲩⲛ ⲛ̄ⲧⲡⲉ, ⲁⲓⲥⲱⲧⲙ̄ ⲉϩⲉⲛ[ⲁⲅ]ⲅⲉⲗⲟⲥ ⲙⲛ̄ ϩⲉⲛⲁⲣⲭⲁⲅⲅⲉⲗⲟⲥ ⲉⲩⲉⲓⲣⲉ ⲛ̄ϩⲉⲛⲧⲃⲁ ⲛ̄ⲧⲃⲁ.
99 On the angels Aftemelouchos and Tartarouchos cf. Jean-Marc Rosenstiehl, "Tartarouchos—Temelouchos: Contribution à l'étude de l'apocalypse apocrpyhe de Paul," in *Deuxième journée d'études coptes: Strasbourg 25 mai 1984*, CBCo 3 (Leuven: Peeters, 1986), 29–56. The word that I translated with "hell," ⲁⲙⲛ̄ⲧⲉ, is the traditional Egyptian name for their version of hell. This term was then later taken up by Christians, as our text shows. For the use of ⲁⲙⲛ̄ⲧⲉ in Egyptian texts such as the Book of the Dead and the Book of Gates cf. Erik Hornung, *Die Unterweltsbücher der Ägypter: Einge-*

(2) *First Visit to the Third Heaven* (*Visio* 19–20). Then the *angelus interpres* who guides Paul, brings him to the third heaven, which the angel calls "the dwelling place of all the holy ones" (ⲉⲡⲙⲁ ⲛ̄ϣⲱⲡⲉ ⲛ̄ⲛⲉⲧⲟⲩⲁⲁⲃ ⲧⲏⲣⲟⲩ, *Visio* 19:1). He places Paul in the decorated gate of the third heaven:

> ⲁϥϫⲓ ⲙⲙⲟⲓ ϣⲁ ⲧⲙⲉϩϣⲟⲙⲧⲉ ⲙ̄ⲡⲉ, ⲁϥⲧⲁϩⲟⲓ ⲉⲣⲁⲧ ϩⲓⲭⲛ̄ ⲟⲩⲡⲩⲗⲱⲛ. ⲁⲓⲛⲁⲩ ⲉⲧⲡⲩⲗⲱⲛ ⲉⲧⲙ̄ⲙⲁⲩ {ⲉⲩ} ⲉⲩⲛⲟⲩⲃ ⲧⲏⲣⲥ̄ ⲧⲉ· ⲁⲓⲛⲁⲩ ⲉⲥⲛⲁⲩ ⲛ̄ⲥⲧⲩⲗⲗⲟⲥ ⲛ̄ⲛⲟⲩⲃ ϩⲓⲣⲛ̄ ⲧⲡⲩⲗⲏ, ⲉⲣⲉ ϩⲉⲛⲡⲗⲁⲝ ⲛ̄ⲛⲟⲩⲃ ϩⲓⲭⲛ̄ ⲛⲉⲥⲧⲩⲗⲗⲟⲥ ⲉⲩⲙⲉϩ ⲛ̄ⲥ<ϩ>ⲁⲓ.
>
> He [the *angelus interpres*] took me to the third heaven, and he placed me next to a gate (πύλη). I saw that the gate (πύλη) was golden in its entirety. I saw two golden pillars (στῦλος) next to the gate (πύλη). Golden tablets (πλάξ) were on the pillars (στῦλος), filled with writing.[100]

On these golden tablets there are written the names of the righteous (*Visio* 19:1–2). Then, the gate opens and Paul meets with Enoch and Elijah, who both reside in this heaven. During this first visit, Paul only visits the gate of the third heaven, and not the third heaven itself. Spatial information is sparse. However, since the *angel interpres* calls it the dwelling place of all the holy ones, it must be quite spacious.

(3) *The Land of Inheritance and the City of Christ* (*Visio* 21–30). Hereafter the *angelus interpres* takes Paul from the gate of the third heaven to the second heaven:[101] "He took me away from that gate, (and) took me to the second heaven" (*Visio* 21:2).[102] The word for "heaven" (ⲙ̄ⲡⲉ) is here not written in the manuscript, and Roig Lanzillotta and van der Vliet have decided to emend the text here by adding it. This addition is justified when comparing the Coptic text with the leading Latin witness, L¹ Paris, which writes: "And he took me down from the third heaven, and brought me in the second heaven" (*Visio* 21:7–8).[103] Furthermore, since there is no real con-

---

leitet, übersetzt und erläutert von Erik Hornung (Zürich: Artemis, 1992). On how ⲁⲙⲛ̄ⲧⲉ was used in Coptic early Christian texts, cf. Frankfurter, "Amente." Cf. here also the Apocalypse of Zephaniah (e.g., *ApocZeph* Akh 14:1), where the text also uses ⲁⲙⲛ̄ⲧⲉ to describe hell.
100 *Visio* 19:1.
101 For more information on gates cf. pp. 201–2. above.
102 ⲁϥⲉⲛⲧ̄ ⲉⲃⲟⲗ ϩⲛ̄ ⲧⲉⲓⲡⲩⲗⲏ, ⲁϥϫⲓ ⲙ̄ⲙⲟⲓ ⲉⲧⲙⲉϩⲥⲛ̄ⲧⲉ <ⲙ̄ⲡⲉ>.
103 *Et deposuit me de tercio celo et induxit me in secundo caelo*. However, compare the other two Latin witnesses edited by Hilhorst and Silverstein: L¹ Sankt Gallen speaks of a first and other heaven: "I exited from the first heaven, and he led me downwards in another heaven" (*inde exiui primum caelum et deduxit me in celum alium*). L³ Arnhem skips this sentence and goes immediately from the third heaven to the place where they view the firmament, leaving a possible reference to other heavens out.

tender for what this "second" could be other than the second heaven, I agree with this emendation.[104]

Having arrived in the second heaven, his angel takes Paul to the firmament and brings him to the east, "the place where the sun rises" (ⲉⲙ̄ⲙⲁ ⲛ̄ϣⲁ ⲙ̄ⲡⲣⲏ, *Visio* 21:2). Paul looks down: "I looked and I saw the foundation of the heaven upon a river of water, and the river of water surrounds the whole inhabited world (οἰκουμένη)" (*Visio* 21:2).[105] Paul asks his angel what this river is, and the angel answers that it is the river Ocean (ⲡⲟⲩⲕⲉⲁⲛⲟⲥ ⲡⲓⲉⲣⲟ, *Visio* 21:2). The river Ocean is first found in Homer's works, where the earth is described as a flat disc with the river Ocean surrounding it.[106] Kirsty Copeland argues that our author's use of the river Ocean is not so much motivated out of cosmological interests, but rather out of narrative ones. Cosmological conceptions changed after Homer: later Greek philosophers started to argue for the sphericity of the earth, with the river Ocean as the divider of continents. This made continents other than the one they lived on inhabited but unreachable. Copeland continues: "Thus, like the [*Visio*], philosophical speculation was primarily concerned with the shore on the far side of Ocean. It was the very inaccessibility of the far shore that made it the ideal site for both philosophical inquiry and revelation."[107] An important aspect of these spaces in *Visio* is that they are only accessible for those who have died, or for those on revelatory journeys like Paul.

Paul then goes beyond the Ocean and enters into this revelatory land on the eastern far shore of the river Ocean, which he learns is called the Land of Inheritance (ⲡⲕⲁϩ ⲛ̄ⲧⲉⲕⲗⲏⲣⲟⲛⲟⲙⲓⲁ [κληρονομία], *Visio* 21:3). It is illuminated by the sun and shines seven times brighter than silver. This land, an overarching spatial frame is divided into three spatial frames. First, the text describes a place with a river flowing with milk and honey, surrounded by fertile grounds on which all kinds of fruit trees are loaden with fruit. The detailed description of date trees with up to ten thousand branches, carrying ten thousand date clusters, is unique to the Coptic

---

104 Cf. Roig Lanzillotta and van der Vliet, *The Apocalypse of Paul*, 263. Budge suggests "the Second [Gate]" (*Miscellaneous Coptic Texts in the Dialect of Upper Egypt*, 1049). He surely seems to mean the gate of the second heaven.
105 ⲁⲓϭⲱϣⲧ̄ ⲁⲓⲛⲁⲩ ⲉⲛ̄ⲥⲛ̄ⲧⲉ ⲛ̄ⲧⲡⲉ ⲉⲩϩⲓϫⲛ̄ ⲟⲩⲉⲓⲉⲣⲟ ⲙ̄ⲙⲟⲟⲩ, ⲉⲣⲉ ⲡⲉⲓⲉⲣⲟ ⲙ̄ⲙⲟⲟⲩ ⲕⲱⲧⲉ ⲉⲧⲟⲓⲕⲟⲩⲙⲉⲛⲏ ⲧⲏⲣⲥ̄.
106 Edward Adams, "Graeco-Roman and Ancient Jewish Cosmology," in *Cosmology and New Testament Theology*, ed. Jonathan T. Pennington and Sean M. MacDonough, LNTS 355 (London: T&T Clark, 2008), 5–27 (7).
107 Kirsty B. Copeland, "Thinking with Oceans: Muthos, Revelation and the *Apocalypse of Paul*" in Bremmer and Czachesz, *The Visio Pauli and the Gnostic Apocalypse of Paul*, 77–104 (87).

text and shows how plentiful the resources in this land are, and how fertile the soil surrounding the river is.[108]

Then, Paul and his angel travel further east, where they see a second river. Paul learns from the angel that this river, with water whiter than milk, is the Acherusian Lake. The sinful people who have repented and want to enter the City of Christ—which is even more eastward—first have to be washed by the angel Michael in order to enter the city. Paul and the angel cross the Acherusian Lake on a golden boat (*Visio* 23:1).

This episode shows interesting parallels to the Apocalypse of Zephaniah, a late second-century apocalyptic text written in Middle- or Upper-Egypt.[109] In the longer Akhmimic Coptic fragment, the seer is also put on a boat with angels: "They helped me and set me on that boat. Thousands of thousands and myriads of myriads of angels (ἄγγελος) gave praise before me" (*ApocZeph* Akh 13:1).[110] The concept of a trip by boat is already known from Predynastic Egyptian religion, where a solar barque was the vessel with which the deceased traveled through the underworld.[111]

The third spatial frame in this part of the text is the "City of the Christ Jesus, Jerusalem" (ⲧⲡⲟⲗⲓⲥ ⲙ̄ⲡⲉⲭⲣⲓⲥⲧⲟⲥ ⲓⲏⲥⲟⲩⲥ, ⲑⲓⲉⲣⲟⲩⲥⲁⲗⲏⲙ, *Visio* 27), and gets the majority of the attention from our text. The city is described as completely made out of gold, with twelve concentric walls of different precious stones encircling it.[112] Each side of it has a gate in which biblical figures reside. Our author has taken inspiration from the canonical apocalypse: In Revelation 21, there is one wall and there are twelve foundations of precious stones. Revelation also speaks of twelve gates, each

---

108 On the Coptic as only witness to these detailed descriptions, and for an argument for why Roig Lanzillotta thinks that this is not a later addition but rather more likely to be original, cf. Roig Lanzillotta, "The Coptic Apocalypse of Paul," 181–83.
109 For the date and place of the Apocalypse of Zephaniah see most recently Michael Sommer, "Roman Tombs in Alexandria and in the Egyptian Chora: A Journey through the After-Life of the Apocalypse of Zephaniah," in *Alexandria: Hub of the Hellenistic World*, ed. Benjamin Schliesser et al., WUNT 460 (Tübingen: Mohr Siebeck, 2021), 207–28.
110 ⲁⲩϯ-ⲧⲟⲟⲧ, ⲁⲩⲧⲁⲗⲁⲉⲓ ⲁⲡⲭⲁⲉⲓ ⲉⲧⲙ̄ⲙⲟ, ⲁⲩϣⲱⲡⲉ ⲉⲩⲥⲙⲟⲩ ϩⲁⲧⲁⲉϩⲓⲉⲓ ϭⲉ-ϩⲉⲛϩⲟ̄ ⲛ̄ϩⲟ ⲙ̄ⲛ̄ϩⲉⲛⲧⲃⲁ ⲛ̄ⲧⲃⲁ ⲛ̄ⲁⲅⲅⲉⲗⲟⲥ.
111 Cf. John Coleman Darnell and Colleen Manassa Darnell, *The Ancient Egyptian Netherworld Books*, WAW 39 (Atlanta: Society of Biblical Literature, 2018), 4: "The locomotive vessel of Re's journey through the Netherworld is the solar bark, whose origins reach back into Predynastic Egypt. The form and crew of the bark can differ between different compositions as well as within a single book." For an example of Predynastic Egyptian depictions of the solar barque cf. John Coleman Darnell, "Iconographic Attraction, Iconographic Syntax, and Tableaux of Royal Ritual Power in the Pre- and Proto-Dynastic Rock Inscriptions of the Theban Western Desert," *Archéo-Nil* 19 (2009): 83–107 (92). For a more detailed comparison of the *Visio* with the *ApocZeph*, cf. Roig Lanzillotta and van der Vliet, *The Apocalypse of Paul*, 114–120.
112 Cf. here also *Visio* 29:1.

one resembling one of the tribes of Israel. In *Visio*, the righteous first need to be washed by the angel Michael in the Acherusian lake. In Rev 22:14, the ones who wash their robes will be blessed and may enter the city.

Surrounding the city in *Visio* are four rivers filled with expensive liquids (see table 1). They all resemble an important river of the fertile crescent moon on earth and refer to the four rivers described in Gen 2:10–14:[113]

Table 1: Rivers in *Visio* 23.

River in *Visio 23*	Liquid	Resembles
Western river	Honey	Phison
Southern river	Milk	Euphrates
Eastern river	Wine	Gihon
Northern river	Oil	Tigris

Each side of the square-shaped city[114] has a gate where biblical figures reside; so for example, Paul finds the minor and major prophets of the Old Testament in the gate next to the western river (*Visio* 25), and the infants that have been murdered by Herod in the gate next to the southern river of milk (*Visio* 26; cf. Matt 2:16–18).[115]

Paul is then taken to the center of the City, where space is used ethically: the better the life someone lived, the closer to the center they are allowed to reside.[116] Golden thrones are put around the twelfth wall, the wall closest to the center. These thrones are reserved for the uneducated people who believed in God without knowledge of or being able to read the Bible (*Visio* 29:2). At the center of the city is an altar with King David standing next to it (*Visio* 29:3).

(4) *The Punishment of the Sinners in the Land of the Wicked* (*Visio* 31–44).[117] Hereafter, the angel takes Paul back to the second heaven and the firmament of the heavens in order to travel to the west. Paul again inquires about the river, and

---

113 On these rivers, as well as their earthly counterparts in *Visio*, see Jacques T.A.G.M. van Ruiten, "The Four Rivers of Eden in the *Apocalypse of Paul* (Visio Pauli): The Intertextual Relationship of Genesis 2.10–14 and the *Apocalypse of Paul* 23," in Bremmer and Czachesz, *The Visio Pauli and the Gnostic Apocalypse of Paul*, 50–76.
114 Cf. Rev 21:16, where the new Jerusalem is described in the shape of a cube.
115 For a more detailed description of the rivers, cf. Roig Lanzillotta and van der Vliet, *The Apocalypse of Paul*, 285–290
116 This is only implied in the Coptic and clearer in the Syriac *Visio*, cf. Roig Lanzillotta and van der Vliet, *The Apocalypse of Paul*, 291.
117 Cf. for more detailed studies into hell in the *Visio* Martha Himmelfarb, *Tours of Hell: An Apocalyptic Form in Jewish and Christian Literature* (Philadelphia: Fortress, 1983); István Czachesz, "Tor-

the *angelus interpres* again tells Paul that it is the river Ocean, indicating that this river indeed encircles the whole inhabited world (*Visio* 31:2). After crossing to the western far shore of the river, they arrive in the Land of the Wicked.[118] It is a terrible place, clearly intended to be *Visio*'s version of hell:

ⲁⲩⲱ ⲛ̄ⲧⲉⲣⲉⲓⲣ̄ ⲡⲃⲟⲗ ⲙ̄ⲡⲟⲅⲉⲁⲛⲟⲥ, ⲙ̄ⲡⲉⲓⲛⲁⲩ ⲉⲗⲁⲁⲩ ϩⲙ̄ ⲡⲙⲁ ⲉⲧⲙ̄ⲙⲁⲩ ⲛⲥⲁ ⲗⲩⲡⲉⲓ ϩⲓ ⲁϣⲁϩⲟⲙ ϩⲓ ⲙ̄ⲕⲁϩ ⲛ̄ϩⲏⲧ ϩⲓ ⲅⲛⲱⲫⲟⲥ ϩⲓ ⲕⲁⲕⲉ ϩⲓ ϩⲧⲟⲙⲧⲙ̄ ϩⲓ ⲧⲁⲕⲟ.

And when I had passed beyond the Ocean, I saw nothing in that place except for grief (λύπη) and groaning and pain and gloom (γνόφος) and darkness and corruption.[119]

This land, a huge parched field (*Visio* 31:3), is filled with pits where all kinds of creatures live and souls get punished: There is a pit filled with dragons, another one with maggots, a third one with ice, a fourth one with fire, and a multitude of other pits of different sizes and contents. In between all these pits there flows a river of fire (*Visio* 31:3–4). To the west of the river of fire there are immensely deep pits, filled with generation upon generation of unbelievers, piled up on each other.

The many groups of people that are punished here are punished according to the principle of *talion*,[120] the idea that the punishment symbolizes the sin.[121] For example, people who had illicit sexual relationships are submerged up to their hips, and those who slandered the church are submerged up to their lips in the fiery river (*Visio* 31:4).[122]

This part of the text makes clever use of space: as a rule of thumb, the more to the West a punishment is located, the worse were the sins committed. The absolute worst sinners are found in the westernmost part of the Land of the Wicked. The so-called Well of the Abyss (ⲧϣⲱⲧⲉ ⲙ̄ⲡⲛⲟⲩⲛ, *Visio* 41:1), is one of those locations, filled with an evil stench and glowing embers.[123] The souls thrown in there have committed the gravest of sins: not believing that Jesus came to earth in the flesh, denying that he was born from the Virgin Mary, not believing in the transfiguration during the eucharist and renouncing their baptism (*Visio* 41:2–3). Most important

---

ture in Hell and Reality: The *Visio Pauli*," in Bremmer and Czachesz, *The Visio Pauli and the Gnostic Apocalypse of Paul*, 130–43; Bremmer, "Christian Hell."
118 This western part of the celestial realm is not named in the text. I follow the name given to it by Roig Lanzillotta in Roig Lanzillotta, "The Coptic Apocalypse of Paul."
119 *Visio* 31:2.
120 Himmelfarb, *Tours of Hell*, 122.
121 Bärbel Beinhauer-Köhler, "Talion, I. Zum Begriff, II. Religionswissenschaftlich," *RGG4* 8:52–53.
122 For a more detailed description of the punishments cf. Bremmer, "Christian Hell."
123 On the importance of smells in the *Visio*, cf. Roig Lanzillotta and van der Vliet, *The Apocalypse of Paul*, 340; 397–398.

here is the absence of the Father, Son, Holy Spirit and all the angels, which makes it the most undesirable space in the whole cosmos: "His resemblance will not go up before the Father, and the Son, and the Holy Spirit (πνεῦμα), and all the angels (ἄγγελος)" (*Visio* 41:2).[124] Other people, who have claimed that Jesus was not raised from the dead and that humanity will not raise from the dead are also punished in the westernmost regions of the Land of the Wicked. They are incapsulated in ice, forever living in cold (*Visio* 42:1).

Seeing these punishments is so overwhelming for Paul that he starts to cry. His crying compels the souls being punished to cry out as well. As a reaction to their cries, the heaven opens, and archangel Michael with all the angels comes down. The damned souls ask Michael for respite (*Visio* 43). They compel Michael to beg Christ for mercy on their behalf. After Michael has begged, Paul sees the heaven moving and shaking like a tree. He then gets to see a glimpse of heaven:

ⲁⲓⲛⲁⲩ ⲉⲡϫⲟⲩⲧⲁϥⲧⲉ ⲙ̄ⲡⲣⲉⲥⲃⲩⲧⲉⲣⲟⲥ ⲙⲛ̄ ⲡⲉϥⲧⲟⲟⲩ ⲛ̄ⲍⲱⲟⲛ ⲉⲁⲩⲡⲁϩⲧⲟⲩ. ⲁⲓⲛⲁⲩ ⲉⲡⲉⲑⲩⲥⲓⲁⲥⲧⲏⲣⲓⲟⲛ ⲙⲛ̄ ⲡⲕⲁⲧⲁⲡⲉⲧⲁⲥⲙⲁ ⲉⲁⲩⲡⲁϩⲧⲟⲩ.

I saw the twenty-four elders (πρεσβύτης) and the four creatures (ζῷον) that lied prostrate. I saw the altar (θυσιαστήριον) and the veil (καταπέτασμα) that lied prostate.[125]

This description of the heavenly throne room with twenty four elders and the four creatures is influenced by the description of the heavenly throne room in Revelation 4–5, where these figures also appear, and also prostrate themselves before and praise God. Jesus descends from heaven to grant the pleading souls rest on the Lord's Day, as well as the first fifty days after his resurrection (*Visio* 44:4).

(5) *The Earthly Paradise* (*Visio* 45–54). After these horrible and gruesome descriptions of what happens to sinners and unbelievers, the *angelus interpres* takes Paul to the earthly paradise, described as "the place where Adam transgressed (παραβαίνω) with his wife" (*Visio* 45).[126] It contains the springs of the rivers Gihon, Phison, Euphrates and Tigris. A tree, with the Spirit of God dwelling upon it, provides the water for these springs. Every time the Spirit blows, water flows out of the roots of the tree (*Visio* 45:3). These rivers are not the same as the four rivers surrounding the City of Christ, because the ones surrounding the City of Christ *resemble* (ⲧⲛ̄ⲧⲱⲛ, *Visio* 23) the ones on earth, and are filled with wine, milk, honey, and oil. These earthly rivers contain water, and combined with the fact that it is the place where Adam and Eve transgressed, it is safe to assume that this paradise

---

124 ⲙⲉⲣⲉ ⲡⲉϥⲣ̄ ⲡⲙⲉⲉⲩⲉ̄ ⲉⲓ ⲉϩⲣⲁⲓ ⲙ̄ⲡⲙ̄ⲧⲟ ⲉⲃⲟⲗ ⲙ̄ⲡⲉⲓⲱⲧ ⲙⲛ̄ ⲡϣⲏⲣⲉ ⲙⲛ̄ ⲡⲉⲡⲛⲉⲩⲙⲁ ⲉⲧⲟⲩⲁⲁⲃ ⲙⲛ̄ ⲛⲁⲅⲅⲉⲗⲟⲥ ⲧⲏⲣⲟⲩ.
125 *Visio* 44:1.
126 ⲡⲙⲁ ⲛ̄ⲧⲁ ⲁⲇⲁⲙ ⲡⲁⲣⲁⲃⲁ ⲛ̄ϩⲏⲧϥ ⲙⲛ̄ ⲧⲉϥⲥϩⲓⲙⲉ.

is located on earth. Two other trees are also located here: the tree of knowledge of good and evil and the tree of life are both found in the middle of Paradise (*Visio* 45:4; cf. Gen 2:9).

The remaining chapters dedicated to the earthly paradise describe the many meetings Paul has with many figures from the Old and New Testaments, such as the Patriarchs, Moses, the Virgin Mary and the Prophets of the Old Testament (*Visio* 46–54). There are no additional spatial descriptions in these chapters, except that Paul sees some of them approaching from a distance which signals that this paradise must be quite large. At this point, *Visio*'s witnesses in the other languages either cut off or end, and the Coptic is the only witness of chapters 52–64.

(6) *Second Visit to the Third Heaven* (*Visio* 55). Paul then is taken up by a cloud and brought to the third heaven again. This time, he enters it: "And after all these things, I was taken up in a cloud and taken towards the third heaven" (*Visio* 55).[127] Here he sees singing eagles and angels surrounding an altar:

> ερε ⲥⲁϣϥ̄ ⲛ̄ⲁⲉⲓⲧⲟⲥ ⲛⲟⲩⲟⲉⲓⲛ ⲁⲁϩⲉⲣⲁⲧⲟⲩ ⲛ̄ⲥⲁ ⲟⲩⲛⲁⲙ ⲙ̄ⲡⲉⲑⲩⲥⲓⲁⲥⲧⲏⲣⲓⲟⲛ ⲁⲩⲱ ⲥⲁϣϥ̄ ⲛ̄ⲥⲁ ϩⲃⲟⲩⲣ ⲙ̄ⲙⲟϥ, ⲉⲩϩⲩⲙⲛⲉⲩⲉ ϩⲛ̄ ⲟⲩⲭⲟⲣⲟⲥ ⲛ̄ⲥⲙⲟⲩ ⲉϩⲟⲩⲛ ⲉⲡⲉⲓⲱⲧ, ⲉⲣⲉ ϩⲉⲛⲧⲃⲁ ⲛ̄ⲧⲃⲁ ⲛ̄ⲁⲅⲅⲉⲗⲟⲥ ⲁⲁϩⲉⲣⲁⲧⲟⲩ ⲙ̄ⲡⲉϥⲙ̄ⲧⲟ ⲉⲃⲟⲗ ⲁⲩⲱ ϩⲉⲛϣⲟ ⲛ̄ϣⲟ ⲉⲩⲕⲱⲧⲉ ⲉⲣⲟϥ.

> There were seven eagles (ἀετός) of light standing to the right of the altar (θυσιαστήριον), and seven to its left, singing hymns (ὑμνέω) in a choir (χορός) of blessing to the father, while myriads upon myriads of angels (ἄγγελος) were standing in front of it, and thousands and thousands around it.[128]

This sight is too much for Paul: "When I saw them, I, Paul, I trembled in every body part (μέλος), and I fell downwards upon my face" (*Visio* 55).[129] The third heaven is too holy for Paul to manage, and that is why he does not enter it the first time, and why the visit is short the second time around. The inclusion of eagles is because of their status as powerful and gracious in the Hebrew Bible (so in Jer 49:16; Obad 4; Ps 103:5; Prov 30:19; Isa 40:31), and their symbolism as divine and royal animals in the Roman Empire. They were the symbols of the highest god Zeus/Jupiter (cf., e.g.,

---

127 ⲙⲛ̄ⲛ̄ⲥⲁ ⲛⲁⲓ ⲇⲉ ⲧⲏⲣⲟⲩ ⲁⲩⲧⲟⲣⲡⲧ̄ ϩⲛ̄ ⲟⲩⲕⲗⲟⲟⲗⲉ ⲁⲩϫⲓⲧ ϣⲁ ⲧⲙⲉϩϣⲟⲙⲧⲉ ⲙ̄ⲡⲉ.
128 *Visio* 55:2.
129 ⲛ̄ⲧⲉⲣⲉⲓⲛⲁⲩ ⲉⲣⲟⲟⲩ ⲁ̄ⲛⲟⲕ, ⲡⲁⲩⲗⲟⲥ, ⲁⲓⲥⲧⲱⲧ ϩⲛ̄ ⲛⲁⲙⲉⲗⲟⲥ ⲧⲏⲣⲟⲩ ⲁⲩⲱ ⲁⲓϩⲉ ⲉϩⲣⲁⲓ ⲉϫⲙ̄ ⲡⲁϩⲟ. Cf. Ezekiel's vision in Ezek 1:1–3:15, esp. 1:28, where Ezekiel sees God: like the appearance of a bow in a cloud on a rainy day, so was the appearance of the brightness all around. This was the appearance of the likeness of the glory of YHWH. "When I saw it, I fell on my face" (BHS: וָאֶרְאֶה וָאֶפֹּל עַל־פָּנָי; LXX: καὶ εἶδον καὶ πίπτω ἐπὶ πρόσωπόν μου). See also 1 En. 71:11, where Enoch falls to the ground when he sees God: "And I fell on my face (*wa-wadaqi ba-gaṣṣya*), and my complete body became relaxed, and my soul became relaxed."

Plin., *HN* 10.5), functioned as his messengers (cf., e.g., Hom., *Il.* 8.247; 24.292, 311), and were the symbol of the Roman army.[130] In early Christianity, the eagle was either a reference to the evangelist John,[131] but here more importantly: the eagle also was a symbol of Christ resurrected.[132]

With this second trip, we learn little more about the spatiality of the third heaven: there is an altar that is surrounded by eagles and an immense amount of angels. The usage of "myriads and myriads" (ϩⲉⲛⲧⲃⲁ ⲛ̄ⲧⲃⲁ) and "thousands and thousands" (ϩⲉⲛϣⲟ ⲛ̄ϣⲟ) suggests a colossal space. When combining the information from both visits, we get an idea of this spatial frame. The third heaven has a beautiful gate as its entrance, it is the dwelling place of all the holy ones (*Visio* 19–20), there is an altar flanked by eagles and angels and it must be enormous in order to contain the number of angels the text describes (*Visio* 55).

(7) *The Celestial/Heavenly Paradise and the Abodes of the Saints* (*Visio* 56–62). Because Paul is so set back from his visit to the third heaven, his *angelus interpres* quickly gets him out of there and takes him to paradise: "And the angel (ἄγγελος) who traveled with me took me to paradise (παράδεισος)" (*Visio* 56:1).[133] However, it seems that they make a brief detour, as they first arrive in the Holy Land of the Lord (ⲡⲕⲁϩ ⲉⲧⲟⲩⲁⲁⲃ ⲙ̄ⲡϫⲟⲉⲓⲥ, *Visio* 56:2), a space filled with many magnificent and beautiful thrones. Paul inquires about the many people that are there, and the angel tells him that these are the prophets, and that these thrones are for them. Then the angel takes Paul to a tabernacle of light (ⲉⲩⲥⲕⲩⲛⲏ [σκηνή] ⲛ̄ⲟⲩⲟⲉⲓⲛ) and shows him his glorious throne, flanked by the angels Uriel and Suriel who sing hymns of praise (*Visio* 56:3). Almost immediately after Paul has seen this throne, however, the angel takes Paul to show him the heavenly paradise, his throne, and his crown: "I will show you the heavenly paradise (παράδεισος) and your throne (θρόνος) and your crown" (*Visio* 58:1).[134] It is unclear to me why they would go visit Paul's throne after they just saw it. Perhaps Paul has two thrones, or perhaps the text is confused.[135]

---

130 T. Schneider and E. Stemplinger, "Adler," *RAC* 1:87–94.
131 This is based on the description of the four creatures described in Rev 4:7. For how these four creatures were related to the four evangelists in early Christianity cf. Craig G. Koester, *Revelation: A New Translation with Introduction and Commentary*, AB 38A (New Haven: Yale University Press, 2014), 351–53.
132 Cf. Schneider and Stemplinger, "Adler," 92. Cf. also on the use of eagles in antiquity Steven L. Bridge, *"Where the Eagles Are Gathered": The Deliverance of the Elect in Lukan Eschatology*, JSNTSup 240 (London: Sheffield Academic Press, 2003), esp. 57–86.
133 ⲁϥϫⲓⲧ ⲛ̄ϭⲓ ⲡⲁⲅⲅⲉⲗⲟⲥ ⲉⲧⲙⲟⲟϣⲉ ⲛⲙ̄ⲙⲁⲓ ⲉⲡⲡⲁⲣⲁⲇⲉⲓⲥⲟⲥ.
134 ⲛ̄ⲧⲁⲧⲣⲉⲕⲑⲉⲱⲣⲉⲓ ⲙ̄ⲡⲡⲁⲣⲁⲇⲉⲓⲥⲟⲥ ⲛ̄ⲧⲡⲉ ⲙⲛ̄ ⲡⲉⲕⲑⲣⲟⲛⲟⲥ ⲙⲛ̄ ⲡⲉⲕⲕⲗⲟⲙ.
135 Cf. here Roig Lanzillotta and van der Vliet, *The Apocalypse of Paul*, 90–93, where they argue that the text is confused, and provide two alternative reconstructions of *Visio* 55–63. Both recon-

During his visit of the heavenly paradise (*Visio* 58–59), Paul is taken aback by the beauty of this paradise, which is described in detail. The text describes detailed measurements of walls and circumferences, as well as precise numbers of pillars (240,000 [!]), plants, and fruits growing, to give off the idea of a beautiful and enormous space.[136] This heaven has three walls, two made of silver and a golden one in between them. Compare here the aforementioned *Tabula Cebetis*, where travelers need to pass three rings of walls in order to reach the castle of eudaimonia.[137] Paul then gets taken back to the Land of the Lord where he gets to see his (second) throne. Paul is being led to "the veil of the Holy Land," and there he sees a throne with a robe and crown lying on it. In close vicinity to this throne are the thrones of his fellow apostles (*Visio* 60),[138] as well as a multitude of thrones that are reserved for martyrs (*Visio* 62).

(8) *The Mount of Olives* (*Visio* 63–64). The *angelus interpres* brings Paul to the Mount of Olives, where the other apostles were gathered. Paul greets them and recounts the journey he made to them. Mark and Timothy write it down. Hereafter, Jesus comes and visits the apostles, and orders a cloud to bring the apostles to their respective countries to evangelize and "preach the gospel (εὐαγγέλιον) of the kingdom of heavens forever" (*Visio* 64:3).[139] Here our text ends.

---

structions assume that *Visio* 58 is intrusive in its current position, that *Visio* 56–57 are original, and that *Visio* 59–60,1 are doublets that should be left out. While they acknowledge that it is difficult to say which scenario is correct, they maintain the following: "Paul's encounters with the various groups of saints who welcome him, culminating in the eulogy of 62,2, must be original. These are a strong structuring element, recurring from chapter 46 onwards, and certainly belong to the primitive text" (93).

136 Cf. for example *Visio* 58:1: "[T]here were two hundred and forty thousand sturdy pillars, and each pillar was seventy-two cubits high. Eighteen hundred kinds of fruit were growing within it and two thousand precious herbs and forty-five kinds of fragrant plants and twelve cypresses. It was encircled by a stone wall in emerald green and within it there were twelve hundred golden lamps, sixteen pillars of silver and marble surrounding it." Translation taken from Roig Lanzillotta and van der Vliet, *The Apocalypse of Paul*, 217.

137 Cf. pp. 201–2 above.

138 Compare here Matt 19:27–28: "Then Peter answered and spoke to him: 'See, we have given up everything and started following you. What is that to us, then?' Jesus said to them [Peter and the other apostles, BL]: 'Amen, I say to you that you who are following me, that in the regeneration, when the Son of Man will be sitting on his throne of glory, you will be sitting on twelve thrones, judging the twelve tribes of Israel'."

139 ⲛⲓⲙ ⲙ̄ⲡⲉⲩⲁⲅⲅⲉⲗⲓⲟⲛ ⲛ̄ⲧⲙⲛ̄ⲧⲉⲣⲟ ⲛ̄ⲙ̄ⲡⲏⲩⲉ ϣⲁ ⲉⲛⲉϩ.

Narrative World of *Visio*

The narrative world in *Visio* is—like the narrative world described in *ApocPaul*—presented as a tripartite and carefully crafted cosmos. It contains an earthly, celestial and heavenly realm, using space to its advantage. Let us consider them in order.

The first realm is the earthly realm. This realm contains the earthly Paradise and the Mount of Olives, where Paul is brought to after his journey at the end of *Visio*. I agree with Robert Casey that it is likely that the now-missing beginning of the Coptic *Visio* had Paul start his journey from the Mount of Olives, and that he returns there to report to the other apostles what he saw. This is based on the *Apocalypse of Peter*, whose author begins and ends his text by having Peter, Christ and the apostles standing on the Mount of Olives.[140] *Visio* most likely knew and used the *Apocalypse of Peter*.[141] Furthermore, a beginning on the Mount of Olives would fit in the concentric narrative structure of *Visio* proposed by Roig Lanzillotta and van der Vliet. The surviving text conforms to an A-B-C-D-C-B-A pattern:

>A: the judgement scene (Visio 15–18)
>>B: the third heaven (Visio 19–20)
>>>C: the Land of Inheritance and City of Christ (Visio 21–30)
>>>>D: the Land of the Wicked and divine mercy (Visio 31–44)
>>>C: the Paradise (Visio 44–54)
>>B: the third heaven (Visio 55)
>A: Reward (Visio 56–62)[142]

Taking both the influence of the Apocalypse of Peter and the concentric narrative structure of the Visio in account, it makes most sense to assume that the text had Paul start and end his journey on the Mount of Olives. This location could be derived from Mark 13 and Matthew 24, where the apostles ask Jesus—on the Mount of Olives—about the signs of his Parousia and the end of the world.[143] That Jesus then sends them away at the end of *Visio* is a motif taken from Matt 28:16–20. Thus, while the text itself does not really provide spatial information about the Mount of Olives, it is likely that the readers of *Visio* would have a clear picture in mind. The earthly realm is separated from the celestial realm by the river Ocean.

---

140 Casey, "The Apocalypse of Paul," 24–25.
141 So, e.g., Casey, "The Apocalypse of Paul," *passim*; Bremmer, "Christian Hell," 302: "The author of the [*Visio*] most likely knew the *Apocalypse of Peter* and borrowed some elements from it." For an argument against this claim cf. Himmelfarb, *Tours of Hell*, 140–47.
142 Roig Lanzillotta and van der Vliet, *The Apocalypse of Paul*, 67–71.
143 Bart D. Ehrman, *Forgery and Counterforgery: The Use of Literary Deceit in Early Christian Polemics* (Oxford: Oxford University Press, 2014), 447.

The second realm is the celestial realm. The two lands in the celestial realm are antithetical parallels. They both are the first location discovered when crossing the river Ocean. They give an indication of what lies ahead, be it abundance, splendor and holiness in the East, or pain and suffering in the West. The detailed description of the trees that are laden with fruit in the Land of Promise are a stark contrast to the detailed description of the many pits in the Land of the Wicked.[144] The two rivers they encounter further in the East are antithetical parallels as well. On the one hand, the river/lake Acherusia in the East is used by the angel Michael to wash and purify the righteous ones in order to enter the City of Christ. On the other hand, the river of fire in the West is used by angels to punish the unrighteous souls. The City of Christ in the East and the abyss in the West are antithetical parallels, because the City is the easternmost location in the realm, filled with splendor and glory. More importantly, it is the location closest to Christ when he returns. The Well of the Abyss and icy plane are the complete opposite. They are the westernmost locations in the celestial realm and they house the sinners that have committed the gravest of sins. These people are as far away from the City of Christ, and thus Christ himself with his mercy and love, as possible. That the Land of Inheritance is found in the East is no coincidence. The East is where the sun rises, and by placing the City of Christ in the easternmost part of the realm, it is closest to the light of the sun and the true light Jesus Christ (cf., e.g., John 1:9) when he returns.[145]

The third and last realm is the heavenly realm. The heavenly realm of *Visio* is made up out of three heavens. The text does mention a seventh heaven once in *Visio* 29:4, but this seems out of order, as already noted by Casey: "This [the mentioning of the seventh heaven, BL] appears to be a different source from the main structure which implies a three-fold division of heaven."[146] The third heaven is clearly the highest realm in *Visio*. It is the abode of God and all his angels, its holiness so great that Paul is not able to reside in it for long. This could very well be based on a careful exegesis of 2 Cor 12:2c: "that such a person was snatched up *as far as* the third heaven (ἕως τρίτου οὐρανοῦ)." The use of ἕως combined with the genitive τρίτου οὐρανοῦ shows that ἕως should be translated with "until" or "as far as."[147]

---

144 Cf. Roig Lanzillotta, "The Coptic Apocalypse of Paul," 175–76.
145 Cf. here Roig Lanzillotta and van der Vliet, *The Apocalypse of Paul*, 77–83.
146 Casey, "The Apocalypse of Paul," 16.
147 LSJ *s.v.* ἕως (B) A. "II b. of Place: ἕ. τοῦ γενέσθαι *up to the point where . . . as far as.*" See also Franco Montanari, *The Brill Dictionary of Ancient Greek*, ed. Madeleine Goh, trans. Rachel M. Costa (Leiden: Brill, 2015), 888c: "*with gen.* up to, as far as, *of time and place.*"

The author of *Visio* thus had no reason to assume that there would be a higher realm than the third heaven, because Paul went *as far as, until* the third heaven.[148]

The heavenly paradise is also located in the third heaven, because the light of God dwells there (*Visio* 59:2), and just as Paul was shaking and fell on his face after seeing all the glorious sights during his second visit to the third heaven (*Visio* 55), so the text describes that Paul feels unworthy to stay in this heavenly paradise (*Visio* 59). Next to the third heaven, there is the second heaven, of which we only learn that it contains the firmament of the heavens which rests on the river Ocean. The text surely also implies the existence of a first heaven, but this one is not mentioned by *Visio*.

The detailed descriptions of where Paul is in the cosmos are not only there for ease of reading, as is aptly observed Roig Lanzillotta and van der Vliet:

> The combination of precise geographical coordinates with cosmographic descriptions does something more, however, than simply orienting the reader in the symmetric conception of the cosmos. It also offers a coherent description of the world that is wholly consistent with the functioning of theodicy. The [Visio's] cosmographical interest and the intertwining of cosmography and theodicy seem to indicate that in the mind of the author both aspects were inseparable parts of God's providential activity.[149]

In other words, the narrative world in the Visio is a carefully crafted cosmos that uses cosmography to show its readers that their lives on earth dictate where they will eventually reside after they pass away: either in the east, close to the City of Christ, or in the west, in pits full of terrible beasts and the well of the abyss.

Conclusion

Having arrived at the end of this chapter, it is time to summarize its findings with a three-fold conclusion:

(1) While both apocalypses based themselves on the same hypotext, namely 2 Cor 12:2–4, it is clear that they used a different approach in writing their receptions. Most of *Visio* consists of filling in the account of Paul, trying to give a comprehensive overview of the realms Paul traveled through, a *horizontali-*

---

148 However, cf. Roig Lanzillotta and van der Vliet, *The Apocalypse of Paul*, 295: "The text apparently uses the seventh heaven as a designation of the highest abode of the Father, similar for instance to the *Ascension of Isaiah* 9 or 2 *Enoch* 9, not as a way of referring to the City of Christ, where Paul is presently."
149 Roig Lanzillotta and van der Vliet, *The Apocalypse of Paul*, 83

zation. *ApocPaul* on the other hand gives next to no details about the heavens Paul through which voyages. Instead of staying close to the cosmological model of 2 Corinthians 12, the Apocalypse of Paul focuses on a *verticalization* of the cosmological model, stretching out the cosmos by adding seven more heavens than described in 2 Cor 12:2–4 to show that Paul ascended to the realm above that of the demiurge.[150] In the context of spatiality, then, *Visio* focuses on the lack of space in 2 Corinthians 12 and goes above and beyond in filling the gaps with long descriptions of Jerusalem, the Land of the Wicked and even heaven. As I already noted, spatial information in *ApocPaul* is more sparse, since giving a complete overview of the cosmos was no main goal of its author. Instead, it wants to show its readers the difficulties that lie ahead for the souls wishing to ascend to the highest heaven. Since this can be done without extensive descriptions of the spaces to which Paul travels, the text keeps descriptions of the heavens to the bare minimum while still making its point.

(2) When this then is seen in the context of Breed's theory of reception history, we come to the following point. "Traditional" biblical studies, as introduced by Breed, differentiates between the possible and the real, where there are many explanations possible, but there is only one acceptable and real one. This assumption, that we as modern scholars are able to discern which interpretation is the correct one, is not justifiable for me, as it is logical that both *ApocPaul* and *Visio* were convinced that their amplification of the Pauline account was good, otherwise they would not have been written. To see these two texts instead as two differing actualizations of the virtual potential within 2 Cor 12:2–4 removes this judgment and makes it possible to accept both apocalypses as they are and helps to analyze them in their own right, as I hope I have done here. By using this text for their own Pauline journeys, they actualized the virtual potential of space in 2 Cor 12:2–4 to write their own reception of the account.

(3) Although both of these actualizations of Paul's account in 2 Corinthians take the form of a journey, the journey aspect is not necessarily the focal point of the texts, nor is their description of the cosmos. Whereas Paul wrote his ascension account to defend his apostolic ministry, both apocalypses took up the sparse details in 2 Corinthians in order to convey an ethical message.

ApocPaul aims to show its readers the dangers of escaping the material realm and the hostilities during the heavenly ascent while attempting to become a psychic being. It does so by calling the material world the "mountain of Jericho", as well as "world of the dead" twice (*ApocPaul* 20:19–20; 23:13–14). Similarly, reincarnation—

---

[150] Cf. Roig Lanzillotta and van der Vliet, *The Apocalypse of Paul*, 77–78; 107.

being sent back into a material body—is the punishment for disobedient and misbehaving souls. On the way to the top they encounter a scene of judgment, toll-collectors functioning as gatekeepers, and the demiurge who is trying to scare Paul with his powers and principalities. Since Paul is being led by the Holy Spirit, and because he has received his "sign," Paul is able to continue onwards to show what the goal of life is: becoming one with God in the highest state of being.

The goals of *Visio* are different, but still ethical in nature. By using the far shores of the river Ocean *Visio* shows that its spatial interests are not primarily cosmological. Rather, in line with ancient philosophical tradition, it uses these spaces as revelatory lands, telling its readers what might wait for them in the afterlife depending on what life they decide to live on earth. These far shores are in other ways meant to convey ethics: the good people are allowed to live in the eastern part of the celestial realm where the City of Christ is waiting to be revealed at the time of judgment. The better the life one has lived, the closer to the center of the city they are allowed to live. On the other, far side of the river, the sinners are placed based on the severity of their sins on earth. The worse the sin, the further away from the east, rising sun, and the true light, Christ. The text thus presents a choice: either live a bad life on earth and end up in the western parts of the celestial realm, or live a good life on earth and have a chance of living close to the temple of Christ in the middle of his city, located in the eastern parts of the celestial realm.

This analysis thus has shown that space itself can be a means to convey ethics: *ApocPaul* does so by having Paul travel *upwards* towards the tenth heaven, and *Visio* by presenting the eastern and western lands of the celestial realm as antithetical parallels.

References

Adams, Edward. "Graeco-Roman and Ancient Jewish Cosmology." Pages 5–27 in *Cosmology and New Testament Theology*. Edited by Jonathan T. Pennington and Sean M. MacDonough. LNTS 355. London: T&T Clark, 2008.
Bal, Mieke. *Narratology: Introduction to the Theory of Narrative*. 4th ed. Toronto: University of Toronto Press, 2017.
Barnett, Paul. *The Second Epistle to the Corinthians*. NICNT. Grand Rapids: Eerdmans, 1997.
Barrett, C.K. *The Second Epistle to the Corinthians*. BNTC. London: Adam & Charles Black, 1973.
Beinhauer-Köhler, Bärbel. "Talion, I: Zum Begriff, II: Religionswissenschaftlich." *RGG4* 8:52–53.
Betz, Hans Dieter. *Der Apostel Paulus und die sokratische Tradition: Eine exegetische Untersuchung zu seiner "Apologie" 2 Korinther 10–13*. BHT 45. Tübingen: Mohr Siebeck, 1972.
Bray, Gerald, ed. *1–2 Corinthians*. ACCS New Testament 7. New York: Routledge, 1999.
Breed, Brennan W. *Nomadic Text: A Theory of Biblical Reception History*. Bloomington: Indiana University Press, 2014.

Bremmer, Jan N. "Christian Hell: From the Apocalypse of Peter to the Apocalypse of Paul." *Numen* 56 (2009): 298–325.
Bridge, Steven L. *"Where the Eagles Are Gathered": The Deliverance of the Elect in Lukan Eschatology.* JSNTSup 240. London: Sheffield Academic Press, 2003.
Buchanan Wallace, James. *Snatched into Paradise (2 Cor 12:1–10): Paul's Heavenly Journey in the Context of Early Christian Experience.* BZNW 179. Berlin: De Gruyter, 2011.
Budge, Ernest A.T.W. *Miscellaneous Coptic Texts in the Dialect of Upper Egypt.* London: British Museum Press, 1915.
Bultmann, Rudolf. *Der zweite Brief an die Korinther.* KEK 8. Göttingen: Vandenhoeck & Ruprecht, 1976.
Burmester, O.H.E. "Egyptian Mythology in the Coptic Apocrypha." *Orientalia* 7 (1938): 355–67.
Burns, Dylan M. "Is the *Apocalypse of Paul* a Valentinian Apocalypse? Pseudepigraphy and Group Definition in NHC V,2." Pages 97–112 in *Die Nag-Hammadi-Schriften in der Literatur- und Theologiegeschichte des frühen Christentums.* Edited by Jens Schröter, Konrad Schwarz, and Clarissa Paul. STAC 106. Tübingen: Mohr Siebeck, 2017.
Carrez, Maurice. *La deuxième épitre de Saint Paul aux Corinthiens.* Commentaire du Nouveau Testament—Deuxième série 8. Geneva: Labor et Fides, 1986.
Casey, Robert P. "The Apocalypse of Paul." *JTS* 34 (1933): 1–32.
Copeland, Kirsty B., "Thinking with Oceans: Muthos, Revelation and the *Apocalypse of Paul*." Pages 77–104 in *The Visio Pauli and the Gnostic Apocalypse of Paul.* Edited by Jan Bremmer and István Czachesz. Studies on Early Christian Apocrypha 9. Leuven: Peeters, 2007.
Crum, W.E. *A Coptic Dictionary.* Oxford: Oxford University Press, 1939.
Czachesz, István. "Torture in Hell and Reality: The *Visio Pauli*." Pages 130–43 in *The Visio Pauli and the Gnostic Apocalypse of Paul.* Edited by Jan N. Bremmer and István Czachesz. Studies on Early Christian Apocrypha 9. Leuven: Peeters, 2007.
Darnell, John Coleman. "Iconographic Attraction, Iconographic Syntax, and Tableaux of Royal Ritual Power in the Pre- and Proto-Dynastic Rock Inscriptions of the Theban Western Desert." *Archéo-Nil* 19 (2009): 83–107.
Darnell, John Coleman, and Colleen Manassa Darnell. *The Ancient Egyptian Netherworld Books.* WAW 39. Atlanta: Society of Biblical Literature, 2018.
DeConick, April D. "Apostles as Archons: The Fight for Authority and the Emergence of Gnosticism in the Tchacos Codex and Other Early Christian Literature." Pages 243–88 in *Codex Judas Paper: Proceedings of the International Congress on the Tchacos Codex Held at Rice University, Houston, Texas, March 13–16, 2008.* Edited by April D. DeConick. NHMS 71. Leiden: Brill, 2009.
Deleuze, Gilles. *Difference and Repetition.* Translated by Paul Patton. New York: Columbia University Press, 1995.
Domeracki, Michael S. "The Apocalypse of Paul (NHC V,2) as a Valentinian Baptismal Liturgy of Ascent." *Gnosis* 2 (2017): 212–34.
Dubois, Jean-Daniel. "What Is 'Gnostic' within Gnostic Apocalypses?" Pages 385–410 in *Dreams, Visions, Imaginations: Jewish, Christian and Gnostic Views of the World to Come.* Edited by Tobias Nicklas, Jens Schröter, and Armand Puig i Tàrrech. BZNW 247. Berlin: De Gruyter, 2021.
Ehrman, Bart D. *Forgery and Counterforgery: The Use of Literary Deceit in Early Christian Polemics.* Oxford: Oxford University Press, 2014.
Ellington, Dustin W. "Not Applicable to Believers? The Aims and Basis of Paul's 'I' in 2 Corinthians 10–13." *JBL* 131 (2012): 325–40.
Feldmeier, Reinhard. "Paedeia Salvatrix: Zur Anthropologie Und Soteriologie Der Tabula Cebetis." Pages 149–63 in *Die Bildtafel des Kebes: Allegorie des Lebens.* Edited by Rainer Hirsch-Luipold,

Reinhard Feldmeier, Barbara Hirsch, Lutz Koch, and Heinz-Günther Nesselrath. SAPERE 8. Darmstadt: Wissenschaftliche Buchgesellschaft, 2005.
Fiori, Emiliano. "A Reactivation of the Apocalyptic Genre in Early Egyptian Monasticism: The *Apocalypse of Paul*." Pages 307–22 in *Wissen in Bewegung: Institution—Iteration—Transfer*. Edited by Eva Cancik-Kirschbaum and Anita Traninger. Episteme in Bewegung: Beiträge zu einer transdiziplinären Wissensgeschichte 1. Wiesbaden: Harrassowitz, 2015.
Fossum, Jarl E. "The Origin of the Gnostic Concept of the Demiurge." *ETL* 61 (1985): 142–52.
Frankfurter, David. "Amente Demons and Christian Syncretism." *ARelG* 14 (2013): 83–102.
Furnish, Victor Paul. *II Corinthians*. AB 32A. New Haven: Yale University Press, 1995.
Gooder, Paula R. *Only the Third Heaven? 2 Corinthians 12:1–10 and Heavenly Ascent*. LNTS 313. London: T&T Clark, 2006.
Goulder, Michael. "Visions and Knowledge." *JSNT* 56 (1994): 53–71.
Gräßer, Erich. *Der zweite Brief an die Korinther: Kapitel 8,1–13,13*. ÖTK 8/2. Gütersloh: Gütersloher Verlagshaus, 2005.
Harrison, J.R. "In Quest of the Third Heaven: Paul and His Apocalyptic Imitators." *VC* 58 (2004): 24–55.
Herrmann, Léon. "Apollos." *RevScRel* 50 (1976): 330–36.
Himmelfarb, Martha. *Tours of Hell: An Apocalyptic Form in Jewish and Christian Literature*. Philadelphia: Fortress, 1983.
Hirsch-Luipold, Rainer. "Einleitung." Pages 11–37 in *Die Bildtafel des Kebes: Allegorie des Lebens*. Edited by Rainer Hirsch-Luipold, Reinhard Feldmeier, Barbara Hirsch, Lutz Koch, and Heinz-Günther Nesselrath. SAPERE 8. Darmstadt: Wissenschaftliche Buchgesellschaft, 2005.
Hornung, Erik. *Die Unterweltsbücher der Ägypter: Eingeleitet, übersetzt und erläutert von Erik Hornung*. Zürich: Artemis, 1992.
Jiroušková, Lenka. *Die Visio Pauli: Wege und Wandlungen einer orientalischen Apokryphe im lateinischen Mittelalter: Unter Einschluß der alttsechischen und deutschsprachigen Textzeugen*. MLST 34. Leiden: Brill, 2006.
Kaler, Michael. *Flora Tells a Story: The* Apocalypse of Paul *and Its Contexts*. Studies in Christianity and Judaism/Études sur le christianisme et le judaïsme 19. Waterloo: Wilfrid Laurier University Press, 2008.
Kaler, Michael. "The Intriguing Absence of God in the *Apocalypse of Paul*." *ETL* 34 (2018): 235–40.
Keener, Craig S. *1–2 Corinthians*. New Cambridge Bible Commentary. Cambridge: Cambridge University Press, 2005.
Klauck, Hans-Josef. *2. Korintherbrief*. NEBNT 8. Würzburg: Echter Verlag, 1994.
Klauck, Hans-Josef. "With Paul through Heaven and Hell: Two Apocryphal Apocalypses." *BR* 52 (2007): 57–72.
Koester, Craig G. *Revelation: A New Translation with Introduction and Commentary*. AB 38A. New Haven: Yale University Press, 2014.
Kuhn, K.H. *A Coptic Jeremiah Apocryphon*. Louvain: Le Muséon, 1970.
Lambrecht, Jan. *Second Corinthians*. SP 8. Collegeville, MN: Liturgical Press, 1999.
Luther, Susanne. "Space." Pages 59–77 in *How John Works: Storytelling in the Fourth Gospel*. Edited by Douglas Estes and Ruth Sheridan. RBS 86. Atlanta: Society of Biblical Literature, 2016.
Luther, Susanne. "Topographies of Conduct? Ethical Implications of the Ekphrastic Description of Jerusalem in Rev 21." Forthcoming in *Vivid Rhetoric and Visual Persuasion: Ekphrasis in Early Christian Literature*. Edited by Meghan Henning and Nils Neumann. Grand Rapids: Eerdmans.
Luttikhuizen, Gerard P. "The Demonic Demiurge in Gnostic Mythology." Pages 148–60 in *The Fall of the Angels*. Edited by Cristoph Auffarth and Loren T. Stuckenbruck. TBN 6. Leiden: Brill, 2004.

Markschies, Christoph J., and Einar Thomassen, eds. *Valentinianism: New Studies*. NHMS 96. Leiden: Brill, 2020.

Montanari, Franco. *The Brill Dictionary of Ancient Greek*. Edited by Madeleine Goh. Translated by Rachel M. Costa. Leiden: Brill, 2015.

Murdock, William R. "The Apocalypse of Paul from Nag Hammad Codex V: A Translation and Interpretation." PhD diss., School of Theology at Claremont, 1968.

Murdock, William R., and George W. MacRae. "The Apocalypse of Paul: V,2: 17,19–24,7." *Nag Hammadi Codices V, 2–5 and VI with Papyrus Berolinensis 8502, 1 and 4*. Edited by Douglas M. Parrott. Brill: Leiden, 1979.

O'Brien, Carl Séan. *The Demiurge in Ancient Thought: Secondary Gods and Divine Mediators*. Cambridge: Cambridge University Press, 2015.

Piovanelli, Pierluigi. "The Miraculous Discovery of the Hidden Manuscript, or the Paratextual Function of the Prologue to the *Apocalypse of Paul*." Pages 23–49 in *The Visio Pauli and the Gnostic Apocalypse of Paul*. Edited by Jan N. Bremmer and István Czachesz. Studies on Early Christian Apocrypha 9. Leuven: Peeters, 2007.

Roig Lanzillotta, Lautaro. "The Apocalypse of Paul (NHC V,2): Cosmology, Anthropology, and Ethics." *Gnosis* 1 (2016): 110–31.

Roig Lanzillotta, Lautaro. "The Coptic 'Apocalypse of Paul' in Ms Or 7023." Pages 158–97 in *The Visio Pauli and the Gnostic Apocalypse of Paul*. Edited by Jan N. Bremmer and István Czachesz. Studies on Early Christian Apocrypha 9. Leuven: Peeters, 2007.

Roig Lanzillotta, Lautaro, and Jacques van der Vliet. *The Apocalypse of Paul (Visio Pauli) in Sahidic Coptic: Critical Edition, Translation and Commentary*. With an appendix by Jos van Lent. SVigChr 179. Leiden: Brill, 2023.

Rosenstiehl, Jean-Marc. "Tartarouchos—Temelouchos: Contribution à l'étude de l'apocalpyse apocrpyhe de Paul." Pages 29–56 in *Deuxième journée d'études coptes: Strasbourg 25 mai 1984*. CBCo 3. Leuven: Peeters, 1986.

Rosenstiehl, Jean-Marc. "La montagne de Jéricho (NH V,2,19,11–13)." Pages 885–92 in *Coptica—Gnostica—Manichaia: Mélanges offerts à Wolf-Peter Funk*. BCNHE 7. Québec: Les presses de l'Université Laval, 2006.

Rosenstiehl, Jean-Marc. "Crime et châtiment au quatrième ciel: NH V,2: 20,5–21,21." Pages 559–83 in *L'Évangelie selon Thomas et les textes de Nag Hammadi*. Edited by Louis Painchaud and Paul-Hubert Poirier. BCNHE 8. Québec: Les presses de l'Université Laval, 2007.

Rosenstiehl, Jean-Marc, and Michael Kaler. *L'Apocalypse de Paul (NH V, 2)*. BCNHT 31. Québec: Les presses de l'Université Laval, 2005.

Roukema, Riemer. "Paul's Rapture to Paradise in Early Christian Literature." Pages 267–83 in *The Wisdom of Egypt: Jewish, Early Christian, and Gnostic Essays in Honour of Gerard P. Luttikhuizen*. Edited by Anthony Hilhorst and George H. van Kooten. AJEC 59. Leiden: Brill, 2005.

Roukema, Riemer. "The Good Samaritan in Ancient Christianity." *VC* 57 (2003): 56–74.

Rowland, Christopher. *The Open Heaven: A Study of Apocalyptic in Judaism and Early Christianity*. London: SPCK, 1982.

Ruiten, Jacques T.A.G.M. van. "The Four Rivers of Eden in the *Apocalypse of Paul* (Visio Pauli): The Intertextual Relationship of Genesis 2.10–14 and the *Apocalypse of Paul* 23." Pages 50–76 in *The Visio Pauli and the Gnostic Apocalypse of Paul*. Edited by Jan N. Bremmer and István Czachesz. Studies on Early Christian Apocrypha 9. Leuven: Peeters, 2007.

Ryan, Marie-Laure. "Space." In *The Living Handbook of Narratology*. Edited by Peter Hühn, John Pier, Wolf Schmid, and Jörg Schönert. https://www-archiv.fdm.uni-hamburg.de/lhn/node/55.html.

Ryan, Marie-Laure, Kenneth Foote, and Maoz Azaryahu. *Narrating Space/Spatializing Narrative: Where Narrative Theory and Geography Meet*. Theory and Interpretation of Narrative. Columbus: Ohio State University Press, 2016.

Sælid Gilhus, Ingvild. "The Gnostic Demiurge—An Agnostic Trickster." *Religion* 14 (1984): 301–11.

Satake, Akira. "Schritt für Schritt: Die Argumentation des Paulus in 2Kor 10–13." Pages 283–99 in *Der zweite Korintherbrief: Literarische Gestalt—Historische Situation—Theologische Argumentation: Festschrift zum 70. Geburtstag von Dietrich-Alex Koch*. Edited by Dieter Sänger. FRLANT 250. Göttingen: Vandenhoeck & Ruprecht, 2012.

Schmeller, Thomas. *Der zweite Brief an die Korinther*. EKK VIII/2. Göttingen: Vandenhoeck & Ruprecht, 2015.

Schneider, T., and E. Stemplinger. "Adler." *RAC* 1:87–94.

Schnelle, Udo. "Der 2. Korintherbrief und die Mission gegen Paulus." Pages 300–22 in *Der zweite Korintherbrief: Literarische Gestalt—Historische Situation—Theologische Argumentation: Festschrift zum 70. Geburtstag von Dietrich-Alex Koch*. Edited by Dieter Sänger. FRLANT 250. Göttingen: Vandenhoeck & Ruprecht, 2012.

Silverstein, Theodore. *Visio Sancti Pauli: The History of the Apocalypse in Latin Together with Nine Texts*. London: Christophers, 1935.

Silverstein, Theodore. "Did Dante Know the Vision of St. Paul?" Pages 231–47 in *Harvard Studies and Notes in Philology and Literature 19*. Cambridge: Harvard University Press, 1936.

Silverstein, Theodore. "The Date of the 'Apocalypse of Paul.'" *Mediaeval Studies* 24 (1962): 335–48.

Silverstein, Theodore, and Anthony Hilhorst. *Apocalypse of Paul: A New Critical Edition of Three Long Latin Versions*. COr 21. Geneva: Patrick Cramer, 1997.

Smith, Morton. "Ascent to the Heavens and the Beginning of Christianity." Pages 403–29 in *Aufstieg und Abstieg—Vorträge gehalten auf der Eranos Tagung in Ascona vom 19. bis 27. August 1981*. Edited by Adolf Portmann and Rudolf Ritsema. Ascona: Eranos Foundation; Frankfurt: Insel, 1982.

Sommer, Michael. "Roman Tombs in Alexandria and in the Egyptian Chora: A Journey through the After-Life of the Apocalypse of Zephaniah." Pages 207–28 in *Alexandria: Hub of the Hellenistic World*. Edited by Benjamin Schliesser, Jan Rüggemeier, Thomas J. Kraus and Jörg Frey, with the assistance of Daniel Herrmann. WUNT 460. Tübingen: Mohr Siebeck, 2021.

Thomassen, Einar. *The Spiritual Seed: The Church of the "Valentinians."* NHMS 60. Leiden: Brill, 2006.

Thrall, Margaret. *The Second Epistle to the Corinthians*. 2 vols. ICC. London: Bloomsbury, 2001.

Touati, Charlotte. "Das Schweigen sprechen lassen: Von 2 Kor 12,2–4 zu den apokryphen Apokalypsen." Pages 301–12 in *Christian Apocrypha: Receptions of the New Testament in Ancient Christian Apocrypha*. Edited by Tobias Nicklas and Jean-Michel Roessli. NTP 26. Göttingen: Vandenhoeck & Ruprecht, 2014.

Twigg, Matthew. "The Mountain of Jericho in the Nag Hammadi *Apocalypse of Paul*: A Suggestion." *VC* 69 (2015): 422–42.

Twigg, Matthew. *The Valentinian Temple: Visions, Revelations, and the Nag Hammadi Apocalypse of Paul*. New York: Routledge, 2022.

Vliet, Jacques van der. "Paul and the Others: Rereading the Gnostic Apocalypse of Paul (NHC V,2)." *Gnosis* 7 (2022): 127–50.

Wolff, Christian. *Der zweite Brief des Paulus an die Korinther*. ThHK 8. Leipzig: Evangelische Verlagsanstalt, 1989.

Tobias Nicklas
The Travels of Barnabas: From the Acts of the Apostles to Late Antique Hagiographic Literature

Abstract: This chapter explores how Christian sources from the New Testament until late antiquity depict the travels of the apostle Barnabas. As shall become clear, the itineraries attributed to Barnabas in various writings cannot be harmonized, but serve specific purposes within each writing.

To this day, we find maps in common editions of the Bible on which Paul's three missionary journeys as well as his journey as a prisoner to Rome are marked. The editors of these Bibles usually adhere to the specifications of the canonical Acts of the Apostles. It is assumed implicitly (at least to readers who are not trained in historical criticism) that it is a matter of secured historical knowledge. I assume fundamentally that Luke's Acts offers in parts quite reliable historical material, although it is of course an idealizing narrative of the origin of the early Christian movement—or rather, of the followers of the "Way."[1] However, the New Testament offers already different itineraries of Paul that cannot be fully harmonized with each other: is Paul's letter to the Galatians addressed to one of the regions that Paul passes through together with Barnabas on his first journey (Acts 13:14–14:25) or to the inhabitants of the *Landschaft* of Galatia, which in turn is mentioned only extremely briefly in Acts (cf. however Acts 16:5)?[2] Or (following the new commentary by Martin Meiser[3]) should an even more complex intermediate solution be constructed? Paul writes Romans with the intention of preparing his planned journey to Spain (Rom 15:22). At the end of Acts we find Paul as a prisoner in Rome, but his fate is not yet decided. That his way could perhaps still lead him to Spain is by no means excluded: the Latin Acts of Peter (in the form of the *Actus Vercellenses*

---

1 For Luke as the theologian of the "Way" see, e.g., Hans Klein, *Lukasstudien*, FRLANT 209 (Göttingen: Vandenhoeck & Ruprecht, 2005), 105–18.
2 This classical problem of New Testament introductory studies has not been solved completely even today, although a large number of exegetes are again turning more to the provincial hypothesis. On this discussion see for example Dieter Sänger, "Die Adresse des Galaterbriefes: Neue (?) Überlegungen zu einem alten Problem," in *Schrift—Tradition—Evangelium: Studien zum frühen Judentum und zur paulinischen Theologie* (Neukirchen-Vluyn: Neukirchener Verlag, 2016), 229–74.
3 Martin Meiser, *Der Brief des Apostels Paulus an die Galater*, THKNT (Leipzig: Evangelische Verlagsanstalt, 2022), 10–21 (including an extensive overview of secondary literature).

https://doi.org/10.1515/9783110717488-012

§§ 1–3) assumes the apostle's mission to Spain. This is also the text that provides us with the reasons Peter went to Rome to suffer martyrdom there.[4] Paul's mission to Spain, initiated by Christ himself (cf. the *Actus Vercellenses* § 1), leads to the intrusion of Simon Magus into the Roman community, which almost completely falls away from the faith because of it. In turn, this forces Peter to travel to Rome, defeat Simon Magus, and lead the congregation back to the right path. In the depiction of the Acts of Peter, Paul's journey to Spain and Peter's journey to Rome (as well as his martyrdom) are thus also logically closely linked. But while the work and the martyrdom of Peter in Rome is still today a fixed role in the memory at least of the Roman Catholic Church,[5] Paul's mission to Spain is usually doubted (for quite good reasons)—and also not reflected in the maps of the Pauline missionary journeys known to me. In addition to these examples, the information of the Pastoral Epistles about Paul's whereabouts cannot be harmonized with that of the Acts of the Apostles:[6] already at first glance it is noticeable that Titus presupposes an initial mission to Crete by Paul (Titus 1:5), which is to be "brought to completion" by Titus. The apostle, on the other hand, is in Nicopolis in Epirus (in the northwest part of today's Greece), where he wishes to spend his winter (Titus 3:12). Even if we do not take into account the information of the other Pastoral Epistles which—in 2 Timothy—have Paul writing from Rome, it is clear that the itinerary of the Pastoral Epistles cannot be reconciled with that of Acts. There, too, Paul arrives in Crete (Acts 27:7–13), but only as a prisoner on a ship headed to Rome, certainly without

---

4 Edition: Marietheres Döhler, *Acta Petri: Text, Übersetzung und Kommentar zu den Actus Vercellenses*, TU 171 (Berlin: de Gruyter, 2018). We also encounter Paul in Spain within the Acts of Xanthippe and Polyxena. For further information about this text see David L. Eastman, "The Life and Conduct of the Holy Women Xanthippe, Polyxena, and Rebecca," in *New Testament Apocrypha: More Noncanonical Scriptures*, ed. Tony Burke and Brent Landau, 3 vols. (Grand Rapids: Eerdmans, 2016, 2020, 2023), 1:416–53 (including an overview of secondary literature). For a historical discussion of the matter see Armand Puig i Tarrèch, "Paul's Missionary Activity during His Roman Trial: The Case of Paul's Journey to Hispania," in *The Last Years of Paul: Essays from the Tarragona Conference, June 2013*, ed. Armand Puig i Tarrèch, John Barclay and Jörg Frey, WUNT 352 (Tübingen: Mohr Siebeck, 2015), 469–506 and Christos Karakolis, "Paul's Mission to Hispania: Some Critical Observations," in Puig i Tarrèch, Barclay and Frey, *The Last Years of Paul*, 507–20.
5 David L. Eastman compiles texts and traditions on the martyrdom of Peter in Rome within his *The Ancient Martyrdom Accounts of Peter and Paul*, WGRW 39 (Atlanta: Society of Biblical Literature, 2015). On the development of these writings cf. also Tobias Nicklas, "Antike Petruserzählungen und der erinnerte Petrus in Rom," in *Petrusliteratur und Petrusarchäologie: Römische Begegnungen*, ed. Jörg Frey and Martin Wallraff, Rom und der Protestantismus 4 (Tübingen: Mohr Siebeck, 2020), 159–87.
6 For more detail on this see, for example, Michael Theobald, *Israel-Vergessenheit in den Pastoralbriefen: Ein neuer Versuch zu ihrer historisch-theologischen Verortung im 2. Jahrhundert n.Chr. unter besonderer Berücksichtigung der Ignatius-Briefe*, SBS 229 (Stuttgart: Katholisches Bibelwerk, 2016), 333–48.

the opportunity to proselytize there or even to winter in Nicopolis. The examples could be continued. I am not interested in deciding which itinerary describes Paul's journeys more reliably. Moreso, there are two observations. On the one hand, the itineraries of the apostles, especially as soon as we include apocryphal texts, cannot be harmonized. They do not form a self-contained network of routes through the Roman Empire (and beyond) that can be coordinated between the various texts, but are often in blatant contradiction to each other. On the other hand, they seem to be so important for many texts about the apostles—even the Pastoral Epistles, for whose teaching they regularly play a role. According to my very simple thesis, there must be reasons for this beyond the level of historical factuality. If we consider the fact that the apostolic narratives often have the function of offering narratives about the origins of regional or local churches that attempt to anchor themselves in apostolic times, this may reveal a way to trace these reasons. I can illustrate the topic, which is extensive enough to fill a monograph, here with only one example: the (in part little known) itineraries that associated with the apostle Barnabas. In this vein, I begin with the canonical Acts of the Apostles and follow the developments up to hagiographical writings at the border of Late Antiquity.

From the Acts of the Apostles to the Acts of Barnabas

The Acts of Barnabas—actually titled The Travels and Martyrdom of Barnabas—is a rather short apostolic narrative (in 26 concise paragraphs) compared to, say, the early Acts of Paul, Acts of Peter, Acts of Andrew, Acts of Thomas, or the Acts of John. Using Acts 13:5 as a point of connection, the Acts of Barnabas is told from the perspective of John Mark. Its subject matter includes Barnabas' and Paul's helpers along with the Cyprus mission.[7] For reasons to which I will return later, the text was probably written in Cyprus in the first half of the 5th century, with some probabil-

---

[7] Edition: Adelbertus Lipsius and Maximilianus Bonnet, eds., *Acta Apostolorum Apocrypha II/2: Acta Philippi et Acta Thoma: Accedunt Acta Barnabae* (Leipzig, 1903; repr., Darmstadt: Wissenschaftliche Buchgesellschaft, 1959), 292–302. For an introduction to the work cf. Enrico Norelli, "Actes de Barnabé," in *Écrits apocryphes chrétiens II*, ed. Pierre Geoltrain and Jean-Daniel Kaestli (Paris: Gallimard, 2005), 617–42 (with a French translation); Glenn E. Snyder, "The Acts of Barnabas: A New Translation and Introduction," in *New Testament Apocrypha: More Noncanonical Scriptures*, ed. Tony Burke and Brent Landau, 3 vols. (Grand Rapids: Eerdmans, 2016, 2020, 2023), 1:317–36; Bernd Kollmann and Burkhard Schröder, *Der Evangelist Markus: Historische Konturen: Altkirchliche Legenden: Hagiographische Zeugnisse*, SBS 257 (Stuttgart: Katholisches Bibelwerk, 2023), 90–97 (Introduction) and 159–67 (German translation) as well as Tobias Nicklas, "Die Akten

ity before the Council of Ephesus (431 CE).[8] Whereas the canonical Acts is interested primarily in the first missionary journey leading Barnabas and Saul, chosen by the Holy Spirit, from Antioch to Cyprus, it is hardly mentioned in the Acts of Barnabas. Instead, the second missionary journey is in the foreground, which Acts mentions only briefly (cf. Acts 15:39). Already the comparison of itineraries of the first missionary journey is highly revealing. In the canonical Acts, the starting point of the journey is especially emphasized: this is not due, however, to a strategic point of view; instead, Barnabas and Saul, who are described as being a part of a group of prophets and teachers in Antioch (on the Orontes), are chosen by the Holy Spirit himself (Acts 13:1–4).[9] In light of this perspective, the connection between Cyprus and Antioch is clearly God-ordained. The journey continues and leads Barnabas and Saul/Paul (as well as John Mark) to Seleucia on the Orontes, i.e., the port city of Antioch (Acts 13:4). They sail to Cyprus, where they disembark at Salamis, i.e., on the southeastern coast of Cyprus (Acts 13:5). From there they "traverse the whole island" (Acts 13:6: διέλθοντες δὲ ὅλην τὴν νῆσον); specific places and events on this part of the journey, however, are not mentioned. Instead, the account focuses on the last stop in Cyprus, Paphos (in the southwest of the island), the meeting with the governor Sergius Paullus,[10] and especially the confrontation with the Jewish magician Bar-Jesus/Elymas, in which Saul proves to be the real sovereign. After the punitive miracle against Bar-Jesus, the account changes: from now on Saul is abruptly called Paul (Acts 13:13), and the group is now no longer led by Barnabas (cf. Acts 13:2) but is referred to as "Paul's people" (Acts 13:13: οἱ περὶ Παῦλον). Afterward, the three leave the island. Nothing is said about missionary successes or other events at the next station, Perge in Pamphylia (on the southern coast of present-day Turkey). The text only reports that here the paths of the three part: John Mark returns to Jerusalem where, as we learned in Acts 12:12, his mother has a house. Paul and Barnabas' journey, however, leads to Pisidian Antioch (Acts 13:14).

---

des Barnabas," in *Zwischen Apokryphen und Hagiographie: Spätantike Apostelerzählungen in ihrer Welt*, ed. Tobias Nicklas, Tria Corda Lectures (Tübingen: Mohr Siebeck, forthcoming).

8 I have justified this in Nicklas, "Akten des Barnabas." Cf. also Tobias Nicklas, "Barnabas Remembered: Apokryphe Barabastexte und die Kirche Zyperns," in *Religion als Imagination: Festschrift Marco Frenschkowski*, ed. Lena Seehausen, Paulus Enke and Jens Herzer (Leipzig: Evangelische Verlagsanstalt, 2020), 167–88 (176–78). This does not rule out a later dating, as has usually been advocated since Lipsius and Bonnet, *Acta Apostolorum*, 290–97 (e.g., Kollmann and Schröder, *Evangelist Markus*, 97). However, the text might have been written well before the year 488 CE, when the complete body of the (alleged) Barnabas was found.

9 This is of course typical for Acts, in which the Holy Spirit is one of the actual protagonists *behind* the narrative.

10 Another way of spelling this name is Sergius Paulus.

Already the depiction of this first Cyprus mission in the Acts of Barnabas differs from that of Acts in some important details: it seems especially important for our question that the journey of the three clearly does *not* take its starting point in Antioch but rather in Iconium, today's Konya in Lycaonia (Acts Barn. § 5). John Mark and Barnabas independently receive a vision of Christ (Acts Barn. §§ 3–4)—here, there is no mention of Paul—which emphasizes the future significance of John Mark. Christ (who is not recognized by John) speaks in this manner to John Mark in Acts Barn. § 3: "Be confident, John! For you will be renamed Mark, and your glory will be proclaimed in all the world." Barnabas, in turn, is not only prophesied to concerning his future martyrdom, he also receives the charge to hold fast to John Mark. Similar to the description in Acts, the three travel from there to Seleucia where they remain for several days before sailing to Cyprus. With this motif, then, the text seems (at least a first glance) to remain true to Acts, while simultaneously altering it in a most subtle way: here, the Seleucia on the Orontes of Acts can hardly be meant, but only the Seleucia on the Calycadnos in Isauria.[11] This not only completely severs the connection to Syrian Antioch, but replaces the itinerary of Acts with an aspect of what we find in the Acts of Paul and Thecla: after all, the reason given for the group's stay in Iconium is that there was a "holy and pious man (there) who had received us and whose house Paul had sanctified" (Acts Barn. § 5). This can basically only be the Onesiphoros of the Acts of Paul and Thecla;[12] the events that are connected in the canonical Acts of the Apostles with the stay in Iconium described there (albeit *after* the first journey to Cyprus), on the other hand, are not mentioned (cf. Acts 13:51–14:5). It is not at all problematic that the Acts of Paul and Thecla do not mention Barnabas and John Mark. The following summarizes the events of the first missionary journey in just a single sentence: we "sailed . . . to Cyprus, and I [John Mark] was their servant as long as we passed through Cyprus" (Acts Barn. § 5). The text does not lose a word about Paul's punitive miracle against Elymas/Bar-Jesus, not a word about the conversion of the governor, does not mention a single specific place in Cyprus, and does not at all hint at the change in the leadership within the group! This does not seem to be primarily because the Acts of Barnabas simply presuppose knowledge of the canonical Acts of the Apostles, for then it would not have to be as precise in other details: the text clearly wants to downplay the importance of the first missionary journey (and simultaneously probably that of Paul) versus that of the second missionary journey (and the role of Barnabas). Even the figure "John Mark" changes: although the

---

11 Thus also Kollmann and Schröder, *Evangelist Markus*, 160 (n. 3) as well as Nicklas, "Akten des Barnabas."
12 Thus also Kollmann and Schröder, *Evangelist Markus*, 160 (n. 3) as well as Nicklas, "Akten des Barnabas."

paths of the group parts in Perge, thus at the place with which this is also connected in Acts, John Mark does *not* simply travel back to Jerusalem but remains for two months in Perge in order to "sail away to the western climes" (and therefore not to Jerusalem!). However, he is prevented from doing so by the Holy Spirit himself, and sets out again in search of the apostles, that is, Barnabas and Paul (Acts Barn. § 5).[13] He finds them in Antioch. Which Antioch is in view here is entirely open: I believe it is probable that the text assumes that John Mark had followed the other two to Antioch, specifically to the Antioch in Pisidia mentioned in Acts 13:14–50! After all, the Acts of the Apostles does not mention in the slightest the length of stay there. Whether Antioch in Pisidia or Antioch on the Orontes is meant, in either case the events from Luke's Acts have been altered. In the first case, the problem arises that Lucius of Cyrene (Acts Barn. § 7; cf. Acts 13:1) is also in this Antioch and that the events recounted in Acts 14 are omitted. However, Acts Barn. § 11 speaks quite clearly in favor of the Pisidian Antioch: there, it is mentioned that Barnabas and John Mark broke off to go to Laodicea. This would be rather unlikely if they were travelling from Antioch on the Orontes. In the second case, i.e., the decision in favor of Antioch on the Orontes, it remains unclear what can be meant by the "end of the teaching activity" of the two apostles in Antioch; at the same time, the separation of Barnabas and Paul is moved to a point in time apparently before the so-called "apostolic council" (Acts 15:1–35). The text also seems to assume that Paul (because of a vision in a dream and not because of the appearance of "people from Judea") left for Jerusalem *alone* (Acts Barn. § 7; cf. instead Acts 15:1–3). Whether this refers to Paul's journey to the apostolic council or to Paul's last journey within Acts with the farewell speech in Miletus (Acts 20:17–38) remains unclear (and should probably remain unclear). After all, the Paul of the Acts of Barnabas already has his death in mind during this journey (Acts Barn. § 10). Above all, the additional itinerary which leads Barnabas and John Mark from Laodicea via Isauria to Cyprus from Acts Barn. § 11 speaks very clearly in favor of the first solution, i.e., against Antioch on the Orontes as attested in the canonical Acts: those who do not think too carefully about geographical possibilities will hardly find the differences between the Acts of Barnabas and what we find in the canonical Acts to be too serious. Only readers who visualize the possible route the apostles would have had to take will more concretely notice the dramatic difference.[14] There is no possibility of harmonizing the itineraries in the canonical Acts and in the Acts of Barnabas. The reason for this is well-known and obvious: the Acts of Barnabas most likely emerged at a

---

[13] It is an important difference between the Acts of the Apostles and the Acts of Barnabas that (using a broad concept of apostles) the latter can easily call Paul and Barnabas apostles.

[14] It would of course be highly interesting to know how ancient readers would have perceived the differences without the maps we take so much for granted today.

time in which the Church of Cyprus was struggling for its independence from the Church of Antioch on the Orontes. The statements in the canonical Acts that the Holy Spirit himself initiated the Cyprus mission from Antioch on the Orontes played into the hands of the ecclesiastical-political opponent. Therefore, the connection to Antioch has to be reduced as far as possible, even virtually excised. Simultaneously, the prominent role Paul plays in the Acts of the Apostles is relativized: he is not described simply as the leader of the group but continues to be on par with Barnabas. In addition, the confrontation between Paul and Barnabas—which is only briefly elaborated in Acts 15:36–39 and which, unlike Paul's desire to continue to take John Mark with him—is described much more broadly in the Acts of Barnabas than in the Acts of the Apostles. Paul proves downright merciless toward John Mark (cf. Acts Barn. §§ 6, 8), while Barnabas takes on the role of conciliator. It is Christ himself who appears to Paul and makes the reconciliation between the apostles possible before their departure.

The second missionary journey to Cyprus, only hinted at in Acts 15:39—this time carried out only by Barnabas and John Mark—now occupies a wide space in the Acts of Barnabas: the itinerary of the two goes from Antioch (apparently the one in Pisidia) to Laodicea, Korasion (in Isauria near Korykos),[15] to Palaia in Isauria and from there to the island of Pityusa, the island of Dana lying on the Isaurian coast (all from Acts Barn. § 1),[16] then to the Akonesian islands (present Babadil Adalari; Acts Barn. § 12).[17] The fact that the mention of none of these locations contributes anything to the plot of the story, but that even places beyond the major centers are mentioned here, makes one sit up and take notice. Does the text wish to establish a special relationship between the Cyprus mission and places in Pisidia (like Antioch, which is obviously perceived as an important center of apostolic activity), Phrygia (Laodicea) and especially Isauria? This seems to me to be at least plausible, although concrete reasons for this seem to be only rudimentarily tangible. A connection to the cult of Thecla, for example, is not made plausible. Does one hope to receive ecclesiastical-political support from this side through the revaluation of these regions? Are concrete places related to the veneration of apostles in the mentioned portions of Isauria in mind?[18] The (geographically) plausible but at the same time rather emphasized itinerary is hardly attributable to coincidence.

---

15 On this see Philipp Pilhofer, "Von Segeltouren und Konjekturen: Die Barnabas-Akten als Quelle zur Topographie der isaurischen Küste," *Orbis Terrarum* 13 (2015): 192–210 (198–202).
16 On this see Kollmann and Schröder, *Evangelist Markus*, 162 (n. 9).
17 On this see Pilhofer, "Segeltouren," 204–205 as well as Kollmann and Schröder, *Evangelist Markus*, 163 (n.10).
18 This idea comes from Arabella Cortese, *Cilicia as a Sacred Landscape in Late Antiquity: A Journey to the Trail of the Apostles, Martyrs and Local Saints* (Wiesbaden: Reichert, 2022), 41–53.

Also in the second missionary journey Barnabas and John Mark traverse the entire island: by way of contrast with the first missionary journey, now the author mentions concrete locations which can be connected to a clear (and also comprehensible) itinerary. The journey goes from Krommyakites (Cape Krommyatikon, Acts Barn. § 14) in the very north slightly southeast of Lapithos, then south to Lampadistos (both Acts Barn. § 15), further south to Tamassos (Acts Barn. § 17), then sharply southwest over the snowy mountains to (Palaia) Paphos (Acts Barn. § 18), to move on from there along the southern coast via Kourion (Acts Barn. §§ 18–19), Amathus (Acts Barn. § 20) and Kition (Acts Barn. § 21) (by ship over the "Nesoi," i.e., the unnamed islands) to Salamis (Acts Barn. § 22). There, Barnabas suffered martyrdom. Of course, first of all this gives the impression that Barnabas and Mark really walk all over Cyprus during their journey and touch as many later ecclesiastical centers as possible. Bernd Kollmann and Burkhard Schröder write: "Die Reiseroute von Barnabas und Johannes Markus führt über die gesamte Insel und bezieht sämtliche Orte mit ein, die Bischofssitze waren."[19] At the same time, however, it is clear that not all of the locations mentioned are ascribed with the same significance: In Krommyakites the two are welcomed by the "temple servants Timon and Ariston" (Acts Barn. § 14), Barnabas cures Timon of a high fever by apparently laying a copy of Matthew's Gospel on him.[20] From then on Timon accompanies the group as well (Acts Barn. §§ 15–16, 21). Only very briefly mentioned are the stays in Lapithos, which is not even entered by the group because of a pagan festival, or Mapadistos, where only a meeting with a certain, not further introduced Herakleios is mentioned (Acts Barn. § 16). Only in Acts Barn. § 17 is it explained who this is, namely a person (not mentioned in Acts) who, according to the text, had already met Paul on the first missionary journey in Kition but only now, during the second missionary journey, is baptized, renamed Herakleides, and appointed bishop of Cyprus with his residence in Tamassos. In Palaia Paphos, the travelers are joined by a temple servant named Rhodon, but the antagonist Bar-Jesus, familiar from the Acts of the Apostles, now reappears and prevents the group from entering Paphos. Something similar happens in Kurion because of an "unholy race" (Acts Barn. § 19). In "some" unspecified village, moreover, the group encounters a certain Aristoklianos, who had already been consecrated as bishop in Antioch (Acts Barn. § 20). While the group is hospitably received here, they again encounter resistance organized by Bar-Jesus in Amathus. In Kition, too, the travelers, welcomed

---

19 Kollmann and Schröder, *Evangelist Markus*, 96.
20 See further on this AnneMarie Luijendijk, "The Gospel of Matthew in the Acts of Barnabas through the Lens of Book History: Healing and Burial with Books," in *From Roman to Early Christian Cyprus: Studies in Religion and Archaeology*, ed. Laura Nasrallah, AnneMarie Luijendijk and Charalambos Bakirtzis, WUNT 437 (Tübingen: Mohr Siebeck, 2020), 169–94.

by no one, do not stop; however, they meet Herakleides again and instruct him "how he should preach the gospel and establish churches and appoint liturgists in them" (Acts Barn. § 21). It is not until Salamis, the terminus of the tour of Cyprus, at the same time the starting point of the first missionary journey, that Barnabas is reported in more detail as teaching in public (Acts Barn. § 22). Despite a promising start, however, Bar-Jesus, who had arrived in the meantime, succeeds in turning the Jewish crowd against Barnabas. The latter suffers martyrdom (related only quite briefly), and his body is burned. But John Mark, Timon and Rhodes manage to save at least the ashes and hide them in a cave near the village of Ledra (near today's Nicosia?). The three succeed in escaping, and they board a ship and reach Alexandria.[21] Already on the basis of this description it becomes clear that although all the mentioned places of Cyprus are touched by the mission of the apostle Barnabas, by no means all of them play the same role: it is striking not only how many towns have no successful preaching at all, but also how few people are converted at all on a lasting basis. Of these, Timon and Rhodes in turn end up leaving the island. Thus, in the perspective of the Acts of Barnabas, the future of the Church of Cyprus rests first and foremost on Herakleides, the bishop of Tamassos, a place where, moreover, the existence of congregations is apparently already presupposed (Acts Barn. § 17).[22] The latter, moreover, receives the right "apostolic" instruction in all that is necessary for the proper spread of the gospel. The second place, marked as particularly important, is of course, but nevertheless clearly more negatively associated, Salamis: only here a more detailed teaching activity of Barnabas is reported, here his martyrdom takes place, and from here the remainder of the group successfully escapes. The precise place where the relics of the apostle are found, however, remains unnamed. And the conclusion is also exciting: the Cyprus that in this origin narrative is completely detached from its relations with Antioch on the Orontes, that instead apparently wishes to be seen in relation to Isauria, that locates a core of its ecclesiastical organization in Tamassos, now connects its origin narrative with that of Alexandria. Mark, the apostle of Alexandria, is also one of the first missionaries of Cyprus. However, the Cyprus mission precedes that of Alexandria.

Of course, there are also historical reasons for all this.[23] Kollmann and Schröder write:

---

21 This is, of course, the place where according to early tradition, John Mark later founded the Christian church. Is a deliberate relationship established here between Cyprus and Alexandria, which plays no role in the founding text of the Church of Alexandria, the Martyrdom of Mark?

22 The relevant text here reads: "We appointed him bishop of Cyprus, and strengthened the churches in Tamassos, and left him to take up his abode with the brethren there."

23 On this see further Young Richard Kim, "Cypriotic Autocephaly, Reconsidered," in Nasrallah, Luijendijk and Bakirtzis, *From Roman to Early Christian Cyprus*, 153–67 (with older secondary

Im Hintergrund der Darstellung steht der Kampf der Kirche Zyperns um ihre Unabhängigkeit. Ab dem 5. Jh. sind Versuche der Patriarchen von Antiochia bezeugt, Einfluss auf die kirchenpolitischen Belange zu nehmen. Das Ansinnen lag wegen der politischen Verwaltungsstruktur im Osten des Römischen Reiches nahe. Mit der im Jahr 293 von Kaiser Diokletian vorgenommenen Reorganisation des Reiches war die bis dahin selbständige Provinz Zypern in die Diözese Oriens eingegliedert worden, deren politisches Zentrum sich in Antiochia befand. Da sich das Hoheitsgebiet des Patriarchen von Antiochia weitgehend mit dem Territorium der kaiserlichen Diözese Oriens deckte, begann dieser eine Herrschaftsgewalt über die Kirche Zyperns zu beanspruchen. Im Jahr 431 gelang es dem zyprischen Bischof Rheginus, den Anspruch Antiochias abzuwehren.[24]

I consider it very likely that the Acts of Barnabas belongs to this period. That in this context any reference to the mission of Cyprus to Antioch on the Orontes had to be put aside against the testimony of the canonical Acts of the Apostles, but in parts based on the apocryphal Acts of Paul and Thecla, does not need a detailed explanation.

From the Acts of Barnabas to the *Encomium on Barnabas* (*Laudatio Barnabae*)

Even when the claim of the Church of Cyprus to ecclesiastical independence from Antioch (which was also co-established by the Acts of Barnabas) was confirmed in the Council of Ephesus (431 CE), Antioch's claims to supremacy over Cyprus were by no means applied *ad acta*. On the contrary, they flared up again around the year 485 under the rule of Patriarch Petrus Fullo (Patriarch of Antioch 471, 476–477, as well as 485–488), at the same time "ein enger Vertrauter von Kaiser Zeno"[25] the Isaurian (474–491 [with interruption in 475–476]). Now, simply put, it was necessary to be able to show a presentable apostolic tomb to prove the independence of the Church of Cyprus.[26] This was not possible with what was narrated in the Acts of Barnabas alone. According to this text, Cyprus was indeed a church founded by an apostle, but this could have been provided with the Acts of the Apostles itself, if need be. It did house the tomb of an apostle, but this could not be located, visited, or even demonstrated. So, in fact, under growing political pressure, the tomb of Barn-

---

literature) as well as Nicklas, "Akten des Barnabas."
24 Kollmann and Schröder, *Evangelist Markus*, 93–94.
25 Kollmann and Schröder, *Evangelist Markus*, 95.
26 On this development see also Nicklas, "Barnabas Remembered."

abas—this time containing an entire corpse—had to be "rediscovered."[27] This, like the deeds of Barnabas more broadly, became the subject of another, later Barnabas text, the *Encomium on Barnabas*,[28] a writing probably from the mid-6th century CE, which is not only interested in the (broadly painted) life and work of Barnabas, but also reports (directed in part highly polemically against Petrus Fullo and the Antiochian claims) on the discovery of Barnabas' tomb. Unlike the Acts of Barnabas, this Barnabas text concentrates not only on the apostle's effectiveness in Cyprus but embeds it into a larger context of life. Itineraries are therefore significant on several levels.

(1) The first of these routes is related to the origin and history of Barnabas before the events mentioned in Acts: starting from Acts 11:23—"But Barnabas was a good man, full of the Holy Spirit and faith"—the text begins with *Encom. Barn.* § 9, a narrative about the origin and youth of Barnabas.[29] Barnabas is from the tribe of Levi, specifically his family traces itself back to that of the prophet Samuel. Due to a war, his family had come to Cyprus. However, his family still possessed rich property and a plot of land near the city of Jerusalem (*Encom. Barn.* § 9).[30] Thus, although Barnabas is described as a Jew born in Cyprus (*Encom. Barn.* § 10), he is at the same time associated with Jerusalem. Already as a "boy" (παῖς), however, he moved with his parents to Jerusalem, where Barnabas had been sent to study "at the feet of Gamaliel" (παρὰ τοὺς πόδας Γαμαλιήλ, *Encom. Barn.* § 11), had behaved in an exemplary manner, and had made great progress, but because of his youth had not yet been assigned to serve as a Levite. Basically, then, Barnabas is already portrayed here as a kind of "better Paul,"[31] of whom it is said that the latter—still called Saul at this point—had been his fellow disciple (*Encom. Barn.* § 11; cf. Acts 22:3). From Barnabas' stay in Jerusalem, the *Encomium* concludes that he also met Jesus there. Jesus recognizes Barnabas' faith and welcomes him, whereupon Barnabas

---

27 Kollmann and Schröder, *Evangelist Markus*, 95 speak in this case of the "fortunate coincidence that in 488 the supposed tomb of Barnabas could be presented with the remains of the apostle and the Gospel of Matthew used by him." I assume that fortune has had a bit of help along the way here.
28 Edition: Peter van Deun and Jacques Noret, eds., *Hagiographica Cypria*, CCSG 26 (Turnhout: Brepols, 1993), 15–122, as well as Bernd Kollmann and Werner Deuse, eds., *Alexander Monachus: Laudatio Barnabae—Lobrede auf Barnabas*, FC 46 (Turnhout: Brepols, 2007) (with a detailed introduction). On this see also Kollmann and Schröder, *Evangelist Markus*, 97–102 as well as Nicklas, "Barnabas Remembered."
29 The first eight paragraphs read like a single, at the same time quite tiring, hymn of praise to the apostle.
30 The text justifies this with a quotation from Isa 31:9.
31 In certain passages, the text recalls Paul's self-description in Gal 1:13–14 without quoting specifically or offering literal allusions.

also leads his aunt Maria, the mother of John Mark, to Jesus (*Encom. Barn.* § 12).[32] From here on, she makes available her home in Jerusalem to Jesus and his disciples, e.g., for the Last Supper during the feast of Passover and also for the period of time after Jesus' ascension up until Pentecost (*Encom. Barn.* § 13). However, Barnabas encounters Christ not only in Jerusalem but also follows him in Galilee and is the first among the seventy who, according to Luke 10:1, were sent out by Jesus.[33] Within this context, he receives the honorary name "son of encouragement" mentioned in Acts 4:36 (*Encom. Barn.* § 14).[34] Back in Jerusalem, he sells his belongings and gives the proceeds to the apostles. The connection to the depiction in the Acts of the Apostles is thereby established (*Encom. Barn.* § 15; Acts 4:37). Finally, he is the one who makes it possible to integrate the former persecutor, Saul (*Encom. Barn.* § 16), into the group of disciples after his vision of Christ in Damascus (*Encom. Barn.* §§ 17–19). The sequence of events of Jesus' life described here is naturally harmonized: it requires that—against the Synoptics—Jesus must have been in Jerusalem several times, and it sets the sending of the seventy after this (at least) initial journey to Jerusalem made by Jesus. In other words, the itineraries of Jesus mentioned in the Gospels are adapted to integrate Barnabas into Jesus' ministry. Even the scenes in which Barnabas convinces the apostles to recognize Paul as the herald of Christ's message take place before the dispersion of believers mentioned in Acts (Acts 8:1b–4). Thus, at the time when Paul is still described as a persecutor in Acts (8:3), he is already converted and on his way to Tarsus on behalf of the apostles according to the *Encomium on Barnabas* (Acts 9:30). In other words, in the description of Barnabas' life up to the point of his stay in Antioch, the connection established in Acts between Barnabas' origins as a Levite from Cyprus on the one hand and Jerusalem on the other is embellished with new details, and a parallel to Paul's life is established. In comparison to Paul, however, Barnabas is the one who follows Jesus from the beginning, which is why his way leads him together with Jesus also to Galilee. Even if it is not possible to place him among the Twelve, he is described as factually equal to them and recognized by them as having the highest worth. Despite the "excursion" to Galilee, however, Jerusalem is the focus in the first part of his ministry.

(2) This changes dramatically at *Encom. Barn.* § 20 and onward. Here, the text follows what is reported in Acts 11:19–20 at first: the focus now turns to Antioch,

---

[32] The thought about the relationship between Barnabas and John Mark is developed via Col 4:10.
[33] As is well known, the text of Luke 10:1 is not clearly handed down. While most critical editions opt for "seventy-two," the *Encomium* follows the tradition that there must have been seventy messengers. However, it is not the number that is important, but rather the special honorary position of Barnabas.
[34] In the *Encomium* this leads to the comparison of him with other disciples who are given specific honorific names (such as the "sons of thunder"; *Encom. Barn.* § 13).

where those scattered because of the persecution of Stephen are gathering again. Hearing of this in Jerusalem, Barnabas is sent "to the very holy congregation there to shepherd the flock of Christ" (*Encom. Barn.* § 20). However, while Acts of the Apostles speaks of Barnabas now going to Tarsus to fetch Paul from there to Antioch where they both work for a year (Acts 11:25–26), the *Encomium on Barnabas* builds in an extensive missionary journey of Barnabas which has no parallels I know of in earlier literature. "Led by the Holy Spirit" (*Encom. Barn.* § 20), he travels through "all cities and countries" and proclaims the gospel. Thus he reaches Rome, even before all the other apostles. There, his proclamation of the "gospel of Christ" is so successful that he finally has to retreat again out of concern that he has become too famous.[35] From there he arrives in Alexandria, where he also proclaims the "word of the Lord" (*Encom. Barn.* § 21). "One after the other" (*Encom. Barn.* § 21) he passes through all cities and finally reaches Jerusalem once again. Only then does he go again to Antioch, to travel from there to Tarsus to fetch Paul (*Encom. Barn.* § 21). This again connects to the plot of Acts (Acts 11:25–26). Thus, in the itinerary of Acts, like a huge arc, a kind of journey around the world is described,[36] touching all the great centers of the early church, which later became the great patriarchates: Antioch, Rome, Alexandria, and Jerusalem—only Constantinople is lacking and for good reasons: the city did not yet exist at the time of Barnabas.[37] Be that as it may, the overall ecclesiastical importance of Barnabas—his role for the mission of Rome, Alexandria, Jerusalem, and Antioch, as well as the many cities not mentioned by name on this journey—could not be presented more impressively. In contrast to the Acts of Barnabas, Antioch on the Orontes is by no means left out. The text largely follows the guidelines of the Acts of the Apostles.[38]

---

[35] The text here obviously plays on the veneration accorded in its time to other apostles like Paul and Peter in Rome, who are thus portrayed as less humble than Barnabas, who actually preceded them. At the same time, of course, it is hardly possible (from Cyprus) to think of imposing against the traditions about the Roman Peter and Paul (or alongside them) a Barnabas tradition that is also significant for Rome. The statements from the *Encomium* remain too vague for that. It seems more important to make Barnabas, who was so important for Cyprus, as big as possible.

[36] Of course, the image of the "arc" owes itself to ideas we form on the basis of modern maps of the Mediterranean, and of course the cities named do not cover the entire world known at that time. That this is nevertheless aimed at a specific goal is clear from the passages that speak of traversing all cities (and countries; see *Encom. Barn.* §§ 20 and 21).

[37] On the founding of Constantinople by Emperor Constantine I in 324 CE (completion of construction in 330 CE) see further, e.g., Albrecht Berger, *Konstantinopel: Geschichte, Topographie, Religion*, Standorte in Antike und Christentum 3 (Stuttgart: Anton Hiersemann, 2011), 1–20.

[38] The preaching of Barnabas in Alexandria, on the other hand, has a parallel in the Pseudo-Clementines, where Clement comes to Alexandria and experiences Barnabas as a preacher. Unlike in the *Encomium on Barnabas*, however, this scene takes place during Jesus' lifetime. On this see Tobias Nicklas, "Jews and Christians? Sketches from Second Century Alexandria," in *Jews and Christians:*

(3) Only after the return to Antioch, the briefly mentioned journey to the apostolic council together with Paul (*Encom. Barn.* § 21), and the renewed return to Antioch, is the first missionary journey to Cyprus reported in almost a shorthand manner:

> But after they were sent out by the congregation of the Antiochians through the Holy Spirit, they came to Cyprus. And they crossed the entire island from Salamis up to Paphos, preaching and working miracles, making Elymas blind and enlightening the proconsul.

In fact, unlike the Acts of Barnabas, the *Encomium* following Acts 13:4 is self-conscious enough to describe the sending out to Cyprus on the first missionary journey from Antioch itself, as willed by the Holy Spirit. Nevertheless, small shifts are still noticeable. Unlike in Acts, it is not Paul alone who performs the punitive miracle against Elymas, but the two of them (or better, the entire group). Thus, no change in the leadership of the group is necessary. The separation from John Mark, which is only briefly hinted at in Acts 13:13, is explained in greater detail in *Encom. Barn.* § 22: the latter returns to Jerusalem to his mother, as in the Acts of the Apostles, but against the testimony of the Acts of Barnabas. The further way of the first missionary journey depicted in Acts is now only hinted at, the text only speaks of the return to Antioch (*Encom. Barn.* § 22). After a detailed (clearly euphemistic) description of the events surrounding the apostles' dispute over whether it was possible to take John Mark back (*Encom. Barn.* § 23),[39] and the eventual separation of the two (*Encom. Barn.* § 24), the journey is not resumed until *Encom. Barn.* § 25. Then *Encom. Barn.* §§ 25–29 tell of the second missionary journey of Barnabas and John Mark to Cyprus: unlike the Acts of Barnabas, however, neither stations of the journey to Cyprus are described, nor an itinerary through Cyprus. This is certainly not only due to the fact that the itinerary of the Acts of Barnabas works from Isauria outward, whereas the apostles in the *Encomium* begin with Antioch. What the Acts of Barnabas describe in several partial chapters and where they line up place by place, the *Encomium* offers only the following sentence:

> After traversing the entire island and teaching a sizable crowd, he arrived in Salamis.

From now on, only events in Salamis are recounted: the apostle's teaching, growing Jewish opposition to him, a detailed farewell speech (*Encom. Barn.* §§ 26–27), a final eucharistic celebration with a special farewell to John Mark (*Encom. Barn.* § 28), and finally the martyrdom of Barnabas (*Encom. Barn.* § 29). Similar to the descrip-

---

Parting Ways in the First Two Centuries C.E.? Reflections on the Gains and Losses of a Model, ed. Jens Schröter, Benjamin Edsall, and Joseph Verheyden, BZNW 253 (Berlin: de Gruyter, 2021), 347–79 (esp. 361–62).

[39] The idea that there may have been such a thing as strife or disharmony among apostles seems to have been intolerable to late texts such as this one.

tion of the Acts of Barnabas, fire is set to the apostle's body, but it miraculously remains unharmed and thus can be buried in a cave not far from the city (*Encom. Barn.* § 29). The journey of Barnabas, which started in the togetherness of Cyprus and Jerusalem, which subsequently made him a follower of Jesus and a preacher in Jerusalem and Galilee, led from Jerusalem to Antioch and from there in a circle to all the extant early church patriarchates in the first century, thus ends in Salamis in Cyprus. And yet, not everything has been said with this.

(4) Due to a persecution and dispersion of the Christians of Salamis, the memory of Barnabas fell into oblivion. Also, Mark, who continues his journey, leaves the island (*Encom. Barn.* § 30).[40] Thus, the location of the grave remained unknown for centuries: finally, with *Encom. Barn.* § 31, the text jumps into the 5th century, that is, the time when the tomb is rediscovered. It speaks first of "unusual miracles" which happened at the place in which the corpse of Barnabas lies unrecognized (*Encom. Barn.* § 31), then of the struggles for the Church of Cyprus' independence that break out under the Antiochian patriarch Petrus Fullo, "a devil as a monk, like Judas among the apostles" (*Encom. Barn.* § 32). Intrigues of the Antiochian at the side of Emperor Zeno the Isaurian (*Encom. Barn.* §§ 33–37) against the Church of Cyprus are described in detail. Barnabas himself intervenes in this situation: he appears in the night several times to Bishop Anthemius of Salamis and shows the bishop the way to his grave (*Encom. Barn.* §§ 38–40). The apostle's grave is of course discovered, the latter is identified by means of the copy of his gospel written by the apostle Matthew himself, and the apostolicity of the episcopal see of Salamis is proven (and likewise the independence of the Church of Cyprus from Antioch confirmed; *Encom. Barn.* §§ 40–44). A church was erected around Barnabas' grave, where "the day of the honorable commemoration of the thrice blessed apostle and noble martyr Barnabas is to be celebrated, according to the Romans three days before the Ides of June, according to the Cypriots at Constantia [= Salamis] on the eleventh of the month of Mesor, which is also called the tenth, according to the inhabitants of Asia or the inhabitants of Paphos on the nineteenth of the month Plethypatos, which is also called the ninth" (*Encom. Barn.* § 46).

The location where Alexander the monk writes his *Encomium on Barnabas*, the Barnabas Monastery not far from Salamis, is thus not only the end point of Barnabas' itinerary but also a worthwhile destination for the journeys of pilgrims who want to meet and remember the apostle of Cyprus and protector of the entire

---

[40] This topos, which goes beyond the Acts of Barnabas, is important in order to justify why the tomb was discovered only in 488 and why one was not aware of it for so long.

fatherland (*Encom. Barn.* § 50), who continues to work miraculously in his tomb.[41] Implicitly, pilgrims are invited not only from Cyprus but also from places where Barnabas was active according to the text, following the cited calendars, e.g., also from Rome or Asia. New itineraries with the destination Salamis or better, the destination "Barnabas' grave," which thus becomes the center of a network of itineraries from different parts of the world known at his time, can arise.

From the *Encomium on Barnabas* to Later Texts on Barnabas from Cyprus

The traditions about the apostle Barnabas (and connected with them, those about John Mark) have still not come to their end. They could be traced far beyond antiquity. Only two more short examples may show what different techniques, which we have already observed in part, show up in later literature.

The *Vita of Auxibios*

The *Vita Auxibii*, which probably dates to the first half of the 7th century, is a legend about Auxibios,[42] the first bishop of Soloi, a place on the northwestern coast of Cyprus. Auxibios was venerated as a saint and miracle worker, who is not mentioned in the canonical Acts, the Acts of Barnbas, or the *Encomium*. Auxibios, who comes from a wealthy family, secretly leaves his homeland of Rome when his parents want him to get married (*Vit. Aux.* §§ 3–5): he sensed the call to become a Christian and made his way to Palestine. He leaves Rome and goes to Rhodos. "From there, they sail across the sea opposite Pamphylia and reached Cyprus." He reaches Cyprus on its northwest coast at a village called Limnetes, "which is about four miles from the town of Soloi" (both citations come from *Vit. Aux.* § 6). This takes place at the same time as when Barnabas undertakes his second missionary journey to Cyprus with Mark (*Vit. Aux.* § 7). Slightly abbreviating the itinerary of the Acts of Barnabas, where the two land at Cape Krommyatikon, the *Vita Auxibii* speaks of

---

[41] The text here alludes to the conclusion of John's Gospel: "But for the miracles which proceed daily from his holy sepulcher, if any man would record them, I think all the paper in the world would not suffice for them" (*Encom. Barn.* § 47).

[42] Edition: van Deun and Noret, *Hagiographica Cypria*, 137–202 (see also there the discussion of introductory questions). On this cf. Kollmann and Schröder, *Evangelist Markus*, 102–105 (introduction) and 168–73 (German translation of *Vit. Aux.* §§ 1–13).

Lapithos as the first station of the apostles. After that, "they wander through the entire island and come, as Mark reports, to Salamis which is now called Constantia." The meeting with Herakleides, who is already referred to as the "archbishop of the island" in the *Vita Auxibii*, associated in the Acts of Barnabas with Lampadistos and Tamassos, is here transferred to Salamis. After Barnabas dies, Mark is forced to flee. He is pursued—as in the Acts of Barnabas—from Salamis to Ledroi, where he hides in a cave. The mortal remains of Barnabas interestingly enough play no role in this depiction. From there, Mark takes the path over the mountains to the northwest and goes to Limnetes where he meets Auxibios (*Vit. Aux.* § 7), instructs him in the faith, baptizes him, consecrates him as bishop, and sends him to the city of Soloi (*Vit. Aux.* § 8). Mark, following the testimony of the Acts of Barnabas, first moves on to Alexandria, and later seeks out Paul, with whom he remains until Paul's death (*Vit. Aux.* § 12; cf. 2 Tim 4:11). Paul, however, hearing about the situation in Cyprus after Barnabas' death, sends "Epaphras and Tychicos and some others to Cyprus, to Herakleides, the archbishop of the island." Thus, on Paul's orders, there emerges an organization of the Church of Cyprus that is once again more complex than that reported in the Acts of Barnabas. Herakleides clearly remains the head of the Church of Cyprus, but now is connected with Salamis; Epaphras becomes bishop of Paphos; Tychicus of Neapolis, now Limassol; the unnamed others receive other episcopal sees.[43] At the end, however, Auxibios, already on the island, is mentioned: "But go also into the city of Soloi and there search a Roman man with the name Auxibios." The itineraries of the *Vita Auxibii* therefore not only bring Mark and Auxibios into contact with each other in the northwest part of the island—very far away from a meaningful route from Salamis to Alexandria. In comparison with the Acts of Barnabas, they move Herakleides from Tamasos to Salamis and thus at least indirectly emphasize the importance of Salamis as the seat of the archbishop. Most importantly, however, they connect the founding of the bishopric of Soloi, which plays no role at all either in the first or the second missionary journeys described in the Acts of Barnabas, to the apostolic period. Although Auxibios does not meet Barnabas, he is baptized and installed as bishop by Mark himself. The organization of the Church of Cyprus is here, however, no longer *only* concerned with the Barnabas but also Paul: from now on, prominent disciples of the apostles also sit in Paphos and Neapolis.[44] It remains unclear to me the exact localization and function of the village of Limnetes, where Mark and Auxibios meet: wouldn't it be easier to

---

[43] The latter is simply to suggest that the ecclesiastical structure of Cyprus is already (largely) complete in apostolic times.
[44] On Epaphras cf. Phlm 23 as well as Col 1:7 and 4:12. On Tychicus cf. Acts 20:4; Col 4:7; Eph 6:21; 2 Tim 6:21 as well as Tit 3:12.

send Mark immediately to Soloi? Was there a special memorial place here in honor of Auxibios or of Mark? I have not gone further with my research on this point.

The Acts of Herakleides

The Acts of Herakleides (probably in essence from the 6th or 7th century), which have come down to us in two quite different versions—one Greek and the other Armenian—revolve around Herakleides, who has already been mentioned several times and who is understood here as the bishop of Tamasos.[45] Although itineraries also play a role here, I am more interested in the fact that the text mentions a letter of Paul and of Barnabas to Herakaleides (and the "teacher" Mnason [cf. Acts 21:16]). The letter is preserved in the only manuscript of the Greek text fragmentarily. Though the Greek version is obviously corrupt, the text can be largely reconstructed on the basis of the Armenian version. In terms of content, not much is lost: it is basically a request to recognize the right in Paphos, made with richly banal statements that have been strung together. What is interesting here is not so much the itineraries that emphasize the supremacy of the diocese of Tamassos over others, as much as the fact that the idea of a joint letter to Bishop Herakleides written by Paul and Barnabas *together* cannot be located in the relative chronology of events: during and immediately after the first missionary journey, when Paul and Barnabas were still acting together, in the logic of the Acts of Barnabas Herakleides, whom the Acts of the Apostles does not mention, is not yet a bishop. During the second missionary journey, Paul and Barnabas do not work together, and after that they never meet again because Barnabas had already died. This easily comprehensible logic, however, did not prevent the author of our text from writing such a letter: the continuing connection of Herakleides with the two apostles of Cyprus, as well as their continuing unity against the testimony of the Acts of the Apostles is more important than chronological.

---

45 Edition of the Greek text: François Halkin, "Les actes apocryphes de saint Héraclide de Chypre, disciple de l'apôtre Barnabé," *AnBoll* 82 (1964): 133–69; edition of the Armenian version: Michel van Esbroeck, "Les Actes arméniens de saint Héraclide de Chypre," *AnBoll* 103 (1985): 115–62. To my knowledge, no translation of the text exists in a modern language. For arguments on the introductory questions see Tobias Nicklas in collaboration with Mari Mamyan, "Paul and Barnabas to Herakleides (and Mnason): An Unknown Apocryhal Letter in the *Acts of Herakleides*," in *Paul, Christian Textuality, and the Hermeneutics of Late Antiquity: Essays in Honor of Margaret M. Mitchell*, ed. David Moessner et al., NovTSup (Leiden: Brill, forthcoming).

Conclusion

The overview of the development of Barnabas itineraries presented here is by no means complete: the development of Barnabas memories extends well beyond late antiquity.[46] However, it is already apparent that the thesis formulated at the outset holds: even in the case of Barnabas, the itineraries of various writings with their various functions cannot be harmonized. Neither geographical logic—although this at least cannot be completely disregarded in texts that originated and wish to be read in the concrete region in which they are set[47]—nor historical accuracy are decisive. Although the Acts of the Apostles must have long been considered a canonical text at the time when the later apocryphal and hagiographical traditions were likely to have originated, it was possible to write itineraries that clearly go beyond or even violate the testimony of the canonical text. This can go so far—as is the case for the Acts of Barnabas—as to (tacitly) replace aspects of the itineraries of the Acts of the Apostles with those from the Acts of Paul and Thecla. This does not seem to have been at all decisive for the success and authority of a text, at least in certain contexts. It is more important to project into the texts the coexistence of places (and thus spatial structures) that are crucial for one's own present and its challenges, for these texts are origin narratives and are crucial for one's own construction of identity in concrete contexts.[48]

References

Berger, Albrecht. *Konstantinopel: Geschichte, Topographie, Religion*. Standorte in Antike und Christentum 3. Stuttgart: Anton Hiersemann, 2011.
Cortese, Arabella. *Cilicia as a Sacred Landscape in Late Antiquity: A Journey to the Trail of the Apostles, Martyrs and Local Saints*. Wiesbaden: Reichert, 2022.
Cosby, Michael R. *Creation of History: The Transformation of Barnabas from Peacemaker to Warrior Saint*. Eugene, OR: Cascade, 2017.
Deun, Peter van, and Jacques Noret, eds. *Hagiographica Cypria*. CCSG 26. Turnhout: Brepols, 1993.

---

46 Information that extends to the present time (with its highly problematic political situation in Cyprus) is provided by Michael R. Cosby, *Creation of History: The Transformation of Barnabas from Peacemaker to Warrior Saint* (Eugene, OR: Cascade, 2017).
47 It would also be interesting to investigate what it means to read texts like the Acts of Barnabas in Cyprus and in connection with the places where they are set. How the imagination of ancient readers must have been who knew these places is hardly comprehensible today. On a similar problem in connection with the Martyrdom of Mark cf. Tobias Nicklas, "Mit heteronomen Texten arbeiten: Beispiele aus der Welt christlicher Apokryphen," *Early Christianity* 14 (forthcoming).
48 This article was translated from German by Jacob Cerone.

Döhler, Marietheres. *Acta Petri: Text, Übersetzung und Kommentar zu den Actus Vercellenses*. TU 171. Berlin: de Gruyter, 2018.

Eastman, David L. *The Ancient Martyrdom Accounts of Peter and Paul*. WGRW 39. Atlanta: Society of Biblical Literature, 2015.

Eastman, David L. "The Life and Conduct of the Holy Women Xanthippe, Polyxena, and Rebecca." Pages 1:416–53 in *New Testament Apocrypha: More Noncanonical Scriptures*. 3 vols. Edited by Tony Burke and Brent Landau. Grand Rapids: Eerdmans, 2016, 2020, 2023.

Esbroeck, Michel van. "Les Actes arméniens de saint Héraclide de Chypre." *AnBoll* 103 (1985): 115–62.

Halkin, François. "Les actes apocryphes de saint Héraclide de Chypre, disciple de l'apôtre Barnabé." *AnBoll* 82 (1964): 133–69.

Karakolis, Christos. "Paul's Mission to Hispania: Some Critical Observations." Pages 507–20 in *The Last Years of Paul: Essays from the Tarragona Conference, June 2013*. Edited by Armand Puig i Tarrèch, John Barclay and Jörg Frey. WUNT 352. Tübingen: Mohr Siebeck, 2015.

Kim, Young Richard. "Cypriotic Autocephaly, Reconsidered." Pages 153–67 in *From Roman to Early Christian Cyprus: Studies in Religion and Archaeology*. Edited by Laura Nasrallah, AnneMarie Luijendijk and Charalambos Bakirtzis. WUNT 437. Tübingen: Mohr Siebeck, 2020.

Klein, Hans. *Lukasstudien*. FRLANT 209. Göttingen: Vandenhoeck & Ruprecht, 2005.

Kollmann, Bernd, and Burkhard Schröder. *Der Evangelist Markus: Historische Konturen: Altkirchliche Legenden: Hagiographische Zeugnisse*. SBS 257. Stuttgart: Katholisches Bibelwerk, 2023.

Kollmann, Bernd, and Werner Deuse, eds. *Alexander Monachus: Laudatio Barnabae—Lobrede auf Barnabas*. FC 46. Turnhout: Brepols, 2007.

Lipsius, Adelbertus, and Maximilianus Bonnet, eds. *Acta Apostolorum Apocrypha II/2: Acta Philippi et Acta Thoma: Accedunt Acta Barnabae*. Leipzig, 1903. Repr., Darmstadt: Wissenschaftliche Buchgesellschaft, 1959.

Luijendijk, AnneMarie. "The Gospel of Matthew in the Acts of Barnabas through the Lens of Book History: Healing and Burial with Books." Pages 169–94 in *From Roman to Early Christian Cyprus: Studies in Religion and Archaeology*. Edited by Laura Nasrallah, AnneMarie Luijendijk and Charalambos Bakirtzis. WUNT 437. Tübingen: Mohr Siebeck, 2020.

Meiser, Martin. *Der Brief des Apostels Paulus an die Galater*. THKNT. Leipzig: Evangelische Verlagsanstalt, 2022.

Nicklas, Tobias. "Antike Petruserzählungen und der erinnerte Petrus in Rom." Pages 159–87 in *Petrusliteratur und Petrusarchäologie: Römische Begegnungen*. Edited by Jörg Frey and Martin Wallraff. Rom und der Protestantismus 4. Tübingen: Mohr Siebeck, 2020.

Nicklas, Tobias. "Barnabas Remembered: Apokryphe Barabastexte und die Kirche Zyperns." Pages 167–88 in *Religion als Imagination: Festschrift Marco Frenschkowski*. Edited by Lena Seehausen, Paulus Enke and Jens Herzer. Leipzig: Evangelische Verlagsanstalt, 2020.

Nicklas, Tobias. "Jews and Christians? Sketches from Second Century Alexandria." Pages 347–79 in *Jews and Christians: Parting Ways in the First Two Centuries C.E.? Reflections on the Gains and Losses of a Model*. Edited by Jens Schröter, Benjamin Edsall, and Joseph Verheyden. BZNW 253. Berlin: de Gruyter, 2021.

Nicklas, Tobias. "Die Akten des Barnabas." In *Zwischen Apokryphen und Hagiographie: Spätantike Apostelerzählungen in ihrer Welt*. Edited by Tobias Nicklas. Tria Corda Lectures. Tübingen: Mohr Siebeck, forthcoming.

Nicklas, Tobias, in collaboration with Mari Mamyan. "Paul and Barnabas to Herakleides (and Mnason): An Unknown Apocryhal Letter in the Acts of Herakleides." In *Paul, Christian Textuality, and the Hermeneutics of Late Antiquity: Essays in Honor of Margaret M. Mitchell*. Edited by David Moessner, Paul B. Duff, Janet Spittler and Robert Matthew Calhoun. NovTSup. Leiden: Brill, forthcoming.

Nicklas, Tobias. "Mit heteronomen Texten arbeiten: Beispiele aus der Welt christlicher Apokryphen." *Early Christianity* 14 (forthcoming).

Norelli, Enrico. "Actes de Barnabé." Pages 617–42 in *Écrits apocryphes chrétiens II*. Edited by Pierre Geoltrain and Jean-Daniel Kaestli. Paris: Gallimard, 2005.

Pilhofer, Philipp. "Von Segeltouren und Konjekturen: Die Barnabas-Akten als Quelle zur Topographie der isaurischen Küste." *Orbis Terrarum* 13 (2015): 192–210.

Sänger, Dieter. "Die Adresse des Galaterbriefes: Neue (?) Überlegungen zu einem alten Problem." Pages 229–74 in *Schrift—Tradition—Evangelium: Studien zum frühen Judentum und zur paulinischen Theologie*. Neukirchen-Vluyn: Neukirchener Verlag, 2016.

Snyder, Glenn E. "The Acts of Barnabas: A New Translation and Introduction." Pages 1:317–36 in *New Testament Apocrypha: More Noncanonical Scriptures*. 3 vols. Edited by Tony Burke and Brent Landau. Grand Rapids: Eerdmans, 2016, 2020, 2023.

Tarrèch, Armand Puig i. "Paul's Missionary Activity during His Roman Trial: The Case of Paul's Journey to Hispania." Pages 469–506 in *The Last Years of Paul: Essays from the Tarragona Conference, June 2013*. Edited by Armand Puig i Tarrèch, John Barclay and Jörg Frey. WUNT 352. Tübingen: Mohr Siebeck, 2015.

Theobald, Michael. *Israel-Vergessenheit in den Pastoralbriefen: Ein neuer Versuch zu ihrer historisch-theologischen Verortung im 2. Jahrhundert n.Chr. unter besonderer Berücksichtigung der Ignatius-Briefe*. SBS 229. Stuttgart: Katholisches Bibelwerk, 2016.

Catherine Hezser
Rabbinic Geography: Between the Imaginary and Real

Abstract: This article discusses rabbinic perceptions of space and geography, showing how geographical information in rabbinic writings reflects the "local color" of these writings or rabbinic perceptions of the Land of Israel or other regions. This leads to the conclusion that geographical references and descriptions in rabbinic literature should be considered a mixture of daily life experiences, biblical reminiscences, hearsay and wishful thinking.

In antiquity as nowadays, spatial perception and identity were closely linked.[1] The way in which an individual and a group perceived the world was an indicator of personal and group identity. Brouria Bitton-Ashkelony uses the term "sacred geography" for the network of pilgrimage sites that early Byzantine Christians visited in the so-called Holy Land.[2] Within that "sacred geography" distinctions were made. Whether one visited the Church of the Holy Sepulchre in Jerusalem or a hermit in the Sinai Peninsula indicated one's religious preferences and affiliations. Of course, visiting both holy places and holy men was possible as well. Particular ideologies and power constellations determined the way in which the geographical space of Roman-Byzantine Palestine was seen. The Christian Holy Land as a network of pilgrimage sites and the rabbinic Land of Israel as a reminder of monarchic times were not simply descriptions of a geographical space. They were geographies of the mind that colluded with the political and geographical realities late antique Jews and Christians would have been familiar with in daily life.

In their book *Geography in Classical Antiquity*, Daniela Dueck and Kai Brodersen point out that "(g)eographical themes appeared in almost every literary genre."[3] Some geographical details were based on everyday life experience while others were mere fantasy. In poetry, epic and drama, "real and mythic geography" are mixed.[4] Some of the literary references may be useful supplements to the information provided by scientifically oriented geographical handbooks. Others tell us

---

[1] See also Eyal Ben-Eliyahu, *Identity and Territory: Jewish Perceptions of Space in Antiquity* (Berkeley: University of California Press, 2019), xi, who refers to "Jewish identity's territorial dimension."
[2] Brouria Bitton-Ashkelony, *Encountering the Sacred: The Debate on Christian Pilgrimage in Late Antiquity* (Berkeley: University of California Press, 2005), 204.
[3] Daniela Dueck and Kai Brodersen, *Geography in Classical Antiquity* (Cambridge: Cambridge University Press, 2012), 1–2.
[4] Dueck and Brodersen, *Geography in Classical Antiquity*, 23.

https://doi.org/10.1515/9783110717488-013

more about the religious and cultural perceptions of specific authors, editors and the groups they belonged to.[5] The ways in which local and foreign territories and people are described reflect the authors' identity. As R. J. Morgan had pointed out in connection with ancient Greek novels, "(t)he exploration of Greek identity is ... provided by the geographical dimensions of some of these stories, which divide the world into a Greek center, where the protagonists start and finish, and a barbarian periphery into which they journey."[6]

These considerations need to be taken into account when investigating the rabbinic perception of the geographical space that surrounded rabbis. The focus will be on Palestinian rabbinic literature here.[7] How did the rabbinic vision of the Land of Israel differ from the political reality of the Roman Empire? How did rabbis orient themselves within the local and inter-regional spaces in which they lived and moved about? What do the literary sources tell us about Palestinian rabbis' knowledge about the world beyond their place of residence? Was their knowledge of more distant places based on experience, hearsay, popular perception, or literary accounts?

It is important not to generalize and assume that the same geographical perspective was shared by all Palestinian rabbis as well as non-rabbinic Jews. The geographical perception of Josephus as a Greek-educated and well-traveled member of the upper strata of society would have been different from that of a rabbi of a lower social status. A rabbi who lived in Caesarea with its harbor, merchant travel and constant flow of visitors would have perceived his surroundings differently than a rural rabbi in Galilee. Josephus' geographical knowledge was based on the study of Greek historical and geographical literature that belonged to the ancient scientific tradition, even if sometimes lacking in accuracy.[8] Rabbis, on the other hand, seem to have been less interested in the precise mapping of the real world. Like Christians, they presented a "sacred geography" based on a particular reli-

---

[5] On ancient geographical handbooks see Duane W. Roller, *Ancient Geography: The Discovery of the World in Classical Greece and Rome* (London: I.B. Tauris, 2015).

[6] R. J. Morgan, "Foreword to the 2008 Edition," in *Collected Ancient Greek Novels*, ed. B.P. Reardon (Berkeley: University of California Press, 2008), ix–xxi (xiii).

[7] Geoffrey Herman has done some initial studies on Babylonian rabbinic geography. See Geoffrey Herman, "There They Sat Down: Mapping Settlement Patterns in Sasanian Babylonia," in *Studying the Near and Middle East at the Institute for Advanced Study, Princeton 1935–2018*, ed. Sabine Schmidtke (Piscataway: Gorgias Press, 2018), 3–10; Geoffrey Herman, "Babylonian of Pure Lineage: Notes on Babylonian Jewish Toponym," in *Sources and Interpretation in Ancient Judaism: Studies for Tal Ilan at Sixty*, ed. Meron M. Piotrkowski, Geoffrey Herman, and Saskia Doenitz (Leiden: Brill, 2018), 191–228.

[8] On Josephus see Yuval Shahar, *Josephus Geographicus: The Classical Context of Geography in Josephus*, TSAJ 98 (Tübingen: Mohr Siebeck, 2004).

gious ideology. Rabbis propagated their own vision of a Land of Israel in which Jewish life should be conducted and in which rabbinic halakah was meant to be followed. Other territories beyond its perceived boundaries were considered foreign, idolatrous, impure and potentially dangerous. In the following, I shall investigate Palestinian rabbinic spatial perception moving from local to more distant geographical regions.

Local Color in the Rabbinic Perception of Their Surroundings

We may assume that rabbis were most familiar with the villages, towns and cities they lived in and with their immediate surroundings. Such familiarity may not be reflected in rabbinic literary sources, however, because it was taken for granted rather than expressed and reflected in individual traditions. Tradents and/or editors may have omitted "local color" from earlier traditions.[9] They may have considered such details irrelevant and detrimental to the transmitted materials' more general goals. Formulations are often very general and abstract. Rabbis are said to have "walked on the road" or "went to visit" a colleague without any geographical specification.[10] Can we nevertheless find traces of local geographical awareness in the texts that came down to us?

Research into "local color" (*Lokalkolorit* in German) has been used by the New Testament scholar Gerd Theissen as an extension of the form-historical approach to the synoptic gospels.[11] The identification of local color was meant to provide evidence of a tradition's geographical origin and/or revision at the editorial stage.[12] It is part of

---

[9] The Cambridge Dictionary defines "local color" as "the special or unusual features of a place, especially as described or shown in a story, picture, or film to make it seem more real" (https://dictionary.cambridge.org/dictionary/english/local-colour, last accessed 14 May 2020). Other definitions are much broader, including customs of specific locations (see, e.g., https://www.collinsdictionary.com/dictionary/english/local-colour , last accessed 14 May 2020). On the various meanings and uses of the term see Vladimir Kapor, *Local Colour: A Travelling Concept* (Bern: Lang, 2009), 1–27.

[10] On rabbis "walking on the road" see Catherine Hezser, *Jewish Travel in Antiquity*, TSAJ 144 (Tübingen: Mohr Siebeck, 2011), 215–34.

[11] Gerd Theissen, *Lokalkolorit und Zeitgeschichte in den Evangelien: Ein Beitrag zur Geschichte der synoptischen Tradition*, 2nd ed. (Freiburg: Universitätsverlag; Göttingen: Vandenhoeck & Ruprecht, 1992), 1–24.

[12] See Theissen, *Lokalkolorit und Zeitgeschichte*, 2: "Die Erforschung von Lokalkolorit und Zeitkontexten ist der Versuch, mit Hilfe von Lokal- und Datierindizien die kleineren Einheiten der synoptischen Tradition und ihre Redaktion zeitlich und räumlich zu lokalisieren."

a historical approach that attempts to link the texts to specific locations. In both the gospels and rabbinic texts traces of local color are rare, however, and may often be too general to be useful for geographical identifications. The approach cannot be used in a positivistic way to identify the geographical origins of specific rabbinic traditions. I am therefore not using the concept to claim the chronological priority or authenticity of particular traditions.[13] Geographical references and place names may reveal ancient perceptions of space, however, and indicate patterns of spatial orientation.

The Relative Location of Villages

References to places in rabbinic narratives sometimes imply that they were located close to each other. For example, the Mishnah transmits a story about R. Yehoshua, who went to R. Yishmael in Kefar Aziz. After he showed him a vine plant that was suspended over a fig tree there, R. Yishmael allegedly "brought him up from there to Bet Hameganiah" to see an alternative horticultural condition that was the basis of his halakhic questions (m. Kil. 6:4). In this narrative the place names are merely incidental and irrelevant for the halakhic discussion the tradition was transmitted for. The geographical scenario implies that the two rabbis were able to walk easily from the village of Kefar Aziz to Bet Hameganiah, and that these villages were located within walking distance from each other. Adolphe Neubauer took the story literally as evidence that R. Yishmael, a Tanna of the second generation, lived in Kefar Aziz, and reads it together with another text (m. Ketub. 5:8) that states that R. Yishmael lived near the province of Idumea.[14] Harmonizing the two traditions he concludes that Kefar Aziz must have been located close to Idumea, in the South of Roman Palestine, or even within it.[15] Neubauer maintains that one part of Idumea, Gebalena, was inhabited by Jews, and elsewhere states that R. Yishmael lived in Idumea itself.[16]

From a historical-critical point of view, such harmonizations cannot be supported. Firstly, the literary traditions cannot be considered to contain historically reliable information about R. Yishmael's whereabouts and/or his hometown. Secondly, the text in m. Ketub. 5:8 merely states that "R. Yishmael was near Edom (שהיה סמוך לאדום)." The meaning may be that he merely sojourned in or passed through this location. Thirdly, rabbinic place names do not correspond to clearly identifiable

---

13 See also Kapor, *Local Colour*, 26.
14 Adolphe Neubauer, *La géographie du Talmud* (Paris: Michel Lévy Frères, Libraires éditeurs, 1868), 117.
15 Neubauer, *Géographie*, 117. See also Michael Avi Yonah, *The Holy Land: A Historical Geography from the Persian to the Arab Conquest (536 BC to AD 640)* (Jerusalem: Carta, 2002), 192.
16 Neubauer, *Géographie*, 235: "Rabbi Ishmael ben Elisa, qui habitait Kefar Aziz, en Idumée."

locations. Edom must not necessarily refer to Idumea but was also used by rabbis as a general term for Rome.[17] Sacha Stern writes: "Whereas in the Bible, Esau is no more than the ancestor and founder of the small kingdom of Edom (Idumaea), by the rabbinic period he is identified as the ancestor of the Romans or as the founder of their city."[18] In the Yerushalmi (y. Ketub. 5:11, 30b) the Mishnah's "near Edom" is understood as referring "to the South (לדרומה)," that is, R. Yishmael is assumed to have been in the southern parts of the Land of Israel when he expressed a specific halakhic rule. Ben-Zion Rosenfeld's suggestion that Kefar Aziz was a "Torah center" at "southern Mount Hebron" seems to be based on a conflation of the Yerushalmi text with the Mishnaic story.[19]

The text in m. Ketub. 5:8 may assume that R. Yishmael lived or stayed temporarily near the border between the rabbinically perceived Land of Israel and the area outside ("Edom"), to which other halakhic rules applied. In m. Ketub. 5:8 the reference to R. Yishmael's location is meant to explain the difference between his and R. Yose's ruling. When taking these methodological considerations into account, the narrative in m. Kil. 6:4 merely suggests that the tradents and editors of this tradition considered the villages of Kefar Aziz and Bet Hameganiah to be in walking distance to each other. The text does not allow us to identify their locations and a harmonization with the separate tradition in m. Ketub. 5:8 ("near Edom"; y. Ketub. 5:11, 30b: "to the South") is methodologically inappropriate.

Landmark-Based Orientation

In antiquity, when the modern address system with street and house numbers did not exist, people used landmarks as clues for orientation. They found their destinations though their relative proximity to known buildings and natural features such as springs. With regard to road and sea travel, Dueck and Brodersen write: "Initial

---

[17] In the Hebrew Bible Edom is associated with Esau. See Carol Bakhos, *Ishmael on the Border: Rabbinic Portrayals of the First Arab* (Albany: State University of New York Press, 2006), 24–25. In Roman times, probably from the first century CE onwards, Edom was equated with Rome. Ian E. Rock, *Paul's Letter to the Romans and Roman Imperialism: An Ideological Analysis of the Exordium (Romans 1:1–17)* (Eugene: Wipf & Stock, 2012), 290, writes: "The eponymous use of Esau/Edom as a term for Israel's enemies seems to have originated during the first century; Feldman maintains that it was circa 100 CE that literary evidence of the equation of Romans = Esau was seen in 4 Ezra 6:8–9" See also the bibliographical discussion at Rock, *Paul's Letter to the Romans*, 290 (n.8).
[18] Sacha Stern, *Jewish Identity in Early Rabbinic Writings* (Leiden: Brill, 1994), 19.
[19] Ben-Zion Rosenfeld, *Torah Centers and Rabbinic Activity in Palestine 70–400 CE: History and Geographic Distribution* (Leiden: Brill, 2010), 68. He even posits an "academy" there that attracted Babylonian scholars.

orientation was provided by referring to a direction relative to some geographical or topographical feature, such as a mountain or an island."[20] On a narrower scale, "short identifiers" were used: "The final means of identifying a site ... was by its name and a short identifier, describing, for example, the quality of the harbour, peculiar topographic features or an ethnographic trait."[21] Ancient itineraries guided travelers from one destination to another based on such a landmark and identifier system.[22]

Rabbinic texts are rife with examples of such spatial orientation. For example, a text in y. Šabb. 6:2, 8a uses landmarks to indicate distances that would have been known to the tradents and their audiences.[23] After the general rule that one should put on new shoes on the Sabbath only if one has walked in them before, the question arises, how long one should have walked in them. According to members of the household (i.e., students) of Bar Qappara, the minimum distance would have been from the study house of Bar Qappara to that of R. Hoshaiah. According to the people of Sepphoris, this distance is from the Synagogue of the Babylonians to the courtyard of R. Hama b. Haninah. People of Tiberias allegedly defined the distance from the Great Synagogue to the shop of R. Hoshaiah.

The text's lack of specification and modern readers' lack of knowledge of these landmarks make identifications of the suggested distances impossible. The fifth-generation Tanna (R. Eleazar) Bar Qappara is sometimes associated with Caesarea.[24] R. Hoshaiah, a first-generation Amora, was his student. The first rule is attributed to the members of Bar Qappara's household or, more likely, his students, representing their perspective, that is, the distance from the rabbi's study house—possibly in Caesarea—to that of one of his best-known students. The other suggestions are attributed to the townspeople of Sepphoris and Tiberias and mention probably well-known local synagogues (the Synagogue of the Babylonians and the Great Synagogue) first and buildings belonging to local rabbis (the courtyard of R. Hama b. Haninah and the shop of R. Hoshaiah) in second place. The R. Hoshaiah of the Tiberias tradition would have been the third-generation Amora R. Hoshaiah II.[25]

---

20 Dueck and Brodersen, *Geography*, 90.
21 Dueck and Brodersen, *Geography*, 92.
22 See Kai Brodersen, "The Presentation of Geographical Knowledge for Travel and Transport in the Roman World: *Itineraria non tantum adnotata sed etiam picta*," in *Travel and Geography in the Roman Empire*, ed. Colin Adams and Ray Laurence (London: Routledge, 2001), 19.
23 On Roman spatial perception see Kai Brodersen, *Terra Cognita: Studien zur römischen Raumerfassung* (Hildesheim: Georg Olms, 1995).
24 See Hermann L. Strack, *Einleitung in Talmud und Midrasch*, 6th ed. (Munich: Beck, 1976), 134.
25 See Strack, *Einleitung*, 142 on this sage.

From a halakhic point of view, the text would have been useful only to those who were familiar with the approximate distances between the mentioned landmarks. For later generations, the tradition merely provided evidence of the existence of variant rulings on the matter. For the study of spatial orientation in ancient Jewish society the type of landmarks identified here are meaningful. Since the texts were formulated by rabbis, they may reflect a rabbinic rather than a local Jewish perspective, though. For rabbis, major local synagogues and buildings associated with their rabbinic colleague-friends, foremost amongst them study houses, served as signifying posts in urban environments in which one would have encountered Roman landmarks such as (amphi)theatres, temples, and bathhouses as well. From a rabbinic perspective, Romanized cities such as Caesarea, Tiberias and Sepphoris remained familiar and Jewish if one focused on their Jewish and rabbinic landmarks only. Thus, a halakhic text that deals with the use of new shoes on the Sabbath may provide evidence of a selective religious and ethnographic landmarking enterprise that blotted out traces of Roman culture and featured secure and well-known Jewish landmarks instead. As sociologists have already pointed out, in cosmopolitan contexts, "(s)ome individuals interact selectively on the basis of kinship; others, on the basis of common interests."[26] While rabbis were well-aware of bathhouses, theatres and statues, they prioritized their own cultural markers and thereby familiarized themselves with life in Greco-Roman *poleis*.

The Roman realities of a place were not always blotted out, however. Sometimes they could even serve halakhic purposes, as in the case of the *eruv* or Sabbath boundary around Tiberias, which Shimon b. Laqish tried to extent to include the village of Bet Maon (y. 'Erub. 5:1, 22b):

> R. Shimon b. Laqish said: I can make Bet Maon to be encompassed (within the Sabbath boundaries) of Tiberias. And you see the stadium as if it were filled with houses (i.e., a residential area). And the (Roman) camp is located within seventy and two thirds (cubits distance) from the stadium. And Bet Maon is located within (a distance of) seventy and two thirds (cubits) from the camp. And if you measure (for Sabbath limits) from Pigma (or: turret),[27] you find that Siriqin (or: monument of the Syrians)[28] is (located) within (a distance of) seventy and two thirds (from Tiberias). And if you measure (for Sabbath limits) from Phorta (or: pottery), you find that Siriqin is within seventy and two thirds cubits (from it).

---

26 Lenore Borzak, *Field Study: A Sourcebook for Experiential Learning* (Thousand Oaks, CA: Sage, 1981), 286.
27 For פיגמא see Marcus Jastrow, *A Dictionary of the Targumim, the Talmud Bavli and Yerushalmi, and the Midrashic Literature* (Jerusalem: Horev, 1985), 1159: "*semicircular turret, Pigma*, a suburb of Tiberias."
28 See Jastrow, *Dictionary*, 1027.

A village called Bet Maon, located close to Tiberias, is mentioned by Josephus (*Vita* 12). Josephus also mentions a stadium in or near Tiberias (*Vita* 92). Manfred Lämmer already suggested that this stadium would have been located to the north of Tiberias, half-way to Bet Maon.[29] During excavations in 2002 and 2005 structures which the excavators believe to be remnants of the stadium of Tiberias have been found "outside the city to the north on the shore in front of the lake."[30] The stadium seems to have existed from the first to the third century CE.[31]

The tradition in the Yerushalmi is attributed to the third-century Amora Shimon b. Laqish. It reckons with the audience's knowledge of the location of the stadium. According to Morten Hørning Jensen, "(t)he structure was eventually covered with mud as a result of flooding by the Sea of Galilee. In the mud, pottery from the third century was found, indicating that the structure was abandoned in that period."[32] Uzi Leibner points to a similar end-date for the existence of Bet Maon: "The results of the survey . . . and extensive excavation indicate that the site was abandoned around the second half of the third century."[33] In rabbinic sources Bet Maon is associated with third-century Amoraim. It may have had a synagogue and a priestly community that was critical of the patriarch in Tiberias (cf. Gen. Rab. 80:1).[34] The Yerushalmi tradition quoted above indicates "the geographical proximity and the strong connections between this settlement and nearby Tiberias."[35] It reflects the "local color" of the area in the third century CE.

For the purpose of extending the Sabbath boundaries of Tiberias to Bet Maon, that is, to allow people to walk between these locations on the Sabbath, the stadium is hypothetically seen as a residential area.[36] Various locations (Pigma, Siriqin, Phorta) that lie within a radius of seventy and two thirds cubits from Tiberias are

---

[29] Manfred Lämmer, *Griechische Wettkämpfe in Galiläa unter der Herrschaft des Herodes Antipas*, Jahrbuch der deutschen Hochschule Köln (Schorndorf: Hoffmann, 1976), 43–54. See also Steve Mason, *Life of Josephus*, vol. 9 of *Flavius Josephus: Translation and Commentary* (Leiden: Brill, 2001), 70 (n. 475).

[30] Morten Hørning Jensen, *Herod Antipas in Galilee: The Literary and Archaeological Sources on the Reign of Herod Antipas and its Socio-Economic Impact in Galilee*, 2nd rev. ed., WUNT 2/215 (Tübingen: Mohr Siebeck, 2010), 145.

[31] See Hørning Jensen, *Herod Antipas in Galilee*, 144.

[32] Hørning Jensen, *Herod Antipas in Galilee*, 144. The salvage excavations were carried out by Moshe Hartal.

[33] Uzi Leibner, *Settlement and History in Hellenistic, Roman, and Byzantine Galilee: An Archaeological Survey of the Eastern Galilee*, TSAJ 127 (Tübingen: Mohr Siebeck, 2009), 294.

[34] On this tradition see Oded Irshai, "The Priesthood in Jewish Society in Late Antiquity," in *Continuity and Renewal: Jews and Judaism in Byzantine Christian Palestine*, ed. Lee. I. Levine (Jerusalem: Dinur Center and Yad Yizhak Ben Zvi, 2004), 67–106 (esp. 77–79) (Hebrew).

[35] Leibner, *Settlement and History*, 294.

[36] See also Samuel Klein, *Beiträge zur Geographie und Geschichte Galiläas* (Leipzig: Haupt, 1909), 60.

mentioned, which serve as an analogy to the Roman camp outside of Bet Maon that lies at the same distance from the town. Through an extension of the radius Bet Maon is included in the *eruv* around Tiberias.

The Roman stadium and camp are not significant in their political and institutional meaning here but are reduced to mere landmarks that allowed rabbis to extend the Sabbath boundaries of Tiberias to neighboring towns and villages. What is also interesting is that locations received their names on the basis of landmarks that existed there at certain times, such as a semicircular turret (Pigma), something (e.g., a monument) associated with Syrians (Siriqin) and a pottery (Phorta). We may assume that the names continued to denote settlements at these places, even when the respective landmarks were no longer there. The stated measures were probably approximate rather than exact. Rabbis would have been familiar with Roman milestones that were set up on the major roads between cities.[37] Perhaps some of the mentioned locations lay on these routes. Otherwise distances could be estimated only.[38] The discussions in the Mishnah and Talmud tractate 'Erubin use real landmarks and geographical distances for religious purposes. The *eruv* creates a fictional space, in which certain activities may be carried out on the Sabbath.[39] It is imposed upon and overrides real spaces and boundaries.

The Rabbinic Land of Israel

Under Hadrian's rule, shortly before or after the Bar Kokhba revolt, the provinces of Judea and Syria were merged into the larger unit Syria-Palestine. No political boundary would have existed between the Galilee, coastal plain, and Judea, where Jews lived and spoke Aramaic amongst themselves, and the Syrian areas further north, in which Syrians and Greeks formed the majority of the population. At the time when the Mishnah and Talmud were composed, rabbis would have lived in this larger province of Syria-Palestine under direct Roman rule. Yet they continued

---

[37] On milestones in Roman Palestine see, e.g., Benjamin H. Isaac, "Milestones in Judaea, from Vespasian to Constantine," *PEQ* 110 (1978): 47–60; Benjamin H. Isaac and Israel Roll, "A Milestone of AD 69 from Judaea: The Elder Trajan and Vespasian," *JRS* 66 (1976): 15–19.
[38] On this issue see Ray Laurence and Francesco Trifilò, "The Global and the Local in the Roman Empire: Connectivity and Mobility from an Urban Perspective," in *Globalisation and the Roman World: Archaeological and Theoretical Perspectives*, ed. Martin Pitts and Miguel John Versluys (Cambridge: Cambridge University Press, 2015), 99–122 (110–11).
[39] On the notion of the *eruv* and its origins in Second Temple times see Lutz Doering, *Schabbat: Sabbathalacha und -praxis im antiken Judentum und Urchristentum*, TSAJ 78 (Tübingen: Mohr Siebeck, 1999), 524–27.

to refer to their home-country as the Land of Israel, a term that had biblical origins and was religiously meaningful.[40]

The Boundaries of the Land of Israel

Already in the Tosefta rabbis are concerned with defining the boundaries of the rabbinically perceived Land of Israel because the distinction between inside and outside of the Land was halakhically relevant:

> What is (considered) the Land (of Israel) and what is considered outside of the Land? All that slopes down from the Mountains of Amanus[41] and inward is (considered) the Land of Israel; from the Mountains of Amanus and beyond is (considered) outside of the Land. The islands which are in the sea (the Mediterranean), they see them as if they were a string extending from the Mountains of Amanus to the Brook of Egypt.[42] (Those) from the string inwards are (considered) the Land of Israel. (Those) from the string outwards are (considered) outside of the Land. R. Yehudah says: Everything opposite the Land of Israel, behold, it is (considered) as the Land of Israel, as it is said, "For the western boundary, you shall have the Great Sea and its coast" (Num 34:6). Islands which are at the sides, they see them as if they were a string from Kaflaria to the ocean (i.e., the Mediterranean Sea), from the Brook of Egypt to the ocean. From the string and inwards is the Land of Israel; from the string and outwards is outside of the Land.[43]

This definition is based on biblical terminology and not very exact from a geographical point of view. It refers to the mountain range of Amanus in the North, the brook of Egypt in the South, and the Mediterranean in the west as the natural boundaries of the Land of Israel. As far as the eastern boundary is concerned, t. B. Qam. 8:19 mentions the river Jordan as the border of Israel with idolatrous "Canaan." The

---

40 On the rabbinic boundaries of the Land of Israel in ancient Jewish consciousness see Eyal Ben-Eliyahu, *The Boundaries of the Land of Israel in the Consciousness of the People of the Second Temple and the Roman-Byzantine Periods* (Jerusalem: Yad Ben-Zvi, 2014), 86–109 (Hebrew).
41 The term "Amanus" already appears in Strabo (*Geog.* 16.1.2) and denotes a mountain pass, "the pass by which the ordinary road from the sea coast of the gulf of *Issus*, leads into the inland parts of Syria, through the mountains behind Alexandretta," see James Rennell, *Illustrations (Chiefly Geographical) of the History of the Expedition of Cyrus* (London: W. Bulmer and Co., 1816), 41.
42 On the Brook of Egypt see Paul K. Hooker, "The Location of the Brook of Egypt," in *History and Interpretation: Essays in Honour of John H. Hayes*, ed. M. Patrick Graham, William P. Brown, and Jeffrey K. Kuan (Sheffield: Sheffield Academic Press, 1993), 203–14 (203): the term was already used in the Hebrew Bible "to designate the boundary between the territory of Judah and either the domains of the pharaohs or a sort of 'no man's land' between Judah and Egypt." Hooker reviews scholarly attempts to locate the Brook of Egypt in the Sinai Peninsula, a region of merchant travel that required particular security measures.
43 t. Ter. 2:12 par. t. Ḥal. 2:11.

references to the Bible and lack of specificity indicate the theological rather than political, historical, and geographical basis of the rabbinic definition.

Elsewhere in the Tosefta, an alternative definition is provided:

> What is (considered) the Land of Israel? From the river south of Keziv and onwards (cf. m. Šeb. 6:1; t. Ḥal. 2:6). (The settlements) close to Ammon and Moav, the land of Egypt, are (divided into) two countries (or: regions): either (the produce) is eaten and (the land) is cultivated, or (the produce) is not eaten and (the land) is not cultivated.[44]

Here Keziv/Akhziv, which seems to have been identical or close to the so-called Ladder of Tyre, is seen as the boundary between the Land of Israel and Syria. The southern area bordering on Egypt is considered ambiguous with regard to its inclusion into the Land of Israel. A part of it, probably the region with more Jewish settlements, was treated halakhically as part of Israel, whereas another region was considered outside, that is, a foreign or diaspora region. Where real political borders were nonexistent, rabbis suggested a Jewish border guard system: "Settlements of the Land of Israel which are close to the border (cf. t. ʿErub. 4[3]:5), they appoint for them a guard, so that gentiles will not break across and steal produce of the Seventh Year."[45]

The discussion of the boundaries and dimensions of the Land of Israel continues in the Yerushalmi and rabbinic suggestions continue to be diverse. One tradition uses water reservoirs to mark Israel's boundaries:

> Seven seas surround the Land of Israel: the Great Sea (Mediterranean), the Sea of Tiberias (i.e. Sea of Galilee), the Sea of Kobev (or: Kokhav), the Salt Sea, the Sea of Helat, the Sea of Shilhat, the Sea of Apamea. The Sea of Hamaz: Diocletian stopped rivers to make it.[46]

Three of these water reservoirs are easily recognizable: the Mediterranean Sea, the Sea of Galilee and the Salt Sea (cf. Gen 14:3, i.e., the Dead Sea). The Sea of Galilee and the Salt Sea are linked by the Jordan river, which is not mentioned here. The rabbis who formulated and transmitted this tradition probably included the Sinai Peninsula and extended the water demarcation to the Gulf of Aqaba and the Red Sea. If so, the Suez Canal would have constituted the western border between Egypt and Israel. Yet, the Suez Canal that links the Red Sea to the Mediterranean was constructed in the nineteenth century only. In the eighteenth century archaeologists

---

44 t. Šeb. 4:6.
45 t. Šeb. 4:7. The internal areas of the Land of Israel are listed in t. Šeb. 4:11.
46 y. Ketub. 12:4, 35b.

allegedly discovered an ancient canal that extended northward from the Red Sea and then westward toward the Nile.[47]

The reference to Diocletian stopping the rivers to make the Sea of Hamaz may refer to "Diocletian's remodeling of Babylon (in Egypt) around AD 300, when the fortress was built to defend, and enclose, the early Roman harbour and the entrance to the Red Sea canal."[48] According to Gawdat Gabra, "(a) seventh-century chronicle from John of Nikiou, a Coptic bishop, attributes to the Roman Emperor Trajan the creation of a canal that connected the Nile and the Red Sea and began in (the Egyptian fortress of) Babylon."[49] John of Nikiou's attribution of the canal to Trajan must be considered legendary, though. Scholars have confirmed that it was Diocletian who built the fortress of Babylon and constructed the canal.[50] Amoraic rabbis seem to have been more correct in their association of the waterway with Diocletian. A canal was not a "sea," however, and the name "Hamaz" does not appear elsewhere in this connection.

In the North, the Roman city of Apamea was located on the bank of the Orontes River in Syria. If the rabbinic Land of Israel reached up to Apamea, it would have been imagined to comprise large parts of (coastal) Syria as well. Rather than being based on the political reality of the Roman Empire, this extension of the rabbinic Land of Israel seems to be inspired by biblical prophesies. In Gen 15:18 God's territorial promise to Abram is mentioned: "On that day the Lord made a covenant with Abram saying: To your offspring I assign this land, from the river of Egypt to the great river, the river Euphrates," followed by a reference to the other ethnic groups whose land this territory comprised (Gen 15:19–21). Y. Qidd. 1:9, 61d comments on this biblical text and provides explanations on the territory and its earlier inhabitants, which are diverse and differ from the biblical list (Hittites, Amorites, Canaanites etc.). R. Judah refers to the Shalamites, Arabs and Nabateans; R. Shimon to Asia, Apamea and Damascus; R. Eliezer b. Yaqob to Asia, Carthage and Thrace; and (anonymous) rabbis to Edom, Moab and the area of the Ammonites. In late antiquity, rabbis had difficulties reconciling the biblical prophecy with the political

---

[47] Mentioned in *Description de l'Égypte, ou Recueil des observations et des recherches qui ont été faites en Égypte pendant l'expédition de l'armée française, publié par les ordres de Sa Majesté l'Empereur Napoléon le Grand* (Paris: Imprimerie impériale, 1809–1828).
[48] Peter Sheehan, *Babylon of Egypt: The Archaeology of Old Cairo and the Origins of the City* (Cairo: The American University in Cairo Press, 2010), 63.
[49] Gawdat Gabra, "The Fortress of Babylon in Old Cairo," in *The History and Religious Heritage of Old Cairo: Its Fortress, Churches, Synagogue, and Mosque*, ed. Carolyn Ludwig and Morris Jackson (Cairo: The American University in Cairo Press, 2013), 16–33 (22).
[50] See Gabra, "The Fortress of Babylon," 22.

and territorial reality they lived in. Yet they held up the belief in a geographically vast Land of Israel whose borders they were unable to define exactly.⁵¹

Rabbinic Perspectives on the Rest of the World

It is not astonishing that the areas outside of the Land of Israel that are most often mentioned by Palestinian rabbis are Syria and Egypt, Babylonia and Rome. These were the places of major significance to Jews in Roman Palestine: Syria and Egypt as the adjacent territories to one's homeland, Babylonia as the land with the largest Jewish community outside of Israel, and Rome as the center of the Roman Empire. At least some rabbis, disciples of sages and other Jews would have traveled to these regions. Upon their return, they would have related their observations to their colleagues, friends and relatives. Travel reports would have merged with hearsay and stereotypes about the respective places and people. To disentangle such reminiscences and establish a historical or geographical kernel is therefore often impossible. In the following, I shall present only one example of this phenomenon: the rabbinic description of a large synagogue in Alexandria in Egypt.

The Tosefta transmits a narrative that describes an Alexandrian synagogue in exaggerated terms:

> R. Yehudah said: Everyone who has not seen the double colonnade (דפלסטון)⁵² of Alexandria of Egypt has not seen Israel's glory in his entire life. It was like a large basilica, one colonnade inside another. Sometimes there were there twice as many (people) as went forth from Egypt. And seventy-one golden cathedras (קתדראות) were there for the seventy-one elders, each one worth twenty-five myriads (of golden denars), and a golden platform (במה) in the middle. And the chazzan of the congregation stands on it and the flags are in his hand. He moved (or: washed his hands) to read (from the Torah), and that one would wave the flags, and they answered "Amen" for each and every blessing. And that one would wave the flags and they answered "Amen." And they did not sit mixed, but goldsmiths by themselves, silversmiths by themselves, (common) weavers by themselves, artistic weavers by themselves, and blacksmiths by themselves. And all this, why? So that when a stranger⁵³ came, he could join his craft (ויטפל לאומנותו), and from there he could make a living⁵⁴

---

51 Ben-Eliyahu, *Identity*, 90, also refers to the "elasticity of the borders of the land in rabbinic literature."
52 Jastrow, *Dictionary*, 304; also: basilica synagogue, cf. y. Sukkah 5, 55a.
53 Or: guest (אכסניי), see Jastrow, *Dictionary*, 64.
54 Literally: "and from there his maintenance would come forth" (ומשם פרנסה יוצאה). t. Sukkah 4:6.

A Jewish building in Egypt is described almost in terms of a tourist attraction here. The building was probably imagined to be a synagogue in the sense of an assembly space for Egyptian Jews. It is said to have been huge, able to accommodate large numbers of congregants. The chazzan and the "seventy-one" elders form the number seventy-two which is reminiscent of the seventy-two elders, six from each tribe, mentioned in the Letter of Aristeas (Let. Aris. 32). The description of the interior splendor of the building ("golden cathedras," "golden platform") is reminiscent of the "golden vessels," "golden bowls" and "golden vials," with which the Ptolemaic king is said to have provided the Torah translators (Let. Aris. 75–79). The chazzan's duties are evocative of those of priests (flags, "amen" for each blessing). The compartmentalization of the sitting area may mimic the Temple's division into courtyards, although professional divisions are not mentioned in that regard. The division into crafts is said to have had a practical purpose, namely the professional integration of visitors from outside the congregation. John Kloppenborg and Stephen Wilson's association of Greco-Roman synagogues with "voluntary associations" is pertinent here.[55]

For his own time, Philo mentions various local synagogues (*proseuchai*) in Alexandria rather than one exceptionally large and splendid building (*Legat.* 132: "there are a great many in every section of the city"). Many of them were allegedly burned or otherwise destroyed by the Romans (*Legat.* 133–134). Throughout his *Legatio ad Gaium* he uses the plural form for these buildings. It is, of course, possible that Alexandrian Jews had built one large synagogue in the city in late antiquity. To take the rabbinic text literally as evidence of the existence of such a synagogue at Philo's time, as Dorothy Sly does, is inappropriate, though.[56]

We should rather ask what the rabbinic text is meant to convey. This becomes clear from the reference to "Israel's glory" at the beginning of the description. The Palestinian rabbis who formulated and transmitted the text wanted to show that "Israel's glory" reached beyond the Land of Israel into Egypt, where many Jews lived at least until the first century CE. Due to the sparseness of the evidence, the size of the Alexandrian Jewish community after 117 CE is impossible to determine.[57] It must have been much smaller than at Philo's time, however, which makes a large and representative synagogue building unlikely. The Tosefta text, which may have been formulated and transmitted in late antiquity, can therefore not be read like a

---

55 See the articles in John S. Kloppenborg and Stephen G. Wilson, eds., *Voluntary Associations in the Graeco-Roman World* (London: Routledge, 1996).
56 Dorothy I. Sly, *Philo's Alexandria* (London: Routledge, 1996), 43–44.
57 Roger S. Bagnall, *Egypt in Late Antiquity* (Princeton: Princeton University Press, 1993), 276: "Whatever remained is largely invisible in the documentation, and the one criterion generally used to identify Jews in the period after 117, nomenclature, cannot bear the weight put upon it."

travel report, based on actual observations and experiences. It seems to have been formulated on the basis of older traditions (some of which also appear in the Letter of Aristeas) about the size, significance and wealth of Alexandrian Jews. Rather than providing historically accurate information, the great Alexandrian synagogue must be seen as the product of rabbinic imagination and wishful thinking. In the Yerushalmi, the quotation of the baraita is followed by an anonymous comment that the synagogue was destroyed by Trajan (y. Sukkah 5:1, 55a–b). The editors of the Talmud would have been aware of its non-existence in their own time period.

Summary

On the basis of this discussion the term rabbinic "geography" needs to be qualified. Rabbis were not interested in scientific geography based on exact observations and measures. Their geographical references and descriptions should rather be considered a mixture of daily life (e.g., travel) experiences, biblical reminiscences, hearsay and wishful thinking. Especially as far as the rabbinical notion of the Land of Israel is concerned, we are dealing with a "geography of the mind" rather than with exact boundaries. The rabbinic notion of the land was based on biblical prophesies and monarchic memories and therefore elusive and uncertain. As Eyal Ben-Eliyahu has already pointed out, different views on how to determine its boundaries circulated.[58] Neither the recurrence to waterways and mountain ranges nor to ethnic groups who once lived within allowed a precise definition of its borders. In late antiquity, when rabbis lived in the province of Syria-Palestine under Roman imperial rule, the notion of the Land of Israel constituted an alternative ideational homeland and territory in which rabbinic jurisdiction applied. The distinction between the Land of Israel and the territory "outside the Land" was primarily relevant for halakhic reasons, to demarcate Palestinian rabbis' religious rulings that applied to fellow-Jews on Jewishly-owned land only. For Jews who lived outside of the Land and/or in areas where the majority were gentiles, different halakhic rules applied.

Rabbinic texts are full of incidental references to towns, villages and features of the landscape such as mountains and waterways. Some of them are well-known from other sources, whereas others appear in rabbinic texts only. In the past, scholars have often taken place names and distances at face value to reconstruct the geography and settlement of the region in the first centuries CE. More recently,

---

[58] Ben-Eliyahu, *Identity and Territory*, 93–97. See my review of this book in *Theologische Literaturzeitung* 10 (2020): 920–22.

scholars have become much more cautious and critical, however, as far as the historical reliability of rabbinic texts is concerned. A historical-critical approach must also be applied to rabbinic geographical information. Each reference has to be analyzed in connection with outside information from Greco-Roman and Christian sources, travelogues and itineraries, and especially archaeological discoveries of recent years. Although a differentiation between imagined and real geographical data is often difficult if not impossible, a new methodologically informed attempt to study rabbinic texts from a geographical point-of-view should nevertheless be undertaken.

From this limited analysis it is already obvious that rabbis were most familiar with and knowledgeable of their local surroundings. When it comes to the Land of Israel as a whole or locations and places outside of it, descriptions are much more imaginative. Rabbinic traditions may contain and should be examined with regard to "local color," that is, reflections of local geographical features supported by archaeological evidence and/or other texts. The identification of local color sometimes allows us to associate texts with specific time periods. Such an analysis also enables us to view the geographical space with the eyes of the ancients and discover how they oriented themselves, which geographical and spatial features they prioritized, and how they moved about in the space they inhabited. The study of rabbinic geography must move forward from its past focus on the identification of localities and the localization of rabbis. What is called for is a much broader holistic approach that examines rabbinic space perception within the context of ancient geographical imagination and daily life experience.

References

Avi-Yonah, Michael. *The Holy Land: A Historical Geography from the Persian to the Arab Conquest (536 BC to AD 640)*. Jerusalem: Carta, 2002.
Bagnall, Roger S. *Egypt in Late Antiquity*. Princeton: Princeton University Press, 1993.
Bakhos, Carol. *Ishmael on the Border: Rabbinic Portrayals of the First Arab*. Albany: State University of New York Press, 2006.
Ben-Eliyahu, Eyal. *The Boundaries of the Land of Israel in the Consciousness of the People of the Second Temple and the Roman-Byzantine Periods*. Jerusalem: Yad Ben-Zvi, 2014. (Hebrew)
Ben-Eliyahu, Eyal. *Identity and Territory: Jewish Perceptions of Space in Antiquity*. Berkeley: University of California Press, 2019.
Bitton-Ashkelony, Brouria. *Encountering the Sacred: The Debate on Christian Pilgrimage in Late Antiquity*. Berkeley: University of California Press, 2005.
Borzak, Lenore. *Field Study: A Sourcebook for Experiential Learning*. Thousand Oaks, CA: Sage, 1981.
Brodersen, Kai. *Terra Cognita: Studien zur römischen Raumerfassung*. Hildesheim: Georg Olms, 1995.

Brodersen, Kai. "The Presentation of Geographical Knowledge for Travel and Transport in the Roman World: *Itineraria non tantum adnotata sed etiam picta*." Pages 7–21 in *Travel and Geography in the Roman Empire*. Edited by Colin Adams and Ray Laurence. London: Routledge, 2001.

Description de l'Égypte, ou Recueil des observations et des recherches qui ont été faites en Égypte pendant l'expédition de l'armée française, publié par les ordres de Sa Majesté l'Empereur Napoléon le Grand. Paris: Imprimerie impériale, 1809–1828.

Doering, Lutz. *Schabbat: Sabbathalacha und -praxis im antiken Judentum und Urchristentum*. TSAJ 78. Tübingen: Mohr Siebeck, 1999.

Dueck, Daniela, and Kai Brodersen. *Geography in Classical Antiquity*. Cambridge: Cambridge University Press, 2012.

Gabra, Gawdat. "The Fortress of Babylon in Old Cairo." Pages 16–33 in *The History and Religious Heritage of Old Cairo: Its Fortress, Churches, Synagogue, and Mosque*. Edited by Carolyn Ludwig and Morris Jackson. Cairo: The American University in Cairo Press, 2013.

Herman, Geoffrey. "There They Sat Down: Mapping Settlement Patterns in Sasanian Babylonia." Pages 3–10 in *Studying the Near and Middle East at the Institute for Advanced Study, Princeton 1935–2018*. Edited by Sabine Schmidtke. Piscataway: Gorgias Press, 2018.

Herman, Geoffrey. "Babylonian of Pure Lineage: Notes on Babylonian Jewish Toponym." Pages 191–228 in *Sources and Interpretation in Ancient Judaism: Studies for Tal Ilan at Sixty*. Edited by Meron M. Piotrkowski, Geoffrey Herman, and Saskia Doenitz. Leiden: Brill, 2018.

Hezser, Catherine. *Jewish Travel in Antiquity*. TSAJ 144. Tübingen: Mohr Siebeck, 2011.

Hezser, Catherine. Review of Eyal Ben-Eliyahu, *Identity and Territory*. *Theologische Literaturzeitung* 10 (2020): 920–22.

Hooker, Paul K. "The Location of the Brook of Egypt." Pages 203–14 in *History and Interpretation: Essays in Honour of John H. Hayes*. Edited by M. Patrick Graham, William P. Brown, and Jeffrey K. Kuan. Sheffield: Sheffield Academic Press, 1993.

Irshai, Oded. "The Priesthood in Jewish Society in Late Antiquity." Pages 67–106 in *Continuity and Renewal: Jews and Judaism in Byzantine Christian Palestine*. Edited by Lee. I. Levine. Jerusalem: Dinur Center and Yad Yizhak Ben Zvi, 2004. (Hebrew)

Isaac, Benjamin H. and Israel Roll. "A Milestone of AD 69 from Judaea: The Elder Trajan and Vespasian." *JRS* 66 (1976): 15–19.

Isaac, Benjamin H. "Milestones in Judaea, from Vespasian to Constantine." *PEQ* 110 (1978): 47–60.

Jastrow, Marcus. *A Dictionary of the Targumim, the Talmud Bavli and Yerushalmi, and the Midrashic Literature*. Jerusalem: Horev, 1985.

Jensen, Morten Hørning. *Herod Antipas in Galilee: The Literary and Archaeological Sources on the Reign of Herod Antipas and its Socio-Economic Impact in Galilee*. 2nd rev. ed. WUNT 2/215. Tübingen: Mohr Siebeck, 2010.

Kapor, Vladimir. *Local Colour: A Travelling Concept*. Bern: Lang, 2009.

Klein, Samuel. *Beiträge zur Geographie und Geschichte Galiläas*. Leipzig: Haupt, 1909.

Kloppenborg, John S., and Stephen G. Wilson, eds. *Voluntary Associations in the Graeco-Roman World*. London: Routledge, 1996.

Laurence, Ray, and Francesco Trifilò. "The Global and the Local in the Roman Empire: Connectivity and Mobility from an Urban Perspective." Pages 99–122 in *Globalisation and the Roman World: Archaeological and Theoretical Perspectives*. Edited by Martin Pitts and Miguel John Versluys. Cambridge: Cambridge University Press, 2015.

Leibner, Uzi. *Settlement and History in Hellenistic, Roman, and Byzantine Galilee: An Archaeological Survey of the Eastern Galilee*. TSAJ 127. Tübingen: Mohr Siebeck, 2009.

Lämmer, Manfred. *Griechische Wettkämpfe in Galiläa unter der Herrschaft des Herodes Antipas*. Jahrbuch der deutschen Hochschule Köln. Schorndorf: Hoffmann, 1976.
Mason, Steve. *Life of Josephus*. Vol. 9 of *Flavius Josephus: Translation and Commentary*. Leiden: Brill, 2001.
Morgan, R. J. "Foreword to the 2008 Edition." Pages ix–xxi in *Collected Ancient Greek Novels*. Edited by B.P. Reardon. 3rd ed. Berkeley: University of California Press, 2019.
Neubauer, Adolphe. *La géographie du Talmud*. Paris: Michel Lévy Frères, Libraires éditeurs, 1868.
Rennell, James. *Illustrations (Chiefly Geographical) of the History of the Expedition of Cyrus*. London: W. Bulmer and Co., 1816.
Rock, Ian E. *Paul's Letter to the Romans and Roman Imperialism: An Ideological Analysis of the Exordium (Romans 1:1–17)*. Eugene: Wipf & Stock, 2012.
Roller, Duane W. *Ancient Geography: The Discovery of the World in Classical Greece and Rome*. London: I.B. Tauris, 2015.
Rosenfeld, Ben-Zion. *Torah Centers and Rabbinic Activity in Palestine 70–400 CE: History and Geographic Distribution*. Leiden: Brill, 2010.
Shahar, Yuval. *Josephus Geographicus: The Classical Context of Geography in Josephus*. TSAJ 98. Tübingen: Mohr Siebeck, 2004.
Sheehan, Peter. *Babylon of Egypt: The Archaeology of Old Cairo and the Origins of the City*. Cairo: The American University in Cairo Press, 2010.
Sly, Dorothy I. *Philo's Alexandria*. London: Routledge, 1996.
Stern, Sacha. *Jewish Identity in Early Rabbinic Writings*. Leiden: Brill, 1994.
Strack, Hermann L. *Einleitung in Talmud und Midrasch*. 6th ed. Munich: Beck, 1976.
Theissen, Gerd. *Lokalkolorit und Zeitgeschichte in den Evangelien: Ein Beitrag zur Geschichte der synoptischen Tradition*. 2nd ed. Freiburg: Universitätsverlag; Göttingen: Vandenhoeck & Ruprecht, 1992.

Paul L. Heck
The Journey of Zayd Ibn ʿAmr: In Search of True Worship

Abstract: This essay reflects on the little-known tale of Zayd Ibn ʿAmr who lived in Mecca, prior to Islam, in the sixth century CE. Breaking with the worship of Quraysh (the leading tribe of Mecca), he set off on a journey in search of true worship in the fashion of Abraham. Reflection on the tale in relation to other literature of the period, including pre-Islamic poetry and the Qurʾan, enriches perspective on the meaning of travel in late antiquity and also, in this case, on the rise of Islam. Before concluding the essay, I look at a selection of examples of Islamic travel literature from more recent centuries. The themes of this literature are not unrelated to the tale of Zayd Ibn ʿAmr, particularly the understanding of travel as a search for true worship and, as well, for signs of the ethical fruits of true worship especially in the Abode of Islam. Thus, despite the diverse journey experiences of Muslims over the ages, it is possible to speak of a coherent understanding of the purpose of travel in Islam. Since the Qurʾan does not fully spell out the meanings of travel, the tale of Zayd Ibn ʿAmr serves as something of a non-sharīʿa precedent in that regard with insight for reading Islamic travel literature across the centuries.

The journey to be considered here is the little-known tale of Zayd Ibn ʿAmr who lived in Mecca, prior to Islam, in the sixth century CE. Along with a small group of fellow Meccans, he rejected the false sacrifices that were being offered at the sanctuary in Mecca—the Kaʿba. Despite his devotion to the Kaʿba as the place where, it was increasingly felt, Abraham had worshipped God, Zayd came to realize that his people were not undertaking worship there according to "the religion of Abraham." Indeed, it was clear to him that they did not even have the knowledge to worship God as Abraham had. Breaking with his people and their rites, he set off to travel across the wider region, Mesopotamia and the Levant, in search of knowledge of true worship. Along the way, he communicates with Jewish and Christian scholars, who were unable to offer him what he was seeking. In the end, he met a monk in the vicinity of Damascus, who informed him that he should return to Mecca, where a prophet would soon appear who could initiate Zayd into the worship of Abraham. However, while making his way home to Mecca, Zayd was set upon by highway robbers and killed.

Even if Zayd wasn't able to worship at the Kaʿba as Abraham had done, his tale is quite revealing not only in terms of the purpose of travelling to shrines in late antique Arabia but also in terms of the origins of Islam as a movement that sought not simply to renew the message of God's oneness—Jews and Christians, among others, were quite aware of the concept[1]—but more so to establish true worship, meaning worship that is productive of devotion to the Glory of God (ʿizzat allah, cf. Q Fāṭir 35:10 and Q al-Ṣāffāt 37:180), the Lord of the Kaʿba (rabb al-bayt), rather than to the glory of one's tribe.

The tale of Zayd is recorded only in early Islamic sources, so there are historiographical concerns. The earliest telling of the tale appears in the life of the prophet (al-sīrat al-nabawiyya) as compiled by Ibn Isḥāq (d. 767) and redacted by Ibn Hishām (d. 833). Since this work was compiled long after the reported lifetime of Zayd, one might ask whether the tale actually happened.[2] Three points can be made in that regard. First, the tale seems to have carried significant meaning for Muslims. It was preserved in several places in works from Islam's early centuries other than Ibn Hishām's redaction of the life of the prophet, for example, in *The Book of the Partisans of the Caliph ʿUthmān* (Kitāb al-ʿUthmāniyya) by al-Jāḥiẓ (d. 869);[3] *The Book of Songs* (Kitāb al-Aghānī), compiled by Abū al-Faraj al-Iṣfahānī (d. 967);[4] and also in a hadith from the collection of al-Bukhārī (d. 870).[5] Second, other figures, who, unlike Zayd, would actually meet the prophet, are depicted as traveling in Arabia in search of true religion, notably Salmān al-Fārisī (d. 656) and Kaʿb al-Aḥbar (d. ca. 655). Of course, one could question the historicity of all such accounts, but history is more than a record of facts on the ground. It also includes moral sentiments. In this regard, the tale of Zayd is part of a collective memory in early Islam that connected pious travel in the region of Arabia with the rise of Islam.[6] Third, in this sense, the tale of Zayd fits well with the moral sentiments that feature in other sources of the day, including pre-Islamic poetry and the Qurʾan,

---

[1] For religion in pre-Islamic Arabia see Valentina A. Grasso, *Pre-Islamic Arabia: Societies, Politics, Cults, and Identities during Late Antiquity* (Cambridge: Cambridge University Press, 2023).
[2] I rely on the earliest account of the tale in the life of the prophet by Ibn Hishām, *al-Sīrat al-Nabawiyya*, ed. Muṣṭafā al-Saqā, Ibrāhīm al-Abyārī, and ʿAbd al-Ḥafīẓ Shalabī, 2nd ed., 4 vols. (Beirut: Dār al-Khabar, 1995), 1:179–87. There is a well-known translation: Alfred Guillaume, trans., *The Life of Muhammad* (Oxford: Oxford University Press, 1955). All citations here are to the Arabic.
[3] al-Jāḥiẓ, *Kitāb al-ʿUthmāniyya*, ed. ʿAbd al-Salām Muḥammad Hārūn (Beiruit: Dār al-Jīl, 1991), 142.
[4] Abū al-Faraj al-Iṣfahānī, *Kitāb al-Aghānī*, 25 vols. (Beirut: Dār Iḥyāʾ al-Turāth al-ʿArabī, 1994), 3:87.
[5] See nos. 3614 and 3615 in *Ṣaḥīḥ al-Bukhārī*. This hadith report, where Zayd meets the prophet (albeit before the beginning of the latter's prophetic mission), seems to contradict the account in Ibn Hishām, where he does not.
[6] In other words, the tale of Zayd should be read as part of a larger narrative that would include all kinds of pious travel in the late antique Near East. For a collection of articles that explore the multiple ways in which a tale of pious travel is remembered (including the way in which it reflects broader religious and political development in the region) see Johannes Hall and Volker Menze,

particularly in terms of the debates over worship at the Kaʿba. This last point is the most significant for our purposes. The tale of Zayd closely aligns with the meanings and moral sentiments around pious travel in late antique Arabia, especially travel to shrines.

The tale of Zayd therefore enriches our understanding of the moral sentiments surrounding the Kaʿba as a site of divine power, before—no less than after—the rise of Islam. As a site of divine power, the shrine is meant to fashion the order that God intends for the world whereby the mighty are humbled and the lowly raised up (cf. Q al-Qaṣaṣ 28:4–5). One is therefore not to visit and offer sacrifice at the shrine for the sake of divine support for one's tribe but to grow in devotion to God. In this sense, sacrifice at the shrine is to be sacrifice for a righteous purpose, offered not in expectation of worldly gain, as if a bargain (*do ut des*), but entirely out of devotion to God. The worship of Abraham, remembered as both the builder of the Kaʿba, along with his son Ishmael (Q al-Baqara 2:127), and exemplar of righteousness par excellence, was the obvious model in this sense.

In what follows, I first discuss the tale of Zayd in its pre-Islamic context, including debates over true worship as they feature in the Qur'an, and then consider later examples of shrine visitation in Islam. On this basis, Zayd's tale, it would seem, is best taken as representative of a travel concept that would feature across the history of Islam. I am not suggesting that his tale was taken by later writers as a model of shrine visitation, only that there's a conceptual through-line.

The group that rejected the false sacrifices being offered in the sanctuary in Mecca, among them Zayd, did so because they recognized that such sacrifices, at least as performed by their tribe, only reinforced its clan chauvinism. Zayd is depicted at the Kaʿba as humbling himself before God, saying that he seeks righteousness (*birr*), not arrogance,[7] whereas, in contrast, the religion of his tribe is described as the idolatry of tyrants (*awthān al-ṭawāghīt*) in the elegy given for Zayd by Waraqa Ibn Nawfal, one of those who, along with Zayd, had abandoned the false clan worship at the sanctuary in Mecca.[8] In echo of this discourse, the Qur'an speaks of such disordered worship as "the fanaticism of ignorance" (*ḥamiyyat al-jāhiliyya*), giving it as the reason for the clan opposition to the sacrifice that Muhammad and his followers sought to offer at the sanctuary—sacrifice that is depicted as effective in bringing about awareness of God's mercy since such sacrifice is offered in devotion to God (Q al-Fatḥ 48:25–26) and not for the glory of one's tribe.

---

eds., *The Wandering Holy Man: The Life of Barsauma, Christian Asceticism, and Religious Conflict in Late Antique Palestine* (Oakland: University of California Press, 2020).
7 Ibn Hishām, *al-Sīrat al-Nabawiyya*, 1:185–86.
8 Ibn Hishām, *al-Sīrat al-Nabawiyya*, 1:187.

The ignorance (*al-jāhiliyya*) mentioned in the above qur'anic verse is often identified as polytheism. Indeed, according to the qur'anic narrative, idols, while powerless, do engender a disordered state in the soul.[9] However, the importance of monotheistic belief to the qur'anic message notwithstanding, the deeper issue at play in relation to the Ka'ba involves the question of worship, namely, harmful worship of a kind that recalls the description of disbelievers at Ps 94:8 as senseless because they fail to take into account God's concern for righteousness: the issue is not that they deny the existence of God but rather that they lack true devotion to God. As a result, their worship results only in the unjust treatment of others.[10] The Qur'an has a similar meaning in mind in the above verse where it attributes ignorance to disbelievers. It is not that they actually deny the existence of the one God but rather that they lack devotion, and so they remain brutish, despite their sacrifices, whereas believers come to know God's mercy because they offer sacrifice sincerely.

The Qur'an describes such "brutish" worship as slandering God. The term for slander (*iftirā*) features with varied nuance in numerous qur'anic verses, but it is generally associated with wrongdoing. In one verse (Q al-Mā'ida 5:103), it is connected with categories of animals, which, early commentary suggests, were exempted from sacrifice, a practice that worked to the glory of one's tribe and its idols, rather than being sacrificed for the good of the people in general.[11] (It seems a clan might take pride in the fact that its beasts were not made available for the wider community.) This verse thus speaks to the very issue that caused Zayd to break with worship at the Ka'ba—animal sacrifices offered to idols (*al-dhabā'iḥ allatī tudhbaḥ li-l-awthān*) that only encourages, as noted above, a spirit of pride and tyranny.[12]

Despite abandoning the false worship at the Ka'ba, Zayd remained devoted to the site itself, the Ka'ba, reportedly clinging to it with his entire body. To distinguish his piety from that of the clan system of worship, he is identified as a *ḥanīf*, a term that is found across varied genres of literature from this period (including the Qur'an) to describe one who is devoted to the religion of Abraham yet neither Jewish nor Christian. Such a person is, then, one of the righteous gentiles who

---

[9] See Paul L. Heck, "Paul and Muhammad: The Challenge of the Convert," *IslChr* 37 (2011): 127–43. For discussion of idolatry as generating a disordered state in the soul see especially pp. 141–43.

[10] See Jaco Gericke, *The Hebrew Bible and Philosophy of Religion* (Atlanta: Society of Biblical Literature, 2012), esp. 343–70.

[11] The idea that a sacrifice would not be for the common good contrasts with one purpose of sacrifice, nourishment of the poor and weak, as described in the Qur'an, for example, at Q al-Ḥajj 22:28, 36.

[12] Ibn Hishām, *al-Sīrat al-Nabawiyya*, 1:181.

formed a minor but noticeable movement in sixth-century Arabia.[13] As such, Zayd knows the God of Abraham but is bereft of the specific ritual knowledge by which to worship God as Abraham had.[14] What is meant by ritual knowledge, it seems, is not the materiality of the sacrifice to be offered at the Ka'ba, which included animals both before and after Islam,[15] but rather the manner in which one was to offer it such that it be counted as righteous sacrifice. As we will see, for sacrifice to be righteous, it would need to be associated with the bodily presence of a righteous person, namely, the Prophet Muhammad as the progeny of Abraham.

Description of Zayd's journey itself receives only a few sentences but is accompanied by several other revealing reports, including excerpts of his poetry, which display a general understanding of the biblical message: he expresses his desire to serve the God who forgives and to reside in paradise. Such poetry suggests that his religious vision differs significantly from that of his own tribe. In his poetry, he refers to Moses and Jonah, doing so in a way that affirms the link between the oneness of God and the mercy of God as the sole object of one's hope. In other words, he comprehends the connection between God as the creator and God as the forgiver of sins. In one poem, he upbraids his wife for scheming to keep him from traveling in search of the religion of Abraham, describing himself as a type of itinerant figure who frequents the gates of kings and whose camel crosses the vast desert.[16] This aspect of his poetry shows him to be part of a pre-Islamic heritage that celebrated the image of caravans crossing the desert.[17]

Of course, the singularly pious purpose of Zayd's journey diverges from the goals of most travel as depicted in pre-Islamic poetry. He is searching for true

---

[13] For only the most recent article on descriptions and interpretations of righteous gentiles (ḥanīfi-yya) in Arabia prior to and after the rise of Islam see Mun'im Sirry, "The Early Development of the Qur'anic Ḥanīf," *JSS* 56 (2011): 345–66.

[14] A similar case is Abū Qays Ibn Abū Anas from Yathrib, a contemporary of Zayd, who apparently lived long enough to become a follower of Muhammad. Before Islam, Abū Qays, like Zayd, had abandoned the worship of idols, claiming to worship the Lord of Abraham. Instead of traveling in search of true worship, he set up a mosque in his home. We are given no details on the nature of this worship, only that he forbade ritually impure people from participating in it. The report offers evidence of one attempt to perform communal worship after the model of Abraham even if in a private home. In this sense, the tale of Abū Qays shows that Zayd wasn't alone in his ritual goal—not only to worship the one God but to do so as Abraham had. For Abū Qays see Ibn Hishām, *al-Sīrat al-Nabawiyya*, 2:116–19.

[15] There is a good deal of scholarly literature on ritual sacrifice in early Islam. See, for example, Gerd Marie Ådna, *Muhammad and the Formation of Sacrifice* (Bern: Lang, 2014).

[16] Ibn Hishām, *al-Sīrat al-Nabawiyya*, 1:185.

[17] One cannot separate pious travel from the vast network of trade across Arabia. For trade in Late Antique Arabia see George Hatke and Ronald Ruzicka, eds., *South Arabian Long-Distance Trade in Antiquity: "Out of Arabia"* (Newcastle: Cambridge Scholars Publishing, 2021).

worship in contrast to the likes of Maymūn Ibn Qays al-Aʿshā (d. 625 CE), a Christian poet who traveled the region not in search of true worship but in hope of financial patronage at the region's courts.[18] Thus, despite the particular nature of Zayd's journey, it would be too facile to see his tale simply as heralding a new prophet. There is enough in the reports about him to suggest that we should read his tale, short as it may be, as part of a cultural milieu that was rich in images of travel of all kinds. One might travel in and beyond Arabia in search of trade at the region's markets or patronage at its courts, but the matrix of such travel would also feature a network of monasteries that shaped the cultural landscape and, indeed, the very meaning of one's travel.

Zayd's devotion to the Kaʿba, despite his rejection of his tribe's manner of worshipping there, points to a centuries-long history of contestation over the purpose of the shrine. Was the shrine to be a place that represented reverence for worldly power or devotion to God? Zayd, of course, supported the latter view but did not have the ritual knowhow—a righteous body to be associated with one' worship of God—to represent it fully. Significantly, he was not the only one in his day who thought to correct the nature of the sacrifice offered at the Kaʿba in a biblical fashion. A pre-Islamic Christian poet by the name of ʿAdī Ibn Zayd (d. 600 CE) associated the cross with Mecca in one of his poems where he invoked "the Lord of Mecca and the Cross."[19]

ʿAdī Ibn Zayd, who hailed from the tribe of Tamīm, was a highly erudite figure who composed a poetic summary of the biblical message—from creation to redemption—in verse that recalls that of the Qurʾan.[20] He also had connections to the courts of the region and is credited with introducing the language of the Arabs into the courts of the Sasanian Empire. His passing association of the cross with Mecca suggests his apparent interest in reforming its clan-associated ritual system, making the redemptive sacrifice of the cross the focal point of its worship. The idea did not take hold, perhaps because of the poet's own ties to worldly power and his reputation for wine-drinking or perhaps because Jesus wasn't linked to the Kaʿba as Abraham was (at least at the dawn of Islam if not before it). It is worth noting that the Qurʾan actually seeks to restore the image of Jesus, declaring that Jesus is

---

[18] For travel in pre-Islamic poetry see ʿUmar Ibn ʿAbdallah al-Sayf, *Bunyat al-Riḥla fī al-Qaṣīda al-Jāhiliyya* (Beirut: Muʾassasat al-Intishār al-ʿArabī, 2009). For al-Aʿshā's poetic claim to travel for patronage, see pp. 149–50.

[19] See Louis Cheikho, ed., *Shuʿarāʾ al-Naṣrāniyya Qabla al-Islām*, 4th ed. (Beirut: Dār al-Mashriq, 1991), 451.

[20] See Kirill Dmitriev, "An Early Christian Arabic Account of the Creation of the World," in *The Qurʾān in Context: Historical and Literary Investigations into the Qurʾānic Milieu*, ed. Angelika Neuwirth, Nicolai Sinai, and Michael Marx (Leiden: Brill, 2010), 349–87.

no wretched tyrant but is blessed by God (Q Maryam 19:31–34). The need to absolve Jesus from any association with tyranny is suggestive. Does it allude to the way in which some Christians in Mecca, partisans of the imperial cult in Constantinople, may have sought to incorporate the shrine in Mecca into the imperial order? Indeed, among those who rejected tribal worship at the Ka'ba along with Zayd was a certain 'Uthmān Ibn al-Ḥuwayrith, who would adopt Christianity and obtain a high rank with the emperor in Byzantium.[21]

If naming Jesus as blessed is a way for the Qur'an to absolve Jesus from disordered worship associated with the imperial cult, then, it can be concluded, being blessed has something to do with true worship. In short, it signals the efficacy of worship, that is, that one's worship of God works to increase one in righteousness rather than in a spirit of wrongdoing (*baghī*) that follows from false worship, as earlier discussed. To draw out the point: the qur'anic description of Jesus as blessed suggests that his body was a candidate to be associated with ritual worship in Mecca (recalling 'Adī Ibn Zayd's invocation of "the Lord of Mecca and the Cross") such that it would be true worship—his righteousness imbuing the worship with a spirit of righteousness and thereby making it ethically productive. However, the association did not stick. The reason that it did not do so may have to do with the qur'anic critique of Christian worship as ethically suspect. (This may also help explain why the Qur'an seeks to disassociate Jesus from the Christians of its milieu.) In the eyes of the Qur'an, Christian worship is ethically suspect, first, because of its association with the imperial cult, as noted above. In addition, the Qur'an charges Jews and Christians with religious pride. They pretend to a religious superiority by claiming exclusive "ownership" of Abraham, who, the Qur'an notes, was actually neither Jewish nor Christian (Q Āl 'Imrān 3:64–68). Again, as with tribal deities, so, too, with the Jews and Christians of Mecca, the charge is false worship, that is, worship that yields arrogance rather than humility.

It is worth noting in this regard that Jesus, in addition to his association with the imperial cult, had come to be perceived—within the religious system of pre-Islamic Arabia—as the equivalent of a partner deity, effectively putting him on par with the partner deities that the clans of Arabia associated with Allah. One qur'anic verse is highly suggestive in this regard: the clans mock Muhammad when referring to Jesus, who, in their view, is no different from the deities to which they offer sacrifice (Q al-Zukhruf 43:57–65). Why, then, should they abandon their deities when Muhammad speaks favorably of Jesus, whom—in their cultural outlook—is

---

21 For the involvement of Byzantium in Arabia see Irfan Shahid, "Byzantium in South Arabia," *DOP* 33 (1979): 22–39. 'Uthmān Ibn al-Ḥuwayrith tried to install himself as King of Mecca with support from Byzantium. For Christians in Arabia see C. Jonn Block, *The Qur'an in Christian-Muslim Dialogue* (New York: Routledge, 2014), 19–34.

the functional equivalent of their deities? The confusion was only made worse by the language used to speak of the sonship of Jesus. The term that the Qur'an attributes to the Christian description of Jesus as Son of God, *walad*, is the same term used to describe the tribal deities as "offspring of God." Thus, to speak credibly against tribal deities, Muhammad was compelled to downplay the stature of Jesus, being a *walad*, as the focus of worship (Q 43:81).

As we will see, it is important for a righteous body, a body like the body of Abraham, to be associated with worship at the Ka'ba for it to be righteous worship, but the figure of Jesus was ambiguous for the reasons just given. The point, it seems, was not lost on Zayd, who is described as rejecting Judaism and Christianity.[22] He may then have viewed these two traditions as ritually ineffective, debased forms of worship that, like his clan's worship, only increase one's arrogance over others rather than increasing one's righteousness. In the end, there was, then, nothing blessed about Jewish and Christian worship in this context. Whose body, then, would be associated with worship at the Ka'ba to ensure its biblical purpose?

Mecca, the Qur'an declares, is blessed for all peoples on account of its status as the first house of worship (Q 3:96). Mecca, then, is to be the site of worship that is true because it bears ethical fruit (i.e., as the effect of its blessedness), endowing its devotees with the righteousness of Abraham. However, as noted above, for worship to yield righteousness, it needs to be associated with the body of a righteous figure. The righteous body that will make worship at Mecca true worship would not be that of Jesus, who, in addition to his association with suspect worship, as discussed above, was not the prophetic figure who had traditionally been linked to the Ka'ba. Thus, at least by the Qur'an's reckoning, Jesus is not obviously the source of its blessed status. Rather, Abraham, as depicted in the Qur'an, not only builds the Ka'ba but also purifies it for worship and also asks God to teach him correct ritual and to send a messenger (*rasūl*) from among his descendants, meaning Muhammad, *who will make worshippers acceptable* (Q 2:124–134), that is, righteous. It is thus the righteousness of Abraham, embodied through his descendant Muhammad, that ensures the blessed status of the Ka'ba as site of true worship. In other words, it will be the righteous body of Muhammad, Son of Abraham through Ishmael, that makes worship at Mecca blessed, known for devotion to God rather than pride in one's group.

Zayd's journey in search of true worship is part and parcel of the contestation over the meaning of worship at the shrine in Mecca in the sense just discussed. His journey across the wider region is thus also a journey into the purpose of shrines, which, in his view, as far as we can surmise, exist to bring about the order of the

---

22 Ibn Hishām, *al-Sīrat al-Nabawiyya*, 1:180.

world as God intended it, that is, in behalf of the people in general and not simply for the prestige of worldly powers. The idea that the shrine exists for "the people" (*al-nās*) features in the qur'anic verse that explains the reason for building "the house"—the Ka'ba as the House of God—and also in the verse that describes Mecca as blessed.[23] In other words, the shrine is blessed because its divine power is in service of the people in general and not the interests of the ruling elite. It is worth emphasizing this point because it clarifies the meaning of Zayd's travel. He is in search of a community that is oriented to divine blessedness and the ethical fruit it bears, not to clan power and the pride and tyranny that it begets, but such a community takes shape only when it offers sacrifice with the right spirit, that is, the right manner of sacrifice, namely, the manner of the worship of Abraham.[24]

The shrine in Mecca was a focus of veneration in pre-Islamic Arabia. Then, too, its meaning was contested. Did it exist to reinforce the stature and interests of those in power? Or to establish righteousness, which benefited "the people"? Shrines in pre-Islamic Arabia had multiple functions. They were "gathering-places for pilgrimages and markets,"[25] making them places of peace and prosperity—refuges from the conflict and violence that hung-over the wider society beyond such sanctuaries. Shrines, then, were the obvious place for tribes to deposit declarations of alliance, meant as a way to mitigate the factors that encouraged volatility in society.[26] In this sense, a shrine was meant to draw worldly powers together only to restrain them by its divine power as recognized in such alliances. Inscriptions in South Arabia from long before the Common Era speak of political communities being founded by pacts that were sealed with sacrifice to the deity.[27] However, with the rise of kingdoms in Arabia, rulers sought to coopt shrines as a way to extend power over "the people" (conquered communities).[28] Such power, of course, presented itself as a divine mandate. For example, a pre-Islamic poem speaks of kingly power as "a grace" upon the people (*faḍl 'alā l-nās*).[29] In other words, rulers sought to establish

---

23 See also Q 22:26, which speaks of the sanctuary as being for the people equally.
24 Zayd is clearly interested in sacrifice that begets ethical community. For example, he describes the practices of his tribe as shameful, noting in particular the practice of killing infant daughters. See Ibn Hishām, *al-Sīrat al-Nabawiyya*, 1:181.
25 See Andrew Marsham, *Rituals of Monarchy: Accession and Succession in the First Muslim Empire* (Edinburgh: Edinburgh University Press, 2013), 36.
26 Marsham, *Rituals of Monarchy*, 27.
27 Marsham, *Rituals of Monarchy*, 26.
28 Marsham, *Rituals of Monarchy*, 36: "The sacred status of these places as sacred enclaves, or *ḥarams* dedicated to particular deities, where taboos prevented the shedding of blood, made them gathering-places for pilgrimages and markets. Tithes and sacrifices allowed their guardians to acquire material wealth as well as sacred charisma."
29 Marsham, *Rituals of Monarchy*, 33.

their sovereignty by reversing the purpose of shrines, which was to strengthen the well-being of the community in general, by associating their power with its divine stature.

The compilation of Ibn Hishām (d. 833), where the story of Zayd was first recorded in writing, includes extensive background on the history of the Ka'ba. Thus, just as the travel of Zayd should be read within its cultural milieu, as discussed above, so, too, it should it be read as part of a single historical narrative, as presented by Ibn Hishām. One focus of this narrative was the contestation over the meaning of the shrine in Mecca, as briefly described above, and its eventual resolution in the message of Islam.

The reports that make up the historical backstory to the rise of Islam, as told by Ibn Hishām, suggest that the shrine in Mecca was a center of pilgrimage—and also a site of contested meaning—long before Islam. It is not entirely clear whether the people of Mecca before Islam connected the Ka'ba to Abraham and his near sacrifice of his son.[30] Still, irrespective of the connection to the story of Abraham, long before Islam, the shrine represented a field of contestation between two concepts of power—one worldly, the other divine. We see this, for example, in the way the narrative frames the interest that the rulers of Yemen took in the shrine of Mecca, which they saw as part of their strategy to extend their sway over the Hijaz in Western Arabia. Their attempts to control it seem to have had the unintended effect of contributing to the centralization of shrine worship in Mecca and the eradication of minor shrines in other parts of Western Arabia. In addition, the rulers of Abysinnia had their eyes on western Arabia, making it right to see Mecca within the clash of powers that unfolded across the broader region.[31]

Within this historical context, it is important to note the rise of Judaism and the impact it likely had on the way in which the shrine in Mecca was perceived. Jewish tribes had settled in the Hijaz before the Common Era and were well-established in the Hijaz long before Islam. Their presence very likely led to the cultural localization of Judaism in Mecca, including the association of the Ka'ba with the story of Abraham and the sacrifice of his son as it had long been associated with the Temple in Jerusalem.[32] In addition, the rulers of Yemen converted to Judaism in the fourth

---

[30] See Mohsen Goudarzi, "The Ascent of Ishmael: Genealogy, Covenant, and Identity in Early Islam," *Arabica* 66 (2019): 415–84.

[31] For more background on Mecca see M.J. Kister, "Some Reports concerning Mecca from Jāhiliyya to Islam," *JESHO* 15 (1972): 61–93; Mahmood Ibrahim, "Social and Economic Conditions in Pre-Islamic Mecca," *IJMES* 14 (1982): 343–58.

[32] 2 Chr 3:1 connects the temple in Jerusalem with Mount Moriah, site of the binding of Isaac. For the ritual connection see Andrew L. Huizenga, *The New Isaac: Tradition and Intertextuality in the Gospel of Matthew* (Leiden: Brill, 2009).

century CE, thereby introducing Judaism into the power clash in the region, which included understandings of the purpose of the shrine in Mecca.

Indeed, the first of the rulers of Yemen to embrace Judaism did so in relation to his interest in controlling the shrine in Mecca.[33] The story in question is that of Abū Karib Tibān Asʿad (r. 378–430 CE), the first ruler of Yemen to convert to Judaism.[34] Abū Karib, having marched northwards to counter the forces of Byzantium in the Hijaz, set up his son as governor of the town of Yathrib, which would later become known as Medina under Islam. Its people, the narrative tells us, would kill the son of Abū Karib, who, in revenge, subdued the city. However, in the process of doing so, he came under the influence of two rabbis of Yathrib. Taking them into his entourage as counselors, he adopts Judaism. On his way back to Yemen, Abū Karib passes by Mecca. A group of its inhabitants, members of the tribe of Hudhayl, try to entice him to take the city, informing him that its shrine contains great treasure that had escaped the notice of former kings. In other words, they seek to trick him into becoming a tyrant who would elevate his own worldly power over the divine purpose of the shrine. In truth, the narrative informs us, rulers who act tyrannically (*baghā*) at the shrine are destined to be destroyed.[35]

Fortunately, the rabbis tell Abū Karib that the shrine is the House of God that Abraham built and advise him to show appropriate devotion to it, and he does so. He makes pilgrimage to the Kaʿba and offers sacrifice for "the people" (*li-l-nās*). In other words, he recognized the moral purpose for which the shrine exists, namely, the security of all. He then has the guardians of the shrine, members of the tribe of Jurhum, purify it (*taṭhīr*). He thereupon acts humbly before the shrine, recognizing it as source of divine power to which he is to submit—rather than using its power to bolster his interests. The narration confirms the point by including a poem of a woman by the name of Subayʿa Bint al-Aḥabb, which she addresses to her son, emphasizing upon him the inviolability of the shrine and the grave offense of tyranny (*baghī*) against it.[36] To summarize her words: those who act unjustly in Mecca will perish, since it is God who secures it, and so no castle (that is, worldly power) is to be built in its vicinity. Indeed, as the poem notes, the rulers of Yemen had in the past sought to attack it, seeking to clothe it in their royal hue, and so God (*rabbī*, literally, "my lord") debased their royal authority there (*adhalla mulkahu fīhā*).

---

[33] See Michael Lecker, "The Conversion of Ḥimyar to Judaism and the Jewish Banū Hadl of Medina," *WO* 26 (1995): 129–36.
[34] Ibn Hishām, *al-Sīrat al-Nabawiyya*, 1:18–25.
[35] Ibn Hishām, *al-Sīrat al-Nabawiyya*, 1:21–22.
[36] Ibn Hishām, *al-Sīrat al-Nabawiyya*, 1:23.

Abū Karib fulfills his vows, walking barefoot in the sanctuary and offering two thousand camels as sacrifice in the courtyard of the shrine. The scene recalls Solomon's inauguration of the Temple in Jerusalem as described at 1 Kings 8. Indeed, the narrative as a whole has a biblical hue: a central shrine where attempts are made to put its worship at the service of royal glory until prophets—or a couple of rabbis—arise to remind the ruler of the meaning of true worship. The pre-Islamic background to the shrine in Mecca as presented by Ibn Hishām is not quite a preparation for Islam, as the Hebrew Bible came to be seen for the gospel, but is part of a single historical narrative that includes—as a central theme—contestation over the meaning of the shrine in Mecca, a contestation that would feature at the origins of Islam and also in the tale of Zayd, as we've seen. Historical narrative here is less a record of past events and more a message to the future, as it were. To be sure, the narrative is not disconnected from actual historical developments, but the details can be elusive, and the attempt to establish them may actually miss the point, which, in our case, is the affirmation of a message about the meaning of worship, both true and false worship, and its relation to "the people," who benefit more from a blessed space and the righteousness it brings than they do from the tribal and imperial powers that would exploit it through false worship. The reports narrate a story of contestation around the main shrine in the Hijaz, a contestation that predates Islam and that includes powerful rulers, rabbinical counselors, and solitary travelers looking for a way to worship God with the righteousness of Abraham.

The narrative reaches its resolution, of course, when Muhammad establishes true worship at the Ka'ba. What needs to be emphasized is that this establishment of true worship depends not simply on having the correct creed (monotheistic belief) but more profoundly on the presence of a righteous body that makes the sacrifice righteous. Islam, in this sense, can be seen as a kind of indigenization of biblical worship in Arabia, including the focus on a righteous body, that is, a prophetic body, such as that of Ezekiel, whose body became a focus of worship after the destruction of the Temple in Jerusalem, as described at Ezekiel 4, or, more clearly, that of Jesus.

The idea is not limited to biblical worship. What is biblical is the presence of a prophetic body of a biblical kind. In the worship practices of pre-Islamic Arabia, people identified their devotions not with prophetic bodies but with the bodily representation of tribal deities, pagan idols, as a way to obtain a share in their character or power, their *baraka* (charisma).[37] Ibn Hishām's compilation includes

---

[37] The concept of blessing (*baraka*) is central to Islam, but the scholarly literature on it is surprisingly sparse. See, for example, Oliver Leaman, "Baraka," in *The Qur'an: An Encyclopedia*, ed. Oliver Leaman (New York: Routledge, 2006), 109–14; and Dietrich von Denffer, "Baraka as Basic Concept of Muslim Popular Belief," *IslSt* 15 (1976): 167–86.

a report about a man who stood by his tribe's idol after having sacrificed to it, seeking its *baraka*.[38] However, his purpose was not to grow in devotion but in wealth. As reported by Ibn Hishām, his sacrifice fails to achieve its purpose. His flock flees before the idol and scatters. He can't be blamed for the worldly nature of his worship before the idol since, after all, worldly profit was the reason for having a tribal deity, as noted above. The point to stress is the bodily nature of pre-Islamic religiosity, which continued under Islam even if with different purpose. Tribes had idols in their homes, which they would reverence with bodily contact, rubbing them when setting off on journey and returning home.[39] The bodily nature of religiosity did not change with Islam; the only difference—one of utmost importance—was that the body of ritual focus was now a prophetic body that enjoyed divine favor rather than the false body of a tribal deity as represented in idolatrous form. Thus, despite the reported association of the Ka'ba with Abraham even before Islam,[40] people seemed not to have known "the religion of Abraham" as the true worship that Zayd had set out to discover.[41]

In light of the foregoing, we are left to ask how the body of Muhammad became the body of ritual focus in Islam, rendering it true worship, and how it was materially represented. We have plenty of reports indicating that the body of Muhammad had a charismatic quality (*baraka*), enabling healing, victory in battle and a blessed death.[42] A hadith describes his cloak as healing the sick who touched it.[43] Similarly, people might rub his saliva onto their own bodies for its blessing, as if mixing his body with theirs. All of this was not mere superstition. Rather, it had ethical import. As a result of his righteousness, Muhammad was seen as uniquely embodying divine power of a kind. A blessing was expected from "taking on" his body in some fashion. A servant of his was "embalmed with a perfume . . . containing the sweat and hair of the prophet," and a companion of his "asked to be buried in a cloak that the prophet had given him and that the prophet's nail clippings be sprinkled over his eyes and into his mouth after his death" as the material representation of the prophetic blessing that would ensure divine mercy in the next life.[44]

---

38 Ibn Hishām, *al-Sīrat al-Nabawiyya*, 1:68.
39 Ibn Hishām, *al-Sīrat al-Nabawiyya*, 1:69.
40 Ibn Hishām, *al-Sīrat al-Nabawiyya*, 1:69–70.
41 Ibn Hishām, *al-Sīrat al-Nabawiyya*, 1:180.
42 See Adam Bursi, "A Hair's Breadth: The Prophet Muhammad's Hair as Relic in Early Islamic Texts," in *Religious Competition in the Greco-Roman World*, ed. Nathaniel P. DesRosiers and Lily C. Vuong (Atlanta: Society of Biblical Literature, 2016), 219–31.
43 See *Ṣaḥīḥ Muslim*, "Kitāb al-Libās wa-l-Zīna," no. 2069.
44 Bursi, "A Hair's Breadth," 224–25.

It is worth emphasizing two points here. First is Islam's adoption of the material nature of religiosity in pre-Islamic Arabia, reorienting it, however, to a prophetic body rather than a tribal idol. Second is the fact that the body of Muhammad was a conduit of the blessed status that the Qur'an attributes to Mecca. Early reports mention this explicitly, speaking, for example, of the transmission of a blessing (*baraka*) through the sweat of Muhammad.[45] Similarly, a blessing from Muhammad over a sparse meal would turn it into a banquet of abundance enough to feed the entire community.[46] Of course, it would be centuries before the relation of the prophetic body to the rest of the community, especially its saintly virtuosi, would be fully elaborated. In later writings, the bodies of righteous members of the community, living and deceased, were taken as representing the prophetic body. Their bodies were extensions of his, thereby transmitting a blessing of righteousness to local communities across the Abode of Islam.[47] The idea, while widespread, was not without controversy. Did saintly bodies have a higher ontological status of their own? Or was such status derivative, that is, realized only when the charismatic status of the saint perfectly represented the prophetic body, as evidenced in the saint's embodiment of the ethical character of the prophet? In any case, the concept—the bodily representation and transmission of the prophetic blessing to the rest of the community—was already present from the start. It should, then, be no surprise that it would continue with the saints.

Muslims, of course, do not worship the prophet, but he has long been taken as object of ritual and ethical identification. In that sense, it is the blessed status of the prophetic body that imbues worship with a prophetic righteousness.[48] Still, it remains to explain how such worship-mediated ethics transference was formulated in the first place. What was the role of the body of Muhammad in establishing true worship at the Ka'ba? On the one hand, his descent from Abraham, as narrated by the Qur'an, designated his body as a prophetic body in a biblical sense. On the other, in the one pilgrimage to the Ka'ba that Muhammad performed, known as the Farewell Pilgrimage, not long before he died, he offered animal sacrifice for the people and distributed his shaven hair and cut nails to his followers so as to trans-

---

[45] See Brannon Wheeler, "Gift of the Body in Islam: The Prophet Muhamad's Camel Sacrifice and Distribution of Hair and Nails at his Farewell Pilgrimage," *Numen* 57 (2010): 341–88 (364).
[46] al-Dārimī, *Kitāb al-Musnad al-Jāmi'*, ed. Nabīl al-Ghumarī (Beirut: Dār al-Bashā'ir al-Islāmiyya, 2013), 106.
[47] For one relatively late example see Paul L. Heck, "Finding New Life among the Dead: The Ethical Mysticism of *The Book of Pure Gold*," in *Mysticism and Ethics in Islam*, ed. Bilal Orfali, Atif Khalil, and Mohammed Rustom (Beirut: American University of Beirut, 2021), 281–300.
[48] Being imbued with a prophetic righteousness is never a onetime event but something one is always to grow in.

mit—from his body to the community—the blessing of righteousness that made worship true worship.[49] The ritual focus, then, is not only the site of the Ka'ba as "the Place of Abraham" (*maqām Ibrāhīm*). Even if the physical body of the prophet lies in his grave in Medina, his body has ritual purpose. This took different forms. Initially, as just described, the righteous body of the prophet, needed for worship to be true worship, was extended to others through bodily relics, such as his hair and nails. Later, ritual identification with the prophetic character of righteousness would be realized not only by bodily contact with relics but more so by bodily imitation of Muhammad's ritual actions as set out in the prophetic texts and also by devotional hymns of praise of the prophet.[50]

Did this ritual gesture of Muhammad amount to a bodily sacrifice, rendering his worship a mirror image of that of Abraham—or at least of his son? In other words, did the bodily relics of Muhammad that featured in his only act of worship at the Ka'ba serve to identify his body ritually with that of the son of Abraham whose near sacrifice, according to Islam, took place at the Ka'ba? There is a well-known tradition that the body of Ishmael is buried at the Ka'ba.[51] In addition, Muhammad apparently referred to himself as scion of the two figures who were called the sacrifice of God (*dhabīḥ allāh*).[52] The first is Ishmael son of Abraham, the second the prophet's own father, 'Abdallah Ibn 'Abd al-Muṭṭalib, whose father, 'Abd al-Muṭṭalib, nearly sacrificed him as a result of a vow he had made.[53] Despite the prophet's descent from each "sacrifice of God," more compelling evidence is needed to conclude that Muhammad saw his offering at the Farewell Pilgrimage as a sacrificial offering of his own body for his community. Still, while he may not have intended to represent his body ritually as a sacrifice (and certainly not to atone for the community's sinfulness), he did present his offering—shaven hair and cut nails—as the bodily representation of the blessing of prophetic righteousness that makes

---

49 See Wheeler, "Gift of the Body in Islam," 341–88. For some details on the historical background to sacrifice and pilgrimage in Mecca see Brannon Wheeler, "Sacrifice and Pilgrimage: Body Politics and the Origins of Muslim Pilgrimage," in *Muslim Pilgrimage in the Modern World*, ed. Babak Rahimi and Peyman Eshagi (Durham: University of North Carolina Press, 2019), 49–67.
50 See Suzanne Pinckney Setkevych, *The Mantle Odes: Arabic Praise Poems to the Prophet Muhammad* (Bloomington: Indiana University Press, 2010).
51 However, while it is widely held by Muslims today that Ishmael, not Isaac, was the son to be sacrificed, the matter was not at all clear among the early qur'anic commentators. See Reuven Firestone, "Abraham's Son as the Intended Sacrifice (*al-Dhabīḥ*, Qur'ān 37:99–113): Issues in Qur'ānic Exegesis," *JSS* 34 (1989): 95–131.
52 The prophet is asked about his being called "son of the two sacrifices" at Ibn Kathīr, *Tafsīr*, ad Q 37:107, which is the qur'anic verse that recounts Abraham's "great sacrifice" as God's redemption of his son.
53 Ibn Hishām, *al-Sīrat al-Nabawiyya*, 1:124–27.

worship true worship.⁵⁴ As noted above, in addition to offering animal sacrifice, he distributed bodily relics to the community as if a means for them to identify their bodies with his. Performed by a righteous descendent of Abraham, Muhammad's "bodily" worship at the Ka'ba was ritually associated with the worship of Abraham, identifying it as true worship.⁵⁵

It is worth recalling that Zayd Ibn 'Amr did not know the ways of true worship at the Ka'ba, despite being aware of its association with Abraham. This point remains enigmatic. How did the people of Mecca, despite knowing of their own descent from Abraham and the association of the Ka'ba with his legacy, not perform worship at the Ka'ba as he did?⁵⁶ All we can say is that knowledge is not enough. That is, a simple instruction manual would not have done the job. As discussed earlier, a righteousness beyond tribal partisanship is also required. To achieve that purpose, one needed a figure with the blessed status of Muhammad, capable of renewing the worship of Abraham at the Ka'ba with the required prophetic righteousness. Without such a figure, Zayd, who did not know Muhammad, was left without a way to worship at the Ka'ba despite his own devotion to it.⁵⁷

In sum, Zayd's travel in search of a way to perform worship at the Ka'ba according to the religion of Abraham suggests that biblical worship, whereby the sacrificial offering of Abraham was the mark of ethically effective ritual, was unknown during Zayd's lifetime—or had been forgotten.⁵⁸ It was this worship that Muham-

---

54 It is worth noting that the idea of atonement (*kaffāra*) is still strongly associated with the pilgrimage rituals in Mecca. See Marion Katz, "The Ḥajj and the Study of Islamic Ritual," *StIsl* 98/99 (2004): 95–129.
55 It is also worth mentioning the poetry in praise of Muhammad during his own lifetime, most famously by Ḥassān Ibn Thābit (d. 674). In one of his poems, he calls Muhammad "blessed" (*mubārak*), the very term that the Qurʾan uses for the shrine in Mecca. See Badr al-Dīn al-Ḥāḍirī, ed., *Ḥassān Ibn Thābit al-Anṣārī*, 2nd ed. (Beirut: Dār al-Sharq al-ʿArabī, 1998), 10, line 25, where Muhammad is also called righteous (*barr*), a ritually significant term. In other words, it is due to the blessed status of the shrine and its prophetic mediator that ritual is ethically effective, that is, that it imbues devotees with a share in prophetic righteousness.
56 The traditional view, represented by Ibn al-Kalbī (*Book of Idols*), is that the religion of Abraham in Mecca had become corrupted over time as people began associating their tribal deities as partners with the God of Abraham.
57 Of course, if Zayd was so devoted to true worship, it could be asked why he did not play the role of the righteous figure whose bodily presence as ritual focus makes worship true worship. In this regard, when asked about Zayd, Muhammad says that he is in paradise, calling him a religious community of his own. Ibn Hishām, *al-Sīrat al-Nabawiyya*, 1:181.
58 For Muslims, Muhammad did not establish but rather restored the worship of Abraham at the Ka'ba. For a scholarly defense of this idea see Khalil Athamina, "Abraham in Islamic Perspective: Reflections on the Development of Monotheism in Pre-Islamic Arabia," *Der Islam* 81 (2004): 184–205.

mad sought to renew as his primary goal, his message of monotheism being secondary to that goal since, again, the peoples of Arabia were not unaware of monotheism. Against the backdrop of the story of Zayd, it becomes possible to see more clearly that pilgrimage to Mecca involved not only travel to a site but also orientation to a prophetic body, that of Muhammad, descendant of Abraham, as the essential element of ethically effective performance of ritual. For this reason, the Qur'an depicts the two—Muhammad and Abraham—with similar language. Both are comely models (Q al-Aḥzāb 33:21 and al-Mumtaḥana 60:4), and both are called Muslims (Q 3:67; al-An'ām 6:163; al-Zumar 39:12). Elsewhere, both are called the Friend of God (khalīl allāh).[59] Such language, we now see, has ritual significance. Bereft of such ritual knowhow, Zayd had to travel in search of it.

Before concluding, it will be useful to offer a glimpse into the narrative of pious travel in Islam, as explored so far, as it unfolds in later centuries. Travel in Islam has meant many things. Pilgrimage to Mecca is central, but the travelogues of pilgrims show variety. Some serve as a guidebook—how to get to Mecca and perform a ritually correct pilgrimage. Others shows a humanistic side, including reports of the pilgrim's interactions with scholars and rulers along the way. In what follows, we look at only two cases that recall the tale of Zayd as a journey in search of true worship. Even if the final destination in the two cases we consider below is known in advance, namely, Mecca, their journeys still include the sense of searching for evidence of true worship, not simply at the shrine in Mecca but, rather, throughout the varied communities that make up the Abode of Islam as the spatial extension of the Ka'ba as its ritual center. In other words, they're not only traveling on pilgrimage to Mecca but also in search of evidence of the blessing of righteousness in the Abode of Islam as mark of its religious integrity.

Both travelogues, as we will see, involve the theme of blessing, as evidenced in righteous behavior and righteous order throughout the wider community of Muslims. Oddly, despite the centrality of the concept of blessing to Islam, there are no comprehensive studies on its history and the nuances it has taken over the centuries. The two cases considered below suggest both continuity and variety. In echo of early Islam as discussed above, blessing in these two cases is tied to the mani-

---

[59] It is well-known that Abraham is called the Friend of God in the Qur'an (Q al-Nisā' 4:125) but less well-known that Muhammad is, too, not in the Qur'an, but in a hadith that says that God took him as friend just as God took Abraham as friend. See Ṣaḥīḥ Muslim, "Kitāb al-Masājid wa-Mawāḍi' al-Ṣalāt," no. 532. The reason why this title for Muhammad is less well-known may have something to do with his title as the Beloved of God, which seems to have superseded the former title. Some commentators, however, suggest that Friend of God is more specific than Beloved of God and therefore a higher honor. The reference to Abraham as Friend of God in Jas 2:21–23 includes mention of his sacrifice. Is this what Muhammad had in mind in using the title for himself?

festation of righteousness across the Abode of Islam and not only at the shrine in Mecca; blessing at these later time periods, as in Islam at its beginnings, continued to be understood in relation to a righteous body, that of the prophet as mediated through his saintly successors.

The author of the first travelogue, Aḥmad Ṭuwayr al-Janna (1787–1849) from Mauritania, makes the connection explicitly: the manifestation of righteousness, as he witnesses it in his travels, is the fruit of the prophetic blessing, which he sees as the central aspect of the journey to Mecca. In other words, his travel is not just physical movement. The entire journey is a ritual venture. The ritual aspect of the journey is, then, not limited to the prescribed acts of pilgrimage that one performs upon arriving to Mecca. The author of the second travelogue, Abū Sālim ʿAbdullah al-ʿAyyāshī (1628–1679) from Morocco, looks to the manifestation of the prophetic blessing in varied places, including the way in which commercial and political business conforms to the sharīʿa, in hymns of praise to Muhammad, and, most notably, in saintly shrines as local expressions of the divine power that extends via the prophetic body to the rest of the community especially through the bodies of its most righteous members, living and deceased.[60]

In the travelogue of Aḥmad Ṭuwayr al-Janna,[61] the prophetic blessing features prominently in the hospitality with which the pilgrims are received by people along the way. By housing and feeding the pilgrims as a show of religious solidarity, one receives a share in the prophetic blessing that the pilgrims will receive as a result of their ritual journey. Failing to show such hospitality is not simply a transgression of local cultural custom. It constitutes a much graver offense, a failure of the righteousness that is supposed to be the distinguishing mark of the Abode of Islam. The result of such a failure, the absence of righteousness, is evidence of being deprived of the prophetic blessing with real consequences. There is, then, a prophetic ethics that is to prevail across the Abode of Islam, that yields a blessing which all believers should desire, and that is ultimately grounded in the blessedness of the prophetic body that validates worship at the shrine in Mecca.

By way of example, soon after Ṭuwayr al-Janna and his fellow pilgrims depart from Mauritania, he relates the kindness (*iḥsān*) shown to them by the elders in the various places where they encamp. He draws attention to one particular expe-

---

[60] For travel connecting the Islamic West and Islamic East see Maribel Fierro and Mayte Penelas, eds., *The Maghrib in the Mashriq: Knowledge, Travel and Identity* (Berlin: De Gruyter, 2021). For one study on the theme of travel in literature from the Islamic West see July Scott Blalack, "Travel Inside and Outside: Maghribi Resistance as a Literary Force" (PhD diss., SOAS University of London, 2021).

[61] Aḥmad Ṭuwayr al-Janna, *Riḥlat al-Munā wa-l-Minna*, ed. Ḥamāhu Allāh Wuld Sālim (Beirut: Dār al-Kutub al-ʿIlmiyya, 2012).

rience without identifying the place. At first, its elder agrees to put them up only for pay, as if it's simply a contractual matter, but over the course of their stay, he is increasingly charitable. When they depart, there's no mention of pay. Ṭuwayr al-Janna credits the change to the impact of the prophetic blessing,[62] the ultimate cause of all righteousness operative in the Abode of Islam.

Another example, a negative one this time, comes from Taroudant in the south of Morocco. Ṭuwayr al-Janna speaks of the leader of the town and his vizier, implying members of the governing class.[63] They fail to show the hospitality due to pilgrims. On the return journey, Ṭuwayr al-Janna hears that only a month or two after their departure from Taroudant, its leader had been imprisoned, presumably for corruption, and the vizier killed in his sleep by his own slaves, presumably in revenge for his ill treatment of them. Ṭuwayr al-Janna reports that his slaves killed him in the name of a local saint famous for his blessing (*baraka*). The point of the narrative is clear: If you neglect "the guests of God's messenger," you'll lose his blessing with tragic consequences. We should not read this story simply as a version of "what goes around comes around." The causality at play is that of the prophetic blessing, which is what enables pilgrims to reach their destination in Mecca, because people are keen not simply to assist them but, more specifically, to share in the prophetic blessing that pilgrims receive and thereby embody in a special way as a result of their travel to Mecca.

According to the logic of Ṭuwayr al-Janna, it is because people want a share in the prophetic blessing that they help pilgrims advance on the journey. (Again, righteous action is due to the prophetic blessing.) The image that comes to mind is that of a vibrant economy of hospitality, revolving around the prophetic blessing. Those who fail to participate in it are cut off from its benefits. Not unlike the contestation over the shrine in Mecca in pre-Islamic Arabia, here, too, "the blessed economy" is set against the metrics of worldly power as represented by the likes of the officials of Taroudant who didn't understand the metrics of righteousness as the fruit of the prophetic blessing, and so they failed to be hospitable.

The vision of Ṭuwayr al-Janna is that of a civilization pulsating with the righteousness of prophetic ethics as enacted in gestures of kindness, perfectly embodied in saintly figures. Of course, this divine power is also quick to exact vengeance on those who fail to meet expectations of kindness (*iḥsān*) as expression of Islam's righteousness (i.e., putting religion before worldly interests). Indeed, such vengeance is appropriate. It's not a personal vendetta but actually defense of the common good (recalling the qur'anic association of the shrine in Mecca with "the

---

62 al-Janna, *Riḥlat al-Munā wa-l-Minna*, 29.
63 al-Janna, *Riḥlat al-Munā wa-l-Minna*, 33.

people"). The local order holds together not by power but by righteousness, allowing people to trust one another, trust being the key to a prosperous society. Ṭuwayr al-Janna is, then, not just traveling in a physical sense. His journey is a witness to the ethical character of the Abode of Islam, which he dramatizes with a contrast of positive and negative examples of character. This contrast was also seen in the tale of Zayd, where his own tribe represented the negative example, as seen in the spirit of tyranny and pride that was the fruit of their false worship, while Zayd, like Ṭuwayr al-Janna, travelling in search of righteousness as the fruit of true worship, represented the positive example.

In the travelogue of Ṭuwayr al-Janna, worldly power, it should be noted, is not condemned outright, only when it is disordered, that is, when it fails to conform to the blessed economy. For example, when Ṭuwayr al-Janna meets the Sultan of Morocco ʿAbd al-Raḥmān (r. 1822–1859), he is struck by his hospitality and humility, which he credits to the power of the prophetic blessing that defines his character and his rule. In other words, power is rightly sovereign when it conforms to the blessed economy.[64] In short, right political order flows from right ritual order, as Ṭuwayr al-Janna sees in the sultan's goodness, recalling the tale of Zayd, who broke not with the Kaʿba but with worship that was not righteously oriented to the well-being of "the people."[65]

The theme of the prophetic blessing bringing success to travelers is consistent throughout the travelogue of Ṭuwayr al-Janna. The blessing is not about a bargain (*do ut des*), devotion in exchange for success. Rather, it is the mark of the ethical integrity—the righteousness—of the community of Muslims. Ṭuwayr al-Janna also speaks of the saintly blessing as cause of success, but it's clear that all blessing, including that of the saint, is foregrounded in the blessedness of the prophet. It is worth noting that when he arrives to Medina, site of the prophetic body, he recalls a saying that he attributes to Muhammad: "Whoever visits me, I guarantee for him the acceptance of the pilgrimage."[66] I have not been able to find this statement in any hadith collection. However, it recalls the idea discussed earlier, namely, that worship is righteous when it is oriented by the bodily presence of a righteous person. Visiting the prophetic grave before the Kaʿba fulfills that role, enabling the acceptance of one's pilgrimage by God.

The lengthy travelogue of al-ʿAyyāshī, seventeenth-century Moroccan scholar, on his experiences to and from Mecca is called *Water of the Tables* or, simply, *The*

---

[64] al-Janna, *Riḥlat al-Munā wa-l-Minna*, 46ff.
[65] It is worth noting that in Arabic blessing (*baraka*) is defined as the constancy of goodness (*thubūt al-khayr*).
[66] al-Janna, *Riḥlat al-Munā wa-l-Minna*, 131–32.

Journey of al-ʿAyyāshī.⁶⁷ The work has different aspects. It details the order of travel and also describes the author's engagement with local dignitaries of various kinds. A main goal—perhaps the main goal—is to document the workings of the prophetic blessing in the Abode of Islam (or their absence). On the one hand, al-ʿAyyāshī focuses not infrequently on the power attached to the shrines of saints, as if they have their own blessed status, but a close reading shows that he foregrounds all instantiations of blessing in the prophet's blessedness. Early in the work, he explains that hymns in praise of the prophet remove all obstacles and smooths all roads in front of the pilgrim.⁶⁸ Indeed, he offers a straightforward definition of blessing as imitating the prophetic example (*baraka imtithāl al-sunna*).⁶⁹ Thus, while the shrines of the saint are depicted as sacred institutions in their local societies, the blessings that issue from them originate in Muhammad.

What is the nature of the blessing that issues from the shrines of the saints? On the one hand, the blessing is a function of the righteousness of the saint occupying the shrine, which is itself the extension of prophetic righteousness, but when requesting a blessing at the shrine, the petitioners were not necessarily seeking growth only in devotion. For example, al-ʿAyyāshī describes a visit to the shrine of Sīdī ʿAbdallāh al-Daqqāq in Sijilmasa. He and his fellow pilgrims, pressed for time, had left aside other shrines but could not pass over this one because "its blessing had appeared" (*ẓaharat barakatuhu*).⁷⁰ What this odd phrase means is that the blessing of the shrine had been proven by experience. People had turned to it with their desires and were answered. While the text doesn't give details, the literature of the period suggests a range of petitions—healing for a sick person, the return of one long absent, success in business or education, increase in wealth, a good marriage, or the birth of child. Of course, the material and the spiritual form a single fabric in this context. Thus, such "worldly" requests might be woven together with spiritual purpose. For example, one might request the birth of a child with the aim of raising him or her in righteousness before God, while another might request increased devotion and nothing more. Similarly, one might ask for a blessing from the saintly inhabitant of the shrine to memorize the Qurʾan or for "spiritual victory" whereby one experiences immersion in the divine presence. The blessing might be realized through a dream or even by supernatural means. In sum, the shrine is a place of divine power, which exists not only to care for the people but also to

---

67 Abū Sālim ʿAbdallah al-ʿAyyāshī, *al-Riḥla al-ʿAyyāshiyya*, ed. Saʿīd al-Fāḍilī and Sulaymān al-Qurashī (Abu Dhabi: Dār al-Suwaydī li-l-Nashr wa-l-Tawzīʿ, 2006).
68 al-ʿAyyāshī, *al-Riḥla al-ʿAyyāshiyya*, 59.
69 al-ʿAyyāshī, *al-Riḥla al-ʿAyyāshiyya*, 67.
70 al-ʿAyyāshī, *al-Riḥla al-ʿAyyāshiyya*, 72.

ensure that worldly power not glory in itself (recalling the story of Abū Karib, ruler of Yemen, as earlier discussed).

For example, at one point in the narrative, the caravan in which al-ʿAyyāshī is travelling alights in a town in Libya, Zliten, about 160 kilometers east of Tripoli. He uses the opportunity to describe what he sees as the most notable feature of the town, namely, the shrine of a sixteenth-century saint by the name of ʿAbd al-Salām al-Asmar (d. 1575), renowned for his ability, when alive, to subdue local tyrants and redeem hostages from the Crusaders; he reportedly continued to have effect on the people of Zliten long after he had passed from this world.[71] As part of his description of the saint, al-ʿAyyāshī mentions his town of origin, al-Fawātir, about a parasang's distance from his shrine in Zliten. That town, al-ʿAyyāshī explains, has from distant times been inhabited by righteous worshippers. Indeed, the town has always been home to seven of the world's most righteous people, who cannot be distinguished from others by their clothing or profession but who are guardians of the shariʿa, that is, custodians of the religious integrity of the town. Because of this, God smashes anyone who seeks to do ill to the people of the town (*ahl al-balda*, recalling "the people" for whom the shrine in Mecca was established). More specifically, as al-ʿAyyāshī relates, anyone who rules tyrannically over the people will be humiliated by God (*adhallahu allāh*, the very language used in the reports of Ibn Hishām to describe what would happen to rulers who attacked the shrine in Mecca).

In other words, the presence of these holy bodies in the town ensures God's intended order for the world. In illustration, al-ʿAyyāshī narrates a story about a potentate by the name of ʿAbd al-Ḥafīẓ (it is not clear who he is). Whenever he would visit the town with his retinue, he would descend from his horse before entering it, conducting his visit on foot in a state of humility (recalling the story of Abū Karib). He is reported to have said that he would fear for his life were he to enter the town as one to be followed (i.e., as a potentate). It is remarkable how closely the story follows the ancient contestation around the shrine in Mecca. The association of the righteous body with the shrine is vital not only to guarantee against the perversion of worship but also against the perversion of power.

In both cases, seventeenth-century Libya and pre-Islamic Arabia, the holiness of the shrine restrains worldly power, thus serving as a blessing for the people. Indeed, in the view of al-ʿAyyāshī, shrines are guarantors of justice in society. This is seen by negative no less than positive examples. He criticizes the various forms of corruption that he witnesses throughout the cities of the Abode of Islam over the course of his travels: arbitrary rule in Mamluk Cairo, the selling of offices in

---

[71] al-ʿAyyāshī, *al-Riḥla al-ʿAyyāshiyya*, 184.

Ottoman Medina, and the bribery at sway over court verdicts.[72] This was not the order that Islam had come to establish. These comments on corruption serve as negative examples of God's intended order, now within the Abode of Islam, risking its standing with God.

We thus see with al-ʿAyyāshī what we saw with Zayd. They both break with the unrighteousness of the day while turning to travel with both ritual and ethical purpose. In the case of Zayd, there is no possibility of a prophetic blessing since he precedes the prophetic mission of Muhammad, the progeny of Abraham, but he travels in search of true worship. In this sense, his tale represents one point in a trajectory that includes not only Abū Karib and the Qur'an but also al-ʿAyyāshī and Ṭuwayr al-Janna many centuries later—and so many others whose travel in search of righteousness directs them towards shrines as centers of a power that is divine yet represented by a human body that is known to be undeniably righteous.

In conclusion, when it comes to travel in Islam, as in other traditions, we are faced with the question of continuity. Can we say that travel in Islam, across the centuries, has a single meaning? Certainly, the travel experiences of the various figures who feature in this article, from late antiquity to the modern period, cannot be reduced to a single type. Nevertheless, there is a pattern. Each case needs to be studied in its own context, but common themes, even terms, recur from one period to another. Our tale of Zayd Ibn ʿAmr is hardly the apex of this centuries-long narrative, but it does offer insight into what is at stake when it comes to the meaning of travel in Islam, especially when such meaning was not clearly spelled out in the Qur'an. Travel here, as exemplified by the story of Zayd, is the search for true worship—for evidence of a ritual order that brings about a righteous order of benefit for all.

References

Ådna, Gerd Marie. *Muhammad and the Formation of Sacrifice*. Bern: Lang, 2014.
Athamina, Khalil. "Abraham in Islamic Perspective: Reflections on the Development of Monotheism in Pre-Islamic Arabia." *Der Islam* 81 (2004): 184–205.
al-ʿAyyāshī, Abū Sālim ʿAbdallah. *al-Riḥla al-ʿAyyāshiyya*. Edited by Saʿīd al-Fāḍilī and Sulaymān al-Qurashī. Abu Dhabi: Dār al-Suwaydī li-l-Nashr wa-l-Tawzīʿ, 2006.

---

[72] See Abderrahmane El Moudden, "The Ambivalence of *riḥla*: Community Integration and Self-Definition in Moroccan Travel Accounts, 1300–1800," in *Muslim Travellers: Pilgrimage, Migration, and the Religious Imagination*, ed. Dale F. Eickelman and James Piscatori (New York: Routledge, 1990), 69–84 (esp. 76–79).

Blalack, July Scott. "Travel Inside and Outside: Maghribi Resistance as a Literary Force." PhD diss., SOAS University of London, 2021.
Block, C. Jonn. *The Qur'an in Christian-Muslim Dialogue*. New York: Routledge, 2014.
Bursi, Adam. "A Hair's Breadth: The Prophet Muhammad's Hair as Relic in Early Islamic Texts." Pages 219–31 in *Religious Competition in the Greco-Roman World*. Edited by Nathaniel P. DesRosiers and Lily C. Vuong. Atlanta: Society of Biblical Literature, 2016.
Cheikho, Louis, ed. *Shu'arā' al-Naṣrāniyya Qabla al-Islām*. 4th ed. Beirut: Dār al-Mashriq, 1991.
al-Dārimī. *Kitāb al-Musnad al-Jāmi'*. Edited by Nabīl al-Ghumarī. Beirut: Dār al-Bashā'ir al-Islāmiyya, 2013.
Dmitriev, Kirill. "An Early Christian Arabic Account of the Creation of the World." Pages 349–87 in *The Qur'ān in Context: Historical and Literary Investigations into the Qur'ānic Milieu*. Edited by Angelika Neuwirth, Nicolai Sinai, and Michael Marx. Leiden: Brill, 2010.
El Moudden, Abderrahmane. "The Ambivalence of *rihla*: Community Integration and Self-Definition in Moroccan Travel Accounts, 1300–1800." Pages 69–84 in *Muslim Travellers: Pilgrimage, Migration, and the Religious Imagination*. Edited by Dale F. Eickelman and James Piscatori. New York: Routledge, 1990.
Fierro, Maribel, and Mayte Penelas, eds. *The Maghrib in the Mashriq: Knowledge, Travel and Identity*. Berlin: De Gruyter, 2021.
Firestone, Reuven. "Abraham's Son as the Intended Sacrifice (*al-Dhabīḥ*, Qur'ān 37:99–113): Issues in Qur'ānic Exegesis." *JSS* 34 (1989): 95–131.
Gericke, Jaco. *The Hebrew Bible and Philosophy of Religion*. Atlanta: Society of Biblical Literature, 2012.
Goudarzi, Mohsen. "The Ascent of Ishmael: Genealogy, Covenant, and Identity in Early Islam." *Arabica* 66 (2019): 415–84.
Grasso, Valentina A. *Pre-Islamic Arabia: Societies, Politics, Cults, and Identities during Late Antiquity*. Cambridge: Cambridge University Press, 2023.
Guillaume, Alfred, trans., *The Life of Muhammad: A Translation of Isḥāq's* Sīrat Rasūl Allāh. Oxford: Oxford University Press, 1955.
al-Ḥāḍirī, Badr al-Dīn, ed. *Ḥassān Ibn Thābit al-Anṣārī*. 2nd ed. Beirut: Dār al-Sharq al-'Arabī, 1998.
Hahn, Johannes, and Volker Menze, eds. *The Wandering Holy Man: The Life of Barsauma, Christian Asceticism, and Religious Conflict in Late Antique Palestine*. Oakland: University of California Press, 2020.
Hatke, George, and Ronald Ruzicka, eds. *South Arabian Long-Distance Trade in Antiquity: "Out of Arabia"*. Newcastle: Cambridge Scholars Publishing, 2021.
Heck, Paul L. "Paul and Muhammad: The Challenge of the Convert." *IslChr* 37 (2011): 127–43.
Heck, Paul L. "Finding New Life among the Dead: The Ethical Mysticism of *The Book of Pure Gold*." Pages 281–300 in *Mysticism and Ethics in Islam*. Edited by Bilal Orfali, Atif Khalil, and Mohammed Rustom. Beirut: American University of Beirut, 2021.
Huizenga, Andrew L. *The New Isaac: Tradition and Intertextuality in the Gospel of Matthew*. Leiden: Brill, 2009.
Ibn Hishām. *al-Sīrat al-Nabawiyya*. Edited by Muṣṭafā al-Saqā, Ibrāhīm al-Abyārī, and 'Abd al-Ḥafīẓ Shalabī. 2nd ed. 4 vols. Beirut: Dār al-Khabar, 1995.
Ibrahim, Mahmood. "Social and Economic Conditions in Pre-Islamic Mecca." *IJMES* 14 (1982): 343–58.
al-Iṣfahānī, Abū al-Faraj. *Kitāb al-Aghānī*. 25 vols. Beirut: Dār Iḥyā' al-Turāth al-'Arabī, 1994.
al-Jāḥiẓ. *Kitāb al-'Uthmāniyya*. Edited by 'Abd al-Salām Muḥammad Hārūn. Beirut: Dār al-Jīl, 1991.
Katz, Marion. "The Ḥajj and the Study of Islamic Ritual." *StIsl* 98/99 (2004): 95–129.
Kister, M.J. "Some Reports concerning Mecca from Jāhiliyya to Islam." *JESHO* 15 (1972): 61–93.

Leaman, Oliver. "Baraka." Pages 109–14 in *The Qur'an: An Encyclopedia*. Edited by Oliver Leaman. New York: Routledge, 2006.
Lecker, Michael. "The Conversion of Ḥimyar to Judaism and the Jewish Banū Hadl of Medina." *WO* 26 (1995): 129–36.
Marsham, Andrew. *Rituals of Monarchy: Accession and Succession in the First Muslim Empire*. Edinburgh: Edinburgh University Press, 2013.
al-Sayf, ʿUmar Ibn ʿAbdallah. *Bunyat al-Riḥla fī al-Qaṣīda al-Jāhiliyya*. Beirut: Muʾassasat al-Intishār al-ʿArabī, 2009.
Sirry, Munʿim. "The Early Development of the Qurʾanic *Ḥanīf*." *JSS* 56 (2011): 345–66.
Stetkevych, Suzanne Pinckney. *The Mantle Odes: Arabic Praise Poems to the Prophet Muhammad*. Indiana University Press: Bloomington, 2010.
Ṭuwayr al-Janna, Aḥmad. *Riḥlat al-Munā wa-l-Minna*. Edited by Ḥamāhu Allāh Wuld Sālim. Beirut: Dār al-Kutub al-ʿIlmiyya, 2012.
Von Denffer, Dietrich. "Baraka as Basic Concept of Muslim Popular Belief." *IslSt* 15 (1976): 167–86.
Wheeler, Brannon. "Gift of the Body in Islam: The Prophet Muhamad's Camel Sacrifice and Distribution of Hair and Nails at his Farewell Pilgrimage." *Numen* 57 (2010): 341–88.
Wheeler, Brannon. "Sacrifice and Pilgrimage: Body Politics and the Origins of Muslim Pilgrimage." Pages 49–67 in *Muslim Pilgrimage in the Modern World*. Edited by Babak Rahimi and Peyman Eshagi. Durham: University of North Carolina Press, 2019.

Reuven Kiperwasser and Serge Ruzer
Nautical Fiction of Late Antiquity: Jews and Christians Traveling by Sea

Abstract: The storms threatening ancient sea-travelers were traditionally supposed to be a sign of divine displeasure. The marine voyage with its tempests, famously featuring in the Jonah story, also became a well-known topos in Greco-Roman storytelling. This essay investigates how some Jewish and Christian narrators reworked that topos in light of their particular religious agendas. Their tales thus turn out to be hybrid creatures composed of both biblical and mythological patterns of narration. Several such mythological patterns can be discerned in late antique sea travelogues, including divine intervention calming a stormy tempest; wondrous birds coming to sailors' rescue; and treasure hidden in the depth of the sea, guarded by a monstrous creature. Our study focuses on the final motif, with the texts under discussion mostly originating in the Syro-Mesopotamian Aramaic-speaking cultural sphere—Jewish rabbinic and Syriac Christian milieus. For all our narrators, the sea maintained its perilous appeal and the voyages provided a meaningful liminal experience that challenged their religious outlook. We outline a variety of strategies in dealing with the tension inherent in the sea adventure, some of them tailored to temper the mythic tenor of the background tradition.

Introduction

If a sea traveler survives tempestuous waters, he is fortunate indeed to arrive in the safe haven of the harbor. Along the way, he encounters the marvels of the sea. Storms are supposed to be a sign of divine displeasure, and the adventures of the biblical prophet Jonah cast a long shadow on the narratives created by both Jews and Christians in Late Antiquity.[1] The marine voyage, with its dramatic outbreak of tempest, was also a well-known topos in Greco-Roman storytelling, as exemplified

---

[1] See discussion in Reuven Kiperwasser and Serge Ruzer, "Sea Voyages Tales in Conversation with the Jonah Story: Intertextuality and the Art of Narrative Bricolage," *Journeys* 20 (2019): 39–57.

Note: This study was conducted as part of an ongoing project on Late Antique Christian and Jewish Travel Narratives: Patterns and Strategies of Intercultural Exchange (№ 755/20) under the auspices of the Israel Science Foundation.

in the mythological encounters of Odysseus during his travels.² Jewish and Christian narrators sometimes invoked that topos, reworking it in accordance with their particular religious agendas. Such narratives, then, while supplying a challenging liminal experience, are hybrid creatures composed of both biblical and mythological patterns of narration.

We can identify several such adopted—and adapted—mythological patterns, including divine intervention calming a stormy tempest; wondrous birds coming to sailors' rescue; and treasure hidden in the depth of the sea, guarded by a monstrous creature.³ This study focuses on the final motif, with the texts under discussion mostly originating in the Syro-Mesopotamian Aramaic-speaking cultural sphere—Jewish rabbinic and Syriac Christian milieus. Differences among the texts notwithstanding, in all of them the sea represents the chaos that is absorbed, according to the mythical worldview, by the universe. It is possible to discern several strategies to deal with the tension inherent in the liminal sea adventure, some of them, along the way, dissipate the mythic flavor of the background tradition. We will see that, with some overlap among the strategies, a distinguishing Jewish motif stands out: the sea as a storage place for treasure destined to play a foundational role during the eschatological era.

The stories we will deal with belong to the well-known genre of "sailors' yarn." Analyzing its attestations in *The Odyssey*, Robert Foulke suggests that

> [They] represent a specialized type of folktale; they spin exaggerations around a core of sea reality, and they share the fluidity of the oral tradition. They are outlandish only in the sense that they build around places that are new and strange, and that realm includes everything beyond the Aegean and Ionian seas known to Greek seafarers in the era of the epic's composition.⁴

---

2 Robert Foulke, *The Sea Voyage Narrative* (Milton Park: Routledge, 2001), 33, 40, 58.
3 See Reuven Kiperwasser and Serge Ruzer, "Aramaic Stories of Wandering in the High Seas of Late Antiquity," in *The Past Through Narratology: New Approaches to Late Antiquity and the Early Middle Ages*, ed. Mateusz Fafinski and Jakob Riemenschneider, Das Mittelalter Beihefte 18 (Heidelberg: Heidelberg University Publishing, 2022), 161–77.
4 Foulke, *The Sea Voyage Narrative*, 54. He is adding there that "[o]nly the first episode of the wanderings—the raid on the Cicones—deals with fully human beings; in the rest, Odysseus and his crews encounter beasts or monsters, immortals, sorcerers, or gods—the stuff of a good yarn. Magic substances and talismans abound, from the intoxicating lotus and the spell that transforms men into swine to the veil that saves Odysseus from drowning." Denys Page (*Folktales in Homer's "Odyssey"* [Cambridge: Harvard University Press, 1973], 74, 76), noting that Aeolus is not divine, ascribes the bag of winds "not to folklore but to life, a particular sphere of life in which magical arts are commonly employed." He, however, also reminds us that *The Golden Bough* by James G. Frazer "documents 50 examples of wind magic, many of them from European sources." See also Foulke, *The Sea Voyage Narrative*, 54.

While the pagan background tradition is most interested in meeting fabulous creatures in the form of monsters and gods, we will highlight, as noted, the motif of a treasure hidden in the depth of the sea, featuring prominently in rabbinic and Syriac Christian tales.

We hope to show that the sea adventure narratives under discussion aim to adjust the traditional sailors' yarn tales to their new religious discourse. Yet, in addition to demonstrating such adjustment strategies, Late Antique Jewish and Christian sources also seem to reflect underlying shared myths. As such, they may nuance our picture of the mythological perceptions of the sea.[5]

Alongside a perhaps universal enchantment with the wonders of the watery abyss, narrators send their protagonists on the high seas in order to test—and eventually confirm and amplify—their cherished religious values. It thus makes sense, in our context, to go beyond classical narratology, which is mainly concerned with the synchronic dimension of the poetics of narrative, to an interdisciplinary angle. Therefore, we will emphasize the changing form and function of narrative patterns and the dialogical negotiation of meaning, pointing to issues of cultural context.[6]

Many of the late antique texts discussed below come from Mesopotamia, a terrestrial region far removed from the sea. One might speculate that the inhabitants of those inland areas, for whom the maritime depths was but a vague notion, were particularly prone to embracing mythological models of the water. Christians and Jews alike may have inherited the imagined contours of a vast threatening space teeming with marvelous creatures and mysterious treasures.

Eschatological Storeroom of Precious Stones

Some of the Babylonian rabbinic sailor yarns originated on the shores of Roman Palestine. Thus, our first example of such stories comes from a source from the Land of Israel. It is already there that we witness the motif of a precious stone stored in the depths of the sea and carefully kept for a specific use in the hereafter.

שמתי כדכוד (ישעיה נד: יב). ר' אבא בר כהנא א' כדין וכדין. ר' לוי אמר כדכדיינון. ר' יהושע בן לוי אמ' אבני כדכודיה . . . ושעריך לאבני אקדח (ישעיהו נד), ר' ירמיה בשם ר' שמואל בר יצחק עתיד הקדוש ברוך הוא לעשות שער מזרחי של בית המקדש הוא ושני פשיפשיו אבן אחת של מרגלית. ר' יוחנן הוה יתיב

---
5 See Kiperwasser and Ruzer, "Aramaic Stories of Wandering".
6 Ansgar Nünning, "Narratology or Narratologies? Taking Stock of Recent Developments, Critique and Modest Proposals for Future Usages of the Term," in *What Is Narratology? Questions and Answers Regarding the Status of a Theory*, ed. Tom Kindt and Hans-Harald Müller (Berlin: de Gruyter, 2003), 243–46.

ודריש גו כנישתא רבתה דציפורין, עתיד הקדוש ברוך הוא לעשות שער מזרחי של בית המקדש הוא ושני פשיפשיו אבן אחת של מרגלית . . . והוה תמן חד מינוי פרוש, א' אפי' כהדא ביעתא דשפנינא לית אנן משכחין, והדין יתיב ואמר הכדין, עם שהוא מפרש בים הגדול שקעה ספינתו בים וירד לעימקי תהום וראה מלאכי השרת מסתתים בו, מגלפים בו, מסרגים בו, וא' להם מי הוא זה, אמרו לו זה שער מזרחי של בית המקדש הוא ושני פשיפשיו אבן אחת של מרגלית, מיד נעשה לו נס ויצא משם בשלום. בשתא חורייתא אתא ואשכח לר' יוחנן יתיב ודריש בההוא עניינא, עתיד הקדוש ברוך הוא לעשו' שער מזרחי של בית המקדש הוא ושני פשיפשיו אבן אחת של מרגלית, א' ליה סבא סבא כל מה דאת יכיל למגלגלא גליג, למשבחה שבח, דאילולי דחמנן עיני לא הוינא מהימן, א' ליה ואילולי דחמון עינך לא הויתה מהימן למיליא דמרתי באורייתא, תלא עינוי ואיסתכל ביה, ונעשה מיד גל של עצמות.

And I will make [your windows of] *kadkod*. R. Abba bar Kahana said: either or that [*kadein u-kadein*]. R. Levi said: *kadkedayyanon*. R. Yehoshua ben Levi said: stones of *kadkodiyyah*. . . .[7]

"And your gates of carbuncles ['*eqdaḥ*]." R. Yirmiyah [said] in the name of R. Shmuel bar Yizṣḥak: "In time to come, the Holy One, blessed be He, will make the Eastern Gate of the Temple and its two wickets from a single stone of pearl."

R. Yoḥanan was expounding inside the Great Synagogue of Sepphoris: "In the hereafter, the Holy One, blessed be He, will make the Eastern Gate of the Temple and its two wickets from a single stone of pearl." A certain *parush*-heretic was there.[8] He said: "We do not even find [pearls] as big as a single egg of a turtle-dove. And how has someone been talking such [nonsense]?"

When he set sail upon the Great Sea, his ship sank in the sea. He went to the valleys of the deep, and he saw the ministering angels chiseling, etching, and hatching it (the stone), and he said to them: "What is this?" They replied: "This is the Eastern Gate of the Temple and its two wickets being made from a single stone of pearl." Immediately a miracle was performed for him and he departed unharmed.

A year later, he arrived and found R. Yoḥanan, who was expounding on the same matter: "In the hereafter, the Holy One, blessed be He, will make the Eastern Gate of the Temple and its two wickets from a single stone of pearl."

---

7 The omitted passage was discussed recently in Kiperwasser and Ruzer, "Aramaic Stories of Wandering."
8 Different suggestions regarding the meaning of *parush* here have been offered. Saul Lieberman (*Tosefta ki-fshuṭah: A Comprehensive Commentary on the Tosefta, Zeraim* [New York: Jewish Theological Seminary, 1955], 1:54 [n. 8] [Hebrew]) believes—in correspondence with what follows in the Tosefta passage—that it marks the heretic as a seafarer. James Adam Redfield ("The Iridescence of Scripture: Inner-Talmudic Interpretation and Palestinian Midrash," in *Studies in Rabbinic Narratives: Volume One*, ed. Jeffrey L. Rubenstein [Providence: Brown Judaic Studies, 2021], 115–75) is of the opinion that the combination of *minaei* (heretic) and *parush* indicates belonging to a Christian sect, the members of which called themselves "sailors" (*pelagies*). However, the enigmatic expression could be understood also as derived from פרישה meaning a wondrous act (see Michael Sokoloff, *A Dictionary of Jewish Palestinian Aramaic of the Byzantine Period*, 3rd rev. and exp. ed. [Ramat Gan: Bar-Ilan University Press, 2017], 507). If so, the protagonist is called here a wondrous heretic on account of what will happen to him later on in the story; it may alternatively indicate that he has already been accustomed to wondrous events.

He said to him: "Elder, Elder! proclaim all you can proclaim, praise all there is to praise. For had my eyes not seen, I would not have believed."

"And had your eyes not seen, you would not have believed the words that I said about Torah!" he replied.

He raised his eyes and looked at him, and immediately he was transformed into a pile of bones.[9]

This exemplary rabbinic sailor's yarn story features the motif of a mysterious stone hidden in the depths of the sea, where it awaits its future use in the construction of the eschatological Temple. The story stands out as a rather literal interpretation of Isaiah's imagery. In parallel to that, the motif of the clash of religious ideologies—with the high seas as the playground for establishing the superiority of rabbinic outlook—might have been inspired by the Jonah story.[10] While our heretic—whether a Jewish insider or a Christian, that eternal Other—could have grasped R. Yohanan's message in the comfort of a synagogue sermon, the narrative sends him on a sea journey to attain understanding through extreme trial. Alas, even that experience does not suffice, and the heretic, lacking in the faith shared by the rabbinic community, ends as a pile of bones at the feet of his master.[11] James Redfield comments about the heretic, "our proverbial Doubting Thomas is struck down by precisely that in which he placed his trust—the eyes."[12] Leaving aside the exact pattern of

---

[9] Pesiq. Rab Kah. 18.5, ed. Mandelbaum pp. 296–98. For a brief analysis of this story and its comparison with the parallel in the Bavli see Richard Lee Kalmin, *Jewish Babylonia between Persia and Roman Palestine* (New York: Oxford University Press, 2006), 88–90. See also Redfield, "Iridescence." We are grateful to James for sharing with us his paper before it was finally published.

[10] Kiperwasser and Ruzer, "Sea Voyages Tales in Conversation with the Jonah Story."

[11] The destructive power of the gaze of some rabbis is a common motif in rabbinic literature, described in great detail by Turán Tamás, "'Wherever the Sages Set Their Eyes, There is Either Death or Poverty': On the History, Terminology and Imagery of the Talmudic Traditions about the Devastating Gaze of the Sages," *Sidra* 23 (2008): 137–205 (Hebrew).

[12] Redfield, "Iridescence," 136. Yoḥanan's saying resembles the words addressed by Jesus to Thomas in John 20:29: "Have you believed because you have seen me? Blessed are those who have not seen and yet come to believe." Note the parallel master-disciple context and the shared problem of vision-belief (as opposed to the episode in the Infancy Gospel of Thomas, where it is the student [Jesus] who punishes his unbelieving teacher by death). The parallel was noticed and treated independently in Marc Hirshman, "Pesikta de-Rav Kahana and Paideia," in *Higayon L'Yona: New Aspects in the Study of Midrash, Aggadah and Piyut in Honor of Professor Yona Fraenkel*, ed. Joshua Levinson, Jacob Elbaum and Galit Hasan-Rokem (Jerusalem: Magnes, 2007), 165–78 (175); Joshua Levinson, "There is No Place Like Home: Rabbinic Responses to the Christianization of Palestine," in *Jews, Christians, and the Roman Empire: The Poetics of Power in Late Antiquity*, ed. Natalie B. Dohrmann and Annette Yoshiko Reed (Philadelphia: University of Pennsylvania Press, 2013), 99–120 (115–16). It was actually addressed already by Hermann L. Strack and Paul Billerbeck, *Kommentar zum Neuen Testament aus Talmud und Midrasch*, 3 vols. (Munich: Beck, 1922–1928), 2:586.

polemic shown here, we will only mention the function of the sea as a liminal space populated by angels who guard wondrous objects destined to serve in eschatology.

This tradition was brought to Babylonia, where it was enthusiastically embraced by the editors of the Babylonian Talmud:

> מאי ושעריך לאבני אקדח כי הא דיתיב ר' יוחנן וקא דריש עתיד הקב"ה להביא אבנים טובות ומרגליות שהם שלשים על שלשים וחוקק בהן עשר ברום עשרים שנ' ושעריך לאבני אקדח ליגלג עליו אותו תלמיד אמ' השתא כי ביעתא דציליצולא ליכא כי האי גונא איכא לימים הפליגה ספינתו בים אזל ואשכח מלאכי דהוו מנסרי אבנים טובות ומרגליות אמ' להו הני למאי אמרו ליה שעתיד הק'ב'ה' להעמידן בשערי ירושלם כי הדר אשכחיה לר' יוחנן דקא דריש אמ' לו ר' דרוש ולך נאה לדרוש כאשר אמרת כן ראיתי אמ' לו ריקה אלמלא לא ראית לא האמנת מלגלג על דברי חכמ' אתה נתן בו עיניו ונעשה גל עצמות.

What is: "And your gates of carbuncles" (Isa 54:12).[13] Just as in the following: Once was R. Yoḥanan sitting and expounding: "In the hereafter, the Holy One, blessed be He, will bring precious stones and pearls that are thirty by thirty [cubits], and carve out [a square from] them ten [cubits wide] by twenty [high],[14] and set them up in the gates of Jerusalem." A certain disciple jeered at him: "Nowadays, we don't find them as big as a turtle-dove's egg; are we to find them that big?!" Some days later, the disciple's ship went off to sea. He saw the ministering angels who were chiseling precious stones and pearls thirty by thirty [cubits] and carving out [a square block from them] ten [cubits wide] by twenty high. He said to them: "Who are these for?" They replied that in the hereafter, the Holy One, blessed be He, would set them up in the gates of Jerusalem. When he came before R. Yoḥanan and found him expounding said to him: "Expound, Rabbi, it is fit for you to expound; yea, just as you have said, thus have I seen." He replied: "Good-for-nothing! If you *hadn't* seen, you *wouldn't* have believed! You jeer at the words of the sages." He cast his eyes at him, and he was transformed into a pile of bones.[15]

Let us note here an illuminating metamorphosis of the story initially composed in the Land of Israel and later brought, as suggested above, by a Palestinian rabbinic tradent to the East. The outsider "sectarian" from the original tale characteristically morphs into a less than diligent disciple, which does not change the Other's sad final fate. The sea, however, of which the terrestrial Babylonians might have not had a first-hand knowledge, still functions primarily as a storage place for items to be revealed at the end of days. We will see that, a bit later in the same tractate, the Babylonian narrators amplify the wondrous aspect of the plot by introducing an additional astounding motif.

---

13 For the partial parallel to this passage, see b. Sanh. 100a.
14 The translation follows the understanding suggested by R. Shmuel b. Meir (12th century) *ad loc.* and the clarifying wording of the repetition below ("twenty high").
15 b. B. Bat.74a. The texts of the Babylonian Talmud quoted here are according to Ms. Hamburg 165g with some emendations.

Sea Treasure and Its Guardian Bird

In *b. Baba Bathra* 74b, we read about a ship threatened by a mighty tempest and rescued through the miraculous intervention of a heavenly bird.[16] The story is related by R. Yehudah Hindu'a (the Indian), a character unknown to us from any other rabbinic tradition:[17]

> רב יהודה הנדואה משתעי זימנא חדא הוה הוה קא אזלינן בספינתא וחזינא לההוא אבן טבא דהוה הדר לה
> תנינא ונחית בר אמוראי רב יהודה הנדואה משתעי זימנא חדא הוה הוא קא אזלינן בספינתא וחזינא לההוא
> אבן טבא דהוה הדר לה תנינא ונחית בר אמוראי לאיתוייה אתא תנינא קא בעי למיבלע לה לספינתא אתא
> פשקנצ' קטעיה לרישיה [ואיתהפוכו מיא והוו דמא] אתא [תנינא] חבריה אותבה [עילויה] וחייה והדר איתא
> קא [בעי למ]בלע לה לספינתא אתא ההוא פשקנצא קטעיה לרישיה שקלה לההיא אבן טבא ופרח בהדי
> דפרח נפל בספינתא והוו הנך ציפרי מליחי בהדן- אותיבנה עלי' דליוה ופרחו.

Rav Yehudah the Indian (Hindu'a) told: "Once we were sailing on a ship and we saw a precious stone with a sea-monster encircling it. A diver descended to bring it up and the sea-monster came and wanted to swallow the ship. Then Paškeza came and bit off his head. [The water turned to blood]. The [sea monster's] fellow came, put it [the stone] on him (the sea monster), revived him and then he [sea monster's fellow] returned. He [the sea-monster] wanted to swallow the ship, but Paškeza came and bit off his head. Then he took the stone and flew away. With Paškeza flying away, the stone was dropped onto the ship, where there were salted birds that we had with us. [Then he] put it (the stone) on them. They lifted it and flew away with it.

Sailors discover an object in the sea, and initially identify it as a common gemstone. But the object is guarded by a monster, *tanina*, indicating that it is destined for an extraordinary assignment, and the daring diver plunges headlong into the water to

---

16 We discussed the appearance of this motif in an instructive parallel from the fifth-sixth century *Vita* of the Christian miaphysite ascetic Barsauma, see Kiperwasser and Ruzer, "Jews and Arameans Wandering in the High Seas of Late Antiquity."
17 His nickname could be translated as "Indian"—but apparently, in the sense of "one who traveled to India." See the new Sokoloff edition of the Brokelmann dictionary (Michael Sokoloff, *A Syriac Lexicon* [Winona Lake, IN: Eisenbrauns, 2009], 346 and Michael Sokoloff, *A Dictionary of Jewish Babylonian Aramaic of the Talmudic and Geonic Periods* [Ramat Gan: Bar-Ilan University Press, 2002], 80). It may indicate, alternatively, his ethnic background (cf. Syriac *gabra hindua* mentioned in Julius Landsberger, *Die Fabeln des Sophos: Syrisches Original der griechischen Fabeln des Syntipas* [Posen: L. Merzbach, 1859], 1–2, where it serves as a substitute for the "African" in the Greek version). On the navigation to India in ancient times, see Lionel Casson, "Ancient Naval Technology and the Route to India," in *Rome and India: The Ancient Sea-Trade*, ed. Vimala Begley and Richard D. De Puma (Madison: University of Wisconsin Press, 1991), 8–11. This and the following story from the Babylonian Talmud were recently analyzed by Daniel J. Frim, "'Those Who Descend upon the Sea Told Me': Myth and Tall Tale in Baba Batra 73a–74b," *JQR* 107 (2017): 1–37. Our understanding of the story however, as well as its translation, are different.

retrieve it.[18] Now enraged, *tanina* attempts to devour the entire vessel. Paškeza,[19] a winged creature, comes to the rescue, slaughtering the monster and saving the ship, which in the meantime has come perilously close to the precious stone.[20] It may be possible to identify this winged creature of the Babylonian Talmud as metamorphosis of the mythical Iranian Baškuč-bird,[21] which in Persian lore resembles the griffon.[22] The wondrous stone is described as able to raise the dead—first the sea monster and then the birds—which, in our view, points to an incorporation of the rabbinic religious agenda into the background sailor yarn. It seems that the motif is also imbued with another item on this agenda: the stone will continue to be hidden, thus indicating the postponement of the general resurrection till the end of days.

Excursus: The Song of the Pearl

A vision of a marvelous stone revealed to the eyes of stunned seafarers from the depths of the abyss is also found in the Song of the Pearl, perhaps a remnant of ancient Syro-Mesopotamian voyage poetry, incorporated into the (gnostic) Christian Acts of Thomas (AoT):[23]

---

18 Sokoloff, *Dictionary of Jewish Babylonian Aramaic*, 234.
19 On this creature in the Babylonian Talmud see Reuven Kiperwasser, "Rabba bar Bar Channa's Voyages," *Jerusalem Studies in Hebrew Literature* 22 (2007–2008): 215–42 (232) (Hebrew).
20 Paškeza has already appeared earlier in this b. Baba Batra chain of stories, where it swallowed the giant serpent who had previously swallowed a giant toad, and after finishing its feast settled down on a gigantic tree. See Kiperwasser, "Rabba bar Bar Channa's Voyages," 233–34. Talmudic commentators identify פשקנצא, as a gigantic raven and this understanding was recorded by Sokoloff, Sokoloff, *Dictionary of Jewish Babylonian Aramaic*, 944 – but corrected in the new 2021 edition, p. 918a. For the additional bibliography, see note 21.
21 Walter B. Henning, "Two Manichean Magical Texts with an Excursus on the Parthian Ending -ēndēh," *BSOAS* 12 (1947): 39–66 (esp. pp. 42–43). The identification proposed by Henning was accepted by others, see Hans-Peter Schmidt, "The Sēnmurw of Birds and Dogs and Bats," *Persica* 8 (1980): 1–86; Daniel E. Gershenson, "Understanding Puškansa," *Acta Orientalia* 55 (1994): 23–36; David Buyaner, "On the Etymology of Middle Persian baškuč (Winged Monster)," *StIr* 34 (2005): 19–30.
22 On its occurrence in Iranian lore see L.C. Casartelli, "Çyena—Simrgh—Roc," *Congrès scientifique international des Catholiques* 6 (1891): 79–86; C.V. Trever, *The Dog-Bird: Senmurw-Paskudj* (Leningrad: I. Fedorov Press, 1938); Wolfgang Fauth, "Der persische Simurg und der Gabriel-Melek Tāwūs der Jeziden," *Persica* 12 (1987): 123–47; Schmidt, "The Sēnmurw of Birds and Dogs and Bats"; Hans-Peter Schmidt, "Simorgh," *Encyclopaedia Iranica*, https://iranicaonline.org/articles/simorg (last accessed 20 April 2023). There is a closeness between Baškuč פשקנצא and Sēnmurw / Simurgh, also an Iranian mythical bird, who is viewed as the king of all winged creatures.
23 The Syriac version translated here is that of Taeke Jansma, *A Selection from the Acts of Judas Thomas* (Leiden: Brill, 1952), 35–40. For the summary of different scholarly approaches to this com-

"If [you would go] down into Egypt and bring [back] the one pearl (ܡܪܓܢܝܬܐ), which is in the middle of the sea (ܒܓܘ ܝܡܐ) surrounded by the hissing serpent (ܚܘܝܐ ܢܫܘܒܐ), then you will put on your glorious garment and your toga which rests (is laid) over it." ... I passed through the borders of Maishan, the meeting-place of the merchants of the East, and I reached the land of Babel, and I entered the walls of Sarbug. I then went down into Egypt, and my companions parted from me. I went straight to the serpent (ܚܘܝܐ ܢܫܘܒܐ), around its lodging I settled until it was going to slumber and sleep, that I might snatch my pearl from it. Then I became alone and lonely, to my fellow-lodgers I became a stranger (ܢܘܟܪܝ).

The function of the poem in the general outline of the AoT is unclear. Scholars who view the AoT as a gnostic composition tend to interpret the hymn along the lines of the gnostic outlook, assuming that the pearl is an allegory of either the hidden light or of the soul's descent into this world.[24] Others discern here a didactic and/ or rhetorical stratagem with no initial link to gnostic ideas. In any case, this poetic fragment, which was likely inserted into the AoT, should be analyzed as a separate unit.[25] If it was the product of a different setting, it might have been based on a sailor story prototype. That prototype would have been transmitted independently, and only eventually put into the mouth of Thomas by the compiler of the AoT. Disconnected from the context of the AoT, the story would then read like a Babylonian fairytale.[26] In such a tale, the stone could have functioned as part of the royal regalia snatched from the Parthian court—thus explaining the need to bring it back.

***

In the talmudic narrative, we have seen that the precious stone acquires a new meaning, correlating with ideas of rabbinic eschatology. It is hidden in anticipation of the end of time, when it will have the power to bring the dead back to life. The winged creature acts as the guardian of the sailors, who are placed under the special protection of God. The wondrous nature of the stone became manifest when the first monster's companion emerged from the bloodied waters and revived his slaughtered mate. The resuscitated monster tried one more time to swallow the ship, ostensibly motivated by revenge and the desire to guard the stone. To properly deal with the danger, the winged creature had to kill the *tanina* again. Having then seized the stone, it carried it away to a new hiding place where it will be safely

---

position see Gerard P. Luttikhuizen, "The Hymn of Jude Thomas, the Apostle, in the Country of the Indians," in *The Apocryphal Acts of Thomas*, ed. Jan N. Bremmer (Leuven: Peeters, 2001), 108–13.

24 See the summary of these scholarly evaluations in Luttikhuizen, "The Hymn of Jude Thomas," 103–108 and Gerard Luttikhuizen, "A Gnostic Reading of the Acts of John," in *The Apocryphal Acts of John*, ed. Jan N. Bremmer (Kampen: Kok Pharos, 1995), 119–52, esp. 133–52.

25 Klaus Beyer, "Das syrische Perlenlied: Ein Erlösungsmythos als Märchengedicht," ZDMG 140 (1990): 234–59 (234–35).

26 This assumption is derived from the discussion by Beyer, "Das syrische Perlenlied," 238–40.

kept until the ordained time. Yet before that could happen, the stone, evidently on purpose, was dropped on the ship, with the result that the carcasses of the birds salted by the sailors came back to life. The birds, having come back to life, took possession of the stone and flew away, seemingly following their leader Paškeza.

Birds Animated

Although detached there from the sea-travel context, the motif of inanimate birds suddenly coming to life and flying away is found in the Infancy Gospel of Thomas (IGT), believed to be of Syriac-language provenance and dated to the first half of the second century.[27] At the start of the composition, we are told how the five-year-old Jesus was playing with other "Hebrew boys" by a running stream and made the muddy waters clean by the power of his word. This display of the child's marvelous powers is complemented by the following pericope (IGT 2):

> He was playing at the ford of a stream . . . [Then] he made soft clay and formed twelve sparrows out of it[28] . . . [But] a certain Jew saw what Jesus did . . . on the Sabbath [day]; he immediately went and announced to his father Joseph: "See, your child . . . has profaned the Sabbath." Then Joseph came to the place, and seeing what Jesus did, he cried out: "Why do you do on the Sabbath what it is not lawful to do?" [Then] Jesus clapped his hands and cried to the sparrows: "Be [alive and] gone!" And the sparrows flew off chirping.[29]

Initially offended by what seemed like Jesus' violation of the Sabbath, the Jews later became flabbergasted and recounted the miracle to the leaders of the community.

***

The motif of animated birds seems to have been popular enough to reach even the Qur'an, where its Jesus-centered variant with one bird only was retold.[30] Suggesting the motif's broader circulation, we see the Babylonian rabbinic narrator as adopting the background narrative plot of the miraculously revived birds to embellish

---

[27] Regarding the history of research of this remarkable text see Reidar Aasgaard, *The Childhood of Jesus: Decoding the Apocryphal Infancy Gospel of Thomas* (Eugene, OR: Cascade, 2009), 1–13. For discussion of later medieval reception of the tradition, see Mary Dzon, "Jesus and the Birds in Medieval Abrahamic Traditions," *Traditio* 66 (2011): 189–230.

[28] For a suggestion that the number twelve here may hint at the mission of the twelve apostles see Dzon, "Jesus and the Birds," 198. However, this motif—as well as other possible meanings of the typological number of twelve—is nowhere spelled out in the composition.

[29] English translation is indebted to Bart D. Ehrman, *The New Testament and Other Early Christian Writings. A Reader* (New York: Oxford University Press, 1998), 127–28.

[30] Q Āl 'Imrān 3:46, 49.

and reinforce the main motif of the wondrous stone. Far from the human gaze, a stone with the capacity to restore life remains a secure secret, until the dawn of the eschatological era. Our conjecture is that it would then be employed for reviving the dead of Israel. Rabbinic literature offers glimpses about how, and through what agency, God will perform the ultimate miracle of resurrection.[31] One of them is exemplified by our story in b. Baba Batra: here the vast dimensions of the sea, the place of primordial chaos in mythological thought, became a storage place for the keys to the eschatological future. In his Babylonian didactic tale, the rabbinic storyteller mobilized the two complementing motifs—a wondrous stone retrieved by a diver and a miraculous bird who rescues sailors.

One may suggest that underlying the various independent stories is the same prototype, in which the sea holds marvelous treasures, guarded by wondrous creatures, destined to be recovered by sailors. Whereas in the Song of the Pearl the function of the treasure remains unclear, in the rabbinic versions it is safeguarded until the days of eschatological redemption, after which it will bring about resurrection of the dead. The next section provides additional evidence for this eschatologically flavored motif.

A Lady's Precious Basket

Following in the steps of our travelers through the sea of the Talmud, we arrive at another example of the eschatologically motivated adoption strategy in the context of rabbinic narrative. It appears in the same sequence of stories about marvelous objects found in the sea depth (b. B. Bat. 74b):[32]

ר' יונתן משתעי זמנא חדא הוה קאזלינן בספינתא וחזינן ההיא קרטליתא דהוו מקבעא בה אבנים טובי' ומרגליו' והוה הדר לה מינא דכוארא דשמיה כירשא והוה נחית בר אמודאי לאיתויה ובעא דנישמטה לאטמיה סליק ושקא זיקא דחלא בהדיה נפקא בת קלא ואמר' לן מאי עיבידתיכו בהדי קרטליתא דביתהו דר' חנינא בן דוסא דעתידא למשדא ביה תכלתא לצדיקי לעלמא דאתי

R. Yonathan relates: "Once we were traveling on a ship and we saw the small basket studded with precious stones and pearls and surrounded by a species of Kara-fish called Karša. There a diver descends, to bring it and (the Karša) wanted to hit him (the diver) on his thigh. (He)

---

31 A common point of view among Palestinian rabbis is that at the end of time, God will resurrect the deceased with the help of the miraculous dew, an indication of which is found in a verse from Isa 26:19. See for example y. Ber. 5:2 [9b] and y. Ta'an. 1:1 [63b]. However, there also existed a belief that some secret agents able to revive the deceased were dispersed out in the mundane world. See for example Lev. Rab. 22:4. See also our discussion on b. B. Bat. 74b further on.

32 The texts of the Babylonian Talmud quoted here are according to Ms. Paris 1337 with some emendations.

ascended and threw (his) skin-bottle of vinegar (on the Karša?). Following that, a *bath-qōl* (heavenly echo?)[33] came forth, saying to us: 'What have you to do with the small basket of R. Hanina b. Dosa's wife who is to store in it the purple-blue for the righteous in the world to come'."

This story should be read in light of other variants of the sea-voyage plot,[34] particularly the one concerning R. Yehudah the Indian, discussed above.[35] Here the narrator relates that while sailing, he and his companions saw in the water a small basket studded with precious stones and pearls, and guarded by a flock of giant *Kara*-fish.[36] Having descended into the water to retrieve the basket, the diver succeeds in outsmarting the guardian sea monsters. However, the heavenly voice (*bath-qōl*) comes forth and demands of the seafarers to stay away from the basket, which, as it turns out, in the post-resurrection era is meant to be in the possession of R. Hanina ben Dosa's wife. "Purple-blue" here is the dye used for coloring the fringes of the traditional four-corner cloak (*talith*); as for the long-lost secret of its preparation,[37] it will be, according to one belief, revealed anew in the last days.[38]

---

[33] Rabbinic term indicating a feminine personification of God's voice in a period when the biblical prophecy is perceived as belonging to a distant past. About the gender politics behind the term see Tal Ilan, *Masekhet Ta'anit* (Tübingen: Mohr Siebeck, 2008), 259–63.

[34] See Raphael Patai, *The Children of Noah: Jewish Seafaring in Ancient Times* (Princeton: Princeton University Press, 1999), 126–27.

[35] b. B. Bat. 74b.

[36] See Reuven Kiperwasser and Dan Y. Shapira, "Irano-Talmudica I: The Three-Legged Ass and Ridyā in B. Taanith: Some Observations About Mythic Hydrology in the Babylonian Talmud and in Ancient Iran," *Association for Jewish Studies Review* 32 (2008): 101–16; Reuven Kiperwasser and Dan Y. Shapira, "Irano-Talmudica II: Leviathan, Behemoth and the 'Domestication' of Iranian Mythological Creatures in Eschatological Narratives of the Babylonian Talmud," in *Shoshanat Yaakov: Ancient Jewish and Iranian Studies in Honor of Yaakov Elman*, ed. Shai Secunda and Steven Fine (Leiden: Brill, 2012), 203–36.

[37] See R. Isaac Herzog, "Hebrew Porphyrology," in *The Royal Purple and The Biblical Blue*, ed. Ehud Spanier (Jerusalem: Keter, 1987), 17–131 (44, 110–12). Chronologically, the latest mention of *tekhelet* in rabbinic literature of Palestinian provenance is found in the Midrash Tanḥuma (Shelaḥ 28, on Num 17:5), with the lament that "and now we have no *tekhelet*, only white." Herzog hypothesized that it was the Arab conquest of the Land of Israel that brought an end to the snail-based dyeing industry among the Jews.

[38] This belief is not emphatically pronounced, but it can be derived from some sources. For example, in the Tanḥuma mentioned above, explaining that *tekhelet* is no longer available, the midrashist uses the expression *nignaz* (stored away or hidden, see Shamma Friedman, "The Primacy of Tosefta in Mishnah–Tosefta Parallels [Shabbat 16.1]," *Tarbiz* 62 [1993]: 313–38 [Hebrew]). He has shown that the verb *g-n-z* is primarily used in the negative sense of making an item unusable without destroying it (Friedman, "The Primacy of Tosefta," 323–24), so that whereas it is currently impossible to fulfil the precept, it will become feasible in the future. Even more explicit in this regard is the passage from b. Baba Batra addressed above.

This dye was once derived from the *hillazon*, a mollusk found on the seashores of the Land of Israel and probably exported to other countries.[39]

The idea that the purple-blue will be rediscovered in the eschatological era seems to have been an innovation of Babylonian Jewry.[40] For the narrator, of course, both R. Hanina b. Dosa, a first-century CE charismatic miracle worker,[41] and his wife have long been dead and thus their mention here refers the audience to the future age of resurrection. It seems that the end-of-days focus of the story should inform our understanding of the function of the precious object in this narrative.

We can see how in the two rabbinic stories a background tall-tale of guarded sea treasure happened upon by sailors, originally lacking explicit religious markers, is imbued with eschatological meaning, thus undergoing a Judaization of sorts. The basic underlying plot brings the protagonist to explore the depths of the sea, relating the wondrous finds and encounters with miraculous creatures. The Judaizing move establishes a link to specific religious values: the eschatological Temple, resurrection, ritual demands transferred to the hereafter, and the involvement of prominent rabbinic figures.

Conclusion

We have discussed a number of sailor-yarn traditions about a treasure hidden in the depths of the sea and guarded by either a monstrous creature or the Divine Presence. They demonstrate attempts to balance the inherited backdrop of mythological motifs and their reworking in light of specific religious agendas of our Late Antique narrators.

---

39 A number of archaeological sites along the northern coast of Israel, extending up to the port city of Sidon, attest to a well-developed Murex-based dyeing industry in the region; see Nira Karmon and Ehud Spanier, "Archaeological Evidence of the Purple Dye Industry from Israel," in Spanier, *The Royal Purple and the Biblical Blue*, 149–57; Israel A. Ziderman, "Reinstitution of the Mitzvah of Tekhelet in Tzitzit," *Tehumin* 9 (1988): 423–46 (438) (Hebrew).

40 See b. Soṭah 46b and Reuven Kiperwasser, "Elihoref and Ahia—The Metamorphosis of the Narrative Tradition from the Land of Israel to the Sassanian Babylonia," in *Rabbinic Traditions between Palestine and Babylonia: From There to Here*, ed. Tal Ilan and Ronit Nikolsky (Leiden: Brill, 2014), 255–73 (268–69).

41 See Joseph Blenkinsopp, "Miracles: Elisha and Hanina Ben Dosa," in *Miracles in Jewish and Christian Antiquity*, ed. John C. Cavadini (Notre Dame: University of Notre Dame Press, 1999), 57–81; David Levine, "Holy Men and Rabbis in Talmudic Antiquity," in *Saints and Role Models in Judaism and Christianity*, ed. Joshua Schwarz and Marcel Poorthuis (Leiden: Brill, 2004), 45–58; Chanah Safrai and Zeev Safrai, "Rabbinic Holy Men," in Schwarz and Poorthuis, *Saints and Role Models*, 59–78; David Flusser, *Jesus* (Jerusalem: Magnes, 2001), 113, 117.

We observed that for Syro-Mesopotamian Aramaic-speaking storytellers, the sea maintained its perilous appeal and the voyages provided a meaningful liminal experience that challenged the narrators' religious outlook. For them all, undeniable differences notwithstanding, the water, the watery abyss represented the chaos embedded in the universe according to its mythical perception. Additionally, various strategies for coping with the tension inherent in sea adventures were set forth—among them, those trying to temper the mythic tenor of the background tradition.

While the Talmud makes use of some of these strategies, one notes the distinguishing Jewish motif of the sea as the storage place for the treasure destined to serve during the era of eschatological resurrection. Meanwhile, an early Christian text, the Hymn of the Pearl, possibly inserted into the AoT to reflect gnostic Christian ideas, unsurprisingly, does not show interest in introducing the resurrection motif. Generally speaking, both Jewish and Christian narrators of sea adventures sought to adjust the traditional sailors' tall tales to their own religious agendas. However, in addition to sharing adjustment strategies, our sources also seem to reflect underlying shared myths. Both Christians and Jews use the meaningful space of the sea as a locus of intense semiotic traffic,[42] in which nothing is thrown into the sea as unnecessary baggage and everything finds its place among the building blocks of the narrative bricolage.

We conclude with an idea attributed to the semiotician Juri Lotman, who considered culture a kind of machine that exists to produce meaning. Under normal circumstances and with identical raw materials, it produces the same products again and again. Under changing circumstances, however, which might be seen as "glitches" in its working mechanism, the machine of culture becomes erratic, and produces ever-new products.[43] In our case, the machine was fed with the motifs of chaos represented by sea and the danger of sea travel, as well as monsters and wondrous objects in the watery abyss, and produced variegated narratives that served the agendas of the different storytellers.

---

[42] This extraordinarily evocative term, which captures the journey as a process of obtaining meaning, is borrowed from Joshua Levinson, "Travel Tales of Captivity in Rabbinic Literature," *Journeys* 17 (2016): 75–95 (76).

[43] For an oral transmission of this opinion see, Michail Gasparov, *Zapiski I Vipiski* (Moscow: Novoye Lit. Obozrenye, 2001), 215. Juri Lotman (1922–1993) was a prominent author in the field of semiotics and cultural research.

References

Aasgaard, Reidar. *The Childhood of Jesus: Decoding the Apocryphal Infancy Gospel of Thomas*. Eugene, OR: Cascade, 2009.
Beyer, Klaus. "Das syrische Perlenlied: Ein Erlösungsmythos als Märchengedicht." *ZDMG* 140 (1990): 234–59.
Blenkinsopp, Joseph. "Miracles: Elisha and Hanina Ben Dosa." Pages 57–81 in *Miracles in Jewish and Christian Antiquity*. Edited by John C. Cavadini. Notre Dame: University of Notre Dame Press, 1999.
Buyaner, David. "On the Etymology of Middle Persian baškuč (Winged Monster)." *StIr* 34 (2005): 19–30.
Casartelli, L.C. "Çyena—Simrgh—Roc." *Congrès scientifique international des Catholiques* 6 (1891): 79–86.
Casson, Lionel. "Ancient Naval Technology and the Route to India." Pages 8–11 in *Rome and India: The Ancient Sea-Trade*. Edited by Vimala Begley and Richard D. De Puma. Madison: University of Wisconsin Press, 1991.
Dzon, Mary. "Jesus and the Birds in Medieval Abrahamic Traditions." *Traditio* 66 (2011): 189–230.
Ehrman, Bart D. *The New Testament and Other Early Christian Writings: A Reader*. New York: Oxford University Press, 1998.
Fauth, Wolfgang. "Der persische Simurg und der Gabriel-Melek Tāwūs der Jeziden." *Persica* 12 (1987): 123–47.
Flusser, David. *Jesus*. Jerusalem: Magnes, 2001.
Foulke, Robert. *The Sea Voyage Narrative*. Milton Park: Routledge, 2001.
Friedman, Shamma. "The Primacy of Tosefta in Mishnah-Tosefta Parallels (Shabbat 16.1)." *Tarbiz* 62 (1993): 313–38. (Hebrew)
Frim, Daniel J. "'Those Who Descend upon the Sea Told Me': Myth and Tall Tale in Baba Batra 73a–74b." *JQR* 107 (2017): 1–37.
Gasparov, Michail. *Zapiski I Vipiski*. Moscow: Novoye Lit. Obozrenye, 2001.
Gershenson, Daniel E. "Understanding Puškansa." *Acta Orientalia* 55 (1994): 23–36.
Henning, Walter B. "Two Manichean Magical Texts with an Excursus on the Parthian Ending-ēndēh." *BSOAS* 12 (1947): 39–66.
Herzog, R. Isaac. "Hebrew Porphyrology." Pages 17–131 in *The Royal Purple and The Biblical Blue*. Edited by Ehud Spanier. Jerusalem: Keter, 1987.
Hirshman, Marc. "Pesikta de-Rav Kahana and Paideia." Pages 165–78 in *Higayon L'Yona: New Aspects in the Study of Midrash, Aggadah and Piyut in Honor of Professor Yona Fraenkel*. Edited by Joshua Levinson, Jacob Elbaum and Galit Hasan-Rokem. Jerusalem: Magnes, 2007.
Ilan, Tal. *Massekhet Ta'anit*. Tübingen: Mohr Siebeck, 2008.
Jansma, Taeke. *A Selection from the Acts of Judas Thomas*. Leiden: Brill, 1952.
Kalmin, Richard Lee. *Jewish Babylonia between Persia and Roman Palestine*. New York: Oxford University Press, 2006.
Karmon, Nira and Ehud Spanier. "Archaeological Evidence of the Purple Dye Industry from Israel." Pages 149–57 in *The Royal Purple and the Biblical Blue*. Edited by Ehud Spanier. Jerusalem: Keter, 1987.
Kiperwasser, Reuven. "Elihoref and Ahia—The Metamorphosis of the Narrative Tradition from the Land of Israel to the Sassanian Babylonia." Pages 255–73 in *Rabbinic Traditions between Palestine and Babylonia: From There to Here*. Edited by Tal Ilan and Ronit Nikolsky. Leiden: Brill, 2014.
Kiperwasser, Reuven. "Rabba bar Bar Channa's Voyages." *Jerusalem Studies in Hebrew Literature* 22 (2007–2008): 215–42. (Hebrew)

Kiperwasser, Reuven, and Dan Y. Shapira. "Irano-Talmudica I: The Three-Legged Ass and Ridyā in B. Taanith: Some Observations About Mythic Hydrology in the Babylonian Talmud and in Ancient Iran." *Association for Jewish Studies Review* 32 (2008): 101–16.

Kiperwasser, Reuven, and Dan Y. Shapira. "Irano-Talmudica II: Leviathan, Behemoth and the 'Domestication' of Iranian Mythological Creatures in Eschatological Narratives of the Babylonian Talmud." Pages 203–36 in *Shoshanat Yaakov: Ancient Jewish and Iranian Studies in Honor of Yaakov Elman*. Edited by Shai Secunda and Steven Fine. Leiden: Brill, 2012.

Kiperwasser, Reuven, and Serge Ruzer. "Aramaic Stories of Wandering in the High Seas of Late Antiquity." Pages 161–77 in *The Past Through Narratology: New Approaches to Late Antiquity and the Early Middle Ages*. Edited by Mateusz Fafinski and Jakob Riemenschneider. Heidelberg: Heidelberg University Publishing, 2022.

Kiperwasser, Reuven, and Serge Ruzer. "Sea Voyages Tales in Conversation with the Jonah Story: Intertextuality and the Art of Narrative Bricolage." *Journeys* 20 (2019): 39–57.

Kiperwasser, Reuven, and Serge Ruzer. "Aramaic Stories of Wandering in the High Seas of Late Antiquity." Pages 161–77 in *The Past Through Narratology: New Approaches to Late Antiquity and the Early Middle Ages*. Edited by Mateusz Fafinski and Jakob Riemenschneider. Das Mittelalter Beihefte 18. Heidelberg: Heidelberg University Publishing, 2022.

Landsberger, Julius. *Die Fabeln des Sophos: Syrisches Original der griechischen Fabeln des Syntipas*. Posen: L. Merzbach, 1859.

Levine, David. "Holy Men and Rabbis in Talmudic Antiquity." Pages 45–58 in *Saints and Role Models in Judaism and Christianity*. Edited by Joshua Schwarz and Marcel Poorthuis. Leiden: Brill, 2004.

Levinson, Joshua. "There is No Place Like Home: Rabbinic Responses to the Christianization of Palestine." Pages 99–120 in *Jews, Christians, and the Roman Empire: The Poetics of Power in Late Antiquity*. Edited by Natalie B. Dohrmann and Annette Yoshiko Reed. Philadelphia: University of Pennsylvania Press, 2013.

Levinson, Joshua. "Travel Tales of Captivity in Rabbinic Literature." *Journeys* 17 (2016): 75–95.

Lieberman, Saul. *Tosefta ki-fshuṭah: A Comprehensive Commentary on the Tosefta, Zeraim*. New York: Jewish Theological Seminary, 1955. (Hebrew)

Luttikhuizen, Gerard. "A Gnostic Reading of the Acts of John." Pages 119–52 in *The Apocryphal Acts of John*. Edited by Jan N. Bremmer. Kampen: Kok Pharos, 1995.

Luttikhuizen, Gerard P. "The Hymn of Jude Thomas, the Apostle, in the Country of the Indians." Pages 101–14 in *The Apocryphal Acts of Thomas*. Edited by Jan N. Bremmer. Leuven: Peeters, 2001.

Nünning, Ansgar. "Narratology or Narratologies? Taking Stock of Recent Developments, Critique and Modest Proposals for Future Usages of the Term." Pages 239–76 in *What Is Narratology? Questions and Answers Regarding the Status of a Theory*. Edited by Tom Kindt and Hans-Harald Müller. Berlin: de Gruyter, 2003.

Page, Denys. *Folktales in Homer's "Odyssey."* Cambridge: Harvard University Press, 1973.

Patai, Raphael. *The Children of Noah: Jewish Seafaring in Ancient Times*. Princeton: Princeton University Press, 1999.

Redfield, James Adam. "The Iridescence of Scripture: Inner-Talmudic Interpretation and Palestinian Midrash." Pages 115–75 in *Studies in Rabbinic Narratives: Volume One*. Edited by Jeffrey L. Rubenstein. Providence: Brown Judaic Studies, 2021.

Safrai, Chanah, and Zeev Safrai. "Rabbinic Holy Men." Pages 59–78 in *Saints and Role Models in Judaism and Christianity*. Edited by Joshua Schwarz and Marcel Poorthuis. Leiden: Brill, 2004.

Schmidt, Hans-Peter. "Simorgh." *Encyclopaedia Iranica*. Https://iranicaonline.org/articles/simorg.

Schmidt, Hans-Peter. "The Sēnmurw of Birds and Dogs and Bats." *Persica* 8 (1980): 1–86.

Sokoloff, Michael. *A Dictionary of Jewish Babylonian Aramaic of the Talmudic and Geonic Periods*. Ramat Gan: Bar-Ilan University Press, 2002.
Sokoloff, Michael. *A Dictionary of Jewish Palestinian Aramaic of the Byzantine Period*. 3rd rev. and exp. ed. Ramat Gan: Bar-Ilan University Press, 2017.
Sokoloff, Michael. *A Syriac Lexicon*. Winona Lake, IN: Eisenbrauns, 2009.
Strack, Hermann L. and Paul Billerbeck. *Kommentar zum Neuen Testament aus Talmud und Midrasch*. 3 vols. Munich: Beck, 1922–1928.
Tamás, Turán. "'Wherever the Sages Set Their Eyes, there is Either Death or Poverty': On the History, Terminology and Imagery of the Talmudic Traditions about the Devastating Gaze of the Sages." *Sidra* 23 (2008): 137–205. (Hebrew)
Trever, C.V. *The Dog-Bird: Senmurw-Paskudj*. Leningrad: I. Fedorov Press, 1938.
Ziderman, Israel A. "Reinstitution of the Mitzvah of Tekhelet in Tzitzit." *Tehumin* 9 (1988): 423–46. (Hebrew)

Clare E. Wilde
Monasteries as Travel Loci for Muslims and Christians (500–1000 CE)

Abstract: This article surveys references to monasteries in various genres of late antique Islamic and Christian literature, demonstrating the ambiguous attitude towards monasteries reflected in these sources. Subsequently, the article discusses possible explanations for the notable lack of extensive descriptions of travel experiences in these sources.

Starting with the Qur'an itself, Christian monks, monasteries and monasticism have been known to Islamic tradition.[1] While the Qur'an does not discuss monks or monasticism in great detail, its allusions assume a familiarity with this Christian institution on the part of its auditors. In later Arabic and Islamic literature, monasteries figure, frequently as waystations of sorts for travelers—pilgrims, merchants, the sick[2] and even caliphs and kings. And, as in the Qur'an (and also Christian tradition), monks and their dwellings have a mixed estimation in Islamic tradition. On the one hand, "good" Christian ascetics have been termed the models of pious Muslim behavior.[3] But, on the other hand—somewhat akin to the *khamriyya* (wine song, which also pre-dates Islam)[4]—there is also a subgenre of Arabic Islamic lit-

---

[1] See, e.g., Elizabeth Key Fowden, "The Lamp and the Wine Flask: Early Muslim Interest in Christian Monasticism," in *Islamic Crosspollinations: Interactions in the Medieval Middle East,* ed. Anna Akasoy, James E. Montgomery, and Peter E. Pormann (Cambridge: Gibb Memorial Trust, 2007), 1–29. For monasteries in and near Arabia see, e.g., Julie Bonnéric, "Archaeological Evidence for an Early Islamic Monastery in the Centre of al-Qusur (Failaka Island, Kuwait)," *AAE* 32 (2021), https://doi.org/10.1111/aae.12182; Joseph Elders, "The Lost Churches of the Arabian Gulf: Recent Discoveries on the Islands of Sir Bani Yas and Marawah, Abu Dhabi Emirate, United Arab Emirates," *Proceedings of the Seminar for Arabian Studies* 31 (2001): 47–57.
[2] For the early history of monastic health care see Andrew Todd Crislip, *From Monastery to Hospital: Christian Monasticism and the Transformation of Health Care in Late Antiquity* (Ann Arbor: University of Michigan Press, 2005).
[3] For discussion of Christian ascetics as paradigms for Muslim heroes, especially *mujāhidūn,* see Thomas Sizgorich, "Narrative and Community in Islamic Late Antiquity," *PaP* 185 (2004): 9–42.
[4] Philip Kennedy, *The Wine Song in Classical Arabic Poetry: Abū Nuwās and the Literary Tradition* (Oxford: Oxford University Press, 1997); Bruno Paoli, "Traders, Innkeepers and Cupbearers: Foreigners and People of the Book in Arabic Wine Poetry," in *Religious Culture in Late Antique Arabia: Selected Studies on the Late Antique Religious Mind,* ed. Isabel Toral-Niehoff and Kirill Dmitriev (Piscataway: Gorgias, 2017), 147–62.

erature, the *diyārāt*,⁵ that describes in flowery detail caliphal sojourns in Christian monasteries (many of which were, seemingly, accompanied by debauchery).⁶ For their part, Christian monasteries house manuscripts (in various languages) of Christian refutations of, or responses to, Islam, many of which feature a monk debating Muslims, occasionally in a monastery. Mindful of the distance from the original authors' intentions and audience reception, as well as the variety of genres in which monks and monasticism (*ruhbān/rahbāniyya*) appear, the following, after an overview of qur'anic allusions to monks and monasticism, explores what can be gleaned from a selection of literary sources (500–1000 CE) about Muslim, or Christian, experiences of "monastic travel loci" in the late antique and early Islamic periods.⁷

Qur'anic Critique of Monasticism

The Qur'an (and later Islamic tradition) has a multifaceted understanding of Christian institutions and doctrines. For example, it knows the late antique Christologi-

---

5 See Hilary Kilpatrick, "Monasteries through Muslim Eyes: The Diyarat Books," in *Christians at the Heart of Islamic Rule: Church Life and Scholarship in 'Abbasid Iraq*, ed. David Thomas (Leiden: Brill, 2003), 19–37. For a reevaluation of the relevant literature, with an emphasis on the devotional aspect of Muslim visits to monasteries, see Brad B. Bowman, "The Monastery as Tavern and Temple in Medieval Islam: The Case for Confessional Flexibility in the Locus of Christian Monasteries," *ME* 27 (2021): 50–77.
6 While mosques and churches were frequently contiguous (see, e.g., Elizabeth Key Fowden, "Christian Monasteries and Umayyad Residences in Late Antique Syria," *AnCr* 21 [2004]: 565–81), and knowledge flowed between Christian and Muslim communities, the reciprocal situation (Christians in Muslim religious/educational centers) is not the focus of this study. For some discussion of Christian-Muslim relations see, e.g., Sidney H. Griffith, *The Church in the Shadow of the Mosque* (Princeton: Princeton University Press, 2012); Mattia Guidetti, "The Byzantine Heritage in the Dār al-Islām: Churches and Mosques in al-Ruha between the Sixth and Twelfth Centuries," *Muqarnas* 26 (2009): 1–36; Mu'nim Sirry, "The Public Role of Dhimmīs during 'Abbāsid Times," *BSOAS* 74 (2011): 187–204; Clare Wilde, "We Shall Not Teach the Qur'an to Our Children," in *The Place to Go To: Contexts of Learning in Baghdad from the Eighth to Tenth Centuries*, ed. Jens Scheiner and Damien Janos (Princeton: Darwin, 2014), 233–59.
7 First, however, a brief caveat on the concept of "travel experience," is in order. "Travel experience" may be understood as the experience (or construction) of a destination, or the "experience" on the road. See Linda Ellis and Frank L. Kidner, eds., *Travel, Communication and Geography in Late Antiquity: Sacred and Profane* (London: Routledge, 2017), which notes that geography is a cultural construct that can be imagined in various ways. Fowden ("Christian Monasteries and Umayyad Residences") reflects this idea of a cultural construction of a geographic space.

cal controversies[8] addressed at the Council of Chalcedon (451 CE). Although monasticism is noted (or criticized) as an innovation (Q al-Ḥadīd 57:27), monks receive a mixed estimation (Q al-Mā'ida 5:82 being favorable, and Q al-Tawba 9:31, 34 being more critical): they are depicted as humble, but also hoarding wealth and "taken as gods besides God." Q al-Fatḥ 48:29 has also been thought as reflecting knowledge of monks engaging in much prayer, leaving the mark of prostration on their heads.[9]

Qur'anic comments on *ruhbān/rahbāniyya* resonate particularly strongly with canons of the Council of Chalcedon (451 CE)[10] that enumerate the abuses of clergy and also some of the errors of monks that have led them to fall under episcopal control. That monasteries are included in the qur'anic list of destroyed places of worship (Q al-Ḥajj 22:42) may reflect awareness of the inter-religious and inter-Nicene struggles of late antiquity, which saw bishops exiled to monasteries[11] or, as with the eponym of the Monophysite/miaphysite churches (Jacob Baradaeus, d. 578 CE), engaging in clandestine ordinations in order to maintain separate "non-Chalcedonian" hierarchies, particularly throughout Syria.[12] Qur'anic awareness of chris-

---

8 Sidney H. Griffith, "The Melkites and the Muslims: The Qur'ān, Christology, and Arab Orthodoxy," *Qantara* 33 (2013): 413–43; Cornelia Horn, "Jesus, the Wondrous Infant, at the Exegetical Crossroads of Christian Late Antiquity and Early Islam," in *Exegetical Crossroads: Understanding Scripture in Judaism, Christianity and Islam in the Pre-Modern Orient*, ed. Georges Tamer et al. (Berlin: De Gruyter, 2017), 27–46.
9 See Johanne Louise Christiansen, "'Stay Up During the Night, Except for a Little' (Q 73:2): The Qur'ānic Vigils as Ascetic Training Programs," *Religion* 49 (2019): 614–35. See also K. Wagtendonk, "Vigil," in *Encyclopaedia of the Qur'ān*, ed. Johanna Pink, http://dx.doi.org/10.1163/1875-3922_q3_EQSIM_00444 (last accessed 26 April 2023).
10 Available in English translation at https://earlychurchtexts.com/public/chalcedon_canons.htm (last accessed 26 April 2023). The Council also attests that the fact of travel (and some of its hardships) were not confined to monks. Canon 19 addresses irregularities in episcopal administration in the provinces, while canon 20 notes the practice of clergy officiating at more than one church, including those "who have been driven by necessity from their own country." Canon 11 provides instruction around the travel of the poor and those in need of assistance.
11 Elisabeth R. O'Connell, "'They Wandered in the Deserts and Mountains, and Caves and Holes in the Ground': Non-Chalcedonian Bishops 'in Exile'," *Studies in Late Antiquity* 3 (2019): 436–71.
12 There were over 100 Monophysite monasteries in the region, mainly located outside the main cities; see Irfan Shahîd, *Toponymy, Monuments, Historical Geography, and Frontier Studies*, vol. 2/1 of *Byzantium and the Arabs in the Sixth Century* (Washington, DC: Dumbarton Oaks, 2002), 186–87. Especially noteworthy is the Christian community in Najran, in the southern part of Arabia—a community that gave the Church its first Monophysite/Miaphysite martyrs, early in the 6th century CE. See Lucas van Rompay, "Society and Community in the Christian East," in *The Cambridge Companion to the Age of Justinian*, ed. Michael Maas (Cambridge: Cambridge University Press, 2005), 239–66. The Qur'an also appears to reference this martyrdom at Q al-Burūj 85. See also Susan Ashbrook, "Asceticism in Adversity: An Early Byzantine Experience," *BMGS* 6 (1980): 1–11. Jeanne-Nicole M. Saint-Laurent, "Hagiographical Portraits of Jacob Baradaeus," in *Missionary Stories and*

tological, as well as ecclesiastical, fallout of Chalcedon is not surprising. For, in addition to other relationships that existed between various semi-nomadic tribes and monasteries, Syrian monasteries served as waystations for caravans from Arabia.[13]

Monastic Visits in Arabic Literature, and the Genres in Which They Appear

Christian and Muslim sources indicate that monasteries continued many of their late antique functions into the Islamic period. For, whether preserving the memories of their ancestors (many of whom would have been Christians who converted to Islam and continued some of the devotions of their forebears[14]), or because monasteries did not limit their hospitality to their coreligionists, monasteries figure frequently in Islamic geographic, cultural and historical compositions as locales that Muslims knew, and visited. Those located in the desert continued to provide hospitality to passersby. Along with desert forts, monasteries could serve a double function as both a seat of power and influence in the steppes, while also being at a remove from the "worldliness" of the cities.[15] Their liminality, arguably, also pro-

---

the Formation of the Syriac Churches (Berkeley: University of California Press, 2015), 96–109; cf. also Pauline Allen, "Religious Conflict between Antioch and Alexandria c. 565–630 CE," in *Religious Conflict from Early Christianity to the Rise of Islam*, ed. Wendy Mayer and Bronwen Neil (Berlin: De Gruyter, 2013), 187–200.

13 For monasteries as caravan waystations in Egypt see Jean-Claude Garcin, "Les traces de l'époque musulmane," in *Kellia I. Kôm 219: Fouilles exécutées en 1964 et 1965*, ed. François Daumas and Antoine Guillaumont (Cairo: Imprimerie de l'Institut français d'archéologie orientale, 1969), 125–34; Wendy Mayer, "Welcoming the Stranger in the Mediterranean East: Syria and Constantinople," *Journal of the Australian Early Medieval Association* 5 (2009): 89–106; Abdulla Al-Shorman et al., "Travel and Hospitality in Late Antiquity: A Case Study from Umm El-Jimal in Eastern Jordan," *NEA* 80 (2017): 22–28. On the relationship between Mar Sabas and semi-nomadic persons see Sean Kingsley and Michael Decker, *Economy and Exchange in the East Mediterranean During Late Antiquity* (Oxford: Oxbow, 2015), 11. For an overview of trade and travel in the region more generally see Olivia Remie Constable, *Housing the Stranger in the Mediterranean World: Lodging, Trade, and Travel in Late Antiquity and the Middle Ages* (Cambridge: Cambridge University Press, 2004).

14 For shared devotions at Rusafa see, e.g., Elizabeth Key Fowden, "Sharing Holy Places," *Common Knowledge* 8 (2002): 124–46. See also Bowman, "Monastery as Tavern." For contemporary examples see, e.g., Maria Couroucli, "Chthonian Spirits and Shared Shrines: The Dynamics of Place among Christians and Muslims in Anatolia," in *Sharing the Sacra: The Politics and Pragmatics of Inter-communal Relations around Holy Places*, ed. Glenn Bowman (Oxford: Berghahn, 2012), 44–60.

15 For these desert forts as more than the "exercise of political power in the steppe" and, rather, "flight from the city in favor of a simpler life" (along the lines of the first ascetics) see Fowden, "Christian Monasteries and Umayyad Residences," 580–81.

vided an ideal setting for transgressive behavior (factual or fictional), whether it be the consumption of alcohol (and its over-indulgence), extra-marital relations or, arguably, theological encounters between Christians and Muslims.

Appearing in a range of genres, from histories to biographies to poems composed for entertainment, Islamic descriptions of monastic sojourns contain portrayals of piety, as well as of debauchery. They depict Christian acceptance of, or deference to, Muhammad and his message—or the worldly delights hidden behind their walls (implicitly or explicitly challenging Christian claims of pious abstinence, or responding to Christian critiques of Muslim worldly excesses). In many Christian compositions, on the other hand, monks or monasteries may be a background feature of an encounter, with little description. But, what—if anything—can be gleaned of the travel *experiences* from such descriptions?

Some Examples of Literary References to Monastic Sojourns

Although there are anecdotes of the monastic visits of the Damascus-based Umayyads (ca 680–750 CE) and early Baghdad-based Abbasids (ca 750–1258 CE), it was well into the Abbasid period, and further north, in the literary circles of Sayf al-Dawla, emir of Aleppo and north Syria from 945–967 CE—who was also a sponsor of the philosopher al-Fārābī[16]—that the Islamic genre of *diyārāt* ("monastery writings") flourished.[17] Given the luxuries of the monumental monasteries in the region, as well as the shrines to Saint Simeon the Stylite (just to the north of Aleppo) and Cosmo and Damian (in Cyrrhus, 70 km northeast of Aleppo), both of which would have been loci of pilgrimage among pre-Islamic Christians, Arabs and others, the emergence of the *diyārāt* in northern Syria is not surprising. Similar to the wine songs (*khamriyya*)[18] that emerged prior to Islam (largely in the vicinity of Hira in southern Iraq), but continued into the Islamic period, these "tales of the monasteries" often detail the delights of Christian monasteries. In addition to entertainment, the compositions give voice to some of the struggles that mark human

---

16 See, e.g., Ian Richard Netton, *Al-Farabi and His School* (London: Routledge, 2005).
17 In addition to their testimonies to revelry, this literature is an indication of the continued popularity of monastic sojourns in the Islamic period. See a list of Arabic works on monasteries (by Muslim authors) in ʿAlī b. Muḥammad al-Shābushtī, *Kitāb al-diyārāt*, ed. Kirkīs ʿAwwād (Baghdad: Maktabat al-Muthanna, 1966), 36–48. See also S. Munajid, "Morceau choisis du livre des moines," *MIDEO* 3 (1956): 349–58; Gérard Troupeau, "Les couvents chrétiens dans la littérature arabe," *La nouvelle revue du Caire* 1 (1975): 265–79.
18 For later wine poems see Geert-Jan van Gelder, "A Muslim Encomium on Wine: The Racecourse of the Bay (Halbat al-Kumayt) by al-Nawagi (d. 859/1455) as a Post-Classical Arabic Work," *Arabica* 42 (1995): 222–34 (222).

existence (love, questions about eschatology). They also highlight the permeable (or impermeable) nature of socially constructed boundaries: (il)licit desires of the body, whether gustatory, sensual or sexual; as well as interpersonal encounters, such as those that cross confessional lines. As such, they may be interpreted as reinforcing, or transgressing, boundaries. In the *diyārāt* and other literary genres, the most prevalent literary trope portrayed monasteries as places to indulge in wine music and flirtation—secularizing the monastery, and turning the sacred Christian space into places of leisure and indulgence for Muslims.[19]

Only one example of the genre of *diyārāt* survives in substantial portions (that of Shābushtī, d. 988 CE). It has 53 sections, describing particular monasteries. The first 39 sections note the location and setting, natural beauty and notable features, including festival days or amenities for visitors. It is followed by poetry composed at or about the monastery. The work contains anecdotes about the visits of caliphs, poets or other notables, as well as information on the history of the region and its people (e.g. Baghdad, Egypt or Syria, or the inhabitants and geography of the area of the Tigris and Euphrates). It concludes with monasteries where miracles occurred. There are numerous poems in which wine, women, youths, flowing streams, etc., figure prominently. While such compositions arguably reflect the author's "construction" of a site, the works do testify to the phenomenon of Muslim visits to monasteries. They are also a sort of travel guide for potential visitors. Similarly, while geographical dictionaries (e.g. the 7th/13th century Yāqūt's *Muʿjam al-buldān* or the 8th/14th century al-ʿUmari's *Masālik al-abṣār fī mamālik al-amṣār*) do provide information on monasteries, the information provided must be used carefully as it chiefly comes from poems, with elite drinking parties forming the core of the references. Some additional details may also be gleaned from other literary genres, such as histories or *adab* works.

The literary genre of a dialogue, sometimes within the compass of a letter-treatise, came to be an apologetical catechism for the use of Christians living in the world of Islam.[20] These Christian debate texts echo understandings of the liminality of monasteries, but tend to gloss over details of the travelers and their experience. Occasional details, however, do appear that give an indication of how a traveler may have experienced a monastery. For example, one debate text (discussed below) not only states illness of the Muslim participant as the pretext for the debate setting, but also specifies the number of days spent at the monastery, giving the reader a

---

[19] See, e.g., Kilpatrick, "Monasteries through Muslim Eyes," esp. p. 22.
[20] On this genre see Sidney H. Griffith, "The Monk in the Emir's Majlis: Reflections on a Popular Genre of Christian Literary Apologetics in Arabic in the Early Islamic Period," in *The Majlis: Interreligious Encounters in Medieval Islam*, ed. Hava Lazarus-Yafeh et al. (Wiesbaden: Harrassowitz, 1999), 13–65.

sense of why a Muslim may have had an extended stay at a monastery. Before discussing the "travel experience," an overview of a sampling of Christian and Muslim descriptions of "monastic sojourns" is in order.

Muhammad and Bahira

Reflecting the role of monastic establishments in the Syrian desert as waystations for caravans from Arabia, Islamic tradition maintains that a monk recognized the sign of prophethood on Muhammad long before the Qur'an would be revealed to him. According to this tradition,[21] as a young boy, Muhammad accompanied his uncle Abū Tālib as part of a caravan that stopped at a monk's dwelling in Bosra (an important city in late antique southwest Syria that housed a bishopric and where, in the 6th century, one of the largest churches in the region had been built: a five-aisled basilica[22]). The monk (Sergius/Bahira[23]) recognized even on the young Muhammad the "sign of prophecy."[24] Christian apologists were quick to develop a literature of their own (albeit not always in Arabic) about the (in their view, renegade) monk who fed Muhammad garbled versions of biblical stories to incorporate into the Qur'an.[25] Indicative of the confessional plurality of the region (although the Bosran episcopate adhered to Chalcedon, in 542 CE, a Miaphysite bishop was appointed for

---

21 This appears in a very early Muslim source, the *Sīrat rasūl Allāh*—biography of the Prophet—by Ibn Isḥāq, who was born in Medina about the year 85/704 CE. For other suggested locations—e.g., Mayfa'a (Umm al-Rasās, south of Amman) and Dayr al-Ba'iqi (20 km southwest of Bosra)—see, e.g., Bert de Vries, "On the Way to Bostra: Arab Settlement in South Syria Before Islam—The Evidence from Written Sources," in *Heureux qui comme Ulysses a fait un beau voyage: Movements of People in Time and Space*, ed. Nefissa Naguib and Bert de Vries (Bergen: BRIC, 2010), 69–92 (71); Shahîd, *Toponymy, Monuments, Historical Geography, and Frontier Studies*, 186–88.
22 See, e.g., Sulaiman A. Mougdad, *Bosra: Guide historique et archéologique* (Damascus: Tarabichi, 1974).
23 For various Christian interpretations of this encounter see Barbara Roggema, *The Legend of Sergius Baḥīrā: Eastern Christian Apologetics and Apocalyptic in Response to Islam* (Leiden: Brill, 2008).
24 On this concept see Sarah Stroumsa, "The Signs of Prophecy: The Emergence and Early Development of a Theme in Arabic Theological Literature," *HTR* 78 (1985): 101–14.
25 For reflections on John of Damascus' intimations that Muhammad was informed by a monk see, e.g., Peter Schadler, *John of Damascus and Islam: Christian Heresiology and the Intellectual Background to Earliest Christian-Muslim Relations* (Leiden: Brill, 2017). For a thoughtful reflection on an architectural analogue (e.g., Christian-Muslim interaction in the construction of mosques and churches) in Rusafa and the Negev see Glenn Peers, "'Crosses' Work Underfoot: Christian Spolia in the Late Antique Mosque at Shivta in the Negev Desert (Israel)," *Eastern Christian Art* 8 (2011): 101–19.

the city, likely residing in nearby Jabiya, a stronghold of the powerful Ghassanid tribe),[26] the Christian versions often identify the monk as adhering to a different Christological understanding from that of the author of the text in question (e.g., Nestorian or Jacobite in a "Melkite" text).

In these accounts, Christian or Muslim, the focus is the exceptional encounter between a monk and Muhammad, rather than the travel experience. While the *Sīra* (biography of Muhammad) does note that, in contrast to previous stops when the monk barely noticed the caravaneers, on the occasion of the meeting with Muhammad a great feast was provided, the nature of the dwelling, how long they stayed and how they were accommodated, let alone how individuals experienced the journey, are not provided.

Umayyads in Rusafa

As in the reports of the caravan of which Muhammad was a part, later Muslims would also find rest or refuge in monasteries. The Umayyad caliph Hishām Abd al-Malik (r. 724–43 CE), for example, reportedly escaped to a monastery during a time of plague. Likely the monastery was in the vicinity of Rusafa (southwest of present-day Raqqa, in north central Syria). Known as Sergiopolis to the Byzantines, after Jerusalem, it had been the major pilgrimage site of Palestine,[27] and the pilgrimage continued well into Islamic times. Significantly, the *qibla* wall (that housing the *miḥrāb*, the prayer niche indicating the direction of Mecca) of the major mosque of the city was adjacent to a courtyard shared with the basilica that housed the remains of Saint Sergius, a Byzantine martyr venerated by Christians and Muslims alike.[28]

Regarding the caliph's visit, the late 12th/early 13th century geographer, Yāqūt, notes that the caliph Hishām frequented Rusafa during a plague, using pre-existing (Ghassanid) constructions. He also describes a monastery in Rusafa that he had seen and considered one of the "wonders of the world as regards its beauty and architecture." He describes it as "a day's march from Raqqa for those who are laden."[29] From this, we can understand it took people with beasts of burden who

---

[26] C. Jonn Block, "Philoponian Monophysitism in South Arabia at the Advent of Islam with Implications for the English Translation of 'Thalātha' in Qur'ān 4.171 and 5.73," *JIS* 23 (2012): 50–75.
[27] Irfan Shahîd, "Arab Christian Pilgrimages in the Proto Byzantine Period," in *Pilgrimage and Holy Space in Late Antique Egypt*, ed. David Frankfurter (Leiden: Brill, 1998), 373–90 (379).
[28] Fowden, "Christian Monasteries and Umayyad Residences," 565–81.
[29] Cited by Fowden, "Christian Monasteries and Umayyad Residences," 576.

were carrying loads a day to travel there. But, the details of the travel experience are not germane to the geographer's purpose.

Even accounts that do attempt to furnish details of a travel experience must be read with caution. The following anecdote about the Caliph Hishām recorded by the ninth-century historian al-Balādhurī, is one such example:

> Hishām fled from the plague and came finally to a monastery (*dayr*). The monk brought him into a garden of his, four *jarībs* in area and began to give him the tastiest and ripest fruits. Hishām said, 'Would you sell me your garden?,' but the monk remained silent. Hishām repeated his question, but the monk was still silent. 'Why do you not speak, O monk? Are you hoping that all the people but you will die?' 'Why?' the monk asked. 'So that you may gain your fill,' Hishām said, 'when everything in the world is left for you'. At that the monk laughed and said, 'Didn't you hear that, O Abrash?'. Abrash said [i.e., to the caliph] 'Aside from him, no free man has ever met you.'[30]

While the geographer's and the historian's accounts together provide details that might give insight to the travel experience (such as the distance of the journey and the size of the monstery: the caliph receives fruit in a large garden, one *jarīb* being a 40m x 40m plot of land[31]), details such as which fruit he was offered, his mode of travel, the manner of his accommodation and the length of his stay are lacking. One also suspects that the detail of the size of the garden is provided as an indication of the monastery's luxury, and the monk's detachment from worldly delights, although surrounded by them.

This Umayyad[32] use of Rusafa echoes the pre-Islamic Ghassanid rulers' use of Christian monasteries.[33] Its water supply and gardens, combined with its intersection of trade and migration routes and its pilgrimage shrine of Sergius, made it a meeting place for tribes from Syria and Mesopotamia—a function that would not have gone unnoticed by Byzantine, Sasanian (or Arab Muslim) rulers. But what can, or do, we know of the "travel experience" of such a visit? Elizabeth Key Fowden has provided one possible reconstruction of a Ghassanid phylarch's—or Umayyad caliph's—visit to the monastery: upon arrival, he would have been respectfully received, likely participating in, or observing, the divine liturgy. Subsequently, he

---

30 Cited by Fowden, "Christian Monasteries and Umayyad Residences," 566.
31 A. Asa Eger, "(Re)Mapping Medieval Antioch: Urban Transformations from the Early Islamic to the Middle Byzantine Periods," *DOP* 67 (2013): 95–134.
32 For further discussion of caliphal visits to monasteries see Robert Hamilton, *Walid and His Friends: An Umayyad Tragedy* (Oxford: Oxford University Press, 1988), 86–91.
33 As noted by Fowden, "Christian Monasteries and Umayyad Residences," 567–68, 576–77, the Christian Arab tribes of the region had a devotion to the soldier saint (Sergius), and both migratory and trade routes of Arab pastoralists, semipastoralists and merchants passed by the walled settlement, including its shrine and monastery.

would have conducted his necessary affairs of state from the rooms that were provided him. In all likelihood, a banquet and considerable wine-consumption would have been part of any phylarch's, or caliph's, monastic visit.[34] But, while such a reconstruction is indeed plausible, it must be emphasized that the sources that recount such visits do not purport to relate the "travel experience" of the ruler or his entourage.

'Abbāsid accounts: al-Hira, Mosul and Samarra

Monasteries figures in accounts of caliphs and other notables into Abbasid times as well—apparently even featuring in wall paintings of an 'Abbāsid residence at Sāmarrā', capital of the caliphate from 836–ca. 892 CE.[35] Caliphs also continue to be portrayed as frequenting monasteries. For example, in the one surviving example of *diyārāt* literature, al-Shābushtī reports that, while on a hunting party, the caliph al-Mu'tazz (r. 866–869 CE) and a few of his companions became separated from the rest. The caliph became thirsty and one of his companions tells of a monk at a nearby monastery (in the vicinity of Sāmarrā') who possesses "wonderful charity" (*muwadda ḥasana*), a "charming spirit" (*khafīf al-rūḥ*)—and that there is wonderful food in the monastery. The caliph agrees to stop there, is refreshed, and, at the conclusion of his visit, orders a donation of money be given to the monastery. The monk accepts it on the condition the caliph returns one day.[36]

Similarly, al-Shābushtī reports that, while visiting Mosul, al-Ma'mūn (r. 813–833 CE) and his entourage sojourned at Dayr 'Al'ā—on Palm Sunday—because they had heard of its beauty and charm.[37] While details of the festival and the caliph's vantage point evoke a festive religious service befitting one of the most dramatic celebrations of the ecclesiastical calendar (the commemoration of Christ's entry to Jerusalem prior to his crucifixion, marking the start of Christianity's holiest week), again details of the "travel experience" of the caliph and his entourage are largely missing.

And it was not only caliphs who enjoyed visiting monasteries. The poet Jaḥẓa (224–324/839–936 CE), for example, provides details similar to those of al-Ma'mūn's visit in his description of a visit to Dayr Hanna, a celebrated monastery near

---

34 Fowden, "Christian Monasteries and Umayyad Residences," 576.
35 See Fowden, "The Lamp and the Wine Flask," 13 for the description left by one visitor to the al-Mukhtār palace at Sāmarrā'.
36 Anecdote and translation provided in Bowman, "Monastery as Tavern," 67.
37 Bowman, "Monastery as Tavern," 68; for further details of the monastery see, e.g., Kilpatrick, "Monasteries through Muslim Eyes," 29.

al-Ḥīra. As Fowden notes, such descriptions may be understood as "a distillation of what monasteries had come by the early ʿAbbāsid period to represent in the Muslim literary imagination: places of sensual beauty and ease, where food, wine, sacred books and sexual titillation converged."[38]

While the details that do emerge from al-Shābushtī's *diyārāt* (wine, aromatic plants, gardens, proximity to the Tigris river) evoke frivolous diversion and pleasurable escape from cares, as Brad Bowman has recently argued,[39] the numerous accounts of Muslim visits to monasteries may also reflect a climate of confessional fluidity,[40] in which Muslims actively—intentionally and willingly—participated in Christian festivals and visited monasteries with devotional intent. If the latter is the case, accounts (especially by detractors) of such visits may have included debauchery (e.g., wine drinking) in order to distract from, or discredit, any semblance of confessional confusion—or to cast aspersions on the character of a caliph who was already subject to criticism (e.g. al-Maʾmūn, as discussed below). But, as Christian religious services (if not monasteries per se) would have allowed for mixing of the sexes, singing and consumption of wine—and as monks both produced and consumed wine (and were not subject to Islamic prohibitions deriving from the Qurʾan—although the extent of Muslim observance of such prohibition is not always clear)[41]—monasteries could also have served as acceptable loci for activities upon which members of the Islamic religious establishment may have frowned.

Christian Accounts, from Harran to al-Hira

Christian literature also depicts monastic sojourns. Even in pre-Islamic times, Christians were at the forefront of the so-called *khamriyyāt*, or wine songs, which frequently highlight the Bacchic potential of monasteries.[42] Monasteries also appear in texts of a more serious nature, however. For example, the debate over whether Christian monks should teach Muslim children is mentioned by one of the first Syriac Christian authors who alludes to Islam, Jacob of Edessa (ca. 640–708

---

38 Fowden, "The Lamp and the Wine Flask," 15.
39 Bowman, "Monastery as Tavern."
40 Suliman Bashear, "Qibla Musharriqa and Early Muslim Prayer in Churches," *MW* 81 (1991): 267–82 (p. 278).
41 For an overview of some of the nuances within Islamic history to this prohibition see, e.g., Kathryn Kueny, *The Rhetoric of Sobriety: Wine in Early Islam* (Albany: State University of New York Press, 2001).
42 See Fowden, "Lamp and Wine Flask," 14 for a discussion of al-Ḥīra and neighboring al-Kūfa as the "mother of the wine song."

CE).⁴³ This question would be picked up in various recensions of the Covenant of Umar.⁴⁴ Although the details of the interactions (for example, where such lessons would take place) are not precised, that both Christian and Muslim sources reference the problem indicates that monks and other Christian clerics were, in fact, involved in the education of Muslim children. Similarly, Christian-Muslims debate texts often feature a monk debating the virtues of Christianity before an emir—but as the guest of the Muslim ruler, rather than the host of the emir (e.g. Theodore Abu Qurra, bishop of Harran, before al-Ma'mun).⁴⁵

And, references to Muslim visits to monasteries do appear in Christian writings. One of the earliest examples is the debate of a Muslim with a monk of Beyt Hale.⁴⁶ Although composed in Syriac, it is likely the conversation occurred in Arabic as the author states that the dialogue went forth without the aid of an interpreter. While the precise identity of the interlocutors, as well as the location of the monastery is uncertain, it has been argued convincingly that the monastery was Dayr Mār 'Abdā near Kūfa and Hīra, and that the Muslim was Maslama b. 'Abd al-Malik (d. 738 CE), who was governor of Iraq in the 720s CE. For our purposes, the account is notable as it states that the debate occurred with a member of the caliphal entourage who was at the monastery for ten days because he was ill. As this note does nothing except to give a justification for the debate (a bedridden delegate)— does it mean that he stayed longer than was usual, or that he had come intentionally because of his illness? Although further details of the travel experience are not provided, the reader is left with the impression that the monastery functioned as a hospital, or guest house, of sorts, for an ill Muslim—and that the environment was sufficiently comfortable to furnish an opportunity for theological discussion while at least one of the participants was ill.

---

43 On whom see, e.g., Bas ter Haar Romeny, ed., *Jacob of Edessa and the Syriac Culture of his Day* (Leiden: Brill, 2008).
44 On which see Wilde, "We Shall Not Teach the Qur'an to Our Children," 233–59.
45 For an indicative overview of such debate texts from the early period (also from Islamic tradition) see, e.g., David R. Thomas and Barbara Roggema, *600–900*, vol. 1 of *Christian-Muslim Relations: A Bibliographical History* (Leiden: Brill, 2009). Other volumes in the series continue this bibliographic history up until the present day.
46 See Sidney H. Griffith, "Disputing with Islam in Syriac: The Case of the Monk of Bēt Hālē and a Muslim Emir," *Hug* 3 (2000): 29–54.

Discussion: Discerning Travel Experiences from Literary Texts

Travel is a commonly attested phenomenon in the late antique and early Islamic period, with somewhat different emphases. In pre-Islamic Arabia, the *qasida* was the Arabic literary form par excellence.[47] Reflecting journeys as a common fact of life for pastoralists, nomads and merchants, these compositions contain detailed descriptions of the difficulties the poet faced while traveling to his destination. The Qur'an, too, references the annual summer and winter journeys of the Qurayš (Q Qurayš 106:2) and appears to distinguish the desert nomads from other qur'anic auditors (e.g. Q al-Aḥzāb 33:20; Q al-Ḥujurāt 49:14). One of the early designations of Muslims is, in fact, *muhājirūn*—those who have migrated (both in the immediate context of Muhammad's followers who left Mecca for the more hospitable Medina/Yathrib in 622 CE, and also as a descriptor of those who left the peninsula to help establish new Arab/Muslim settlements in nearby regions).[48] Later Islamic compositions such as the *maqāmāt* and *riḥla* would also elaborate upon the travel experiences of various individuals, lending themselves to the observation that one of the "core attitudes" of "pre-modern Arabic, indeed Islamic, culture" was "geographic and cultural mobility."[49]

Unlike contemporaneous pre-Islamic Arabic literature that includes journeys as part of life, even extolling them, late antique literature frequently depicts people who travel in an unsavory manner (e.g., the marauding Arabs who cause the martyrdom of pious Christians).[50] Reflecting a settled, urban bias, even wan-

---

47 For an overview of the history of the *qasida* see, e.g., Beatrice Gruendler, "The Qasida," in *The Literature of Al-Andalus*, ed. María R. Menocal, Raymond P. Scheindlin, and Michael Sells (Cambridge: Cambridge University Press, 2000), 211–31 (esp. 212).
48 Ilkka Lindstedt, "Muhājirūn as a Name for the First/Seventh Century Muslims," *JNES* 74 (2015): 67–73.
49 Angelika Neuwirth, "*Ayyu harajin ʿalā man anshaʾa mulahan*? Al-Ḥarīrī's Plea for the Legitimacy of Playful Transgressions of Social Norms," in *Humor in der arabischen Kultur: Humor in Arabic Culture*, ed. Georges Tamer (Berlin: De Gruyter, 2009), 241–54 (241). For an overview of Arabic travel writing, e.g. the *riḥla*, which emerges in north Africa and al-Andalus a few centuries after the *diyārāt*, see Daniel Newman, "Arabic Travel Writing," in *The Cambridge History of Travel Writing*, ed. Nandini Das and Tim Youngs (Cambridge: Cambridge University Press, 2019), 143–58; for an overview of classical Arabic poetic descriptions see Akiko Motoyoshi Sumi, *Description in Classical Arabic Poetry: Waṣf, Ekphrasis, and Interarts Theory*, Brill Studies in Middle Eastern Literatures 25 (Leiden: Brill, 2004). On poetry in the early Islamic period in general see Stefan Sperl, "Islamic Kingship and Arabic Panegyric Poetry in the Early 9th Century," in *Early Islamic Poetry and Poetics*, ed. Suzanne P. Stetkevych (London: Routledge, 2017), 79–94.
50 For an overview of their depiction see Konstantin M. Klein, "Marauders, Daredevils, and Noble Savages: Perceptions of Arab Nomads in Late Antique Hagiography," *Der Islam* 92 (2015): 13–41; for

dering holy men who are portrayed as saintly are depicted as coming into conflict with established powers.⁵¹ Despite the aforementioned mobility, such bias arguably continued among the urban-based populations in the Islamic period, where "illicit encounters" (e.g., inter-confessional debates, or various sexual relations or other behaviors that did not fall within societal norms) frequently are portrayed as occurring outside of the city limits: on the road, in the fortified castles of the deserts,⁵² and even in monasteries.

But these monasteries, while in the desert, were also adjacent to main roadways, including caravan or pastoralist routes. (A similar observation could be made about the desert palaces of the Umayyads.) And, if the population in question was relatively mobile, with adequate connections to facilitate travel between cities and villages (and even to outlying monasteries), might a journey to a monastery represent a relatively common journey, devoid of excessive hardships, that the journey itself merited little comment?

The paucity of the details of the travel experience in both Christian and Muslim texts, however, deserves deeper reflection. Especially when compared to other literary genres (both pre-dating and continuing into the Islamic period) that do contain details of travel, many of the texts examined here are striking for the dearth of details of the travel experience itself. For example, even when a particular encounter is mentioned in an independent historical source,⁵³ as in the Christian debate texts or even the *diyārāt*, details such as the means of transportation, the length of the journey, or how many people were in the traveler's entourage are frequently missing. Is this because they were not germane for the purpose of these texts (indicating that these were not travel logs, but were rather catechetical exercises, or designed for entertainment)—or is it because the details of travel would be already

---

depictions as Christians came to write in Arabic see David Vila, "The Struggle over Arabisation in Medieval Arabic Christian Hagiography," *Masāq* 15 (2003): 35–46.

51 For an overview of their conflicts with the political and ecclesiastical establishment see Daniel Caner, *Wandering, Begging Monks? Spiritual Authority and the Promotion of Monasticism in Late Antiquity* (Berkeley: University of California Press, 2002). On the portrayal of travel as difficult see, e.g., Maribel Dietz, *Wandering Monks, Virgins, and Pilgrims: Ascetic Travel in the Mediterranean World, AD 300–800* (University Park: Pennsylvania State University Press, 2005), 135. For a nuanced interpretation of the urban-rural (including wandering ascetic) divide see David Frankfurter, "Urban Shrine and Rural Saint in Fifth-Century Alexandria," in *Pilgrimage in Graeco-Roman and Early Christian Antiquity: Seeing the Gods*, ed. Jas Elsner and Ian Rutherford (Oxford: Oxford University Press, 2007), 435–49.

52 See Fowden, "Christian Monasteries and Umayyad Residences" for discussion on various parallels between Umayyad residences and Christian monasteries located outside the cities.

53 Theodore Abū Qurra's encounter with the caliph al-Ma'mūn is one such example. See, e.g., Sidney H. Griffith, "Reflections on the Biography of Theodore Abu Qurrah," *ParOr* 18 (1993): 143–170 (156).

known, or uninteresting, to the intended audience? For, unlike the perils faced by pre-Islamic nomads traveling through the deserts, or the adventures awaiting later Muslims who traveled far from their own cultural zones,[54] the authors and subjects of the aforementioned compositions likely journeyed along familiar routes—monasteries frequently being located in the vicinity of well-traveled routes or roads, many in Syria being of Roman design.[55] While highway robbery and other such dangers were not unknown, Hugh Kennedy's observations[56] on the early Islamic period, including the shift to city government, opening up of land routes and also the building of palaces and accompanying agricultural developments in the countryside lends itself to such a reading.[57]

Despite the relative dearth of descriptions of the "travel experience," Christians and Muslims have used, and written about, monasteries as travel loci, although the compositions arguably have very different purposes and audiences. Christian debate texts may be set in monasteries, or contain a Christian monk traveling to a Muslim notable's residence. Islamic sources, in a variety of genres, also reference Christian monasteries. While such places were in fact outside of the cities, thus providing an illusion of liminality, they were also easily within reach of society. Does this imply that the liminality of such encounters was also only illusory? That the debate text was the most common genre of Christian apologetics indicates that it resonated with people: Christians and Muslims *did* interact. Whether the monastic setting was a construction (drawing upon late antique tropes) intended to establish the liminality of such encounters, or whether traveling enabled (more relaxed) encounters than one might have within the societal restrictions of one's normal habitus, is difficult to determine.

We are far removed from the authors and initial audiences of (let alone the encounters depicted in) the texts discussed here. Nevertheless, the differences between Christian and Muslim accounts of monastic sojourns also merit some reflection. The differences among the details found in the various accounts of

---

54 On rihla accounts see, e.g., Houari Touati, *Islam and Travel in the Middle Ages* (Chicago: University of Chicago Press, 2010); Methal R. Mohammed-Marzouk, "Knowledge, Culture, and Positionality: Analysis of Three Medieval Muslim Travel Accounts," *Cross-Cultural Communication* 8/6 (2012): 1–10.
55 On Roman roads in the region see, e.g., Katia Cytryn-Silverman, "The Fifth mīl from Jerusalem: Another Umayyad Milestone from Southern Bilād al-Shām," *BSOAS* 70 (2007): 603–10; David Kennedy, "Roman Roads and Routes in North-East Jordan," *Levant* 29 (1997): 71–93.
56 Hugh Kennedy, "From Polis to Madina: Urban Change in Late Antique and Early Islamic Syria," *PaP* 106 (1985): 3–27.
57 On the "borderless" nature of the 7th century Roman Empire see David Olster, "From Periphery to Center: The Transformation of Late Roman Self-Definition in the Seventh Century," in *Shifting Frontiers in Late Antiquity*, ed. Ralph W. Mathisen and Hagith S. Sivan (Aldershot: Ashgate Variorum, 1996), 93–101 (98), cited in Bowman, "Monastery as Tavern," 53.

monastic sojourns of the early Islamic period, such as the relative silence in Christian texts on monastic luxuries, leaves us with some questions as to the fact, and nature, of the travel experience. How comfortable were monasteries—for monks or their guests? How did the monks or their guests experience the travel to, or from, the monastery? Despite these lingering questions, the presence of monasteries as travel destinations of caliphs and other Muslims indicates that, far from seclusion, monasteries frequently served as hospitality centers for Christians—and, eventually, for Muslims.[58] Further, the prevalence of the trope of the monk (or other Christian cleric) traveling to the Muslim official's residence to participate in debates indicates that the tendency that troubled late antique bishops—the peripatetic leanings of some monks—also seems to have continued well into Islamic times.

The differences between the descriptions of Christians (especially the monastery hosts) and Muslim (visitors) may also simply be due to an emic/etic divide. Polemic or apologetic intent aside, an insider (monk) may simply not think to comment on aspects of the monastery visit that coincide with his routine; the outsider (visiting Muslim, for example) may, due to the novelty of the experience, find many more things upon which to comment.

Nevertheless, while the different texts and authors do not furnish us with identical details of a monastery or a journey,[59] a similar picture emerges from the various literary references: monasteries as desert waystations that could serve as host to dignitaries, pilgrims, the ill or merchants. Continuing the trend begun in late antiquity, monasteries appear as privileged sites that rulers (Christian or not) enjoyed. Archaeological findings confirm the descriptions in literary sources of monasteries situated by water supplies, providing a green relief to the desert landscape. The food was of better than average quality. Some had beautiful churches and luxurious decorations (lamps, tapestries). As such, also under Muslim rule, the monasteries of Greater Syria and Iraq, at least, continued to serve the same role in hospitality they had had in late antiquity.

To summarize, both Christian and Muslim compositions from the early Islamic period reflect pre-Islamic understandings of monasteries (and also churches) as a network of privileged sites. But, given their source material (e.g., poems from drinking parties), even the Islamic geographic or administrative dictionaries are unlikely to have been intended as providing a literal recounting of the details of actual historic encounters. Any such details that might emerge are more likely to

---

[58] On this see Kilpatrick, "Monasteries through Muslim Eyes," 23–24.

[59] And sometimes interreligious encounters are preserved by only one tradition. See, e.g., Sidney H. Griffith, "Disputes with Muslims in Syriac Christian Texts: From Patriarch John (d. 648) to Bar Hebraeus (d. 1286)," in *Doctrine and Debate in the East Christian World: 300–1500*, ed. Averil Cameron and Robert Hoyland (London: Routledge, 2011), 173–96.

be incidental (e.g. the four-jarīb garden of Hishām's visit). The *diyārāt* and debate texts are even further removed from a pretense of annales-style historical record keeping. But, each of these compositions would likely have had enough verisimilitude to actual, or possible, encounters—to be convincing enough to hold the attention of their intended audience. Thus, while attempting to match a single known historical figure or historical encounter (as attested in other biographical or chronological sources) to individuals named in such literature might result in inconclusive identifications (at best), the descriptions of the encounters may indeed give some insight to contemporaneous society and culture.[60]

Conclusions

A recent (pre-Covid) popular article on people's lack of interest in vacation stories[61]— even those of their own friends—identifies a number of factors affecting people's interest (or lack thereof) in the travel experiences of other people. The biggest obstacles are the joy people derive from speaking of themselves (substantiated by a Harvard study that demonstrated speaking of oneself activates the pleasure center of the brain) and the misplaced belief that people enjoy being told new information (when, in fact, as another study revealed, people are much more likely to enjoy a story whose material was familiar to them). This study of people's interest in the travel of others reflects the importance of both the narrator's and the audience's subjectivity in the reception of a "travel narrative." Even were we somehow able to control for chronological and cultural differences, how possible is it to attain an understanding of the experience itself from the report of the journey? In contrast to a casual conversation of acquaintances, literary reports, especially those that have passed through various editorial redactions, are constructed with an intended audience and designated purpose. Whether the initial travelers anticipated their intended audiences' lack of interest in the mundane details of their journeys, or whether they were constrained by a sense of humility, or whether later editors excised details they considered extraneous (such as any descriptions of the travel experience itself), the texts discussed here are remarkably lacking in details of the travel experience. Details of the location and participants are provided for verisimilitude, but the focus is the conversation.

---

60 For this argument see, e.g., Bowman, "Monastery as Tavern."
61 Aditi Shrikant, "Why we Hate Hearing about Other People's Vacations," *Voxmedia*, 18 Oct 2018, https://www.vox.com/the-goods/2018/10/18/17994238/vacation-travel-stories-boring (last accessed 26 April 2023).

Nevertheless, the fact remains that both Christian and Islamic sources attest to Muslim visits to monasteries, indicating that such journeys likely did occur (even taking into consideration the possibility that later editors may have introduced details to give a semblance of accuracy, or fact, to otherwise fictional encounters). While we are unlikely to be understand their travel experiences, that such visits (and conversations between Christians and Muslims) were reported—by both Christian and Muslim authors—to have occurred in Christian monasteries in areas under Muslim rule nuances historical and contemporary narratives of the difficulties faced by the dhimmis (religious minorities) in *dār al-Islām*.

While pre-Islamic Arab notables are known to have used churches as banquet halls for state functions, the liminality of monasteries arguably permitted a greater range of encounters, or served as a plausible background for liminal encounters. For, following late antique stereotypes, boundary-crossing is a prevalent theme in allusions to monasteries in Arabic and other literature coming from Islamic times—monasteries as (desert) locations in which (at least in the eyes of their critics) sometimes transgressive encounters might occur. Particularly if Muslims did continue to honor some of the devotions of their ancestors (such as to Christian saints),[62] and confessional boundaries were not as clearly defined as the portrayal of (later) prescriptions mandating separation from (and, at times, the subservience of) the *dhimmī* (religious minorities "protected" by the caliphate),[63] how do we best understand the accounts of Muslims in monasteries as they were understood at the time of composition, rather than through the preconceptions of our chronological (and geographic) remove?

Another important question is whether the surviving reports of monastery visits reflect the opinions of larger society, or particular factions or individuals. For example, the geographer al-Yāqūt preserves a report of the oft-vilified Umayyad caliph al-Walīd b Yazīd (d 744 CE),[64] who is frequently depicted as engaging in debauchery, as taking communion at Dayr Bawannā, a monastery near Damascus. That his actions were commemorated in verse suggests they were told widely, for instructional and/or entertainment purposes. But, as with the early Abbasid caliph,

---

[62] On Muslim appreciation for Christian monasteries and churches see Gérard Troupeau, "Les églises d'Antioche chez les auteurs arabes," in *L'Orient au coeur*, ed. Floréal Sanagustin (Paris: Maisonneuve & Larose, 2001), 319–27; Troupeau, "Les couvents chrétiens dans la litterature arabe"; for a theory of confessional fluidity as a result of widespread theological ignorance on the part of most of the population see Jack Tannous, *The Making of the Medieval Middle East: Religion, Society, and Simple Believers* (Princeton: Princeton University Press, 2018).

[63] Wadi Zatoan Haddad, "Ahl al-dhimma in an Islamic State: The Teaching of Abū al-Hasan al-Mawardi's *Al-ahkam al-sultaniyya*," *ICMR* 7 (1996): 169–80.

[64] Steven Judd, "Reinterpreting al-Walīd b. Yazīd," *JAOS* 128 (2008): 439–58. Discussed also in Bowman, "Monastery as Tavern," 68–69.

al-Maʾmūn (r. 813–833 CE), whose short-lived attempt to influence theological interpretations[65] placed the eponym of the "traditionalist" *madhhab* (law school) Ahmad b. Hanbal (d 241/855 CE), in prison, is it also possible that later portrayals of the "transgressions" of these caliphs were as much the constructions (in their lifetimes, or subsequently) of their political, or theological, opponents as a reflection of their behaviors? For, as with a travel experience, even if the actions did in fact occur, how well can we know how they themselves, or their contemporaries, perceived their actions? Although, Islam is commonly portrayed[66] as forbidding intoxicants, the qurʾanic and later Islamic approaches to *khamr* and related substances is more nuanced.[67] Similarly, the practices of individual Christians and Muslims, past and present, do not conform to official prohibitions on Muslims in Christian churches (and Christians in Muslim places of worship) that are currently enforced in some areas (e.g. the "cathedral-mosque" of Cordoba,[68] or the Islamic holy sites at Mecca and Medina[69]).

We may well ask whether the descriptions discussed above were intended to portray the intimate details of actual encounters; to highlight the piety and worldly detachment of the "good" monks (or Muslims); or to underscore the hypocrisies of Muslim rulers who "command the good and forbid the wrong"—yet engaged in activities permitted to Christians but forbidden to Muslims, or of Christians who profess a life of abstinence, yet clearly have all the necessities (and luxuries) available in their day.[70] While neither the intent of those who portrayed such visits nor the

---

65 On al-Maʾmūn and mihna see, e.g., John Nawas, "A Reexamination of Three Current Explanations for al-Mamun's Introduction of the Mihna," *IJMES* 26 (1994): 615–29.
66 See, e.g., Yusuf al-Qaradawi, *The Lawful and the Prohibited in Islam:* الحلال والحرام في الإسلام, first published in Arabic in 1960, and now widely available in English translation, e.g., at http://www.genderi.org/pars_docs/refs/76/75338/75338.pdf (last accessed 26 April 2023).
67 Kueny, *The Rhetoric of Sobriety*; Pooyan Tamimi Arab, "Islamic Heritage versus Orthodoxy: Figural Painting, Musical Instruments and Wine Bowls at the Dutch National Museum of World Cultures," *Journal of Material Culture* 26 (2021): 178–200; for a similar fluidity regarding images of the Prophet and popular perceptions of Islamic bans on this practice see Christiane Gruber, "Between Logos (Kalima) and Light (Nūr): Representations of the Prophet Muhammad in Islamic Painting," *Muqarnas* 26 (2009): 229–62.
68 Jessica R. Boll, "Irony Made Manifest: Cultural Contention and Córdoba's Mosque-Cathedral," *Journal of Cultural Geography* 34 (2017): 275–302; Brian Rosa and Jaime Jover-Báez, "Contested Urban Heritage: Discourses of Meaning and Ownership of the Mosque-Cathedral of Córdoba, Spain," *Journal of Urban Cultural Studies* 4 (2017): 127–54.
69 Harry Munt, "'No Two Religions': Non-Muslims in the Early Islamic Ḥijāz," *BSOAS* 78 (2015): 249–69.
70 For one Christian response to Muslim critiques of chastity see Thérèse-Anne Druart, "An Arab Christian Philosophical Defense Of Religious Celibacy Against Its Islamic Condemnation: Yaḥyā Ibn ʿAdī," in *Chastity: A Study in Perception, Ideals, Opposition*, ed. Nancy van Deusen (Leiden: Brill, 2008), 77–85.

"travel experiences" of those involved may ever be known with certainty, literary attestations to Muslim visits to Christian monasteries have echoes in contemporary practices. Thus, the observations of contemporary social scientists such as anthropologists and sociologists, coupled with the significant findings of archaeologists attesting to the proximity of Muslim and Christian places of worship, may help us interpret both legal statutes concerning, and literary attestations to, Muslim visits to Christian monasteries.

While the early Islamic confessional "confusion" (or fluidity) may well be attributed to the theological ignorance of the masses, might insights into human culture and society from disciplines such as sociology and anthropology (and politics), as well as critical reflection on the nature, intention and reception of historical "texts," influence our understanding of the development of theological and legal norms? Similarly, social sciences (sociology, including politics and economics; anthropology) may better explain contemporary prohibitions on Muslims "prostrating" in the Cordoba cathedral, or the strict regulations around the sale and consumption of alcohol in some Muslim-majority countries, than scriptural or theological references. Finally, might the study of (contemporary) human behavior (such as Muslims frequenting Christian churches in Iraq) also contribute to our understanding of details provided in historical texts that are at variance with official (Christian and Muslim) narratives and norms around the separation of the confessions?

References

Allen, Pauline. "Religious Conflict between Antioch and Alexandria c. 565–630 CE." Pages 187–200 in *Religious Conflict from Early Christianity to the Rise of Islam*. Edited by Wendy Mayer and Bronwen Neil. Berlin: De Gruyter, 2013.
Ashbrook, Susan. "Asceticism in Adversity: An Early Byzantine Experience." *BMGS* 6 (1980): 1–11.
Bashear, Suliman. "Qibla Musharriqa and Early Muslim Prayer in Churches." *MW* 81 (1991): 267–82.
Block, C. Jonn. "Philoponian Monophysitism in South Arabia at the Advent of Islam with Implications for the English Translation of 'Thalātha' in Qurʾān 4.171 and 5.73." *JIS* 23 (2012): 50–75.
Boll, Jessica R. "Irony Made Manifest: Cultural Contention and Córdoba's Mosque-Cathedral." *Journal of Cultural Geography* 34 (2017): 275–302.
Bonnéric, Julie. "Archaeological Evidence for an Early Islamic Monastery in the Centre of al-Qusur (Failaka Island, Kuwait)." *AAE* 32 (2021). https://doi.org/10.1111/aae.12182.
Bowman, Brad B. "The Monastery as Tavern and Temple in Medieval Islam: The Case for Confessional Flexibility in the Locus of Christian Monasteries." *ME* 27 (2021): 50–77.
Caner, Daniel. *Wandering, Begging Monks? Spiritual Authority and the Promotion of Monasticism in Late Antiquity*. Berkeley: University of California Press, 2002.
Christiansen, Johanne Louise. "'Stay Up During the Night, Except for a Little' (Q 73:2): The Qurʾānic Vigils as Ascetic Training Programs." *Religion* 49 (2019): 614–35.

Constable, Olivia Remie. *Housing the Stranger in the Mediterranean World: Lodging, Trade, and Travel in Late Antiquity and the Middle Ages*. Cambridge: Cambridge University Press, 2004.
Couroucli, Maria. "Chthonian Spirits and Shared Shrines: The Dynamics of Place among Christians and Muslims in Anatolia." Pages 44–60 in *Sharing the Sacra: The Politics and Pragmatics of Inter-communal Relations around Holy Places*. Edited by Glenn Bowman. Oxford: Berghahn, 2012.
Crislip, Andrew Todd. *From Monastery to Hospital: Christian Monasticism and the Transformation of Health Care in Late Antiquity*. Ann Arbor: University of Michigan Press, 2005.
Cytryn-Silverman, Katia. "The Fifth mīl from Jerusalem: Another Umayyad Milestone from Southern Bilād al-Shām." *BSOAS* 70 (2007): 603–10.
Dietz, Maribel. *Wandering Monks, Virgins, and Pilgrims: Ascetic Travel in the Mediterranean World, AD 300–800*. University Park: Pennsylvania State University Press, 2005.
Druart, Thérèse-Anne. "An Arab Christian Philosophical Defense Of Religious Celibacy Against Its Islamic Condemnation: Yaḥyā Ibn ʿAdī." Pages 77–85 in *Chastity: A Study in Perception, Ideals, Opposition*. Edited by Nancy van Deusen. Leiden: Brill, 2008.
Eger, A. Asa. "(Re)Mapping Medieval Antioch: Urban Transformations from the Early Islamic to the Middle Byzantine Periods." *DOP* 67 (2013): 95–134.
Elders, Joseph. "The Lost Churches of the Arabian Gulf: Recent Discoveries on the Islands of Sir Bani Yas and Marawah, Abu Dhabi Emirate, United Arab Emirates." *Proceedings of the Seminar for Arabian Studies* 31 (2001): 47–57.
Ellis, Linda, and Frank L. Kidner, eds. *Travel, Communication and Geography in Late Antiquity: Sacred and Profane*. London: Routledge, 2017.
Fowden, Elizabeth Key. "Christian Monasteries and Umayyad Residences in Late Antique Syria." *AnCr* 21 (2004): 565–81.
Fowden, Elizabeth Key. "The Lamp and the Wine Flask: Early Muslim Interest in Christian Monasticism." Pages 1–29 In *Islamic Crosspollinations: Interactions in the Medieval Middle East*. Edited by Anna Akasoy, James E. Montgomery, and Peter E. Pormann. Cambridge: Gibb Memorial Trust, 2007.
Fowden, Elizabeth Key. "Sharing Holy Places." *Common Knowledge* 8 (2002): 124–46.
Frankfurter, David. "Urban Shrine and Rural Saint in Fifth-Century Alexandria." Pages 435–49 in *Pilgrimage in Graeco-Roman and Early Christian Antiquity: Seeing the Gods*. Edited byJas Elsner and Ian Rutherford. Oxford: Oxford University Press, 2007.
Garcin, Jean-Claude. "Les traces de l'époque musulmane." Pages 125–34 in *Kellia I. Kôm 219: Fouilles exécutées en 1964 et 1965*. Edited by François Daumas and Antoine Guillaumont. Cairo: Imprimerie de l'Institut français d'archéologie orientale, 1969.
Gelder, Geert-Jan van. "A Muslim Encomium on Wine: The Racecourse of the Bay (Halbat al-Kumayt) by al-Nawagi (d. 859/1455) as a Post-Classical Arabic Work." *Arabica* 42 (1995): 222–34.
Griffith, Sidney H. "Reflections on the Biography of Theodore Abu Qurrah." *ParOr* 18 (1993): 143–170.
Griffith, Sidney H. "The Monk in the Emir's Majlis: Reflections on a Popular Genre of Christian Literary Apologetics in Arabic in the Early Islamic Period." Pages 13–65 in *The Majlis: Interreligious Encounters in Medieval Islam*. Edited by Hava Lazarus-Yafeh, Mark R. Cohen, Sasson Somekh, and Sidney H. Griffth. Wiesbaden: Harrassowitz, 1999.
Griffith, Sidney H. "Disputing with Islam in Syriac: The Case of the Monk of Bēt Ḥālē and a Muslim Emir." *Hug* 3 (2000): 29–54.
Griffith, Sidney H. "Disputes with Muslims in Syriac Christian Texts: From Patriarch John (d. 648) to Bar Hebraeus (d. 1286)." Pages 173–96 in *Doctrine and Debate in the East Christian World: 300–1500*. Edited by Averil Cameron and Robert Hoyland. London: Routledge, 2011.

Griffith, Sidney H. *The Church in the Shadow of the Mosque*. Princeton: Princeton University Press, 2012.
Griffith, Sidney H. "The Melkites and the Muslims: The Qur'ān, Christology, and Arab Orthodoxy." *Qantara* 33 (2013): 413–43.
Gruber, Christiane. "Between Logos (Kalima) and Light (Nūr): Representations of the Prophet Muhammad in Islamic Painting." *Muqarnas* 26 (2009): 229–62.
Gruendler, Beatrice. "The Qasida." Pages 211–31 in *The Literature of Al-Andalus*. Edited by María R. Menocal, Raymond P. Scheindlin, and Michael Sells. Cambridge: Cambridge University Press, 2000.
Guidetti, Mattia. "The Byzantine Heritage in the Dār al-Islām: Churches and Mosques in al-Ruha between the Sixth and Twelfth Centuries." *Muqarnas* 26 (2009): 1–36.
Haar Romeny, Bas ter, ed. *Jacob of Edessa and the Syriac Culture of His Day*. Leiden: Brill, 2008.
Haddad, Wadi Zatoan. "Ahl al-dhimma in an Islamic State: The Teaching of Abū al-Hasan al-Mawardi's *Al-ahkam al-sultaniyya*." *ICMR* 7 (1996): 169–80.
Hamilton, Robert. *Walid and His Friends: An Umayyad Tragedy*. Oxford: Oxford University Press, 1988.
Horn, Cornelia. "Jesus, the Wondrous Infant, at the Exegetical Crossroads of Christian Late Antiquity and Early Islam." Pages 27–46 in *Exegetical Crossroads: Understanding Scripture in Judaism, Christianity and Islam in the Pre-Modern Orient*. Edited by Georges Tamer, Regina Grundmann, Assaad Elias Kattan, and Karl Pinggéra. Berlin: De Gruyter, 2017.
Judd, Steven. "Reinterpreting al-Walīd b. Yazīd." *JAOS* 128 (2008): 439–58.
Kennedy, David. "Roman Roads and Routes in North-East Jordan." *Levant* 29 (1997): 71–93.
Kennedy, Hugh. "From Polis to Madina: Urban Change in Late Antique and Early Islamic Syria." *PaP* 106 (1985): 3–27.
Kennedy, Philip. *The Wine Song in Classical Arabic Poetry: Abū Nuwās and the Literary Tradition*. Oxford: Oxford University Press, 1997.
Kilpatrick, Hilary. "Monasteries through Muslim Eyes: The Diyarat Books." Pages 19–37 in *Christians at the Heart of Islamic Rule: Church Life and Scholarship in 'Abbasid Iraq*. Edited by David Thomas. Leiden: Brill, 2003.
Kingsley, Sean, and Michael Decker. *Economy and Exchange in the East Mediterranean During Late Antiquity*. Oxford: Oxbow, 2015.
Klein, Konstantin M. "Marauders, Daredevils, and Noble Savages: Perceptions of Arab Nomads in Late Antique Hagiography." *Der Islam* 92 (2015): 13–41.
Kueny, Kathryn. *The Rhetoric of Sobriety: Wine in Early Islam*. Albany: State University of New York Press, 2001.
Lindstedt, Ilkka. "Muhājirūn as a Name for the First/Seventh Century Muslims." *JNES* 74 (2015): 67–73.
Mayer, Wendy. "Welcoming the Stranger in the Mediterranean East: Syria and Constantinople." *Journal of the Australian Early Medieval Association* 5 (2009): 89–106.
Mohammed-Marzouk, Methal R. "Knowledge, Culture, and Positionality: Analysis of Three Medieval Muslim Travel Accounts." *Cross-Cultural Communication* 8/6 (2012): 1–10.
Mougdad, Sulaiman A. *Bosra: Guide historique et archéologique*. Damascus: Tarabichi, 1974.
Munajid, S. "Morceau choisis du livre des moines." *MIDEO* 3 (1956): 349–58.
Munt, Harry. "'No Two Religions': Non-Muslims in the Early Islamic Ḥijāz." *BSOAS* 78 (2015): 249–69.
Nawas, John. "A Reexamination of Three Current Explanations for al-Mamun's Introduction of the Mihna." *IJMES* 26 (1994): 615–29.
Netton, Ian Richard. *Al-Farabi and His School*. London: Routledge, 2005.
Neuwirth, Angelika. "*Ayyu harajin 'alā man ansha'a mulahan*? Al-Ḥarīrī's Plea for the Legitimacy of Playful Transgressions of Social Norms." Pages 241–54 in *Humor in der arabischen Kultur: Humor in Arabic Culture*. Edited by Georges Tamer. Berlin: De Gruyter, 2009.
Newman, Daniel L. "Arabic Travel Writing." Pages 143–58 in *The Cambridge History of Travel Writing*. Edited by Nandini Das and Tim Youngs. Cambridge: Cambridge University Press, 2019.

O'Connell, Elisabeth R. "'They Wandered in the Deserts and Mountains, and Caves and Holes in the Ground': Non-Chalcedonian Bishops 'in Exile'." *Studies in Late Antiquity* 3 (2019): 436–71.

Olster, David. "From Periphery to Center: The Transformation of Late Roman Self-Definition in the Seventh Century." Pages 93–101 in *Shifting Frontiers in Late Antiquity*. Edited by Ralph W. Mathisen and Hagith S. Sivan. Aldershot: Ashgate Variorum, 1996.

Paoli, Bruno. "Traders, Innkeepers and Cupbearers: Foreigners and People of the Book in Arabic Wine Poetry." Pages 147–62 in *Religious Culture in Late Antique Arabia: Selected Studies on the Late Antique Religious Mind*. Edited by Isabel Toral-Niehoff and Kirill Dmitriev. Piscataway: Gorgias, 2017.

Peers, Glenn. "'Crosses' Work Underfoot: Christian Spolia in the Late Antique Mosque at Shivta in the Negev Desert (Israel)." *Eastern Christian Art* 8 (2011): 101–19.

al-Qaradawi, Yusuf. *The Lawful and the Prohibited in Islam:* الحلال والحرام في الإسلام. http://www.genderi.org/pars_docs/refs/76/75338/75338.pdf.

Roggema, Barbara. *The Legend of Sergius Baḥīrā: Eastern Christian Apologetics and Apocalyptic in Response to Islam*. Leiden: Brill, 2008.

Rompay, Lucas van. "Society and Community in the Christian East." Pages 239–66 in *The Cambridge Companion to the Age of Justinian*. Edited by Michael Maas. Cambridge: Cambridge University Press, 2005.

Rosa, Brian, and Jaime Jover-Báez. "Contested Urban Heritage: Discourses of Meaning and Ownership of the Mosque-Cathedral of Córdoba, Spain." *Journal of Urban Cultural Studies* 4 (2017): 127–54.

Saint-Laurent, Jeanne-Nicole M. "Hagiographical Portraits of Jacob Baradaeus." Pages 96–109 in *Missionary Stories and the Formation of the Syriac Churches*. Berkeley: University of California Press, 2015.

Schadler, Peter. *John of Damascus and Islam: Christian Heresiology and the Intellectual Background to Earliest Christian-Muslim Relations*. Leiden: Brill, 2017.

al-Shābushtī, ʿAlī b. Muhammad. *Kitāb ad-diyārāt*. Edited by Kirkīs ʿAwwād. Baghdad: Maktabat al-Muthanna, 1966.

Shahîd, Irfan. "Arab Christian Pilgrimages in the Proto-Byzantine Period." Pages 373–90 in *Pilgrimage and Holy Space in Late Antique Egypt*. Edited by David Frankfurter. Leiden: Brill, 1998.

Shahîd, Irfan. *Toponymy, Monuments, Historical Geography, and Frontier Studies*. Vol. 2/1 of *Byzantium and the Arabs in the Sixth Century*. Washington, DC: Dumbarton Oaks, 2002.

al-Shorman, Abdulla, Abdelqader Ababneh, Akram Rawashdih, Ahmad Makhadmih, Saad Alsaad, and Monther Jamhawi. "Travel and Hospitality in Late Antiquity: A Case Study from Umm El-Jimal in Eastern Jordan." *NEA* 80 (2017): 22–28.

Shrikant, Aditi. "Why we Hate Hearing about Other People's Vacations." *Voxmedia*, 18 Oct 2018. https://www.vox.com/the-goods/2018/10/18/17994238/vacation-travel-stories-boring.

Sirry, Muʾnim. "The Public Role of Dhimmīs during ʿAbbāsid Times." *BSOAS* 74 (2011): 187–204.

Sizgorich, Thomas. "Narrative and Community in Islamic Late Antiquity." *PaP* 185 (2004): 9–42.

Sperl, Stefan. "Islamic Kingship and Arabic Panegyric Poetry in the Early 9th Century." Pages 79–94 in *Early Islamic Poetry and Poetics*. Edited by Suzanne P. Stetkevych. London: Routledge, 2017.

Stroumsa, Sarah. "The Signs of Prophecy: The Emergence and Early Development of a Theme in Arabic Theological Literature." *HTR* 78 (1985): 101–14.

Sumi, Akiko Motoyoshi. *Description in Classical Arabic Poetry: Waṣf, Ekphrasis, and Interarts Theory*. Brill Studies in Middle Eastern Literatures 25. Leiden: Brill, 2004.

Tamimi Arab, Pooyan. "Islamic Heritage versus Orthodoxy: Figural Painting, Musical Instruments and Wine Bowls at the Dutch National Museum of World Cultures." *Journal of Material Culture* 26 (2021): 178–200.

Tannous, Jack. *The Making of the Medieval Middle East: Religion, Society, and Simple Believers*. Princeton: Princeton University Press, 2018.

Thomas, David R., and Barbara Roggema. *600–900*. Vol. 1 of *Christian-Muslim Relations: A Bibliographical History*. Leiden: Brill, 2009.

Touati, Houari. *Islam and Travel in the Middle Ages*. Chicago: University of Chicago Press, 2010.

Troupeau, Gérard. "Les couvents chrétiens dans la littérature arabe." *La nouvelle revue du Caire* 1 (1975): 265–79.

Troupeau, Gérard. "Les églises d'Antioche chez les auteurs arabes." Pages 319–27 in *L'Orient au coeur*. Edited by Floréal Sanagustin. Paris: Maisonneuve & Larose, 2001.

Vila, David. "The Struggle over Arabisation in Medieval Arabic Christian Hagiography." *Masāq* 15 (2003): 35–46.

Vries, Bert de. "On the Way to Bostra: Arab Settlement in South Syria Before Islam—The Evidence from Written Sources." Pages 69–92 in *Heureux qui comme Ulysses a fait un beau voyage: Movements of People in Time and Space*. Edited by Nefissa Naguib and Bert de Vries. Bergen: BRIC, 2010.

Wagtendonk, K., "Vigil." In *Encyclopaedia of the Qur'ān*. Edited by Johanna Pink. http://dx.doi.org/10.1163/1875-3922_q3_EQSIM_00444.

Wilde, Clare. "We Shall Not Teach the Qur'an to Our Children." Pages 233–59 in *The Place to Go To: Contexts of Learning in Baghdad from the Eighth to Tenth Centuries*. Edited by Jens Scheiner and Damien Janos. Princeton: Darwin, 2014.

Sachregister

Abraham 11–13, 15–17, 20–21, 24–27, 29, 64–65, 148, 150–151, 269, 271–285, 291
Acts
- Apocryphal 229–239, 241–247, 302–303
- Canonical 6, 51, 74, 83, 87–88, 90–91, 97, 99–107, 109–110, 146, 169, 194, 229–236, 238–242, 244–247

Afterlife 7, 37, 40, 44–49, 66, 210, 224
Alexandria 43, 89, 108, 119–120, 132–133, 167, 172, 175, 176, 237, 241, 245, 263–264
Analogy 7, 38, 41–43, 47, 259
Antioch 89, 104, 119–120, 132–136, 167, 175, 232–238, 240–243
Apocalypse 7, 66–67, 70, 148, 189–224
Apocalyptic
- Early Christian 63, 67, 151, 197, 200, 206, 213
- Jewish 63–64, 157
- Greco-Roman 69–70
Apocalypticism 157–158

Arabia 269–271, 273–275, 277–278, 280, 282, 285, 287, 290, 319, 325
- Jews and Christians of Arabia 313, 315–320, 322–324, 326–332

Athens 89, 91, 105, 114
Authority 45, 67–68, 70, 74, 81, 91, 133, 151–152, 164, 189, 247, 279

Babel
- Tower of Babel 6, 11, 14–16, 18, 20–21, 23–28

Border 27, 67, 108, 135, 231, 255, 260–261, 263, 265, 303, 327
Border Crossing 16, 21, 57–58, 69
Boundaries 47, 98, 101, 132, 253, 257–261, 265, 318
Boundary Crossing 55, 58, 330

Comparative Method 2–3, 5, 7, 33–34, 37, 47–48, 50–53
Comparison 33–34, 47, 50–52, 63, 68, 74, 79, 157, 164, 173, 200, 209, 213, 232, 240, 245, 299
Consolation 7, 33–34, 36–37, 44–47

Consolatory 37, 42, 46–49, 51
Cosmic City (Stoicism) 38, 42, 46
Cosmopolitanism 45, 108–109, 127, 137, 257
Cyprus 6, 231–246
Costs (→ Travel)

Dangers (→ Travel)
Dedication 147, 182, 185, 187
Dialogical Self Theory 5, 6, 97, 99–102, 106, 108–109
Diaspora 25, 82, 114, 117, 119, 135, 261
Diaspora Letter 130, 131, 138
Dionysius the Elder 39–40
Dispersed Persons 11, 13, 18, 20, 26, 28, 305
Dispersion 14–16, 18–19, 23, 25–28, 240, 243
Do ut des 186–187, 271, 288

Earthly Journey (→ Journey)
Economy 24, 113, 116–117, 125–128, 181, 183, 287–288
Education/*Paideia* 73–74, 81–82, 87–90, 100, 130, 201–202, 252, 289, 324
Educational Center(s) 314
Educational Journey (→ Journey)
Egypt 24, 36, 43, 167, 172, 208, 213, 260–264, 303, 316, 318
Emotion 51, 161–164, 168, 171–172, 176–177, 186
Epistemology 145, 148, 153, 154, 156, 205
Ethics 38, 68–70, 81–82, 115–124, 129–138, 204–206, 214, 223–224, 275–277, 281–291
Etiology 15, 22, 25
Exemplum 74, 91
Exile 11, 17, 23, 25–26, 36, 39, 84, 149
Experience
- Liminal Experience 296, 308
- Religious Experience 4, 12, 60
- Travel Experience 3–8, 12, 28, 41–43, 46–47, 64, 97, 109–110, 115, 118, 162, 164, 169, 176, 266, 288, 291, 314, 317–323, 325–332

Flavius Josephus 6, 135, 161–177, 252, 258

Genesis 6, 11–29, 104, 148, 214, 217, 261, 262
Genre 56, 60, 78–81, 83, 88–89, 121, 123, 130, 251, 272, 296, 313–314, 316–318, 327–328

Sachregister

Geography 4, 6–7, 77, 80, 86, 88, 90–91, 103, 125, 130, 132, 134, 146–147, 162, 175, 191, 198, 222, 234–235, 247, 251–256, 258–262, 265–266, 314, 316, 318, 325, 328, 330
Geography of the Mind 251, 265
Global culture 125, 126, 128, 136–137
Globalization 98–99, 101, 109, 124–132, 136–138
Globalization studies 129–138
Globalized world 113–115, 120, 124–129, 132, 136–138
Glocalization 126–127
Gospel of John
– Johannine Epistemology 145–155
– Johannine Spirituality 145–148, 154–158
– Johannine Travel 145–158
Gospel of Luke 6, 64–65, 68, 73–79, 83, 85–88, 91, 97, 106, 146, 169, 199, 229, 240
Gospel of Mark 73, 75–79, 84–87, 91, 169, 219–220
Götterverschmelzung 183
Group identity 100, 106, 109, 251
Group/traveling in groups (→ Traveler)

Hades 55–56, 58, 60–65, 68–70
ḥanīf 272–273
Heaven 4, 7, 26–27, 55, 58, 61–70, 102, 145–153, 155–156, 189, 192–194, 198, 200–202, 204–212, 214, 216–224
Heavenly journey (→ Journey)
Herod 82, 127, 164–165, 171–173, 176, 214,
History/Historiography
– Primeval History 13–16, 19–21, 25, 28
– Classical Historiography 81, 171, 176,
Homeland 117, 131, 244, 263, 265
Homogenization 126, 128, 131, 132

Identity
– Construction of Identity 5–6, 18–23, 88–89, 99–101, 106–110, 122, 124–128, 131–133, 147, 153, 229–247, 251–252, 272–273, 280–281
– Identify Formation 6, 23–26, 28–29, 97–106
Idolatry 71, 104, 271–272
Infrastructure 79, 113, 137
Interconnectivity 66, 101–102, 114, 117, 122, 124–125, 127, 129, 131, 132, 136
Interdependence 124, 128
Interpretatio Romana 182–183

Iraq 317, 324, 328, 332
Islam
– Islamic Travel Literature 270–291, 313
– Origins of Islam 269–291, 313–314
Itinerary 6, 12–14, 16–17, 23–24, 28, 43, 229–237, 239–247, 256, 266, 273

Jerusalem 73–77, 82–84, 86–87, 90–91, 102, 132, 135, 146–148, 154, 166–168, 171–172, 191–192, 194, 198–200, 206–208, 213–214, 223, 232, 234, 239–243, 251, 278, 280, 300, 320, 322
Journey
– Earthly Journey 11, 13, 14, 17, 23–26, 28–29, 34, 41, 43, 47, 67–68, 76, 78–81, 83, 97–100, 102, 105–109, 146, 162, 167, 173, 198, 229–237, 240–246, 320–321, 325–328, 330
– Educational Journey 41, 83, 87–91, 107, 114, 118, 119, 201–202
– Heavenly Journey 45, 68, 145–146, 152, 190, 192–194, 197–198, 200, 204–205, 207, 208–209, 212, 219–220, 223
– Journey to Hades 55, 58–61, 63–64, 68
– Journey to Heaven 55, 61–64, 66–67
– Marine Voyage 295–301, 303–308
– Otherworldly Journey 55–58, 64–65, 68–70, 151
– Sea Journey 37, 38, 162–163, 177, 183, 185
– Spiritual Journey 145–158, 269, 273–274, 276, 281, 285–289
– Underworld Journey 58–59, 61, 213
Judaea 97, 102, 108–109, 127, 146–147, 163, 167–168, 171–173, 176, 191, 234, 259
Judaean (or Jewish) War 82, 162–168, 171–177

Knowledge 4, 6–7, 25, 52–53, 55, 57, 64, 82, 99, 101–103, 107, 114, 116, 118, 120, 125–126, 129, 149, 152–158, 191, 205, 214, 217, 229, 233, 252, 256, 258, 269, 284, 300, 314–315

Landmarks 90, 191, 255–277
Legatio 108–109, 170
Liminal Experience (→ Experience)
Liminality 316, 318, 327, 330
Lokalkolorit/Local Color 253–254, 258, 266
Lucian 56, 59–60, 62, 65, 89
Lukan Travel Narrative (→ Narrative)
Luke-Acts 74, 83, 87–88

Map 131, 136, 183, 191, 229-230, 234, 241, 252, 319
Marine Voyage (→ Journey)
Memory 39-40, 230, 243, 270
Menippean Literature 3, 5, 55-70
Travelers
- Merchant Travelers 1, 3, 113-119, 130, 183, 186, 252-253, 260, 303, 313, 321, 325, 328-329
Merchant(s) (→ Travelers/Merchant Travelers)
Mesopotamia 17-18, 25-26, 296, 302, 308
Metaphor 13, 33, 49-51, 83-85, 87, 90, 119, 131, 155, 199-200, 206
Migration 1, 12-14, 118, 125, 127, 129, 164, 321
Mobility
- Mobility of Discourses 116, 129-137
- Mobility of Ideas 113-116, 120, 125, 137
Monastery 3, 243, 274, 313-332
Mucianus 164-165, 167, 172, 175-177

Narrative
- Adventure Narrative 297
- Islamic Travel Literature (→ Islam)
- Lukan Travel Narrative/*Reisebericht* 73-78, 83-84, 87-88, 91
- Travel Narrative 5-6, 12, 34, 37, 44-49, 79-82, 97, 98, 100, 107-110, 148, 165, 285, 330
- Travel Accounts 5, 56-58, 64-65, 68-70, 81, 83, 88, 107, 148, 189-190, 193, 195
Nature 11, 18, 26, 41-42, 44-48, 51, 56, 81, 97, 108, 163-164, 176, 192, 197, 224, 273-274, 281-282, 289, 303, 318, 320, 323, 327-328, 332
Nemeton 182
Nomad 18-19, 23-25, 28, 325, 327
Nomadic Life 23-24, 316
Nomadism 34
Numen 182

ὁδός 73-74, 83-91
Odyssey 55, 81-82, 168, 171, 296
Oikoumene 127-130
Origins of Islam (→ Islam)
Ostia 43
Otherworldly Journey (→ Journey)

Paideia (→ Education)
Parable 64-65, 67-69, 86-87

Patriarch 13, 16, 23-24, 217, 238, 243, 258
Paul of Tarsus 3, 7, 33-34, 48-52, 83, 85, 87, 90-91, 100, 102, 105-106, 132, 135, 169, 189-190, 192-200, 202-224, 229-236, 240-246
Πεπαιδευμένος 6, 74, 87, 91
Perception 114-116, 124, 126-130, 133, 138, 251-254, 266, 297, 308, 331
Pilgrim 3, 244, 285-287, 289, 313, 328
Pilgrimage
- Christian 2, 3, 243-244, 251
- Jewish 2, 82-84
- (Pre-)Islamic 277-280, 282-289, 317, 320-322
Place
- Holy Places 146, 150, 211, 217-219, 251, 269, 320-322
- Sacred Space (→ Space)
Plato 39, 45, 60, 130, 157
Pluralism, religio-philosophical 47
Poetry, Pre-Islamic 270, 273-274, 284
Prosopopoeia 41-42, 45-48

Qur'an 270-276, 282, 284-285, 289, 291, 304, 313-315, 319-321, 323, 325

Rabbinic Writings 3, 5, 149, 251-254, 256, 258, 263-266, 297, 299, 301-302, 305-307
Reasons for Travel
- Pilgrimage (→ Pilgrimage)
- Profit/Merchandise (→ Merchants)
- Sickness 289, 313
- Tourism (→ Tourism)
- Wisdom (→ Wisdom)
Reciprocity 52, 314
Reisebericht (→ Narrative)
Religio 185-186
Religion 1-3, 88, 91, 121, 127, 129, 184-186, 213, 269-273, 281, 284, 287, 316
Religious Experience (→ Experience)
Revelation 64, 66-71, 146, 151-152, 155, 203, 212-213, 216, 218
Rhetoric 48, 121, 138, 163, 303
Ritual Knowledge 273
Road Network 4, 114
Rome 6, 36, 83, 89, 91, 105-109, 114, 127, 132-133, 135, 163-170, 172-177, 191, 229-230, 241, 244, 255, 263

Sacrifice 82, 269, 271–275, 277–281, 283–285
Sage 4, 81, 91, 108, 256
Sailor 5, 181, 296–299, 301–305, 307–308
Sanctuary 146, 270–271, 277, 280
Sea journey (→ Journey)
Sea Storm (→ Storm)
Sea voyage (→ Journey)
Seneca 3, 7–8, 33–52, 56, 61–63, 69, 130
Ship 43, 116, 169, 173, 183, 230, 236–237, 298, 300–305
Shipwreck 43, 52, 98, 113, 169, 173
Shrine 2, 181–184, 269–271, 274–280, 284–291, 317, 321
Shrine Devotion 183–184, 269–271, 276–280, 285–286, 289–290
Sicily 38, 43
Socrates 44
Space
– Liminal space 300
– Sacred Space 99, 114
– Spatial frames 191–192, 198–204, 209–219
– Spatial theory 190–192
Status Reversal 59–60–62, 64–65, 68–69
Stoic 36–38, 42, 45–48, 52
Stoicism 34, 38, 50
Storm 97, 113, 168–171, 295–296
Syracuse 7, 8, 37–43, 47
Syria 104, 119–120, 134–136, 175, 233, 259–263, 265, 315–319, 321–322, 323–324, 327, 328

Teacher 4, 74, 79, 84, 87, 89, 91, 114, 152–154, 157, 232, 246, 299
Tourist(s)/Touristic travels 7, 39, 43, 107, 114, 264
Trade
– Trade Diaspora 117–118
– Trade Networks 98, 115–116, 273
– Trade Voyage 119, 274, 316
Traditions 2–3, 5, 8, 20, 24, 45, 62, 80, 85, 87, 108, 115, 119–120, 122, 124, 128, 130–134, 136–138, 149–153, 157, 201, 206, 210, 223–224, 230, 237, 240–241, 244, 247, 252–258, 261, 265–266, 276, 283–284, 291, 296–297, 300–301, 304, 306–308, 313–314, 319, 324, 328

Transience 12, 18, 23, 26, 28
Transportation 79, 113–114, 125, 326
Travel
– Costs of Travel 113–114, 125, 127–128, 286–287
– Dangers of Travel 4, 6, 38, 47, 113–115, 117–119, 168–171, 176–177, 206, 223–224, 295–297, 299–302, 307–308, 327
– Reasons for Travel (→ Reasons)
Travel Accounts (→ Narrative)
Travel Experience (→ Experience)
Travel Narrative (→ Narrative)
Traveling deity 14, 26–27
Traveling sage 81, 91, 107–108
Traveler
– Individual 6, 26, 100, 118–119, 148, 183, 280, 295
– Group 3, 14, 16–19, 21–23, 26, 28, 59, 69, 97–98, 106, 115–119, 129, 183–185, 201, 204, 219, 236, 256, 288, 306, 313, 318, 327, 330
Travelogue 266, 285–286, 288
Triplication 182

Uncertainty 5–6, 41, 97–103, 105–107, 109, 115, 124, 134
Underworld Journey (→ Journey)

Vespasian 6, 162–177, 259
Vitellius 162, 164, 166–168, 170, 173–177
Votum 183, 185
Vow 185, 186, 280, 283

Wanderradikalismus 85
Way 97, 100–101, 103–106, 109
Wayfarers 181
Wisdom 4–7, 107–108, 115–119, 123, 125, 131, 136, 138, 201
World Consciousness 127, 129, 137
Worship 3, 6, 66–68, 70, 269–286, 288–291, 315, 331–332

Year of the Four Emperors 162, 164–168, 174, 176

Ziqqurrat 27

Stellenregister

Hebrew Bible

Genesis		10:8–19	20
1–11	13, 15, 17, 20, 22, 25	10:16–18	21
1:28	13, 27	10:21	20
2–3	15, 22	10:21–24	11
2–13	17	10:25–30	20
2:8	13, 17, 25	10:30	17
2:9	217	10:32	13
2:10–14	214	11	12, 14–15, 18–23, 25–29
2:14	17	11–13	17
2:15	13	11:1	19
3:8	13, 26	11:1–4	15
3:22–24	13	11:1–9	14–15, 20, 22, 28
3:24	17	11:2	14, 16–19, 28
4:1–16	23	11:2–4	14, 17
4:12	13	11:3–4	16
4:12–16	12	11:3–9	17
4:14	13	11:5	13–15, 16–19, 22
4:16	13, 17	11:5–7	21, 26
4:17	23	11:5–9	15
4:17–24	23	11:6	16, 19
4:17–26	21–22	11:6–9	14, 17
5	13	11:7	13–14, 16
5:21–24	12–13	11:7–9	18
5:22	148	11:8–9	18
5:24	148	11:9	14, 16, 18, 28
5:29	21	11:31	13
6	14, 21	12	11
6–9	14, 17	12–13	12
6:1–4	15, 21–22	12–50	15
6:4	21	12:1–3	12
6:9	12–13	12:1–4	12, 24
8–9	104	12:1–9	13
9–11	20	12:1–20	24
9:1	27	12:8	17, 24
9:18–27	20	12:8–9	24
9:19	13, 19, 21–22	12:9	16
9:20–27	21	12:10ff	24
9:20–28	21	13	12
10	20–21	13:3	16
10:5	13	13:10–11	17
10:8–12	17, 23, 25	13:11	16–17

13:11–12	13	33:18–23	26
13:14	17	33:20	149–150
13:17	24	34:2	149
13:18	13, 24	34:28	149
14:3	261	34:29–35	149
15:18	262		
15:19–21	262	Leviticus	
16:6–8	13	17–26	104
17:1	12		
18	26	Numbers	
18–19	23	9:18	16
18:21–22	13, 26	12:8	150
19:1	13	12:16	16
20:1	16	17:5	306
24	11	33:3–48	16
24:4	13		
24:64	13	Deuteronomy	
25:6	17	32:49	198–199
26:1–23	13	34:1	199
27:43ff	12		
28:10–20	17	1 Kings	
28:12–13	13, 26	8	280
28:14	17	18:12	84
29:1	17	18:46	84
32	26		
33:12	13, 16	2 Kings	
33:17	16	2:11	148
35:1–7	17		
35:5	16	2 Chronicles	
35:16	16	3:1	278
35:21	13, 16		
37:12–17	12	Psalms	
37:17	15–16	67:19 (LXX)	203
37:28, 36	12	94:8	272
42:3	11	103:5	217
46:1	16		
46:1–4	12	Proverbs	
		16:9	115
Exodus		30:19	217
12:37	16		
14:10	16	Isaiah	
14:19	16	6	146, 151
17:1	16	6:1–5	150
19:3	149	14:13–15	151
19:20–25	149	26:19	305
20	150	31:9	239
20:21	149	40:3	84–85

40:31	217		1:28	217
42:16	84		4	280
43:16	84			
43:19	84		Daniel	
48:17	84		7–8	146
49:11	84		7:9–10	150, 203
51:10	84			
54:12	300		Joel	
			3:1	109
Jeremiah				
49:16	217		Amos	
			9:11–12	109
Ezekiel				
1	146		Obadiah	
1:1–3:15	217		4	217
1:26–28	150			

New Testament

Matthew			Mark	
2:16–18	214		1:1–2	85
3:3	85		1:2	83–85
5:10–12	123		1:3	83–85
5:21–22	123		1:9	83
5:25	86		1:14–15	84
5:34–37	123		1:17–18	85
6:13	123		1:18	85
6:19	123		1:35–8:26	84
6:34	123		1:38	84
7:16–20	123		2:14	85
8:18	86		2:15	85
8:23–27	169		2:23	83–84, 86
12:33	123		3:7	85
12:36	123		4:4	83–84, 86
12:1	86		4:15	83–84, 86
15:1	123		4:35–41	169
19:16–30	123		5:24	85
19:27–28	219		6:1	85
21:21	123		6:8	83–85
22:9	87		6:45–8:26	75
24	220		8:3	83–84
28:16–20	220		8:27	83–84, 86

8:31	87	9:51	74–77, 91
8:34	85	9:51–56	91
9:31	87	9:51–18:14	76, 78
9:33–34	83, 86	9:51–19:27	73–75
9:33	84, 86	9:51–19:28	77
9:34	84, 86	9:51–19:48	73, 76
10	84	9:52	77, 91
10:1	77	9:53	91
10:17	83–84, 86	9:56	91
10:21	85	9:57	86
10:28	85	10–12	87
10:32	83–86	10:1	240
10:32–34	87	10:1–18:14	75
10:32–52	91	10:4	85–87
10:33	84	10:19	199
10:46	83–86	10:25	91
10:52	83–86	10:25–37	87, 97
11:1	73	10:30	199
11:8	83–84, 86	10:31	86
11:19	85	10:33	77
12:13	84	10:38	91
12:14	83–84, 86	11:1	91
13	220	11:1–18:30	79
15:41	85	11:5–8	87
		11:6	86
Luke		11:29	91
1:1–4	83	11:45	91
1:76	85–86	12:1	91
1:79	86	12:13	91
2:1–21	83	12:16–21	87
2:22–39	83	12:58	86
2:41	83	13:10	91
2:42–51	83	13:22	91
2:44	86	13:23	91
3	85	13:23–33	87
3:4	85	14:23	86–87
3:4–5	86	14:25	91
6:1	86	15–19	87
6:45–8:26	86	15:8–9	87
7:27	85–86	15:11–32	87
8:3	86	16	68
8:5	86	16:1–13	87
8:12	86	16:19–31	55, 64, 87
8:22–25	169	16:23	65
9:3	86	16:25	65
9:18	86	16:26	65
9:46	86	16:27–31	65

17:7–10	87	2:12	146
17:11	77, 91	2:13	146–147
17:16	77	2:21	147
17:25	86	2:21–22	157
18:1–8	87	2:23	153
18:8	86	2:24	154
18:9–14	87	3	145, 148, 155
18:14	76	3:1–9	154
18:15	74–75, 77	3:5	152
18:18	91	3:8	156
18:30	74, 91	3:10	152
18:31	86, 91	3:11	152, 154
18:31–34	86	3:12	152
18:35	74, 77, 86	3:13	145, 147–148, 151–153
18:43	86	3:14	152, 156
19:1	91	3:22	146
19:10	74	3:31	153
19:11	91	3:32	154
19:27	74	4:3	146
19:28–40	74	4:20	146
19:28–41	76	4:21	147
19:28	74, 91	4:22	146
19:28ff	75	4:23	147
19:36	86	4:36	240
19:44	74	4:37	240
19:46	74	4:44	146
19:48	74	4:46	146
20:21	86	4:54	146, 153
21:38	74	5	156
24	146	5:1	146
24:32	86	5:39	147
24:34–35	86	6:1	146
24:35	86	6:1–5	157
		6:27	152
John		6:32–35	147
1:1–18	145	6:42	148, 154
1:9	221	6:44–46	154
1:10–11	154	6:46	149
1:12–13	153, 156	6:62	147, 152
1:14	147	6:65	154
1:17	147	7–8	147
1:18	145, 149	7:1	146
1:23	85	7:2	146–147
1:26	154	7:8	146–147
1:51	147, 152	7:10	146
2:1	146	7:14	146
2:11	153	7:27–29	154

7:33	147	14:17	152
7:33–36	147	15:19	156
7:50–52	154	15:20	156
8:1b–4	240	15:20–21	156
8:3	240	15:21	154
8:14	148	15:24	153
8:14–15	154	16:13	152
8:19	154	17:6	156
8:21	147	17:11	147
8:21–22	147	17:13	147
8:28	152	17:14	156
8:39–59	154	17:16	156
8:43	147	19:39–40	154
8:56–58	151	20:7	145
9	156	20:17	146–147
9:30	240	20:19	154
9:30–33	153	20:29	299
9:35	152	20:30	153
10	147	21:11	146
10:1	146		
10:22	147	Acts	
10:40	146	1	146
11:1	146	1:8	102
11:15	146	2:5	102
11:19–20	240	2:28	109
11:25–26	241	8:1–4	102
11:54	146	8:4–8	102
11:55	146	8:14–18	102
12:10	156	8:25	102
12:12	146–147	8:26–40	102
12:20	146	9	194
12:23	152	9:1–9	51
12:24–26	156	9:2	74, 83
12:34	152	10–11	102
12:34–36	151	11:23	239
12:35–36	155	12:12	232
12:39	147	13–14	102
12:41	151	13:1	234
12:55	147	13:1–3	102
13:1	145	13:1–4	232
13:1–3	147	13:2	232
13:3	145	13:4	232, 242
13:30	154	13:5	231–232
13:31	152	13:6	232
14:2	148	13:13	232, 242
14:6	85, 147–148	13:14	232
14:9	149	13:14–14:25	229

13:51–14:5	233
15	97, 102–106, 109
15:1–3	234
15:1–35	101, 234
15:5	103
15:16–17	109
15:20	103–104
15:21	105
15:23	104
15:29	103
15:36–39	235
15:36–17:22	102
15:39	232, 235
16:5	229
16:6–10	105
16:10–17	83
16:12ff	83
17:16–34	105
17:25–28	105
19:9	83
19:23	83
20:4	245
20:5–21:18	83
20:17–31	234
20:18–35	100
21:16	246
21:25	103
22:3	90, 239
22:4	83
22:6–11	51
24:14	74
24:22	74, 83
27	169
27–28	51, 83
27:7–13	230
27:9–12	169
28:11–31	105
28:16–31	83
28:30–31	91

Romans
9:14–24	51
15:22	229

1 Corinthians
13:9–12	49

2 Corinthians
10–13	189, 193
10:17	193
11	49
11:25–26	51
12	223
12:2	193, 205, 221
12:2–4	189–190, 192–194, 197, 222–223
12:4	193, 205

Galatians
1–2	194, 208
1:13–14	239
1:15	203
4:13–14	50

Ephesians
4:8	203
6:12	203
6:21	245

Philippians
1:19–25	50
3:7–11	50
3:10–14	49
3:20	34

Colossians
1:7	245
4:7	245
4:10	240
4:12	245

1 Thessalonians
2:9	49

2 Thessalonians
3:6–11	49

2 Timothy
4:11	245
6:21	245

Titus
1:5	230
3:12	230, 245

Philemon

23	245

James

1:1	115, 117, 130
1:5	119
1:6	119, 123
1:19–20	123
2:1–13	123
2:21–23	285
3:1–12	123
3:4	119
3:7	119
4	116
4:13	116
4:13–15	115, 119
4:13–5:6	123
4:17	115
5:12	123

Revelation

1	66
1–3	66
1:19	67
4	66, 68
4–5	203, 216
4:1	64, 66
4:1–11	55, 66
4:2	66
4:7	218
4:9	66
4:10	66
4:11	66
5:12	66
5:13	66
7:12	66
19:1	66
20:11	67
21	213
21:16	214
21:23	66
22	66
22:4	66
22:7	67
22:10	67
22:14	214
22:18–19	67

Greco-Roman Literature

Appian
The Civil Wars

2.56–58	169

Arrian
Anabasis

5.28.1–29.1	108

Caesar
Civil War

3.5.2	169
3.6	169
3.6.1	169
3.6.3	169

Cassius Dio
Roman History

41.46	169
64.22	176
65.8	174

Cicero
Letters to Atticus

7.22.1	169–170
8.9.2	169–170

On the Republic

6.9–26	151

Demetrius
On Style

288	163

Herodotus
Histories

1.29–33	81

Hesiod
Works and Days
617–695   168
618   168

Homer
Iliad
8.247   218
24.292   218
24.311   218

Odyssey
1.1–3   82
1.5.3   82

Lucan
Pharsalia
5.403–460   169
5.504–677   169
5.577–593   169
5.653–671   169
5.671–677   169

Lucian
Cataplus
4   59
13   59
15   59
19   59
22   59
24   59, 65
28   60, 65

Icaromenippus
2–3   61
15–17   61
20   61
33   61
34   61

Necyomantia
6–7   60
8   60
9   60, 65
11   60
14   60

17   60
20   60

Philostratus
Life of Apollonius
1.19   90
1.35   108
2–3   107
2.27   108
2.27–28   108
3.18   108
3.25   108
5.2   90
8.31   90

Lives of the Sophists
480–481   89

Plato
Apology
40–41D   44

Republic
10.14–15   60

Phaedo
114C–115   44

Pliny the Elder
Natural History
5.70   82
10.5   218

Plutarch
Caesar
37–38   169

Consolation to His Wife
611C–F   44

On the Fortune of the Romans
319B–D   169

Polybius
Histories
10.32.7–10   170
10.33.2   170

Quintilian
Institutes of Oratory
9.2.65　　　　　163

Seneca
On Consolation to Marcia
16.2　　　　　36
16.5　　　　　50
16.8　　　　　35, 37–38
17.1　　　　　38, 41
17.2　　　　　38
17.2–4　　　　38
17.2–18　　　　37
17.5　　　　　39
17.6　　　　　40
17.6–7　　　　41–42
17.7　　　　　42
18.1　　　　　41
18.8　　　　　41–42
19.4–21.1　　　44
23.1　　　　　44
24.5–26.7　　　37, 44
25.1　　　　　44
25.2　　　　　44–45
25.3　　　　　45
26.5–7　　　　45

Apocolocyntosis
1.1–3　　　　62
4.2–3　　　　62
8.1　　　　　62
10.3–4　　　62
11.6　　　　62
14.2　　　　62
15.2　　　　62

Statius
Silvae
4.3　　　　　80

Strabo
Geography
1.1　　　　　80

Suetonius
Life of Julius Caesar
58　　　　　169

Life of Vespasian
5.1　　　　　174
7.1　　　　　176

Consolation to Helvia
19.2　　　　43

Tacitus
Histories
2.6–7　　　　174
3.78　　　　176
4.1–11　　　176
4.4　　　　　176

Thucydides
Histories
4.14–15　　　168

Tabula Cebetis
4.2–3　　　　201
12.1–3　　　201
18.2　　　　201
21.3　　　　201

Valerius Maximus
9.8.2　　　　169

Vegetius
Epitome of Military Science
4.39　　　　97

Vergil
Aeneid
3.57　　　　82
5.704ff　　　82
8.530ff　　　82

Josephus and Philo of Alexandria

Josephus		4.605	172, 175
Jewish Antiquities		4.616	167–168
1.109–110	18–20	4.616–619	175
		4.619	175
Jewish War		4.620	167
1	171	4.620–621	175
1.204–430	171	4.630	167–168, 175
1.274–276	172	4.630–632	167
1.274–285	164	4.631	175
1.277	172	4.631–657	166
1.277–278	171	4.632	175
1.277–285	171	4.633–644	167
1.278	172	4.645–649	167, 175
1.279	172	4.647	168
1.281	173	4.650	175
1.282–285	173	4.650–654	167
2.649	175	4.652	167–168
3.29	135	4.654	175
4	161, 164, 171, 174, 176	4.654–655	167
4.39	168	4.654–656	168
4.318	168	4.656	167, 176
4.440–441	166	4.656–663	175
4.449–511	168	4.658	167, 176
4.486	167	5.291–387	168
4.494–502	166	7	167
4.497	172	7.21–22	167
4.498–502	167	12.403–25	168
4.501	167		
4.544	168	*Life of Flavius Josephus*	
4.545–549	166	12	258
4.550	167	13–16	169
4.550–555	167	92	258
4.583–587	173		
4.585–588	166	Philo of Alexandria	
4.588	167	*On the Life of Abraham*	
4.588–589	172	65	118
4.588–591	162, 166, 168		
4.588–663	162	*On the Confusion of Tongues*	
4.589	167	76–82	23
4.591	168	95–97	149
4.592–604	172	134–139	26
4.593–594	168		
4.596	167–168	*On the Migration of Abraham*	
4.603–604	175	216–218	118

Against Flaccus
125   170

On the Embassy to Gaius
97–103   149
132   264
133–134   264
190   97, 171

On the Life of Moses
2.71   149

On the Posterity of Cain
13–16   149

Questions and Answers on Exodus
2.44   149

Early Jewish Texts: Hebrew Bible Apocrypha; Jewish Hellenistic Literature, Qumran

Apocalypse of Abraham
16   150

Apocalypse of Zephania
13:1   213
14:1   211

Ascension of Isaiah
3:8–9   150
9   222
9:37–38   150
10:24–27   201

1 Enoch
1–36   148
17–19   150
19:3   150
37–71   148
39:5–6   150
71:1   150
71:11   217
91:5   150
91:10   150

2 Enoch
9   222
22:1–6   150

3 Enoch
15B:2   149
18:3–4   201

Ezekiel the Tragedian
68–81   149

4 Ezra
6:8–9   255

History of the Captivity in Babylon
25   199

Jubilees
10:19   19
10:19–36   20
10:23   26

Letter of Aristeas
32   264
75–79   264

Orphica
20–24   149

Pseudo-Philo
Book of Biblical Antiquities
11:4   150

Qumran
4Q491   149

Sirach
1:11–20   119
8:15   118

11:18–19	115	Testament of Levi	
26:12	118	2–5	148
33:2	118	2:6	66
34:9–13	118	5:1	150
34:14ff	118		
36:31	118	Wisdom of Solomon	
40:26–27	119	10:10	152
42:3	118		

Rabbinic Literature

Mishnah
Kil.
6:4   254–255

Šeb.
6:1   261

Ketub.
5:8   254–255

Tosefta
Šeb.
4:6   261
4:7   261
4:11 261

Ter.
2:12 260

Ḥal.
2:6   261
2:11 260

ʿErub.
4[3]:5 261

Suk.
4:6   263

B. Qam.
8:19 260

Midrashim
Gen. Rab.
30:10 12
36:1   19
38:1–9 19
80:1   258

Lev. Rab.
2:4   305

Pesiq. Rab. Kah.
18.5   299

Tanḥuma Shelaḥ
28   306

Jerusalem Talmud
Ber.
5:2, 9b   305

Šabb.
6:2, 8a   256

ʿErub.
5:1, 22b 257

Suk.
5:1, 55a   263
5:1, 55a–b 265

Taʿan.
1:1, 63b 305

Ketub.		B. Bat.	
5:11, 30b	255	74a	300
12:4, 35b	261	74b	301, 305–306

Qidd.		Sanh.	
1:9, 61d	262	100a	300

Babylonian Talmud
Soṭah
46b   307

Early Christian Texts (Patristics, Apocrypha, Nag Hammadi)

Acts of Paul (Actus Vercellenses)		19:3–5	203
1	230	19:10–14	198
1–3	229–230	19:17–18	207
		19:17–19	198, 206
Acts of Barnabas		19:18–20	207
1	235	19:20–25	200
3	233	19:29	204
3–4	233	20:2–21:22	200
5	233–234	20:4	204
6	235	20:5–11	200
7	234	20:16	201
8	235	20:19–20	204, 223
10	234	21:5	204
11	234	21:26–28	201
12	235	22:2–4	202
14	236	22:11–13	201
15	236	22:19–24	202
15–16	236	22:20	201
16	236	22:23–30	202
17	236–237	23:2–4	203
18	236	23:9–10	203
18–19	236	23:13–14	204, 223
19	236	23:13–17	203
20	236	23:27	204
21	236–237	23:29–24:4	207
22	236–237	23:29–24:8	204
		24:6–8	207
Apocalypse of Paul (NH V,2)			
18:6	198	Encomium on Barnabas	
18:8	198	9	239
18:13–14	198	10	239
18:16–17	203	11	239

12	240	21:2	211–212
13	240	21:3	212
14	240	23	216
15	240	23:1	213
16	240	25	214
17–19	240	26	214
20	240–241	27	213
21	241–242	29:1	213
22	242	29:2	214
23	242	29:3	214
24	242	29:4	221
25	242	30–44	209
25–29	242	31–44	214–216, 220
26–27	242	31:2	215
28	242	31:3	215
29	242–243	31:3–4	215
30	243	31:4	215
31	243	41:1	215
32	243	41:2	216
33–37	243	41:2–3	215
38–40	243	42:1	216
40–44	243	43	216
46	243	44–54	220
47	244	44:1	216
50	244	44:4	216
		45	216

Infancy Gospel of Thomas
2	304

45–54	209, 216–217
45:3	216
45:4	217

Origen
Contra Celsum
6.30–31	210

46	219
46–54	217
52–64	217
55	209, 217–218, 220, 222

Treatise of the Sethians
56:25–26	202

55–63	218
55:2	217
56–57	219
56–62	209, 218–219, 220

Visio Pauli (Coptic)
15–18	209, 220
16–18	210
16:2	210
16:4	210
16:7	210
18:2	210
19–20	209, 211, 218, 220
19:1	211
19:1–2	211
21–30	209, 211–214, 220

56:1	218
56:2	218
56:3	218
58	219
58–59	219
58:1	218–219
59	222
59–61	219
59:2	222
60	219

62	219	Vita of Auxibios	
62:2	219	1–13	244
63–64	209, 219	3–5	244
64:3	219	6	244
		7	244–245
Visio Pauli (L¹ Paris)		8	245
21:7–8	211	12	245

Qur'an

Qur'an		22:36	272
2:124–134	276	22:42	315
2:127	271	28:4–5	271
3:46	304	33:20	325
3:49	304	33:21	285
3:64–68	275	35:10	270
3:67	285	37:107	283
3:96	276	37:180	270
4:125	285	39:12	285
5:82	315	43:57–65	275
5:103	272	43:81	276
6:163	285	48:25–26	271
9:31	315	48:29	315
9:34	315	49:14	325
19:31–34	275	57:27	315
22:26	277	60:4	285
22:28	272	106:2	325